PERSPECTIVES IN COMPANY LAW AND FINANCIAL REGULATION

This collection of essays has been compiled in honour of Professor Eddy Wymeersch on the occasion of his retirement as professor at Ghent University. His main international academic peers explore developments on the crossroads of company law and financial regulation in Europe and the United States, providing a unique view on the dynamics of regulatory competition in an era of economic globalization, whether in the fields of rule making, organizing the mobility of capital or the enforcement of rules. The deepening of European financial integration and the transatlantic regulatory dialogue has generated new paradigms of rule setting in a multinational framework and reinforced the need to develop adequate instruments for cooperation between regulators. Regulators increasingly use concepts such as equivalence or mutual recognition to regulate cross-border relations.

MICHEL TISON, HANS DE WULF, REINHARD STEENNOT and CHRISTOPH VAN DER ELST are professors at the Financial Law Institute at Ghent University.

INTERNATIONAL CORPORATE LAW AND FINANCIAL MARKET REGULATION

Recent years have seen an upsurge of change and reform in corporate law and financial market regulation internationally as the corporate and institutional investor sector increasingly turns to the international financial markets. This follows large-scale institutional and regulatory reform after a series of international corporate governance and financial disclosure scandals exemplified by the collapse of Enron in the United States. There is now a great demand for analysis in this area from the academic, practitioner, regulatory and policy sectors.

The *International Corporate Law and Financial Market Regulation* series will respond to that demand by creating a critical mass of titles which will address the need for information and high-quality analysis in this fast-developing area.

Series Editors
Professor Eilis Ferran, University of Cambridge
Professor Niamh Moloney, London School of Economics
Professor Howell E. Jackson, Harvard Law School

Editorial Board
Professor Marco Becht, Professor of Finance and Economics at Université Libre de Bruxelles and Executive Director of the European Corporate Governance Institute (ECGI).

Professor Brian Cheffins, S.J. Berwin Professor of Corporate Law at the Faculty of Law, University of Cambridge.

Professor Paul Davies, Cassel Professor of Commercial Law at the London School of Economics and Political Science.

Professor Luca Enriques, Professor of Business Law in the Faculty of Law at the University of Bologna.

Professor Guido Ferrarini, Professor of Law at the University of Genoa and Honorary Professor, Faculty of Law, University College London.

Professor Jennifer Hill, Professor of Corporate Law at Sydney Law School.

Professor Klaus J. Hopt, Director of the Max Planck Institute of Comparative and International Private Law, Hamburg, Germany.

Professor Hideki Kanda, Professor of Law at the University of Tokyo.

Professor Colin Mayer, Peter Moores Professor of Management Studies at the Saïd Business School and Director of the Oxford Financial Research Centre.

James Palmer, Partner of Herbert Smith, London.

Professor Michel Tison, Professor at the Financial Law Institute of the University of Ghent.

Andrew Whittaker, General Counsel to the Board at the UK Financial Services Authority.

Professor Eddy Wymeersch, Chairman of the Committee of European Securities Regulators (CESR); Co-Chair of the CESR-European Central Bank Working Group on Clearing and Settlement.

PERSPECTIVES IN COMPANY LAW AND FINANCIAL REGULATION

Essays in Honour of Eddy Wymeersch

EDITED BY

MICHEL TISON, HANS DE WULF,
CHRISTOPH VAN DER ELST AND
REINHARD STEENNOT

CAMBRIDGE
UNIVERSITY PRESS

CAMBRIDGE UNIVERSITY PRESS
Cambridge, New York, Melbourne, Madrid, Cape Town, Singapore, São Paulo, Delhi

Cambridge University Press
The Edinburgh Building, Cambridge CB2 8RU, UK

Published in the United States of America by Cambridge University Press, New York

www.cambridge.org
Information on this title: www.cambridge.org/9780521515702

First published 2009

Printed in the United Kingdom at the University Press, Cambridge

A catalogue record for this publication is available from the British Library

Library of Congress Cataloguing in Publication data
Perspectives in company law and financial regulation : essays in honour of
Eddy Wymeersch / [edited by] Michel Tison ... [et al.].
p.   cm. – (International corporate law and financial market regulation)
ISBN 978-0-521-51570-2 (hardback)   1. Corporation law.   I. Wymeersch, E.
II. Tison, Michel.   III. Title.   IV. Series.
K1315.P47 2009
346'.066–dc22
2009002692

ISBN 978-0-521-51570-2 hardback

CONTENTS

v

LIST OF CONTRIBUTORS

Paul Krüger Andersen

Paul Krüger Andersen is professor in company law at Aarhus School of Business, University of Aarhus. He holds a PhD in marketing law (1976) and Dr jur. (1997) (studies in Danish corporate group law) and is co-founder of the Nordic Research Network for Company Law and co-founder and editor of the Nordic Journal of Company Law (*Nordisk Tidsskrift for Selskabsret*). Member of the board of the Danish Association of Corporate Governance (DACP). In 2003 he was legal adviser for the Latvian Company Register. In 2004 he was appointed Distinguished Professorial Fellow at the British Institute of International and Comparative Law, London. In 2005 he was appointed Dr h.c. at the Turku School of Economics and Business Administration, Finland. He is chairman of the European Model Company Law Group and author and co-author of several textbooks and numerous articles in Danish and international journals on private law, marketing law, company law and securities law.

Harald Baum

Harald Baum is Senior Research Fellow and Head of the Japan Law Department at the Max Planck Institute for Comparative and International Private Law, Hamburg, Germany. He graduated from Freiburg University and practiced law as a member of the Hamburg bar before joining the Institute in 1985. Dr iuris, Hamburg, 1985; Habilitation, Hamburg 2004. He teaches at the University of Hamburg and is Research Associate at the European Corporate Governance Institute, Brussels. Dr Baum is the Founding Editor of the *Journal of Japanese Law*. In 2005 he served as Visiting Professor at the University of Tokyo. He has authored numerous books and articles on business law, corporate governance, takeovers, and capital markets regulation in Germany, the EU, Japan and the US.

Theodor Baums

Theodor Baums holds an endowed chair for business law at Goethe Universität Frankfurt and is a Director at the Institute for Law and Finance (ILF). His academic career comprises positions at the universities of Bonn; Münster; Osnabrück; Frankfurt/Main (since 2000); visiting professorships at UC Berkeley; Vienna; Stanford/CA; Columbia/ New York and Luxembourg. He has frequently advised public institutions (World Bank; EU Commission; German Federal Parliament and Government) on company and securities market regulation. He was the chairman of the Federal Government's Commission on Corporate Governance and Company Law Reform. Currently he is a member of the advisory boards of the EU Commission (on company law); of the German Capital Markets Supervisory Agency (BAFin); and of the German Accounting Enforcement Agency (DPR); an adviser on corporate governance issues to the Vorstand of the Deutsche Bundesbank; and serves on several boards of private companies. Theo Baums is fellow of the ECGI, a member of the European Model Company Law Group and has written more than 140 books and articles on corporations, civil and antitrust law. He has been awarded the Order of Merit 1st class of the Federal Republic of Germany.

Marco Becht

Marco Becht is a Professor of Finance and Economics at Université Libre de Bruxelles, a Resident Fellow at the European Centre for Advanced Research in Economics and Statistics at ULB and the Executive Director of the European Corporate Governance Institute. Teaching at the ULB, his research currently focuses on law and finance, with particular emphasis on corporate governance. In 2003, he was Visiting Professor at the Saïd Business School, University of Oxford and in 2008 Max Schmidheiny Visiting Professor for Entrepreneurship and Risk at the University of St. Gallen.

He has been instrumental in launching the Transatlantic Corporate Governance Dialogue (TCGD) and is the scientist in charge of the European Corporate Governance Training Network (ECGTN).

Jean Nicolas Druey

Jean Nicolas Druey (born 1937) is an Emeritus of the University of St Gallen (Switzerland) and lives in Basel. He was a student of law at the Universities of Geneva and of Basel and at Harvard Law School. He served in the legal office of the pharmaceutical company of Hoffmann-La Roche 1968–1974 and in the auditing firm known today as Ernst & Young, Zurich branch, 1974–1980 and as a consultant up to the present day. In 1980 he was elected to a teaching chair in the fields of private and commercial law at the University of St Gallen which he held until his retirement in 2000.

His book publications include a thesis on moral damage (1966) and on the right of privacy of enterprises (1976), then books on developments of the law on corporate groups (Zeitschr. f. schweiz. Recht 1980 II), securities (1985, with Jäggi and v. Greyerz), inheritance law (1986, 1988, 1992, 1997, 2002, next edition due in spring 2009), Swiss commercial law (in the context of the law of obligations treatise by Guhl, 1991, 1995, 2000, next edition due in 2009), information as a subject of law (1995) and on Swiss court practice in matters of corporate groups (1999). All books are in German.

He served from 1991 to 2000 on the board of the Swiss Association of Jurists, 1997 to 2000 as chairman.

Luca Enriques

Luca Enriques joined the Faculty of Law at the University of Bologna in 1999. A Full Professor there since 2007, he is now on leave to serve as a Commissioner at Consob (the Italian SEC). Before entering academia, Professor Enriques worked for the Bank of Italy in Rome. He has published two books and several articles in Italian as well as international law reviews on topics relating to corporate law, corporate governance, takeovers, institutional investors and corporate groups. He has been adviser to the Italian Ministry of Economy and Finance from 2000 to 2006 and, from 2005 to 2007, a member of the Forum of Market Experts on Auditors' Liability set up by the European Commission.

Eilís Ferran

Professor Eilís Ferran is Professor of Company and Securities Law at the University of Cambridge and co-director of the University's Centre for Corporate and Commercial Law (3CL). Her recent publications include *Principles of Corporate Finance Law* (OUP, 2008) and *Building an EU Securities Market* (CUP, 2004), as well as numerous articles and other pieces. She has been a visiting professor in Hong Kong and New Zealand and has spoken at conferences in Europe, Asia and North America. She is an editor of the *Journal of Corporate Law Studies* (Hart Publishing), a contributing editor of *Palmer's Company Law* (Sweet & Maxwell, looseleaf) and a research associate of the European Corporate Governance Institute. She is Series Editor (with Professor Niamh Moloney and Professor Howell Jackson) of the Cambridge University Press monograph series *International Corporate Law and Capital Market Regulation*.

Guido Ferrarini

Guido Ferrarini graduated from the Genoa Law School in 1972, and obtained an LL.M. from Yale Law School in 1978. He is Professor of Business Law at the University of Genoa and Director, Centre for Law and Finance.

He is Independent Director of Atlantia s.p.a. and Chairman of TLX (an Italian MTF and investment exchange). He is Vice-Chairman of the European Corporate Governance Institute (ECGI), Brussels.

He was Lead Independent Director of Telecom Italia s.p.a. and a member of the Board of Trustees of the International Accounting Standards Committee (IASC), London.

He is the author of various books and articles in the fields of financial law, corporate law and business law. He was a Visiting Professor at Bonn University (Graduate College of European Law), Columbia Law School, Frankfurt University (Institute for Law and Finance), Hamburg University (Law Faculty), NYU Law School and University College London (Faculty of Laws).

Stefan Grundmann

Professor Dr Stefan Grundmann LL.M. has been Professor at Humboldt University, Berlin, for German, European and International Private and Business Law since 2004. He heads the Institute for banking and capital market law and is the deputy of the faculty for the European Law School. From 1995 to 2001 and 2001 to 2004 he was professor for the same subjects at Halle-Wittenberg and at Erlangen, where he initiated and was responsible for study courses on International Business Law.

After studies in Munich, Aix-en-Provence, Lausanne, Lisbon and Berkeley he wrote a dissertation on the basic theme 'Qualification' (1985). He then concentrated on conflicts of law within integrated markets (Common Market). Today he specializes in the areas of business law, banking and capital market law, and European contract and private law, always including interdisciplinary aspects. He is the author of various books in all of these areas: 'Fiduciary Relationships' (1997); 'European Bank Supervisory Law' (1990); 'European Contract Law' (1999, 2009); 'European Company Law' including Capital Market Law (2nd edn in 2007). He also wrote numerous papers and commentaries on about half of the banking laws for the large Commentary Ebenroth/ Boujong/Joost (2001 and 2008). Professor Grundmann also founded the Society of European Contract Law (SECOLA). Since 2005 he is editor-in-chief of the *European Review of Contract Law*. Stefan Grundmann also studied philosophy and the history of art and has written three books in this area.

Jesper Lau Hansen

Jesper Lau Hansen was educated as a lawyer (Candidatus Juris) at the University of Copenhagen, Denmark, in 1989 and as a Master of Law (LL.M.) from the University of Cambridge in 1993. He worked for six years for a major law firm, where he was admitted to the appeals court bar in 1992. He returned to the University of Copenhagen in 1995, where he became Doctor Juris in 2001 on a dissertation on the regulation of information in stock exchange law. He has held the chair of Professor in Financial Markets Law since 2003. He is currently serving as the head of the research centre FOCOFIMA at the University of Copenhagen Law Faculty. Further information is available at www.jur. ku.dk/jlh.

Douglas W. Hawes

Retired from Dewey & LeBoeuf LLP, international law firm in 2005, where he specialized in mergers and acquisitions and other corporate and securities matters. He became a partner in 1964 and was based in the New York office. During part of that time he taught full time at Vanderbilt University School of Law from 1972–4 and as an adjunct there and later at New York University School of Law until 1989 when he moved to France. Author of *Utility Holding Companies* (1985, Clark Boardman) and numerous law review articles.

Douglas Hawes is currently involved in non-fiction writing and venture capital. He published *Oradour – The Final Verdict* (2007) in English; to be published in French in 2009 by Editions de Seuil.

Peter Hommelhoff

Professor Dr Dres. h.c. Peter Hommelhoff (born 1942) was Director of the Institute of German and European Corporate and Economic Law at the University of Heidelberg from 1991 until his retirement in 2007. During his last years at the University of Heidelberg he also served as its Rector (Chancellor) and was executive director of the Association of German-speaking Civil Law Instructors. Before his time at the University, Hommelhoff served as judge at the Higher Regional Court of Hamm/Westphalia and later in Karlsruhe. Over several decades he was a member of the board of examiners for certified accountants in North Rhine-Westphalia and Baden-Wuerttemberg. He is honorary doctor of the universities of Krakow and Montpellier and a member of the Chilean Academy of Sciences. Hommelhoff was awarded the German Federal Cross of Merit in 2007.

Klaus J. Hopt

Director Max Planck Institute for Private Law, Hamburg/Germany; formerly professor of law Tübingen, Florence, Bern, Munich. Professional: Judge Court of Appeals Stuttgart 1981–5; member of: High Level Group of Company Law Experts, board of the ECGI; vice-president of the German Research Foundation; expert: German Parliament, European Commission, BIS, World Bank. Visiting prof.: Paris, Rome, Brussels (ULB), Tilburg, Chicago, NYU, Harvard, Kyoto, Tokyo. (Co-)Author: *Corporate Group Law for Europe*, 2000; *Anatomy of Corporate Law*, 2004. (Co-)Ed.: *Comparative Corporate Governance,* 1998; *Capital Markets and Company Law*, 2003; *Reforming Company and Takeover Law*, 2004; *Corporate Governance in Context*, 2005 (all Oxford and together with Wymeersch). Honors: Dr iur. h.c. mult. (U. Libre de Bruxelles 1997, U. Catholique de Louvain 1997, Paris Descartes 2000, Athens 2007). Various prizes.

Howell E. Jackson

Howell Jackson is the James S. Reid, Jr, Professor of Law at Harvard Law School. His research interests include financial regulation, international finance and consumer protection. He is a member of the National Academy on Social Insurance, a trustee of the College Retirement Equities Fund (CREF) and its affiliated TIAA-CREF investment companies, a member of the panel of outside scholars for the NBER Retirement Research Center, and a senior editor for Cambridge University Press Series on International Corporate Law and Financial Regulation. Professor Jackson was a law clerk for Associate Justice Thurgood Marshall and practiced law in Washington, DC. Professor Jackson received JD and MBA degrees from Harvard University in 1982 and a BA from Brown University in 1976.

Hideki Kanda

Professor of Law at the University of Tokyo, Japan. His main areas of specialization include commercial law, corporate law, banking regulation and securities regulation. Mr Kanda served as Visiting Professor of Law at the University of Chicago Law School in 1989, 1991, 1993 and 2006 and Visiting Professor at Harvard Law School in 1996.

Roberta S. Karmel

Roberta S. Karmel is Centennial Professor of Law and Co-Director of the Dennis J. Block Center for the Study of International Business Law at Brooklyn Law School. She was engaged in the private practice of law in New York City for over thirty years at Willkie Farr & Gallagher, Rogers & Wells, and Kelley Drye & Warren. She was a Commissioner of the Securities and Exchange Commission from 1977–80, a public director of the New York Stock Exchange, Inc. from 1983–9, and a member of the National Adjudicatory Council of the NASDR from 1998–2001.

She received a BA cum laude from Radcliffe College in 1959 and an LLB cum laude from New York University School of Law in 1962.

Professor Karmel is a Trustee of the Practising Law Institute. She is Co-Chair of the International Coordinating Committee of the Section of Business Law of the American Bar Association and a member of the Advisory Committee on capital markets law to Unidroit, a member of the American Law Institute, a Fellow of the American Bar Foundation, and on the Boards of Advisors of Securities Regulation and Law Report, The Review of Securities and Commodities Regulation, and the World Securities Law Report. She was a Fulbright Scholar in 1991–2.

Professor Karmel is the author of over fifty articles in books and legal journals, and writes a regular column on securities regulation for the *New York Law Journal*. She is a frequent lecturer on financial regulation. Her book entitled *Regulation by Prosecution: The Securities and Exchange Commission vs. Corporate America* was published by Simon and Schuster in 1982.

Veronika E. Korom

Veronika E. Korom, dr iur. (Budapest), lic. droit (Aix-Marseille), MJur (Oxford), LLB is a PhD candidate at the Centre de Droit Economique (Aix-Marseille), member of the START-Project II 'Legal Evolution – European Company Law Harmonisation' at the Vienna University of Economics and Business Administration and trainee solicitor at Clifford Chance LLP, London.

Friedrich Kübler

Studied law and history in Tübingen, Lausanne, Reading/Berks. and Bonn. Teaching assistent in Tübingen and Paris. In 1961 doctor iuris and 1966 Habilitation in Tübingen. Professor of law in Giessen (1966–71), Konstanz (1971–6) and Frankfurt (since 1976, emeritus since 1998). In 1968 visiting lecturer Harvard Law School; 1975 and 1982 visiting professor Pennsylvania Law School; since 1985 Professor of Law at Penn. In 1973–86 member of the Board of Deutsche Gesellschaft für Rechtsvergleichung; 1974–86 member of the board of Deutscher Juristentag. 1997–2003 member of the (German) Commission for the Assessment of Concentration in the Broadasting Industry. In 1998–2006 counsel Clifford Chance, Frankfurt am Main. Member of the American Law Institute, of the European Shadow Financial Regulatory Committee and of the Frankfurt Academy of Sciences. Areas of interest and research: contracts and property, corporations and securities regulation, banking and international finance, mass media, comparative law, modern legal history, law and economics.

Donald C. Langevoort

Donald C. Langevoort is the Thomas Aquinas Reynolds Professor of Law at Georgetown University Law Center, Washington, DC. He joined the Georgetown faculty in 1999 after eighteen years at Vanderbilt University School of Law, where he had been the Lee S. & Charles A. Speir Professor. He has also been a visiting professor at the University of Michigan, Harvard Law School and the University of Sydney in Australia. Professor Langevoort graduated from the Harvard Law School in 1976, and went into private practice with the law firm of Wilmer, Cutler & Pickering in Washington. Later, he joined the staff of the US Securities & Exchange Commission as Special Counsel in the Office of the General Counsel, where he served until 1981.

Ruben Lee

Ruben Lee is the CEO and Founder of the Oxford Finance Group, a research and consulting firm which concentrates on business, economic, legal, regulatory and strategic aspects of financial markets. From 1989 to 1992, Dr Lee was a Fellow of Nuffield College, Oxford University, where he specialized in financial economics and law. He worked from 1980 to 1984 in the capital markets in New York and London for Salomon Brothers International. Dr Lee has published widely on many topics concerning financial markets, including exchanges, clearing and settlement, and EU securities regulation. He is the author of the book *What is an Exchange? The Automation, Management, and Regulation, of Financial Markets*, and is currently leading a project on the governance of market infrastructure institutions. Ruben Lee is a member of the Conseil Scientifique of the Autorité des Marchés Financiers in France, and was previously on the Advisory Panel of Financial Services Experts, established by the Economics and Monetary Affairs Committee, European Parliament.

Marcus Lutter

Born 1930 in Munich, Prof. Dr Dr h.c. mult. Marcus Lutter got his PhD from the University of Freiburg and his Habilitation from the University of Mainz. He was then Professor for German and European Company Law at the University of Bochum and later at the University of Bonn. He is now speaker of the Centre for European Economic Law at the University of Bonn. He received a Doctor honoris causa from the Wirtschaftsuniversität Wien, the University of Warszawa and the University of Jena.

Joseph A. McCahery

Joseph A. McCahery is Professor of Corporate Governance and Innovation at the University of Amsterdam Faculty of Economics and Econometrics and Professor of Financial Market Regulation at Tilburg University Faculty of Law and the Tilburg Law and Economics Centre. He is co-director of the Amsterdam Centre for Corporate Finance and a Research Associate of the European Corporate Governance Institute.

Michel Menjucq

Professor at the University of Paris 1 Panthéon-Sorbonne since 2000 and Director of the center of research 'Sorbonne-affairs'. Doctor in International and European Company Law, he is the author of books on *La mobilité des sociétés dans l'espace européen* (LGDJ, 1997), *Droit international et européen des sociétés* (Précis Domat, Montchrestien, 2nd edn, 2008) and also has directed a book on *Droit du commerce international* (Traité Litec, 2005). His recently published articles in European journals include 'Regulation no 1346/2000 on Insolvency Proceedings and the groups of companies' (*ECFR,* June 2008, 135*),* and 'The European company under French Law : main features' (with Fages and Vuidard, *EBOR* 9(1), 2008, 137*).*

Hanno Merkt

Professor of Law and Director of the Institute for Foreign Law and International Private Law at the University of Freiburg i. Br., Germany and Judge at the Court of Appeals of Karlsruhe. He received law degrees from the University of Bonn, the University of Chicago, the University of Münster i.Westf. (doctor iuris) and the University of Hamburg. In 1990 he was admitted to the New York Bar. He teaches German, European and international commercial and corporate law and securities regulation. He is author of various books, commentaries and articles on German commercial, company and accounting law as well as on American law of corporations. He is also co-editor of the *European Company and Financial Law Review* (*ECFR*) and various other business law journals.

Niamh Moloney

Niamh Moloney is Professor of Capital Markets Law at the University of Nottingham; from January 2009 she is Professor of Financial Markets Law at the London School of Economics. She is a graduate of Trinity College Dublin and Harvard Law School. Her research field is EC company law and securities regulation and her major publications include *EC Securities Regulation*, OUP, 2nd edn 2008. She is a board member of the *European Business Organisation Law Review*, a Series Editor of the Cambridge University Press Series on *International Corporate Law and Capital Market Regulation*, Consultant Editor on EC Company Law to D. Vaughan and A. Robertson (eds), *Encyclopedia of EC Law* (OUP), and consultant editor on corporations and finance and investment to the *New Oxford Companion to Law* (OUP).

Peter O. Mülbert

Professor of Corporation Law, Securities Law and Banking Law, and Director of the Centre for German and International Law of Financial Services, Johannes Gutenberg-Universität, Mainz; Member, Panel of Financial Services Experts of the Committee on Economic and Monetary Affairs of the European Parliament; Member, Administrative Protest Committee of the Federal Financial Supervisory Authority; Research Fellow, European Corporate Governance Institute; Member, Management Board of 'Bankrechtliche Vereinigung e.V – wissenschaftliche Gesellschaft für Bankrecht e.V.'; Co-Editor, 'Zeitschrift für das gesamte Handelsrecht und Wirtschaftsrecht', Co-Editor, 'Neue Zeitschrift für Gesellschaftsrecht'; Member, Advisory Board of 'Wertpapiermitteilungen'; 1976, Universities of Tübingen and Genf; 1984, PhD Degree in Law, University of Tübingen; 1994, Habilitation, University of München; 1994, Professor of Law, Universities of Heidelberg, Trier and Mainz; books and articles in the area of corporation law, groups of corporation, capital market law, banking law.

Peter Nobel

Prof. Dr rer. publ., Attorney at Law in Zurich since 1980 (own law firm since 1982); Professor for Private, Trade and Commercial Law at the University of St. Gallen since 1984. Professor in ordinary ad personam for Swiss and International Trade and Commercial Law at the University of Zurich since March 2007. Substitute judge at the Court of Commerce of the Canton of Zurich since 1998; member of the Swiss Federal Banking Commission 1988 until 2000. Frequently appointed as arbitrator or mediator in international and domestic arbitration; various assignments as chairman. Editor-in-chief of the Swiss Review of Business and Financial Market Law since 1995; co-editor of Jusletter. Author to numerous publications in various legal areas of commercial law and litigations.

Dan Prentice

Allen & Overy Professor of Corporate Law, University of Oxford; Fellow of Pembroke College; author of various texts and articles on company law, insolvency and the law relating to financial markets; barrister, Erskine Chambers, Lincoln's Inn.

André Prüm

Nominated professor of the French universities in 1995, André Prüm joined the University of Luxembourg in 2005 where he holds the chair in financial and business law. He is also visiting professor at the University of Paris 1 Panthéon-Sorbonne and Paris 2 Panthéon-Assas teaching European banking and financial law. In 1996, he created the Laboratory of Economic Law in Luxembourg that has contributed to the preparation of several draft bills in the field of company law, the law of trust and fiduciary contracts, the law on securitization, competition law, the law of electronic commerce and others. In October 2005, André Prüm was elected Dean of the Faculty of Law, Economics and Finance of the University of Luxembourg. His teaching and research activities are enriched by his work as an adviser and arbitrator.

Theo Raaijmakers

Theo Raaijmakers is professor of the law on business organizations (Tilburg University) since 1986 and director of its Center for Company

Law. Until 2001 he was also Legal Adviser to Royal Philips Electronics NV and Executive Vice President of Philips International. Other functions *inter alia*: part-time judge District Court Den Bosch (1980–93), part-time Justice Court of Appeals Arnhem (since 1994), Chairman Netherlands Association of Corporate Lawyers (1985–89), chairman UNICE Committee Company Law (1982–97), chairman Advisory Committee on Modernization of Bankruptcy Law, member Committee on Capital Markets of Netherlands Autoriteit Financiële Markten. PhD thesis was on character and group relationships of joint ventures. Other publications: books and articles on corporate reorganizations, partnerships, corporate governance, securities law and a major comment on Netherlands law on business organizations.

Jonathan Rickford

Jonathan Rickford has been Visiting Professor in European corporate law at the London School of Economics since 2003.

He was: Project Director of the UK's independent Review of Company Law in 1998–2001; a member of the Commission's High Level Group ('Winter' Group) on company law in 2001–2 and Unilever Professor at Leiden in 2002.

He has also been: a member of the UK Competition Commission (1997–2004); successively Chief Legal Adviser, and Director of Regulation and Corporate Strategy with British Telecommunications plc (1987–96); and in the UK Government Legal Service (1972–87), including Head of Company Law and Solicitor (General Counsel) to the Department of Trade and Industry. From 1968–72 he taught at Berkeley (California) and the London School of Economics.

Mark J. Roe

Mark J. Roe teaches corporate law and corporate bankruptcy at Harvard Law School. He wrote *Strong Managers, Weak Owners: The Political Roots of American Corporate Finance* (Princeton, 1994), *Political Determinants of Corporate Governance* (Oxford, 2003), and *Bankruptcy and Corporate Reorganization* (2nd edn, Foundation Press, 2007). Recent articles include 'Legal Origins, Politics, and Modern Stock Markets', *Harvard Law Review* 120, 460 (2006), 'Regulatory Competition in Making Corporate Law in the United States – And Its Limits', *Oxford Review of Economic Policy* 21, 232 (2005), 'Delaware's Politics', *Harvard Law Review* 118, 2491

(2005), 'The Inevitable Instability of American Corporate Governance', in American Academy of Arts and Sciences (eds), *Restoring Trust in American Business* (MIT Press, 2004), 'Delaware's Competition', *Harvard Law Review* 117, 588 (2003), and 'Corporate Law's Limits', *Journal of Legal Studies* 31, 233 (2002).

Marie-Claude Robert Hawes

Marie-Claude Robert Hawes served at the French Commission des Operations de Bourse (current title Autorité des Marchés Financiers) from April 1968 to November 2000: Section head of the Legal Department (1968–79); Deputy head of the Research Department 1979–85); Head of the International and Public Relations Department (1985–91); Head of the Public Relations Department (1991–97); First Mediator appointed by the Commission (1997–2000).

She was Adjunct Professor, University of Paris School of Law (II) (1979–91) and Associate member of the International Faculty for Capital Markets and Corporate Law (1976–95).

She is currently a member of the Consultative Committee of the Autorité des Marchés Financiers on Protection of Investors.

Honours : Knight of the Order of Legion d'Honneur, January 2000.

Wolfgang Schön

Wolfgang Schön is since 2002 a Director at the Max Planck Institute for Intellectual Property, Competition and Tax Law (Department of Accounting and Taxation) in Munich and Honorary Professor at Munich University. He was appointed Anton Philips Professor at Tilburg/NL University's Centre for Company Law for the Academic Year 2004/2005 and was invited to join the Global Law Faculty at NYU in 2006. Since 2008 he has served as Vice-President of the Max Planck Society.

Joëlle Simon

Juris Doctor (*magna cum laude*), Paris II University – 1982; Director for Legal Affairs, MEDEF – French Business Confederation; *Chevalier, Ordre National du Mérite (France)*. Member of the Advisory Group on Corporate Governance and Company Law (since May 2005); Member of the High Level Group of Company Law Experts, European Commission (2001–2); Member of the technical committees of the VIENOT (1999) and BOUTON Committees (2002) on corporate governance.; Member of the Commission on 'Landmine destruction' (CNEMA /OTTAWA Convention) (1999–2005); Vice-chairperson, Company Affairs Committee, UNICE (1997–2001); Member of the French Economic & Social Committee (1989–91, 1995–97); Member of the Unfair Trading Terms Committee (1992–3); General Secretary of the French Association of Business Lawyers (until 1993).

Levinus Timmerman

Levinus Timmerman was professor in commercial law and company law at the University of Groningen in the Netherlands. He is since 2003 advocate-general with the Dutch Supreme Court and professor in the principles of company law at the Erasmus University in Rotterdam. He was editor-in-chief of the Dutch periodical *Ondernemingsrecht* and acts as chairman of the Dutch commission on company law.

John Vella

John Vella is Norton Rose Career Development Fellow in Company Law at the Faculty of Law, University of Oxford. He first studied law at the University of Malta, obtaining a BA and an LLD. He was admitted to the Maltese bar and practised briefly. He then obtained an LLM and a PhD from the University of Cambridge. He has been a visiting researcher at the Oxford University Centre for Business Taxation and has acted as a co-arbitrator on a tax dispute before the ICC International Court of Arbitration. His main research interests and publications are in corporate finance and tax law. At Oxford, he teaches company law, corporate finance law, EC law and Roman law.

Erik P. M. Vermeulen

Erik Vermeulen is Professor of Financial Market Regulation at the Tilburg Law and Economics Centre (TILEC) and Professor of Law and Management at Tilburg University Faculty of Law. He teaches corporate law, corporate finance, corporate acquisitions and joint ventures. He has written articles on a variety of subjects in corporate law, corporate governance, securities regulation, and private equity and venture capital contracts. Erik Vermeulen is also a vice-president at the corporate legal department of Philips International B.V. in the Netherlands. He is the author of *The Evolution of Legal Business Forms in Europe and the United States* (Kluwer, 2003) and co-author of *The Corporate Governance of Non-Listed Companies* (Oxford University Press, 2008).

Rebekka M. Wiemann

As a fellow of the German National Academic Foundation, Rebecca Wiemann studied law at the Universities of Passau (Germany), Concepción (Chile) and Mainz (Germany), where she graduated in 2006. In 2006–7 she worked as a research assistant with Professor Peter O. Muelbert (University of Mainz). Currently she is pursuing her legal clerkship (German Referendariat) at the European Commission in Brussels. Her academic and professional focus is on international economic law and European law.

Jaap Winter

Jaap Winter is partner at the law firm De Brauw Blackstone Westbroek in Amsterdam. His practice areas include mergers and acquisitions, corporate governance and corporate litigation. He is also Professor of International Company Law at the University of Amsterdam and visiting professor at Columbia Law School in New York.

He was chairman of the High Level Group of Company Law Experts set up in 2001 by the European Commission to advise it on a modern regulatory framework for company law in Europe. The Group in January 2002 first advised on issues related to takeover bids. The final report of the Group on a Modern Regulatory Framework for Company Law in Europe (November 2002) was the basis for the Commission's Company Law Action Plan.

He was a member of the Dutch Corporate Governance Committee, chaired by Morris Tabaksblat, that has drafted the Dutch Corporate Governance Code of December 2003.

Jaap Winter is a member of the European Corporate Governance Forum set up by the European Commission in 2004 to advise it on corporate governance developments in Europe. He received the 2004 International Corporate Governance Award from the International Corporate Governance Network. He is also a member of the Supervisory Board of the Dutch securities regulator AFM.

FOREWORD

The wide-ranging content of this book can be seen as a reflection of the academic career of the person it is dedicated to, Eddy Wymeersch. After receiving a Law degree at Ghent University in Belgium and a Master of Laws degree at Harvard Law School in the USA, Eddy Wymeersch ventured into academia as an assistant to Professor Jean Limpens at Ghent University. He briefly worked for the Belgian banking supervisor, then called Banking Commission, but soon left, only to return as the chair of its executive committee in 2001. In 1972 he was appointed professor at the newly established University of Antwerp. In 1984 he returned to his alma mater, Ghent University, to remain there until his retirement in 2008. At Ghent University, Wymeersch and his colleague Guy Schrans founded the Financial Law Institute in 1990, as a research center but also as a forum where (Belgian) academics and practitioners can meet to discuss new developments in company and financial law. Professor Wymeersch is still a source of inspiration to all members of the Institute and we all hope he will continue to stimulate younger members with his direct and critical but always constructive comments.

Speaking and/or reading Dutch, English, French, German and Italian and, being from little, outward-looking Belgium, Wymeersch has always closely monitored legal developments internationally, both in Europe and the USA, at a time when many were only interested in the technical intricacies of their national legal systems. This partly explains his exceptionally good nose for what would become the topics of future legal research in European company and financial law. He was a pioneer in many fields related to securities, corporate and banking law. In the 1970s the European Commission charged him with a seminal study on "The Control of the Securities Markets in the European Community" (published in 1978). Hardly anything had been written on the topic at that time, but Eddy Wymeersch revealed a wealth of important issues, many of which were only dealt with in European regulation at the start of the twenty-first century, by which time he had become the chairman of the Committee of European Securities Regulators (CESR). He established contact with Klaus Hopt and together they would embark on a series of groundbreaking conferences, which were always accompanied by important and widely consulted conference volumes and which brought together many of the leading, internationally minded scholars in areas such as banking, securities and corporate law from across Europe and the USA. The first two such conferences dealt with Insider dealing and takeover bids in Europe. Later Guido Ferrarini would transform the couple into a triumvirate of close friends. They would continue to meet each other in various fora and locations. The award of the prestigious Max Planck Research Prize in 1998 enabled Eddy Wymeersch to fund some of the later conferences. Other fora, such as the International Faculty for Corporate Law and Securities Regulation, or the Forum Europaeum, which worked on principles of group law, were equally productive in terms of academic output.

In 1992 Eddy Wymeersch spoke about corporate governance at Cambridge, at a (still just pre-Cadbury) time when hardly any scholar, board member or institutional investor on the Continent had heard about the concept. He would soon start spreading the gospel, leading to him more or less single-handedly writing the Belgian Corporate Governance Act of 2002, being involved in the drafting of every official Belgian corporate governance Code for listed companies and being chosen as a member of the European Corporate Governance Forum. At that time he already had years of consulting for, among others, the IMF and World Bank behind him, which had given him the opportunity to advise several eastern European states on the introduction of stock exchange regulation and other aspects of what was for these countries, in the immediate aftermath of the fall of the Berlin Wall, the new capitalist system of funding companies. Eddy Wymeersch also chaired the European SLIM-working group (which stands for Simpler Legislation for the Internal Market) that had a significant impact on the modernization and simplification of the First and Second Company Law Directives related to legal capital and disclosure.

For European legal academics under 45 years old who write in English – still a small but rapidly expanding minority – some knowledge of basic law and economics concepts is self-evident. This was certainly not always the case, and Wymeersch was an early, although always cautious enthusiast of the movement and even more of purely economic literature and attention to empirical data. For Professor Wymeersch, multidisciplinarity is essential for the legal scholar: legal research must be open to other disciplines like economics and even politics. But one should avoid meta-analysis of rules without first familiarizing oneself with their often important technical details, and think twice about developing grand theoretical schemes that stand no chance whatsoever of being applied to real world situations. He also force-fed the *Financial Times*, the *Economist* and *Harvard Business Review* to anyone who wanted to write a doctoral thesis under his guidance – and being prepared to write a PhD was a requirement if you wanted to become a full-time researcher at the Financial Law Institute. Another requirement was learning enough German to understand the German literature that is often two or three years ahead of the rest of Europe. Not a year went by in which Eddy Wymeersch did not visit at least two or three German universities and academic conferences and from the beginning of the 1990s onwards he published more in German and other foreign journals than in Belgian ones, turning him into one of the most downloaded European authors on SSRN and making some junior Belgian colleagues wonder whether he was actually truly Belgian. Anyone familiar with Eddy Wymeersch knew, though, that for him an international outlook had never been incompatible with an interest in local developments. On the contrary, awareness of what was going on elsewhere seemed to him to be essential if one wanted to intervene in a useful way in national debates. In his fare-well speech at the academic session organized to mark his official retire-ment as a professor at Ghent Law School in October 2008, he expressed his worries about the decline of the knowledge of French among Flemish professionals, including academics. It would prevent them, he warned, from performing the bridge function his generation had tried to play between the "Germanic" and "Latin" worlds of northern and southern Europe – worlds that meet in places like Brussels, 50 kilometers from Ghent.

While his roots and interests are certainly in the academic sphere, Eddy Wymeersch never limited his academic research to a purely dog-matic, positivist dissection of texts, as is still rather common in Europe. After he had given a solid foundation to his academic career, Wymeersch placed his knowledge and insights at the disposal of practice and policy: to name only a few of them, he was appointed to the Belgian Council of State (which vets Bills before they are introduced into Parliament); became a member of the board of Governors of the National Bank of Belgium; chairman of the board of BIAC, the national airport com-pany; chairman of the executive committee of the Belgian banking and securities supervisor, which he transformed into the Belgian Banking,

Finance and Insurance Commission (CBFA) by incorporating the previously independent insurance supervisor; followed by the chairmanship of the supervisory board of this CBFA. In 2007 he was elected as chairman of the Committee of Securities Regulators (CESR).

This book is dedicated to Eddy Wymeersch. It was accompanied by an international conference, 'Perspectives in Company Law and Financial Regulation', held in December 2008 in Ghent in honour of Eddy Wymeersch. This conference was an attempt by Eddy Wymeersch's successors at Ghent Law School to emulate the success of the Siena and Syracuse conferences and to fruitfully combine intellectual work and food for thought in an atmosphere of friendship.

This collection of essays is the result of the collective effort of Eddy Wymeersch's main academic peers and friends worldwide. We are extremely grateful to every one of the contributors for having freed scarce time to participate in this tribute to Eddy Wymeersch. Eilis Ferran, Howell Jackson and Niamh Moloney kindly hosted the collection of essays in the *International Corporate Law and Financial Market Regulation* series they edit at Cambridge University Press. We are also grateful to the publishers at Cambridge University Press, notably Kim Hughes and Richard Woodham, and to Jamie Hood at Out of House Publishing Solutions for their relentless efforts and patience through all the productions stages of this volume. Finally, the assistance of the researchers at the Financial Law Institute (Filip Bogaert, Diederik Bruloot, Isabel Coppens, Wendy Dammans, Sarah De Geyter, Delphine Goens, Evelyne Hellebuyck,, Kristof Maresceau, Sara Pauwels, Fran Ravelingien and Lientje Van Den Steen), and of its secretariat (Nicolle Kransfeld and Annelies Rademaker) in the editing and proof-reading of the manuscripts was critical in meeting the production deadlines.

The more than 30 contributions in this volume highlight a wide range of current issues in company law and financial regulation in various jurisdictions, both in Europe, the USA and Japan. Most contributions were finalized during Spring 2008, and could not, therefore, incorporate the most recent market and regulatory developments that have characterized the current financial crisis since the second semester of 2008. We hope this volume will provide some more inspiration for future research to Eddy's no doubt already overflowing list of things to do once CESR and officialdom give him back some time – although we will not stop him if he prefers to take his cue from Voltaire and dedicate himself to the most civilized of all tasks, tending his magnificent garden – where he also produces some of the most red and fleshy tomatoes north of the Alps.

We wish Eddy Wymeersch all the luck for his future activities and other new inspiring challenges and ventures. We also hope and are convinced he will continue to spend some of his valuable time to share his views, ideas and inspiration with the Financial Law Institute at Ghent.

Hans De Wulf
Reinhard Steennot
Michel Tison
Christoph Van der Elst

PART I

Perspectives in company law

SECTION 1

European company law:
regulatory competition and free
movement of companies

1

The European Model Company Act Project

THEODOR BAUMS AND
PAUL KRÜGER ANDERSEN

I. Introduction

On 27 and 28 September 2007, a commission formed on the initiative of the authors[1] held its first meeting in Aarhus, Denmark to deliberate on its goal of drafting a European Model Company Act (EMCA). This project, outlined in the following pages, aims neither to force a mandatory harmonization of national company law nor to create a further, European corporate form. The goal is rather to draft model rules for a corporation that national legislatures would be free to adopt in whole or in part. Thus, the project is thought of as an alternative and supplement to the existing EU instruments for the convergence of company law. The present EU instruments, their prerequisites and limits will be discussed in more detail in Part II, below. Part III will examine the US experience with such 'model acts' in the area of company law. Part IV will then conclude by discussing several topics concerning the content of an EMCA, introducing the members of the EMCA Working Group, and explaining the Group's preliminary working plan.

---

[1] See P. Krüger Andersen, 'Regulation or Deregulation in European Company Law – a Challenge', in U. Bernitz (ed.), *Modern Company Law for a European Economy – Ways and Means*, (Stockholm: Norstedts Juridik Förlag, 2006), 263 *et seq.*; T. Baums, 'The law of corporate finance in Europe – an essay', *Nordic Company Law*, 31 (2008), *et seq.*; also see Ebke's earlier proposal to set up a 'European Law Institute' modelled on the American Law Institute in order to draft a European Model Company Law Statute; W. Ebke, 'Unternehmensrechtsangleichung in der Europäischen Union', in *Festschrift für B. Großfeld*, (Heidelberg: Recht und Wirtschaft, 1999), 189, 212 *et seq.*, and J. Wouters, 'European Company Law: Quo Vadis?', *Common Market Law Review*, 37 (2000), 257–307, especially 298.

II. European company law legislation: traditional instruments and a new tool

A. *The limits of European company law legislation*

Until now, the European Union has employed three tools to ensure that the legal rules in the area of company law are compatible with the goal of a functioning internal market: first, the *harmonization of national company law* through directives adopted under art. 44(2)(g) Treaty Establishing the European Community (EC Treaty) that national legislatures must implement; second, the *creation* of new *supranational organizational forms* on the basis of art. 308 EC Treaty, forms which exist alongside their national counterparts as alternative vehicles for companies; and third, the *judicial policing of national company law under the right of free establishment* (arts. 43 and 48 EC Treaty) as performed by the European Court of Justice (ECJ), which in a series of landmark decisions since 1999 – among them the well-known *Centros*, *Überseering* and *Inspire Art* cases – has rejected a number of national limitations and thus triggered a 'regulatory competition' among national corporate laws, the results of which are not yet foreseeable.

Each of these methods of structuring the law has its own prerequisites and conditions of application – which here will be mentioned only summarily[2] – that make supplementation through a uniform, albeit non-mandatory, European Model Company Act both meaningful and desirable.

Harmonization by means of directives is understood as a technique for achieving less than full unity of law and is subject to the Treaty condition that the measure be implemented only if and to the extent required for reaching the goal of a common market (arts. 3(1)(h) and 44(2)(g) EC Treaty). This approximation of laws presupposes the existence of a variety of individual national legal systems that will continue to exist, and also of diverse, possible legal solutions. As a form of 'harmonization *lite*', it seeks merely to ensure that each member state enacts provisions that do not disrupt the internal market. Beyond that floor, each member state remains free to shape its company law in any way it chooses, provided the result conforms to the minimum needs of the Union. Although this

---

[2] See the detailed discussion by C. Teichmann, *Binnenmarktkonformes Gesellschaftsrecht* (Berlin: de Gruyter Recht, 2006), pp. 73 *et seq.*, and e.g. K. Engsig Sørensen and P. Runge Nielsen, *EU-retten*, (Copenhagen: Jurist- og Økonomforbundets Forlag, 2004), 675 *et seq.*

solution effectively allows the use of 'states as laboratories' to develop competing corporate models[3] and helps counteract a petrification of a status quo reached by centrally developed norms,[4] beyond the minimally harmonized area a basic tension remains with the expectations of corporations operating on a European scale, which rather ask for standardization of operating rules and seek uniformity in laws on investor protection and the disclosure of information, so as to reduce their information and transaction costs.

Supranational organizational forms like the European Company (SE), the European Co-operative (ECS) or the European Economic Interest Grouping (EEIG) would only meet these needs if the statutes of the individual member states in which they are based had substantially similar content. This is a condition that the current state of affairs does not meet, given that the statutes creating supranational entities contain

---

[3] For a detailed discussion of competition between legislatures, *see* E. M. Kieninger, *Wettbewerb der Privatrechtsordnungen im Europäischen Binnenmarkt*, (Tübingen: Mohr Siebeck, 2002); K. Heine, *Regulierungswettbewerb im Gesellschaftsrecht*, (Berlin: Duncker & Humblot, 2003); Teichmann, *Binnenmarktkonformes Gesellschaftsrecht*, (note 2, above), 330 *et seq.*; J. Armour, 'Who should make Corporate Law? EC Legislation versus Regulatory Competition', *ECGI- Law Working Paper*, 54 (2005), available at http://ssrn.com/abstract=860444; J. Andersson, 'Competition between Member States as Corporate Legislator', in U. Bernitz (ed.), *Modern Company Law for a European Economy – Ways and Means* (Stockholm: Norstedts Juridik Förlag, 2006), 143 *et seq.*; H. Søndergård Birkmose, 'Regulatory Competition and the European Harmonisation Process', *European Business Law Review*, 17 (2006), 1079–97. The discussion on competition is particularly related to the European Legal Capital Regime as determined by the Second Company Law Directive. Thus, there is a debate on what the directive allows – is it possible for the member states to create a competitive new model for regulations within the framework of the directive, or is it necessary to create an alternative system? In a newly published contribute to that debate (P. Santella and R. Turrini, 'A contribution to the debate on the legal capital regime in the EU: What the Second Company Law Directive allows', in P. Krüger Andersen and K. Engsig Sørensen (eds.), *Company Law and Finance*, (Copenhagen: Thomson, 2007), 85 *et seq.*), the authors argue that the Second Company Law Directive is a very flexible instrument which to a very large extent allows member states to develop new and efficient capital rules. An example to illustrate this could be the new (2006) and liberal Finnish Company Act. See J. Mahönen, 'Capital Maintenance and Distribution Rules in Modern European Company Law', in Andersen and Sørensen (eds.), *Company Law and Finance*, p. 119; and M. Airaiksinen 'The Delaware of Europe Financial Instruments in the new Finnish Company Act', in Andersen and Sørensen (eds.), *Company Law and Finance*, 311.

[4] On the disadvantages of centrally developed norms (keywords: elimination of regulatory competition; 'petrification' of the law because of the EU legislative process; costs of change) see C. Teichmann, 'Wettbewerb der Gesetzgeber im Europäischen Gesellschaftsrecht', in E. Reimer et al. (eds.), *Europäisches Gesellschafts- und Steuerrecht*, (Munich: Beck Juristischer Verlag, 2007), 313, 329 with further references.

numerous references to national laws as gap-fillers. In this way, the enacted company forms by no means create uniform rules, but rather each member state presents a different mosaic of supranational and national rules to the market. In the case of the SE, above all, EU law creates a mere torso of a corporation. There are undisputable advantages to this type of form (e.g., combining free structuring with a uniform 'European Trademark'). However, the advantages of a truly unified corporate form remain beyond reach. It remains to be seen whether it will be possible to develop a genuinely European company in the planned 'European Private Limited Company' (EPC).

Judicial policing of national company law for conformance with the right of free establishment can in the final determination only clear away barriers on a case-by-case basis, but cannot serve to positively create workable forms. Although offending national norms are removed, they are not replaced with provisions serving the internal market. Rather, ECJ company law decisions have since 1999 launched a competition for corporate charters in which member states have started to adopt differing measures within the open area left by the ECJ. In this respect it has been argued that the establishment of a market for corporate charters does not necessarily lead to regulatory competition as the supply side (the member states) lack sufficient incentives to compete for charters.[5] The work of the Group might help to improve this as its procurement of detailed information on national company law will create the transparency that is a prerequisite for competition.

B. *The present aims of EU regulation: from harmonization to convergence*

The objectives of EU regulation in the area of company law have changed substantially over time – in spite of their unchanged basis in Article 44(3)(g) of the EC Treaty. In an article on the subject, Jan Wouters analysed the development from the 1960s (the adoption of the first series of directives) until the year 2000.[6] During the 1960s, the ambitious goal was to harmonize company law, comprising all aspects of such law from the formation of companies to investment, dividends, mergers and liquidations. After adoption of the first series of harmonization directives, this

---

[5] See H. Søndergård Birkmose, 'A Race to the Bottom in the EU', *Maastricht Journal of European and Comparative Law*, 1 (2006), 35–80.

[6] Wouters, 'European Company Law: Quo Vadis?', (note 1, above), 257–307.

development gradually stopped. It turned out that it was impossible to realize full harmonization in several areas, and the goal of harmonization was subjected to debate. *Wouters* describes the EU's activity in company law around the turn of the millennium as characterized by a four-fold crisis: conceptually (e.g. participation versus consultation of employees), in relation to competence (i.e., an emphasis on subsidiarity), questioning legitimacy (i.e., a new preference for a decentralized development of the law) and a growing local loyalty (member states' resistance to implementation of EU norms).[7] He argued that the Commission did not have any coherent vision or agenda in the field of company law. Shortly after the publication of this article, the Commission (on 4 September 2001) set up a Group of Company Law Experts. This Group was due to provide recommendations for creating a modern framework for European company law. Based on the Group's final report,[8] the Commission elaborated its Action Plan in 2003.[9] To use the words of *Rolf Skog*,[10] one might well say that EU's work with company law gained new wind in the sails.

Although the initial Action Plan of 2003 has been reviewed and developed further meanwhile,[11] the three 'guiding political criteria' that the regulatory activity at the European level needs to respect remain important also in the context of the Model Law Project.[12] These criteria are (1) the *subsidiarity* and *proportionality principle* of the Treaty, (2) that the regulatory response is *flexible in application, but firm in principles*, and (3) that it should shape *international regulatory developments*.

To sum up, the present aim of the EU regulation is *not* to harmonize the companies acts of the member states. Directives are not the primary regulatory tool. Better regulation can include alternative tools – such as a model law that can foster convergence and best practice on a European level. Creating a European Model Company Act is completely in line with this view expressed by the Commission.

---

[7] Wouters, 'European Company Law: Quo Vadis?', (note 1, above), 275.

[8] *Report of the High Level Group of Company Law Experts on a Modern Regulatory Framework for Company Law in Europe*, Brussels, 4 November 2002.

[9] *Modernising Company Law and Enhancing Corporate Governance in the European Union – A Plan to Move Forward* (COM(2003) 284 Final).

[10] See R. Skog, 'Harmoniseringen af bolags- og börsrätten indom EU – ny vind I seglen?', *NTS (Nordisk Journal of Company Law)*, (2001), 331; R. Skog, 'Harmoniseringen af bolagsrätten indom EU – fortfarende vind i seglen?', *NTS*, 1(2007), 66.

[11] See T. Baums, 'European Company Law beyond the 2003 Action Plan', *European Business Organization Law Review*, 8 (2007), 143 *et seq.*

[12] See *Modernising Company Law and Enhancing Corporate Governance in the European Union – A Plan to Move Forward* (COM(2003) 284 Final), 4.

C. Concluding thoughts on the EU company law programme

As has been shown above, today member states have a significant amount of legislative free space in the area of company law. This area is limited only in certain areas by the ECJ's decisions protecting freedom of establishment, and has been – and will continue to be – harmonized only in certain other areas by EU directives. On the one hand, this free space should, in light of the disadvantages of centrally harmonizing substantive law[13] and the advantages of decentralized, competing legislative efforts,[14] be retained and defended. On the other hand, as said, certain disadvantages are connected with relinquishing further substantive harmonization of national company law. Thus, the abandonment of central harmonization can cause three conceivable losses: first, the standardization of norms creates economic savings by eliminating the costs of obtaining information about diverse laws and adapting business to them;[15] second, a regulatory competition which is driven primarily by the preferences of managers and investors may not always lead to optimal results for the affected third-party constituencies;[16] third, legislation promulgated from a central government can break through impediments to reform that are well entrenched at the level of individual states.

The potential loss of these benefits does not, however, speak unconditionally for a programme of central harmonization. For example, it does not seem that the competition for corporate charters in Europe that has only just begun has injured third parties to an extent which would call for the prompt creation of harmonized norms for private limited companies. It is also the very purpose of regulatory competition to subject to market competition those local particularities seen by one party as an impediment to reform while valued by the other as desirable options, rather than simply either eliminating or perpetuating them through centralized rules. However, the fact remains that a basic tension exists between the goal of a unified, internal market and the continued existence of different systems of corporate law, a tension that entails both advantages and disadvantages. Can a unified,

---

[13] Note 4, above.　　　　[14] Note 3, above.

[15] See E. Kitch, 'Business Organization Law: State or Federal? – An Inquiry into the Allocation of Political Competence in Relation to Issues of Business Organization Law in a Federal System' in R. M. Buxbaum et al. (eds.), *European Business Law: Legal and Economic Analyses on Integration and Harmonization* (Berlin: de Gruyter, 1991), pp. 35, 40 *et seq.*

[16] On this point see the literature and references note 3, above.

voluntary model law serve to preserve the advantages of decentralized legislative energy and imagination while assuring most advantages of centralized harmonization? The following paragraphs consider this possibility.

D. The functions of an EMCA

A European Model Corporation Act[17] would not lead to a legal instrument issued by the European Union: the member states would neither be ordered to implement an EU directive nor would the Union create yet another European business form. To this extent, the concept of a European Model Company Act must not be misunderstood. Emphasis should be on the word '*model*'. The project is to develop a model for a companies act that the member states are free to adopt or reject. The content of the model should include broadly acceptable uniform rules, building on the common legal traditions of the member states and the existing *acquis communautaire*, but also contribute to developing best practice based on experiences from the modern companies acts of various member states. The draft should both leave individual states free space for their own take on the model, so as to account for local and national particularities, and offer incorporators maximum flexibility with which to structure the ultimate business enterprise.

Of course, even now every carefully prepared amendment of law is preceded by a thorough comparative analysis. Nevertheless, such comparative analyses are often restricted to the most economically important jurisdictions and are often performed in a perfunctory way. Alone on the basis of having a member from each of the twenty-seven EU member states,[18] the EMCA drafting commission will incorporate experience from all the legal traditions found in the European Union within its comparative study and draft a model act that takes this experience into account. This should be of use not only for the smaller member states – which are often pressed to staff and dispatch a team of legal experts for the drafting of such measures – when it comes time to consider adopting the EMCA. In addition, it may be hoped that national legislatures, including those of the larger member states, will hesitate before evoking national particularities in order to deviate from

---

[17] Regarding the type of corporations that should be regulated by the EMCA, see *infra* Part IV.A.

[18] See *infra* Part IV.B.

the European 'benchmark' when faced with a model act that has been specifically designed for uniform use throughout the Union. Lastly, a provision of national law that restricts freedom of establishment will likely be scrutinized even more strictly when it is not compatible with a model act that has been designed and adopted by all member states.

In addition to the advantages discussed above, the development of a model companies act fits nicely within the current legislative plan of the European Commission, see also Part II.2, above. On the one hand, the Commission is currently examining the existing EU norms in the area of company law for possible simplification and deregulation, where this is possible and meaningful.[19] A model act that could replace the imperative command of a directive or regulation with an informed recommendation to the member states could prove a workable alternative to the current EU regulatory mix. On the other hand, by developing genuinely European forms for business organization (SE, SCE, EEIG, and, probably, the EPC) the European Commission is also trying to enrich the assortment of available options for users. For this reason as well, the Commission sees with interest and favour the attempt to develop a model company form on the basis of a thorough comparative analysis that can – unlike existing supranational company forms – operate largely independently from references to other national laws. The next part of this article will discuss the US experience with model laws.

III. Model acts in the United States

Comparative analyses often refer to the work of the National Conference of Commissioners on Uniform State Laws (NCCUSL) in the United States[20] as an example of unifying law through the

---

[19] See in this regard the reports by Baums, 'European Company Law beyond the 2003 Action Plan', (note 11, above), 143–160; and D. Weber-Rey, 'Effects of the Better Regulation Approach on European Company Law and Corporate Governance' *European Company and Financial Law Review*, 3 (2007), 370, 374 *et seq.*

[20] For a general discussion see K. Zweigert and H. Kötz, *An Introduction to Comparative Law*, third edition (Oxford: Clarendon, 1998), § 17.III; specifically on company law see R. Romano, *The Genius of American Corporate Law* (Washington: American enterprise institute for public policy research, 1993), 128 *et seq.*; J. von Hein, 'Competitive Company Law: Comparisons with the USA', in U. Bernitz (ed.), *Modern Company Law for a European Economy – Ways and Means*, (Stockholm: Norstedts Juridik Förlag, 2006), 25 *et seq.*

formulation of recommendations at a central source in spite of legislative competence remaining lodged with decentralized, individual states. For the purposes of this paper, a brief sketch of the US experience should suffice.[21] The EMCA drafting commission will seek to benefit from the experience gained in the United States by bringing in a US legal expert as a consultant.

US attempts to draft a corporation statute to unify the laws of the individual US states date back to the 1920s. The NCCUSL completed a Uniform Business Corporation Act (UBCA) in 1928. The UBCA was conceived as a *uniform* act governing all corporations, and was to be uniformly adopted in identical form without change by the states. However, the UBCA was not a success (it was adopted by only a few small states, such as Louisiana, Washington, and Kentucky) and in 1943 the NCCUSL changed its status into the more flexible form of a *model* act, although this did not bring about an improvement in its fortunes and the Act was withdrawn in 1958. During this period, the American Bar Association (ABA) had independently set out to develop its own 'Model Business Corporation Act' (MBCA), which it released in 1946, and it eventually took over the NCCUSL's project, which has since that time been carried forward by the ABA's Committee on Corporate Laws of its Section on Corporation, Banking, and Business Law.[22] In contrast to the UBCA, the MBCA has been a great success and has been adopted by the majority of US states and has served as a resource of company law doctrine for state legislatures and courts.[23] The MBCA was thoroughly revised in 1984, and released as the 'Revised Model Business Corporation Act (RMBCA).[24] The Model Business Corporation Act is

---

[21] For a more detailed discussion, see R.W. Hamilton, 'The Revised Model Business Corporation Act: Comment and Observation. Reflections of a Reporter', *Texas Law Review*, 63(1985), 1455; J. Macey, *Macey on Corporation Laws* (Aspen Publishers, 2002), Introduction.

[22] See Hamilton, 'The Revised Model Business Corporation Act', (note 21, above), 1457.

[23] See R. A. Booth, 'Model Business Corporation Act – 50th Anniversary', *Bus. Law.*, 56 (2000), 63. The article discusses statistics proving that the MBCA has been remarkably influential not only for state statutes, but also for court decisions. The Act has also been cited or discussed in numerous law review articles. See also J. A. Barnett et al., 'The MBCA and state corporation law – a tabular comparison of selected financial provisions', *Bus. Law.*, 56 (2000), 69. In US law schools corporate courses are usually based on the Model Act, often combined with, e.g., the Delaware General Corporation Law. Similar developments could arise in the EU with respect to EMCA/national law.

[24] Reprinted in M. A. Eisenberg, *Corporations and Other Business Associations. Statutes, Rules, Materials, and Forms* (New York: Foundation Press, 2007), 677.

revised every year, and proposed revisions are published in the ABA's *Business Lawyer* magazine.

The basic entity intended to be created under the RMBCA is a publicly held corporation. To this end, the RMBCA is accompanied by a Model Statutory Close Corporation Supplement, which was first released in 1982. Beginning in the 1990s, however, small entrepreneurs came for tax and other reasons to favour the Limited Liability Company (LLC), and all of the fifty US states now have some form of LLC statute. The NCCUSL published a 'Uniform Limited Liability Company Act' in 1995, and this model was revised in 2006.[25]

In addition to these model acts, the American Law Institute's 'Principles of Corporate Governance', which were first released in 1994, have great importance for company law.[26] The Principles are not recommendations to the states for possible implementation, but rather restate leading judicial decisions and scholarship in the field of corporate governance, synthesizing best practice behaviour for boards and shareholders in a form of 'soft law'.

IV. Individual issues

Here we discuss answers to individual questions that are currently being raised regarding the EMCA project. The first question, which will be discussed in Section A, regards the EMCA's contents, i.e., the definition of the topics and areas that are currently expected to be regulated by the draft EMCA. The second question, discussed in Section B, is on the drafting commission itself, its members, *modus operandi* and relation to the European Commission. Lastly, the preliminary plan for drafting the Act itself will be discussed in Section C.

A. *The content of the EMCA*

The drafting commission will initially occupy itself with public companies limited by shares (*Aktiengesellschaft, société anonyme, società per azioni*, etc.), including listed companies. Private limited companies will be drawn into the project at a later date. This does not imply any

---

[25] Reprinted in Eisenberg, *Corporations and Other Business Associations.* (note 24, above), 418.

[26] American Law Institute, *Principles of Corporate Governance: Analysis and Recommendations*, 1994.

recommendation that a unified law on business corporations, as exists in some member states, should be offered.

A further question regards those areas that, through EU directives, have already largely been harmonized, such as the disclosure of market relevant information and capital contributions and maintenance. This existing harmonization and the fact that national legislatures may not deviate from existing directives in force speaks for the position that the EMCA should not include proposals deviating from the existing *acquis communautaire*. Exceptions may present themselves in cases where change is being discussed at the EU level, so that a concrete possibility would exist that member states could legally adopt EMCA provisions deviating from outgoing EU law.

The stock of norms that are grouped together under the rubric 'company law' is defined differently in the various member states. Functional analysis shows that a number of rules from tort law, civil procedure, insolvency law, securities regulation, and international private law (conflict of laws) can be seen as integral to company law. A convincing, conceptual distinction between company law and these overlapping areas can only be achieved through examination of the individual fact patterns addressed by the provisions, evaluation of the solutions currently used by member states for such situations, and formulation of the most appropriate, proposed boundary – irrespective of whether this rule would be considered part of company law in one legislation and part of, e.g., tort law or insolvency law in another.

A similar method or approach seems to recommend itself for the law of corporate groups. Legal issues in connection with the domination of a group of companies, information problems within the group, and the liability of the dominant company and its management, *inter alia*, must all be examined in the respective context. The extent to which a separate set of legal rules on company groups would be found advisable will then be a technical question.

Options will have to be preserved for the seating of employee representatives on boards and the division of the board into management and supervisory components for those member states that currently have co-determination or a two-tier board structure, or may be interested in adopting one of these governance tools. This would not exclude the possibility of formulating recommendations in this area, such as with regard to the size of the supervisory board or the board of directors.

B. The Drafting Commission

Each of the twenty-seven EU member states is represented by a company law expert in the drafting commission.[27] This Commission is chaired by Professor *Paul Krüger Andersen* of the Aarhus School of Business, University of Aarhus, and the Group's secretariat is situated at that location and headed by Associate Professor *Hanne Søndergård Birkmose*. The drafting commission will, as needed, consult experts in specialized topics for assistance as such questions arise. The EMCA project is not sponsored by the European Commission, although the two bodies have agreed to regular exchanges of information, and the European Commission may dispatch its own people to represent it at working group meetings.

C. The preliminary working plan

As one would expect, the work on the EMCA will proceed in a number of individual stages that correspond to the individual chapters of the Act. Each member of the drafting commission will prepare a report on his or her national law to accompany the drafting of each chapter of the Act. A general reporter for each chapter will analyse the national reports and prepare a summary report, setting forth the various solutions and making recommendations, which the drafting commission will then discuss, supplement and adopt. It is expected that there will be plenary meetings every six months. The proposals, i.e., the recommended provisions with explanatory comments and references to national rules, will be published chapter by chapter so that the entire academic and business community can take part in the process of developing the EMCA.

Chapters currently in progress are the rather technical provisions for the formation of companies (whether through incorporation or reorganization) and the central chapter on 'directors' duties', the drafting of which is an exploration of whether a common position can

---

[27] As of January 2008, the following persons comprise the Commission: Susanne Kalss (AT); Hans de Wulf (BE); Alexander Belohlávek (CZ); Theodor Baums (DE); Paul Krüger Andersen (DK; Chair); Juan Sanchez-Calero (ES); Matti Sillanpää (FI); Isabelle Urbain-Parleani (FR); Evanghelos Perakis (GR); András Kisfaludi (HU); Blanaid Clarke (IR); Guido Ferrarini (IT); André Prüm (LU); Harm-Jan de Kluiver (NL); Stanislaw Soltysinski (PL); José Engrácia Antunes (PT); Rolf Skog (SE); Maria Patakyova (SK); Paul Davies (UK).

indeed be found in this very important but hitherto unharmonized area.

The difficulties standing in the way of successfully completing this project are not few and should not be underestimated, but we believe that the EMCA drafting commission can overcome such difficulties, and we also believe that the project will contribute to the efficiency and competitiveness of European business.

2

The *Societas Privata Europaea*: a basic reform of EU law on business organizations

THEO RAAIJMAKERS

I. Introduction

It is a great pleasure to contribute to this *liber amicorum* in honour of Eddy Wymeersch. His vast and seemingly unlimited interest in company and securities law offered an equally broad choice of subjects for this article. Working with a team of researchers in Tilburg's Center for Company Law on a broader project aiming at revealing the basic elements and guiding principles of reform of company and enterprise law, I decided to carve out from this project some observations on the intended introduction of a statute for European Private Companies.

The idea for an EPC is not new. Shortly after publication of the first draft for the SE Statute, Mme Boucourechliev published her 'Pour une SARL Européenne'. Together with Drury, Hommelhof *inter alia*, she was involved in drafting a proposal that was published by CREDA/Medef in 1998. The High Level Group of Company Law Experts reiterated the case for an EPC and the EC in its 2003 Action Plan and gave it a mid-term priority. In 2006 a consultation document was published focusing on the scope and nature of an EPC statute: (a) should it be available to single-owned firms and quasi-partnerships or also to private firms with 'dispersed' ownership?; (b) should the statute be standalone and exhaustive or – like the SE statute – build on and refer to national law? Though the responses are somewhat diffuse, respondents focus on enhancing start-ups and cross-border activities of SMEs and almost unanimously plead for contractual freedom and flexibility, avoidance of complexities for subsidiaries and time-consuming, costly procedures and formal requirements (like notarization of documents) as well as for introduction of a stand-alone statute that does not create twenty-seven different statutes by referring to national law. The emphasis is on organization, not on *re*-organization. Meanwhile the EC announced that it would take further decisions on a Statute (regulation) for a Societas Privata Europaea (SPE).[1]

The SPE project should be placed against the background of EU constitutional law, the Lisboa agenda (2000, as amended), the prevailing case law of the European Court of Jusitce (ECJ), the regulatory competition fuelled thereby and the reforms of the law on private (close) companies as now being scheduled and/or discussed in several member states. In the perspective of global competition, it is equally important to assess the regulatory actions in other jurisdictions, more specifically the Limited Liability Corporation and the Limited Liability Partnership, since both combine a high degree of contractual freedom with limitation of liability. This combination seems to cause one of the main obstacles to reform towards more flexible business forms for SMEs. This article therefore aims to contribute to the forthcoming debate by an analysis of the combination of contractual and corporate devices as developed in the LLC using the text of the US Model Act (ULLCA).

Taking the constitutional aspects first, the annex to the revised Roman Treaty follows the Social Charter (2000) and proclaims the freedom of entrepreneurship, the freedom of association (not excluding commercial cooperation) and the protection of property. These constitutional principles evidently do not prevent the EU nor its member states from protecting the business community and general public by rules on business organizations and their activities in providing goods or services, but it forces them to respect such limitations and contrast them to the overall societal objective of enhancing entrepreneurship by means of an advanced law on business organizations for SMEs and large firms. The ECJ plays an important role. It held that the freedom of establishment prevents member states from refusing to recognize (pseudo) foreign corporations (business organizations, firms) on the mere ground that these do not meet the protective standards that member states have set for their *national* business forms or pseudo-foreign corporations. Such restrictions by member states and others to prevent clear fraud are not completely foreclosed but their reach can be challenged before the ECJ. Its case law allows entrepreneurs to freely select business forms of *other* member states – the choice shall in principle be recognized in the case where registered office and real seat are not located in the same member

---

[1] See: http://ec.europa.eu/internal_market/company/epc/index_en.htm

state. The prohibition of such a 'split' in art. 9 of the SE Statute seems to be obsolete now.

The ECJ case law fuelled a certain degree of regulatory competition within the EU and an acceleration of reform initiatives for national statutes for close corporations, e.g. the amended French SàS regime and the Netherlands project to revise the BV statute. Since an SPE Statute would enlarge the menu of business organizations available to entrepreneurs in the EU, it would therefore also and *per se* have a competitive effect in the selection of business forms. The discussion on the outlines of an SPE Statute therefore is also relevant for such reforms of national law on business organizations. Reforms continuously appear to be burdensome, 'path dependent' as they are. The eligibility of close corporations providing limited liability and the concern to prohibit abuse and fraud is closely linked to the basic principles of company and partnership law or – in a wider sense – of the law on business organizations, including the most common form of sole ownerships. An SPE Statute offers the challenge to be drafted from scratch, but also at EU level this may be constrained by the *acquis communautaire* that effectively fixes starting conditions as an EU path of its own and prevents the creation of a competitive business vehicle for European entrepreneurs fitting into and serving the Lisbon agenda, the constitutional freedoms and the Treaty's principles of freedom of establishment and capital.

The Lisbon ambitions urge the development of the law on business organizations in the EU and also the SPE project as part thereof to be placed in the wider context of global regulatory competition and strengthening the EU common market. Furthering the integration of the EU common market as well as enhancing entrepreneurship and competitiveness in a globalizing economy, urges benchmarking with developments outside the EU to enable sharper identification of constraints to, as well as of, opportunities for change and the impact thereof. Specifically the development of the very successful Limited Liability Corporation (LLC) in the US offers such a fresh look to regulatory concepts as being developed over centuries in different jurisdictions. This modest contribution therefore contrasts the ideas on a possible SPE statute with these business forms. This article respectfully builds on research dedicated by many scholars who, I hope, will appreciate that the limited size of this article caused me to refrain from documenting these sources. This will follow in a more extensive publication anticipated by the Tilburg research team.

II. Preliminary observations: the need for a European flexible, cost-effective (corporate) vehicle for entrepreneurs in small- and medium-size enterprises

Entrepreneurs, whatever the scope of their business activities, usually start as sole proprietors but may soon be confronted with the need to select a corporate vehicle from the menu of business organizations to incorporate their business. Usually they will select a form from the menu of their home state, but may also select this from another member state's menu. If they develop permanent cross-border activities in other member states they have to decide whether to organize their business as a separate corporate vehicle ('sister', in a horizontal structure held by themselves), a branch of their home state firm or as a subsidiary. An SPE Statute should clearly envisage each of these organizational segments of cross-border activities and the practical need for *all* SMEs to organize their cross-border activities as a group of companies: a parent (SPE or other form) to be selected from the menu of the home or another member state and one or more subsidiaries in other member states. For the parent the European label of an SPE may enhance its image in the business community of other member states, also if cross-border activities are organized as branches, but less so in case the latter would be incorporated as 'local' SPE subsidiaries. The major concern that seems to drive the SPE initiative is to facilitate and enhance the organization of a multi-state business in the EU. The design of the SPE Statute should, however, clearly reflect that the structure of the European common market substantially differs from that of other major markets, such as in the US, China, Russia and India, that allow a simple single business entity to operate in other states or provinces in their own market. The EU will remain to consist of different jurisdictions characterized by different languages, cultures, traditions, commercial and societal customs, financing possibilities for SMEs, private and commercial law, taxation, insolvency rules and principles, labour relations, customer protection, environmental and other rules. These differences will in many cases urge EU entrepreneurs to separately incorporate as a subsidiary their permanent business activities in other member states. Thus they typically will prefer or be *de facto* forced to organize their multi-state business as a group of companies. This remains a disadvantage in comparison with other large multi-state markets where a multi-state business can be organized as a single entity headquartered in one state (province) and operating through local branches in other states (provinces). Size does not make a decisive difference: although the initial and marginal costs of creating such a structure will be higher for SMEs, these have to be offset against the continuous costs and management risks of operating through branches in other jurisdictions.

An SPE Statute therefore should equally serve (the shareholders base and governance of) a stand-alone SPE as an entity that enshrines incorporation of a single-person company, quasi-partnership or family company, as well as an SPE that (also) operates as the parent of a group of SPEs (or other entities) and, moreover, looking from the perspective of a subsidiary SPE in relation to its parent to preserve the coherent and unified control of the parent over its operational and legal group structure in its multi-state group strategy and management. Hence the SPE Statute should explicitly take into account that expectedly an SPE will often be used to create cross-border subsidiaries, quasi-partnerships and joint ventures for cross-border cooperation. The Statute should envisage the use of an SPE as parent as well as at subsidiary level. Therefore the eligibility of an SPE should not be limited to multi-state cases.[2] If the 'European label' should allow the enhancement of cross-border marketing and business, also nationals should be able to benefit from the SPE in pursuing cross-border activities. Evidently the plea for flexibility and contractual freedom equally applies to the use of the SPE as cross-border subsidiary and as a vehicle for start-ups and quasi partnerships.

The main deciding elements for the initial selection of a business form to be considered in designing a flexible SPE Statute remain:

a) to partition the business-related assets and liabilities (enterprise) from the rest of his private property to enhance separate management thereof as a propriety interest under full control of the entrepreneur, e.g. distinct from matrimonial property and facilitating a transfer thereof;

b) in cross-border activities: similarly to partition his business abroad from that in his home country by creating a subsidiary to be party to all contracts and transactions in the other member state and to assume all the liabilities thereof;

---

[2] It would require complicated requirements and enforcement rules if the promoter should be resident in another member state and question the validity of the subsidiary's SPE form if he would be dissolved or acquire the same nationality as a subsidiary. Unnecessary set-up of special vehicles to meet requirements of multi-nationality should be avoided.

c) to manage business activities and fully control strategy, policies and management by a statutory off-the-peg organization model, which will be most relevant in case of a cross-border subsidiary to incorporate a permanent organization of activities in one or more member states;

d) to insulate entrepreneurial risks and protect non-scope private assets from bankruptcy of the firm by shielding off liability for its liabilities (again, also in case of subsidiaries in other member states);

e) to optimize taxation (corporate and personal income tax) under national law and in cross-border relations;

f) to facilitate financing of the business (equity, loans, credit) and to attract new business or financial partners by issuing (transferable or non-transferable) shares or rights thereto (this again relates both to a parent as to a subsidiary in other member states). In case of creating a quasi partnership or joint venture decisive factors may be:

   (i) flexibility to enter into enforceable agreements with one or more partners/shareholders (including venture capitalists and private equity firms) on the internal control and exercise of formal shareholder rights and obligations within the firm and

   (ii) contractual freedom to arrange for or – alternatively – fall back on flexible and cost-effective *default* rules on internal disputes, sell out, buy out and appraisal.

While these elements focus on the initial selection of a single business vehicle, the dynamics of business activities urge the promoter/entrepreneur also to consider the possibilities and degree of flexibility to *re*-organize the legal organization of the firm and its activities. Initially the question arises whether a business can be incorporated as going concern *uno actu* by operation of law. In the life cycle of the firm other reorganizations may present themselves and it should be considered whether and to what the extent the SPE Statute offers flexible opportunities for, amongst others, extension of the shareholders base to (new) partners or financiers, conversion into another business form, merger, split, takeover transaction and also going public.

An SPE typically would offer the additional advantage of a European label in cross-border activities. This may become more important in view of the increased multi-cultural character of the EU after the extension of the EU to – at present – twenty-seven member states with their different legal traditions and company law.

In the selection from the menu of business organizations (home state and other member states) the above elements should be balanced against constraints to full control and costs of incorporation (initial and continuous) both under national law (parent) as under the law of the other member states involved:

a) costs of incorporation: procedures, notarization, registration, professional advice (legal, tax, accountancy);
b) initial and ongoing taxation (as well as possible choice between income and corporate tax);
c) administrative burdens of formalization of internal procedures (formal division of powers as – single or joint – shareholder(s) and manager; need for formal resolutions, e.g. on instructions/approvals of shareholders meeting; 12th directive);
d) constrains to control over strategy and management of the parent and 'foreign' subsidiaries respectively;
e) initial and ongoing administrative costs, fees and levies of registration;
f) costs of disclosure duties and audit services as provided for under the 1st, 4th and 7th EU directive or other statutory requirements; contractual monitoring requirements set by banks or other financiers (venture capitalists); again, both at the level of the parent and its 'foreign' subsidiaries;
g) costs of legal and other advice in the ongoing operations and any subsequent internal and external disputes at the level of the parent as well as of its 'foreign' subsidiaries.

Evidently the success of the SPE Statute will largely depend on its ability to shape an effective group organization consisting of an SPE-parent that will be in full control of its 'local' SPE-subsidiaries.

The EC's synthesis of the comments on the consultation document on a possible statute for an EPC[3] largely reflects the above elective elements both implicitly and explicitly. Asset partitioning and limited liability are apparently assumed, but the responses do not clarify the position on the 'price' in terms of (national or EU) protection of third parties, like capital protection, statutory disclosure of accounts and audit, liability of directors and shadow directors or wrongful trading rules.

---

[3] See: http://ec.europa.eu/internal_market/company/epc/index_en.htm

The most remarkable observations are in line with the earlier recommendations of the High Level Group of Company Law Experts (November 2003, Ch. VII) and can be summarized as follows:

a) The diversity of company laws and regimes are a significant source of costs and legal uncertainty. The existing legal framework is insufficient for cross-border activities. Providing a European label is regarded to be helpful as a marketing tool in a global environment. An SPE would allow significant costs savings by using the same legal form across the EU;

b) The SPE statute should be as open as possible and offer maximum flexibility. Even though a majority would still support a single shareholder SPE, most consider that the SPE should be open to single and multiple shareholders (legal and natural persons alike) and be allowed to have headquarters and registered office in different member states. A single shareholder model, however, would allow for a more simple and uniform SPE statute. A majority clearly favours a stand-alone and exhaustive SPE statute without reference to national law to provide for a set of unambiguous rules, prevent high legal costs and the emergence of twenty-seven different rather than one single EPC. This would be the real added value of the statute.

c) In a single shareholders SPE statute more matters could be left to the articles of association than in a multiple SPE; many matters pertaining to the management of an SPE should be left to contractual freedom.

d) Respondents' reactions were split on the issue of employee participation regimes, some opting for uniform rules and others believing that opting for the rules applicable in the member state where the SPE has its seat would be the only feasible solution.

Since the Lisboa ambitions, as rephrased, are formulated in a global, rather than internal European perspective, we should compare with developments in other important jurisdictions. Since the aims formulated by the EC to consider an SPE Statute evidently closely resembles those that lead to the introduction of the very successful business organizations of the LLC and LLP in the US and other jurisdictions, a closer comparative analysis of these regulatory innovations seems highly relevant for the design of a brand new SPE as a European business organization. These business forms offer starters and entrepreneurs a flexible business form in a start-up to incorporate their business activities. The check-the-box rules allow a choice between corporate and income taxation.

III. Overall regulatory approach by the EU and starting conditions

The preamble of the EPC Statute should clearly lay down the legal basis for the nature of the Statute and its purpose in the socio-economic framework of our societies as reflected in the European Treaty for Human Rights, the Roman Treaty (as amended), the Social Charter (2000) and the Lisbon statements. Freedom of enterprise and association and protection of property shall be respected and undue state interference shall be avoided. Similarly the freedom of establishment (and recognition of pseudo-foreign corporations) as established by the ECJ in *Centros*, *Überseering* and *Inspire Art* shall be reflected. These basic concepts and policies should guide EU regulatory action to enhance entrepreneurship and private initiative as indispensable generators of wealth and innovation. The design of the Statute should strengthen the competitiveness of the EU business climate and environment in the global competition. Present but sometimes ineffective concepts to prevent and sanction abuse and fraud should be reconsidered in close connection with insolvency law since the ultimate test of such corporate behaviour emerges practically always in bankruptcy/insolvency. *Capitis deminutio* and *mort civile* may have been abolished but lifelong stigmatization replaced these sanctions and the approach of a 'fresh start' after insolvency is not common in Europe.

The *constitutional starting points and freedoms* can be summarized as follows:

a) the basic constitutional freedom of entrepreneurship as the autonomy of persons (citizens) to become and operate as an entrepreneur by starting, organizing, financing and operating a business under own control and discretion, accrue and receive earnings (salary and profits) therefrom and create value on top of the net asset value, which can be disposed of as a propriety interest by sale to third parties, by will or otherwise;

b) the constitutional freedom to *associate* with others (entrepreneurs and/or financiers) to pursue a joint enterprise by contract, partnership or any other form of joint ownership and association, and to *share* propriety interests (control, earnings and the accrued value of the joint firm);

c) the freedom to select without state intervention (or concession) any business form available within their own or any other (EU) jurisdiction;

d) the freedom to re-incorporate a business in another EU jurisdiction;

e) the freedom to *organize* the 'internal affairs' of the business organization as they think fit for their firm and resolve on matters concerning the firm upon the agreed upon scheme;

f) the freedom to reorganize the firm's business form and/or the members relationship thereto by changing its internal affairs, merger, split, conversion or any other such mechanism, including going public by issuing (tradable) securities in the market;

g) the freedom to *dissolve* the firm with or without continuation of the business.

These basic freedoms are guiding principles in our free market economy based on liberal democracy. On the other hand the general and public interest of our complex societies urges proper regulation of amongst others economic activities of entrepreneurs. They have to pay direct and indirect taxes, observe strict quality and safety standards in manufacturing and sale of products and services under public oversight, e.g. production/sale of food and drugs, banking, insurance, traffic, all kinds of professionals services, environmental risks. Regulators thus discharge their public tasks with respect to much more: care for personal health, quality of drinking water, food, medical and other professional care, personal and general safety and security, prevention and reduction of environmental risks et cetera.

However, such rules on *market activities* of entrepreneurs should be sharply distinguished from those on the *organization of their business form as such*, i.e. the law on business organizations. It is here that we encounter (diverging) historical roots that until today do influence our concepts and – often unveiled – assumptions. Free entrepreneurship was restricted by the medieval guilds, that were abolished in/after the French Revolution. Today membership of professional organizations is required for certain regulated professions only. Restrictions to free association did occur throughout history and recognition of associations as legal persons in The Netherlands required until 1976 Royal Approval which regularly was withheld. Cooperative associations were long distrusted for their 'political' aims. In commercial law over time *contractual* joint enterprises developed for cooperation between entrepreneurs and/or financiers in the form of (limited) partnerships giving the (general) partners joint control and ownership and limited liability to 'silent' partners. Companies emerged as *continuous* partnerships with fixed capital divided in (tradable) shares and limited liability for the holders thereof. The Dutch East Indian Company (1602), created by Act of Parliament, received a concession to trade 'with the East' to act 'in the common wealth' under public oversight. Only after more than a century such a concession was gradually replaced by 'free covenant': promoters themselves without such approval could create a company-legal person, but the Napoleonic codification re-introduced a moderated form of state approval (non-objection). In the UK the South Sea Bubble caused parliament (in 1720) to ban public companies altogether, which remained effective until 1840. German 'Konzessionszwang' and public interest objectives were replaced in the 1892 Aktiengesetz by a set of detailed mandatory substantive rules ('materielle Normativbestimmungen') to protect shareholders, creditors and others. While the flexible and sober Netherlands statute also allowed the NV to be tailored for flexible closely held NVs, Germany created next to its strict AG statute a *separate* 'light' contract-based GmbH statute, which was copied in many countries. In The Netherlands such a separate BV form was only introduced as late as 1971 to avoid mandatory disclosure of accounts for closely held NVs as still allowed by the 1st EU directive.[4] The statute was copy pasted from

---

[4] Until 1976 company and partnership law were integrated in the Commercial Code (no separate form for private companies). 'Public' companies were *'corporate* species' of partnership, essentially based – at least its internal organization – on contract, albeit that a notarization and a ministerial decree of non-objection were required (public oversight). The statute was very flexible and at the start of the EU The Netherlands were feared to become the Delaware of Europe. In 1971 the BV, i.e. the 'close' corporation, was introduced to enable privately held companies to be exempted from the duty of the 1st Directive to disclose audited annual accounts. Its statute was, however, copy-pasted from the then modernized and institutionalized NV with employee participation for 'large' companies. NV *and* (!) BV were disconnected from partnership law and enacted in Book 2 Civil Code under the heading Legal Persons (together with public entities, churches, associations, cooperatives and foundations) and with overall general rules. Hence, until today, even single-owned BVs and quasi-partnership BVs are characterized as 'institute' and legal person in the first place. The original notion of contract is absent, but a broad rule establishes that all directly related parties should observe rules of equity. Anti-abuse provisions against acts contravening the 'own interest of the company' have been piled up in company law (minimum capital, capital protection, disclosure of accounts, directors' liability for non-compliance with disclosure duties also in bankruptcy, the duty to properly resolve and record resolutions in case of related party transactions and conflicts of interest also in one-man companies). Case law shows that non-observance of company law rules are used by receivers to hold directors and shadow directors liable in bankruptcy. The pending Bill to reform the BV deletes some rules on minimum capital and capital protection, but leaves many others in place and adds a new solvency test in case of distributions.

the NV statute and hence the BV inherited the influx of the stakeholders approach that characterized the amended 1970 NV statute.

The 'Rheinland' (stakeholders) model is well known from the debate on the governance of *public* issuers. It regards companies as an *institution* with a variety of stakeholders and interested parties, rather than as an *instrument* of entrepreneurs and/or shareholders. Creditors should be protected not only by means of general private law and specific insolvency law provisions, but also by company law itself (*inter alia* protection of capital, rules on external liability of directors and disclosure of annual accounts to allow assessment of the solvency of the company as – potential – debtor). After World War II, Germany and various other countries introduced rules on participation and co-determination of employees (not only at shop floor, but also at board level).

Thus close companies became a derivative of 'public' companies rather than of contractual 'partnership' or of sole ownershipship. So the stakeholders concept over time influenced close companies as well, including schemes of participation of employees. Creation of close companies as legal persons providing limited liability to shareholders in The Netherlands until recently required a ministerial declaration of 'non objection' and it is still subject to notarization. The latter requirement will be even extended to partnerships that elect to be 'legal person' (a status that thus be attributed rather than *recognized*). Moreover the close company law statute over time has been filled with strict mandatory rules to prevent abuse and fraud, not the least to protect collection of taxes. Further, companies regulation follows the regulatory concept of 'associations' of capital providers (*universitas personarum*) rather than that of contractual cooperation (*societas*) between entrepreneurs and financiers or a *universitas iuris* with particular beneficial interests (incorporation of sole ownership). The 'institutional' concept of companies shifts regulatory concern to the variety of stakeholders and mandatory rules to protect their interests. Applied to 'private' businesses it constrains their contractual character. The regulatory claim of this legislative approach necessarily tends to a closed shop (*numerus clausus*) of business organizations with mandatory

---

Co-determination for large BVs will not be changed. The Explanatory Notes to the Bill specifically state that the 'institutional' character of (also) the BV remains the guiding principle for reform. No contract, no split between memorandum of incorporation and articles of association, shareholders agreements remain non corporate contracts, still quasi-NV rather than quasi-partnership, mandatory law. Faced with requests to consider a Netherlands LCC and LLP the Minister of Justice recently responded in the same way. It illustrates the importance of going back to basics.

regulations, resulting in restrictions to the menu of possible reorganizations (conversions, mergers, splits, transfer etc.). The recent ECJ decisions (*Centros, Uberseering, Inspire Art* and *Sevic*) does however breach
such ban.

Thus the statutory concepts and objectives for different 'legal
persons'–business organizations – raises the basic question whether
these forms are instrumental to the entrepreneur or rather institutional.
This is not a soft, philosophical issue, but one that is highly relevant to
guide regulation on a number of issues. Prevailing answers indeed form
part, also in reform debates in member countries, of path-dependent
directions and should therefore be unveiled. This is also true for the
present debate on the SPE Statute.

Netherlands company law is framed in a broad regulation of 'legal
persons', disconnected from partnership and commercial law. Also
other jurisdictions do not have a coherent statute for business organizations but rather a dispersed variety of codes and statutes. Belgium and
Austria did recently integrate their regulation.[5]

Overlooking EU company law the picture is not different. To achieve one
common market the Roman Treaty established the freedom of establishment (arts. 42–49). Cross-border corporate mobility was hardly existent
and regulatory competition restricted by the aim to harmonize corporate
law (art. 44(g)) which reflects a broad 'institutional' and 'stakeholders'
concept of companies/entities/legal persons (art. 48–2 and art. 44(g)).

The 1st (and for branches: the 11th) directive created a EU-style corporate
disclosure system to facilitate access to basic data of '*companies*': instrument
of constitution (incorporation) and amendments, (powers of) managers,
subscribed and authorized capital *and* annual accounts as required by the
4th and 7th Directive (audited single and consolidated accounts). Initially
'private' companies were exempted, but were later included by extending
their scope. The 2nd Directive introduced mandatory rules on protection and
maintenance of capital and assets (minimum capital, evaluation and audit
of contribution in kind, mandatory reserves, limits to distributions of profit
and reserves; some member countries extended these rules to 'private' companies to prevent fraud and abuses of limited liability. The 4th and 7th directive require all companies (incl. private and one-man corporations; see 12th
Directive) to draft single and consolidated annual accounts (balance sheet,
P&L account and management report) in accordance with its standards,

---

[5] Belgian Wetboek van Vennootschappen and Austrian Unternehmensgesetzbuch
(2007).

statutory audit and disclosure (filing with the commercial register/registrar). They thus typically reflect an institutional (stakeholder- rather than shareholder-oriented) approach. Specific disclosure rules are applicable in case of changes of capital and other incidental corporate reorganizations: (cross-border) legal mergers and splits (3rd, 6th and 10th Directive). The system focus at *disclosure* of accounts (and specific reports) to serve the public at large. The draft 5th Directive intended to harmonize corporate governance of 'large' formal public companies: board structure, co-determination, division of powers between management, non executive directors and GMS and other governance issues, but no agreement was reached on the choice between shareholder and employee orientation. The 9th Directive on the law on groups of companies,[6] *inter alia* providing for a special report on related party transactions between parent and a public type subsidiary, did not even reach the status of an official draft. Most of the scope and subject matters of the directives and regulations focus on the type of *public* companies and issuers. The directives are implemented into national corporate law, sometimes with voluntary extension to close and pseudo-foreign corporations.

The EU did not itself develop a clear concept of, nor a coherent statute for, *private companies* or partnerships (the EEIG resembles both partnerships and (cooperative) associations). It allows the EU to make a fresh start, deviate from and set aside the 'acquis communautaire' that largely originated as a top-down (from large enterprises to SMEs) rather than as bottom-up design, i.e. starting with small and medium-sized enterprises and building on such rules towards larger and big firms. The present EU company law in fact is very dispersed in concept as well as in substance. It reveals the opportunity to create a new, flexible and innovative SPE that avoids the petrification of existing EU company law.[7]

---

[6] This subject was covered in paras. 291–328 of the new Aktiengesetz (1965) and was copied into the first drafts for the SE Statute (Title VII of the 1970 draft). The text of the provisional draft for a directive was published in M. Lutter, *Europäisches Unternehmensrecht, Sonderheft Zeitschrift für Unternehmens- und Gesellschaftsrecht* (1991), 279–289.

[7] The societal and, hence, legal extension of the concepts of entrepreneur and enterprise caused a gradual linkage of traditional private and classical commercial law regulation. The basic 'entity', the sole ownership, in which the entrepreneur 'owns' his enterprise and acts as party to all contracts and transactions, is not generally but only incidentally addressed (e.g. EU Directive protection of employees in case of transfer of business). 'Civil' and commercial partnerships may be regulated in civil and commercial codes and/or in separate statutes, sometimes as specimen of joint ownership, sometimes as specific contracts and yet in other times as separate entities. Similarly *corporate* business organizations are sometimes linked to 'associations', sometimes to partnership or to trustlike devices or simply to artificial persons (e.g. Book 2 DCC), each time – though not necessarily exclusively – addressee of all assets and liabilities.

The overriding question for the SPE statute – and more generally for the development of the EU and national law on business organizations – appears to be how it can contribute to enhancing economic and innovative strength of EU enterprises in the rapidly changing global economy. At the level of regulatory design an equally relevant question is how in this changing reality of our EU market and society the primary freedoms and proprietary interests of entrepreneurs shall be respected and balanced against the interests (an appropriate protection) of other interested parties. The most promising approach seems to be to think bottom-up or – as was the device in the UK – to think small first.

Entrepreneurship should be enhanced, its imminent entrepreneurial risks should be acknowledged and divided properly, acquired and accrued value in business should be properly protected as a propriety interest, creditor self-help should in business be the lead theme, not accumulation of statutory protective rules that are ineffective and burdensome.

If these elements are taken as starting points for drafting the statute it allows a sharper view on where and to what extent such specific corporate law protection should be provided for. It would also urge a reassessment of concepts and substantive rules of prevailing EU company law directives and regulations to allow a fresh view on the regulatory function and border zones between company and insolvency law. Taking another route may result in piling up or even cherry picking rules without assessing their ratio and effectiveness. Protection of associates, members and third parties should be based on contractual freedom to agree on the 'internal affairs' between them as associates, not as anonymous investors. General private law (contract and property) should be tested on their ability to cope with fraud and abuse of the corporate device, e.g. by distributing funds causing the company to become unable to pay its tax and other bills without recourse for creditors in bankruptcy. It urges to seek borderline solutions between strict company law and general private and insolvency law (like the *actio Pauliana*). Prevailing regulations should be meticulously assessed (e.g. asset and capital protection, disclosure of accounts, statutory audits, mandatory division of powers, general and specific (insolvency law) liability of directors and shadow directors, derivative or direct actions of creditors and other enforcement mechanisms. At least in the Netherlands case law reveals that receivers in bankruptcy did (successfully) attempt to construe directors' liability on alleged non-observance of *internal* company law rules.

IV. Basic issues to be addressed in the SPE Statute

Thinking bottom-up – like the ULLCA did – would cause the basis for the SPE Statute to be the freedom of enterprise and contract and the protection of propriety interests to enshrine the economic and legal organization of single-owned enterprises (incl. subsidiaries), quasi-partnership, firms financed with venture capital and family holdings with 'dispersed' ownership. The Statute should focus on minimum mandatory requirements and provide as well – in one form or another – off-the-peg models and solutions (default rules) for different, also more complicated firms like family holdings. It should allow partnership-like patterns for cooperation between business partners and tailor-made financing by venture capitalists and merchant banks. It should be apt to become a standard form in its own right. State concessions and similar requirements ('birth control') should be avoided and formal requirements (notarization) be minimized. Regulation of internal affairs (to protect shareholders) should be left to contractual freedom of promoters/partners and shareholders. In view of the many single-person companies and quasi-partnerships the statute should not be overloaded with superfluous rules that de facto address patterns with a multitude of 'outside' shareholders. The SPE should be recognized as a legal person the internal affairs of which are regulated by contract. The 'owners' of an SPE (shareholders) will have limited liability. Protection of employees, creditors and other interested third parties should be addressed primarily by non-corporate law rules, like contract and labour law, that can provide more effective and tailor-made tools for the protection of their interests. Tort victims are usually not specifically protected by the law on business organizations. (Future) Creditors should be more clearly confined to the principle of creditor self-help. Trust is indispensable in the business community, but should not be – at least not primarily and exclusively – be gained by a multitude of detailed and complicated statutory rules that later may and often do appear to be costly but ineffective.

A. *The character of the SPE Statute*

The choice for an SPE from the available menu(s) of business organizations should offer a reliable, cost effective business organization. The SPE Statute should therefore be drafted – in contrast to the SE Statute – as a real stand-alone statute. A Regulation would provide the proper instrument. It should be comprehensive and exhaustive, i.e. without references to national law to fill gaps and without additional national requirements. Disputes are to be resolved by applying the rules of the statute in accordance with their ratio. Official comments should offer guidance. Ultimate interpretative questions will be submitted to the ECJ. Arbitration and mediation should be recognized as appropriate means which partners or shareholders can freely select to resolve their disputes. To prevent petrification of the Statute an official experts committee should be appointed to monitor practice and advise the EC on amendments or additions that may become necessary or desirable.

1. The character of the SPE

The focus on SMEs implies a bottom-up approach. Hence the SPE should be instrumental rather than institutional to enable and facilitate incorporation of small and medium-size sole ownerships, partnerships, family holdings and venture capital financed firms. The SPE should not be designed as a derivative of 'public' companies, but rather build on the contractual and proprietary concepts of partnership and sole ownership (see S. 202 ULLCA). Complicated internal governance and shareholder protection rules for public type companies should be avoided. The SPE should offer a simplified company form which is recognized as a separate legal entity (see S. 112, 201 and 501 ULLCA), grant limited liability to its owner(s)/shareholder(s) (see S. 303 ULLCA) and allows contractual freedom to organize its internal affairs. To prevent uncertainty and legal costs the Statute should provide for proper default rules and attach various off-the-peg models for the internal organization. Transfer of shares need not be excluded; the main rules can be adapted to those applicable in partnership law.

To enable the reality of SPE-patterns to be reflected the Statute should enable an SPE to be structured as 'shareholders managed' or as 'management managed' corporations.

2. Eligibility of an SPE

Perhaps the major advantage of an SPE in the enlarged and culturally diversified EU will be its European label, particularly in cross-border business activities developed from the home state. A requirement of being 'international' (or – like an SE – to be created by promoters from different member states) would unnecessarily limit the eligibility of the SPE. Promoters should not be forced to create artificial, 'formal' cross-border structures. An SPE should rather be eligible for every EU citizen-entrepreneur or firm, irrespective of the nature of their activities: merchants (Kaufleute), providers of professional services (lawyers, auditors, docters), securities industry, farmers and others, including existing companies or other entities (also other than an SPE). A plurality of promoters will not be required (12th Directive). Limitations to the objects and operations like art. 3 of the EEIG Regulation should be avoided (S. 112 ULLCA).

B. *The creation of an SPE*

An SPE should be created by signing a memorandum of incorporation and filing that memorandum with the Commercial register (Registrar or similar national agency) which filing will vest legal personality (see S. 202 and 205–7 ULLCA and art. 1 EEIG). The Statute should – like the EEIG Statute – provide its own rules without reference to the 1st Directive. The creation will not be subject to any (form of) state consent or approval, nor quasi-public oversight like notarization of documents. Registration of the memorandum will inform and protect the business community and disclose its existence, scope, whether it is shareholder managed or management managed, the identity of the promoter(s), the power of managers – or in case of a shareholder-managed SPE, of shareholders to represent the SPE (see S. 202/203 and 301 ULLCA). The contractual internal organization and division of powers need not be disclosed. An SPE may also be created by conversion of existing corporate entities and partnerships without limitation to 'companies' as meant in art. 1 of the 1st Directive (as suggested in art. 5 EPC) and by a 'going concern' contribution in kind of a sole ownership (transfer by operation of law and therefore a quasi-conversion).

1. Capital and shares

The capital of the company will be divided in shares and the rights attached thereto will be laid down in the agreement between promoters. Shares may vary in terms of nominal value, control, income and value. Whether shares are transferable or may be pledged will depend on the operation agreement. The ULLCA takes another approach and explicitly provides that members are not co-owners of nor have a transferable interest in an LLC's property. It avoids the qualification 'share' and uses the term 'transferable interest' distinct from any (further) rights members in the organization of an LLC. Only that transferable interest may be transferred and the transferee consequently will not be a member (S. 501–3 ULLCA). That transferable interest may be pledged or be the subject of a lien ordered by the court. In case of dissociation of a member in a continuing LLC only this interest will be purchased by the LLC against its value as agreed upon or fixed by the court (see 504, 602–3, 701 and 702 ULLCA).

2. Contribution

The SPE rules on contribution shall not be governed by the 2nd Directive and no minimum capital will be required. They should rather focus on partnership like rules and hence allow movable and immovable assets, money, but also services of any kind to be contributed (S. 401 ULLCA). The obligation to contribute will be governed by the agreement and be enforceable on behalf of the company (derivatively) by every shareholder-promoter and – in case he relied upon the obligation to contribute – a creditor (see S. 402 ULLCA). Since SMEs very often start as sole ownerships, contribution is in kind as a 'going concern' by operation of law and thus preserving its 'identity'.

C. *Internal organization*

The Statute's rules on internal organization should offer both the freedom to members to lay down such rules by (operating) agreement, off-the-peg choices and default rules. To reflect and follow the reality of single-owned companies, quasi-partnerships, subsidiaries and family-owned structures the Statute should follow the ULLCA example and allow SPEs to be organized both as a *shareholder-managed* SPE and as a *management-managed* SPE. The latter could serve cases with a wider circle of shareholders or delegated organizational structures. Mandatory provisions on the creation of and the division of powers between bodies corporate become obsolete; default rules on the consequences of such a choice do not. Because the choice directly affects the authority of members/managers to represent the SPE the choice should be disclosed in the memorandum of incorporation. An operating agreement regulates the affairs of the EPC and the conduct of its business and governs the relations among its members, managers and the company. It should include the following elements.

A *member-managed SPE* would effectively operate as a quasi partnership with each member having power to represent the SPE in its normal course of business, but also – as 'partner' – to be accountable to his fellow members and to observe duties of care and loyalty vis-à-vis the SPE (S. 103 and 404 ULLCA). Therefore the operating agreement cannot unreasonably withhold information and inspection rights of members, duties of loyalty and care, eliminate obligations of good faith and fair dealing, vary the right to expel members in specified events or to wind up an SPE, as specified. It may specify the procedure to be observed in case of conflicts of interest (S. 103 ULLCA). Each member is agent of the SPE for the purpose of its business. He binds the SPE unless the third party with whom he was dealing knew or had notice of the lack of authority. In case of acts outside the ordinary course of business will be binding only if all other members did authorize such act. The SPE will be bound by wrongful acts in the ordinary course of the SPE's business (S. 301–302 ULLCA). Liability solely by reason of being or acting as member (or manager) is excluded. Members *may* by consent and disclosure assume liability for the debts of an EPC (S. 303 ULLCA).

With respect to the *management* each member would have equal rights and, unless otherwise provided, matters relating to the business of the SPE could be decided by majority vote (S. 404 ULLCA).

Each member shall properly account for his management to the company and its members. Each member has the right to be informed and access to the records of the company (S. 408 ULLCA). The 4th and 7th Directives would not be applicable to the SPE. Public disclosure would be limited to the memorandum of incorporation, irrespective specific information duties to tax authorities and other public agencies or contractual rights of financiers or other third parties.

Fiduciary duties of members in a member-managed SPE would be limited to the following duties of loyalty: to account to the SPE and hold as trustee assets and business opportunities; to refrain from self-dealing in case of a conflict of interest; refrain from competition with the SPE. Duties of care would be limited to refraining from engaging in grossly negligent or reckless conduct, intentional misconduct or a knowing violation of law. His assignment should be exercised with the obligation of good faith and fair dealing. These duties are not violated merely because the member's conduct furthers his own interest (S. 409 ULLCA).[8]

In a *management-managed SPE* managers will be elected by (a majority of) the members. The rules on binding the SPE would follow *mutatis mutandis* for a member-managed company and the same would be the case for the management-managed company. Management would exclusively decide on any matter related to the business; major matters

---

[8] See for the position of a member-non-manager in member-managed company: S. 409 (g) ULLLCA.

concerning the organization of the EPC would require approval by the members (S. 404 ULLCA).

Payments made by members made in the ordinary course of the business will be reimbursed and indemnified for any liability so incurred (S. 403 ULLCA). Accounting and information to the company and its members follow *mutatis mutandis* the rules for a member-managed SPE.

D. The limits of limited liability

The limits of limited liability are a delicate and heavily 'path dependent' topic since regulators – also at EU level – over time have designed a series of general and detailed rules to prevent and sanction abuse of limited liability (and non-liability of directors) by mandatory *company* and also private or insolvency law provisions. In drafting a 'light' SPE Statute a fresh analysis is needed of the relationship between recognition/grant of corporate personality as such, the conditions for limited liability, the allocation of the *per se* existing entrepreneurial risks between entrepreneur and third parties, the ability of the latter to protect their risks by contract (banks, suppliers/customers, tax collectors) and the entrepreneurial assignment of managers. Prevention of fraud and criminal use of the corporate device (e.g. for laundering) should be addressed separately in the context of crime prevention and penal sanctions.

The EU 2nd Directive for 'public' companies aims to protect the company's capital by a series of detailed and complicated rules (which were extended by some member states to 'close' companies). Non-observance of internal organization rules (often copied from public company statutes) have sometimes been interpreted as to cope with agency problems in close corporations as well and hence be extended (derivatively, by tort law or otherwise) to protection of third parties, thus blurring border lines between (internal) corporate and insolvency law. The 4th/7th Directives require 'private' companies to prepare and disclose audited single and consolidated accounts to enable (potential) creditors to assess their solvency.[9] As stated above an LLC is not subject at all to such duties

---

[9] Non-observance of these requirements under Netherlands law (art. 2:248 Civil Code) vest an assumption of causation in case of bankruptcy and hence liability of (shadow) directors for the company's deficit. This is far from rational and reality although these ongoing requirements are costly and burdensome. They tempt receivers to out-of-context interpretations. Starting from the inherent risk of any business venture, the crucial test should rather be whether shareholders in the face of insolvency risks divert assets from the company or managers knowing/intending to induce new creditors to find recourse.

of drafting, auditing and disclosure of its accounts. The directives in their 'institutional' approach thus deviate from the mere traditional accounting to members who evidently can design their own rules for accounting and inspection of records (with proper default rules). Since the ultimate test materializes in insolvency the variety of specific insolvency rules[10] developed in various member states have to be taken into account as well and preferably the SPE Statute should provide exhaustive rules.[11]

The focus should be (again) on the basic issue of withdrawing (by whatever technique) assets from the SPE's patrimony causing the SPE to be or become unable to pay its debts as becoming due in the ordinary course of its business or the SPE just becoming insolvent. This is the core of many existing rules and it should preferably be the core provision in the Statute as well. Its application would involve directors' liability vis-à-vis the SPE to be also enforceable derivatively.

For the LLC the following rules have been established. S. 406/407 ULLCA prohibit distributions to shareholders if (a) the company would be unable to pay its debts as they become due in the ordinary course of business. be made and liability for unlawful distributions or – in summary – (b) total assets would be less than total liabilities upon dissolution of the company. Members/managers failing to meet the standards of conduct and vote for or assent to unlawful distributions will be personally liable for the portion of the distribution that exceeds the maximum amount that could have been lawfully distributed. The recovery remedy extends to the company only, not to creditors.

E. Dissociation and expulsion of members

Regulation of dissociation and expulsion of members in SPE's with more than one member would be primarily subject to the operating agreement between the members. For quasi-partnerships and joint ventures members should envisage that the basis of personal cooperation and commitment (*affectio societatis*) may disappear and result in frustration of the operations of the company or even a deadlock in its management and strategy. Members may provide for dispute resolution but if unsuccessful dissociation should be allowed. They therefore should explicitly provide for – like in a partnership – the terms and conditions for expulsion and for voluntary dissociation and, equally important, for the

---

[10]   E.g. wrongful trading and thin capitalization.
[11]   S. 807–8 ULCCA: procedures to settle claims against dissolved LLC.

settlement of the exit price. In view of possible incomplete contracts or a change of the shareholders base, the Statute should provide for default rules to be applied in such case. Although continuity of the SPE's business should be the guiding principle, complete dissolution of the SPE will follow upon occurrence of an event or consent of (number/percentage of) members as specified in the operating agreement, inability to pursue the business or on a substantiated application of a member or transferee of a member's interest (S. 801 ULLCA).

The default rules providing the reasons and grounds for dissociation should include a (lawful)[12] notice of a member to withdraw, agreed upon event, expulsion according to the operating agreement or by unanimous vote under substantiated circumstances, dissolution of a corporate member or partnership, judicial expulsion, bankruptcy, death or appointment of a guardian or conservator (cf. S. 601 ULLCA).

The effect of dissociation of a member is that his 'organizational' rights as most of his fiduciary duties ceases to exist and that he becomes entitled to a purchase by the LLC of his transferable interest against the agreed-upon value or – upon application – as being fixed by the court (S 603, 701–2 ULCCA).

F. Corporate reorganizations

Corporate reorganizations are important for SPEs as they are for other business forms. The 3rd, 6th and 10th Directives harmonized (cross) border mergers and splits and the SEVIC decision of the ECJ extended the reach of facilitating national rules, like German Umwandlungsgesetz to 'foreign' firms wishing to use these. Seat transfer, conversion and cross-border merger are also addressed in the SE Statute.

The dynamics of SMEs equally require a flexible regime for corporate reorganizations which should be addressed separately in the SPE Statute by extending the existing facilities to include SPEs. In view of the very nature of the LLC, allowing contractual cooperation between its members as quasi-partnership, it would be important to also allow for conversion of partnerships into an LLC and vice versa as well as to convert an LLC in other forms, including a 'public' company, e.g. in view of going public of a successful start-up of a firm financed with venture capital. Apart from the existing EU rules reference is made to the flexible rules as provided by Article 9 ULLCA on conversions of partnerships

---

[12] S. 602 ULLCA.

into an LLC and merger of entities with or resulting in an LLC. For completeness sake it should be noticed that an amendment of an SPE from a member-managed into a management-managed SPE does not constitute a conversion of business form in the strict sense.

V. Concluding remarks

The main purpose of this article in honour of Eddy Wymeersch was to address the possibility of combining corporate and contractual (partnership-like) notions into one and the same statutory business organizations. Faced with the intention of the European Commission to come up with an innovative design of an SPE to facilitate SMEs and taking notice of the desires as expressed in the consultation, the danger should be faced and addressed that the project will stand on the dogmatic resistance of combining what according to some scholars can simply not be combined: contract and corporation. This idea seems to be definitely outdated but continues its life as 'unveiled assumption'. Since my 1976 PhD thesis on joint ventures I have been fascinated with the question whether one can be a partnership *inter sese* and a corporation to the rest of the world. The question was positively resolved in the US at the beginning of the last century and the LLC, the highly successful offshoot of this development, provides us with a statutory example how to combine contract and corporation. I sincerely hope that Eddy Wymeersch will continue to enrich the academic debate as he did so devotedly for so long!

Post scriptum

After completion of this article the European Commission published a draft Statute for a European Private Company (SEC/2008/2098/2099). Time and space only allow a very brief overview. The Statute largely follows the 'standard' form for private companies in the EU. Its formation is free and includes transformation/conversion of an existing business as well as merger/division (art. 5). Registered office and real seat may be in different states (art. 7). Articles of association shall be published, not only a memorandum of incorporation; legal personality will be acquired upon registration (art. 8–11). Capital divided in shares, no minimum capital required, contribution in kind allowed (art. 14–15, 19–21). Transfer regulated by articles; expulsion and withdrawal of shareholder envisaged (art. 16–17). Solvency certificate required before distributions to shareholders (art. 21). Preparation, filing, auditing and publication of accounts according to art. 25 follow applicable national law, i.e. essentially the 4th and 7th Directives. The Statute does not envisage a shareholder-managed EPC and sticks to the model of centralized management acting in the interest of the EPC (art. 30/31) albeit with broad collective powers for the AGM (art. 27). Individual (group) rights of information and calling a meeting are covered by art. 29/29. Transfer of registered office is regulated separately (incl. employee participation). Transformation, merger, division and dissolution follow national law (art. 39–40). The Statute should be in force by July 1, 2010.

The draft takes an important step towards a stand-alone 'federal' business form for all member states. In view of its focus on SMEs and its use as cross-border subsidiary further simplifications as allowed by ULLCA should be considered.

3

Ius Audacibus. The future of EU company law[1]

JAAP WINTER

> An Elf shall go
> Where a Dwarf dare not?
> Oooh, I will never hear the end of it.
>
> Gimli in Lord of the Rings, Tolkein

I. Introduction

The European Union originally was conceived as creating an economic community between Member States. A key pillar of the European Community is the principle of free movement as expressed in the free movement of persons, goods, services and capital. Together with the EU rules on competition they form the European Community's economic constitutional law.[2] Part of the free movement of persons is the freedom of establishment. This freedom includes 'the right to take up and pursue activities as self-employed persons and to set up and manage undertakings, in particular companies or firms...under the conditions laid down for its own nationals by the law of the country where such establishment is effected, subject to the provisions of the Chapter on capital' (Article 43 Treaty of Rome). In order to attain freedom of establishment the Council and the Commission are required to 'co-ordinate to the necessary extent the safeguards which, for the protection of the interests of members and others, are required by Member States of companies or firms...with a view to making such safeguards equivalent throughout the Community' (art. 44 (2) (g)). This Treaty provision is the basis for the harmonization of company law in the European Union. It is a rather

---

[1] This contribution is an adaptation of my inaugural lecture at the University of Amsterdam held on 14 April 2007.

[2] J. Baquero Cruz, *Between Competition and Free Movement. The Economic Constitutional Law of the European Community* (Oxford: Hart Publishing, 2002).

peculiar basis. It takes a specific angle to the harmonization process: the protection of shareholders and others which is required by Member States' company laws. The protection of shareholders and others, in particular creditors, was very much in the minds of the original authors of the Treaty. There was a concern among Member States in those days, we speak of 1957, that shareholders and creditors would not invest in companies from other Member States or do business with them, as they would not be familiar with the company laws to which such companies would be subject and particularly with the protections afforded to them under these company laws. In addition, Member States feared that without a rigorous harmonization programme, Member States would race to the bottom by creating company laws with ever-reducing protection for shareholders and creditors in order to compete with other Member States for the incorporation or registration of companies in their jurisdictions. The Netherlands were seen as Europe's bottom in those days, not only geographically but also in terms of company law. Dutch company law was very flexible in those days, with a minimum of mandatory rules. Regulatory arbitrage that would lead other Member States to race to that same bottom was to be avoided. I will not go into the question whether such a race to the bottom would have ever occurred without article 44 (2) (g) and the harmonization programme. For now I just note that approaching company law legislation with the primary objective to make protections for shareholders and creditors equivalent across the EU is indeed a peculiar approach to company law. I will come back to this at the end of this chapter.

On the basis of article 44 (2) (g) in the meantime eleven directives have been adopted. They primarily deal with formalities of company law such as incorporation, publicity, capital formation and protection, (cross-border) legal mergers and split-ups, accounting, branches etc. Some call the resulting EU company law trivial.[3] Member States have discovered fundamental differences of opinion on such core issues as the organization of the board, the role and rights of shareholders, group relationships, employee co-determination and corporate control. In these areas nothing of substance has been agreed by Member States, projects were either abandoned (the fifth Directive on the structure of the company dealing with board structures and the rights of shareholders,

---

[3] L. Enriques, 'EC Company Law Directives and Regulations: How Trivial Are They?', in J. Armour and J. McCahery (eds.), *After Enron, Improving Corporate Law and Modernising Securities Regulation in Europe and the US*, (Oxford: Hart Publishing, 2006), 641–700.

and the ninth Directive on group law) or Member States have agreed to disagree and to leave it to Member States individually (e.g. the Statute for the Societas Europea on board structures and the thirteenth Directive on takeover bids).

II. Political process

In light of the political decision making in the EU process we should perhaps be surprised that so many directives have actually made it to their adoption. The right of initiative lies with the Commission which has a primarily, but maybe not exclusively European agenda. But the key decisions are made by the Council of Ministers. The Council consists of representatives of the current twenty-seven Member States' governments. Decisions in the Council are often, perhaps more often than not, driven by each Member State's government negotiating to preserve and further national Member State interests. They are doing this on a number of files which are discussed simultaneously and which should all lead to some form of regulation or action at EU level. Member States find it difficult to suppress the inclination to make deals across files, to agree to certain other Member States' wishes, say on an agricultural issue, in order to get their agreement on a company law issue. The compromises that follow often have little to do with the merits of the issues dealt with. Directives then require approval from the European Parliament. The Parliament functions mainly along party lines, but MEPs sometimes are sensitive to national issues and particular concerns of the Member States they are representing. In some cases all MEPs from a particular Member State vote in a certain direction to protect perceived national interests, as is said did the German MEPs from left to right when voting down the Takeover Bids Directive in June 2001.

A complicating factor in this political process is that on many files the question is raised whether it is really for the EU to regulate or whether regulation should be left to Member States. Member States have become sensitive to this question when after some decades they witnessed that many of their powers had effectively been transferred to the EU and would need to be shared with other Member States. In the Maastricht Treaty of 1992 article 5 was introduced, providing that in areas which do not fall within its exclusive competence, the Community shall take action, in accordance with the principle of *subsidiarity*, only if and insofar as the objectives of the proposed action cannot be sufficiently achieved by the Member States and can therefore, by reason of the scale or effects of the proposed action, be better achieved by the Community. The words 'cannot be sufficiently achieved' and 'be better achieved' leave ample opportunity to challenge EU interference in almost any area. Subsidiarity is an argument often heard and used when Member States do not like the possible outcome of an EU regulatory process.

Linked to these factors troubling the political decision-making process is the fact that Member States' governments also make up the key decision maker at EU level, the Council of Ministers. This has the effect that these governments, but also everybody else who has a role or an interest in the subject matter to be regulated, can and often needs to play chess on two chess boards: national level and EU level. If for example a certain national legislative development is not desired by a Member State government, or by those who lobby that government, it or they can argue that this is a matter for the EU to regulate and not for any single Member State. This often serves as an efficient delaying tactic as agreement at EU level is difficult to achieve. Or, vice versa, a deadlock at national level can sometimes be broken by forging an agreement with other Member States at EU level. Playing simultaneous chess on two boards is what the vast lobbying industry in Brussels is all about.

All these factors contribute to the political decision-making process in the EU being highly complex and its outcomes highly unpredictable. The focus and efforts of the EU to improve its legislative process through the Better Regulation initiatives[4] are not suited to dealing with these fundamental complicating factors, which lie at the root of the political structure of the EU. They have caused three somewhat overlapping trends in EU legislation of company law in this century.

III. Three trends

The first trend is a strong emphasis on *subsidiarity*. This trend can be seen from abandoning the fifth and ninth Directives on the structure of the company and on group law, which are now no longer issues where the EU seeks a legislative role for itself. This trend is also clear from the efforts to simplify current directives, in particular the second Directive on capital maintenance. The thrust is to remove from the Directives anything which is not really necessary or clearly helpful.[5] Finally we see this

---

[4] See http://ec.europa.eu/enterprise/regulation/better_regulation/index_en.htm.
[5] See Directive the European Parliament and of the Council of 6 September 2006 amending Council Directive 77/91/EEC as regards the formation of public limited liability

trend from the development to not impose certain elements of legislation on Member States but to either give them options to apply or not apply certain EU rules (see the thirteenth Directive on Takeover Bids and the opt-outs that Member States have been given from the rules on defence against takeovers, provided they give opt-in rights to companies)[6] or to leave out of an EU legislative instrument core elements of regulation (see the SE Statute, leaving anything contentious to Member States to regulate themselves in their legislation implementing the SE Statute).[7]

The second trend is the *privatization of company law.* This trend is visible at national and at EU level. The SE Statute for example leaves the choice for a one-tier board structure or a two-tier board structure to those incorporating the SE themselves, see articles 39 and 42 SE Statute. Similarly, companies have the right to opt-in to application of articles 9 (board passivity) and 11 (break-through) of the thirteenth Directive on Takeover Bids, if the Member State does not impose application of these rules, see article 12. Finally, and perhaps most importantly, the regulation of corporate governance to a large extent is left to companies and their shareholders. Codes of corporate governance are to be adopted at Member State level and in most if not all Member States these codes have been drafted by committees consisting of representatives of companies, shareholders and other private entities. Furthermore, these codes are not binding upon companies, but companies must explain to what extent and for what reasons they do not comply with the code to which they are subject, see article 46a (1) (a) and (b) of the fourth Directive on annual accounts, as amended by Directive 2006/46/EC, L 224/1. The enforcement is primarily in the hands of shareholders.[8]

companies and the maintenance and alteration of their capital 2006/68/EC [2006] OJ L 264/32. See for the general thrust to simplify company law, the report on the public consultation on the future priorities of the company law action plan, http://ec.europa.eu/internal_market/company/consultation/index_en.htm.

[6] G. Hertig and J. McCahery, 'An Agenda for Reform: Company and Takeover Law in Europe', in G. Ferrarini, K. Hopt, J. Winter and E. Wymeersch (eds.), *Reforming Company and Takeover Law in Europe,* (Oxford University Press: 2004), 21–49, who advocate the option-approach for EU company legislation. My concern with this approach is that the design and effects of the options to be given to Member States will be subject to the same political factors I described above and are likely to be used particularly to protect national interests.

[7] See L. Enriques, 'Silence is Golden: The European Company As a Catalyst for Company Law Arbitrage', *Journal of Corporate Law Studies* (2004), 77.

[8] See the Statement of the European Corporate Governance Forum on the comply-or-explain principle of 22 February 2006, see, http://ec.europa.eu/internal_market/company/ecgforum/index_en.htm.

The third trend is that where Member States do reach an agreement in spite of conflicts between national interests and perceptions, the outcome is typically an *ugly compromise* creating problems for companies that have to apply the resulting rules. The Directive accompanying the SE Statute on the involvement of employees, in particular the rules on participation of employees in a board of the company, are a fine example. The Directive is wrought with provisions whose only purpose is to avoid that by merging into an SE a German company subject to German co-determination rules could escape those rules. The rules create a complex set of provisions detailing what majorities of employees of participating companies can in different circumstances outvote German employees to not apply the German co-determination rules to the SE. If no agreement is reached a set of standard rules apply, the interpretation of which would be a tough challenge for the European Court of Justice and some of which actually are mutually conflicting.[9] Another example is offered by the opt-out and opt-in rules combined with the reciprocity rule of article 12 of the thirteenth Directive on takeover bids. These rules result in preserving the existing situations in Member States with respect to takeovers and defence instead of creating a level playing field for takeover bids, which is the stated objective of the Directive. They also create rules which are either easy to circumvent and manipulate or incredibly difficult to apply and which are possibly in breach of the Treaty itself and with the EU's obligations under the WTO as they by definition exclude non-listed and non-EU companies from obtaining as good as a position as a bidder as EU-listed companies can obtain.[10]

IV. EU's legislative remit in company law

In light of all this, I believe the remit of the EU's involvement in company law should be modest, at best. In line with the principle of subsidiarity, it should focus on those issues where individual Member States cannot provide solutions, and, in addition, on those issues where the evidence of a benefit of a solution at EU level over a solution by individual Member States is clear. These issues are most likely to arise with companies whose shares are listed on a regulated market. The securities laws to which these listed companies have become subject in Europe are to a very large extent

---

[9] See J. Winter, 'De Europese Vennootschap als sluis voor in- en uitvoer van vennootschapsrecht', *Nederlands Juristenblad* (2002), 2034–40.

[10] J. Winter, 'You must be joking', *Ondernemingsrecht* (2004), 367.

harmonized, if not uniform across the EU following the many far-reaching Directives and secondary regulations that have been adopted under the Financial Services Action Plan. A key aspect of the new rules is to ensure that companies in Europe have efficient access to capital markets across Europe and that their investors are offered equivalent protections on these markets. As a result, a key feature of listed companies, i.e. their relation to the capital markets, is regulated practically uniformly across the EU. It is more likely that there are issues for these companies that require EU solutions or where EU solutions are clearly preferable over Member States solutions than for non-listed companies.

Finally, the subject of corporate governance warrants EU attention. Not in the traditional way of trying to regulate the substance of corporate governance at EU level, as was intended with the fifth Directive, but in a more distanced way. The substance of corporate governance is linked directly to the core of company law: the structure and operation of boards of companies and the relationship with their shareholders. As this core of company law is designed differently across Member States, based on different legal, social, financial and cultural traditions, it is unlikely that Member States at EU level will reach agreement on a single model to be applied across the EU. It is also very doubtful whether creating and imposing such a model would really be efficient. But the EU can coordinate the efforts of Member States to protect and where necessary improve the integrity of their corporate governance models. This is particularly so because of the warm reception the so-called comply-or-explain model has received in Member States. This model avoids mandatory legislation on the substance of corporate governance by implementing corporate governance codes, compliance with which or proper explanations for non-compliance are to be enforced primarily by shareholders. The High Level Group that I chaired and the European Corporate Governance Forum recommend this model as a means to create and improve corporate governance in the EU.[11] But if we are honest, we should admit this is one big experiment. There is little or no experience with corporate governance codes and comply-or-explain in most Member States. There is also little understanding of what type of regulatory environment is required for such a system to function properly. What can or should

[11] See the report 'A Modern Regulatory Framework for Company Law in Europe' of November 2002, http://ec.europa.eu/internal_market/company/modern/index_en.htm#background. See also the Statement of the Forum on comply-or-explain, (note 8, above).

be done to ensure sufficient explanation for non-compliance? The systems assumes that shareholders can exercise certain rights effectively in order to enforce proper compliance or explanation, but it is not clear that shareholders actually have these rights in all Member States and it is certainly clear that most shareholders cannot exercise their rights efficiently across borders. The Directive on Shareholders Rights, which has been adopted to solve problems of cross-border voting in the EU, is precisely not doing that.[12] There are also questions in cases where the company is controlled by a major shareholder and the (non)compliance with the code fulfils the major shareholder's wishes (possibly to the detriment of minority shareholders), particularly if the major shareholder is able to exercise more control rights than are proportionate to his ownership of share capital. Comply-or-explain works fundamentally differently in those circumstances.[13] These are issues where the EU should at least coordinate the efforts of Member States. By using instruments such as the Recommendation the Commission would create a sort of comply-or-explain environment for Member States, which may create incentives to actively improve the national corporate governance system while retaining some flexibility between Member States.[14]

V. A new avenue for progress: the free movement of capital

The legislative remit for the EU in company law may be limited; this does not mean to say that the EU will not have an important impact on the company laws of Member States in different ways. The European Court of

---

[12] Directive of the European Parliament and of the Council of 11 July 2007 on the exercise of certain rights of shareholders in listed companies 2007/36/EC [2007] OJ L 184/17; see also the recommendations made by the European Corporate Governance Forum on solutions for cross-border voting, see statement of 24 July 2006, http://ec.europa.eu/internal_market/company/ecgforum/index_en.htm.

[13] After having called for substantial research into whether there is a need to regulate structures which create disproportionate control rights, EU Commissioner McCreevy abandoned this in October 2007. See for the reports on disproportionality http://ec.europa.eu/internal_market/company/shareholders/indexb_en.htm. The European Corporate Governance Forum did recommend several measures to be taken, including a higher level of disclosure of disproportionate control structures, see the statement of the Forum and the paper of the Forum's working group on proportionality on

[14] See for example the Commission's Recommendations on the role of independent directors and on director remuneration, http://ec.europa.eu/internal_market/company/independence/index_en.htm and http://ec.europa.eu/internal_market/company/directors-remun/index_en.htm.

Justice has proven to be a particular driving force, with its judgments on the freedom of establishment. The *Centros*, *Überseering* and *Inspire Art* judgements[15] have established that, where Member States have not agreed on harmonization of certain aspects of company law, a Member State may not impose barriers to the freedom of establishment merely because a company with an establishment in that Member State is incorporated in another Member State in which it does not perform any real business activities. Restrictions imposed on such a company, such as not allowing registering the establishment in the Member State, denying legal standing in court and imposition of additional administrative and substantive legal burdens, are not justified by the fact that the company does not adhere to the same capital maintenance rules as companies incorporated in the Member State itself. This case law has had at least three effects: (i) an increased trend to use English limited liability companies instead of the national form of limited company for doing business in other Member States, in particular Germany,[16] (ii) a fundamental discussion on whether the real seat theory is still a viable theory on the basis of which to apply company law of a Member State to a company incorporated in another Member State,[17] and (iii) some Member States have initiated proposals to deregulate their laws on limited companies, like the Netherlands and Germany.[18] This may lead to a convergence of company law from the bottom up, by incorporation choices of companies and by legislative actions by Member States without any EU legislation.

The case law on freedom of establishment is now well understood and its effects are becoming clear. The question is whether the other freedom

---

[15] Case C-212/97, *Centros Ltd* v. *Erhvervs- og Selskabsstyrelsen*, [1999] ECR I-1459 Case C-208/00, *Überseering BV* v. *Nordic Construction Company Baumanagement GmbH*, [2002] ECR I-9919 Case C-167/01, *Kamer van Koophandel en Fabrieken voor Amsterdam* v. *Inspire Art Ltd*, [2003] ECR I-10155.

[16] M. Becht , C. Mayer and H. Wagner, 'Where do firms incorporate? Deregulation and the cost of entry', *ECGI Law/Working Paper 70*(2006), http://papers.ssrn.com/sol3/papers.cfm?abstract_id=906066.

[17] E. Wymeersch, 'The transfer of the company's seat in EU company law', *ECGI Law/ Working paper 08*(2003), http://papers.ssrn.com/sol3/papers.cfm?abstract_id=384802.

[18] In the Netherlands a proposal to simplify and make more flexible the law applicable to *the besloten vennootschap* (limited company) has been submitted to parliament. According to this proposal the minimum capital requirement of currently €18,000 will be abolished. See for the German proposal to change the law applicable to the Gesellschaft mit beschränkter Haftung www.jura.uni-augsburg.de/prof/moellers/ materialien/materialdateien/040_deutsche_gesetzgebungsgeschichte/momig/. The German proposal does not abolish minimum capital altogether but reduces it from €25,000 to €10,000.

relevant to company law will have similar effects. This is the free movement of capital. The ECJ by now has established important case law based on the free movement of capital in the area of so-called golden shares. Golden shares refers to arrangements, either in law or in the company's constitution, made by Member States with respect to companies in their jurisdiction, typically companies that have been privatized, and that confer to a Member State certain powers of control over those companies, or the ability to prevent certain shareholders to acquire control over those companies. This is a crucial issue in the development of the EU. It is about striking the right balance between the EU's objective to create a single market without artificial barriers imposed by Member States and the Member States' concerns about losing control over business that are crucial to their economy and national infrastructure. The case law shows that the ECJ leaves Member States only very little scope to fence off companies with golden-share structures, which are quickly considered to hinder the free movement of capital as they are liable to dissuade investors (either direct investors interested in participating in control or portfolio investors not interested in participating in control)[19] from investing in the company. As with the freedom of establishment, the ECJ accepts only limited justifications of any impediment to the free movement of capital.[20]

So far, the case law on the free movement of capital is related to Member States and state actions, rather than to companies and citizens. However, the recent Volkswagen case may open up new avenues for development of EU company law on the basis of the free movement of capital.

VI. Volkswagen

The *Volkswagen* case[21] deals with the so called Volkswagen Act, a special Act of the German legislator dealing with certain governance arrangements for Volkswagen AG. After World War II the trade unions had started up the car-making business of Volkswagen, without it being clear who

---

[19] The ECJ has repeatedly ruled that both types of investors, distinguished in the Commission's statement of 19 July 1997 relating to certain legal aspects of intra-Community investments, Pub nr C 220, are protected by the free movement of capital.

[20] Case C-367/98, *Commission v. Portugal* [2002] ECR I-04731; Case C-483/99, *Commission v. France* [2002] ECR I-04781; Case C-503/99, *Commission v. Belgium* [2002] ECR I-04809; Case C-463/00, *Commission v. Spain* [2003] ECR I-4581; Case C-98/01, *Commission v. United Kingdom* [2003] ECR I-4641; Case C-174/04, *Commission v. Italy* [2005] ECR I-4933 and Cases C-282/04 [2006] ECR I-9141 and 283/04, *Commission v. the Netherlands* [2006] ECR I-9141.

[21] Case C-112/05, *Commission v. Germany* [2007] ECR I-8995.

actually owned the business. In 1959–60 the Federal German government and the government of the state of Lower Saxony discussed and agreed with the trade unions on the ownership of the business. It was decided that Volkswagen was to be a publicly held company, an Aktiengesellschaft, in which both the Federal State and Lower Saxony would each hold 20% of the company's share capital and the rest would be offered to the public. To date, Lower Saxony has maintained a stake of approximately 20% in Volkswagen, by subscribing for and investing in new shares whenever they were issued by the company. The Federal State has sold its shares. Part of the deal struck in 1959–60 was that minority shareholders would be protected against a party trying to take control of the company without acquiring the full share capital. At the same time this would protect employees against a possible hostile bid that could lead to lay-offs in Germany. The parties agreed to the adoption of three key governance provisions:

- the voting rights of each Volkswagen shareholder are limited to a maximum of 20% of the total votes that can be cast, even if the shareholder holds more than 20% of share capital;
- special resolutions of the general meeting of shareholders of Volkswagen that require a 75% majority under standard German law, require a majority of 80%;
- Germany and Lower Saxony may each, as long as they are Volkswagen shareholders, appoint two members to the Volkswagen supervisory board.

These provisions have not only been incorporated in the articles of association of Volkswagen AG, but have also been imposed on the company and its shareholders by the Volkswagen Act. As a practical result, Lower Saxony by maintaining its 20% in Volkswagen could veto important resolutions in the general meeting and no other shareholder could acquire more voting rights than Lower Saxony.

Germany had argued that all of this was nothing more than a private agreement between parties who had disputed the ownership of the company, which private agreements have merely been confirmed by the Volkswagen Act. The Court rejects this argument. The Volkswagen Act, a state measure, imposes these arrangements on the company and its shareholders and does not allow for the shareholders to decide to change them.[22]

---

[22] In the cases against the Netherlands, the Court considered putting certain clauses in the articles of association granting it special rights in companies the Netherlands was

Germany then argued that the voting cap and the super-majority requirement did not restrict the free movement of capital, because they apply without distinction to all shareholders, including Lower Saxony, and work both to the benefit (reduced chance of a third party acquiring cheap control with a relatively low percentage) and detriment (reduced ability to exercise control yourself with a relatively low percentage) of all shareholders, including Lower Saxony. The Court rejected this argument as well. But in doing so and by arguing that the Act does restrict the free movement of capital, the Court took a new turn. The Court basically argued that the 80% super-majority requirement created an instrument for Lower Saxony, as an approximately 20% shareholder, to procure for itself a blocking minority allowing it to oppose special resolutions on the basis of a lower level of investment than would be required under general company law. The 20% voting cap supplements this legal framework and enables Lower Saxony to exercise considerable influence on the basis of such a lower investment. The combination of the 80% super-majority requirement and the 20% voting cap, the Court ruled, diminishes the interest in acquiring a stake in the capital of Volkswagen as it is liable to limit the possibility for other shareholders to effectively participate in the management and control of Volkswagen. By arguing in this way, the Court made instrumental to its reasoning the investment Lower Saxony held in Volkswagen and continued to maintain at around 20% by subscribing for newly issued shares. The Court uses vague words in this respect. It does not rule that the provisions of the Act as such are liable to deter investors, but states: this 'situation', i.e. rules combined with a private investment by Lower Saxony, is liable to deter investors from other Member States. This raises at least two interesting questions: how would the Court have ruled if Lower Saxony had not maintained its investment at around 20% and its investment would have dropped significantly as a result of share issues to others? Could the Volkswagen Act still be saved if Lower Saxony was to sell a significant part or all of its shares in Volkswagen?[23]

privatizing, as taking a state measure. In Volkswagen the 20% voting cap and the 80% majority requirement did not create special rights, but there was a clear state act in the form of the Volkswagen. It would be interesting to see how the Court would rule if the state acts as a shareholder to include certain restrictive clauses in the articles of association of a company, which do not grant special rights to the state. See on this J. van Bekkum, J. Kloosterman and J. Winter, 'Golden Shares and European Company Law: the Implications of Volkswagen', *European Company Law* (2008), 9.

[23] Interestingly, Porsche, which in the meantime has acquired a 30% stake in Volkswagen sought to get shareholder approval from removing the provision copying the Volkswagen Act from the Articles of Association of Volkswagen in the Volkswagen annual general

By drawing Lower Saxony's investment decisions into its reasoning, the Court at least conceptually opens the door to applying the free movement of capital to the private sphere. In *Volkswagen* the Court did not have to dwell on this, as the Volkswagen Act itself is clearly a state act. But broadening the scope of the free movement of capital by bringing it into the private sphere would not be surprising, in light of the trends in the case law of the Court on the other Community freedoms. The free movement of capital case law has traditionally trailed the case law on the other freedoms but has picked up quite a bit over the last decade. And recent case law shows only few differences between the doctrinal features of this freedom compared with the others.[24]

VII. Free movement and the private sphere

For the other freedoms, the Court has already addressed the question whether and to what extent they could be applied to private person. In particular the free movement of workers has triggered Court rulings that apply the freedom into the private realm. In cases such as *Walrave*[25] and *Bosman*[26] the Court held that provisions limiting the free movement of workers were adopted in a collective manner (e.g. by international cyclist and football organizations), these provisions should be caught by Article 39 and 49 EC and should be subjected to the same standards applicable to state measures. In *Ferlini*[27] the Court went a little further by arguing that the discrimination prohibition of article 12 EC also applies to a case where an organization (in this case an organization of Luxembourg hospitals) exercises a certain power over individuals and is able to impose conditions upon them as a result of which the exercise of fundamental freedoms guaranteed under the Treaty is made more difficult. And in *Agonese*[28] the Court ruled that the requirement imposed by a private bank in Northern Italy for candidates applying for a job at the bank to prove their bilingual capabilities (Italian–German) by a

---

meeting held on 24 April 2008. The resolution was rejected as 'it did not obtain the required majority' (i.e. still 80% under the Articles of Association), the Volkswagen website announces, see http://www.volkswagenag.com/vwag/vwcorp/info_center/en/news/2008/04/AGM.html.

[24] L. Flynn, 'Coming of Age: the free movement of capital case law', *Common Market Law Review* (2002), 773–805.
[25] Case C-36/74, Walrave and Koch [1974] ECR 1405.
[26] Case C-415/93, Bosman [1995] ECR I-4921.
[27] Case C-411/98, Ferlini [2000] ECR I-8081.
[28] Case C-281/98, Angonese [2000] ECR I-4139.

diploma that can only be obtained in one province of Italy, constitutes a prohibited discrimination on the basis of nationality. The precise extent of this case law is not yet clear. One interpretation is that the prohibition against discrimination may be applied against any person (as shown in *Angonese*), while the prohibition against restrictions on the free movement of workers only applies to measures of a collective character with semi-public implications (*Walrave, Bosman, Ferlini*).[29]

For the free movement of goods, the Court traditionally takes the view that articles 28 and 29 only apply to measures taken by Member States and not by private persons.[30] There is backdoor, however, through which even this freedom may have its effects on the actions of private persons. In *Commission v. France*[31] French farmers repeatedly and violently obstructed Spanish farmers from selling their strawberries in France. The Court ruled that the actions undertaken by the French government were manifestly inadequate to ensure freedom of intra-Community trade in agricultural products on its territory by preventing and effectively dissuading the perpetrators of the offences in question from committing and repeating them. It is for the Member State concerned to adopt all appropriate measures to guarantee the full scope and effect of Community law so as to ensure its proper implementation in the interests of all economic operators. The actions of the French farmers were extreme, but the case may provide the basis for a more general rule that if private persons repeatedly and consistently obstruct the exercise of the Treaty freedoms by others, Member States may have to take measures to guarantee that these freedoms can be exercised.

VIII. Let's speculate: cross-border voting

There is no reason why the extension of the Treaty freedoms to the private sphere as follows from the case law referred to above could or should not also apply to the free movement of capital.[32] Speculating about the

---

[29] P. Oliver and W.-H. Roth, 'The Internal Market and the Four Freedoms', *Common Market Law Review* (2004), 423.

[30] Oliver and Roth, 'The Internal Market' (note 29, above), 422, with references to relevant case law.

[31] Case C-265/95, *Commision v. France* [1977] ECR I-6959.

[32] Oliver and Roth refer to the complication of the justifications that may be available for Member States under the Treaty may not be available for private persons. In particular, private autonomy, protected by national constitutions and the very essence of the European market economy, does not show up as a justification, see note 28, above, 423. The justification for private persons to restrict the Treaty freedoms is indeed

application of the free movement of capital into the private realm, one example comes to mind where this could have a salutary effect.

Europe is struggling with the exercise of voting rights by shareholders in companies located in another Member State. Today, shareholders typically hold their shares through securities accounts with intermediaries such as banks and brokers. When holding shares in a company in another Member State usually a chain of intermediaries in various jurisdictions exists between the shareholder and the company, each holding shares for the next intermediary until the ultimate shareholder is reached. It is often not clear legally and practically whether the ultimate shareholder, as the person who has invested in the shares and, in principle holds the economic risks attached to the shares, is entitled and able to vote the shares. The chain of intermediaries leads to multiple contractual and ownership claims in various jurisdictions and there is no EU or other rule clarifying that the entitlement of the ultimate shareholder at the end of the chain allows him to control the exercise of the voting rights. And practically, the securities intermediaries do not have systems in place allowing for the swift identification of ultimate shareholders, or the passing on of voting instructions or powers of attorney along the chain. For the intermediaries, facilitating the exercise of voting rights by their clients is a burdensome service to their clients and most intermediaries simply do not provide the service, or at least will not ensure that the next intermediary down the chain will also provide the service.[33]

---

problematic. But in this respect the free movement of capital is no different than the other freedoms where the Court has brought them into the private sphere. For a different view, B.J. Drijber, 'De Dertiende Richtlijn tussen Europese politiek en Europees recht', *Ondernemingsrecht* (2004), 140, holding that art. 56 EC does not have any horizontal effect. See for further speculation into the possible horizontal effect of the free movement of capital I. van der Steen, 'Horizontale werking van de vier vrijheden en van het discriminatieverbod van artikel 12 EG', *Nederlands tijdschrift voor Europees recht* (2001), 8, relating to the effect the free movement of capital on the ability of companies to defend against hostile takeover bids. See also the report of the European Corporate Governance Forum working group on proportionality, referring to cases in which foundations hold control over listed companies through mechanisms that allow for control rights disproportionate to the investment made by the foundation to further different stakeholder and societal interests. The report suggests that the free movement of capital may offer a fruitful avenue that can be explored to restrict the use of disproportionate mechanisms by such foundations to situations which are acceptable and justified under the Treaty, see p. 19 of the report of June 2007, see the posting on the website of 12.09.2007 http://ec.europa.eu/internal_market/company/ecgforum/index_en.htm.

[33] See for a description of the problems underlying cross-border voting J. Winter, 'Cross-border voting in Europe', in K. Hopt and E. Wymeersch (eds.), *Capital Markets and Company Law* (Oxford University Press: 2003), 387–426.

A typical cross-border problem is one that cannot be solved by Member States individually and therefore calls for an EU solution. The EU has identified such problems and sought to address them. The Shareholders Rights Directive[34] is aimed at solving problems of cross-border voting. Recital 11 states:

> Where financial intermediaries are involved, the effectiveness of voting upon instructions relies, to a great extent, on the efficiency of the chain of intermediaries, given that investors are frequently unable to exercise the voting rights attached to their shares without the cooperation of every intermediary in the chain, who may not have an economic stake in the shares. In order to enable the investor to exercise his voting rights in cross-border situations, it is therefore important that intermediaries facilitate the exercise of voting rights.

But then, typically for EU Member States not agreeing and the Commission for whom agreement on a Directive is often preferable over a Directive which makes sense, the Directive completely fails to provide any useful content that would allow shareholders to effectively exercise their voting rights along a chain of intermediaries. Securities intermediaries are not required to exercise voting rights according to the instruction of their clients or to pass on such voting instructions to the next intermediary in the chain or to provide powers of attorney to their clients to vote directly.[35] Instead, the real issue is moved to a possible Recommendation from the Commission to Member States, which in itself, by definition, will not be able to solve the problem as Member States can choose to ignore it and to not impose any obligation on securities intermediaries.

What good could the application of the free movement of capital do here? Banks and brokers are instrumental to the holding of shares by investors today. The vast majority of investors, big and small, hold their shares through securities accounts with these intermediaries. As a result, investors generally fully depend on these securities intermediaries to facilitate the exercise of their voting rights. Without the

---

[34] Directive of the European Parliament and of the Council of 11 July 2007 on the exercise of certain rights of shareholders in listed companies 2007/36/EC [2007] OJ L 184/17.

[35] The European Corporate Governance Forum had recommended to include such obligations for intermediaries in the Directive, see its recommendation of 24 July 2006, see http://ec.europa.eu/internal_market/company/ecgforum/index_en.htm.

banks and brokers no investor can identify themselves as shareholders to the companies in which they own shares and provide evidence of their share ownership. In chains of intermediaries, voting instructions or powers of attorney to vote need to be passed on by all intermediaries in the chain until they reach the company or the investor in question. Through their essential role in the international system of shareholding in book-entry form banks and brokers have become indispensable for the exercise of voting rights by investors. In the words of the Court in *Ferlini* the banks and brokers exercise a certain power over individuals and are able to impose conditions upon them as a result of which the exercise of fundamental freedoms guaranteed under the Treaty is made more difficult. This is precisely what banks and brokers do by not facilitating the exercise of voting rights by their clients through the chains of intermediaries across borders. The resulting inability to exercise voting rights across borders is liable to dissuade investors to invest in companies in other Member States and therefore a restriction on the free movement of capital. A different approach, based on the *Commission* v. *France* ruling, could be that Member States, allowing that banks and brokers in their jurisdiction facilitate the exercise of voting rights of their clients in their own jurisdiction but consistently refuse to facilitate (i) the exercise of voting rights by their clients on shares held in companies in another Member State, and (ii) the exercise of voting rights by investors from other Member States on shares in companies within the jurisdiction of the banks and brokers, failing to adopt all appropriate measures to guarantee the full scope and effect of the free movement of capital so as to ensure its proper implementation in the interests of all economic operators. The first, *Ferlini*-based reasoning, would allow for a case against the banks and brokers directly by investors, with the possibility of the national court to request the European Court to give a ruling on the interpretation of art. 56 EC on the basis of art. 234 EC. The second, *Commission v. France*-based reasoning, would allow for the Commission to adopt a policy not unlike its policy on golden shares, directed at ensuring that Member States require their banks and brokers to facilitate cross-border voting by their own clients and by investors from other Member States. Where a Member State fails to do so, the Commission could bring an action against that Member State with the European Court. Both avenues would allow for creating solutions to the problem of cross-border voting without legislation at EU level.

IX. *Ius audacibus*: company law and EU law

Capitalism isn't for the faint hearted, it is said. It is based on people who are willing to take risks in order to reap the fruits if they succeed. This is what produces wealth and wealth allows us to prosper as a society.

Both company law and EU law are instrumental to this objective. Company law first of all facilitates entrepreneurship, the risk-taking by business in order to generate profits. But it also seeks to protect those who are affected by companies against careless exploitation.

EU law creates a European space for entrepreneurship, where people and capital can move freely to create optimal results without artificial restrictions. Company law and EU law therefore have a common characteristic: they are both law for the brave, *ius audacibus*. It is only natural that they meet, for example in the free movement of capital.

Eddy Wymeersch has made numerous contributions to both these fields of law. It is always a delight to discuss, write and work with him and it is an honour for me to contribute to this book of his friends.

4

Free movement of capital and protectionism after *Volkswagen* and *Viking Line*

JONATHAN RICKFORD[1]

I. Introduction

It is a particular honour to provide an essay in tribute to Eddy Wymeersch. Just ten years ago I was appointed, after over fifteen years without involvement in company law matters, as project director of the UK Company Law Review.[2] Very shortly thereafter I received a generous invitation[3] from Eddy (whom I had never met) to attend a very high powered international corporate law conference convened by him in Siena. The contrast between the European approach of fifteen years before and those discussions was remarkable: the former mechanical, ideological harmonization *per se*, with the law of one Member State at its core; the new approach scientific and openly comparative, heavily law-and-economics in style, and purposive, concerned for efficiency and economic welfare. Soon afterwards I found this now generally characterized Commission and Brussels work. The responsibility for that change lay very much with Eddy and a group of colleagues[4] successfully dragging EU company law into enlightenment.[5]

---

[1] The paper develops thoughts offered at a conference marking the Finnish presidency of the EU in October 2006.

[2] Now largely embodied in the Companies Act 2006.

[3] The generosity extended to my wife also!

[4] Perhaps most notably, if another name is to be mentioned, Professor Klaus Hopt.

[5] The Siena papers were published as K. Hopt and E. Wymeersch (eds.), *Capital Markets and Company Law* (Oxford University Press, 2003). There is much more: perhaps most significantly K. Hopt, H. Kanda, M. Roe, E. Wymeersch (eds.), *Comparative Corporate Governance, the State of the Art and Emerging Research* (Oxford University Press, 1998); G. Ferrarini, K. Hopt, J. Winter and E. Wymeersch (eds.), *Reforming Company and Takeover Law in Europe* (Oxford University Press, 2004); K. Hopt, E. Wymeersch, H. Kanda and H. Baum (eds.), *Corporate Governance in Context* (Oxford University Press, 2005) and G. Ferrarini and E. Wymeersch (eds.), *Investor Protection in Europe, Corporate Law Making, the MiFID and Beyond* (Oxford University Press, 2006).

Two years later there emerged proposals at the highest political level, for opening up European law and related corporate service markets to free competition and restructuring.[6] The objective was an efficient structure and financial base for European business, exposed to open market forces, with a view to global competitiveness – the right objective for our law of business organization.

Ever since Siena I have derived enormous pleasure and satisfaction from cooperative work with Eddy, friends and colleagues met there, on occasions too numerous to enumerate. So I write in both admiration and gratitude.

However, while over the intervening decade enormous strides, both legislative[7] and jurisprudential,[8] have been made in developing EU law in that direction, recently problems have emerged at market, Member State and Community level. Member States pursued protectionist policies at community level in the Directive on Takeover Bids,[9] and implemented them with protectionist effects at market level. The Commission, too, seems to have lost confidence in new legislative projects addressing closed markets, notably on 'shareholder democracy', pre-bid takeover defences and proportionality.[10]

But the biggest concern is that the objectives of Member State governments have become more widely and overtly, and no doubt also covertly, protectionist – to achieve a 'national solution', 'economic patriotism', and

---

[6] Lisbon European Council Presidency Conclusions 23, 24 March 2000 EU see Press Release library at www.europa.eu.

[7] Including: Statute for a European Company: Directives on Employee Involvement; Cross Border Mergers and Takeover Bids; Regulation on International Accounting Standards; Directives on Company Accounts, on Audit and on Shareholder Rights; Corporate Governance Recommendations; and Financial Services Action Plan initiatives opening markets in financial services and capital.

[8] Cases C-212/97, *Centros*, [1999] ECR I-1459; C-208/00, *Ueberseering*, [2002] ECR I-9919; C-167/01, *Inspire Art*, [2003] ECR I-10155; C-411/03, *SEVIC*, [2005] ECR I-10805.

[9] Directive of the European Parliament and the Council 2004/25/EC [2004] OJ L142/12 – see article 12 (optionality for neutrality and pre bid defences).

[10] In October 2007 Commissioner McCreevy abandoned further action on 'shareholder democracy' (1 share:1 vote) and on the 14th Directive (corporate migration). In February 2008 he also abandoned work on capital maintenance (2nd Company Law Directive) reform. The original announcement relied on a false analogy between international best practice on binding balance sheet tests and EC law and a misrepresentation of the 'Rickford' Report on Reforming Capital, *European Business Law Review*, (2004), 919. The errors were corrected in March 2008, but the conclusion was maintained nevertheless.

so on.[11] This is particularly worrying, even distressing, for an observer from a Member State with open markets. One sees domestic businesses being acquired from foreign states (perfectly acceptably if the market so concludes) but then locked into closed corporate and national legal structures which lock out subsequent open restructuring – not so much the notorious 'unlevel playing field', of the football metaphor, as a kind of tilted billiard board where the balls are progressively sliding off the table and into pockets where they are destined to remain out of play. This irreversible progression of the market from open to closed represents not only a stifling but a reversal of the spirit of Lisbon.

In the face of this Member State hostility to basic principles of the European economic constitution, and the current unwillingness of the Commission to pursue its responsibilities, this paper considers the extent to which a reversal of these trends, and even progress, can be looked for from the Court of Justice, as champion by default of Community principles. The paper will focus on the impact on state interventions in the market for corporate control of the developing law on free movement of capital, mainly in the 'Golden Shares' cases and in particular the recent *Volkswagen*[12] decision, on the one hand, and the relevance in that context of the developing jurisprudence in the area of horizontal application of the fundamental freedoms,[13] on the other.

The paper thus falls into four parts:

- first, a selective survey of the free movement of capital as a constraint on state interference in the market for corporate control, based on the case law before *Volkswagen*;
- second, an examination of the implications of *Volkswagen*;
- third, examination of recent cases on the horizontal effect of fundamental freedoms and their implications for such state interference, beyond the traditional golden share public law mechanisms, and also for private law managerial entrenchments, which often complement state protectionism; and
- fourth, some conclusions and a proposed solution.

---

[11] Too frequently reported in the financial pages to require enumeration. Similarly K. Hopt, 'Concluding Remarks, ECFR Symposium on Cross-border Company Transactions', *European Company and Financial Law Review*, 4 (2007), 169.

[12] Case C-112/05, *EC* v. *Germany*, [2007] ECR, I-8995.

[13] *Viking Line* and *Laval* Cases (notes 88 and 89, below).

II. Free movement of capital

Free movement of capital ranks equally with the other three freedoms as a fundamental principle of Community[14] (soon to be EU)[15] law and as a component of the internal market which is the foundation of the Community. In many respects it corresponds in shape and effect to those freedoms (of goods, persons and services). But it presents special problems, because of the detail of the text and because capital transactions tend to be engaged in for ulterior or connected purposes (such as in pursuit of investment transactions – a service – or company control transactions – establishment), rather than in their own right.

As for the text, Article 56(1) EC simply states:

> Within the framework of the provisions set out in this chapter all restrictions on the movement of capital between Member States and third countries shall be prohibited.

Unlike freedoms of establishment or services,[16] for capital the beneficiary of the obligation need not be a community national. The transaction itself is required to be free regardless of the parties, as for free movement of goods.[17] But goods applies only to inter-State transactions: the territorial scope of the capital prohibition applies also to transactions between Member States and third countries. The capital freedom thus has a wider range than the others both as to beneficiaries and territorial scope.

Second, there are also issues about the transactions which fall within the prohibition – what is a 'movement of capital'? In particular what is the distinction between such a movement (which, as we shall discover, includes an investment in a share and the exercise of the managerial rights attaching to a share) and an exercise of freedom of establishment, which includes 'the right to … set up and manage undertakings, in particular companies or firms'?[18]

---

[14] EC Treaty Articles 2, 3(1)(c) and 14 (abolition of obstacles to free movement of capital, one of the four freedoms characterizing the common market, as a means for achieving the Community task).

[15] The Reform Treaty, agreed in October 2007 but not yet ratified, renders the internal market an aim of the Union – Treaty on European Union, article 3(2) and defines it in article 22a, Treaty on Functioning of the European Union (which replaces the EC Treaty), substantially restating article 14, EC. Article 3(1)(c) EC is repealed. The ECJ's approach to the fundamental freedoms should be unaffected.

[16] Articles 43, 49 EC.

[17] Restrictions are prohibited 'between Member States' – articles 25 (customs duties) and 28 (quantitative restrictions and their equivalents).

[18] Article 43, 2nd paragraph EC.

Third, where a capital transaction is engaged in as an ancillary part of another transaction governed by a fundamental freedom, such as a movement of goods, the provision of a service, or an exercise of a right of establishment, to what extent is the right in question constrained by the limits which attach to those other rights?[19]

A fourth, perhaps most significant, area of difficulty is the need to characterize the kinds of Member State intervention in the markets for corporate control which are likely to fall foul of the prohibition on restricting capital movement.

All these issues are of concern for my purpose, which is to determine the extent to which Member States and others are and should be constrained by article 56 in their ability to engage in protectionist policies and operations.

A. *Beneficiaries and territorial scope*

Evidently on its face the capital freedom extends to non-Member State nationals and to transactions between third countries and Member States as well as to the normal scope of the EU freedoms (inter-state trade).[20] Also, since the beneficiary need not be a national, the qualifications (community incorporation, commercial character and perhaps additional requirements) for companies and firms as beneficiaries of freedoms of establishment and services[21] do not apply.[22] Such extended territorial, transactional and personal scope of the freedom would be significant for state protectionism – different considerations apply to protection against 3rd countries (as opposed to inter-State transactions and those done by Member State nationals). This might argue for a less extensive scope for the freedom in other respects. However it will be argued below that this is not justified.

---

[19] Further uncertainties arise as to the interference with the freedom prohibited in terms of the means used and the nature of the obligees, whether public, semi-public, private but performing some public law function, or private.

[20] Thus covering some ground normally within the common commercial policy – Article 113 EC.

[21] As explained in *Ueberseering* (note 8, above). *Quaere* also whether even a nationally incorporated firm must have a real economic link with a Member State economy – a concept originally developed in the General programme on Establishment and reserved in *Ueberseering* (note 8, above) at 74, 75.

[22] Thus a charitable body has the benefit of the freedom for an investment in land, Case C-386/04, *Centro di Musicologia v. Finanzamt Muenchen*, [2006] ECR I-8203 – article 48 applies only to 'profit-making' bodies.

B. Movement of capital

The treaty does not define 'movement of capital' but it has been established since 1999[23] that the nomenclature in Annex I (including important clarifications in its explanatory notes) to the Capital Directive of 1988[24] is 'indicative'. This, in brief, makes it clear that investments in companies whether direct (i.e. to establish or maintain lasting economic links) or portfolio (i.e. broadly speaking passive) investments are covered. Direct investment includes the power 'to participate effectively in the management of the company or its control'.[25]

C. Ancillary character of capital movements

It is clear, as already noted, from this definition that free movement of capital in some cases (but not all) covers transactions also subject to freedom of establishment: the right to 'set up and manage an undertaking', under article 43 EC, necessarily involves and coincides with, subscription for or purchase of shares.[26] So, so far as the definition of

---

[23] Case C-222/97, *Trummer and Mayer* [1999] ECR I-1661, para 20, 21. Repeated in all the Golden Share cases (see below) most recently in C-112/05 *Commission* v. *Germany* (*'Volkswagen'*) [2007] ECR at para 18.

[24] Council Directive 88/361/EEC [1988] OJ L178/5, providing for direct implementation of the original capital provision, old article 67 EC, which was not directly effective in itself. Remarkably, old article 67 was materially different from article 56 EC enacted by the Treaty of Amsterdam; it applied only to 'movements of capital belonging to persons resident in Member States' - repeated in article 1 of the Directive.

[25] For a company share a rigid distinction between direct and portfolio investments is unsatisfactory since any share carries rights of control and influence and an investment which is intended to be passive may at any time become active, for example in a public offer - a good reason for rejecting (as the Court did) the arguments of Maduro AG in *EC* v. *UK ('BAA')* and *EC* v. *Spain*, (note 34, below), that direct investment issues should be resolved solely under the establishment chapter - but not of direct concern here, as in the context of state protectionism only direct investments are relevant.

[26] The Capital Directive Annex I nomenclature specifically includes in direct investment 'establishment of branches or new undertakings belonging solely to the person providing the capital and the acquisition in full of existing undertakings' as well as more limited participation - para I, 1 and 2. This is 'to be understood in its widest sense', explanatory note para 1. It has been suggested, relying on *Baars*, C-251/98 [2000] ECR I-2787 at para 21, 22, that acquisitions of shares providing a 'definite influence over a company' and allowing the shareholder to 'determine its activities' are a matter for freedom of establishment *and not for capital* - see C-208/00 *Ueberseering* v. *Nordic Construction* (note 8, above) at 77. But this now seems unsustainable. *Baars* decided that influence was required for establishment, not that it was a disqualifier for capital. The alternative question on capital in *Baars* was not reached.

movements of capital is concerned, the chapter would extend to the control transactions in companies which are of concern to protectionist Member States and would in that context extend the freedom to third country transactions and to non-nationals and companies and firms which do not qualify as nationals for establishment purposes.[27] However article 58(2) provides that the chapter is to be 'without prejudice to the applicability of restrictions on the right of establishment which are compatible with this Treaty'. Apparently[28] that exemption will allow Member States to deny a right of direct investment under the chapter to individuals and firms which could not take advantage of the chapter on establishment – a position confirmed by dicta in the *Volkswagen* case.[29]

It seems therefore that in spite of its wider territorial and personal extent the capital freedom does not extend, for transactions which involve establishment, to persons and territories beyond the establishment chapter. Therefore there is no need, in determining the appropriate scope of the capital freedom, to take account of the need of Member States in developing their mercantile policies to take special precautions against transactions involving third countries.[30]

As already noted, it is sometimes argued that where capital movements are ancillary to other transactions (e.g. investment services, such as life insurance, collective investment or brokerage, or lending, or establishment, as discussed above) it is appropriate to treat the capital right as no more extensive than the 'primary' right under consideration. It may be argued similarly that third country nationals who seek to make direct investments in a Member State are exercising their right of establishment as a primary matter and free movement of capital is really secondary in relation to that. This is an alternative route to the

---

[27] Article 48 EC – also article 55 for services.

[28] Unfortunately the argument is not completely free from doubt – article 57(1) provides that article 56 is without prejudice to certain restrictions which exist under national or community law on 31 December 1993 on capital movements to or from third countries involving direct investment, establishment, financial services and admission of securities to listing. But this specific transitional derogation must be without prejudice to the later general derogation for establishment restrictions in article 58(2).

[29] Case C-112/05, at para 17: 'article 56(1) generally prohibits restrictions on movements of capital between Member States', citing C-282/04, *EC* v. *Netherlands* (KPN) [2006] ECR I-9141 at para 18, which introduced this qualification.

[30] *Centro di Musicologia*, (note 22 above), which applies capital *ratione personae* beyond the beneficiaries of the establishment and services chapters, did not involve direct investment or establishment.

conclusion above. The Court has recently made such a finding for credit services provided in Germany from Switzerland.[31]

However that line seems precarious. It may (perhaps) be possible by the light of nature to conclude that in a credit transaction the receipt of the service by the borrower predominates in importance over the making of the investment by the lender. But how is it to be determined, in the case of the acquisition of a share conferring control powers, where the acquisition of the share and of the rights that go with it is both a capital right and an establishment right, which of the two predominates? Moreover the Golden Share cases, to which we now turn, are not consistent with this approach. They were generally decided on the basis that both establishment and capital were in issue, but determined in practice on the basis of capital, either because the Court regarded it as unnecessary also to decide on establishment, or because the Commission failed to press that charge.[32]

D. Nature of the prohibited state interventions

Having characterized a capital movement for Treaty purposes as including direct investment in companies, at first impression it seems easy enough to identify the obligation of Member States – surely any kind of state measure, legislative or administrative, which has the potential, object or effect of restricting the enjoyment of the freedom should be prohibited, on the analogy of the other freedoms?[33] Matters are however not so simple. The cases so far have focused on Member States' reservations of control powers over companies on privatization by means of so-called 'Golden Shares' powers.[34]

---

[31] Case 452/04, *Fidium Finanz*, [2006] ECR I-09521. The Court concluded that where one of the freedoms is 'entirely secondary in relation to the other and may be considered together with it' then the state measure will be considered in relation to that other freedom only (at 34); the effect on cross-border financial traffic was 'merely an unavoidable consequence of the restriction on the freedom to provide services' and 'the predominant consideration is freedom to provide services rather than the free movement of capital' (at 48, 49).

[32] As in *Volkswagen* C-112/05 (note 23, above) at para 14, 15.

[33] See the familiar jurisprudence on goods based on Case 8/74, *Dassonville*, [1974] ECR 837 at 5: 'all rules … which are capable of hindering, directly or indirectly, actually or potentially, intra community trade'.

[34] Key cases are: Cases C-367/98, *EC* v. *Portugal*, [2002] ECR I-04731 (privatization of a wide range of enterprises); C-483/99, *EC* v. *France* (Elf Aquitaine), [2002] I-4781; C-503/99, *EC* v. *Belgium* (Distrigas) [2002] ECR I-4809, ('1st generation cases'); similar is Case C-463/00, *EC* v. *Spain* (petroleum, telecommunications, banking, tobacco and

Typically such powers attach to special shares giving Member States rights enabling them to retain control over such enterprises in order to prevent their operation contrary to national interests and/or prevent undesirable persons obtaining control. Member States may accordingly take powers to veto certain strategic transactions, such as disposals of core assets, and certain acquisitions of shareholdings and/or of voting powers by persons, or groups of persons, above a percentage ceiling. In some cases they also take powers to nominate board members, so as to secure influence over ongoing operations, or at least to provide information.

Such powers may be acquired under public law provisions, or under public law provisions authorizing or requiring issue of shares to Member States conferring ostensibly private law powers to the same effect, or through issue of such shares under private law.

In 1997 the Commission, viewing such measures as liable to infringe Community law, issued a Communication to that effect[35] and took legal proceedings.

1. First generation Golden Share cases – powers under public law

The first three cases[36] all involved public law provision. The issue was made simpler because the powers in question were conceded to amount to restrictions on capital. France and Portugal did argue that the provisions were not discriminatory and did not involve any particularly restrictive treatment of nationals of other Member States; but the court ruled that they were 'liable to impede the acquisition of share in the enterprises concerned' and 'as a result to render free movement of capital illusory' thus restricting the right to make direct investments as defined by the capital directive.[37] The court thus, implicitly at least, refused to accept the argument that the provisions were not prohibited restrictions because they did not bear differentially on investors from outside the home Member State, i.e. inhibit 'access' to the state market.[38] So there were restrictions conflicting with the freedom.

---

electricity) [2003] ECR I-4581; C-98/01 *EC* v. *UK (BAA)* [2003] ECR I-4641; C-463/00, and C-282/04 and -283/04, *EC* v. *Netherlands* (KPN/TPG), [2006] ECR I-9141 ('2nd generation').

[35] Communication of the Commission On Certain Legal Aspects Concerning Intra-EU Investment [2007] OJ C 220/15, 19.7.1997.

[36] I.e. the first generation cases cited at footnote 34 above.

[37] *EC* v. *Portugal* (note 34, above) at para 30 and 45–46; *EC* v. *France* (note 34, above) at para 37–42.

[38] See the discussion in P. Oliver and W. Roth, 'The Internal Market and the Four Freedoms', 41 (2004), *Common Market Law Review*, 407.

The issue then turned on whether these (to the extent they were not actually discriminatory)[39] were justifiable by reference to the 'rule of reason' or 'general interest/proportionality' tests familiar from the other freedoms.[40] The Court made three important rulings on what could be regarded as legitimate general interests and proportionate protection thereof: first, such interests would include protection of the national petroleum and gas supply or other vital public services such as telecommunications and electricity but did not include retention of state controls over other enterprises such as banking, or tobacco[41]; second, national economic policy could not be invoked as a general interest, so an attempt to uphold restrictions, as necessary to secure that national industry was restructured satisfactorily after the mass privatizations, could not be sustained[42]; and third, where the powers were discretionary, procedural safeguards were required to ensure transparency of the grounds on which the powers were exercised and recourse to legal challenge to secure this. This is an important point – even where such powers constraining or encumbering investment are exercisable on legitimate grounds they may in fact be abused. Transparent grounds and legal recourse must be available to meet this risk.

The effect of this first generation of cases was that where special powers to intervene in strategic decision making or to disallow acquisition of strategic stakes were conferred by or under public law on Member States, then if the effect was to render investment less attractive (inevitably so given the operational constraints and limits on realisation of investment, e.g. in takeovers), the provisions would be prohibited restrictions and not justifiable except in defence of such vital national interests as the protection of energy supply, and then only if the powers in question were transparent and subject to judicial scrutiny.

---

[39] As some of the restrictions in *EC* v. *Portugal* were.

[40] E.g. Case C-55/94 *Gebhard*, [1995] ECR I-4165 – restrictions to be justifiable must be imposed in order to serve a (*sc* legitimate) general interest, must be non-discriminatory, must be appropriate for the purpose, and must impose no greater restriction than is necessary to achieve the objective.

[41] *EC* v. *Spain* (note 34, above), at para 70; but in *Volkswagen* the Court seems to have accepted that the general interest could be served in the context of a particular manufacturing company – see below.

[42] *EC* v. *Portugal* (note 34, above) at para 52, 53. 'It is settled case law that economic grounds can never serve as justification for obstacles prohibited by the Treaty'. Portugal claimed the powers were necessary to enable it to ensure appropriate strategic partners, to strengthen the competitive market and to modernise and increase efficiency of production.

2. Second generation Golden Share cases – powers under private law

However the powers in these cases were conferred by or under public law provisions and created special exceptions to the normal company law provisions. In two later cases the powers were conferred by vesting the special share in a government official under private law, these powers were consistent with general company law and their legal source was the company's (private law) constitution.

The first of these was the *BAA* case, concerning a Golden Share in the company owning the major UK airports.[43] The UK government made two important arguments:

- First, that the constraints in question (which conferred a prior approval power on Government for disposals of major airports and for acquisitions of more than a 15% voting stakes) could not amount to restrictions because they bore equally on all shareholders and thus did not constrain access to the market.[44] The court responded, following the Commission, that the restrictions 'affected the position of a person acquiring a shareholding as such and are thus liable to deter investors from other Member States and, consequently, affect access to the market'. This amounts to an assertion that any deterrence of other Member States investors amounts to an effect on access regardless of whether it is greater than the effect on domestic investors; this is difficult to follow and open to challenge.[45] Any provision of a company's constitution, or indeed any provision of mandatory company law, may deter an investor – for example a limitation on the company's objects or a provision which restricts the extent to which the constitution can be changed or which enables directors to be removed. If the provision is there for private purposes then *ex hypothesi* there will be no general interest to be invoked by way of justification. If it is there for public purposes it will also

---

[43] Case C-98/01, *EC* v. *UK* (note 34, above). BAA is now wholly owned by the Spanish company Ferrovial SA.

[44] At 24–7, citing the well known cases on goods, Cases C-267 and 268/91 *Keck and Mithouard* [1993] ECR I-06097.

[45] In *EC* v. *Netherlands* (KPN Case) (note 34, above). Maduro AG at para 24 suggested that where any shares confer special rights they are likely to inhibit access because those rights are likely to be vested in nationals, thus deterring investment by non-nationals. This point clearly applies *a fortiori* to cases where the shares are vested in national governments. It suggests a way forward – see below.

require justification; but does all mandatory company law require justification?

- Second, the UK argued the powers were private-law powers, compatible with UK company law (albeit unusual) and thus not 'repugnant to company law'. The Commission responded that this made no difference because the powers were exercisable exclusively by the UK Government *qua* State. The Court rejected the UK argument on somewhat different grounds: that the articles 'do not arise as the result of the normal operation of company law' but had to be approved under the privatization Act; the UK thus acted 'in its capacity as a public authority'.[46]

The ruling on access was not a surprise.[47] Although the issue had been obscured in the previous cases by the concessions by the Member States the Court had found a restriction in each case in spite of equal applicability. This point apart, the decision turned on whether there was a state measure.[48] This was resolved on the basis of the statutory authorization. But that was essentially an accident: the same result could have been achieved by the UK as shareholder adopting the relevant articles before privatization, exercising normal shareholder powers. While the method of restriction would have been different, the effect would have been the same.

This issue presented itself in the second of the cases about the use of private law powers, *EC* v. *Netherlands*. Shortly before their privatization the Netherlands postal and telecommunications companies resolved[49] to issue to the Dutch government special shares which enabled it to require prior approval of a wide variety of transactions, including share issues and repurchases, distributions, mergers and demergers, and articles changes, but not acquisition of shares; the government also agreed that it would not use its powers to defeat a hostile takeover. It argued that these provisions did not result from exercise of public power but from

---

[46] *Ibid*. 47. The Commission itself suggested a 'derogation from company law' test in 1999 (note 35 above).

[47] Although Colomer AG protested, arguing that in the interests of uniformity of application of all the freedoms the Court 'should temper the rigour with which it applied its principles on restrictions applicable without distinction … as it did … in *Keck*', opinion at para 36 footnote 10.

[48] The restriction on acquisition of more than 15% of voting rights bore equally on all shareholders (except the Government which had powers to allow its removal) but nothing was made of this in the case. Compare the discussion of *Volkswagen* below.

[49] The resolution was carried by the Dutch government as shareholder – see the following footnote.

its powers as a shareholder, as a market operation, and did not therefore fall within article 56.[50] The court had no difficulty, following established jurisprudence, in finding that the provisions constituted restrictions on capital, as likely to deter investors. To the argument that they were not public measures, it responded that they were 'state measures', because they were 'the result of decisions taken by the Netherlands state in the course of the privatization of the two companies with a view to reserving a certain number of special rights under the companies' statutes'.[51] But, unlike the UK case, the Court found it necessary to go on to add two points: that the special shares conferred on the State important powers and a *disproportionate influence* – i.e. one 'not justified by the size of its investment and greater than that which an ordinary shareholding would normally allow it to obtain'[52] and thus 'limited the influence of other shareholders in relation to the size of their holding'; and that they created *a risk* that the Netherlands might pursue interests which did not coincide with the economic interests of the company, thus discouraging direct (and portfolio) investors.[53]

Thus the ruling turned on three points, apart from the familiar point that the powers attached to the shares deterred investors (albeit equally applicable as between those from the Netherlands and other Member States): i.e. that they:

- constituted a '*state measure*' because they were taken for privatization purposes,
- conferred *disproportionate powers* at the expense of other shareholders; and
- created *a risk* of state interference with operation of the company in its own best economic interests.

This deserves closer examination. The argument alleging existence of a state measure amounts to one that use by a Member State of private law powers may be regarded as a state measure where the purpose for their use is a public purpose of a certain kind – *in casu* a privatization policy. Such a 'public purpose' test will probably be satisfied whenever a state takes a shareholding with a view to exercising influence. Only where the state is investing as a portfolio investor is it likely that it is not exercising

---

[50] See speech of Maduro AG at para 19; cf. the ruling at para 16, characterizing the argument as that the powers were 'not State measures'.

[51] *EC* v. *Netherlands* (note 34, above), at para 22.

[52] *Ibid.* 24.

[53] *Ibid.* 28.

some industrial or other public policy objective. So the state measure requirement looks weak – it is likely always to be satisfied.

The nature of the disproportionality test is obscure. It may rely on some idealized vision of what level of shareholding entitles a company member to any particular level of influence. But, as the UK Government pointed out in *BAA*, national company law often allows shareholders autonomously to determine the allocation of powers between them, a freedom allowed by the Community legislators to continue in the context of the Takeover Bids Directive. A subsequent Commission study led in turn to the conclusion that departures from proportionality could not on the evidence be regarded as contrary to the general interest and that no further work should be done on the issue.[54] So the idealized view of proportionality is neither defined nor agreed.

An alternative view of proportionality, not open to these objections and conceivably what the Court had in mind, would be by reference to the default rules of the national company law applicable; a departure from these being not 'normal'.[55] It is true that default rules in all Member States seem to provide for a 'one share: one vote' rule and a standard level of minority blocking power in relation to decisions of major importance. However the decisions which require special majority approval (and thus confer a disproportionate blocking power on dissenters) are by no means uniform in their nature in all Member States, nor are the majorities required the same. Moreover ordinary default rules are by no means uniform. So reference to departure from such rules would produce different results in different Member States. Again, it by no means follows from the existence of a default rule that it is 'normally' followed – a conclusion which would require a statistical examination of national practice. So this 'non-idealized' version of the proportionality rule would have a subjective effect as between Member States, producing an absence of uniformity in the measures permitted to deter capital

[54] Commission announcement of October 2007 (note 10, above) referring to a Report by KPMG.
[55] *EC* v. *Netherlands* (note 34, above), at para 24. Compare the Commission assertion in its Communication of 1999 that even provisions of general application allowing state veto of certain operational decisions and state board nominations for that purpose are offensive as 'in derogation of company law'. This however seems to posit some single Platonic ideal, so to speak, of company law, rather than one that varies between Member States. Of course no such ideal model exists and special veto or nomination rights for particular shareholders or others are quite lawful under general law in many States.

movement as between different States.[56] It is not evident why company law rules should have this differential effect on the operation of a fundamental freedom, nor why national rules should determine whether capital movement is restricted.

The third test, relating to risk of abuse, is of course the heart of the matter. The concern is always the risk that powers may be exercised for purposes contrary to EU principles, particularly in pursuit of economic policies designed to achieve nationalist industrial policies and protectionism. The Court puts this argument in different terms however – i.e. of the risk that the State will depart from *the economic interests of the company* – following the Advocate General, who suggested that the principle should be that once the state places an enterprise in the market place it must live by the laws of the market place and in consequence must respect the company's economic autonomy, justifications by reference to security of public services apart.[57] But this is too wide – it is not in fact a universal principle of States' company laws that shareholders' powers must be exercised in the economic interest of the company (whatever that means) and even when such a principle operates it is no part of the competence of the Community to ensure that it is upheld. On the other hand, exercise of discretionary powers *to impede the common market* is of course highly offensive to Community principle and this is the risk of abuse which should be considered here.

Two further comments can be made about this risk test (whether or not the narrower scope for it argued for here is accepted):

- First, it will be satisfied in all cases where a Member State holds powers conferred by a company constitution or by public law to determine or influence a company's control, operations or strategy. Thus, while vital, it does not provide a useful criterion for determining which powers amount to a restriction – it suggests that all do.
- Second, the essence of the matter is the risk, or potential, for abuse. This suggests that, short of outlawing all such powers, the appropriate response is to outlaw those that conflict with community principles on the face of it and to ensure that the remainder are not abused in that way.

[56] The same can be said of reference to departures from mandatory, as opposed to default, company law rules, not in issue in the *BAA* or *KPN* cases, but which may be implicit in the first generation cases and as we shall see below were relevant in *Volkswagen*.

[57] ECJ at para 27–28, Maduro AG at para 27–30. Cf. D. Wyatt, A. Dashwood and others, *European Union Law*, 5th Edn. (London: Sweet and Maxwell, London, 2005) 860–1, suggesting that this is the meaning to be attached to the Commission's 'derogation from company law' test.

It was with this in mind that the High Level Group on Company Law and Corporate Governance ('Winter Group') in its first report, recommended that Golden Share powers should be subjected to public law due process principles – i.e. transparency and judicial review.[58] This calls to mind the approach to discretionary powers conferred by public law and the concern about the assertion of Member States' 'economic policy', considered by the Court at the level of justification in the first generation cases, discussed above. The Court there required that discretionary powers should be subject to due process and seems to have rejected economic policies contrary to the market.[59]

This is a key to the problem. But it is appropriate, before developing it, to complete the picture by considering the recent *Volkswagen case* and cases suggesting community freedoms apply to private law measures, whether or not states (or other bodies with public law functions) are involved.

A further question arises from the *Netherlands (KPN)* case. To what extent are the three grounds in the case independent? Would it have been decided the same way on the basis of any one or more, or are all three required, at least in cases where private law powers are in play? Is it enough that investment is deterred either by state measure, or by 'disproportionate' powers conferred on a state, or by powers which create a risk (whether to the company as the Court asserts or to the common market, as is argued here)? This question too is best examined after considering *Volkswagen*.

III. The effects of *Volkswagen*[60]

The notoriety of this case is such that it is likely to be much relied upon. But it does not give clear guidance to Member States and investors concerned with the liberty of investment across frontiers in the Community.

Volkswagen was founded in the 1930s to manufacture the people's car. It was largely controlled by government and trades unions and financed by deposits from prospective car purchasers. After World War II it fell to the German government to determine how the enterprise

[58] Report of the High Level Group of Company Law Experts, Report on Issues Related to Takeover Bids, Brussels 10 January 2002, 34.

[59] The scope of the ECJ's economic policy objection is vague. For a similar suggestion as to its scope see Wyatt and Dashwood, *European Union Law* (note 57, above). Compare Case C-174/04, *EC* v. *Italy* [2005] ECR I-04933 ('golden share' to achieve interstate competition policy).

[60] Case C-112/05, *EC* v. *Germany* ('Volkswagen'), [2007] ECR I-8995.

(now essentially *bona vacantia* but with various moral claims on its ownership) was to be owned and controlled. Under a historic compromise, after long debate between Federal Government, the Land of Lower Saxony (where the enterprise and its factory was based), the trades unions and other claimants, the matter was settled by federal legislation in 1960 privatizing Volkswagen. This Act incorporated the statutes of the new Volkswagen AG, and enabled 60% of the shares to be sold to the public while 20% each were retained by the Federal Government (sold at the time of the proceedings) and Lower Saxony.[61]

The legislation contained three provisions which the Commission argued were unlawful restrictions on free movement of capital and freedom of establishment:[62]

- a voting rights cap of 20% – i.e. provision that any holding in excess of 20% was disenfranchised to that extent;
- special board nomination powers – i.e. power for The Federal Government and the Land of Lower Saxony each to appoint two members of the supervisory board;
- a 20% enhanced blocking minority power – i.e. special company resolutions normally requiring a 75% majority were to require 80%.

Two general arguments were dealt with by the court for all three restrictions:

- First, Germany argued that this was not a state measure as required for liability by previous cases. The Court assumed that such a measure was needed but had no difficulty in concluding the restrictions, as imposed by legislation were 'a manifestation par excellence of State power'.[63]
- Second, the Court concluded that the provisions satisfied the requirement that they deterred investors from other Member States by restricting their ability to participate effectively in management. This conclusion was reached for the board appointment power independently;[64] for the enhanced minority and voting cap provisions it was taken in combination – i.e. that the two provisions taken together had this effect.[65]

---

[61] This settlement has been widely regarded in Germany as epitomizing the German post-war 'economic miracle' and its 'social market' model. For a fuller account see Colomer AG, footnote 47.

[62] The Commission failed to pursue the establishment charge which was on that ground dismissed by the Court, at paras 13–16.

[63] *Volkswagen* para 27.

[64] *Ibid.* para 66.

[65] *Ibid*, paras 51–5.

However apparently these two conclusions were not enough to settle the case.

On the board appointment provisions, the Court noted that these enabled the Land and Federal Government to appoint more members by such special powers than was permitted under general law (which limited such rights to one third of shareholders representatives)[66]. This was thus a specific right which derogated from general company law, enabling the two governments 'to participate in a more significant manner in the ... supervisory board than their status of shareholders would normally allow'. This possibility would continue even if they held only one share each. So the provision gave these authorities 'the possibility of exercising influence which exceeds their levels of investment'.[67]

It is not clear whether the two points – that the appointment powers (i) were greater than normally allowed (i.e. conflicted with general mandatory company law) and (ii) 'exceeded the level of their investment' (i.e. were disproportionate to the potential level of shareholding which conferred them) – were separate points. If the Land had only been entitled to appoint one of the ten shareholder members would this have been disproportionate, albeit company law would have allowed it, or would the provision have needed to require that the Land should for this purpose retain 10% of the share capital (corresponding to 10% of the shareholder members) to satisfy the proportionality criterion? The decision indeed reads on first impression as if the Court regarded a level of representation corresponding to shareholding ('proportionate') as both necessary and sufficient,[68] but this is by no means a principle of the generality of community law. In many EU states, including the UK and Ireland (and I believe France and Belgium), directors can only be securely maintained

---

[66] Art. 101(2) AktG (which makes express exception for Volkswagen). German law sets the size of the supervisory board (which appoints and dismisses the management board and thus ultimately controls both strategy and operations) for companies of this size at twenty, with ten to be appointed by or on behalf of employees (art. 7 MitbestG). The maximum number of shareholder representatives allowed to be appointed by such special appointment powers was therefore three. The effect of the power even when exercised only by Lower Saxony was to confer a blocking majority on a combination of Lower Saxony and the employee representatives thus creating an effective veto on takeovers for Lower Saxony.

[67] *Volkswagen*, paras 61–4.

[68] A position adopted by Colomer AG at 72 'this exclusive power is totally detached from the importance of their respective shareholdings ... and *ruptures the symmetry between the power of capital and the possibilities of management*' (author's translation, emphasis added).

in office by a simple majority.[69] It is also unclear whether if the power had been proportionate but had conflicted with mandatory company law it would have been acceptable. For example, suppose that the case had arisen in the UK, would it have been sufficient for the law to have allowed a power of appointment proportionate to the holding, even though this would have conflicted with the normal UK mandatory provision allowing a bare majority to dismiss *ad nutum*?

It may be argued that this ruling creates a Community proportionality principle, in the generally recognised sense, for shareholder powers exercisable by states by virtue of state measures.[70] This seems doubtful in view of the above points. Nor does the test seem apt to address the mischief in hand. The proportionality of the powers held by a state by reference to the size of its holding bears no relation to the risk that the powers held will (be used to) deter investors. The mere fact that a holding is proportional to the powers of a state can hardly be regarded as allowing those powers to be exercised in a discriminatory fashion. Why should such proportionality allow powers to be used to impede access by investors from other Member States? Yet if satisfaction of this test renders a power no longer a restriction its potential or actual use to hinder access to the State market is presumably not open to challenge.

The remaining two provisions in question, the voting cap and the enhanced minority provision, the Court considered together, as the Advocate General had done. Germany argued that these provisions could not amount to restrictions because, unlike all the earlier cases, they bore equally on all shareholders conferring burdens and (allegedly) benefits on all, rather than conferring special privileges on the two state authorities. While the voting cap was contrary to mandatory German law (which imposes a 'one share, one vote' rule for listed companies),[71] nothing in Community law prevented Germany from adapting this rule for particular companies. This was a formidable line of argument. If provisions which bear equally on all shareholders are objectionable, where is the limit to the powers exercisable by Member States as shareholders which are objectionable? Any normal company law power could be so.

The Advocate General considered the two provisions together, maintaining that it was their combined effect which was to be considered (without

---

[69] Companies Act 2006 sections 168, 169.
[70] As argued by J. van Bekkum, J. Kloosterman and J. Winter, 'Golden Shares and European Company Law – the Implications of Volkswagen', *European Law Review*, (2008) (forthcoming).
[71] Art 134(1) AktG.

explaining what special effect the combination achieved) and relied on two points (apart from the general deterrent effect of the provisions on investors seeking to exercise management control): that the provisions were imposed by a special law by the Government itself and that the special minority position entrenched the Land by virtue of its particular shareholding, which conferred the very blocking minority required to secure its use.

The Court accepted the German assertion that the cap provision was applicable without distinction to all shareholders and was a 'recognised instrument of company law',[72] but noted that it was an infringement of German mandatory company law. However, it clearly did not regard this as sufficient to outlaw it. So it turned, like the Advocate General, to consider the cap and the enhanced minority provisions together.

The relevant German special resolution provisions to which the special minority rule applied were those on various key strategic issues including amendment of the statutes and certain decisions relating to capital and financial structures.[73] While the 75% majority was the default rule nothing prevented companies from adopting articles with a higher requirement. However the Court noted that for Volkswagen the provision had been made mandatory by legislation and could not be revoked by the shareholders.[74] The provision was thus an exception to mandatory German company law in that sense; however the Court did not explicitly take that point.

But the critical aspect in this connection seems to have been that at the time of the enactment both state authorities, and still at the time of judgment the Land, held an approximately 20% holding – i.e. perfectly fitted to take advantage of the blocking minority provision – and were thus able to ensure, once the legislation was enacted, that no structural changes of the relevant kind could ever take place without the consent of each of them – a position which was bound to deter direct investors and particularly takeover bids.[75] This enabled the court to hold that the

---

[72] Case C-112/05, *EC* v. *Germany*, (note 60, above), paras 42, 38. German law allows voting caps for unlisted companies and they are common in certain other European states: see the Report of Institutional Shareholder Services on Proportionality between Ownership and Control in the EU, EC Brussels April 2007, 31. Note that the Court accepted this argument although the cap infringes any 'ideal' notion of proportionality of holding to voting power.

[73] This is all that is mentioned by the Court but a 75% majority is required for a number of other matters including mergers and voluntary dissolution.

[74] Case C-112/05, *EC* v. *Germany*, (note 60, above), para 45.

[75] The Court noted that takeover bids were in issue, though somewhat curiously, it mentions this in the context of the establishment issue, at paras 14, 15. For Porsche SE's current attempts to acquire control, see G.-J. Vossestein, 'Volkswagen, The State of Affairs of Golden Shares', 5:1 (2008), *European Company and Financial Law Review*, 132.

provision thus enabled the Federal and State authorities 'to procure for themselves a blocking minority on the basis of a lower level of investment than would be required under general company law'.[76] In other words *on the facts* the effect of the provision was to confer *a special right* on Lower Saxony (and allegedly on the Federal Government, which was true at the time of the legislation but was however no longer true). While the court did not say so, and perhaps implies otherwise,[77] a further shareholder could take a 20% holding (or a smaller one sufficient for the necessary blocking minority de facto) and would in so doing be able also to exercise the same right of veto; but in practice such a second right of veto would be of little value given the first mover advantage of the Land and would depress the value of the shares generally.

What of the voting cap? The Court held that 'by capping voting rights at the same level of 20% [the cap] supplements a legal framework which enables [these] authorities to exercise considerable influence on the basis of such a reduced investment (i.e. 20%)' and this situation (the combination of powers) was likely to deter investors.

This combined ruling is problematic. It clearly implies that each of the two powers would have been lawful without the other, and that there was some synergy between them which rendered them unlawful.

So apparently the Court did not believe that either provision, the cap or the enhanced blocking power, were sufficient in themselves to constitute a restriction. This was so although the former was contrary to German mandatory law (and clearly made the company a less attractive target for direct investors seeking to exercise control or influence) and the latter was contrary to default law (and excluded a mandatory consensual power, though it would have been lawful as a consensual provision), and also conferred on Lower Saxony de facto a special blocking power over constitutional change and other strategic decisions based on a lower than normal level of investment. The reason why the Court felt unable to find against the cap seems to have been that it conferred no special right on the authorities. The enhanced blocking power did do so de facto. Why did the Court not regard this as sufficient to find against this power in isolation? Perhaps the Court believed or assumed that a special *legal* power was needed to do so, but the factual result was to confer a special right which would be a wholly effective deterrent for strategic investors, as the Court clearly recognised. That is the concern of European law.

---

[76] Case C-112/05, *EC* v. *Germany*, (note 60, above), para 50.
[77] *Ibid.* 'enabling the authorities to procure for themselves'.

We need therefore in order to understand the Court's objection to the two powers in combination to understand the objectionable synergy between them. In what way was the operation of the two powers in combination offensive? Each provision deters direct investors, but separately – the cap, because it makes it difficult for them to exercise influence *outside* the field of the special minority decision – and the special minority provision, because it makes influence impossible (without state consent) *within* that field. The Court drew attention to the fact that the cap and the minority provision both applied at 20%[78] but that was incidental. There therefore seems to have been no legal synergy between the two provisions. One conferred a veto on certain strategic decisions; the other made investment less attractive in relation to the remaining, mainly operational, decisions because it made collective action more difficult – a difficulty increased by the Lower Saxony 20% holding, but there was no magic in that context in the 20%. If there was no legal synergy we are driven to consider synergy on the facts. The two provisions taken together did deter investors more than each provision separately. Perhaps this point about the degree of deterrence taken together founded the Court's conclusion.

But this rationale is unsatisfactory. If the fact that provisions confer no special powers on Member States excludes them, then how can two such provisions be objectionable taken together? If on the other hand the de facto special benefit of the enhanced minority provision rendered it objectionable (as is strongly arguable if we accept the general rationale, although an alternative approach will be suggested below) then why was that provision (which absolutely barred direct investors from power over the constitution, for example) not objectionable in isolation? Why was it necessary that there should have been a voting cap as well? Finally, if the objection to a power depends on the degree of deterrence de facto, then how is the objectionable degree to be calibrated?

The Court would apparently have had little difficulty in finding against the enhanced minority in isolation as a de facto special veto power conferred on the basis of a lower shareholding than normal. It clearly felt the need to find against the cap as well. But what was the real objection to the cap? Surely that, although it applied equally to all shareholders, in practice it made direct investment less attractive, thus enhancing the control powers of Lower Saxony.[79]

---

[78] *Ibid.* 'at the same level' paragraph 51 cited in full above.

[79] The enhanced majority looks objectionable per se. It is reported at the time of writing that the German government proposes relying on the combined nature of the ruling to

The case thus leaves us with the conclusion that for powers over company control and operations to be objectionable they must be:

i. likely to deter investors (perhaps particularly investors from other Member States);
ii. be exerciseable by states; and
iii. be operable in pursuance of a state measure[80] or state power[81] (though how significant this is, is debatable).[82]

Further factors regarded by the Court as relevant are whether the measure:

iv. creates a special power for the state authority;
v. infringes mandatory state law,
vi. departs from default state law; or
vii. infringes proportionality principles (which may be by reference to state law or to some abstract ideal of proportionality).[83]

More sense needs urgently to be made of this catalogue. Items (i) to (iii) seem to be necessary in all cases on the basis of the cases. But the extent to which (iv) to (vii) are needed and in what combination is far from clear. But before considering this task we need to examine the recent jurisprudence on horizontal effect, which brings into question the extent to which (i) to (iii) are required.

IV. Horizontal effects

There is no doubt that the obligation not to obstruct movement of capital, like the other freedoms, binds Member States and other state bodies. It has for many years been debated whether these obligations also bind private persons exercising autonomous private law powers.

Extension of the freedoms to bind private bodies exercising autonomous powers under private law would, if it applies to capital, exclude *a fortiori* any requirement that Member States exercising such powers

---

leave this in place while repealing the cap and the appointment power, blocking Porsche control. See *Financial Times* 26 January 2008, 19, and 15 March 2008, 21.

[80] *KPN* (note 34, above), at para 22.
[81] *Volkswagen* (note 60, above), at para 27.
[82] See the discussion of the *KPN* case (note 34, above).
[83] There is also an important (but beyond our purpose) ruling in Volkswagen that the restrictions were not justified by protection of employees from strategic or control changes, *Volkswagen* (note 60, above) at para 74.

must do so under a state measure or must be in some sense exercising sovereign power.

A series of cases on free movement of workers and services have imposed the obligation on bodies exercising rule-making functions under private-law powers, including bodies making rules about sports[84] and this case law has been applied to professional services and establishment[85]. In one case (*Angonese*)[86] freedom of movement of workers has been held to bind a private employer, even though not exercising any rule-making function,[87] but only in respect of discriminatory practices.

This case law has been extended by two recent cases: *Laval*[88] and *Viking Line*[89]. Both involved trade union industrial action under private law powers. In *Laval* Swedish trades unions sought, by 'blockading' Laval work sites in Sweden staffed by Laval, a Latvian company providing workers in Sweden to work on building sites operated by a subsidiary of Laval, to force Laval to sign the Swedish building sector collective agreement, and to pay a certain hourly wage. Laval claimed this was an unlawful restriction of its freedom to provide services in Sweden and sought a declaration and damages.[90] The Court held compliance with article 49 EC, on freedom of services 'is also required in the case of rules which are not public in nature but which are designed to regulate collectively provision of services' and applies to 'exercise of their legal autonomy by associations or organizations not governed by public law';[91] so

---

[84] Case 36/74, *Walrave* v. *Union Cycliste Internationale*, [1974] ECR 1405 (discriminatory rules governing cycle racing – affecting workers and services); Case 13–76, *Dona* v. *Mantero*, [1976] ECR 1333 (discriminatory rules of a football association affecting workers and services); C-415/93, *Union Royale Belge des Societes de Football Association* v. *Bosman*, [1995] ECR I-4921 (Belgian National football association imposing transfer fees on cross-border transfers and discriminating on eligibility to play for other nation clubs – affecting workers and services); C-51/96 C-191/97, *Christelle Deliège* v. *Ligue francophone de Judo et al*, [2000] ECR I-02549 – to similar effect.

[85] C-309/99, *Wouters* v. *Algemene Raad van Nederlands Orde van Advocaten*, [2002] ECR I-1577 (professional rules on cross-professional partnerships for advocates – affecting services and establishment).

[86] C-281/98, *Roman Angonese* v. *Cassa di Risparmio di Bolzano*, [2000] ECR I-4139.

[87] The practice was permitted but not required by a collective agreement so the decision to apply it was that of the individual defendant employer, *ibid*. at para 11, 36, 37.

[88] C-341/05, *Laval un Partneri Ltd* v. *Svensaka Byggnadsarbefoerbundets et al*, [2007] ECR I – not yet reported.

[89] C-438/05, *International Transport Workers Union and Finnish Seamens' Union* v. *Viking Line ABP*, [2007] ECR I – not yet reported.

[90] The terms sought by the union went beyond those the host state was entitled to impose on services operators under the relevant Community Directive.

[91] *Laval* (note 88, above), at para 98.

that article precluded the union from forcing Laval to enter negotiations on rates of pay and to sign the agreement.

In *Viking Line* Viking proposed to re-register in Estonia a ship registered in Finland, and thus crewed at Finnish rates of pay, in order to subject it to the lower Estonian rates. The unions sought by collective action to prevent this. Viking claimed a declaration that this interfered with its freedom of establishment, and injunctive relief. The referring court asked the European Court if 'article 43 has horizontal direct effect so as to confer rights on private undertakings which may be relied on against another private party and, in particular a trade union in respect of collective action'. The Court ruled that it was clear from the case law that 'abolition of obstacles to free movement of persons and services would be compromised if the abolition of state barriers could be neutralized by obstacles resulting from the exercise by associations or organizations not governed by public law of their legal autonomy [citing the cases mentioned above[92]]'.[93] It added that 'it does not follow [from that case law] that that interpretation applies only to quasi public organizations or to associations exercising a regulatory task and having quasi legislative powers. There is no indication in that case law that could validly support the view that it applies only to [such organizations and associations]'; but the court then added 'furthermore it must be pointed out that in exercising their autonomous power pursuant to their trade union rights ... trade unions participate in the drawing up of agreements seeking to regulate paid work collectively'.[94]

Three questions are prompted by this body of case law in the present context:

- Does the case law apply to freedom of capital?
- What are the implications for the restriction applied in the Golden Share cases that, for the obligation to apply, the state must pursue a 'national measure' or exercise 'state power'?
- What are the implications for private persons in the company law context with powers which enable them to impede free movement of capital?

There can be no doubt that this case law applies to free movement of capital. It applies to establishment and the two freedoms are consistently

---

[92] *Walrave, Bosman, Deliege, Angonese* (note 84, above).
[93] *Viking Line* (note 89, above), at para 57.
[94] *Ibid.* at para 33 'articles 39, 43 and 49 [freedom of workers establishment and services] do not apply only to the actions of public authorities but extend also to rules of any nature aimed at regulating in a collective manner gainful employment, self-employment and the provision of services'.

treated in the Golden share cases as subject to the same rules. Moreover, since the cases of concern also involve establishment this case law will apply by that route anyway.

On the second question, it seems strongly arguable that since the case law applies to private persons exercising private powers it follows *a fortiori* that it does to public persons exercising private powers. This is wholly in conformity with community principles. As the Advocate General pointed out in the *KPN* case, Member States are bound by the treaties *qua* signatories and not *qua* state authorities.[95] Moreover, Member States are obliged by article 10 EC to ensure fulfilment of the obligations arising out of the Treaty, to facilitate the achievement of the Community's tasks and to abstain from any measure which could jeopardize the attainment of the objectives of the Treaty. Where a State can exercise a power in a way which has the object or effect of restricting a fundamental freedom it is bound to comply with the treaty, whatever the legal basis of that power. If a state may exercise powers by virtue of a shareholding in a company then it must not do so in a manner which discriminates, nor in a manner which restricts the fundamental freedoms of others, however that share was acquired. Similarly if a share is acquired with the object of restricting such freedoms or its acquisition would tend to have that effect, that is a breach of the Treaty by that State.

It may be argued that this reasoning neglects the point that the cases apply the law to private persons exercising quasi-regulatory functions. Very considerable doubt at the least is cast on this by the ruling in *Viking* quoted above (although it does then emphasize that the union in question had powers to seek to draw up agreements that regulate work collectively). But in any case this restriction is clearly intended to limit the nature of the private bodies who are to be subject to the case law; it is very doubtful that the court would apply it to a public body.[96]

On the third question, how far can *private persons* engaging in protectionist activity intended to inhibit free movement of capital be bound by the horizontal effect of the freedom? This is more speculative. It is doubtful whether where a private party engages for private purposes

---

[95] 'Treaty provisions on free movement of persons services and capital impose obligations on national authorities regardless of whether these authorities act as public powers or private law entities': Maduro AG in *EC* v. *Netherlands* (note 89, above), at para 22 (author's translation) and again in cases C-463 and 464/04 *Federconsumatori et al* v. *Comune di Milano* [2007] ECR I – not yet reported, at para 22.

[96] Perhaps company constitutions, given the breadth of their effect, do regulate a matter collectively.

in conduct which falls short of discrimination (which is probably out-lawed by *Angonese*)[97] the freedoms can be invoked. But there is room for development of a principle, and some authority, that where such a party engages in such conduct for public purposes, then on the analogy of a trade union which is entrusted by private law with the function of negotiating collective agreements with general effect, that party should be subject to the obligation not to obstruct the operation of the freedoms except in conditions permitted by community law. Where a private party is entrusted with public functions under private law the treaty freedoms apply to that party because he acts as a surrogate for the state.[98]

Two examples of the application of this principle in the context of private persons exercising company powers impeding freedom of capital come to mind:

- First, in the case of some companies a special shareholding is vested in a private body entrusted with functions for the general good. A UK example is the Reuters Trust which has the responsibility of ensuring through a private law Golden Share that control changes in Reuters plc do not endanger editorial independence. Similar is the position of certain foundations in Nordic countries which hold voting shares, often with enhanced powers, exercisable for the benefit of the company in the widest sense, including its continuity, the interests of the employees and the community in which it operates.
- Second, the company laws of some States confer public functions on company boards in the sense that their fidelity obligation requires that they serve not only interests of shareholders but also a wider range of constituencies and the public interest. Such boards are similarly acting as surrogates for the state. A particular context is where boards exercise powers to frustrate the success of takeover bids under authority allowed them under the Takeover Bids Directive[99] and in particular the so-called 'reciprocity' power to block a bid from a company with a less open structure than their own.[100] It is clear from the legislative

---

97 Note 86, above.
98 Cases 266 and 267/87, *The Queen* v. *Royal Pharmaceutical Society*, [1989] ECR I-1295; Case C-16/94, *Édouard Dubois et Fils SA and Général Cargo Services SA* v. *Garonor Exploitation SA*, [1995] ECR I-2421.
99 Directive 2004/25/EC, article 12.
100 The legality of the Directive is beyond the scope of this paper – see J. Rickford, 'The Emerging European Takeover Law from a British Perspective', *European Business Law Review,* (2004), 1379, 1402 ('contrary to well recognized Treaty principles'), developed in 'Takeovers in Europe: a UK Perspective', in T. Baums and A. Cahn (eds.), *Die*

history that this has a public purpose – to level the regulatory playing field. Boards exercising such powers should be subject to Treaty freedoms.

V. Conclusion – proposed way forward

How are the uncertainties attaching to Golden Share cases and horizontal-effects cases to be resolved? As in every game it is important to keep our eye on the ball. As Eddy Wymeersch has himself pointed out more than once,[101] it is not the concern of the Court of Justice or European lawyer to create company law. Nor is it therefore to impose some idealized version of company law on Member States, nor their own company law default rules, nor even their mandatory rules – it is to ensure that States do not adopt powers or actions which conflict with Treaty principles – i.e., here, which have the object or effect of deterrence of inter-State investment.

We must address realities: it is notorious that Member States, in taking powers over companies, whether by public law or private law and whether by special provision or by acquisition of shares in the market place, often (perhaps always) intend to use those powers in pursuit of their industrial policies, frequently for protectionist or other purposes conflicting with Treaty principles. The issue is not the legal means by which those powers are obtained, nor the nature of legal provisions under which they are exercisable, but the actual or potential effect of their existence and actual or potential use. It follows from this reasoning, and, as we have seen, from the implications of the *Netherlands (KPN)* case and the authorities on the horizontal effects of the freedoms, that insistence that States are only subject to Treaty principles if they are acting under State measures is unsustainable. It is sufficient if they are pursuing political objectives. Or to put it another way, the 'state measure' requirement in *KPN* is met wherever states have or may have an industrial policy objective – privatization is merely an example. Similarly insistence on qualifications by reference to actual

---

Umsetzung der Uebernahmerichtlinie in Europa (Berlin: De Gruyter, 2006) 88, 89; cf. Wyatt, Dashwood and others, *European Union Law* (note 57, above), Chapter 20.

[101] 'Cross-Border Transfer of the Seat of a Company', Chapter 6 in J. Rickford (ed.), *The European Company* (Antwerp: Intersentia, 2003) 83, 84; and again, E. Wymeersch, 'The Transfer of a Company Seat in European Company Law', 40 (2003) *Common Market Law Review*, 661, 674.

or ideal company law provisions would only be justifiable if compliance with such provisions were an indicator of absence of the mischievous effect (or even conceivably an indicator that it would be less likely). As a matter of common experience, that is not so – whatever the character of a State's control power it has the potential for protectionist abuse; in some states such abuse is very likely, not disguised and even publicly paraded to deter unwelcome investors. Moreover what applies to States also applies to bodies acting as surrogates of States, such as nationalized industries and state investment banks.[102]

All this is wholly consistent with the general principles of the European economic constitution and far from original. More difficult is how to carry it through in terms of legal consequences in this sensitive context. Clearly where States *exercise* such powers in ways which are discriminatory or deter cross-border investment such exercises are open to challenge. But, as the Court recognizes, the problem lies deeper. The very *existence* of the powers carries the risk of abuse. Such powers are objectionable as such unless they are subject to a transparent and enforceable regime at domestic level which ensures that they are only used for legitimate purposes. If such a regime is in place then investment will not be unlawfully deterred because there is an assurance of the absence of abuse. The burden is on Member States to show that such regimes are effective as the Court itself ruled in the *France* and *Belgium* cases. In the absence of such regimes the powers exercisable by States should be void as contrary to Community law; if they are attached to shares, the shares should remain valid, but be shorn of control rights.

There will be strong political opposition to this proposal and the Commission may well be unable to summon the necessary internal conviction to pursue it before the Court. But fortunately that is not necessary. Any shareholder in a company subject to such powers may pursue it. A suitable test case might be brought by such a shareholder wishing to pursue or facilitate a takeover bid. A shareholders' association has already successfully challenged a Golden Share in this way.[103] Damages will be available, as well as enforcement orders.[104]

---

[102] Such as the Caisse des Depots et Consignations in France.

[103] Cases C-463 and 464/04 *Federconsumatori et al* v. *Comune di Milano* (disproportionate, but lawful, control power reserved by local authority in articles under private law powers).

[104] As in the *Laval* and *Viking* cases (notes 88 and 89, above). Cases C-46 and 48/93, *Brasserie du Pecheur/Factortame III* [1996] ECR I-1029.

Similar conclusions can be applied to company organs exercising public law powers. It is often argued that private persons are subject to Treaty principles even when exercising private powers. This seems a step too far[105] and one the Court deliberately did not take in *Volkswagen, Laval* and *Viking*. It is not necessary for the purposes examined here. And it is sufficient to leave the discipline of true market players to the market, to autonomous regulation and to competition law.

---

[105] See van Bekkum, Kloosterman and Winter, 'Golden Shares and European Company Law – the Implications of Volkswagen', (note 70, above). Many *contra,* e.g. Wyatt, Dashwood et al., *European Union Law* (note 57, above), 861–863; M. Andenas, T. Guett and M. Pannier, 'Free Movement of Capital and National Company Law', *European Business Law Review*, 16 (2005) 757, 775.

5

Centros and the cost of branching*

MARCO BECHT, LUCA ENRIQUES AND
VERONIKA KOROM

Following the *Centros*, *Überseering* and *Inspire Art* decisions of the ECJ a thriving market for incorporations has developed in the European Union. Round-trip incorporation is competing with domestic incorporation. Entrepreneurs can set up a shell company in any EU jurisdiction and branch back to their home country to operate a business. The UK Limited is a popular choice in many countries because it is rapidly and cheaply available online with minimum formalities. We develop a taxonomy for measuring the cost of Limited round-trip incorporation. The cost of setting up a Limited is directly observable in the market while the cost of branching is not. We run field experiments to measure the cost of branching. Our analysis reveals that despite the ECJ rulings, branching remains costly or impractical in many cases. Incorporation agents play an essential role in overcoming the limitations to branching.

I. Introduction

To incorporate a business at a lower cost than required by domestic company law, a Danish couple set up a UK shell company, Centros Limited, to operate a business exclusively in Denmark via a branch. Technically this was achieved by registering Centros Limited with Companies House in the United Kingdom and by applying for registration of a branch with the Danish companies register. After the Danish companies

* We are very grateful to Thomas Bachner, Niklas Cornelius, Francesco Dagnino, Aniek Hos, Michael Karakostas, Johanna Kumlien, Theo Lynn, Wilhelm Niemeier, Juan Pablo Felmer Roa, Katarzyna Stuczynska and Beate Sjåfjell for participating in the country experiments. Without them, this research would not have been possible. We are also grateful to John Favaro, Paul Farrell, Vito Gianella and David Mitzman for comments. Financial support was received from the Business Register Interoperability Throughout Europe (BRITE) project under European Commission contract number 027190.

register refused registration of the branch, the case was brought to the ECJ, which declared the refusal of registration as being against the EC Treaty.[1] *Überseering*[2] and *Inspire Art*[3] confirmed and strengthened the *Centros* ruling. In all three cases the ECJ made it clear that the Treaty grants entrepreneurs the right to choose where to set up their company within the EU and to use that as their business form in the country of operation. It also made it clear that the Court strictly scrutinizes attempts to restrict that right.

These European Court rulings have created an active incorporation market in the European Union. Especially in some countries, entrepreneurs are increasingly aware that they can freely choose among all the limited liability vehicles in the Union to run a business in their home state. In Germany, agents selling the UK Limited are omnipresent in newspapers, on television and on websites. The Limited is discussed on television and in parliament. Scores of legal self-help books on the Limited written in German are on display in bookshops. Between 2003 and 2006 more than 40,000 residents of Germany have incorporated a UK Limited.[4]

In this article we show that incorporation from a distance in the United Kingdom is easy and the cost is the same, no matter in which EU country the founding directors of the UK Limited live. By contrast, the direct and indirect cost of branching for a UK Limited company varies greatly across countries, which helps explain why '*Centros* incorporations' are more frequent in some countries than in others.[5]

---

[1] ECJ, Case C-212/97 *Centros Ltd* v. *Erhvervs- og Selskabsstyrelsen* [1999] *ECR* I-1459. See E. Wymeersch, '*Centros*: A Landmark decision in European Company Law', in Th. Baums, K. J. Hopt and N. Horn, *Corporations, Capital Markets and Business in the Law. Liber Amicorum Richard M. Buxbaum* (London, 2000), 629.

[2] ECJ, Case C-208/00 *Überseering BV* v. *Nordic Construction Company Baumanagement GmbH*, [2002] ECR I-9919.

[3] ECJ, Case C-167/01 *Kamer van Koophandel en Fabrieken voor Amsterdam v Inspire Art Ltd*, [2003] ECR I-10155.

[4] See M. Becht, C. Mayer and H. Wagner, *Where do firms incorporate? Deregulation and the cost of entry*, ECGI Law Working Paper N°.70/2006, August 2007.

[5] To be sure, Member States do not usually provide for stiff sanctions against foreign companies that fail to register their branch in the country of operations. So, for instance, in Austria, § 107 GmbHG (Austrian limited liability company act) requires registration of the branch of a foreign company in the Austrian companies register. § 24 FBG (Company registry act) provides that in case of non-registration the court can impose a maximum fine of €3,600. In Germany, § 13d HGB (German Commercial Code) provides that a company, the seat of which is abroad, must register a branch in Germany. Under § 14 HGB, the penalty for non-registration is a maximum fine of €5,000. In the case BGH 14.03.2005 II ZR 5/03, the German Federal Court of Justice considered the question of whether the sanction for the non-registration of the Limited branch could be to make

We make two contributions to the literature: one, we devise a new experimental methodology that allows us to measure the actual cost of branching, comprising the cost of incorporation in the United Kingdom and the cost of branching;[6] two, we conduct experiments and report the empirical results.

Our experiments show that the total cost of *Centros* incorporation differs considerably across countries. It cost a mere €551 to set up a UK Limited and branch back to Ireland. *Centros* incorporation also proved to be relatively cheap for entrepreneurs from Austria (€698), the Netherlands (€759) and Norway (€947). In contrast the cost has proved to be much higher in Poland (€1631) and Sweden (€2146), and prohibitive in Italy (€5007).

The main driver of the cost differences is the cost of translation and of certification. In the Italian case the cost exploded because Italy requires additional UK documents that also needed to be translated, like a letter of good standing and a decision of the board of directors of the UK Limited to open a branch. In addition we detected country idiosyncrasies that were somewhat surprising, like Sweden requiring the appointment of an auditor before branch registration (€1062). Greece wanted to impose Greek minimum capital requirements on the branch, simply ignoring the existence of the *Centros* case law.

The cost of branching is substantially reduced by the presence of an incorporation agent. Private intermediaries play a central role in overcoming existing administrative hurdles. The 'do-it-yourself' cost of obtaining an *Apostille* might require a trip to London. German agents typically charge less than €30 for an *Apostille* that certifies the authenticity of their standard incorporation documents. The agents can obtain *Apostilles* for hundreds of documents at the same time. The agents can also offer low-cost translations because they use a standard document

---

the director of the Limited personally liable for the company's debts (as it was held by the lower courts). The BGH held that in the case of non-registration only a fine under § 14 HGB could be imposed on the company and that in no case could the director be made personally liable for the company's debts, the directors' liability being governed by English law. No matter how little dissuasive sanctions for non-registration are, branch registration is, however, de facto necessary to deal with banks, State offices or major suppliers.

6 There are other projects measuring the cost of incorporation in different countries, for example the World Bank's 'Doing Business (Washington, January 2008), www.doingbusiness.org. At the moment this project only measures the cost of domestic, not of foreign incorporation. Also, the cost measurement is based on a questionnaire filled out by country correspondents, not on the actual cost of incorporating a real business.

with its standard translation. The marginal cost of translating their 'boilerplate' UK documents is almost zero. In contrast, the translation cost in our Italian experiment was approximately €1800.

The results we obtain help explain why the UK Limited is widely used in the Netherlands while it is practically non-existent in Greece, despite the equal amount of paid-up minimum capital for national private limited liability companies in the two countries (€18,000); or, again, widely used in Norway while almost unheard of in Italy, again despite an approximately equal amount of minimum capital in the two countries (€10,000). The cost of setting up the UK Limited is the same in all cases, but the cost of branching is not; branching to Greece or Italy from the UK is very costly, branching to Norway and the Netherlands is not.

Despite the rulings of the European Court and flanking measures adopted by the European Commission, branching to some EU countries is still more limited than to others. The results of our experiments provide clear indications of where further public or private enforcement of the freedom of establishment principle enshrined in the Treaties is required and of what steps the Commission could take to make branching less costly.

II. *Centros* incorporation terminology

The *Centros* idea of using a legal vehicle in another EU member state to run a local business is well established in the mutual fund industry. Most 'Undertakings for Collective Investment in Transferable Securities' (UCITS) in the European Union are incorporated in Luxembourg or Ireland, although the promoter of the fund resides in another Member State. A fund set up by a Belgian promoter under Luxembourg law and intended to be sold back into Belgium is referred to as a 'round-trip fund'. We use this travel-industry-inspired terminology for *Centros* incorporations.

An entrepreneur wanting to set up a UK Limited from outside the UK to operate a business in his or her home jurisdiction through branching is confronted with three options offered by incorporation agents: 'full round trip', 'incorporation and half-way back' and 'incorporation-only'. The first two options are available in some Member States only.

A. *Full round trip*

The easiest way to set up a *Centros*-type Limited is to purchase a 'full round trip' incorporation package. This service includes everything from registration of the UK Limited to registration of the branch in the entrepreneur's home country.

The 'Foratis Limited' sold in Germany is an example of this service. For €2,500 Foratis AG will create and register a UK Limited with a capital of £120, deliver a Certificate of Incorporation, Memorandum and Articles of Association and a certified translation of these into German with *Apostille*.[7] Foratis will also take care of the branch registration in Germany and open a German bank account. The Limited is registered at an address in Birmingham and Foratis provides a Company Secretary for one year. A one-year service package is included in the purchase price and features an application to the UK Inland Revenue for the Limited to be exempted from filing a UK tax return, a mail forwarding service from the registered office of the Limited to an address in Germany (against a supplementary fee of €2 per letter) and reminders for important dates, like filing obligations with Companies House. After the first year an extension of the service pack subscription is available for €250.[8]

The full round trip service is not widely available and some agents do not offer it at all. Instead, entrepreneurs have to take care of the branching themselves or they are brought 'half-way back' by the incorporation agent.

B. Incorporation and half-way back package

This package differs from the full round trip one in that it does not include the branch registration in the home state and the opening of the bank account. It does provide instead for the registration of a Limited in the UK, plus the documents required to register the branch: the official UK documents with certification (*Apostille*) and certified translations. When the package is offered by a local agent it usually includes instructions. In the ideal case, the national entrepreneur simply needs to take the documents and translations received from the agent to the local companies register and apply for the branch registration.[9]

---

[7] The UK is not a signatory of the Hague convention and the *Apostille* is required to certify the authenticity of the UK documents.

[8] www.foratis.com/thema/000130/foratis_deutsche_limited.html.

[9] An interesting legal question arises when a Belgian resident uses the 'half-way back' service of an agent in the Netherlands to obtain the branch registration documents in Dutch, but certified by an official translator from the Netherlands. Current practice appears to be that the Belgian companies register will not accept official translations from the Netherlands, Germany or France, although Dutch, French and German are official languages in different parts of the country. For cost reasons we did not explore this issue in our empirical research.

C. Incorporation-only package

In the worst case, neither the 'full round trip' nor the 'half-way back' option is available in the country of residence of the entrepreneur. We found, for example, that this was the case in Hungary. A Hungarian entrepreneur has to resort to the services of a UK agent to set up the Limited company and take care of the branching herself. A variety of incorporation services are offered by a broad spectrum of providers. A fully-fledged offering again includes an incorporation package bundled with one year of compliance services, including a 'virtual' registered office, a company secretary and mail forwarding.

After incorporation via the UK agent the Hungarian resident receives the UK documents and has to undertake the branching procedure on her own. This means that she has to arrange for legal representation for the registration procedure,[10] for a board resolution of the Limited to set up a branch in Hungary,[11] the notarization of the signature specimen of the branch representative(s),[12] the payment of all fees[13] and the translation of all required company documents into Hungarian.[14] As one would expect, the requirement to undertake 'do-it-yourself' branching poses serious limits on the relative attractiveness of the UK Limited.

III. Experimental design

The total cost of *Centros* incorporation is directly observable for the 'full round trip' package, but not in the other cases. To obtain a direct measure of the cost of 'Limited round tripping' from countries where a full service is not available we conducted field experiments with the help of country correspondents. We supplied them with a 'Guideline for country correspondents'. The Guideline gave an explanation of the procedural steps

---

[10] For the branch registration process legal representation is compulsory in Hungary, § 32(4) of the Law V of 2006; costs of the legal representation may range between €400 and €4,000, as our country correspondent found out during our experiment.

[11] Appendix I, Law V of 2006.

[12] Appendix I, Law V of 2006, notarization of the signature specimen is regulated by Law XLI of 1991; the cost of notarization is a standard €6 per signature.

[13] Under Law XCIII of 1990 the branch registration fee is 250.000 Ft (€200) and under Law V of 2006 and Decree Nr. 22 of 2006 of the Minister of Justice the publication fee is 14.000 Ft (€56).

[14] Appendix I, Law V of 2006; according to Decree Nr 24. of 1986 the 'National Translation and Translation Authentication Office' has the exclusive right to produce official translations (the rate is approx. €17 per page).

of the branch registration as well as a checklist of information that we required our correspondents to record.

We found country correspondents from ten EEA states: Austria, France, Germany, Greece, Ireland, Italy, the Netherlands, Norway, Poland and Sweden.[15] We asked our country correspondents to put themselves into the shoes of a small local entrepreneur who intends to incorporate and branch back a UK Limited at the lowest possible cost. We thus instructed them to search for a local incorporation agent selling the UK Limited online. In case they could not find local agents we suggested they use Jordans, a reputable UK agent that had been recommended to us. After incorporating the Limited, the correspondents were asked to register a branch in the local companies register and to record the number of procedures they had to undergo, the costs incurred, the time it took them, and any obstacles they encountered.

IV. Results

Of the ten experiments our country correspondents undertook, five were performed until branch registration, while two were abandoned at an early stage (France and Greece), one (Austria) was only recently resumed to obtain registration after some difficulties had emerged, and two were abandoned just before the final steps for cost reasons (Poland and Sweden).

A. Choice of incorporation agent matters

Our French correspondent decided to break off the experiment after experiencing problems with his chosen incorporation agent ('Agent A'), one of the cheapest providers on the UK market with a website in English, French, German, Polish, Italian, Spanish, Arabic and Chinese. Our correspondent reported that incorporation of the private limited company in the UK took place in March 2007. However, despite promises of a prompt delivery (within 10–14 days) of the French translations of the company documents, Agent A posted the translations with a delay of two months (the correspondent also complained about their poor quality). When in May the correspondent tried to apply for branch registration, the French register refused to accept the company documents

---

[15] Freedom of establishment extends to EEA countries. Hence the inclusion of Norway.

issued in March and asked for more recent certificates. Agent A was ready to supply these, but requiring additional payment of course. At this point, the correspondent broke off the experiment.

B. *Further ECJ Rulings might be required*

The Greek experiment was abandoned as soon as our correspondent found out that under Law 3190/1955, for a branch of a foreign private limited liability company (Limited) to be registered in Greece, the foreign company must meet the minimum capital requirements set by Greek law for the Greek private limited liability company, i.e. have a minimum paid-up capital of €18,000.

This requirement of course undermines the basic rationale behind incorporation shopping and might explain why the number of UK-incorporations from Greece is very low, although Greece ranks close to the top of the list of countries in terms of minimum capital requirements and length of incorporation procedures.[16] This requirement constitutes a serious (and, in light of *Inspire Art*, illegitimate) barrier to freedom of establishment, quite aside from the fact that it is also in breach of the Directive 89/666/EEC of 21 December 1989 (Eleventh Company Law Directive on Disclosure Requirements in respect of Branches: hereinafter, the Eleventh Directive).

C. *Italy – a case study in incorporation market closure*

Of the other experiments, the Italian one proved to be of particular interest, both in itself and for the entrepreneurial activity it inspired. In fact, as the Appendix fully details, it uncovered what is probably one of the most tedious and expensive branching procedures in Europe. Further, it gave our country correspondent the idea of setting up an Italian incorporation service provider, 'Italian Limited'.[17] So far, Italian Limited has incorporated thirty Limiteds for Italian entrepreneurs, and there seems to be high potential for further growth. In the face of an actual cost of more than €5,000, Italian Limited offers the full round trip service package for €2,490.

---

[16]   See Becht, Mayer, and Wagner, *Where do firms incorporate?* (note 4, above), 31.
[17]   See www.italianlimited.it.

D. *Proving the existence of the branch*

The Austrian experiment is also interesting. In fact, it was temporarily broken off due to two problems raised by the Vienna Company Court during the registration procedure. First, the Court required that evidence of the actual existence of the branch in Vienna be adduced (e.g. lease of business premises, website, business contacts, etc.) for registration to take place.

In fact, Austrian law provides that, in order for registration to take place, evidence must be given as to the existence of the branch.[18] Austrian Courts have clarified in several cases involving Limiteds incorporated in England under English law and applying for the registration of a branch in Austria.[19] According to this case law, evidence has to be produced that an appropriate business structure is in place which permits the branch to do business permanently and independently form the company itself. The courts concede that also planned measures can be taken into account when determining the existence of the branch, if their implementation can be held to be highly likely in the given circumstances. Examples of accepted evidence are a webpage of the branch, rented premises and facilities, a bank account, the existence of funds, business contacts, etc.

In our case, since the branch was only to be registered for the purposes of the experiment, its real existence was hard to prove. Incidentally, we note that this point should not be a serious obstacle in the case of a local entrepreneur who indeed intends to do business through a Limited.

E. *Objects clause restrictions*

More importantly, the Company Court also required the amendment of the objects clause because the standard English objects clause which the memorandum of the Limited contained included financial activities which under Austrian law need specific authorization.

The Vienna Court of Appeal has held that in the absence of the required authorizations by either the Financial Services Authority in the UK or the equivalent body in Austria the registration of the branch has to be refused.[20]

---

[18] § 12 Austrian Commercial Code (UGB).
[19] OGH 29.4.2004, 6 Ob 43/04y; OGH 29.4.2004, 6 Ob 44/04w; OLG Wien 29.12.2006, 28R 233/06z.
[20] OLG Wien 5.12.2003, 28 R 338/03m, OLG Wien 30.11.2004, 28 R 217/04v.

The objects clause was an obstacle not only in Austria, but also in Poland and Norway. In these two countries minor amendments had to be made to the objects clause to obtain registration.

Apparently, it is frequent for member states to require the disclosure of the memorandum and articles of the foreign company, as Art. 2(2)(b) of the Eleventh Company Law Directive allows them to do. Furthermore, under Art. 2(1)(b) the member states may require the disclosure of the 'activity' of the branch. How these two interact is unclear. While Austrian courts seem to focus on the objects clause of the Limited and pay no attention to the 'activities' of the branch, German courts have come to the conclusion that it is solely the 'activity' carried out by the branch and not the objects clause of the foreign company that the German company courts are called upon to scrutinize when considering the registration of a branch.[21]

F. Agents reduce cost

In the case of Germany, the Netherlands, Norway and Sweden the branching procedure ran fairly smoothly and our correspondents encountered no major obstacles. In Germany the notary fees are heavily regulated with a cap of €19 that can be charged for authenticating the signature specimen of the branch representative. Therefore, although traditionally the application procedure was taken care of by the notaries, with the maximum fee of €19 now applicable, they are reluctant to get involved in branching procedures. Hence, the burden of lodging the application documents at the court falls back on the entrepreneurs. In the Netherlands our correspondent was questioned by the clerk at the Chamber of Commerce (the office in charge of the branch registration) why she decided to use a Limited instead of a Dutch legal form.

In respect of the Irish experiment it must be borne in mind that our correspondent chose to order the 'full round trip' instead of the 'half-way back' service, used by most other country correspondents. Both because of this and because the foreign company concerned was a UK Limited, the process was more straightforward than anywhere else. Of course, a

---

[21] OLG Thüringen, 22.4.1999 – 6 W 209/99; LG Bielefeld, 8.7.2004 – 24 T 7/04; LG Ravensburg, 14.2.2005 – 7 T 1/04 KfH 1; LG Kassel, 18.3.2005 – 13 T 13/04; LG Chemnitz, 24.3.2005 – 2 HK T 54/05; LG Chemnitz, 12.5.2005 – 2 HK T 427/05; OLG Hamm, 28.6.2005 – 15 W 159/05; OLG Frankfurt a.M., 29.12.2005 – 20 W 315/05.

cost advantage for the Irish entrepreneur is that no translation has to be made of incorporation documents.

V. Conclusion

Our field experiments show that there are substantial differences in the cost and feasibility of 'round trip incorporation' between Member States. Incorporating a Limited company in the United Kingdom is cheap, fast and can be done from a distance. When problems arise they stem from branching.

In part, this is explained by the presence of incorporation agents in only some of the Member States. By standardizing the procedural steps that are needed they can cut down on the costs significantly, the most telling difference being between the cost of the required translation where incorporation agents offer this service (€30 in Germany), and where they do not (€1,800 in Italy).

Once the document translation and certification hurdle has been overcome, the ease of branching depends on national idiosyncrasies. Branching can be made more cumbersome and costly by requiring, de jure or de facto, the intervention of a public notary, as in Italy or Germany, or by insisting on evidence that the branch really exists (a requirement that is absent from those the Eleventh Directive allows member states to impose), as in Austria, or by meddling with the contents of the object clause, as in various countries. In Sweden the requirement to appoint an auditor for the branch places an important extra cost burden on branching (although to be sure a similar requirement also exists for domestic companies), while in Italy, Hungary and Poland the requirement to enclose a company resolution setting up the branch will cause additional hurdles since this resolution does not form part of the standard documents provided by incorporation agents.

Of course, such obstacles discourage incorporation agents to begin with, because the arbitrage surplus to be gained by incorporating a business as a Limited will be lower in countries where such obstacles exist, making the supply of a standardized and less costly Limited product less likely.

Our experiments have also highlighted patent violations of EC law, as in the case of Greece, that requires a minimum capital for foreign companies branching in Greece as high as that of a Greek company.

To conclude, our research shows that a lot could be done to facilitate freedom of establishment in the form of branching. First of all, the 11th Directive should be revised, at the very least by introducing mutual recognition of objects clauses: a given object clause should be of no obstacle to branching, no matter whether it includes activities for which an authorization is required in the state of branching. This would not mean that the registered branch would be free to exercise that activity, for which it would have to obtain the required authorization anyway.

The 'European Commission proposals for fast track administrative burden reductions in 2008'[22] presented on 10 March 2008 recognizes that unnecessary and disproportionate administrative costs severely hamper economic activity and aims at cutting administrative costs for entrepreneurs. The Proposals are the second package of an overall programme to reduce the administrative burdens for entrepreneurs in the EU by 25% in 2012.

With respect to cross-border branching the Proposals contain two important measures: one, the possibility of re-using translations of company documents that have already been certified in one member state when the same language is used and second, the abolishment of the obligation to publish business data in the national gazettes.[23] Instead, company information will be made available online which not only saves costs for entrepreneurs, but makes access to the information easier. As a next step the planned integration of the national company registers in the EU could ensure more clarity and easier registration procedures as well as a more efficient information exchange between the register of the country where the company was incorporated and that where it intends to set up a branch.

APPENDIX – COUNTRY EXPERIMENT REPORTS

I. Austria – START Unternehmensberatung Limited

A. Preliminary investigation

There is a vast number of online service providers that offer UK incorporation services in Austria. They are almost exclusively run from

---

[22] MEMO/08/152, http://europa.eu/rapid/pressReleasesAction.do?reference=MEMO/08/152&format=HTML&aged=0&language=EN&guiLanguage=en

[23] For an example of a dispute on the cost aspect of publishing company information in the Official Journal on the occasion of branch registration: see ECJ, Case C-453/04 *Innoventif Limited* v. *Landgericht Berlin*, [2006] ECR 4929.

Germany. Given the fact that there are no language barriers between Germany and Austria, and that the branch registration procedure is very similar in the two countries, German incorporation agents have expanded and now cover the Austrian market too.

The country correspondent for Austria spent approximately half a day on the internet searching for the cheapest incorporation provider and decided to order the 'half-way back' package ('Offizielles Deutschland-Paket') and a one-year company secretary service from Ganz Einfach Ltd.[24] for €348. The package included the Certificate of Incorporation, the *Apostille* for the Certificate of Incorporation, the Memorandum and Articles of Association and their certified German translations.

B. UK incorporation

The correspondent ordered the incorporation of the 'START Unternehmensberatung Limited' on 12 February 2007 by filling in the online order form of Ganz Einfach Ltd. On the same day, Ganz Einfach Ltd. confirmed by email that the START Unternehmensberatung Limited was incorporated. Attached to the email were the Certificate of Incorporation and the Memorandum and Articles of Association.

The next day, *Ganz Einfach* Ltd. provided the country correspondent with a detailed explanation of the incorporation procedure in England, setting out which incorporation documents and translations were still to be sent to the correspondent and when.

On 16 February, only four days after placing the order for the incorporation service, the correspondent received hard copies of the certified translation into German of the Certificate of Incorporation, the Memorandum and the Articles by ordinary mail. On 22 February these were followed by certified copies of the original English language documents.

On 15 March our correspondent received the Companies House Certificate of Incorporation issued by the Officer of the Companies Registration Office in Cardiff.

Unfortunately an error occurred in the mention of the subscriber shareholder which had to be rectified, thus retarding the branch incorporation by more than two weeks. Had this error not occurred, the Austrian correspondent would have had all the necessary documents,

---

[24] www.yoffi.net.

translations and certifications ready for the branch registration within three weeks. Even with the delay, the procedure took just over five weeks.

C. Registration of the branch in the Austrian Companies Register

The country correspondent called the Company Court in Vienna to find out about the required steps for the branch registration. In Austria, the company director is entitled to undertake the registration of the branch herself, there being no requirement for legal representation.

In order to prepare for the registration, our correspondent had to draft an 'application for registration' and a 'signature specimen form'.[25] The director's signature on both these documents must be certified either by a public notary or by the Company Court. Our correspondent chose to have her signature certified by the Court for the cheaper €18/signature as opposed to €30/signature charged by public notaries.

On 4 April 2007 our correspondent handed in the application form for branch registration at the Viennese Company Court. Attached to the form were the English language Certificate of Incorporation and the *Apostille*, the Memorandum and Articles in English and their certified translations into German. The application fee was €34.

On 10 April 2007 the Company Court informed our correspondent by letter that in order to have the Limited branch registered in Austria she had to: (i) prove that the branch was actually and factually established in Austria; (ii) amend the objects clause or provide proof of specific authorization by a financial regulatory authority, because certain paragraphs of the objects clause contained activities which in Austria fall under 'regulated financial activities' and therefore need specific authorization. Unless these requirements were complied with and evidence of the compliance adduced to the Court within eight weeks of the date of the Court's letter, the application would be rejected.[26]

---

[25] In order to do this, our correspondent relied on the following manuals: C. Fritz, *GmbH-Praxis I, Vertragsmuster und Eingaben, Mustersammlung für Gründung, Geschäftsführung, Umwandlung und Auflösung* (Wien: Linde, 2003); A. Kostner/M. Umfahrer, *Die Gesellschaft mit beschränkter Haftung. GmbH-Handbuch für die Praxis* (Wien: Manz, 1998).

[26] It appears to be a general practice of the company courts in Austria to require both evidence of the actual establishment of the branch and the amendment of the object clause for branch registration in the case of UK Limiteds. It is hoped that thereby some control over the pseudo-foreign companies can be exercised. See OLG Wien 5.12.2003, 28

At this point the branching experiment was broken off. Had registration taken place, a registration fee of €180 and a publication fee for publication in the Official Journal of approximately €100 would have been payable (publication fees depend on the length of the published information about the Limited branch).[27]

D. Summary

Cost item	Cost
Incorporation service (incl. company secretary)	€348
Certification of signature	€36
Application fee	€34
Registration fee	€180
Publication fee	€100
Total	€698

Time spent	Time
Search for an incorporation service provider	5h
Prepare application form for registration and signature specimen	3h
Certification of signature and handing in application form at the Company Court	5h
Total	13h
Estimated elapsed time in total for branch registration (from first contact with incorporation agent until branch registration)	approx. 5 weeks

R 338/03m; OLG Wien 30.11.2004, 28 R 217/04v; OGH 29.4.2004, 6 Ob 43/04y; OGH 29.4.2004, 6 Ob 44/04w.

[27] In February 2008 we decided that the experiment should be resumed and full registration of the branch attempted to be attained. Therefore, our correspondent approached the incorporation service provider she had previously used and asked for an amended memorandum that would omit from the objects clause the specific financial activities that would have needed authorisation in Austria. The new memorandum of course had to be translated into German as well. Furthermore, our correspondent took steps to ensure that evidence of the actual establishment and existence of the branch could be established. At the time of writing this part of the experiment is still in progress.

II. Germany – Weiler Unternehmensberatungs Ltd.

Our correspondent ordered 'the incorporation and half-way back' package from GoAhead Limited[28] on 15 December 2006 and the branch was registered on 3 May 2007. There were a number of factors that caused this delay:

A. Delay in document delivery by agent

Our correspondent ordered the Limited on 15 December 2006 and although the GoAhead website states that incorporation would take a week normally, the notification of the incorporation together with the electronic documents were only sent to our correspondent on 28 December. Our correspondent was on holiday until 16 January 2007 and therefore did not receive the documents before that date.

B. Dispute with GoAhead over objects clause

When reviewing the documents, our correspondent discovered that the company's objects clause had not been drafted as ordered. Our correspondent had specifically described the object as 'strategic non-legal advice in M&A', whereas GoAhead used the standard form describing the object of the company as being engaged in any trade. Our correspondent requested a change of the articles and the memorandum, but GoAhead refused and our correspondent let go. This dispute lasted from 18 January to 16 February 2007.

C. Notary

Next, our correspondent contacted his local notary for registration of the branch, but the notary was not responsive and failed to provide a draft of the application form to be handed in to the court in order to register the branch. The correspondent therefore produced the draft form himself and finally received the authentication of his signature on the application form on 12 April from the notary.

While a German notary would normally then submit the application to the court and deal with any inquiries the court might have, the notary refused to do so for a Limited. His explanation was quite

---

[28] www.go-limited.de/.

simple and telling. For the required authentication of the signature, the legal cap for the fee would be approximately €19. For such a low fee he said he would not take it upon himself to submit the application to the court. Our correspondent therefore lodged the application himself.

In our correspondent's words, 'the reluctance of the local notary to handle the matter swiftly is not to be understood as an intention to discriminate against foreign companies. It is mainly influenced by economic factors, that is, the low fee the notary can charge'.

D. Court

The local court registered the branch within a relatively short period of time (18 days).

E. Overall assessment

In our correspondent's view, 'from the four and a half months that it took to register the Limited's branch, more or less two could have been saved had I not been on holiday, not entered into the dispute with GoAhead and urged the local notary more actively'. One should also add that our correspondent lives in the countryside and it is well known in Germany that companies registries in the countryside are slower than elsewhere.

F. Summary

Cost item	Cost
Incorporation with 'half-way back' service	€694.00
Notary	€19.56
Registration fee of Court	€170.00
Total	€883.56

After the company was registered, the local companies register charged €408 as compulsory membership fees.

III. Italy – FRADA Limited

A. Preliminary investigation

After a three-hour internet search the country correspondent for Italy discovered that there were no Limited incorporation service providers offering the 'incorporation and half-way back' or the 'full round trip' services in Italy. He thus decided to choose the 'one-way only' service.

The correspondent then limited his search to the ten most popular results in the internet inquiry (writing 'uk limited companies' in the search engine). Prices ranged from £30 (incorporation only) to £340 (for a full-compliance package). The entrepreneur decided to use Jordans (£340 + VAT): although Jordans was slightly more expensive than its competitors its service was more reliable.

B. UK incorporation

Our correspondent sent an order form to Jordans by e-mail. Within 24 hours, he received by e-mail a copy of the 'certificate of incorporation'. Three days later, our correspondent received a letter with: *a*) documents certifying that the incorporation had taken place; *b*) the company secretarial service agreement (which the correspondent had to sign and return); *c*) a two-page form to be filled in and returned to the Inland Revenue; *d*) a request for the following documents: *i*) a certified copy of the page of a current signed passport which contains the photograph of the correspondent; *ii*) either a certified copy or original of a recent utility bill (not more than three months old and not a mobile telephone bill) or bank or building society statement (not more than three months old) showing the correspondent's current address. The copies of company documents had to be certified, preferably in English, as a true copy of the original and signed and dated by a lawyer, accountant, notary, bank manager, doctor, teacher or embassy official, whose name, address, status or capacity the correspondent had to supply together with the copy documentation.

C. Registration of the branch in the Italian Companies Register

Once FRADA Limited was incorporated, the correspondent called the competent company registry in order to gather information about the registration procedure. According to the registry's officer, the usual procedure requires a notary deed in order for the branch to be registered (although Italian law does not expressly assign a role to notaries for this purpose).[29]

The entrepreneur then contacted twenty notaries in order to register the branch. This part of the procedure was the most cumbersome. Only six out of the twenty notaries were willing to send a cost estimate (€1,500–2,000 on average). One of these six notaries required, in order for the branch to be registered, an extraordinary general meeting conducted pursuant to Italian law (thus ignoring the *lex incorporationis* principle). The remaining five notaries asked for a translation of a board resolution – adopted according to English law – establishing a branch in Italy and appointing a representative in Italy (i.e. the single shareholder). The resolution had to be deposited with Companies House by the company secretary of Frada Limited.

The resolution above, the statute of incorporation, a certification attesting that the Limited still exists, the personal data of the board members have to be deposited at a notary's office in Italy. The documents also have to be translated into Italian by a sworn expert. The notary then takes care of the registration at the company registry. Most of the notaries also required that our correspondent apply for a tax number for the Limited in Italy in order for the registration to be accomplished.

In general, notaries were reluctant to undertake the registration of a Limited branch in Italy. They were apparently not used to this procedure. Since under Italian law a notary is struck off the register whenever she commits two errors during her professional career, notaries may be unwilling to bear the risk of making an error in a not particularly profitable procedure, such as a Limited branching.

After having gathered the above information, the entrepreneur went back to Jordans to obtain the certification attesting that the Limited was still in force and the company's resolution establishing the Italian branch. The next day he received en e-mail containing the resolution which he had to return signed to the company secretary for the registration at Companies House. The cost of the resolution was £50. Ten days later, he received the certificate attesting the Limited was still in

---

[29] See L. Enriques, *Società costituite all'estero*, (Bologna-Roma: Zanichelli-Il Foro Italiano, 2007), 69–70 (according to whom the notary should not be involved if there is no similar requirement in the state of incorporation, but also noting that the contrary view is dominant among scholars and practitioners).

force. This procedure could have been shortened (two days overall) by paying a £30 extra fee.

To obtain the certified translation of the documents for the registration required twelve days and cost €1,801. Our correspondent decided to engage an authorized translator, but the Italian legislation also allows a certified translation to be made by the person applying for registration. In such a case, an €80 registration fee is required. The tax number was obtained in a couple of days and involved a fee of €251.

Our correspondent then contacted the first notary again. The notary took five days to check that the documents were formally complete. Another six days were spent on drafting the application deed for the registration. In the meantime, our correspondent had to convince the notary that the whole procedure was lawful, since the notary apparently was not aware of the *Centros* case law. The notary was eventually convinced, but although his cost estimate had at first been €1,500, he asked for a fee of €3,000 once he understood that the Limited was a 'mailbox company'.

Our correspondent therefore decided to contact another notary, who prepared the application deed in five days for a fee of €2,014. Under Italian law, the branch is formally set up as soon as the notary's deed is registered in the Companies Register. The notary must register the deed within forty-five days after issuing it, but this second notary informally undertook to fulfil this obligation within three days.

D. Summary

Cost item	Cost
Incorporation service (incl. company secretary)	€558.37
Documents provided by Jordans for the registration	€381.54
Translation costs	€1801.22
Opening of tax position	€251.36
Registration and notaries fee	€2014.42
Total	€5006.91

Time spent	Hours
Obtaining information from the Companies' Register	1
Finding a notary and assuming information on the procedure to follow and the documentation required under the Italian law	3
Obtaining from the agent the documentation requested by the notary	1
Finding and dealing with the translator	2
Opening VAT in Italy	1
Meeting and dealing with the first notary	3
Meeting and dealings with the second notary	7
Others (emails, phone calls, post office etc.)	1
Total	19
Estimated elapsed time in total for branch registration (from first contact with incorporation agent until branch registration)	52 days

IV. Ireland – ECGIBRITE Limited

A. Preliminary investigation

The Irish correspondent performed a Google search and selected and ordered a 'full round trip' service from 'Company Bureau',[30] a service which includes both the registration of a UK Limited and the registration of its branch in Ireland. Company Bureau charged €550 for this package.

B. Ordering the 'full round trip' incorporation service

Our correspondent ordered the package on 27 February 2007 by phone. On the same day, Company Bureau emailed him a company formation order form. Besides filling in the form, our correspondent was asked to provide a second, UK-based director and a UK-registered address for the ECGIBRITE Limited.

---

[30] www.companyformations.ie.

Our correspondent completed and returned the form together with the above mentioned additional documents on 5 March. Company Bureau confirmed the incorporation of ECGIBRITE Limited in England on 8 March 2007. The Certificate of Incorporation, the Articles and the Memorandum, the share certificate, minutes of the first board meeting and the company seal were posted to the correspondent on 14 March. He received them on 20 March.

C. Registration of the branch at the Irish Companies Registration Office

On 7 March 2007 Company Bureau emailed the correspondent the F12 Form (requiring personal details of the director). The correspondent filled in the Form and returned it by fax and by post the next day.

Company Bureau applied to the Irish Companies Registration Office to register the Irish branch of ECGIBRITE Limited on 30 March 2007. It had to hand in a certified copy of the Certificate of Incorporation, certified copies of the Memorandum and the Articles, a certified copy of the recent accounting documents and the F12 Form.

The Companies Registration Office confirmed the registration of the branch on 5 April 2007. However, the incorporation service provider only informed our correspondent two weeks later, on 20 April 2007, that the branch registration had taken place.

D. Summary

Cost item	Cost
Incorporation service ('full-round trip') service fee	€300
registration fee and documentation fee	€187
VAT	€67
Fax and postage	€1
Total	€551

Time spent	Time
Researching the internet and filling in various forms	40 min
Total	40 min
Estimated elapsed time in total for branch registration (from first contact with incorporation agent until branch registration)	approx. 5 weeks

V. Netherlands – Expletus Limited

A. Preliminary investigation

The Dutch country correspondent spent approx. two and a half hours on the internet searching and comparing incorporation service providers and decided to order the 'half-way back' package from Haags Juristen College (HJC')[31] for €600. The package included the Certificate of Incorporation, the Memorandum and Articles, a certified Dutch translation of the Articles, the Current Appointments Report and Companies House Forms 10 and 12.

B. Ordering the 'half-way back' incorporation service

Our correspondent made first contact with HJC on 31 January 2007. She received the same day their order form by email which she had to fill in and return by post together with a copy of her passport and a proof of residence for herself (the director of the Limited) and for the company secretary.

Our correspondent posted the above documents on 5 February and on 7 February she received by post the Memorandum of Association of Expletus Limited and Forms 10,[32] 12[33] and 255.[34] Due to some delay in settling HJC's invoice, our correspondent received the Articles of Association with the certified Dutch translation,[35] the Current Appointments Report and once again the Memorandum and Forms 10 and 12 only on 16 March by email. Three days later the Certificate of Incorporation arrived by post.

---

[31] See www.hjc.nl; the *Inspire Art* case was initiated by this specialist in company law.
[32] First directors and secretary and intended situation of registered office.
[33] Declaration on application for registration.
[34] Change of accounting reference date.
[35] For branch registration in the Netherlands, only the Articles of Association have to be translated to Dutch.

C. Registration of the branch at the Dutch Chamber of Commerce

On 19 March our correspondent contacted the Chamber of Commerce of Tilburg to find out about the branch registration procedure and the general requirements that have to be fulfilled prior to registration. She was informed that there were no particular requirements for the branch registration and that she did not need an appointment to hand in the registration documents at the Chamber of Commerce either.

Our correspondent thus went to the Chamber on 22 March to undertake the registration. She handed in the Certificate of Incorporation, the Memorandum and the Articles, the certified Dutch translation of the Articles, the Current Appointments Report and Forms 10 and 12 along with the registration form, which she downloaded from the website of the Chamber of Commerce.

The branch registration went through fast and smoothly, taking about one hour. The clerk of the Chamber of Commerce checked our correspondent's personal identity and carried out a search against the company name 'Expletus'. Upon the payment of the annual registration fee of €148 the branch was registered. Our correspondent had to pay an additional €11 for the Dutch extract of the branch registration of Expletus Limited. She then was given a 'welcome package' containing a welcome letter and a brochure with further information about the Chamber of Commerce.

The registration of Limited branches is not published in an Official Journal or Gazette in the Netherlands, but information about such registrations can be obtained from the website of the Chamber of Commerce.

After registration, our correspondent was advised to apply for a tax identification number to the tax authority.

D. Summary

Cost item	Cost
Incorporation with 'half-way back' service	€600.0
Registration fee	€148.5
Company extracts	€11.0
Total	€759.5

Time spent	Time
Research incorporation services provider and fill in order form	3h
Registration at the Chamber of Commerce	5h
Total	8h
Estimated elapsed time in total for branch registration (from first contact with incorporation agent until branch registration)	approx. 5 weeks

VI. Norway – Ringilihorn Limited

A. Preliminary investigation

There are a large number of agents offering UK Limited incorporation services in Norway.[36] Our country correspondent for Norway searched the internet for an incorporation service provider and also consulted online forums which rate and provide feedback on the agents. She then decided to use Stron Group,[37] which offered the cheapest incorporation service in Norway. For 3,234 NOK (approx. €400) Stron Group offered a 'half-way back' package comprising the Certificate of Incorporation, the Memorandum and Articles of Association, the Current Appointments Report and the certified Norwegian translation of these documents. Furthermore, a board resolution setting up a branch in Norway and appointing our correspondent as the director of the branch, as well as a declaration by the director accepting the nomination were also included in the package. These latter documents were supplied in Norwegian. The one-year company secretary service was also provided by Stron Group, at an additional cost of 2,313 NOK (approx. €247)

B. Ordering the 'half-way back' incorporation service

The correspondent ordered the 'half-way back' package by filling in the online order form on 9 March 2007. On the same day as our correspondent ordered the incorporation service, Stron Group confirmed that the

---

[36] Our correspondent reported that the Limited is a popular means of avoiding the Norwegian minimum capital requirements.

[37] www.stron-group.com.

Ringilihorn Limited was incorporated and emailed all the necessary documents for the branch registration, including the Norwegian translations, to our correspondent.

C. *Registration of the branch in the Norwegian Company Register*

On 10 March the correspondent posted all the above documents together with the registration form, which was also provided by Stron Group, to the Norwegian Company Registry. She had to pay a registration fee of 2,500 NOK (approx. €300). The registration fee for a branch of a foreign company is less than half of the fee (6,000 NOK, or approx. €726) payable upon registration of a Norwegian limited liability company.

Although according to Stron Group the registration of a Limited branch usually only takes about 7–10 days, our correspondent received a letter on 22 March from the Company Registry informing her that for the registration to go through, further information had to be supplied to the Registry about the business objectives of the branch. In accordance with the ECGI BRITE Experiment guidelines, our correspondent had stated 'consultancy; economics and business' in the objects clause of the Limited, which mention however proved to be not specific enough under Norwegian law and had to be amended to 'economics and business consultancy'. The amendment was faxed to the Registry.

In little over a week the Norwegian correspondent finally received a letter from the Company Registry confirming the registration of the branch.

D. *Summary*

Cost item	Cost
Incorporation with 'half-way back' service, including one year of company secretary	€647
Registration fee	€300
Total	€947

Time spent	Time
Researching incorporation service provider, filling in order form, registration	3h 40 minutes
Total	3.66 h
Estimated elapsed time in total for branch registration (from first contact with incorporation agent until branch registration)	approx. 2.5–3 weeks

VII. Poland – Ksanta Limited

A. *Preliminary investigation*

Using the usual keywords 'Limited' and 'UK incorporation' in Google search prompted no Polish results at first, so the country correspondent for Poland decided to instruct Jordans and order the 'one-way only' package.[38] However, our correspondent found out later that there exist also Polish Limited incorporation service providers.[39]

Jordans charged £441 (approx. €581) for the 'Annual Compliance Package' which included the incorporation of Ksanta Limited in England, the one-year company secretary service and a board resolution to set up the branch in Poland. This was needed because in addition to the usual company documents a resolution of the foreign company setting up the branch and appointing a representative is also required for the branch registration in Poland.

The translation of the company documents was not taken care of by Jordans and had to be arranged and paid for by our correspondent herself.

B. *Ordering the 'incorporation only' service*

Our Polish correspondent ordered the Limited incorporation on 31 January 2007. The next day Jordans confirmed that Ksanta Limited

---

[38] www.jordans.co.uk.
[39] E.g.: www.companyinuk.pl, www.form-online.net/_pl/index.php.

was incorporated and emailed the Certificate of Incorporation to the correspondent.

On 5 February 2007, she received the certified copies of the Certificate of Incorporation, the Memorandum and Articles of Association by post together with a) the company secretarial service agreement (which the correspondent had to sign and return); b) a two-page form to be filled out and returned to the Inland Revenue in England; c) a request for the following documents: *i*) a certified copy of the page of a current signed passport which contains the photograph of the entrepreneur; *ii*) either a certified copy or original of a recent utility bill (not more than three months old and not a mobile telephone bill) or bank or building society statement (not more than three months old) showing the entrepreneur's current residential address.

The Memorandum supplied by Jordans contained a mistake; the authorized share capital was marked £1,000 instead of £100. This had to be rectified before the registration process could begin. Our correspondent received the correct Memorandum with three days' delay.

C. Registration of the branch at the Polish Company Court

The following documents are needed for the registration of the branch of a foreign company in Poland: an application form, different forms detailing the appointed representative(s) for the branch and the trading activities of the branch, a board resolution establishing the branch and appointing a representative together with its certified Polish translation, the Memorandum and the Articles together with their certified translations, the Certificate of Incorporation and its certified translation, a signature specimen of the branch representative certified by a notary and the payment of the registration fee and the publication fee.

Our correspondent had to search for a certified translator who would translate the Certificate, the Memorandum, the Articles and the board resolution into Polish. The translations were ordered on 9 February 2007 and cost 935.1 PLN (€266). They were ready by 23 February.

The correspondent also had to arrange for her signature specimen to be certified by a public notary. The certification cost an additional 24.40 PLN (approx. €7).

On 4 April 2007 our Polish correspondent handed in the application form for registration at the Polish Company Court together with the required documents. As she had not received any documents from Jordans confirming her as the director, she was advised by the Court secretary to hand in her share certificate (plus certified translation) instead.

Our correspondent had to pay in advance the registration fee of 1000 PLN (approx. €284) and a publication fee of 500 PLN (approx. €142) for the publication of the branch registration in the Official Journal of the Court.[40]

About three weeks later, the Court wrote to the correspondent requiring her to present documents confirming her status as the director of the company within seven days or else the registration could not take place. Furthermore, the correspondent was asked to make two minor corrections in the application form, one relating to the method of representation and the other to the business activity of the company, so as to bring them into line with the Memorandum of Ksanta Limited.

The correspondent made the requested two changes and turned to Jordans for help in connection with her status as the company director.

Jordans offered to supply a certified extract from Companies House (notarized and legalized for use in Poland) confirming our correspondent as the director of Ksanta Limited for £ 275.

At this point, given the additional costs involved, the branching experiment was broken off.

D. Summary

Cost item	Cost
Incorporation service (incl. company secretary service)	£ 441
Certified translations	PLN 935.1
Notarisation of signature	PLN 24.40

---

[40] The publication in the Official Journal is restricted to the name of the foreign company, its registration number abroad, the Polish registration number of the branch, the activities and the name of the authorised representative of the branch; the Memorandum and the Articles are not published in full.

Registration fee	PLN 1,000
Publication fee	PLN 500
Certified extract confirming director	£ 275 (n.a.)
Cost of Polish translation for director's extract	n.a.
Total	€1631

Time spent	Time
Completing the forms, scanning, mailing, telephones, information, visits to the notary, translator, courts etc.	12h
Travelling – to and from notary, court, translator	12h
Total	24h
Estimated elapsed time in total for branch registration (from first contact with incorporation agent until branch registration)	9 weeks

VIII. Sweden – J&N Consultancy Limited

A. Preliminary investigation

The country correspondent for Sweden conducted a Google search on the internet looking for Swedish Limited incorporation service providers. He found Consab[41] that offered the 'half-way back' incorporation service for 8,112 SEK (approx. €872).

Our correspondent ordered the incorporation package from Consab which included the registration of the Limited in England and the documents needed for the branch registration in Sweden: a certified copy of the Certificate of Incorporation and of the Articles of Association, proof that the Limited had not been declared insolvent in the UK, a power of attorney authorizing the director to act on behalf of the branch and to receive service of process, and the one-year company secretary service.

[41] www.starta-aktiebolag.se

B. *Ordering the 'half-way back'*
incorporation service

Payment to Consab was made on 31 July 2007. Consab confirmed the same day that the J&N Consultancy Limited was incorporated. Our correspondent received the documents needed for the Swedish branch registration within a week, on 6 August.

According to Swedish law, it is mandatory to appoint a certified auditor for the branch.[42] The auditor must be appointed officially after the incorporation of the Limited in the UK and before the branch registration in Sweden. This usually takes a few days. The annual cost for an auditor is approx. 10,000 SEK (approx. €1,062).

C. *Registration of the branch at the Swedish*
Companies Registration Office

The registration procedure is very simple and very flexible in Sweden. No Swedish translation of any of the English company documents is required for the registration of the Limited branch, only a short description of the business activity of the branch must be provided in Swedish. The latter was taken care of by Consab.

According to our correspondent, normally all company documents can be handed in to the Swedish Companies Registration Office in their original language (documents in Danish, Norwegian, German, Spanish, French are usually accepted if the handling officer is able to understand them; however, she can at any time request that any of the documents be translated into Swedish), and all communications with the Registration Office can be in English.

The application for registration is made by email, but the company documents must be sent by post to the Companies Registration Office. It takes usually about a week or one and a half weeks before applications for registration are processed by the Office. The registration fee is 2,000 SEK (approx. €212).

However, the Swedish experiment was broken off before the branch registration could take place because of the high costs involved in the appointment of a branch auditor.

---

[42] This rule applies to all branches of all types of limited liability companies, i.e. to branches of foreign companies (Limiteds) as well as to branches of Swedish companies.

D. Summary

Cost item	Cost
Incorporation and 'half-way back' service (incl. company secretary service)	€872
Registration fee	SEK 2,000 (~€212)
Mandatory Appointment of Auditor	SEK 10,000 (~€1,062)
Total	SEK 20,112 (~€2,146)

Time spent	Time
Search for incorporation service provider	4h
Search for and appointment of an auditor	8h
Total	12h
Estimated elapsed time in total for branch registration (from first contact with incorporation agent until branch registration)	approx. 4 weeks

Table 1. *Summary of country results*

Country	Total cost of incorporation, one year service and branching	Total time spent by correspondent (in hours)	Time in total until branch registration (in weeks, approx.)
Austria	€ 698	13.00	5
Germany	€ 1,302	n.a.	10
Italy	€ 5,007	19.00	7.5
Ireland	€ 551	0.66	5
Netherlands	€ 759	8.00	2
Norway	€ 947	3.66	2.5–3
Poland	€ 1,631	24.00	9
Sweden	€ 2,146	12.00	4

Source: Branching experiment country reports

Table 2. *Comparison of cost items across countries*

Item	Austria	Germany	Italy	Ireland	Netherlands	Norway	Poland	Sweden
UK Incorporation with one-year compliance package	€348	€694	€939.91	€550	€600	€647	€581 (+£275 for director's appointment report)	€872
Notary fee	–		€2,012.42				€7	
Certification of signature	€36	€19						
Translation cost			€1,801.22				€266 (+ translation of director's appointment report)	
Application fee	€34							
Registration fee	€180	€170			€148.50	€300	€284	€212
Publication fee in Official Journal	€100						€142	
Compulsory membership fee		€408						
Tax registration			€251.36					
Administrative cost (fax, post)				€1				
Company extract					€11			
Appointment of certified auditor								€1062
Total	€698	€1,291	€5,006.91	€551	€759.50	€947	€1,631	€2,146

6

Towards the end of the real seat theory in Europe?

MICHEL MENJUCQ[*]

I. Introduction

The mobility of companies has increased significantly over the last decade[1] but, after the *Daily Mail*[2] decision of the European Court of Justice in 1988, the method of company mobility has not been via the transfer of seat.[3] Moreover, recently, Mr McCreevy said 'no to the 14th Company Law directive'[4] on the transfer of registered seat from a Member State to another Member State. In fact, the mobility became a reality in Europe after the revolution realized by the ECJ in the field of the European conflict of corporate laws.[5] Referring to Articles 43 and 48 of the EC Treaty, the ECJ emphasized in its *Centros,*[6] *Überseering,*[7] *Inspire Art*[8] and *Sevic*[9] decisions the freedom of companies to create establishments and to implement cross-border mergers within the EU.

---

[*] Chapter completed in April 2008.

[1] *See* R. Dammann, 'Mobilité des Sociétés et Localisation des Actifs', *JCP-Cahiers de Droit de l'Entreprise*, (2006), 41. See also: M. Menjucq, *La Mobilité des Sociétés dans l'Espace Européen* (Paris: LGDJ 1997); M. Menjucq, 'La Mobilité des Entreprises', *Revue des Sociétés* (2001), 210; H. Le Nabasque, L'Incidence des Normes Européennes sur le Droit Français Applicable aux Fusions et au Transfert de Siège Social, *Revue des Sociétés* (2005), 81.

[2] Case C-81/87, *Daily Mail and General Trust*, [1988] ECR 5483.

[3] See E. Wymeersch, 'The Transfer of the Company's Seat in European Company Law', *Common Market Law Review*, 40 (2003), 661.

[4] Speech by Commissioner McCreevy at the European Parliament's Legal Affairs Committee, Brussels, 3 October 2007. See, K. E. Sorensen and M. Neville, 'Corporate Migration in the European Union: an analysis of the proposed 14th EC company law directive', *Columbia Journal of European law*, 6 (2000), 181.

[5] See, W. Ebke, 'The European Conflict of Corporate Laws Revolution: Überseering, Inspire Art and Beyond', *The International Lawyer*, 38 (2004), 813.

[6] Case C-212/97, *Centros Ltd* v. *Erhvervs- og Selskabsstyrelsen*, [1999] ECR I-1459.

[7] Case C-208/00, *Überseering BV* v. *Nordic Construction Company Baumanagement GmbH*, [2002] ECR I-9919.

[8] Case C-167/01, *Kamer van Koophandel en Fabrieken voor Amsterdam* v. *Inspire Art Ltd*, [2003] ECR I-10155.

[9] Case C-411/03, *SEVIC Systems AG*, [2005] ECR I-10805.

These ECJ decisions in favour of the incorporation theory, raise the question about the future of the real seat theory in Europe. Is it the end of this theory?

As is well known, where the incorporation theory 'recognizes all foreign legal entities according to the rule applicable in the State of origin',[10] the real seat theory in private international law considers the location of the central administration (or effective centre of management) of the company which cannot be dissociated from the location of its registered office.[11] In that case, according to the real seat theory, the company should be no longer recognized as a legal person under the law of the state of its central administration. This was exactly the *Überseering* case which applied the German conflict of laws rule.

A less dogmatic interpretation can be found in the interpretation of Article L. 210–3 of the French commercial code, which provides that the location of the registered office determines the *lex societatis*. However, such place of the registered office cannot be invoked against third parties if the effective centre of management of the company is located elsewhere.[12] The classical French doctrine[13] considers that this provision reflects the theory of *siège réel*. Modern doctrine has suggested replacing this principle by the criterion of the statutory office, corresponding to the State of incorporation, unless the registered office is fraudulent.[14] That said, it appears that French law is less dogmatic than the '*Sitztheorie*' in German private international law.[15]

The real seat theory has, however, been viewed as an obstacle to the freedom of establishment in Europe guaranteed by Articles 43 and 48 EC Treaty. In its *Centros, Überseering, Inspire Art* and *Sevic* decisions the ECJ judged that the prohibition on dissociating the place of

---

[10] Wymeersch, 'The Transfer of the Company's Seat', (note 3, above), 661.

[11] H.J. Sonnenberger, *Münchener Kommentar zum Bürgerlichen Gesetzbuch, Internationales Privatrecht* (München: Beck, 2005), 163, 181 et seq.

[12] Art. 1837 para. 2 of the French civil code provides for a similar provision.

[13] *See* H. Batiffol, and P. Lagarde, *Droit international privé* (Paris: LGDJ, 1981) No. 196, Y. Loussouarn, P. Bourel and P. de Vareilles-Sommières, *Droit international privé, Précis Dalloz*, (Paris: Dalloz, 2007), No. 707.

[14] See Menjucq, *Droit international et européen des sociétés, Précis Domat*, (Paris: Montchrestien, 2001), No. 71 et seq.; also J. Béguin and M. Menjucq (ed.), *Droit du commerce international*, (Paris: LexisNexis Litec, 2005), No. 470; P. Mayer and V. Heuzé, *Droit international privé*, 9th edn, (Paris: Economica, 2006), No. 1037.

[15] In the *Überseering*-case, German lower courts held that a company incorporated in the Netherlands with an effective seat located in Germany does not exist as a legal person under German law. This jurisprudence was reversed by the BGH after the *Überseering* decision of the ECJ.

incorporation from the administration or business activities of a company was contrary to the EC Treaty. This jurisprudence constitutes 'the victory of the Anglo-Saxon incorporation theory pursuant to which the founders of a corporation freely choose the place of incorporation of a company and hence the law applicable to its organization (*lex societatis*)'.[16] Once incorporated, the company can develop its business activities without any geographical restriction within the European Community. Consequently, the company is also free to choose the place of its headquarters and its central administration. The generalization of the incorporation theory will favour the mobility of companies in Europe. Following the jurisprudence of the ECJ, an increasing number of companies have been incorporated in the United Kingdom, despite exercising their activities exclusively in Germany.

II. What are the direct consequences of *Centros, Überseering, Inspire Art* decisions?

The *Centros, Überseering, Inspire Art* and *Sevic* decisions have provoked a 'legal earthquake' in Germany. After years of discussions, German doctrine and jurisprudence has drawn the following conclusion: the real seat theory is, *de facto*, contrary to the EC Treaty and needs to be abrogated and replaced by the incorporation concept. Therefore, in early 2006, the German government prepared a proposal for a Council Regulation (CE) regarding conflict of law issues with respect to companies adopting, *inter alia*, the theory of incorporation.[17] The purpose of this proposal is to harmonize the private international law regarding companies in Europe. Even if this proposition is not adopted in the form of an EC Regulation, in any event, the German legislator plans to amend its private international law accordingly.

In France, the modern doctrine mostly agrees with the ECJ decisions but insists on the need to take into consideration the fraud or abuse as it is evoked in the *Centros* and the *Inspire Art* cases.[18] With this

---

[16] See R. Dammann, 'Mobility of Companies and Localization of Assets – Arguments in Favour of a Dynamic and Teleological Interpretation of EC Regulation no 1346/2000 on Insolvency Proceedings', in G. Affaki, *Cross-border Insolvency and Conflict of Jurisdictions, a US-EU Experience*, (Brussels: Bruylant, 2007), 105.

[17] See the proposal of the German Council for Private International Law under the presidency of Prof. H. J. Sonnenberger, *Revue Critique de Droit International Privé* (2006), 712.

[18] See M. Menjucq, 'La notion de siège social : un unité introuvable en droit international et en droit communautaire', *Mélanges en l'honneur de J. Béguin* (Paris: Litec, 2005), 499.

consideration of fraud or abuse, articles L. 210–3 of the commercial Code and 1837 of the civil Code could be read in conformity with articles 43 and 48 EC Treaty: indeed, if a third person could invoke the real seat only in case of fraud or abuse, the interpretation of articles L. 210–3 of the commercial Code and 1837 of the civil Code would comply with the ECJ jurisprudence.

But the problem is the definition of fraud or abuse in the field of conflict of corporate laws. Merely circumventing the application of Member State companies law is not fraudulent or abusing as the ECJ stressed in the *Centros* decision, except perhaps if the purpose of the founders is to realize a fraud or an abuse of third-party interests. But the ECJ had not given any concrete elements to determine what are fraud and abuse against third-party interests.

Finally, in the field of Community freedom of establishment, if there is a place for the real seat theory, it is only for a much reduced real seat theory, limited only to the consideration of the real seat when there is a fraud or an abuse against third-party interests.

However, this is obviously paradoxical, as the real seat theory is applied in the status of all Community legal persons European Economic Interest Grouping,[19] European Cooperative Society[20] and especially the European Company.

III. The real seat theory and the European Company: a paradox?

A paradox can be drawn with the European Company (*Societas Europea – SE*) that is governed by Council Regulation (EC) no. 2157/01 of 8 October 2001. Pursuant to Article 7 of this Regulation, the registered office must always be situated at the place of its central administration.[21] This provision, which reflects the real seat theory, has been imposed by Germany in the first draft Regulation in the seventies, when German company laws were the model for Community corporate Regulations.[22]

---

[19] Council Regulation 2137/85/EEC on the European Economic Interest Grouping (EEIG), Article 12.

[20] Council Regulation 1435/2003/EC on the Statute for a European Cooperative Society (SCE), Article 5.

[21] See also art. L. 229–1 paragraph 3 C. com.

[22] The first draft Regulation on European Company also contained provisions on groups of companies inspired by German law. About the opportunity of such rules, see, E. Wymeersch, 'Do We Need a Law on Groups of Companies?', in K. J. Hopt and E. Wymeersch, *Capital Markets and Company Law*, (Oxford University Press, 2003).

Consequently, according to Article 8, the transfer of the registered office of an *SE* to another Member State is only possible, provided that a transfer of its central administration occurs simultaneously in order to comply with the provisions of Article 7.

In view of the foregoing, Council Regulation (CE) no. 2157/01 of October 8, 2001 regarding the *SE* appears to be somewhat anachronistic.[23] That said, Article 69 provides for a reassessment of the effective business seat rule by the Commission within five years after the entry into force of the Regulation. Hence, it would appear rather likely that the Regulation will be revised in the future by adopting the incorporation theory in order to increase the attraction of the *SE*. Likewise, the Report on the *Societas Europeae*, written in 2007 by Mrs Lenoir,[24] former French Minister of European affairs, suggests to modify the status of the SE to introduce the incorporation doctrine.

Hence, it is not sure that the real seat doctrine has a future in the European Company. But in the field of insolvency, the presumption in favour of the registered office is losing ground. Is it the revenge of the real seat theory?

IV. The Insolvency Regulation: the revenge of the real seat theory?

Council Regulation (EC) no. 1346/2000 of May 29, 2000 on insolvency proceedings was conceived in the sixties.[25] At the time the location of the registered office was stable and corresponded to the place where the headquarters and the main activities of the company were located. Consequently, save in exceptional circumstances, the centre of main interests of a company was always located at the place of its registered office.

But, nowadays, as we said before, after the *Centros, Überseering, Inspire Art* and *Sevic* decisions of the European Court of Justice, the mobility of companies has increased significantly. In particular, the discussion has focused on the famous term 'centre of main interests' – COMI – which

---

[23] See M. Menjucq, 'Rattachement de la société européenne et jurisprudence communautaire sur la liberté d'établissement : incompatibilité ou paradoxe?', *Recueil Dalloz* (2003), 2874.

[24] See N. Lenoir, Rapport au Garde des Sceaux sur la *Societas Europeae (SE)*. Pour une citoyenneté européenne de l'entreprise, *La documentation Française* (2007).

[25] It is based on the text of a draft treaty of 1995 which was the fruit of a difficult compromise, but which never entered into force because the United Kingdom refused to ratify it. *See* for the historical genesis of the Regulation, C. Saint-Alary-Houin, *Droit des entreprises en difficulté* (Paris: Monchrestien, 2001), n°1147 et seq.

determines the court with jurisdiction to open the main insolvency proceedings and, hence, in accordance with Article 4(1) of the Regulation, the law applicable to such proceedings.

Moreover, most of the cross-border insolvencies falling within the scope of the Regulation involve groups of companies, a phenomenon that needs to be addressed. Unfortunately, the Regulation does not deal with this topic. In order to efficiently address the insolvency of groups of companies, a vast majority of European jurisdictions have adopted a rather wide interpretation of Article 3(1) of the Regulation, judging that the COMI of each entity of the group can be located at the registered office of the controlling (parent) company if such parent company is directly involved in the management of its subsidiaries.[26] This case law has been severely criticized by some authors.[27] It is accused of triggering forum and law shopping, legal uncertainty for third parties and conflicts of jurisdictions. Others have favoured a more teleological approach of Regulation 1346/2001 which enables the application of the Regulation to groups of companies.[28]

After the *Eurofood* decision of the ECJ dated 2 May 2006[29] and despite the restrictions of ECJ, the application of the Regulation on groups of companies has become an established fact, as it appears from the *Eurotunnel* decision of the Court of Paris[30] dated 2 August 2006.

---

[26] For a synthesis of this jurisprudence *see* R. Dammann, 'L'évolution du droit européen des procédures d'insolvabilité et ses conséquences sur le projet de loi de sauvegarde', *Lamy Droit des Affaires* (2005), 18 and M. Raimon, 'Centre des intérêts principaux et coordination des procédures dans la jurisprudence européenne sur le règlement relatif aux procédures d'insolvabilité', *Journal de Droit International* (2005), 739.

[27] See e.g. M. Menjucq, *JCP – Cahiers de Droit de l'Entreprise* (2006), 10089.

[28] *See* R. Dammann, '*Mobility of Companies and Localization of Assets*', *(note 16, above)*, 105.

[29] Case C-341/04, *Eurofood*, [2006] ECR I-3813. See *Recueil Dalloz* (2006), 1286 note A. Lienhard; *Recueil Dalloz* (2006), 1752 note R. Dammann; *JCP-Cahiers de Droit de l'Entreprise* (2006), 10089 note M. Menjucq; *Bull. Joly* (2006), 923 note D. Fasquelle; *Revue des Sociétés* (2006), 360 note Rémery; *JCP-Cahiers de Droit de l'Entreprise* (2006) n° 2071 note J.-L. Vallens; *Lamy droits des affaires* (2006), 29 note Y. Chaput.

[30] *See Recueil Dalloz* (2006), 2329 note R. Dammann and G. Podeur, 'L'affaire *Eurotunnel*, première application du règlement CE n° 1346–2000 à la procédure de sauvegarde'. The judgment was confirmed by the Commercial Court of Paris on January 15, 2007, *Recueil Dalloz* (2007), 313; *Bull. Joly* (2007), 459 note Jault-Seseke and D. Robine. The appeal was rejected by the Court of appeal of Paris in a judgment dated November 29, 2007, *Recueil Dalloz* (2007), 12 note A. Lienhard; M. Menjucq, 'Réflexions critiques sur les arrêts de la Cour d'appel de Paris dans l'affaire *Eurotunnel*', *Revue des procedures collectives* (2008), 9.

The risk of forum and law shopping is real since judges have a large discretion when interpreting the notion of COMI. Consequently, questions arise as to whether an interested party taking the view that COMI is situated in a Member State other than that in which the main insolvency proceedings were opened could effectively challenge the jurisdiction assumed by the court which opened proceedings. In the *Eurofood* decision, the ECJ emphasized the principle of mutual trust among the jurisdictions of the Member States. Consequently it held that any review of jurisdiction must be done by the court of the opening State in accordance with the remedies prescribed by national law of that Member State.[31]

Recent decisions illustrate however some practical problems. In the *Hans Brochier* case, on 4 August 2007, the London High Court of Justice opened administration proceedings. The appointment of the joint liquidators occurred in the framework of the so-called out-of court-appointment proceedings at the request of the management of *Brochier*. In such proceedings, the court does not verify the underlying facts establishing jurisdiction. Consequently, in the *Brochier* case the court relied on the representations made by the management stating that the COMI of *Hans Brochier* Ltd. was located at its registered office in the UK. A fortnight later, German employees filed a bankruptcy petition for *Brochier* with the insolvency court of Nürnberg. In its order of 15 August 2007, the German bankruptcy court held that the COMI of *Brochier* was clearly located in Germany and that the UK main proceedings had been fraudulently opened. Thus the Tribunal of Nürnberg refused to recognize the opening of the UK main proceedings on the grounds that they were contrary to public order in accordance with Article 26 of the Regulation.[32] The principal of mutual trust is difficult to apply if a foreign court is not obliged as a matter of national insolvency law to verify the underlying facts establishing the COMI. In the *Brochier* case, the conflict of jurisdiction was rather quickly resolved. At the request of the UK joint liquidators of *Hans Brochier*, on 15 August 2007, the High Court retracted its judgment opening main proceedings in favour of *Brochier*.[33]

Finally, the question arises under what circumstances the simple presumption of the competence of the jurisdiction of the Member State where the registered office of the debtor is located, could be rebutted. Is there a place for the real seat doctrine in the Insolvency Regulation?

---

[31] See recitals 43 *et seq.* of the *Eurofood* decision (note 29, above).
[32] *Zeitschrift für Wirtschaftsrecht* (2007), 81.
[33] *Neue Zeitschrift für das Recht der Insolvenz und Sanierung* (NZI) 3/2007 p. 137.

The answer can be found in the *Eurofood* decision of the ECJ:[34]

> It follows that, in determining the centre of the main interests of a debtor company, the simple presumption laid down by the Community legislature in favour of the registered office of that company can be rebutted only if factors which are both objective and ascertainable by third parties enable it to be established that an actual situation exists which is different from that which locating it at that registered office is deemed to reflect.
>
> That could be so in particular in the case of a 'letterbox' company not carrying out any business in the territory of the Member State in which its registered office is situated.
>
> By contrast, where a company carries on its business in the territory of the Member State where its registered office is situated, the mere fact that its economic choices are or can be controlled by a parent company in another Member State is not enough to rebut the presumption laid down by the Regulation.

There is no doubt: the COMI is not the real seat of the debtor because it does not refer to the effective centre of management but to the place where the company carries on its business. In fact, the ECJ refers to an economic criterion. Consequently, there is no 'revenge' for the real seat doctrine in the field of Insolvency Regulation.

V. Conclusion

In sum, it seems that there is no future for the real seat theory in the European area even if 'it will remain applicable in the relation to third States'.[35] Actually, this theory was conceived in a different economic and legal environment which is now over. But the possible end of the real seat theory in a few years does not mean that the real seat criterion has absolutely no future. Indeed, if, referring to the *Centros* and *Inspire Art* ECJ decisions, there is a place for fraud or abuse, especially towards third persons, the real seat criterion could be the evidence of such fraud or abuse. However, it is a very small place[36] for a criterion and a theory which were dominant in most of the Member States laws: it is probably the symbol of the new leadership of Anglo-Saxon rules.

---

[34] Recitals 34, 35 and 36 of the *Eurofood* decision (note 29, above).
[35] See Wymeersch, 'The Transfer of the Company's Seat', (note 3, above), 695.
[36] In the same way, see Wymeersch, 'The Transfer of the Company's Seat', (note 3, above), 661.

7

The Commission Recommendations of 14 December 2004[1] and of 15 February 2005[2] and their implementation in Germany

MARCUS LUTTER

I. Introduction

By virtue of their law-making powers European Union institutions may enact Regulations and Directives. During the past forty years, the Commission has made extensive use of both these powers particularly concerning company law.[3] Over the course of this time the Commission's actions were accompanied by remarkable changes in its general policy on a number of occasions. Starting off with the idea of a widespread harmonization of the law,[4] this policy was virtually abandoned by the Commission in 1990. However, under the impact of the capital markets and under the banner of Corporate Governance, the Commission discovered its own original policy at the turn of the millennium. One of the key role players in this realignment of the Commission's policy was the so-called High Level Group and

---

[1] Commission Recommendation of 14 December 2004 fostering an appropriate regime for the remuneration of directors of listed companies 2004/913/EC [2004] OJ L 264/32.

[2] Commission Recommendation of 15 February 2005 on the role of non-executive or supervisory directors of listed companies and on the committees of the (supervisory) boards 2005/162/EC [2005] OJ L 52/51

[3] Cf. detail list in M. Lutter, *Europäisches Unternehmensrecht*, (Berlin: de Gruyter, 1996, 4th Edn). Since then, the Directive of the European Parliament and of the Council of 21 April 2004 on takeover bids 2004/25/EC [2004] OJ L 142 and the Directive of the European Parliament and of the Council of 26 October 2005 on cross-border mergers of limited liability companies 2005/56/EC [2005] OJ L 310/1 have been issued in addition.

[4] The famous Structure Directive (reform proposal of 20 November 1991, [1991] OJ C 321) has altogether undergone three reform changes since its original presentation on 9 October 1972 but has never been issued formally. The same is true of a directive modelled on the German group law regime ('Konzernrechts-Richtlinie'), which has never been taken further on from the stage of its preliminary drafts in 1974 and 1984.

their report dated from 4 November 2002.[5] The Commission warmly welcomed this report by the High Level Group, which had in fact been set up by the Commission itself, and implemented a corresponding EU Action Plan.[6] At the same time, the Commission began reviewing further options as to how the proposals made by the High Level Group might be implemented as law in a form other than a Directive. It was during this reviewing process that the Commission came to regard the Recommendation as a viable alternative for the Directive, since they, too, are listed as in Art. 249 (5) of the EC Treaty as an option for action by the Commission. Yet Recommendations are not binding (Art. 249 (5) EC Treaty) and therefore do not constitute law, at least in the German sense of the word. Nevertheless, the Recommendation can be of quite some interest to the Commission when it comes to using it as a strategic device in order to influence Member States towards its own ends. This is particularly true if the Commission combines a Recommendation with a threat to the effect that a legally binding Directive with an equivalent content shall be enacted should Member States not observe the Recommendation in the first place. In fact, this is exactly what happened with respect to both of the aforementioned Recommendations. Alas for the Commission, combining a Recommendation with a threat of enacting identical rules in the form of a Directive in case of the former's non-observance is easier said than done. The option of acting by way of Recommendation has such great appeal for the Commission because the Commission may enact the Recommendation on its own without having to consult either the European Parliament or the European Council of Ministers. By comparison, with respect to the Directive, the Commission only reserves the power of initiative, the power of enactment itself remaining with the Parliament and the Council. The difficulties which thus lie behind this balance of power have only been too visible for observers of the recent enactment of the Directive on Takeover Bids.[7]

With regard to the transformation into national law of its two Recommendations, the Commission has not ruled out from the start the possibility for member states to bring about harmonization by other

[5] The report may be downloaded from http://ec.europa.eu/internal_market/company/docs/modern/report_en.pdf; an abstract in German language may be found here: Maul, *Der Betrieb* (DB) 2003, 27.

[6] Communication from the Commission to the Council and the European Parliament of 21 May 2003, COM (2003), 284 final.

[7] Directive 2003/25/EC, (*supra* note 3).

means than legislation, but instead has talked of 'appropriate actions' which the Member State must undertake. Accordingly, harmonization may also be resolved through the respective national Corporate Governance Codes.

The Commission therefore attaches most importance to the effective implementation of the Recommendations as such, insofar as this can be reasonably expected. The implementation of both Commission Recommendations in Germany is going to be the topic of this contribution.

II. Remuneration policy and publication of directors' remuneration (Recommendation of 14 December 2004)

This Commission Recommendation deals with the concept of a general remuneration policy for the board directors of listed (stock) companies as well as the publication of each director's respective remuneration, with a special focus on stock-option programmes.

A listed company is therefore required to publish a *report on remuneration* annually, providing information as to the concrete concept according to which remuneration is determined. Further to this, a listed company is required to publish each director's individual annual remuneration. And thirdly, remuneration by way of stock options requires an approving decision of the shareholders' meeting.

In Germany, this Commission Recommendation for the most part was a case of preaching to the converted.

A. Approval of shareholders' meeting in case of remuneration by way of stock-options

Since its introduction in 1937, the German Stock Companies Act (*'Aktiengesetz'*) contains provisions on authorized capital (*'bedingtes Kapital'*) which serves the hedging of conversion rights (*'Umtauschrechte'*), bonds and debentures (*'Wandelschuldverschreibungen'*) and stock-options (*'Bezugsrechte'*). Stock-options such as these may be granted to employees since 1965, and since 1998 to members of the board of directors (*'Mitgliedern der Geschäftsführung'*) also.

Pursuant to §§ 192–3 of the German Stock Companies Act, authorized capital as well as the specific terms and conditions of corresponding conversion rights and stock options may only be granted by a decision of the shareholders' meeting. To this extent the Commission

Recommendation had been fulfilled long before its enactment in Germany.

However, according to the wording of Section 2.1 of the Commission Recommendation the term 'members of the board of directors' ('*Mitglieder der Unternehmensleitung*') also refers to members of the supervisory board, which in Germany is called '*Aufsichtsrat*'. In Germany, the legislative[8] and the judicial[9] branch have reached a common view that supervisory directors may not receive remuneration in the form of stock options as a matter of law – contrary to the view regarding management directors. This understanding has been adopted due to fears for their independence, for example concerning enterprise strategy and valuation policy.[10]

B. Publication of directors' individual annual remuneration

In Germany, this particular Commission Recommendation also was a case of teaching the pope Latin. This was largely due to the fact that the debate on such publication requirements had by 2002 developed as follows.

As a consequence of the insolvency of giant construction firm Philipp Holzmann AG, Chancellor Schröder appointed a commission with the following mandate:[11]

> It shall be the commission's task to review the Philipp Holzmann Case, and on the basis of its findings, the commission shall then deal with possible areas of improvement concerning Corporate Governance and Corporate Control. Furthermore, against the backdrop of constant fundamental change in our companies and market structures owing chiefly to globalization and internationalization of the capital markets, the Commission shall make recommendations for a modernization of our present legislation.

---

[8] Official Reasoning in connection with the Government's Proposal for the Company Control and Transparency Act ('*Gesetz zur Kontrolle und Transparenz im Unternehmensbereich*') (KonTraG), Bundestag printing matter ('*Drucksache*') 13/9712, Annex ('*Anlage*') 1, p. 24.

[9] German Federal Court (BGH), 16 February 2004, II ZR 316/02, BGHZ 158, 122.

[10] Opinions from the scientific community show that this issue is still highly controversial; see Bezzenberger, in K. Schmidt and M. Lutter (eds.), *Kommentar zum AktG, 2008*, (Köln: Schmidt, 2007), § 71, NO. 49.

[11] T. Baums (ed.), *Bericht der Regierungskommission Corporate Governance*, (Köln: Schmidt, 2001), 1.

The commission dealt with its task within only ten months and produced a volume of more than 130 recommendations, most of which were targeted at reforming or amending the German Stock Company Act. Two of these recommendations were concerned with developing a Corporate Governance Code and to compel German stock companies by law to report annually on the compliance or non-compliance therewith.[12] And so it happened. Two months later, the Minister of Justice appointed a second commission and assigned to it the task of developing a German Corporate Governance Code and amending it at regular intervals (standing commission). Again this assignment took the standing commission only six months to fulfil, and in February 2002 the newly developed Code was published.[13]

Parallel to this development, in June 2002 the Bundestag passed a law introducing a new Section 161 to the German Stock Company Law which compels both the directors of the management board and of the supervisory board to annually publish a declaration concerning their compliance or non-compliance with the Code in the respective past year, as the case may be, and their intention whether or not to comply with it in the future.[14]

The Code differentiates between *recommendations* and *suggestions*, and this difference was taken into account by the legislature when it decided upon the wording of Section 161. The law therefore requires members of both the management and the supervisory board to annually declare themselves on the compliance or non-compliance of *recommendations* only, while the same duty does not exist for *suggestions*.

Much to the astonishment of the general public and executive directors of about 800 listed companies alike, the 2002 first version of the

[12] Baums (ed.), *Bericht der Regierungskommission*, NO. 5–15 (*supra* note 11).
[13] The Rules may be downloaded from www.ecgi.org/codes/code.php?code_id=217.
[14] Section 161 of the German Stock Company Act reads as follows:

> Directors both of the management board and of the supervisory board of a listed company shall declare annually whether or not in the past they complied and in the future intend to further comply with the recommendations as laid down by the Government Commission German Corporate Governance Code ('*Regierungskommission Deutscher Corporate Governance Kodex*') and published by the Ministry of Justice in the Official Journal of the Electronic Federal Gazette ('*Bundesanzeiger*'), or, which of these recommendations were not or will not be applied. This declaration shall be made permanently accessible to the company's shareholders. [NB: English version by author]

For more detail see H.M. Ringleb, T. Kremer, M. Lutter, A. von Werder, *Deutscher Corporate Governance Kodex,* (Munich: Verlag C.H. Beck, 2008, 3rd edn.).

Code under Section 4.2.4 already comprised a *suggestion* for each director to individually publish their annual remuneration. The said section read:

> the individual remuneration of each director of the management board shall be reported in the annex to the consolidated accounts ('*Konzernabschluss*'), divided into the following categories: fixed salary, components according to performance and components based on the concept of long-term incentive. The report shall be personalized.

The reaction of the general public was very welcoming, whereas companies and management directors reacted in a rather reserved or even hostile manner. By some the said suggestion was even viewed as an unlawful interference with the personal integrity and privacy of management directors, and therefore to be regarded as unconstitutional.[15]

The suggestion failed to achieve much success. Because of this modest success, and because of the general public's growing displeasure with high salaries and compensation payments following the termination of manager's contracts, the Code commission reviewed the very same provision only one year later, and after heated debates upgraded it to the level of *recommendation* in June 2003. From then on, companies were compelled by law to *publish* their compliance or non-compliance, as the case may be, and moreover, in case of the latter, to publish their reasons as well.[16]

This measure's success started hesitantly all the same; two years later (by 2005) only two-thirds of the DAX-30 companies and only half of the rest of all listed companies had published their directors' remuneration details. At this point in time politicians had had enough, and the Bundestag passed the Publication of Directors' Remuneration Act ('*Vorstandsvergütungs-Offenlegungsgesetz*') (VorstOG), which came into force on 11 August 2005.[17] The Act compels listed companies to publish each of their directors' remuneration in a personalized and detailed

---

[15] In favour of this view: W. Porsch, 'Verfassungs- und europarechtliche Grenzen eines Gesetzes zur individualisierten Zwangsoffenlegung der Vergütung der Vorstandsmitglieder', *Betriebsberater (BB)* (2004), 2533; S. Augsberg, 'Verfassungsrechtliche Aspekte einer gesetzlichen Offenlegungspflicht für orstandsbezüge', *Zeitschrift für Rechtspolitik (ZRP)* (2005), 105; opposed to this view: G. Thüsing, 'Europarechtlicher Gleichbehandlungsgrundsatz als Bindung des Arbeitgebers?', *Zeitschrift für Wirtschaftsrecht (ZIP)* (2005), 1389, 1395.

[16] Code Sec. 3.10.

[17] Publication of Directors' Remuneration Act ('*Gesetz über die Offenlegung von Vorstandsvergütungen*') of 3 August 2005, Federal Law Gazette ('*Bundesgesetzblatt*') (BGBl.) I, S. 2267.

manner in either the annex to the balance sheets ('*Anhang zur Bilanz*') or in the management report ('*Lagebericht*') and the group management report ('*Konzern-Lagebericht*') following *due examination by the annual auditor.*

In short, at the time when the Commission issued its Recommendation concerning the remuneration of management directors on 14 December 2005, the German Corporate Governance Code already comprised an equivalent provision. A few months later, this Code provision was elevated to the status of Act of law, as can be seen in Section 285 Sentence 1 No. 9 of the German Commercial Code (HGB).

III. The composition and independence of supervisory board directors as well as the formation of committees according to the Recommendation of 15 February 2005

A. The election of supervisory board members

Section 11.1 of the Recommendation reads:

> It is recommended that the supervisory board define, and review at regular intervals, its own ideal composition in light of the company's structure and field of activity in order to guarantee well-balanced diverse professional competence among its ranks. It is further recommended that the supervisory board ascertains that its members as a team can command the necessary professional competence, soundness in decision making and expertise.

In Germany, this topic has a story of its own.

The supervisory board as formed by German law ('*Aufsichtsrat*') has always, from its very inception, been assigned the task of supervising the management, and – with hindsight – has never shied away from this task. However, its self-image had widely been quite different all the same: the average supervisory board was part of a nationwide entrepreneurial network: management directors of one company often acted as supervisory directors of many other companies. In this respect, the integration of banks as helpers in need into supervisory boards and the establishment of links with suppliers and recipients was of crucial importance. Supervision ranked only second to networking, and was of a merely reactive nature. In cases of economic disaster, more than one company's supervisory board was unable to accomplish anything more than to simply grin and bear.

This attitude has changed drastically since the mid-1990s, i.e. since the international capital markets conquered the hitherto sealed-off German system. The idea of Corporate Governance was being put at the top of the agenda then, and the German legislature gradually awarded the *Aufsichtsrat* its fair share of entrepreneurial responsibility. As if over-night, the *Aufsichtsrat* was given co-responsibility for general planning and strategy, and it also became its task to give advice to the management board and even to make joint managerial decisions. In short, the active, co-entrepreneurial *Aufsichtsrat* today is a matter of law. Network relations were replaced by personal competence. More than one company's *Aufsichtrat* was not prepared for this change, and many more have not caught up with the development even now. Cases where there is a lack of personal competence to a degree as to render the *Aufsichtsrat* deficient in terms of personal competence when compared to the management board have been and continue to be numerous.[18]

Since that time, scientific writers have zoomed in on this issue,[19] and have postulated the exact same recommendations as are the Commission's, that is:

(i) an abstractly termed outline of a composition scheme as to how shareholders' representation on the supervisory board ought ideally be organized, for example:

- one financial expert
- one accounting and controlling expert
- one expert with technical knowledge
- one marketing expert
- one law and tax expert
- one expert for overseas business activity;

(ii) a hunt for the most qualified candidates to meet the requirements of this composition scheme.

---

[18] M. Lutter, 'Der Aufsichtsrat im Wandel der Zeit – von seinen Anfängen bis heute', in W. Bayer and M. Habersack (eds.), *Aktienrecht im Wandel*, (Tübingen: Mohr Siebeck, 2007), 389.

[19] M. Lutter, 'Auswahlpflichten und Auswahlverschulden bei der Wahl von Aufsichtsratsmitglieder, *Zeitschrift für Wirtschaftsrecht (ZIP)* (2003), 417; M. Lutter, 'Legal Success', *Handelsblatt*, 27 March 2008, No. 60, 9; S. Maul,' Gesellschaftsrechtliche Entwicklungen in Europa – Bruch mit deutschen Traditionen?', *Betriebsberater (BB)* (2005), special issue, 19, 2; D. Bihr and W. Blättchen, 'Aufsichtsräte in der Kritik: Ziele und Grenzen einer ordnungsgemäßen Aufsichtsratstätigkeit – Ein Plädoyer für den 'Profi-Aufsichtsrat', *Betriebsberater (BB)* (2007), 1285.

Yet, Germany is still light years away from arriving at the utopia of a seamless operationalization of these recommendations by listed companies. At least, the first version Code under Section 5.4.1 already showed a similar tendency:

> Upon the proposal of candidates for the election as member of the supervisory board, special attention shall be paid to ensuring that board members as a team command the knowledge, the abilities and the expertise necessary for the sound execution of the board's lawful tasks at all times.

Here, the Code clearly tackles the issue of an ideal composition of the supervisory board from the perspective of the required personal competence; even so, the recommended solution is of an ad hoc nature, not a systematic approach.

A step forward, the Code as amended by 2007 under Section 5.3.3 now recommends the formation of a *nomination committee* (see below).

B. The formation of committees

According to Section 5 the commission recommends the formation of three committees to the supervisory board:

- a nomination committee
- a remuneration committee
- an audit committee.

Section 107 paragraph 3 of the German Stock Company Act provides that a company may, at its discretion, form advisory and co-deciding committees. In practice, the so-called *President Committee* has been prevalent up till now, the task of it being to make recommendations to the plenum with regard to the appointment of new management directors, and upon appointment, to conclude, on its own responsibility, the corresponding manager's contract including remuneration details.

Since its early beginnings, the Code has always recommended the formation of an *audit committee* under Section 5.3.2. This recommendation has widely been put into practice; these days, almost every listed company has an audit committee.[20]

---

[20] The formation of an audit committee was made mandatory by the EU's 8th directive, Directive 2006/43/EC of the European Parliament and of the Council of 17 May 2006 on statutory audits of annual accounts and consolidated accounts, amending Council Directives 78/660/EEC and 83/349/EEC and repealing Council Directive 84/253/EEC, [2006] OJ L 15.

In June 2007, the Code commission amended its said recommendation by adding to it the nomination committee (Sect. 5.3.3), to which it assigned the task of making recommendations to the plenum regarding the composition of the supervisory board. On the one hand, according to Section 101 Paragraph 1 of the German Stock Company Act, the election of supervisory directors from among the group of shareholders is reserved to the shareholders' meeting. On the other hand, according to Section 124 Paragraph 3 of the German Stock Company Act, it is the acting supervisory board's task to make candidate proposals to the shareholders' meeting. In practice, the shareholders' meeting almost always follows these proposals, to the effect that a de facto co-optation is established.

Since the nomination committee is compelled to give reasons for its recommendations in a plenary session, hopefully the system of due selection as discussed above will more and more become standard practice.

C. *The independence of the supervisory board*

In dealing with this topic, the Commission puts a decided emphasis on it by not only drawing up a principle under Section 4, but also a number of detailed recommendations, as in:

- Section 13.1 a definition
- Section 13.2 the establishment of criteria on Member State level
- Section 13.3 publication of these criteria.

Additionally, the Commission set up nine criteria in Annex II to the said Recommendation, which, if fulfilled, are assumed to have a detrimental effect on the independence of supervisory directors, one of them reading: 'd) The person in question may in no case be a controlling stockholder, or its representative.'

The fate of this recommendation in Germany has been markedly different from those already discussed above. This is due to the fact that controlling stockholders are a less rare phenomenon in Germany than elsewhere (BMW, Porsche, VW, Dresdener Bank, METRO etc.), and it comes as no surprise that they usually strive for and in fact do exert influence on 'their own' company. Furthermore, it is common practice in Germany for professionally successful and personally esteemed management directors to take up a seat on the supervisory board at the time of their age-related withdrawal from management functions.

There are virtually no legal rules on independence in Germany, apart from the law stating that no person may be a member of the management board and the supervisory board at the same time. It thus comes as a bit of a surprise that even the first version Code (2002) comprised a provision on this very matter. The very first version of Section 5.4.1 reads:

> Upon the proposal of candidates for the election of members of the supervisory board, special attention shall be paid to…ensuring candidates' sufficient independence.

Also from the 2002 first version onwards, this was put into rather more concrete terms by Section 5.4.2, which states:

> Independent advice to and supervision of the management board by the supervisory board is facilitated by the stipulation that the supervisory board may comprise no more than two members who have been in a managerial position in the same company at some time or another, and that members of the supervisory board may neither act in a managerial position of nor provide advisory service to another company which is a substantial competitor.

After the publication of the Commission Recommendation of 15 February 2005 on the independence of supervisory board members, the next plenary session of the Code commission dealt with this very issue and decided on amending the Code. The wording 'sufficient independence' under Section 5.4.1 was eliminated, and under Section 5.4.2 the following two sentences were added:

> In order to facilitate independent advice to and supervision of the management board by the supervisory board, the latter shall comprise a sufficient number of independent members, at its own discretion. A member of the supervisory board is to be viewed as independent, if he or she is in no way connected with the company or its management board either business-wise or personally in a way that entails a conflict of interests

whereas the limitation on two members who have been in a managerial position in the same company at some time or another and the non-competition requirement remained unamended.

The Code thereby almost verbally adopted the general wording of the Recommendation (Section 13.1). This is nothing to write home about, though. The general wording of both the Recommendation and the Code more or less states what is self-evident anyway. What was of an explosive nature about the recommendation was not its general wording, but a list contained in its Annex, by which the Commission declared who, in its opinion, may *not* be viewed as *independent*. This is where opinions differ. So what is the specific meaning of independence in this context? (Almost) every human being is in some way or another dependent some thing or another. That is not what this is about. What is essential is the *independence from the management board*, be it personal or business-wise. The Code stresses this understanding by its sentence 2 of Section 5.4.2 just cited above.

So is the holder of a controlling stake to be viewed as not independent – as the Commission suggests – or indeed independent? In my opinion, and this is in accordance with the general opinion in Germany, the *management board* is dependent on the controlling stockholder, but not the other way around. Incidentally, this is equally congruent with what the German law states in Sections 17 and 311 of the Stock Company Act. Indeed, the boot is on the other foot: if one can righteously call anybody *independent* from the company and the management board at all, it certainly is the controlling stockholder and its representatives.

This is at least a general rule. There may be exceptions to this rule, i.e. in case business relations are intertwined to such a degree that the controlling stockholder must actually be called dependent – after all, it is the exception which proves the rule.

Consequently, the reception of the Commission Recommendation of 15 February 2005 on the independence of supervisory board members has been ambivalent in Germany. We accept its main principal, and we also accept the principal view that the heart of the whole issue is the independence of supervisory board members from the company and the management board. The German Code has therefore adopted these principles.

Then again we beg to differ, and to differ clearly and decidedly, on a number of sub-issues contained in the list of examples as published in the Annex to the Recommendation. This is why none of these examples have been adopted by the Code: the interpretation of the meanings of *dependence* and *independence* is focused solely on business relations with the company and social and business relations with the management board, but not illustrated with specific examples.

III. The manner of implementation in Germany

When the Recommendation on a regime for the remuneration of directors was published, the German Code already comprised an equivalent recommendation. Shortly afterwards, the Publication of Directors'

Remuneration Act was passed, thereby completing implementation of the Recommendation.

While the legislature did not react to the Recommendation on the role of supervisory directors, the Code did, as described above. There nevertheless remains a difference concerning the interpretation. The Code has almost verbally adopted the general wording of the Recommendation. However, as the examples in the Annex of the Recommendation clearly illustrate, our understanding of the supervisory board directors' independence from the company and the management board is not entirely reconcilable with the Commission's view. In Germany, a general view has developed according to which controlling stockholders and their representatives are to be viewed as independent. That is where we do not find the Commission Recommendation convincing at all, and in this respect we are not going to follow it in the future, either.

8

The Nordic corporate governance model – a European model?

JESPER LAU HANSEN

I. A need for further harmonization?

Depending on your temper, there may be something slightly saddening about looking at the European directives on company law; a feeling that a great momentum has ground to a halt. Then again, you may feel relief.

In the beginning harmonization appeared to be as easy as one, two, three: the First Company Law Directive on publicity and company formation,[1] the Second Company Law Directive on capital[2] and the Third Company Law Directive on mergers.[3] But there soon came the first major stumble, when the proposal for a Fifth Company Law Directive on corporate governance[4] was first brought to a halt, then forgotten and finally abandoned.[5] Although new directives would continue to be adopted with

---

[1] First Council Directive 68/151/EEC of 9 March 1968 on coordination of safeguards which, for the protection of the interests of members and others, are required by Member States of companies within the meaning of the second paragraph of Article 58 of the Treaty, with a view to making such safeguards equivalent throughout the Community [1968] OJ L65.

[2] Second Council Directive 77/91/EEC of 13 December 1976 on coordination of safeguards which, for the protection of the interests of members and others, are required by Member States of companies within the meaning of the second paragraph of Article 58 of the Treaty, in respect of the formation of public limited liability companies and the maintenance and alteration of their capital, with a view to making such safeguards equivalent [1977] OJ L26.

[3] Third Council Directive 78/855/EEC of 9 October 1978 based on Article 54 (3) (g) of the Treaty concerning mergers of public limited liability companies [1978] OJ L295.

[4] Proposal COM/72/887 for a fifth Directive on the coordination of safeguards which for the protection of the interests of members and outsiders, are required by Member States of companies within the meaning of Article 58, second paragraph with respect to company structure and to the powers and responsibilities of company boards [1972] OJ C131.

[5] See the Commission's decision to withdraw this proposal and others in OJ C 5, 9.1.2004, 2.

the Sixth Company Law Directive on the division of companies, this was not quite the same, as this Directive was optional in its entirety.[6] Later, a proposal for a Ninth Company Law Directive on corporate groups was never even adopted by the Commission,[7] which left a gap between the Eighth Company Law Directive on auditing[8] and the Eleventh Company Law Directive on branches,[9] a gap that was widened by the stalling of the proposal for a Tenth Company Law Directive on cross-border mergers.[10] And when that Directive was eventually passed[11] – due, as is so often the case, to the gentle but firm assistance of the European Court of Justice[12] – it no longer carried a number in its title, leaving a permanent gap in the numbering. In omitting its number, it emulated the Directive on takeover bids[13] which had originally been presented as a proposal for a Thirteenth Company Law Directive[14] before suffering a humiliating defeat at the

[6] Sixth Council Directive 82/891/EEC of 17 December 1982 based on Article 54 (3) (g) of the Treaty, concerning the division of public limited liability companies [1982] OJ L378.

[7] The lack of European harmonization within this area was lamented by the Forum Europaeum, *Corporate Group Law for Europe*, (Stockholm: Corporate Governance Forum, 2000).

[8] Eighth Council Directive 84/253/EEC of 10 April 1984 based on Article 54 (3) (g) of the Treaty on the approval of persons responsible for carrying out the statutory audits of accounting documents [1984] OJ L126.

[9] Eleventh Council Directive 89/666/EEC of 21 December 1989 concerning disclosure requirements in respect of branches opened in a Member State by certain types of company governed by the law of another State [1989] OJ L395.

[10] Proposal for a tenth Directive of Council based on Article 54(3)(g) of the Treaty concerning cross-border mergers of public limited companies, COM(84) 727, later revised as COM(1993) 570 final. The proposal was withdrawn in 2004, see footnote 5 *supra*.

[11] Directive 2005/56/EC of the European Parliament and of the Council of 26 October 2005 on cross-border mergers of limited liability companies [2005] OJ L310.

[12] The right to carry out a cross-border merger in accordance with provisions in national law was upheld by the ECJ on the basis of Articles 43 and 48 of the EC Treaty (i.e. primary European law) in its decision of 13 December 2005 in Case C-411/03, *SEVIC Systems*, [2005] ECR I-10805, making the adoption of the Directive the only way for the Member States to regulate this activity under secondary European law. On this judgment, see M. M. Siems, 'SEVIC: Beyond Cross-Border Mergers', *European Business Organisation Law Review*, 8 (2007), 307–16, noting the further implications of the judgment on related problems such as the transfer of a company registered office.

[13] Directive 2004/25/EC of the European Parliament and of the Council of 21 April 2004 on takeover bids [2004] OJ L142.

[14] Proposal for a thirteenth Council Directive on company law concerning takeover and other general bids in COM(88) 823 final, which was revised in COM(90) 416 final of 10 September 1990, and revised again more thoroughly in COM(95) 655 final of 7 February 1996.

hands of the European Parliament,[15] and it was only passed after all its controversial parts had been made optional,[16] leaving it vulnerable to the accusation that it did not comply with the principle of subsidiarity enshrined in Article 5 of the EC Treaty.[17] With the recent declaration by Commissioner Charlie McCreevy that the proposal for a Fourteenth Company Law Directive on the cross-border transfer of a company's registered office will not be proceeded with, as no further action is deemed necessary in this area,[18] it would appear that the Twelfth Company Law Directive on single-member companies adopted in 1989 will be the last of the line.[19] Indeed, when the Directive on shareholders' rights was adopted, it was not presented as a Company Law Directive, but more as an appendix to the regulation of publicly traded (listed) companies as it does not apply to all companies, or even to all companies of the PLC type, but only the sub-set of companies whose securities are admitted to trading on a regulated market.[20] Regulation of company law *per se* seems to have been superseded by the regulation of publicly traded companies in order to enhance the working of the financial markets.

As the harmonization of national company law has ground to a halt, the situation has hardly been any better with European company law

[15] On the defeat of the proposal by the European Parliament in 2001 and the preparation of a new proposal that was eventually passed, see J. L. Hansen, 'When less would be more: The EU Takeover Directive in its latest apparition', *Columbia Journal of European Law*, 9 (2003), 275–298.

[16] The controversial parts are Article 9 (requiring the board of a target company to remain passive in face of a takeover bid) and Article 11 (providing a 'breakthrough rule' which allows a bidder, upon acquiring at least 75% of the capital, to call a general meeting at which all shares carry votes in proportion to their capital and all other limitations on voting are set aside). Article 9 conflicts with the German corporate governance model which allows management considerable discretion to decide on the welfare of the company. Article 11 conflicts with the ubiquitous use of multiple voting shares in the Nordic Member States. Both Articles 9 and 11 are optional for the Member States, though a Member State cannot prevent a national company from applying these provisions, see Article 12.

[17] Article 5, second paragraph reads: 'In areas which do not fall within its exclusive competence, the Community shall take action, in accordance with the principle of subsidiarity, only if and in so far as the objectives of the proposed action cannot be sufficiently achieved by the Member States and can therefore, by reason of the scale or effects of the proposed action, be better achieved by the Community.'

[18] Speech by Commissioner McCreevy on 3 October 2007 at the European Parliament's Legal Affairs Committee in Brussels, (SPEECH/07/592).

[19] Twelfth Council Company Law Directive 89/667/EEC of 21 December 1989 on single-member private limited-liability companies [1989] OJ L232.

[20] Directive 2007/36/EC of the European Parliament and of the Council of 11 July 2007 on the exercise of certain rights of shareholders in listed companies [2007] OJ L184.

as such. For many years the only truly European company entity was the European Economic Interest Grouping (EEIG) adopted in 1985.[21] As an entity without limited liability and without the capacity to conduct business, the EEIG remained unwanted by many and unknown to most. What should have been the flagship of European harmonization, the creation of a European public limited liability company to challenge the various national forms of company while sailing under the grand Latin name of *Societas Europaea* (SE), remained unfinished for more than forty years while successive rounds of negotiations chipped away at it until the resulting hulk was so diminished and so full of holes that the SE could not possibly keep itself afloat above the jurisdictions of the Member States, as originally envisioned.[22] Thus the true European SE does not exist; what exists is a national SE, e.g. a Danish SE as opposed to a German SE, and so far very few SEs have been formed.

A survey of the harmonization efforts so far reveals that it is the issue of corporate governance that most often has delayed or even hindered harmonization. In particular the participation of workers (co-determination) appears to have been a contentious issue. Although a solution of sorts has been provided by the model invented for the SE company,[23] the organization of a company and the internal distribution of powers remain controversial and thus remain unharmonized.

This is not to belittle the extent of the harmonization that has been achieved over the years, but compared to the high degree of harmonization of financial market law on banking, insurance and securities trading, it is undeniable that the harmonization of company law so far is considerably more modest.

The lower level of harmonization of company law than of financial market law is not necessarily a failure. A similar distinction has been observed in the United States of America, where securities trading and exchange law has been harmonized to a great extent by federal law, while company law remains a matter of state jurisdiction, with

---

[21] Council Regulation (EEC) No 2137/85 of 25 July 1985 on the European Economic Interest Grouping (EEIG) [1985] OJ L199.

[22] Council Regulation (EC) No 2157/2001 of 8 October 2001 on the Statute for a European company (SE) [2001] OJ L294. Article 5 in particular springs a major leak in the vessel as it refers all questions of capital to national law. Although some harmonization of capital requirements has been provided by the Second Company Law Directive (note 2, above), this broad reference to national law means that an SE is stuck in the jurisdiction where it is formed.

[23] Council Directive 2001/86/EC of 8 October 2001 supplementing the Statute for a European company with regard to the involvement of employees [2001] OJ L294.

only some harmonization by way of the Model Business Corporation Act (MBCA).[24] It has been argued that the distinction between federal securities regulation and state company law mirrors the distinction in Continental European law between public and private law.[25] This has some merit, as private law is characterized by having less extensive regulation, because individual parties are expected to be able to negotiate in their own interests, whereas public law relies on more extensive regulation, because the parties and interests involved are not equally capable of protecting themselves. Thus, the distinction between more harmonized financial market law and a less harmonized company law may reflect the fact that harmonization is required for financial market law but is unwarranted for company law.

Support for this proposition can be found in the fact that the company law of most European jurisdictions is traditionally of an enabling nature, leaving considerable discretion to the participants in the company to negotiate the arrangements between them, except for provisions on capital where the protection of creditors as 'outsiders' is deemed necessary. To the extent that the national jurisdictions of the Member States abstain from regulating corporate governance issues to allow for greater flexibility, then the EU should follow suit, in compliance with the principle of subsidiarity.

The brief survey of harmonization at the start of this article is a reminder of something else. All secondary European law must have a basis in primary European law. In the case of the harmonization of company law that used to be Article 54 of the EEC Treaty, now Article 44 of the EC Treaty, notably its subsection (3)(g) which concerns 'safeguards' for the protection of the interest of members and others, that is, creditors. However, since the Single European Act of 1986 had the aim of introducing an 'internal market' in lieu of the 'common market' that had eluded the politicians of the Member States, the aim of harmonization appears to have been broadened. A case in point is the Directive on shareholders' rights, which refers both to Article 44 on 'safeguards' and Article 95 on the establishment and functioning of the internal market.[26] Where Article 44 is more modest in scope and strives to harmonize these

---

[24] The MBCA and the revised MBCA is prepared by the Committee on Corporate Laws of the Section of Business Law of the American Bar Association. It has been adopted by many states, but some jurisdictions of major importance for company law have not adopted it, notably Delaware.

[25] See A. N. Licht, 'International Diversity in Securities Regulation: Some Roadblocks on the Way to Convergence', *Cardozo Law Review*, 20 (1998), 227–85.

[26] On the Directive, see note 20, above.

'safeguards', Article 95 is much more open to the argument that any difference, no matter what, should be subject to harmonization in order to iron out any hindrances to cross-border activity. The principle of subsidiarity and the related principle of proportionality, both laid down in Article 5 of the EC Treaty, would prevent this kind of argument. When it comes to corporate governance, there is even more reason to object to a harmonization aimed at creating a single European model. There is no empirical evidence to suggest that a superior corporate governance system exists. Nor is it likely that one could be identified by academics or lawmakers when the market participants themselves have been unable to do so through generations of competitive market behaviour. Indeed, as noted by the Commission, all available expert evidence cautions against imposing one model of corporate governance to fit all.[27]

Consequently, the fact that the harmonization of company law appears to have slowed down and may even have stopped altogether (except for issues pertaining to regulated markets and listed companies) may be due to the fact that the necessary harmonization has been achieved and that those parts where national jurisdictions differ, notably in the field of corporate governance, should remain unharmonized, as there is no single model that would be best for all. Different corporate governance models may suit different needs. If there is any need for harmonization, it ought to be in providing flexibility for the citizens of the EU, so that different jurisdictions should offer a choice of the different corporate governance models available throughout Europe. However, even here there may be no need for European legislation, as the ECJ has already provided such flexibility by its judgments granting the freedom to choose any jurisdiction for the formation of a company and the freedom to move that company within the EU.[28]

---

[27] Communication from the Commission to the Council and the European Parliament – Modernising Company Law and Enhancing Corporate Governance in the European Union – A Plan to Move Forward, COM(2003) 284 final of 21 May 2003, pp. 10–12.

[28] The landmark decision was the judgment of 9 March 1999 in Case C-212/97, *Centros Ltd.*, [1999] ECR I-1459. The judgment relied on previous decisions, notably Case 270/83, *Commission* v. *France*, [1986] ECR 273 and Case 79/85, *Segers*, [1986] ECR 2375. The judgment in the earlier Case 81/87, *The Queen* v. *Treasury and Commissioners of Inland Revenue, ex parte Daily Mail and General Trust*, [1988] ECR 5483, established that a company had no right to transfer its registered office as this was not in accordance with Article 220 of the EEC Treaty (now Article 293 of the EC Treaty). However, in its judgment of 5 November 2002 in Case C-208/00, *Überseering BV v. Nordic Construction Company Baumanagement GmbH*, [2002] ECR I-9919, the ECJ pointed out that *Centros* concerned recognition of foreign companies and the resulting freedom of establishment, whereas *Daily Mail* concerned a transfer of registered office, see paragraph 40. See

II. A distinct Nordic model?

The corporate governance debate in Europe is dominated by the distinction between the one-tier model known in English law, where there is only one company organ (the board of directors) below the general meeting of shareholders, and the two-tier model where there are two company organs below the general meeting (the management board and the supervisory board) known in German law. At first glance, the Nordic model would appear to be a two-tier model, because there are two company organs below the general meeting (the board of directors and the management board, that is, a dual executive system). However, if the purpose is to place the Nordic system in relation to this prevailing dichotomy, the model must be seen as belonging to the one-tier group.[29]

The model was first developed in the reform of the Danish Companies Act of 1930. Before the reform, the prevailing corporate governance model was the one-tier model with a single administrative company organ: the board of directors. During the deliberations on reform of the law, it was argued convincingly that liability should follow capability, and in very large companies the board of directors was not alone in running the company; the senior management headed by the chief executive officer (CEO) would effectively decide all the daily business, subject of course to the instructions of the board, but often with considerable autonomy. Consequently, the Act of 1930 provided that large companies[30] should have another company organ below the board of directors, that of the management board. This model was adopted by Sweden in the reform of its Companies Act in 1944, and later spread to the other Nordic countries, Finland, Norway and Iceland. As the Nordic countries entered either the EU or the EEA,[31] they had to introduce the originally German distinction between public companies and private companies.[32]

---

on this distinction, J. L. Hansen, 'A new look at Centros – from a Danish point of view', *European Business Law Review*, 13 (2002), 85–95. With its judgment in the *SEVIC* case, the ECJ has in effect made it possible to transfer the registered office by way of a cross-border merger, see footnote 12 *supra*.

[29] On the Nordic corporate governance model, see J. L. Hansen, *Nordic Company Law*, (Copenhagen, DJØF Publishing, 2003), 57 – 141.

[30] Companies with a paid up share capital of DKK 100,000, a considerable sum at the time.

[31] Denmark joined the European Community along with the United Kingdom and Ireland in 1973. Finland, Iceland, Norway and Sweden joined the European Economic Area in 1994. Finland and Sweden later joined the EU in 1995.

[32] The distinction was introduced in Germany in 1892 with a separate law on the GmbH, a private limited liability company, that was to be regulated more lightly than the AG,

At that time, the dual executive system became mandatory for all public companies, whereas it remained optional for private companies.[33] In its present form, the corporate governance model of the public company is identical in all five Nordic countries, except for the minor fact that the management board in Denmark and Iceland can be a collective body with more than one member, while in Finland, Norway and Sweden it is a one-member body comprising the CEO.

Several features indicate that, in a European context, the Nordic dual executive system is a one-tier model. The system is strictly hierarchical. The general meeting of shareholders is the supreme company organ with all the residual powers not explicitly denied it by legislation. However, the general meeting does not have executive powers and must thus rely on the two executive organs to carry out its instructions. Of the two executive organs, the board of directors is the senior organ and can instruct the management board. The management board deals with the day-to-day running of the company, under the instructions of the board of directors and submits to the board of directors any extraordinary or far-reaching decisions. To ensure the hierarchical nature of the model, the upper level appoints and dismisses members of the lower level. Thus, the general meeting of shareholders appoints the directors and may dismiss a director at any time and the board of directors hires and fires the managers.[34] Others may also have a right to appoint directors, if the articles of association so provide, and the employees may appoint

---

a public limited liability company. The stricter regulation of public limited companies compared to private companies is reflected in the European directives, notably the Second Directive on capital (footnote 2 *supra*) which only applies to public companies. In order to avoid the stricter regulation of all limited companies, new Member States had to introduce a similar distinction. It should be noted that a public company is public by its choice of company form and not because it is publicly traded on a stock exchange (regulated market), as would be the understanding in US law. Since most of the protection afforded to investors is given in respect of publicly traded companies, and since the revision of the Second Company Law Directive by Directive (2006/68/EC) has eased the strict regulation of capital, the distinction in company law between a 'public' company and a 'private' company is moot and should be replaced by a distinction between publicly traded companies and other companies with limited liability.

[33] If a private company is subject to co-determination, it may be obliged to have both a board of directors and a management board.

[34] The power to dismiss a director at any time prevents the occurrence of 'staggered boards' which may curtail shareholder influence, as is known in some American jurisdictions. The power to dismiss a director or a manager without reason is different in German company law, where a member of a management board (*Vorstand*) can only be dismissed for good reason, see AktG § 84, subsection 3.

directors according to legislation on co-determination,[35] but the majority of directors must always be appointed by the shareholders in a general meeting. As the board of directors decides by simple majority, this mandatory provision ensures that the shareholders enjoy actual power over the board. The strict hierarchy of the dual executive system is very different from the two-tier model known in Germany, where the power of shareholders is limited and the management board is entrenched. Another difference is that under the Nordic system, managers may serve as directors (dual capacity), which is unlawful in the German model. However, in the Nordic model, managers may only constitute a minority on the board of directors and a manager cannot serve as a chairman of the board of directors, which enhances the supervision of the management board by the board of directors.

Although clearly related to the one-tier model and quite distinct from the two-tier model, the Nordic model also has characteristics which set it apart from the one-tier model. Most notable is the allocation of powers between the board of directors and the management board, both being independent company organs with distinct powers and responsibilities. It may be argued that the English corporate governance model has evolved in the same direction since the Cadbury Report of 1992, which emphasized the need to separate the functions of executive and non-executive directors to enhance supervision of the former by the latter.[36] However, there is still a greater emphasis on this separation in Nordic law than in English law. Another minor difference is that the Nordic model is governed by legislation, while the English model relies much more on the soft-law recommendations of the Combined Code of the London Stock Exchange. However, here it is the Nordic countries that appear to be emulating the English approach in providing more regulation by soft law, in the form of codes rather than by legislation.[37]

That the Nordic corporate governance model is different from the models more commonly known in the European corporate governance debate is apparent from the Regulation on the SE statute, where it is difficult to fit the Nordic dual executive system in between the Regulation's

[35] Co-determination, where employee representatives serve as directors, is known in Denmark, Norway and Sweden, and to some extent in Finland, but not in Iceland.

[36] Report of the Committee on the Financial Aspects of Corporate Governance, 1 December 1992.

[37] See J. L. Hansen, 'Catching up with the crowd – but going where? The new codes on corporate governance in the Nordic countries', *International Journal of Disclosure and Governance*, 3 (2006), 213–32.

two corporate governance models of either a one-tier or a two-tier system.[38] It is also evident that the Commission's Recommendation on the role of directors relies on the distinction between a unitary board system and a dual board system akin to the one-tier/two-tier and not the Nordic dual executive system.[39]

However, what really sets the Nordic model apart is not the law but the reality on the ground. There is a predominance of controlling shareholders who either on their own or together with a few others hold enough votes to control the decisions of general meetings; this is even the case in publicly traded companies. In the Nordic corporate governance debate, the active governance of shareholders is seen as a good thing, something to be encouraged, because shareholders will strive to make the company as profitable as possible. As there will only be profits when all other stakeholders have been paid their dues, shareholders are considered to be the best ultimate decision makers. It is sometimes argued that shareholders may pursue short-term gains and that it would be better for a company to pursue long-term gains. However, as at any given time the value of a share depends on the discounted future earnings, there is no difference between the short and the long term when investing in shares, because the price of the share reflects its long-term value and even short time variations reflect changed expectations about the future consequences of present decisions on long-term performance. The problem of shareholder power is more that shareholders enjoy an asymmetrical risk profile with a limited downside and an unlimited upside, which may make then dangerously risk-willing. However, this problem is solved by removing all executive powers from the shareholders in the general meeting and vesting them in the management who are then held personally liable for their executive decisions. Hence, the shareholders may govern the company but cannot

---

[38] On the Regulation, see note 22, above. The Nordic corporate governance model with its dual executive system is made available by Article 43, Subsection 1, that permits the appointment of a 'managing director' under the same conditions that are known in the national company law of the home Member State. Whether this reference to national (Nordic) law is enough to provide for at separate company body for day-to-day management remains doubtful.

[39] Commission Recommendation 2005/162/EC of 15 February 2005 on the role of non-executive or supervisory directors of listed companies and on the committees of the (supervisory) board, [2005] OJ L52/51. Section 2 relies on the distinction between a unitary board and a dual board, which leaves out the non-executive director (dual board) known in the Nordic model. Nonetheless, the overall distinction between executives and non-executives or between supervisory directors and managing directors makes it clear that the Recommendation aims at the directors who are not also serving as managers.

run it without the acceptance of the management who are personably liable for not abusing the limited liability of the company.[40] Consequently, in the Nordic corporate governance debate dominant shareholders are viewed favourably and the legislation is fine-tuned to provide for their dominance, while protecting minorities against any abuse of power.

III. Challenges to the Nordic model

Although the one-tier and two-tier models appear to represent two very different approaches to corporate governance, in reality they combine to form a quite threatening hegemony when viewed from a Nordic perspective. In the two-tier model shareholders are afforded a very limited role and the management is entrenched to prevent shareholders having undue influence; in other words, shareholders are viewed with considerable suspicion. In the one-tier model shareholders are formally on top, and even the latest reform of the English Companies Act in 2006 was based on the idea of 'enlightened shareholder value'. However, where publicly traded companies are concerned, dominant shareholders are equally viewed with suspicion. Because dominant shareholders are relatively unknown in the UK, and especially so in the USA, their presence is considered highly unusual and possibly harmful. Apparently the suspicion is that the only justification for dominant shareholders not diversifying their investments like everybody else must be that they want to use their powers over the company to extract private benefits from the company to the detriment of the other shareholders. The fact that monitoring and disciplining of management may sufficiently increase the reward on the investments of dominant shareholders, even if they have to share some of that reward with the minority shareholders, appears not yet to have been fully appreciated in the corporate governance debate. Consequently, both sides of the one-tier/two-tier debate consider that dominant and influential shareholders are potentially harmful and possibly illegal.

The few measures on corporate governance that have been adopted at European level have mostly been directed at publicly traded companies. But this is exactly the area in which the Nordic model, with its reliance on

---

[40] Strictly speaking, there is no such thing as limited liability for a company, but only for the shareholders who invested in the company. And limited liability is always accompanied by private liability by those who can decide on behalf of the company, that is, the management. In Nordic company law, as in many other jurisdictions, the personal liability of the management may be extended to shareholders if in fact they act as managers (shadow director liability).

dominant shareholders, is most at odds with the major European powers.
A brief overview will show the challenges that have appeared so far.

A. *Proportionality of votes and capital*

Votes are a way of providing security by reducing risk in an investment in shares. As such, it is similar to a mortgage or a pledge, as the
preferred security of lenders. How many votes you get for your share
depends on how much you are willing to pay and how eager the company is to get your money; it is a business transaction like any other.
To invoke the concept of 'shareholder democracy' is just plain wrong;
votes can be bought and sold, and even in a company with only one
class of shares, one person may hold more votes than others. To argue
that there must be proportionality between capital and votes in order
to provide an incentive for the proper governance of the company disregards the fact that shares may be bought at different times and prices
and consequently there is hardly ever proportionality between the
prices different shareholders have paid for their shares and the associated voting rights even in companies with only one class of shares. To
consider shares with multiple votes unfair compared to shares of the
same size but carrying fewer votes is as unfounded as to find it unfair
that some lenders enjoy collateral for their loans while others do not.

As shares with multiple voting rights are often used to maintain concentrated control, it is a measure that enhances the position of dominant
shareholders. As such it is viewed favourably in the Nordic countries.
Nonetheless, for a long time the Commission has argued in favour of
a one-share/one-vote regime. Commissioner McCreevy initiated a
major report to investigate control-enhancing mechanisms.[41] As the
report found no clear link between these mechanisms and economic
performance,[42] Commissioner McCreevy announced that there was no
reason for further action.[43] It is all too rare to see a politician refrain
from action simply because it is unwarranted, and there is all the more
reason to praise the courage and good sense of the Commissioner.

[41] Report on the proportionality principle in the European Union – ISS Europe, ECGI,
Shearman & Sterling, 18 May 2007.
[42] Economic surveys of this kind are notoriously difficult to undertake. One may wonder
whether it is at all possible to compare the economic performance of companies with control-
enhancing mechanisms and those without, as the former have little incentive to value their
assets highly, and the latter have every incentive to inflate their assets to avoid takeovers.
[43] See speech of 3 October 2007 (footnote 18 *supra*).

However, the assault on multiple voting rights is not over. Article 11 of the Directive on takeover bids contains a breakthrough rule that is intended to set aside multiple voting shares under certain conditions. The rule is made optional according to Article 12, because it was fiercely resisted by the some Member States, notably the Nordic Member States. As the Directive is up for revision, a survey has been conducted to investigate the use of the opt-out in Article 12.[44] The survey concluded that the vast majority of Member States had not imposed or were unlikely to impose the breakthrough rule. It could be argued that this calls for the rule to be made mandatory, in order to ensure compliance by all Member States. However, it could equally be argued that a rule which most Member States would not apply voluntarily should not be made mandatory. It rather depends on whether you believe that the Member States are capable of making a sound decision.

Since the Directive already exempts shares where different voting rights are not assigned on issue but accrue over time,[45] even though such shares do actually hinder takeovers contrary to ordinary multiple voting shares that are covered by the Directive[46], and since the Directive also exempts non-voting shares and thus accepts a deviation from proportionality between capital and votes,[47] it would be better to give up this campaign against multiple voting shares altogether and accept

---

[44] Report on the implementation of the Directive on Takeover Bids, SEC(2007) 268, 21 February 2007. On Article 12 of the Directive, see footnote 16 *supra*.

[45] According to Article 2, Subsection 1(g) the Directive only covers shares of different classes with different voting rights, in other words where the difference was already present when the shares were issued and as such known to the investor and publicly by way of the articles of association. In the case of shares where multiple voting rights accrue over time, it is not possible for investors or the public in general to know the distribution of votes, because this depends on how long the shares have been owned by the individual shareholders.

[46] Shares that always carry multiple voting rights can be acquired with their full votes by a bidder as part of a takeover. Shares where multiple voting rights accrue over time would lose their extra votes if acquired by a bidder, which creates a lock-in effect.

[47] Article 11, Subsection 6 exempts 'securities where the restrictions on voting rights are compensated for by specific pecuniary advantages'. The reach of this provision is unclear. It may aim at voteless shares which carries a preferential right to dividends. However, as shares with no (or less) voting rights are always compensated by a lower price upon subscription and in later market transactions compared to shares with the same right to dividends but carrying better voting rights, all non-voting shares could be covered by this Article. Either way, the acceptance of that fact that sometimes shareholders accept less votes than other shareholders if they like the business investment offered should have been applied to all other shares with different voting rights rendering the breakthrough rule unnecessary.

that it is up to the company and its investors to determine what rights should be carried by shares issued by the company and subscribed by the investors.[48]

B. Independent directors

The Commission's Recommendation on the independence of directors could be viewed as yet another challenge to the Nordic corporate governance model.[49] The Nordic model is very specific in making each director directly accountable by ensuring that whoever appoints them may dismiss them again without notice and without reason. Furthermore, the legislation mandates that the majority of directors must be appointed by the shareholders in a general meeting, and as dominant shareholders are ubiquitous at least half and possibly all of the board will often have been appointed by a dominant shareholder. In the Nordic model there is no room for an independent director, as each director is appointed by some person or persons and accountable to them and is liable to be removed if they fail to fulfil their expectations. Independent control of management is provided by the auditor who is also elected at the general meeting, and there is no need to insert yet another controller inside the board. That at least is the law as it stands, but recent Nordic corporate governance codes have now followed the Commission Recommendation and recommend the appointment of independent directors to the board.[50]

The reasoning behind the Recommendation, the prevention of mismanagement, is sound, but the chosen solution defers to the corporate governance models which distrust major shareholders and it is difficult to reconcile it with the Nordic model. One may ask how a director can be truly 'independent' when they are appointed by a dominant shareholder and are conscious of that fact that they are subject to immediate removal by that shareholder? And if a director really feels independent,

---

[48] If the breakthrough rule were abandoned, it would probably be wise to abandon the 'board passivity' rule in Article 9 as well. It would make the shareholders vulnerable to the conflict of interest of a management faced with a takeover bid, but if the Germans and others have chosen a corporate governance model where management is entrenched and the interests of shareholders deferred, then there is little reason to challenge that choice in the absence of firm empirical evidence of the existence of a problem.

[49] On the Commission's Recommendation, see footnote 39 *supra*.

[50] On the Nordic corporate governance codes, see note 37, above. All codes have, at the very least, implemented the Commission Recommendation, and some have gone further, notably the Danish code.

will the director then feel accountable to the shareholders or to the other directors they are supposed to monitor?

From a Nordic perspective, it would appear that the Recommendation has overlooked how these problems are solved in the Nordic model. A director is accountable to the shareholders, but owes a duty of loyalty to the company and all its stakeholders; directors are personally liable if they set the interests of 'their' shareholders above those of others. If a conflict of interest arises, a director cannot participate in the decision and the decision is voidable if they do. Control of daily management, that is, the executives of the company, is guaranteed by the requirement that a majority of the board of directors cannot be made up of managers. That is what is understood by independence in Nordic company law.

C. Insider dealing

The ban on insider dealing in the securities of a publicly traded company is well justified and was part of the law in the Nordic countries long before it was mandated by European law.[51] It is also sensible to prevent selective disclosure of inside information, because the less inside information is disseminated before its publication to the securities market, the less risk there is of insider dealing.[52] There is an exception to the ban on selective disclosure where the disclosure is 'made in the normal course of the exercise of [a person's] employment, profession or duties'. The exception is necessary as it is often important that inside information is passed on to others, even if there is a risk of abuse of the information.

In the Nordic corporate governance model, where active participation by shareholders in the governance of the company is encouraged and where the presence of dominant shareholders ensures that there is such participation, it is normal to inform major shareholders of issues relevant to the running of the company even in publicly traded companies. This is especially the case where decisions would ultimately be made at the general meeting and thus depend on the consent of the majority shareholders. For example, it would be a waste of time to negotiate a

---

[51] A ban was introduced by Council Directive 89/592/EEC of 13 November 1989 coordinating regulations on insider dealing [1989] OJ L334. The Directive was replaced by Directive 2003/6/EC of the European Parliament and of the Council of 28 January 2003 on insider dealing and market manipulation (market abuse) [2003] OJ L96 (hereinafter: MAD).

[52] The ban on selective disclosure of inside information is found in Article 3(a) of MAD (note 51, above).

merger if the dominant shareholder is going to veto it, so it is better to inform the dominant shareholder confidentially in advance. The right to appoint and in particular to dismiss a director at will is a clear indication that the directors are accountable to the shareholders. Dominant shareholders may appoint themselves to serve as directors or appoint somebody else on their behalf, either way their right to govern the company is the same.[53]

However, the corporate governance debate is dominated by the UK and USA where the experience is that shareholders are small and dispersed, which leaves the board isolated or even 'independent' of them. Communication between a director on the board and a shareholder is viewed as highly unusual, and perhaps even downright illegal. This approach, however, risks a too-narrow interpretation of the exception to the ban on selective disclosure of inside information that may effectively sever communication between directors and shareholders, and by extension prevent the participation by shareholders in the governance of the company which the Nordic model relies upon.

Fortunately, when a case came before the ECJ on the interpretation of the ban on selective disclosure,[54] the Court wisely chose to point out that what constituted 'normal' disclosure for the purposes of the exception to the ban would depend on the national corporate governance model and for that reason the Court limited itself to stressing that where such disclosure was normal, the ban would require a strict understanding of

---

[53] Only natural persons can serve as directors, so legal persons are dependent on appointing a natural person as director on their behalf which only underlines the need to receive information in confidentiality.

[54] See Judgment of 22 December 2005 in Case C-384/02, *Grøngaard and Bang*, [2005] ECR I-9939. The case concerned Danish criminal proceedings against an employee representative serving on the board of a publicly traded company who had disclosed to his union president that a merger offer was imminent. The director was also a vice-president of the union and had learned of the news both from serving on the board and from his participation on a cooperation committee. The union president disclosed the information to a union employee who used the information for trading and was convicted of insider dealing. Both the employee representative and the union president were convicted by the City Court of Copenhagen for violating the ban on selective disclosure of inside information. The conviction was upheld by the Eastern Division of the High Court in its judgment of 15 January 2008, but contrary to the City Court, the High Court accepted that disclosure could be made confidentially between a director and his 'constituency', i.e. the union, in order for the union to prepare for the merger and the expected lay-offs. However, the disclosure had been made to a greater extent than necessary, hence the conviction. The judgment may be appealed to the Danish Supreme Court.

whether the disclosure really was necessary, taking into account the risk of insider dealing. The judgment has thus made it possible to uphold the Nordic corporate governance model, but there is a risk that national supervisory authorities or even national courts may be influenced by the international corporate governance debate and construe the sound limitations put forward by the ECJ to narrowly and thereby prevent the Nordic model from functioning.

IV. Conclusion

The Nordic corporate governance model, with its dual executive system, is closely related to the English one-tier model but has unique features. The most distinctive feature is probably the dominant role given to the shareholders, and the prevalence of major shareholders ensures that this role is taken up even in publicly traded companies. The risk of dominant shareholders, that they may pursue private aims and exploit the minority, has been countered by the provisions of companies legislation. Over the years, a highly sophisticated and investor-friendly model has evolved and major scandals have been few and far between.

Although the harmonization of company law has been carried on for many years and covers many areas, the area of corporate governance has largely remained outside the scope of harmonization. The few examples of harmonization have proved to be of limited value and some measures are difficult to reconcile with the Nordic model.

It is argued that the harmonization of corporate governance should only be pursued with great care and only to the limited extent necessary to protect parties who cannot be expected to fend for themselves. There is no need to seek a single European model to replace the many different national models of corporate governance. The existence of a variety of different corporate governance models should not be viewed as an obstacle to the internal market, but as an asset. The recent case law of the ECJ has made this asset available to all investors in the European Union, so there is even less reason to legislate in this area. Better to have many different European corporate governance models than just one.

SECTION 2

Corporate governance, shareholders' rights
and auditing

9

Stakeholders and the legal theory of the corporation

PETER NOBEL

I. Introduction

It is a pleasure for me to write for the lively Eddy, always full of a variety of fertile thoughts, combining eloquence with rapidity. He has worked and published many learned treatises on the law of corporations and the field of finance, which has become more and more integrated in the study of corporations. This is because the capital markets need the producers of their 'deal objects' and continuously try to reshape these objects according to their wishes. For Eddy, I shall endeavour to go off the beaten track in search of a better theory of the corporation. My proposal also contains an incomplete inventory of areas where the science of corporate law is somewhat mired down.

II. Phenomenological analysis

A. The notion of a 'stakeholder'

When I am unsure about the exact meaning of a word like 'stake', I consult the Oxford English Dictionary, bearing in mind that a mad professor has made many contributions to it.[1]

A 'stake' is essentially a pole to which something is attached; historically, it might be a convicted person condemned to death by fire or other means, but when I hear 'stakeholder' I initially think of a situation of gaming where an independent party holds the prize money. This meaning is then extended to a person who holds an interest or concern in something, especially a business.

In the business of commercial law, the term 'stakeholder' is customarily used to show that we are not deprived of a social conscience;

---

[1] H. Sudermann, *The Mad Professor* (London: John Lane The Bodley Head Ltd., 1929).

when we point to the shareholders' interest, we have been taught to add, already routinely, that the corporation is also run in the interest of the stakeholders,[2] and here – in lacking any exact knowledge – we designate all classes of persons or functions – contractual or otherwise – that our imagination produces as being affected by corporate behaviour: workers, creditors, customers, the state, the environment, etc. Obviously, the shareholders are also stakeholders as the corporation's residual income belongs to them.

In this respect and as an example, the OECD Code of Corporate Governance provides that the 'corporate governance framework should recognize the rights of stakeholders established by law or through mutual agreements and encourage active cooperation between corporations and stakeholders in creating wealth, jobs and the sustainability of financially sound enterprises'.[3]

A further examination of who may be included in the circle of stakeholders leads to the question of the relationship between the different groups of stakeholders: what is the relationship of these stakeholders to the corporation if we do not merely characterize it as 'contractual'?

B. Approaches in economic theory

Digging deeper into the phenomenon of a corporation, we are not helped very much by the abstract constructions of the economists. The 'nature of the firm', based on the idea of transaction costs,[4] is indeed applicable to all participants in the production process. The 'bundle' or 'nexus' of contracts notion[5] is helpful to integrate many participants, but it does not provide a design for the relationship between shareholders and stakeholders. Also the idea of 'incomplete contracts', and hence the need of good corporate governance, does not lead us further.[6] Moreover, the view on the 'institution' is not able to say what the right stake of the stakeholders is, even though the institutional approach is seen as a remedy against decline.[7] 'Property rights' as a theory is developed when the choice for shareholder dominance has already been

---

[2] P. Forstmoser, Wirtschaftsrecht im Wandel', *Schweizerische Juristenzeitung*, 104 (2008), 133, 140.

[3] OECD, *OECD Principles of Corporate Governance* (2004), 21.

[4] R. H. Coase, 'The nature of the firm', *Economica*, vol. 4, 16 (1937), 386–405.

[5] O. Hart, *Firms, Contracts and Financial Structure* (Oxford University Press, 1995), 1–12.

[6] Hart, *Firms, Contracts and Financial Structure*, (note 5, above), 3–5.

[7] A. O. Hirschman, *Exit, Voice and Loyalty – Responses to Decline in Firms, Organizations and States* (Harvard University Press, 1970).

made. Economic property rights were defined as the individual's ability, in expected terms, to consume merchandise (or the services of an asset) directly or to consume it indirectly through exchange. According to this definition, an individual has fewer rights over a commodity that is prone to restrictions on its exchange.[8] Bearle and Means have shown that the focus of this view is circling around the relationship between shareholders and assertive managers.[9] Law and Economics give us tools to play with, but no legal clues.

1. Corporate governance discussion

The discussion about corporate governance was very helpful to open our eyes. It actually came out of the shareholder value chain of thought trying to tie down the 'selfish' managers:

> How do the suppliers of finance get managers to return some of the profits to them? How do they make sure that managers do not steal the capital they supply or invest it in bad projects?[10]
>
> Characterized by principal-agent issues, the problems addressed by corporate governance have been manifest in their impact on economic and efficiency and, at times, in the self-serving and/or abusive behaviour by management that jeopardizes company viability and the welfare of shareholders.[11]

Originally, it was the shareholder–manager relationship which seemed to be the main source of preoccupation; but now eyes are open wider:

> Pure shareholder wealth maximization fits poorly with a modern democracy. Everywhere democracies put distance between strong shareholder control and the day-to-day operations of the firm, shielding employees from tight shareholder control...How a nation settles social conflict and distances shareholders from the firm's day-to-day operation can thereafter deeply affect that nation's institutions of corporate governance.[12]

[8] Y. Barzel, *Economic Analysis of Property Rights* (Cambridge University Press, 1997), 3.
[9] A. A. Berle and G. C. Means, *The Modern Corporation and Private Property* (New York: The Macmillan Company, 1932), 188.
[10] A. Shleifer and R. W. A. Vishny, 'Survey of Corporate Governance', *The Journal of Finance,* vol. LII/2 (June 1997), 737.
[11] B. Shull, 'Corporate governance, bank regulation and activity expansion in the United States' in B. E. Gup (ed.), *Corporate Governance in Banking* (Cheltenham: Edward Elgar, 2007), 7.
[12] M. J. Roe, *Corporate Governance: Political and Legal Perspectives* (Cheltenham: Edward Elgar, 2005), 12.

> A firm has many stakeholders other than its shareholders: employees, customers, suppliers, and neighbours, whose welfare must be taken into account. Corporate governance would refer them to the design of institutions to make managers internalize the welfare of stakeholders in the firm.[13]

This widening of horizons could have led to an integrated theory of the firm, but destiny was, unfortunately, not kind with these efforts. The attention of the shareholder discussion was drawn in another direction. The discussion on stakeholders has shifted away to takeovers and their potential impacts on the various groups. On one side, takeovers were considered as an effective means to control inefficient, underperforming managers: a bad stock price was supposed to attract the sharks cleaning out the second tier people. On the other side, such actions were seen as a social challenge, mainly for the employees not having a golden parachute, or for not having any parachute at all. But, a defence also developed here, and an important argument was often brought forward (at least in Europe) that the corporation was not only prey for greedy stockholders, but also for an entire economic community of different stakeholders.

It is not only the national interest in certain key industries that created ideas of anti-takeover rules (ironically accompanying the realization of the 13th Directive – an unlucky number?),[14] but also (although perhaps less outspoken) the fear that enterprises might move to other locations on the planet.[15] The idea has been formulated that corporate decision-making centres involving important economic assets should be bound to given political communities and should not have the freedom to relocate elsewhere. The issue of the day is the (possible) impact of SWFs on sovereign states affairs.

2. Anatomy of the corporation

A recent structural elaboration, the anatomy of the corporation,[16] is also founded on the principal-agency theory. This is a characteristic

---

[13] V. Xavier, *Corporate Governance: Theoretical & Empirical Perspectives* (Cambridge University Press, 2000), 1.

[14] Directive 2004/25/EC of the European Parliament and of the Council of 21 April 2004 on takeover bids [2004] OJ L 142.

[15] Nokia, 'Nokia plans closure of its Bochum site in Germany', *press release* (January 15, 2008), www.nokia.com/A4136001?newsid=1182125.

[16] R. Kraakman et al., *The Anatomy of Corporate Law: a Comparative and Functional Approach* (Oxford University Press, 2006).

of almost all theoretical undertakings since the seminal work of Berle and Means.[17] The agency discussion is almost as old as the discussion on economic organization, which already occupied the ancients and is also found in Adam Smith's work.[18] The anatomy, however, goes a step beyond to include into the agency theory the shareholder–manager relationship and the concepts of majority and minority in the corporation; significantly, it also encompasses the relationship between the corporation and the stakeholders. With regard to the aim of corporate law, it has been noted that

> the appropriate goal of corporate law is to advance the aggregate welfare of a firm's shareholders, employees, suppliers, and customers without undue sacrifice – and, if possible, with benefit – to third parties such as local communities and beneficiaries of the natural environment.[19]

But all non-shareholders are merely 'contractual' partners or even exist only 'in fact'. Here, we get to a practically new age differentiation between 'status' and 'contract', a concept known since Maitland.[20] This might be justified because we also find severe warnings that the notion of agency should not be enlarged for political reasons.[21] Nevertheless, none of this is a sufficient theoretical foundation for the law of the modern enterprise.

C. Legal doctrine

In searching for a theoretical foundation, legal theory is of even less use than economic theory; this is attributable to the fact that the era of the 'grand' theories of the corporation as a legal person is over. For a long time, German legal thought tried to come to terms with the 'reality' of the legal person. A legal person is not a tangible reality, but a social phenomenon. Otto von Gierke demonstrated a strong sense of this idea

---

[17] Berle and Means, *The Modern Corporation*, (note 9, above).

[18] A. Smith, *The Wealth of Nations* (New York: The Modern Library, 2000; first edition 1776), translated into German by H. C. Recktenwald, *Der Wohlstand der Nationen* (Munich: Deutscher Taschenbuch Verlag, 1978), 629–30.

[19] Kraakman et al., *The anatomy of Corporate Law*, (note 16, above), 18.

[20] Cf. F. W. Maitland, *Introduction to Gierke's Political Theories of the Middle Age* (Translation), (Cambridge and New York: Cambridge University Press, 1987; first edition 1900).

[21] H. C. von der Crone, 'Verantwortlichkeit, Anreize und Reputation in der Corporate Governance der Publikumsgesellschaft', *Zeitschrift für Schweizerisches Recht*, vol. 2, 119 (2000), 239–75.

in his monumental works centring on the cooperative type of mutual interdependence.[22] At the end, from the idea of a 'legal person', it was only the farsighted concept of a bundle of assets and liabilities, separate and subject to specific governance for specific purposes, that prevailed.[23]

The endeavour in the 1970s and 1980s, namely to substitute the corporation by the 'enterprise' – a productive entity composed of all participating interests – did not succeed.[24] The main reason was that the discussion got stuck for more than twenty-five years with the conflicting (but beloved in Germany) aim of introducing workers' co-determination in the board rooms.[25] Thomas Raiser's most inspiring book[26] about the enterprise as an organization remained a lonely star, hinting at the neglected necessity of opening up legal thinking towards economic notions and tools.

If a corporation is not a tangible reality, it is an abstract legal construct. The famous Dartmouth case describes a corporation as

> an artificial being, invisible, intangible and existing only in contemplation of law. Being the mere creature of law, it possesses only those properties which the charter of its creation confers upon it, either expressly, or as incidental to its very existence. These are such as are supposed best calculated to effect the object for which it was created.[27]

I would not hesitate to elevate the idea of a legal person to that of a real legal invention.[28] It enables the organization of both assets and people in an efficient manner. If we dig into legal history and notions, we find the idea of an 'Anstalt' in German legal doctrine, which is defined as a composition of material forces and personal means.[29] This legal concept, still

---

[22] O. von Gierke, *Das deutsche Genossenschaftsrecht*, 4 vols. (Graz: Akademische Druck- und Verlagsanstalt, 1954), vol. III.

[23] F. Wieacker, 'Zur Theorie der juristischen Person des Privatrechts' in *Festschrift Ernst Rudolf Huber* (Göttingen: Schwartz, 1973), 339 ff.

[24] P. Nobel, 'Das "Unternehmen" als juristische Person?', *Wirtschaft und Recht*, (1980), 27–46. Now looking again at the enterprise as a whole, composed of various interests, see M. Amstutz and R. Mabillard, *Fusionsgesetz (FusG), Kommentar* (Basel: Helbing, 2008).

[25] See M. Lutter, 'Societas Europaea' in P. Nobel (ed.), *Internationales Gesellschaftsrecht* (Bern: Stämpfli, 2004), vol. V, 35–8; G. Mävers, *Die Mitbestimmung der Arbeitnehmer in der Europäischen Aktiengesellschaft* (Baden-Baden: Nomos, 2002).

[26] T. Raiser, *Das Unternehmen als Organisation: Kritik und Erneuerung der juristischen Unternehmenslehre* (Berlin: de Gruyter, 1969).

[27] Trustees of Dartmouth College v. Woodward, 4 Wheat. 518, 636 (1819).

[28] H. Dölle, *Juristische Entdeckungen*: Festvortrag (Tübingen: Mohr, 1958).

[29] P. Tschannen and U. Zimmerli, *Allgemeines Verwaltungsrecht*, 2nd edition (Bern: Stämpfli, 2004), § 7 nos. 3–4.

used in the domain of public law today, combines both of these latter aspects, and it might also prove useful as a theoretical tool.[30]

The 'legal person' also allows for the preparation of preconditions for the creation of a great work in a structural manner; this comprises a setting in which we no longer have commanding kings and princes and must assure control through organizational means. It also signifies a setting that is acceptable for a democratic society.

It might be added here that, after we had overcome early (American) restrictions, we were able to create whole 'families' of legal persons, groups of companies or *Konzerne*. Their law still presents one of the really unfinished challenges of modern corporation law. Any major bankruptcy case shows this clearly.

The concept of the legal person was a prerequisite for the development of modern corporate law. However, it is of limited value for the development of a theory of the firm. Corporate law itself is probably not able to deliver a theory of the firm as it is (only) concerned with the structure of main command over the firm.

III. Reaching out for a new theoretical foundation of the firm

A. Traditional model of the entrepreneur

The entrepreneur, his ideas and his talent, in combination with other people and assets are still the basic ingredients of a capitalist market economy. There are, as we have seen, the property rights that continuously move the 'creative destruction'.[31] As in statistics, however, the reliability of results depends on large numbers, evening out the outliers; here, we must consider that the model of individual entrepreneurs is only true for a part of the economy. Although it is still an important part,[32] it is not the part where public attention is nowadays focussed. This comprises the part of the big enterprise, the group of companies, the firm, the *Konzern* and the listed corporation, usually multinational. For these, legal theory is somewhat at a loss.

---

[30] P. Nobel, *Anstalt und Unternehmen: Dogmengeschichtliche und vergleichende Vorstudien* (Diessenhofen: Rüegger, 1978), chapter 4.

[31] J. A. Schumpeter, *Theorie der wirtschaftlichen Entwicklung,* (Leipzig: Springer, 1912), 525–33.

[32] 99.7% of all enterprises in Switzerland are small and medium-sized businesses (up to 249 employees); 87.6% employ nine employees at most and are considered as micro enterprises. See Bundesamt für Statistik, Betriebszählung 2005, www.bfs.admin.ch.

B. Groups of companies

The model of the company law codes is still the single corporation. A few countries have tried to enact rules for groups of companies. The success was more limited than the ensuing academic discussion on the law of company groups. It also remained national and no (European) country could embrace the whole of its multinational corporations with a law of company groups, making one enterprise out of it. There is one major and main exception: the groups have to present 'consolidated accounts', making the economic unit more transparent. This is, to a large extent, sufficient as there are no downstream 'external' shareholders; but in case of financial difficulties, the creditors of subsidiaries remain as a major problem.

Here, the law and the legal scholars cope with a considerable number of instruments in order to come to terms with such problems. We are, however, far from a consistent approach in this matter. Corporate law has somewhat abdicated here; and the lawyers also seem to have gotten tired of the discussion on this issue.

For some time there was a short but emotional discussion in Switzerland as to whether a group of companies is a company itself.[33] In European law, things have not developed further than an aborted attempt to a (9th) Directive, and the proposals of the Forum Europaeum based on the French *Rozenblum* case, which only suggests a somewhat vague standard.[34] This proposal was recently commented on by Klaus J. Hopt in a friendlier manner. Hopt does not anticipate that there will be a European law of groups of companies in the near future; in his opinion, it is more likely that there will be a capital markets law, which takes the dimensions of groups of companies into account.[35] There are also a series of rules relating to groups of companies where the regulation and supervision of the capital markets are concerned;

---

[33] H. Peter and F. Birchler, 'Les groupes de sociétés sont des sociétés simples', *Swiss Review of Business and Financial Market Law,* 70 (1998), 113–124; R. von Büren und M. Huber, 'Warum der Konzern keine einfache Gesellschaft ist – eine Replik', *Swiss Review of Business and Financial Market Law,* 70 (1998), 213–220.

[34] Forum Europaeum Konzernrecht, 'Konzernrecht für Europa – Thesen und Vorschläge', *Zeitschrift für Unternehmens- und Gesellschaftsrecht,* (1998), 672–772, 705; The Rozenblum-concept is based on the point of view that the self-interests of the individual companies within a group have to be aligned with the overall interest of the group, i.e. with the group interest.

[35] K. J. Hopt, 'Konzernrecht: Die Europäische Perspektive', *Zeitschrift für das gesamte Handels- und Wirtschaftsrecht,* 171 (2007), 232, 235.

together with take-over rules, these are contributing to the creation of a European Capital Markets Law for large corporate groups.

The conclusion remains that we have no European law for groups of companies. The regulation of the SE, contrary to earlier proposals, no longer contains such rules. In view of the fact that the SE is becoming a preferred statute by big corporations; it is a pity that the occasion was missed.

C. *The corporate governance discussion*

During the past few years, the big issues in corporate law have concerned shareholder value and corporate governance, including the role of the auditors.[36] The corporate governance discussion has been somewhat stuck, continuously turning the same wheel with the hope that it might stop at a lucky number. There is, however, one issue that has politicized the corporate governance discussion: the discussion on executive compensation. In many countries, this topic caused a public outcry, which corporate lawyers were not really able to respond to, except with a considerable amount of political bias. The phrase 'pay without performance'[37] expressed the criticism of executive pay arrangements and the corporate governance processes producing them.

The response of the business circles was very clever and in the relevant corporate governance codes the links to performance were introduced as an obligation.[38] However, as 'performance' is difficult to measure, the appropriate question is whether this is the solution or not, at least in the long term. For a shorter period, it might be a ratio, combining share price and profit.

D. *Underdeveloped shareholder governance*

In my opinion, we have to take a second look at the basics: here we see that the corporation is built on the idea of the shareholder–proprietor who attends the general assembly as if it were a democratic political arena, in spite of the fact that voting rights are regulated in relation to capital

---

[36] F. H. Easterbrook and D. R. Fischel, *The Economic Structure of Corporate Law* (Harvard University Press, 1991).

[37] L.Bebchuk and J. Fried, *Pay without Performance: the Unfulfilled Promise of Executive Compensation* (Harvard University Press, 2004).

[38] Swiss Business Federation, *Swiss Code of Best Practice for Corporate Governance*, new edition (Dielsdorf: Lichtdruck AG, 2007), 17.

and not per capita. All in all, we are still far away from 'one share, one vote'. All endeavours of the more or less recent developments of corporation law were nevertheless directed at the improvement of shareholders' rights. Have we been successful? I do not think so. The fact remains that shareholders do not do what they could do. Academians have to learn to live with the reality that the majority of shareholders allow things that could be changed or disapproved to continue. The shareholders are entitled to select the company's chief executives, reject accounts, sue the directors, etc. But, they simply do not do this. It might thus be the case that the model is wrong. Shareholders can distribute their risk and they can also walk away. They are also not 'real' owners of the corporate assets, only economic beneficiaries.

It is true that I paint a kind of black and white picture here and that one could make finer distinctions. For instance, the American situation is somewhat different because the orientation of the federal security laws has caused many differences and has also had a very strong impact on the SEC.

All this has not prevented the big anti-fraud reaction of the US Congress through the Sarbanes–Oxley legislation, especially its section 404.[39] Another example is the necessity to distinguish between ordinary and institutional shareholders. The emergence of the latter has not only brought changes, but also problems related to their governance.

E. The firm as a result of varying bargaining power

Already the seminal work of Berle and Means (a lawyer and an economist) has described the modern corporation in terms of its transformation of private property.[40] In the New Economy, property rights correspond to the ability of an agent to capture the present cash-flow value that a given asset is expected to generate.[41]

In civil law countries this is even more difficult because we cling to the notion of undivided property and only allow, under strong Anglo-American influence, a distinction between property in the legal sense and 'economic property'. Here, we encounter systemic impediments because the whole of civil law is construed with the idea of a free individual able

---

[39] *Sarbanes–Oxley Act of 2002* (Pub.L. 107–204, 116 Stat. 745, enacted 2002–07–30).
[40] Berle and Means, *The Modern Corporation*, (note 9, above).
[41] U. Cantner, E. Dinopoulos and R. Lanzillotti, *Entrepreneurship, The New Economy and Public Policy* (Springer, 2005).

to contract and dispose of property in the sense of using it as an economic tool. There is no doubt that this individual might sell his shares; if he wants to have a say in the way that his money is invested, he has only one vote out of many. The decisive feature is that the individual shareholder cannot only sell but can also spread his risk over a number of corporations, whereas the employee-insiders are fully bound by their 'job'.

For lawyers the idea of a 'legal person' is a great achievement. A corporation can behave in economic matters, legally speaking, like a natural person. Legal theory, however, has had a hard time to come to terms with the development of such a 'person'. It is very difficult to bridge the gap to the economists, as they describe the firm as a bundle of contracts. In my opinion, the agency theory is in fact a legal notion taken up by the economists to support the lawyers' model, which was prone for derailment.

The bundle of contracts' approach is visibly also an abstract construction of legal elements, but for lawyers it is hard to re-integrate this idea back into the legal system. We might call a certain situation 'a bundle of contracts', but this will not be a legal term. Trying again, a 'bundle of contracts' is a plurality of contracts, maybe of the same contracts or of different contracts. With the idea of 'same contracts', we are not getting further than an unknown number of contracts. With different contracts we might see contracts with the state, contracts with investors, contracts with managers, labour contracts, creditors, etc. But, here we soon realize that the law is much further developed in that it already contains models to combine such contracts institutionally. What is the lesson to learn here? Perhaps it is the idea, as suggested by the economists, that everything should be based on the contract model. Then, the whole institution of the firm becomes a result of the relevant bargaining power.

Even though the contract model (the bundle of contracts) and the idea of bargaining power are closely linked together, bargaining power goes further in that not all bargaining power necessarily leads to a contract; therefore, it is more precise to talk about a 'negotiation model'. In this respect, an open system is formed because all stakeholders may have bargaining power, which is determined by a large number of parameters. In comparison with the principal-agent theory, a model that puts the bargaining power into the centre is able to give a more comprehensive picture of the reality of the firm. Even though the agency model (in its broad interpretation) may capture a large number of different stakeholders, it can only explain a certain part of the reality of the firm. As it focuses on the information asymmetry and the difference of interests between the principal and the agent, it leaves out many aspects that may influence the relationship of the stakeholders. The negotiation model, on the other hand, may easily incorporate these two elements of the agency model: an informational advantage improves the bargaining power of a contractor, and it is virtually a standard situation in negotiations that the contracting parties have non-homogenous interests.

The proposed model may also include other elements that strengthen or weaken the bargaining power such as interrelations or coalitions among the relevant players, acceptance of a position in society or the law of supply and demand.

Bargaining power is not only the relevant criterion in the situation of actual ongoing negotiations among the stakeholders of a company. It remains the core factor in a corporation, even when the various stakeholders of the firm have committed themselves to follow certain rules for an agreed period of time. Contracts are to be seen as nothing but 'frozen' bargaining power. They show a picture of the moment. Corporate reality tells us that the principle of *pacta sunt servanda* does not prevent stakeholders from violating treaties. Once their negotiating power reaches certain strength, they may attempt to renegotiate a compromise to make it more favourable for them or simply behave contrary to the contractual terms.

Hierarchies and delegations are commonly found in corporations, and they are in line with the negotiation model: both regularly derive from concluded contracts. If they are established by non-contractual means, they may still influence the individual bargaining power of the involved persons and respectively have an effect on contracts.

Tangible and non-tangible assets of a company may be included in the contractual model as well. Assets may be owned or rented by the company or, e.g., licensed from IP owners. (If one understands contracts in a broad Rousseauian sense, even the so-called social obligation of property that is recognized in some states may be seen as contractual.) The ownership of assets may have an impact on the bargaining power as well, be it on the side of the suppliers or on the side of the shareholders/ managers vis-à-vis the workers.

F. *Implications of the negotiation model*

When bargaining power is found to be the core factor of all activity within the corporation, the question of legitimacy of the individual power and respectively of the validity of the results of the negotiations among the stakeholders may arise. A number of theories of the firm consider the criteria of legitimacy as an attribute for stakeholder identification and salience. In the negotiation model, legitimacy is only one of many aspects that may raise or limit the bargaining power. It may be a parameter that strengthens the position of a stakeholder. However, it may not serve as an additional factor next to bargaining power, which forms the basis of the theory of the firm.

The concept of the 'one share, one vote' is very much in line with the idea of legitimacy. The implementation of this approach was lately abandoned by the European Commission. Within the negotiation model, this concept of 'one share, one vote' is not helpful as it takes a – possible – result of a negotiation and turns it into a prerequisite of the negotiation.

Another question concerns the role of the law or regulation within the negotiation model. In this context, it is important to distinguish carefully between regulation and legitimacy. The law may be seen as the major external effect on the corporation. While the law sets clear limits to the bargaining power, legitimacy is somewhat an unclear element. It is the function of the law to limit the negotiation power of the contractual partners, who act without legitimacy. For example, as soon as monopolistic structures are identified, the negotiation power has to be looked at from the viewpoint of competition law. As we have seen, corporate law is not useful to develop a theory of the firm. However, the shift to a negotiation model also has legal consequences.

G. Bargaining power of stakeholder groups

Without going into any depth about the position of creditors, it is sufficient to mention that banks, if corporations need them at all, are usually quite able to bargain their position. It is even the case that industry is somewhat disadvantaged when facing investment bankers because their command of the channels to the capital markets as well as the 'customs duty' is often substantial.

Concerning labour, there is already a long tradition of examining bargaining power and establishing rules for negotiations, strikes and lockouts. Very often, instruments of state assistance are also involved.[42] It seems, all in all, that the law is able to come to terms with this aspect of 'social unrest', even though the power of the unions is very different in the various countries. And, all of this is customarily based on

---

[42]   See for Switzerland: 28 III BV, for Germany: 9 III GG.

the contract model, enlarged, it is true, by the instrument of 'collective labour agreements'.

In Germany[43] (and in other countries, e.g. France, Great Britain, Italy, Sweden),[44] the workers entitlement to co-manage is well established.[45] This was the social model of compromise after the Second World War. Nowadays, co-determination is heavily criticized[46] and corporations try to evade it (e.g. by using the SE), but its abolishment is unlikely. It was, however, not possible to export the model into the European law as a general model, with the exception of the directive accompanying the SE statute.[47]

The bargaining powers have indeed changed in other places. The managers are much more powerful and they are much better organized than the shareholders. I am of the opinion that they have a large amount of bargaining power at their disposal, which is not matched by the shareholders.

A question arises as to who belongs to the management? I think that all people, except auditors, elected by the shareholders to hold office in the corporation, belong to the management group. This also comprises the Swiss Board of Directors (*Verwaltungsrat*), even though the management might be separate. Even the German *Aufsichtsrat*[48] belongs here, despite the contrary opinion of doctrine (and the courts)[49] still viewing it to some extent in the historical role as the shareholders' representative committee. In fact, one must concede that, compared with the management or the committee, the German *Aufsichtsrat* does not have the same degree of competence to govern the corporation.

---

[43] See German Montan-Mitbestimmungsgesetz (MontanMitbestG) of 21 May 1951; German Mitbestimmungsgesetz (MitbestG) of 7 May 1976 and German Drittelbeteiligungsgesetz (DrittelbG) of 18 May 2004.

[44] See J. Brown, 'Implications for the Disclosure of Financial Information', *Employment Law Bulletin*, 25 (1999).

[45] R. Göhner und K. Bräunig, ,Bericht der Kommission Mitbestimmung', unpublished Report, Berlin, November 2004, 23–6.

[46] See criticism of the German Institut für Arbeitsmarkt und Berufsforschung, www.iab. de/de/195/section.aspx/Publikation/k051227n15.

[47] Directive 2002/14/EC of the European Parliament and of the Council of 11 March 2002: establishing a general framework for informing and consulting employees in the European Community, [2002] OJ L 80/29. See also P. Hommelhoff and Ch. Teichmann, 'Die Europäische Aktiengesellschaft – das Flaggschiff läuft vom Stapel', *Swiss Review of Business Law*, 74 (2002), 6 and M. Lutter, 'Societas Europaea' in P. Nobel (ed.), *Internationales Gesellschaftsrecht*, (Bern: Stämpfli, 2004), vol. V, 19–45.

[48] See §§ 98–116 AktG of Germany; P.C. Leyens, *Information des Aufsichtsrats* (Tübingen: Mohr Siebeck, 2006).

[49] See BGH II ZR 316/02 of 16 February 2004, *Zeitschrift für Wirtschaftsrecht und Insolvenzpraxis* (2004), 613 (MobilCom).

Furthermore, careful analysis is required. It must first be stated that the economic system of free enterprise requires a fair amount of free action of management, which it must then account for in a transparent manner. Then, a careful examination is needed of the aspect of the shareholder passivity. It is maybe 'rational' not only because of the cost–benefit relationship, but also because shareholders know that large incentives might produce large results. Generally, people are much more open-minded about a profit distribution than a situation where they see an asymmetrical loss bearing.

Here, we might see an inequality of weapons. The general meeting of shareholders is not an ideal bargaining arena. The model is flawed. The shareholders should be able to bargain with the management and then make recommendations to the AGM.

The bargaining model is a good model for the future and, currently, the agency model is outdated. Such a bargaining procedure requires an appropriate forum. A large hall with a fancy screen that only offers the possibility to accept or reject the motions presented is not constructive. Sadly, the only other alternative is disruptive activist action.

IV. Legal future of the enterprise

A. Organizational scheme

It can be anticipated that large enterprises will also play an important role in the future. These large enterprises need (and have) a legal organization. The legal organization consists of a number of legal persons, usually incorporated in various jurisdictions. An enterprise is therefore an international legal organization of decision making over assets. This is the economic reality for which we have to find solutions. The theory of the firm must be, above all, holistic and then duplex: it must encompass the corporate control of assets and the notion of the corporation as a social organization.

Already at this point we have to note that reality is further developed than the law. There is no truly (unitary) international organizational scheme. Not even the Societas Europea could succeed without deep integration and incorporation in the national law of the domicile. We must therefore make use of the existing instruments; but, we should cease to stick to fictitious concepts such as handling the responsibility of the (poor) board of a subsidiary as if there would be no 'boss'.

B. Creditors

Concerning creditors, I would distinguish between 'trade' creditors, belonging to the business, and 'financial' creditors. Trade creditors should be protected throughout the whole group. Financial creditors are sufficiently sophisticated to negotiate the securities they consider as necessary.

C. Workers

Workers are probably the most difficult subject. Their bargaining power comes primarily from the skills they can offer combined with the extent to which they form coalitions.

As far as the skills are concerned, it is the law of supply and demand that decides on the bargaining power of the workforce. In a globalized world, workers find themselves in competition with all workers, on a universal level. In a situation where the skills of the workers are of equal quality, the bargaining power is somehow reduced to the price of their labour. There is no right to maintain production in a place when a new combination of assets and a workforce at other locations is more efficient. This is the price of globalization of the economy. Structural changes cannot be avoided. A high level of specialization may be the best way to strengthen the bargaining power of the workforce. When negotiating on compensation schemes, the asymmetry of information between the management and the workers on the true financial situation of the company may strengthen the management's position. As far as groups of companies are concerned, the design of the compensatory schemes must take the situation of the whole group into consideration, and not only that of the relevant subsidiary.

The other aspect, the bargaining power that results from coalition structures, is declining as the influence of trade unions is constantly receding. This holds true for at least a number of branches and a number of jurisdictions.

Workers may be able to compensate their loss of bargaining power by getting another stake in the corporation. Regularly, workers are also consumers and consumers are also workers, which may result in a potentially high amount of bargaining power. However, this bargaining power is only potential as workers behave very differently in their role as consumers, and vice versa; e.g., as consumers they hunt for the product with the lowest price and as workers they ask for high incomes. The fact remains that the bargaining power of the workforce may improve once the workforce buys shares of their own company. For that, however, a shift in the mentality of many nations is needed. We are still very far away from the worker as an employee–shareholder.

D. Consumers

From a theoretical point of view, consumers should have the most bargaining power of all stakeholders as they are the buyers of the products or services produced by the firms. However, their level of integration is very low. They act through the 'agent' of the consumers' associations. Their bargaining power will depend to a large extent if they manage to form more forceful coalitions.

Legal measures may improve their situation and lead to a more powerful position in the negotiation situation with corporations. As an example, class actions or legal remedies can be mentioned here.

E. Shareholders

Listing of a corporation means that shareholders and potential shareholders get much closer to the economic activity because a whole additional set of information is required to increase transparency. 'Corporate governance' then becomes a major issue here because for many people managers are per se suspicious persons. This leads (somewhat) to a temptation: the shareholders think that they are called to participate in the management; such a notion is, however, prone to lead to a lot of inefficiency and should be avoided at all costs. It should be crystal clear that the management is in charge of the firm. The management is also accountable for its acts and can be dismissed by the board of directors.

Shareholders are a disorganized group of individuals and often have only one opportunity in a year to express their opinion. Institutions like the 'supervisory board' or even auditors were, at one time, supposed to defend shareholders' interests. Nowadays, all being institutionalized with other directional goals, it would be worthwhile to study the idea of electing a shareholders' committee to negotiate certain items reflected in the AGM agenda with the management. A hot topic here is manager compensation. I do not think that the prevailing types of compensation, mainly in banks, have contributed much to the current crisis in the financial world. It is by far not natural law that gross profits are evenly distributed between staff and shareholders. The compensation system should be a matter of negotiation, especially when it also comprises share (or option) allocations, usually at favourable rights; under these circumstances, the compensation system may dilute the position of the other shareholders and, in the medium or long run, may even have the effect of a transfer of control to the employee–shareholders.

F. Management

The principal-agent model does not hold true any more. It sounds nice, however, in a society of property owners. The historic origin is somewhat darker and must be attributed to a master–slave environment rather than to that of a modern democratic society. The agent has not only natural self interests, but is also the master of economic performance. His nomination is maybe the most important task of a board. Such agents are no longer simple executors of instructions given from above but business partners open to negotiations. It would also be the shareholder committee's task to accompany and supervise such negotiations.

V. Summary

Neither legal doctrine nor the theories of the economists offer a comprehensive theory of the firm. The agency model is outdated as we have moved from a structure of order and obedience to a world of pluralistic interests. As a consequence, we need to shift from a commandeering model to a negotiating model. This enables us to get to a theory of the firm that takes into account all different kind of stakeholders and to map all their differing interests. All the parameters that strengthen or weaken the bargaining power of the various stakeholders characterize the reality of the firm. Negotiations may result in contracts in the legal sense or not. The bargaining power is the key element that shapes the corporation in all its aspects.

The shift to a negotiation model has also legal consequences. We should come to solutions which also look at the legal person as a contract, which is to some extent performed by company law, but nevertheless open to negotiation results. The negotiating parties should be the shareholders, the management, the workers and – as far as credits are concerned – the banks. For various purposes (permits, tax) the State is a necessary partner as well.

10

The renaissance of organized shareholder representation in Europe

STEFAN GRUNDMANN

I. Renaissance of shareholder voting rights and organized shareholder representation

A. Renaissance

When Eddy Wymeersch retires, like a good farmer, he leaves us with plenty of crops. Although this is of course not the last harvesting season, these years are certainly particularly rich years in his garden. They are years of a renaissance of shareholder voting rights in Europe and, very prominent among them, shareholder voting via organized shareholder representation. There are at least three reasons for making such a statement.

The first is that one of Wymeersch's core statements in his extensive input to the large stream of European and worldwide corporate governance debate[1] has proven to be impressively right: he was one of the rather few who contributed to this debate in a truly international manner, based on the very extensive comparative law corpus, and who nevertheless did not succumb to the temptation to bet only on mechanisms of external corporate governance. Many of his writings on corporate governance – also early writings – could be summarized in short words as follows: despite the power of external corporate governance mechanisms, despite Wall Street rule and accounting law, 'do not forget

[1] See E. Wymeersch, 'Unternehmensführung in Westeuropa – ein Beitrag zur Corporate Governance-Diskussion', *Aktiengesellschaft,* 40 (1995), 299–316; K. Hopt and E. Wymeersch (eds.), *Comparative Corporate Governance – Essays and Materials,* (Berlin: Walter De Gruyter, 1997); K. Hopt, H. Kanda, M. Roe, E. Wymeersch and S. Prigge (eds.), *Comparative Corporate Governance – the State of the Art and Emerging Research,* (Oxford University Press, 1998); E. Wymeersch, 'Gesellschaftsrecht im Wandel – Ursachen und Entwicklungslinien' in S. Grundmann and P. Mülbert (eds.), *Festheft Klaus J. Hopt,* 'Corporate Governance – Europäische Perspektiven', *Zeitschrift für Gesellschaftsrecht,* 2 (2001), 294–324; *Id.* 'Factors and Trends of Change in Company Law', *International and Comparative Corporate Law Journal,* 4 (2000), 476–502.

shareholder voting rights'.[2] This is indeed the lesson to be learnt from the balance sheet scandals in the United States and then in various Member States.[3] The more mechanisms of external corporate governance show their flaws, the more a combination of external and internal mechanisms of corporate governance becomes attractive – and voting rights are paramount in this respect. The first reason for a renaissance of shareholder voting rights can therefore be summarized as 'back to Wymeersch's early *monita!*'

The second reason is that, of course, this trend has found its way into European legislation as well, and this in a prominent and in an astonishingly rapid way. It did not take more than one and a half years (from proposal to adoption), to enact the EC Directive on 'certain rights of shareholders', all related to shareholder voting (EC Shareholder Voting Directive).[4]

---

[2] See last footnote, *passim*, and, of course as well T. Baums and E. Wymeersch (eds.), *Shareholder Voting Rights and Practices in Europe and the United States*, (Kluwer Law International, 1999). On the other side, focusing mainly on mechanisms of external corporate governance: K. Hopt and E. Wymeersch (eds.), *Capital Markets and Company Law*, (Oxford University Press, 2003). For a large survey on the question which approach is stronger in which Member State(s), see early E. Wymeersch, 'Unternehmensführung in Westeuropa – Ein Beitrag zur Corporate Governance-Diskussion', *Aktiengesellschaft*, (1995), 299, 309–15 (namely Germany on the one hand, the United Kingdom on the other, France and Belgium in between).

[3] In this sense as well, for instance, early the *OECD Principles of Corporate Governance*, Part 1 II and 2 II; Committee on Corporate Governance, *The Combined Code – Principles of Good Governance and Code of Best Practice*, E 1, available at www.fsa.gov.uk/pubs/ ukla/lr_comcode.pdf; and recently M. Siems, *Die Konvergenz der Rechtssysteme im Recht der Aktionäre*, (Tubingen: Mohr Siebeck, 2005), 102–5; N. Winkler, *Das Stimmrecht der Aktionäre in Europa*, (Berlin: De Gruyter, 2006), 1.

[4] European Parliament and Council Directive 2007/36/EC [2007] *OJ* L 184/17; Proposal of 5 Jan. 2006, *COM*(2005) 685 final. On this directive, see, among others: S. Grundmann and N. Winkler, 'Das Aktionärsstimmrecht in Europa und der Kommissionsvorschlag zur Stimmrechtsausübung in börsennotierten Gesellschaften', *Zeitschrift fürWirtschaftsrecht*, (2006), 1421–8; U. Noack, 'Der Vorschlag für eine Richtlinie über Rechte von Aktionären börsennotierter Gesellschaften', *Neue Zeitschrift für Gesellschaftsrecht*, (2006), 321–7; U. Noack and M. Beurskens, 'Einheitliche "Europa-Hauptversammlung"? – Vorschlag für eine Richtlinie über die (Stimm-) Rechte von Aktionären', *Gemeinschaftsprivatrecht*, (2006), 88–91; E. Ratschow, 'Die Aktionärsrechte-Richtlinie – neue Regeln für börsennotierte Gesellschaften', *Deutsches Steuerrecht*, (2007), 1402–8; J. Schmidt, 'Die geplante Richtlinie über Aktionärsrechte und ihre Bedeutung für das deutsche Aktienrecht', *Betriebs-Berater*, (2006), 1641–6; P. Wand and T. Tillmann, 'EU-Richtlinienvorschlag zur Erleichterung der Ausübung von Aktionärsrechten', *Aktiengesellschaft*, (2006), 443–50; D. Zetzsche, 'Virtual Shareholder Meetings and European Shareholder Rights Directive – Challenges and Opportunities', http://papers.ssrn.com/sol3/cf_dev/AbsByAuth.cfm?per_id=357808;

The third reason is one more focused on organized shareholder representation already – not so much only on shareholder voting in general: For sceptics, it comes somehow as a surprise that, indeed, shareholder voting seems to increase considerably again. At least in Germany, over the last three years, the percentage of voting stock in the thirty largest listed companies which is in fact voted on general assemblies rose from 45.87% to 56.42%.[5] This increase is due to a large extent to organized shareholder representation.

B. The overall picture

The EC Shareholder Voting Directive aims at enabling informed shareholder voting (see namely recitals 2, 4–6 and 9–12). The legislative history shows that this scope has received a more positive reaction throughout Europe than, for instance, such fundamental principles as 'one share one vote' – which the new Directive leaves untouched while the EC Takeover Directive, in its Arts. 10 and 11, had been only partially successful in establishing this principle as a European one at least in the more specific arena of takeovers.[6]

Instead, the EC Shareholder Voting Directive deals with more 'procedural' issues – some, however, of high practical importance and some of which had received an astonishingly high variety of answers before. The variety is evident in all three bundles of issues approached by the directive. The first bundle is about the preparatory phase, namely

D. Zetzsche, 'Shareholder Passivity, Cross-Border Voting and the Shareholder Rights Directive', *Journal of Corporate Law Studies*, 8 (2008), 283–336; critical M. Siems, 'The Case against Harmonisation of Shareholder Rights', *European Business Organization Law Review*, 6 (2005), 539–52.

[5] Deutsche Schutzvereinigung für Wertpapierbesitz, *HV-Präsenz der DAX-30-Unternehmen (1998–2007) in Prozent des stimmberechtigten Kapitals*, http://www.dsw-info.de/uploads/media/DSW_HV-Praesenz/2007_02.pdf. For figures in other countries, see for instance, Shearman&Stearling/ISS/ECGI, *Report on the Proportionality Principle in the European Union*, External Study Commissioned by the European Commission, http://ec.europa.eu/internal_market/company/docs/shareholders/study/final_report_en.pdf.

[6] European Parliament and Council Directive 2004/25/EC [2004] OJ L 142/12. On the long history (and importance) see e.g. S. Grundmann, *European Company Law – Organization, Finance and Capital Markets*, (Antwerp/Oxford: Intersentia, 2007), para. 995–1004. See also G. Ferrarini, 'One share – one vote: A European rule?', *European Company and Financial Law Review*, (2006), 147–77; for a short comparative law survey on the deviations from this principle in the large Member States see Grundmann, *ibid.*, paras. 452–54 (deviations stronger in France, the United Kingdom, and Scandinavia than in Germany and Italy).

questions of record date, information, and timing (see Arts. 4–7, also 9). The second is about voting by the shareholder himself. In these two bundles, the directive deals with: rendering information about the items on the agenda more easily accessible also from abroad; eliminating rules which block stock between the record date and the date of the general assembly; abolishing unnecessary requirements of physical presence in the general assembly (voting in absentia and voting via electronic media). The third bundle is about reducing restrictions to shareholder representation (proxies), and, of particular importance, (restrictions to) organized shareholder representation.

The variety existing so far in the Member States can well be shown by concentrating on just one bundle, the second one which, functionally, is already highly related to the third one: both voting in absentia (also by electronic means) and voting via (organized) shareholder representation allow for voting without shareholder presence, which, of course, often is excluded by reasons of costs, time etc.[7] Voting in absentia or by electronic means has, however, been extremely restricted so far even in countries which, such as Germany, were rather liberal with respect to shareholder representation and vice versa. This status could not really be justified by reasoning that one of the two ways of participation was already sufficient: a shareholder may rather opt for the expertise of the representative (and therefore not be satisfied by the possibility to vote in absentia) or he may rather mistrust him because of the danger of conflicts of interests (and therefore not be satisfied by the possibility of shareholder representation). The EC Directive, in principle, forces Member States to allow companies to take all measures necessary to enable shareholders to vote in absentia, by electronic means or by letter (Art. 8, 12), and it forces the Member States to allow for a free choice among the different forms of organized shareholder representation and impose this as well on the companies (Arts. 10, 11, 13).

There is quite considerable change required – in various Member States – already with respect to the second bundle of rules named above.

---

[7] G. Bachmann, 'Verwaltungsvollmacht und "Aktionärsdemokratie" – Selbstregulative Ansätze für die Hauptversammlung', *Aktiengesellschaft*, (2001), 635, 637; W.W. Bratton and J.A. McCahery, 'Comparative Corporate Governance and the Theory of the Firm: The Case against Global Cross Reference', *Columbia Journal of Transnational Law*, 38 (1999), 213, 260; T. Baums and Ph. v. Randow, 'Der Markt für Stimmrechtsvertreter', *Aktiengesellschaft*, (1995), 145, 147; J.C. Coffee, 'Liquidity Versus Control: The Institutional Investor As Corporate Monitor', *Columbia Law Review*, 91 (1991), 1277; U. Noack, 'Die organisierte Stimmrechtsvertretung auf Hauptversammlungen', *Festschrift for Lutter*, (2000), 1463.

The comparative law status so far shows substantial variety and can be summarized as follows: in Germany, voting in absentia is not permitted today, neither by letter nor by electronic media. Functionally, however, it can be seen as an equivalent to have a representative in the general meeting, follow the meeting on the internet and give instructions to the representative contemporaneously via electronic media.[8] Also in the United Kingdom, electronic means could be used only to give proxy. Conversely in France, voting by letter is possible.[9] In Italy, at least in listed companies, a vote is possible in absentia if the statutes so provide (Art. 127 Testo Unico), probably also by electronic communication or via videoconference.[10] The EC Shareholder Voting Directive now forces Member States to allow companies to choose themselves whether they want to provide the facilities for voting in absentia, by electronic means and/or by letter (Art. 8, 12).[11] The scope of these rules is summarized in its 6th Recital saying that all 'shareholders should be able to cast informed votes at, or in advance of, the general meeting, no matter where they reside'.

II. Organized shareholder representation as a centre-piece of the development

The following will show that there is quite considerable change required as well – in other Member States – with respect to organized shareholder representation (third bundle of rules named above, see below). A legislature may, however, opt as well for reforming quite substantially his law on organized shareholder representation more generally. This is so in the case of the proposal now discussed in Germany in the

---

[8] Permissible, see, for instance: G. Spindler, in K. Schmidt and M. Lutter (eds.), *Aktiengesetz*, (2007), § 134 para. 56.

[9] Art. L 225–107 [L = Code de Commerce (Loi, L), Annexe à l'ordonnannce n° 2000–912 du 18 septembre 2000, Livre II, Des Sociétes Commerciales et des Groupements d'interêt économique, last amendment (Nouvelles Régulations Économiques) J.O. 2001, 7776]; M. Cozian, A. Viandier and F. Deboissy, *Droit des Sociétés*, (Paris: Litec, 2001), para. 847; Y. Guyon, *Droit des affaires, vol. 1: Droit commercial général et Sociétés*, (Paris: Economica, 2001), para. 301–1 and 301–2 (for the Code de Commerce as legal basis see there para. 27, 95); since 2001 electronic voting and voting via video conference are accepted (Art. L 225–107 para. 2).

[10] On all this (and on the disputed question whether this rule applies to other PLCs as well): L. Picardi, 'L'articolo 127 del Tuf', in G.F. Campobasso (ed.), *Testo Unico della Finanza – Commentario*, (Utet, 2002), Art. 127 para. 10.

[11] The Proposal for a Fifth EC Company Law Directive still did not contain rules on voting in absentia; see e.g. M. Pannier, *Harmonisierung der Aktionärsrechte in Europa – insbesondere der Verwaltungsrechte*, (Duncker & Humblot, 2003), 136.

context of the transposition of the EC Shareholder Voting Directive.[12] This proposal concerns the parts which will play a role in the following. Indeed, the German legislature proposes to do more than is required in the directive and this mainly with respect to organized shareholder representation. Eddy Wymeersch has always had a particular eye on new developments – and often has initiated them himself. Therefore, it may not bother him too much that it is still highly uncertain whether the parts of this proposal discussed in the following will be enacted at all (or only the parts strictly necessary for the transposition).

A. High density of regulation and admission of all forms

The reason why the focus is on organized shareholder voting representation in the following is simple. In practice, this is by far the most important way of shareholder voting.[13]

This finding is by now means new. Already, the Proposal for a Fifth Directive, had dealt with this issue rather extensively. This is true even though organized proxy – the proposal calls it 'publicly invit[ing] shareholders to send their forms of proxy to him and . . . offer[ing] to appoint agents for them'[14] – is not yet prescribed as a possibility in this

---

[12] See, on the one hand: [Ministry of Justice] *Referentenentwurf eines Gesetzes zur Umsetzung der Aktionärsrechterichtlinie (ARUG)*, www.bmj.bund.de/files/-/3140/ RefE%20Gesetz% 20zur% 20Umsetzung%20der%20Aktionärsrechterichtlinie.pdf; on this proposal U. Seibert, 'Der Referentenentwurf eines Gesetzes zur Umsetzung der Aktionärsrechterichtlinie (ARUG)', *Zeitschrift für Wirtschaftsrecht*, (2008), 906–10. See, on the other hand: [Federal Government] *Entwurf eines Gesetzes zur Umsetzung der Aktionärsrechterichtlinie (ARUG)*, BR-Drs. 847/08, as of 7 November 2008. This second proposal could be taken into account only after this chapter was completed.

[13] In 1992, up to 99% of the capital present at the general meeting was represented by financial institutions which typically acted as proxies for their clients, see T. Baums, 'Vollmachtstimmrecht der Banken – Ja oder Nein?', *Aktiengesellschaft*, (1996), 11, 12. The newest trend would seem to be that independent service providers (ISS, ECGS, IVOX) offer proxy voting services, see U. Schneider and H.M. Anziger, 'Institutionelle Stimmrechtsberatung und Stimmrechtsvertretung – "A quiet guru's enormous clout"', *Neue Zeitschrift für Gesellschaftsrecht*, (2006), 88–96.

[14] This refers to proxies given to banks, the management or shareholder associations: J. Temple Lang, 'The Fifth EEC Directive on the Harmonization of Company Law – Some Comments from the Viewpoint of Irish and British Law on the EEC Draft for a Fifth Directive Concerning Management Structure and Worker Participation', *Common Market Law Review*, 12 (1975), 345, 366; Pannier, *Harmonisierung der Aktionärsrechte in Europa*, 135 *et seq.*; G. Schwarz, *Europäisches Gesellschaftsrecht – ein Handbuch für Wissenschaft und Praxis*, (Baden-Baden: Nomos, 2000), para. 767; C. Striebeck,

proposal.[15] If, however, a Member State allowed organized shareholder voting, already the Proposal of a Fifth Directive would have imposed certain important conditions (Art. 28)[16] with a view to increase the chances that the intentions of shareholders really come to bear: when making the public offer, the representative would have had to propose one method of voting for each item on the agenda, diverging instructions by the shareholder would have had to be rendered possible for each item separately and this would have had to be mentioned explicitly. Moreover, the proxy would have had to be restricted to one meeting only (as formerly in Germany the proxy to banks, the so-called 'deposit-bank voting right') and revocable. This would already have constituted a framework – despite the considerable differences between the (big) Member States.[17]

Today, long after the Proposal has been withdrawn, this only helps to understand which importance has been attached to organized shareholder representation since very early on the European level. In the EC Shareholder Voting Directive, even the starting point has changed and it has done so very radically: this Directive now obliges Member States to allow all forms of organized shareholder representation. In fact, Art. 10 of the directive eliminates all obstacles to organized shareholder representation which are not specified in its first two paragraphs (legal capacity and maximum number of representatives, with further specifications in Art. 13) and, in addition, allows certain restrictions of the use of the proxy in case of conflicts of interests in its para. 3 – not more. Thus, the EC legislature goes further than for

---

Reform des Aktienrechts durch die Strukturrichtlinie der Europäischen Gemeinschaften, Broschiert, (1992), 85–99.

[15] EC Commission's explanation to Art. 28 (*COM*(72) 887 final). This is now a core ingredient in the EC Shareholder Voting Directive 2007/36/EC, [2007] *OJ* L 184/17.

[16] In more detail on these conditions see EC Commission's explanation to Art. 31 (*COM*(72) 887 final); Lang, 'The Fifth EEC Directive on the Harmonization of Company Law', 345, 366; Schwarz, 'Europäisches Gesellschaftsrecht', (note 14, above), para. 767; Striebeck, 'Reform des Aktienrechts', (note 14, above), 87 *et seq.*

[17] Short comparative law surveys in the following text; and T. Baums, 'Shareholder Representation and Proxy Voting in the European Union: A Comparative Study' in K. Hopt, H. Kanda, M. Roe, E. Wymeersch and S. Prigge (eds.), *Comparative Corporate Governance – the State of the Art and Emerging Research*, (Oxford University Press, 1998), 545–64; Th. Behnke, 'Die Stimmrechtsvertretung in Deutschland, Frankreich und England', *Neue Zeitschrift für Gesellschaftsrecht*, (2000), 665–74; and also *DSW-Europastudie – 15 europäische Länder im Vergleich, eine rechtsvergleichende Studie über Minderheitenrechte der Aktionäre sowie Stimmrechtsausübung und -vertretung in Europa*, (1999), 86 *et seq.*; and many contributions to T. Baums and E. Wymeersch (eds.), *Shareholder Voting Rights*, (note 2, above) (entry: proxies).

voting in absentia (second bundle of rules) where it obliges Member States only not to hinder companies from installing such possibilities (Arts. 8 and 12).

B. High diversity in member state laws so far

Proxy rules (both on general and organized proxy) are regulated quite differently in different Member States so far. In Germany, proxy has always been regulated in quite a liberal way, and as of 2002 the NaStraG has admitted board members as proxies as well (§ 134 para. 3(3) *Aktiengesetz*; however, probably not the PLC itself).[18] Proxy has to be given in writing (the company statutes can deviate, § 134 para. 3(2) *Aktiengesetz*), may be given without time limits, but may not be irrevocable.[19] The NaStraG also abolished the time limit for proxies given to banks (see § 135 para 2(2) *Aktiengesetz*).[20] This is ambivalent: banks are subject to conflicts of interests (albeit often not more than management), but the presence of shareholdings in

---

[18] See, for instance G. Bachmann, 'Verwaltungsvollmacht und "Aktionärsdemokratie" – Selbstregulative Ansätze für die Hauptversammlung', *Aktiengesellschaft,* (2001), 635–44; S. Hanloser, 'Proxy-Voting, Remote-Voting und Online-HV – § 134 III 3 AktG nach dem NaStraG', *Neue Zeitschrift für Gesellschaftsrecht,* (2001), 355–58; U. Seibert, 'Aktienrechtsnovelle NaStraG tritt in Kraft – Übersicht über das Gesetz und Auszüge aus dem Bericht des Rechtsausschuses', *Zeitschrift für Wirtschaftsrecht,* (2001), 53, 55 *et seq.*; see also U. Noack, 'Die organisierte Stimmrechtsvertretung auf Hauptversammlungen', *Festschrift for Lutter,* (2000), 1463, 1474–80; comparative law investigations into (organized) proxies: Baums, 'Shareholder Representation', (note 17, above), 545–564; B.C. Becker, *Die Institutionelle Stimmrechtsvertretung der Aktionäre in Europa,* (Frankfurt am Main: Lang, 2001); Behnke, 'Die Stimmrechtsvertretung', (note 17, above), 665–74; M. Hohn Abad, *Das Institut der Stimmrechtsvertretung im Aktienrecht – ein europäischer Vergleich,* (1995); also J. Hoffmann, *Systeme der Stimmrechtsvertretung in der Publikumsgesellschaft – eine vergleichende Betrachtung insbesondere der Haftung des Stimmrechtsvertreters im deutschen und US-amerikanischen Recht,* (Nomos, 1999).

[19] U. Hüffer, *Aktiengesetz* (8th edn 2008), § 134 AktG para. 21; J. Reichert and S. Harbarth, 'Stimmrechtsvollmacht, Legitimationszession und Stimmrechtsausschlußvertrag in der AG', *Aktiengesellschaft,* (2001), 447–55.

[20] See U. Seibert, 'Aktienrechtsnovelle NaStraG tritt in Kraft – Ubersicht über das Gesetz und Auszüge aus dem Bericht des Rechtausschusses', *Zeitschrift für Wirtschaftsrecht,* (2001), 53, 54–6; M. Weber, 'Der Eintritt des Aktienrechts in das Zeitalter der elektronischen Medien – das NaStraG in seiner verabschiedeten Fassung', *Neue für Zeitschrift Gesellschaftsrecht,* (2001), 337, 343; not very common in other countries, see references in Grundmann, *European Company Law,* (note 6, above), § 14 N. 66.

the meeting is increased.[21] Today, there is another restriction on the proxy given to a bank: the bank may not use it if the bank itself holds (and votes) 5% of the company's capital (§ 135 para. 1 (3) *Aktiengesetz*, except for those proxies containing explicit instructions). Moreover, under specific information rules it is made clear how the bank will vote and that the client can deviate for each item individually (§§ 128 para. 2, 3, 135 para. 5 *Aktiengesetz*). In any case, the bank must take the client's interest as a guideline and try to avoid conflicts of interests as far as possible.[22] The French solution is much more restricted: proxies can be given only to other shareholders or the spouse[23] and only for one meeting and in writing, and revocation must remain possible.[24] Organized proxy is typically given to management (mostly in blank).[25] Proxy given to banks – if they do not own stock – would contradict the basic principle of accepting only other shareholders as proxies, in any case, the law does not provide for it.[26] Particularly developed are the bases for organized shareholder representation in the United Kingdom where proxy is not confined to other shareholders (although possible only for polls).[27] Proxy can be given in writing or (as of 2000) in electronic form.[28] Organized proxy is possible without giving specific instructions (general proxy) or with them, and also

---

[21] On this advantage (and on the problem of concentrating power in banks and conflicts of interests): Baums, 'Germany' in T. Baums and E. Wymeersch (eds.), *Shareholder Voting Rights* (note 2, above), 127; and more extensively Hohn Abad, *Das Institut der Stimmrechtsvertretung*, 109 (note 18, above), 13–17; Behnke, 'Die Stimmrechtsvertretung in Deutschland, Frankreich und England', (note 17, above), 667. On existing conflicts of interests see also short explanations in Grundmann, *European Company Law*, (note 6, above), para. 504 *et seq*.

[22] § 128 para. 2 (2) *Aktiengesetz* (German PLC-Code); in the event of unavoidable conflicts there is a duty nevertheless to act in the sole interest of the client, see references in Grundmann, *European Company Law*, (note 6, above), § 12 N. 78.

[23] Art. L 225–106 [L = Code de Commerce, see above N. 9]; critical Guyon, *Droit des affaires*, (note 9, above), para. 301.

[24] Art. D 132 [D = Décret (D) n° 67–236 du 23 mars 1967 sur les sociétes commerciales; see note 3, above]; Guyon, *Droit des affaires*, (note 9, above), para. 301; Behnke, 'Die Stimmrechtsvertretung ', (note 17, above), 668.

[25] Art. L 225–106; Cozian, Viandier and Deboissy, *Droit des Sociétés,* (note 3, above) para. 838; Guyon, *Droit des affaires*, (note 9, above), para. 301.

[26] Y. Guyon, in T. Baums and E. Wymeersch (eds.), *Shareholder Voting Rights*, (note 2, above), 35, 106.

[27] Sec. 372 (old) Companies Act (C.A.), sec. 59 Table A; P. Davies, *Gower's and Davies' Principles of Modern Company Law*, (4th edn, Thomson, 2003), 361 and 363; J. Farrar and B. Hannigan, *Farrar's Company Law*, (7th edn, Lexis Law Publishing, 1998), 315, 322 *et seq*.; R.R. Pennington, *Pennington's Company Law*, (8th edn, LexisNexis UK, 2001), 766, 779 *et seq*.

[28] Sec. 372 II para. 2 (old) C.A.; sec. 60 *et seq*. Table A.

for only a few of the items on the agenda (two-way proxy).[29] In listed companies, only the latter is accepted.[30] When management asks for proxies (i.e. unless the initiative came from the shareholder) it must ask all shareholders.[31] In Italy, there are rather rigid formal require-ments for proxies (in written form, not in blank). Moreover, a proxy can represent only small capital and the company statutes can provide for more restrictions; as of 1998, banks may ask for proxies (within these limits), board members and auditors still not; and in listed com-panies, (associations of) shareholders holding more than 1% of the stock, can broadly ask for proxies.[32]

Summarizing the status quo so far, the starting point is similar: prox-ies are possible in all countries. There are, however, substantial differ-ences so far in very important single questions: in Germany and the United Kingdom, the proxy can be chosen freely, in France only from among other shareholders and spouses and in Italy only for small capital being represented. A proxy without time limits is possible in Germany, and also in the United Kingdom if the statutes so provide. Organized proxies follow different traditions – in Germany proxies are typically given to banks, in France and Great Britain to management and in Italy only to a very restricted extent. Proxies given to depositary banks are, however, more important for bearer shares[33] and registered stock, which predominates in France and the United Kingdom, may well become more important in Germany as well.

---

[29] Sec. 60 *et seq.* Table A; Davies, *Gower's and Davies' principles*, (note 27, above), 360 *et seq.*; Farrar and Hannigan, *Farrar's Company Law*, (note 27, above), 315 *et seq.*; also Pennington, *Pennington's Company Law*, (note 27, above), 782.

[30] On this question (and on the duty to vote which then probably exists): Davies, *Gower's and Davies' principles*, (note 27, above), 360–63; Farrar and Hannigan, *Farrar's Company Law*, (note 27, above), 315 *et seq.*; Pennington, *Pennington's Company Law*, (note 27, above), 782 *et seq.*; Behnke, 'Die Stimmrechtsvertretung ' , (note 17, above), 670.

[31] Davies, *Gower's and Davies' principles*, (note 27, above), 361; Farrar and Hannigan, *Farrar's Company Law*, (note 27, above), 316; Pennington, *Pennington's Company Law*, (note 27, above), 767.

[32] The relevant rules are Art. 2372 Codice Civile and Art. 136–144 Testo Unico della Finanza; on all this P. Marchetti, G. Carcano and F. Ghezzi, 'Shareholder Voting in Italy' in T. Baums and E. Wymeersch (eds.), *Shareholder Voting Rights*, (note 2, above), 171–79.

[33] T. Baums, 'Corporate Governance in Germany: The Role of the Banks', *American Journal of Comparative Law*, 40 (1992), 503, 506; M. Hüther, 'Namensaktien, Internet und die Zukunft der Stimmrechtsvertretung', *Aktiengesellschaft*, (2001), 68, 69 *et seq.*; Noack, 'Die organisierte Stimmrechtsvertretung', (note 18, above), 1466.

III. Structuring organized shareholder representation –
three Cartesian rules

For a 'market order' for organized shareholder representation, three types of rules would seem to develop in Europe – all of them aimed at containing dangers resulting from this type of proxy while profiting from its advantages. The trend is to allow for competition between all forms of organized shareholder representation, i.e. admit them all and subject them to the same or similar safeguards, and to target safeguards more carefully. The German scheme of deposit-bank voting right (§ 135 *Aktiengesetz*) and the English scheme of proxies given to management would seem to be particularly refined. For the former, as has been mentioned, the Ministry of Justice and now also the Federal Government have published reform proposals (N. 12) with three major changes. The English scheme is brand-new anyhow after the adoption of the Company Law Reform.[34] The three basic types of rules developing in Europe are about (i) having an uninterested, professional representative, (ii) providing, as far as possible, the full picture of the market of proposals (proxies) to the shareholder, and (iii) reducing the representative's strategic options via a mandatory vote:

A. *Striving for an uninterested, professional representative*

1. Impartiality v. specific shareholder instructions

The first Cartesian rule developing in Europe for organized shareholder representation would seem to be that it is advisable and permissible for national law to strive for an uninterested, professional representative. The EC Shareholder Voting Directive, while not regulating safeguards in this respect positively, does nevertheless foster them in Art 10 para. 3. In fact, professional representatives are more likely to have the knowledge to cast the vote in the best interest of the shareholder represented. This advantage of the use of an information intermediary[35] has to be set off against the disadvantage that there is often a danger of conflict of interests.

---

[34] See, for instance, P. Davies, *Gower and Davies, Principles of Modern Company Law*, (7th edn, London: Sweet & Maxwell, 2008), 53–62.

[35] For the concept of information intermediaries, advantages and disadvantages (chances and dangers) of their use see more in detail S. Grundmann and W. Kerber, 'Information Intermediaries and Party Autonomy – the example of securities and insurance markets' in: S. Grundmann, W. Kerber and S. Weatherill (eds.), *Party Autonomy and the Role of Information in the Internal Market*, (Berlin: De Gruyter, 2001), 264–310 (and literature quoted there).

Theoretically, two rules seem feasible: either a rule which requires the absence of conflicts of interests (impartiality) and excludes all representatives who do not satisfy this requirement; or a rule which asks for specific instructions on the side of the shareholder in cases where there is a considerable conflict of interests. Already before the adoption of the EC Shareholder Voting Directive, the rule named first would seem to have been a rather theoretical option only. Both Germany and the United Kingdom where this problem was approached with particular intensity opted for the second rule in principle.

In Germany, this was done in § 135 para. 1 (2) *Aktiengesetz* for any proxy given to management in the general assembly of PLC: While this rule applies directly only to (general assemblies of) credit institutions which adopt the form of a PLC, it is increasingly held to apply by analogy to all types of enterprises adopting the form of a PLC.[36] Moreover, § 135 para. 1 (3) *Aktiengesetz* asks for special instructions – i.e. two-way proxies in the English terminology – in cases where proxy is not given to management of the PLC, but to the deposit-bank , if this bank owns in addition 5% of the stock subscribed.

Deposit bank voting is, however, not possible so far in France (unless it owns stock itself), only to a very limited extent in Italy and not usual in the United Kingdom either. Here, as has been said, proxies are given to management (as in France). The peculiarity of the English development is, however, that proxies can be given without specific instructions (general proxies) only in PLCs which are not listed, while in listed companies two-way proxies are needed: Proxies can be voted here only for those items on the agenda where such instructions exist.

2. Management, credit institutions, and shareholders' associations as potential representatives

The question thus arises not so much whether there should be the requirement of a specific instruction by the shareholder but whether all forms of organized representation should be admitted in parallel and

[36] See only (also for the opposing view) C. Bunke, 'Fragen der Vollmachtserteilung zur Stimmrechtsausübung nach §§ 134, 135 AktG', *Aktiengesellschaft,* (2002), 57, 60; M. Habersack, 'Aktienrecht und Internet', *Zeitschrift für das gesamte Handelsrecht,* 165 (2001), 172, 187–89; S. Lenz, *Die gesellschaftsbenannte Stimmrechtsvertretung (Voting) in der Hauptversammlung der deutschen Publikums-AG,* (Berlin: Duncker & Humblot, 2005), 285; U. Noack, 'Stimmrechtsvertretung in der Hauptversammlung nach dem NaStraG', *Zeitschrift für Wirtschaftsrecht,* (2001), 57, 62; G. Spindler, in K. Schmidt and M. Lutter (eds.), *Aktiengesetz,* (2007), § 134 para. 56; opposite, for instance, P. Kindler, 'Der Aktionär in der Informationsgesellschaft', *Neue Juristische Wochenschrift,* (2001), 1678, 1687.

how to define the conflict of interests which gives rise to the requirement of a specific instruction by the shareholder.

While this seems rather simple in the case of proxies given to management or to representatives named by the company – at least in PLCs which are listed – the German rule described above is more problematic. It basically assumes that there is a strong conflict of interest whenever the deposit bank owns 5% of the stock subscribed, but does not take into consideration loans (although in 1998 this had been discussed as well). This rule which has been introduced after long policy debate in the 1990s about the power of banks and their role within the then highly 'cartelized' system of stock-holdings in Germany, the so-called 'Deutschland AG' (PLC Germany), was aimed at combating a different type of conflict of interests: while the potential of bias in the case of management is obvious, that of the bank is seen in four phenomena: deposit banks do not only act as representatives of their clients, but, in a universal bank system, act as well as providers of loans, as owners of their own stock and via their presence on the supervisory board, potentially as well as counsellors.[37] Their conservative – risk averse – attitude in the PLCs which they influence by their votes has often been highlighted. Moreover, interests of large block-holders often diverge from that of small capital represented.

Two developments in the last two years are interesting. The German legislature would like to increase the threshold from which specific instructions are required from 5% to 20% (Federal Government) or even 50% (Ministry of Justice). In fact, the 5% threshold has often been criticized as being much too low and meaningless.[38] Another argument advanced by the legislature is that deposit banks have lost quite substantially the multifold power described.[39] While the German legislature has admitted proxies given to management (only) in 2002, the legislative trend would now seem to be that deposit bank voting is seen (again) as the alternative which should be fostered. Banks are seen

---

[37] D. Charny, 'The German Corporate Governance System', *Columbia Business Law Review*, 1 (1998), 145; K. Hopt, 'Gemeinsame Grundsätze der Corporate Governance in Europa?', *Zeitschrift für Gesellschaftsrecht*, (2000), 773, 802–6.

[38] See, for instance, G. Spindler, in K. Schmidt and M. Lutter (eds.), *Aktiengesetz*, (2007), § 135 para. 20–22.

[39] Even in the 1990s, the share banks owned in listed companies on average was only at about 10% of the stock subscribed: E. Wymeersch, 'A Status Report on Corporate Governance Rules and Practices in Some Continental European States' in K. Hopt, H. Kanda, M. Roe, E. Wymeersch and S. Prigge (eds.), *Comparative Corporate Governance*, (note 1, above), 1176 *et seq.* (similar, however, only in Italy).

(again) as potentially less biased than management – as an interesting balancing factor in a general assembly.

The second development occurred on the European level. The EC Shareholder Voting Directive does not accept a general exclusion of certain types of (organized) shareholder representation, namely not requirements as to which person may be chosen as a proxy. An exclusion of banks is thus no longer admissible (see Art. 10). Moreover, the requirements which may be imposed are channelled now: apart from exclusion based on questions of capacity (para. 1) and restrictions as to numbers (para. 2), only conflicts of interests may be taken as a criterion for restrictions (para. 3). In addition, these restrictions then may not take any form, namely not outright exclusion: it may only be forbidden to pass on the proxy or prescribed to give information on the conflict of interests. The third – and last remaining – tool is that specific instruction by the shareholder may be asked. Finally, also a definition of conflict of interests is given. Although this definition is open ('in particular'), it shows a trend: it would seem as if only (direct or indirect) majority holdings were seen as serious enough a danger. Thus, what the German legislature now proposes may even be required by the Directive (although the German legislature does not think he is bound).

Shareholders' associations would certainly be the least problematic alternative – if there was not the problem that a high level of professional action requires funds as well. Therefore, the real alternative is commercial representation, ISS, ECGS and IVOX being the most prominent players in this respect (see Fn. 13).

3. Striving for a full picture of the market of proposals (proxies)

Specific instructions given by the shareholder are seen as the first best choice in all national laws and in the EC Shareholder Voting Directive. This follows from the fact that such instructions are required in situations where shareholder protection is seen to be particularly important (see, for instance, Art. 10 para. 3 of the directive) and from the fact that they always take precedence over proposals made by management or organized shareholder representatives (Art. 10 para. 2 of the directive). The EC Shareholder Voting Directive does, however, not specify how and which proposals should be made and which effect they have in the absence of such specific instructions.

This is perhaps the most interesting aspect of the reform proposal made by the German Ministry of Justice for the German deposit bank voting scheme, and deserves close attention – even though the chance for this model to become law has now considerably decreased, as it is no longer part of the Federal Government's draft.[40] The first rule proposed is that the credit institution is no longer forced to make its own proposal of how to vote in the absence of a specific shareholder instruction, but that it is still allowed to do so. The second rule is that if the credit institution chooses not to make its own proposal, it may not only propose to follow management's proposals. This is interesting because the rule clearly starts from the assumption that the risk of biases in management's proposals is the strongest. This shows that with respect to the question of who is the ideal proxy, the dividing line within Europe is probably not less prominent than with respect, for instance, to co-determination. The credit institution may refer to the proposal made by any shareholders' association, but if it refers to the proposals made by management, it always has to offer as an alternative at least one proposal made by a shareholders' association as well. The bottom line is that – absent a specific instruction made by the shareholder – credit institutions may act as proxies only if they offer an alternative to management's proposals – which, of course, can also coincide with these proposals in large parts – but they have to make the choices made explicit. In other words, the credit institution has to offer its own alternative to management's proposals or an alternative proposed by another independent 'professional' actor – because this should have ex ante a disciplining effect on management.[41] Weakening this responsibility of the credit institution is a major back-step in the recent Government's *Entwurf* (see note 12, above). The third rule in the Ministry's *Entwurf* is that the credit institution may even choose to offer the shareholder the whole picture of proposals. This goes even further than just disciplining management. A (relatively) independent professional actor gathers all alternative proposals for the shareholder[42] (even so far, credit institutions had to inform about the existence of alternatives and this remains the mandatory rule also in the future). The Ministry's *Entwurf* would have had more control than the Government's *Entwurf*.

[40] On the model, see [Ministry of Justice] *Referentenentwurf* (note 12, above), 48 *et seq.*; first comment by M. Sauter, 'Der Referentenentwurf eines Gesetzes zur Umsetzung der Aktionärsrechterichtlinie (ARUG)', Institute for Law & Finance, Frankfurt, Working Paper Series No. 85, 06/2008, www.ILF-Frankfurt.de, 4 *et seq* and 17 (overall positive). [Federal Government] *Entwurf* (see note 12, above), provides for a different model, see S. Grudmann, 'Das neue Depotstimmrecht nach der Fassung im Regierungsentwurf zum ARUG', forthcoming in *Zeitschrift für Bank- und Kapitalmarktrecht*, issue 1 (2009).

[41] See [Ministry of Justice] *Referentenentwurf*, (note 12, above), 48.

[42] See [Ministry of Justice] *Referentenentwurf*, (note 12, above), 49.

B. Striving for the reduction of representative's strategic options – the mandatory vote

More questionable may be another proposal of deregulation made in Germany.

So far, § 135 para. 10 *Aktiengesetz* forced credit institutions, if at all they offered themselves as organized shareholder representatives, to do so for all their clients. A very similar rule – now for the management – is to be found in English Company Law where management, if it asks for proxies (i.e. unless the initiative came from the shareholder), must ask all shareholders (see Fn. 31). Conversely in Germany, most authors are opposed to an analogous application of said § 135 para. 10 *Aktiengesetz* to management's solicitation of proxies.[43] Thus in Germany, there is no equal treatment or level playing field between these two forms of organized shareholder representation. The rationale behind the rules in the United Kingdom and in Germany is similar: the organized shareholder representative should not be able to exclude those shareholders in fact who are likely to be opposed to the proposals made by the representative.[44] As there is an offer to act as a proxy already, the burden of this duty is low. In Germany it is even further reduced by the fact that the duty is owed only to other clients – not all shareholders – and only if the credit institution has an establishment at the place where the general assembly takes place. Thus, additional burden is in fact avoided. Under these circumstances, the gains from deregulation would seem to be minimal and the policy considerations in favour of equal treatment of shareholders and the trend in Europe go into the opposite direction.

IV. Conclusions

With the transposition of the EC Shareholder Voting Directive, Europe not only develops some basic rules for a level playing field in the core area of organized shareholder representation, namely: (i) any outright exclusion of one or the other type of organized shareholder representation is prohibited (open competition between the different forms); (ii) the grounds on which regulation or restrictions for such organized

---

[43] U. Hüffer, *Aktiengesetz*, (2008), § 135 AktG para. 32; G. Spindler, in K. Schmidt and M. Lutter (eds.), *Aktiengesetz*, (2007), § 135 para. 45; W. Zöllner, in *Kölner Kommentar Aktiengesetz*, (1979), § 135 para. 103.

[44] Explanation to the *Aktiengesetz* 1965, Regierungsbegründung Kropff, 200; U. Hüffer, *Aktiengesetz*, (2008), § 135 AktG para. 32; G. Spindler, in K. Schmidt and M. Lutter (eds.), *Aktiengesetz*, (2007), § 135 para. 44.

representation may be based are substantially reduced; (iii) there is a clear priority rule for specific instructions made by shareholders. With the transposition of the EC Shareholder Voting Directive, however, Europe also seems to enter into a new phase of competition between different designs of organized shareholder representation. Germany has made highly interesting reform proposals for its deposit bank voting scheme which deserve discussion in their underlying rationale. They are an original input to a debate which follows Eddy Wymeersch's *monitum*: 'do not forget shareholder voting rights'.

11

In search of a middle ground between the perceived excesses of US-style class actions and the generally ineffective collective action procedures in Europe

DOUGLAS W. HAWES[1]

I. Introduction

There is a general recognition in Europe that the existing methods of compensating the victims of consumer fraud, anti-competitive behaviour, fraud on investors and other actions with multiple victims are inadequate. Some look longingly at the results obtained in the US class action system but in Europe most people recoil at what are viewed as its excesses.

As the limited survey in Section IV in this chapter shows, two countries in Europe have new class action laws and several others have been working around the edges of the apparent bars to class actions, both legal and cultural, in their countries to provide some effective means for large groups of claimants to obtain damage relief. Most European countries and the European Union itself allow collective or representative actions for injunctions. Even the US role of lawyer's financing class actions on a contingent fee basis is being filled in a limited way by third-party funders (albeit to date mostly in normal commercial litigation). The question remains whether these various substitutes for US class actions ('class actions lite') will provide an adequate and efficient basis for compensating large numbers of claimants without impairing procedural fairness or otherwise suffering any of the maladies associated with the US system.

Class actions have existed for a long time in the United States but were given a significant boost in 1938 when the Federal Rules of Civil

[1] The author wishes to acknowledge the help of the following: Damian Cleary, Alain Hirsch, Thomas Schmuck, George Williams and my wife, Marie-Claude Robert Hawes. However, the views expressed in this article are solely those of the author.

Procedure were amended to codify the process. US class actions have been brought primarily in securities, product liability and anti-trust actions, but are generally applicable. In the securities field, the principal focus of this essay, in 2007 there were 175 securities class actions filed – somewhat below the average of the last ten years.[2] Since 2005 there have been seven settlements of such actions for over $500 million each topped by Enron at over $7 billion.

In brief, the US class action procedures are as follows. First, an action is filed on behalf of one or more named plaintiffs. The plaintiffs' representative then must prove the class satisfies Rule 23 (see discussion of the requisites in the *Vivendi* case in Section III). After a class is certified, notice must be given to the class by direct mail and/or advertising. A class member can then 'opt out' of the class either because the member wants to bring a separate action or is not interested. Those not opting out are foreclosed from bringing their own case and are bound by the outcome of the class action whether by judgment or settlement.

Because US law permits contingent fees, most class action cases are initiated by experienced plaintiffs' counsel who underwrite all the expenses of the litigation in exchange for a percentage of the recovery which tends to be around one-quarter or one-third but can be higher and must be approved by the court at the end of the process.[3] Why are there so many US class actions? First, it has proven to be a lucrative business for plaintiffs' counsel. Second, there is a well-recognized and organized class action process including advertising for claimants. Third, there is a possibility of punitive damages which while rarely applied can influence settlements. Fourth, there is no loser pays rule as in England and other European countries so plaintiffs risk nothing and their counsel only their own expenses and time (which of course can be considerable in a protracted case). Fifth, jury trial is available, which, as a kind of wild card, presents defendants with a serious risk of losing even where they have a strong defence; such risk adds to the pressure to settle. Sixth, the fraud-on-the-market theory allows a presumption that investors relied on corporate misrepresentations even if not specifically aware of them. Seventh, derivative suits allow shareholders to sue on behalf of the corporation, albeit the recovery goes to the company but plaintiffs' counsel receives a fee. Eighth, the Securities and Exchange Commission is active in investigating and taking action against securities violations

[2] Stanford Law School Securities Class Actions, http://securities.stanford.edu/
[3] See note 6.

thus paving the way for civil suits.[4] Ninth, there are extensive discovery obligations on defendants.

The principal perceived excesses of the US class action are: (1) the contingent fee aspect which encourages lawyers to stir up litigation especially given the absence of a regime of loser pays the fees and expenses of the other side; (2) the risks associated with jury trials and the possibility, however remote, of punitive damage actions; and (3) the methods by which some counsel have obtained the clients to bring the case (resulting in at least one prominent criminal indictment brought against plaintiffs' lawyers for giving kick-backs to obtain lead clients)[5] and the bringing of frivolous class actions to obtain settlements (a practice considerably reduced since the passage of the Private Securities Litigation Reform Act of 1998 (PSLRA).[6] One of the failures of the US class actions system in securities cases that is not enough talked about in my opinion is the fact that the forms sent to potential claimants are extremely burdensome so that an individual investor with little or no idea of how much he or she might be entitled to, just dumps the forms in the wastebasket.

Using two US class actions involving European defendants, Shell and Vivendi, as a jumping-off place, this paper first examines the Shell settlement with its non-US shareholders under a relatively new Netherlands Settlement Act (Section II), and then the US District Court's analysis in *Vivendi* that led it to conclude that certain European countries inhospitable to opt-out procedures would not enforce a US court's judgment in an opt-out class action (Section III). Finally, in Section IV, I provide a brief overview of some recent developments in Europe and discuss middle

---

[4] Indeed in this case, Shell had agreed to pay the SEC $120 million for securities law violations and the UK Financial Services Authority £47 million for market abuse.

[5] The leading US class action securities law firm, Milberg Weiss Bershad & Shulman and two of its partners were indicted on 18 May 2006, and charged with making more than $11 million of secret payments to three individuals who served as plaintiffs in more than 150 lawsuits. Bershad and Shulman subsequently pleaded guilty and in February 2008 William Lerach, a former partner of the firm was convicted and sentence to two years in jail for his role in the scandal. On 20 March 2008, Melvyn Weiss himself pleaded guilty.

[6] Under the PSLRA, the court not only selects the lead plaintiff and thereby its counsel (mostly on the basis of the financial interest of the plaintiff) it also scrutinizes the fees in relation to reasonable hours spent and a reasonable hourly basis times some multiple (generally around 2.5 to 3.0 times but depending also on the amount of the recovery for the class – so-called lodestone test). Before the 1998 Act, there was a race to the courthouse with the winner being designated lead counsel, which explains why Milberg Weiss needed a stable of ready plaintiffs each of whom owned a few shares in many public corporations.

grounds between the perceived excesses of the US class action system and the generally ineffective collective action procedures in Europe.

As shown by my wife's companion essay in the next chapter, 'Some modest proposals to provide viable damage remedies for French investors', there also may be other interim solutions available. In her example of France, she advocates remedies for investors by: (1) utilizing the existing injunctive powers of the French *Autorite des Marches Financiers* (AMF) to order restitution to investors in exchange for not sanctioning the violators; or (2) after additional legislation, empowering the AMF through its Mediator function to determine and require restitution to investors after the AMF Commission on Sanctions has condemned persons subject to the AMF's jurisdiction.

II. The Shell Settlement

In January, 2004 and again in March, Royal Dutch Shell announced drastically revised estimates of its proven oil reserves.[7] By September 2004, domestic and foreign shareholders had filed a class action in the US.[8] In December 2004 Shell moved to dismiss the claims asserted by the non-US purchasers for lack of subject matter jurisdiction. In April 2007, Shell reached a several hundred million dollar settlement with a substantial group of European shareholders under a new Netherlands law.[9] The settlement was conditioned on the foreign shareholders being denied jurisdiction in the US case. That occurred in November 2007 in a decision by the US District Court in New Jersey.[10]

I will use the *Shell* case to illustrate: (1) the US law relative to the access of such foreign plaintiffs to the US courts; and (2) the operation of this unusual new Netherlands law that permits settlements to bind parties who do not opt out, such as shareholders, but does not permit claims for damages. In part III, I will utilize the *Vivendi* case[11] to illustrate how, when access is granted in the US, the court must still determine if shareholders from particular countries should be excluded where the opt-out provisions of US law are not likely to be enforced.

---

[7] See press releases by Royal Dutch Shell dated 9 January 2004 and 18 March 2004.
[8] US D.Ct. Dist. of New Jersey, Civ. No. 04–374 (JAP) (Consolidated Cases).
[9] Wet Collectieve Afwikkeling Massaschade, BW Art. 907–10 (the Civil Code of the Netherlands) and 14 Rv Art. 1013–18 (the Code of Civil Procedure of the Netherlands).
[10] In re Royal Dutch Shell Transport Securities Litigation (Royal Dutch II) 2007 US Dist. LEXIS 84434 (D.N.J. 13 November 2007).
[11] In re Vivendi Universal, SA Securities Litigation, Case 02 Civ. 5571, 23 March 2007.

A. Jurisdiction of US Courts in securities class actions over non-US plaintiffs

As noted above, there is a general feeling in Europe among both enterprises and shareholders, especially institutional ones, that the US class action system is excessive. Therefore, some European institutional investors are reluctant participants in class action suits in the US, and some would prefer, as happened in the *Shell* case, to find a European mechanism for just compensation for any securities fraud. Indeed, the European investors who participated in the Netherlands settlement opted out of the US class action. At the same time, as illustrated by the *Shell* decision of the District Court denying jurisdiction, the US courts may be narrowing the gate through which foreign plaintiffs must pass. That gate was also narrowed for foreign and US investors alike by the decision of the Supreme Court on 15 January 2008, in the *Stoneridge* case.[12] The Supreme Court held that a securities fraud lawsuit against suppliers and customers of Charter Communications, Inc., who allegedly agreed to arrangements that allowed Charter to mislead its auditors and issue a false financial statement affecting its stock price, was not tenable because the investor plaintiffs did not rely on statements or representations by such secondary actors.[13]

I now turn to the law on subject matter jurisdiction as found by the New Jersey District Court in *Shell*. After Shell petitioned the District Court to deny jurisdiction over the non-US purchasers of Shell securities, the Court appointed a retired judge as a special master to determine if the Court had jurisdiction. He issued his report in September 2007 suggesting the Court did not have subject matter jurisdiction over these claims. The District Court thereafter adopted his report and dismissed those claims.

The Securities Exchange Act of 1934 (the '34 Act) does not in any way limit the availability of its remedies for foreign purchasers. However, the courts have applied a standard test of such availability in which they seek to determine whether it was the intent of Congress to utilize the 'precious resources of the United States courts to be devoted to

---

[12] *Stoneridge Investment Partners, LLC* v. *Scientific-Atlanta, Inc.*, No. 06–43, 2008 WL 123801 (U.S. 15 January 2008) ('Stoneridge').

[13] See also, *Regents of the Univ. of California* v. *Credit Swiss First Boston (USA), Inc.*, No. 06–1341, *cert. denied* (US 22 January 2008) ('Enron') where the timing of the denial of certiorari after the decision in the *Stoneridge* case impliedly rejected the *Enron* plaintiffs' contention that the ruling in *Stoneridge* did not extend to financial professionals like banks.

such transactions'.[14] Although two tests have emerged for determining whether a federal court has subject matter jurisdiction over a foreign plaintiff's claim under the antifraud provisions of the securities laws, the 'conduct test' and the 'effects' test, in this case the conduct test was found to be controlling. The conduct test asks whether the 'defendant's conduct in the United States was more than merely preparatory to the fraud, and particular acts or culpable failures to act within the United States directly caused losses to foreign investors abroad'.[15] The effects test 'asks whether conduct outside the United States has had a substantial effect on American investors or securities markets'.[16] Since these non-US plaintiffs purchased outside the US there was no effect on American investors or securities markets so the effects test was not applicable.

The conduct test requires detailed attention to the facts. In the *Shell* case, the motion to dismiss for lack of subject matter jurisdiction was denied at the pleading stage of the proceeding,[17] but after extensive depositions and document production, the Special Master was able to determine that, although he had considered 'a multitude of boxes overflowing with transcripts and other exhibits . . . [he could not conclude that the plaintiffs had] satisfied the "conduct test" under the operative analysis'.[18] It is the plaintiff that bears the burden of proof. The primary areas cited by plaintiffs to support jurisdiction were: (1) Shell's investor relations activities in the US; (2) the use of a US-based Shell service organization in the estimation and calculation of proved reserves; and (3) services performed by another US-based Shell service organization which permitted Shell operating units either to maintain proved reserves bookings or to book additional proved reserves.

Although a limited amount of activity in those three areas was found, the Court determined that: (a) Shell did not engage in any fraud-related activity targeted at non-US purchasers within the US by virtue of its investor relations activities; and (b) that the activities of Shell's US-based service organizations were not related to either reporting of proved reserves or maintaining the reserves. In sum, the District Court found that plaintiffs had not shown that 'Shell engaged in conduct that amounted to more than mere preparatory acts in furtherance

[14] *Alfadda* v. *Fenn*, 935 F.2d 475, 478 (2d Cir. 1991), *cert. denied*, 502 US 1005 (1991).
[15] *Ibid.*
[16] *Robinson* v. *TCI/US West Commc'n*, 117 f.3d 900, 905 (5th Cir. 1997).
[17] Royal Dutch Shell I, 380 F. Supp. 2d at 548. (2005).
[18] Special Master's Report, 3.

of the alleged fraud as to the Non-U.S. Purchasers'.[19] Put another way, the Court held that there was insufficient evidence to show that Shell's 'conduct occurring within the borders of this nation was essential to the plan to defraud [the Non-U.S. Purchasers]'.[20]

Note that nothing in the conduct test relates to whether a finding of no jurisdiction would leave the foreign plaintiffs without a remedy. However, the District Court immediately followed its finding of 'no jurisdiction' with the observation below:

> The Court also emphasizes that this holding does not leave the Non-U.S. Purchasers without an alternative recourse to address their alleged injuries. Significantly, the Non-U.S. Purchasers can seek recovery through the [Netherlands] Settlement Agreement entered into before the Amsterdam Court of Appeals or through procedures available within their respective jurisdictions. Therefore, the result reached here does not prejudice the Non-U.S. Purchasers and ultimately serves to preserve 'the precious resources of the United States Court'. (Opinion p. 19)[21]

In short, while the Amsterdam settlement was not a requisite, the Court's finding of no jurisdiction under the conduct test, appeared to have had some influence on that determination. Accordingly, I now turn to a discussion of the Netherlands Settlement Agreement.

B. The Netherlands Settlement Agreement

The Netherlands Act on Collective Settlement of Mass Damages[22] had an unusual origin. Netherlands pharmaceutical manufacturers were faced with a flood of individual suits by victims and their families related to injuries suffered from using a synthetic hormone DES. In many cases it was not clear which pharmaceutical company's product was used by a person.[23] The manufacturers and their insurers went to the legislature

---

[19] Royal Dutch Shell Transport Securities Litigation (Royal Dutch II) 2007 US Dist. LEXIS 84434 (D.N.J. 13 November 2007), 19.

[20] Citing *Sec. and Exch. Comm'n v. Kasser*, 548, F.2d 109, at 115 (3d Cir.), *cert. denied*, *Churchill Forest Indus. Ltd v. Sec and Exch. Comm'n*, 431 U.S. 938 (1977).

[21] Citing *Alfadda*, (note 14, above), 935 F.2d, 478.

[22] Wet van 23 juni 2005 tot wijziging van het Burgerlijk Wetboek en het Wetboek van Burgerlijke Rechtsvordering teneinde collectieve afwikkeling van massaschades te vergemakkelijken (Wet Collectieve Afwikkeling Massaschade).

[23] The original claim was made by six daughters whose pregnant mothers had used DES. A registry was established and 18,000 people signed up out of a possible estimated 440,000 potentially affected. Interestingly, 24,700 people opted out of the settlement although it was not clear how many of them intended to pursue individual actions.

and asked for an act that would permit them to settle all the suits at the same time. After the legislature obliged, and seven years of negotiation, they settled for €38 million which was approved, as required, by the Amsterdam Court of Appeals in June 2006. Since the law was not restricted to the specific DES case, it was then used to settle a case involving retail sales of securities by Dexia Bank. That opt-out settlement was for €400 million and was approved in January 2007. The *Shell* settlement was filed in April 2007. It has not yet been approved by the Amsterdam Court of Appeals as required by the Act because it was conditioned on the US Court denying jurisdiction, which only occurred in November.

The *Shell* settlement was for $352 million plus an agreement with the US Securities and Exchange Commission to distribute $96 million of its $120 million fine to the non-US purchasers. When you add in the legal fees of $47 million agreed to in the settlement the total is about $500 million. The Netherlands Act binds all members of the class (i.e. non-US purchasers) unless they opt out of the settlement. If the deal is approved by the Netherlands court later this year as expected, it is likely to be enforceable throughout the European Union under its regulations relating to enforcement of judgments.[24] Moreover, it will establish an important precedent that is quite likely to attract other large European class action settlements because of the certainty of recovery of some damages in a relatively short time versus an uncertain wait in the US action and the cost and uncertainty of litigation in Europe.[25]

The flaw in the Netherlands Act from a plaintiff's point of view is that it only allows for settlements, not class actions for damages. Presumably, in the negotiations for such settlements, that factor will weigh in the equation. However, on the other side of the coin, if the US becomes ever more hostile to such non-US plaintiffs (and generally less open to securities law actions), the incentive for plaintiffs to settle in Europe will certainly increase. Equally, for defendants if collective actions become more prevalent, they will be more open to settlement especially if otherwise they might have to defend actions in several countries.

---

[24] See Council Regulation on jurisdiction and recognition and enforcement of judgments in civil and commercial matters EC No 44/2001 [2001] OJ L12/1.

[25] In fact in terms of the US Shell litigation for US plaintiffs, Shell announced on 6 March 2008, that it had reached an agreement in principle to settle that action for $79.9 million plus $2.95 million in interest. The deal is subject to the approval of the District Court of New Jersey. An additional $35 million would be paid collectively to the participants in the US class action and the Dutch settlement. See Reuters, 6 March 2008.

III. The Vivendi Case

In addition to the *Shell* decision of the District Court, there are other signs of a narrowing of the door for such plaintiffs to participate in US class actions under the securities laws. Two important decisions of the US District Court for the Southern District of New York in the *Vivendi* class action litigation provide indications, albeit in opposite directions, for non-US purchasers. In 2003 the *Vivendi* Court found that despite the fact that most of the Vivendi shares were traded on European exchanges and Vivendi was not a reporting company under the '34 Act (its securities were traded in ADR form on the NYSE), its conduct in the US[26] affected the American market for their shares which in turn was a substantial factor in the decisions of foreign investors to purchase abroad. Accordingly, non-US purchasers were entitled to bring US securities law claims.[27]

In 2007, in the same litigation, the *Vivendi* court, having decided it had subject matter jurisdiction (contrary to the finding in *Shell*), had to determine whether the claims of the non-US purchasers could proceed as part of the class action. The answer to that question was governed by Sections 23(a) and 23(b) of the Federal Rules of Civil Procedure which also had to be satisfied as to the US part of the class generally. The Court first found that the tests under Section 23(a) were satisfied. That is: numerosity of plaintiffs, commonality of questions of law or fact, typicality of claims and the adequacy of the class representatives. Under Section 23(b) the Court also was satisfied as to the predominance of common issues and generally as to the superiority of class action treatment over other forms. However, it found that the inclusion of non-US purchasers raised a question under the superiority criterion, namely whether foreign jurisdictions would preclude shareholders in such jurisdictions who had not opted out of the US action from pursuing their claims.[28] The Court determined that the standard for exclusion was 'the closer the likelihood of non-recognition is to being a "near certainty", the more appropriate it is for the court to deny certification of foreign claimants'.[29]

---

[26] Including statements made to analysts and investors in New York and the key fact that the CEO and CFO moved to the US allegedly to better direct operations and to correct misleading perceptions on Wall Street.

[27] In re Vivendi Universal, S.A. Securities Litigation, 381 f.Supp.2d 158 (S.D.N.Y.2003).

[28] In re Vivendi Universal, S.A. Securities Litigation 2007 WL. 861147 (S.D.N.Y. 22 March 2007) and 2007 WL 1490466, FN (S.D.N.Y. 21 May 2007).

[29] In re Vivendi Universal, S.A. Securities Litigation, 2007 WL 1490466 at 18 (S.D.N.Y., 21 May 2007).

After consideration of competing affidavits by the parties concerning the foreign law on that subject for France, England, the Netherlands, Germany and Austria, the Court concluded that Germany and Austria were not sufficiently certain to enforce such a US judgment for damages although the other countries would. Therefore it excluded investors from those two countries from the class in fairness to the defendant.

First, I summarize the *Vivendi* court's finding of likely enforceability in France, England and the Netherlands.

A. *France*

Given that Vivendi was based in France and the majority of the non-US shareholders were French, the Court devoted most of its attention to the law of that country. The *Vivendi* court's finding as to France illustrates how a US court is likely to approach the issue. The main points the *Vivendi* court made in deciding that French courts would give preclusive effect to a US class action judgment were:

1. While there is no treaty between the US and France for the enforcement of judgments and there has been no decision in France on any foreign class action judgment, there are French decisions enforcing foreign judgments generally (p. 38).
2. Before a foreign judgment can be enforced in France it must be subject to an *Exequatur* procedure, whereby, if recognized, the foreign judgment is incorporated in the *Exequatur* and then enforced.
3. The leading case on the grant of *Exequatur* is the *Munzer* case decided by France's highest court, the *Cour de cassation*.[30] Pursuant to that case, the four conditions that must be met are: (1) the foreign court must have proper jurisdiction; (2) the foreign court must have applied the appropriate law; (3) the decision must not contravene public policy; and (4) the decision must not be a result of *fraude a la loi* (evasion of the law) or forum shopping.
4. With respect to the jurisdictional prong, among other things, the defendants' experts pointed out that in 2002 an association of minority shareholders ('ADAM') petitioned the Paris Commercial Court to investigate the claimed fraudulent actions of Vivendi. That court found the claims were 'ill-founded' and dismissed them. Subsequently, the defendants said, the head of ADAM [Mme. Colette Neuville] stated

---

[30] In re Munzer, 7 January 1964, *Bull. Civ.* 1, °15.

that the dismissal caused her to introduce a class action in the US on behalf of ADAM's shareholders. Defendants argued that these events showed an attempt to evade French law. However, the *Vivendi* court ruled that because the French substantive law on securities fraud was similar to that of the US the jurisdictional prong was satisfied.

5. As to the appropriate law prong, the Court concluded that while there were procedural differences between French and American law, that aspect should be considered under the public policy prong. As to the rest, the Court held that the substantive similarities were sufficient under the doctrine of equivalence to satisfy the appropriate law prong.

6. The *Vivendi* court next addressed the public policy issue. It conceded that the fact that opt-out class actions are not currently permitted in France was some indication that such actions were contrary to French public policy. But it said the issue is whether such actions infringe the principles of universal justice. The defendants' experts argued that a number of procedural rules in France gave very clear rights to parties that required their participation individually (the 'right to be heard'). Plaintiffs' experts countered that France already authorized group actions by unions on behalf of employees. They also pointed out that shareholder associations have the right to sue companies and directors and to solicit proxies from individual shareholders (using mail and public notice) to act on their behalf.[31]

The Court said that these types of collective actions 'do not evince a fundamental hostility to the concept of collective actions'.[32] Accordingly, the Court concluded that an opt-out class judgment would not offend French concepts of international public policy. The Court went on to say that while such class actions are currently not permitted, 'it is equally clear the ground is shifting quickly'. The Court referred to then President Chirac's creation of a commission in April 2005 to study the introduction of a sort of 'class action' for relationships with consumers. Defendants pointed out that the majority of the commission members had viewed the opt-out class action as contrary to French law although

---

[31] In fact, during the 1990s, provisions for collective actions were enacted or amended for consumers (Art. L. 422–1 of the Consumer Code), for victims of environment violations (Environmental Code L.142–3) and for investors (Financial and Monetary Code L.452–2). However, in the case of investor associations there has been almost no activity. ADAM itself is not under that regime but under the general association law of 1901.

[32] *Vivendi*, 49.

some favoured it. The Court concluded that the views of the President and the debate on the subject 'is strong evidence that the class action model is not so contrary to public policy that its use would likely be deemed an infringement of "principles of universal justice" or contrary to "international public policy"'.[33]

The issue of the enforceability in France of a US judgment in a securities class action is probably academic in the *Vivendi* case since Vivendi has substantial assets in the US against which to satisfy any claim for damages. The situation that would be likely to present that issue would be where the defendant has insufficient assets in the US but has such assets in France.

B. *England*

As there is no convention or statute on the *res judicata* effect of a US class action judgment in England, the issue must be addressed under the common law. The Court concluded that 'English courts are more likely to find US courts are competent to adjudicate with finality the claims of absent class members and therefore would recognize a judgment or settlement in this action.'[34] That determination was based largely on the fact that English representative actions will bind those on whose behalf a claim is brought including persons who are not parties to the claim with the court's permission.[35]

C. *Netherlands*

Based on an unopposed affidavit of Professor Smit that Netherlands courts would give binding effect to a judgment in or settlement of a US class action, the *Vivendi* court included Netherlands investors in the class. As a further basis for that determination, the Court referred to recently enacted class action legislation 'in other contexts', undoubtedly a reference to the Netherlands Act on Collective Settlement of Mass Damages discussed above in relation to the *Shell* case.

Now I turn to those countries whose plaintiffs the *Vivendi* court excluded from the class because of doubts about enforceability of its judgment.

---

[33]   *Vivendi*, 51.   [34]   *Vivendi*, p. 55.
[35]   Rule 19.6 of the 1998 Civil Procedure Rules and Section 4(b).

D. Germany

The first hurdle for the enforcement of a US opt-out class action judgment in Germany would be Article 103 of the German Constitution, which establishes the right of a citizen to be heard and to participate in a legal proceeding. Based on the views of the parties' experts the Court concluded that there are reasonable means available to give actual notice of opt-out rights to class members, but that a US judgment would not be enforced against a class member who did not receive actual notice. The Court went on to note that, unlike France and England, Germany does not have collective actions. Even the recent Capital Markets Model Case Act does not provide for collective actions.[36] Rather, where there are multiple plaintiffs in a securities law matter, a test case can be used whose outcome will be binding on the other individual shareholder actions. Non-party shareholders, however, are not bound by the results. Thus the Court determined that 'the formalities of German law may well preclude the recognition of a judgment in the instant case'.[37]

E. Austria

Austrian law requires formal reciprocity between the foreign state and the Republic of Austria as a condition of recognition of a foreign judgment. No such treaty exists with the US, so the Court concluded that Austrian investors should be excluded from the class.[38]

The *Vivendi* court's voyage into foreign law produced determinative distinctions as to the enforceability of a US opt-out class action judgment in the five countries examined. However, the differences relied on between, for example France (would enforce) and Germany (would not), seemed to be neither apparent nor real. Both countries respect almost universally the 'right to be heard', which is enshrined in the European Convention for the Protection of Human Rights and Fundamental Freedom (ECHR) to which Germany and France are parties. Undoubtedly the fact that Vivendi was a French-based entity and the majority of its non-US shareholders were French, exerted pressure to

---

[36] KapMuG (16 August 2008). The Act was adopted in response to the fact that in 2003, some 15,000 shareholders of Deutsche Telecom flooded a court in Frankfurt with 2,500 suits brought by 700 attorneys alleging false statements related to its real estate in a share offering; the stock had fallen over 80%.

[37] *Vivendi*, 58.   [38] *Vivendi*, 58.

include its plaintiffs in the class. As noted in part IV, the validity of that holding has been questioned by a French academic specialist who was not one of those whose affidavits were proffered by a party.

IV. Selected collective action developments in Europe

It is perhaps useful to offer a few general observations about collective actions before discussing specific developments by country:

1. The distinction between collective actions and class actions is that the former are opt-in and the latter are opt-out thus creating a class.
2. The concept of collective actions has existed for varying periods of time in many European countries. However, (a) such collective actions almost universally are limited, often to particular subject matter such as consumer fraud or unfair competition, (b) either the law itself or the government determines what organizations are authorized to bring such actions, and (c) such actions are only for injunctive relief and not damages.
3. Such collective actions for injunctive relief are of limited use and are regarded as a neither very important supplement to nor a substitute for government enforcement of the law.
4. In some situations and with increasing frequency, there has been pressure from organizations and academics to broaden the scope of collective actions to include claims for damages since government enforcement generally does not result in restitution to those injured.
5. Almost universally, those seeking to broaden the scope of collective actions also make plain their desire to avoid the perceived excesses of the US-style class action system.
6. Two European countries, Italy and Denmark have attacked the matter head on effective this year: they have enacted class action laws. What remains to be seen is if a real system for pursuing such actions will evolve especially in the absence of the contingent fee incentive which is the engine of the US system.

Some of the more recent variations short of class action laws devised to overcome the existing obstacles to collective actions include: (1) the German model case concept currently being employed in actions against Deutsche Telecom; (2) the Netherlands collective settlement law used in Shell referred to above; (3) the ad hoc attempt by a Belgium company, CDC, to pursue in Germany the claims of twenty-nine cement buyers who have assigned their claims to them; and (4) the launch of a fund in the UK by Allianz, the German insurance company, to finance certain kinds of actions. These and other developments are discussed below.

A. Denmark's new class action law

The Danish law on class actions which went into effect on 1 January 2008, along with the new Italian law referred to next, goes a long way towards meeting the need for redress of multiple victims without any of the perceived disadvantages of the US system. Basically the law provides for a full opt-out class action where a public authority such as the Consumer Ombudsman brings the claim and an opt-in collective action by all other authorized representatives of the claimants.[39]

Thus the Ombudsman 'can sue a business on behalf of hundreds or even thousands of consumers . . . where[by] the consumer is [a] member of the group unless he or she chooses to opt our of the claim', provided the court has allowed it.[40] The court's decision in a class action has a binding effect (i.e. is *res judicata*) on the class members covered by the action, that is, all who opt in or who fail to opt out in an action where the opt-out procedure is authorized. Class actions can be brought in almost any area of the law including securities, torts, consumer fraud and anti-competitive behaviour but not family law.

The manner in which the new Act deals with the loser pays risk is instructive: unless a member of a class action group has insurance or is entitled to legal aid, the court can decide that participation is conditioned upon each member providing security for costs. However, such security will be the maximum cost that can be assessed to such member (plus any damages received if there is a partial victory). Unlike England where legal fees of a winning defendant may represent a substantial risk to plaintiffs, the costs assessed in many Continental countries such as France tend to be relatively low and more like court costs in the US.

As to who will take on such class actions in Denmark, Professor Werlauff notes that one legal chain of over seventy firms as well as one of the biggest firms have registered domain names looking to be involved in these new class actions.[41]

---

[39] See, 'Class Actions in Denmark – From 2008', by Professor Erik Werlauff, Aalborg University, Stanford/Oxford Conference on 'The Globalization of Class Actions' (13–14 December 2007, 'Stanford Conference').

[40] *Ibid.*, 3.   [41] *Ibid.*, 7–8.

B. Italy's new class action law

In Italy, a new law goes into effect on 1 July 2008 allowing for collective actions for damages by consumer organizations.[42] A class action can be brought by an accredited association (there are currently sixteen) against any commercial, financial or insurance enterprise for damages arising from (1) standard form contracts, (2) tort liability, (3) unfair trade practices and (4) anticompetitive practices affecting a group of consumers.

To participate, consumers must opt in by writing to the association and the court decision will only be binding on those who do so. Since a consumer can opt in until the last hearing on appeal, there is a possibility consumers will wait to the last minute creating a potential substantial increase in the damages.

The court in such class actions does not award a specific amount of damages but it sets out the criteria for determining the amount to be awarded. The defendant has sixty days from the court's decision to make an offer. If either it does not make an offer or the consumers do not accept the offer, it will go to binding arbitration. One consumer organization, Adusbef, has already announced it plans to file an action against banks for using compound instead of simple interest on loans which Adusbef claims violates Italian law.[43]

C. France

In 2006, bills were introduced in the legislature for a system of collective actions for consumers. The legislation was abandoned at the end of 2007 in the light of the coming presidential and legislative elections. In July 2007 after he was elected President, M. Sarkozy instructed his Minister of Economy, Finance and Employment Mme. Lagarde and the Minister for Consumer Affairs and Tourism M. Luc Chatel (the author of one of the 2006 bills) to prepare legislation that would permit collective actions based somewhat on the American model but denominated 'class actions à la Francaise'. He did warn against class actions that could lead to the bankruptcy of an enterprise (perhaps like the asbestos cases in the US).

---

[42] Amendment to Italy's Consumers Code §140bis enacted 21 December 2007. There is a story that the law was passed in the Senate only because one of its opponents pushed the wrong button and voted for it – providing the crucial margin. See, Dewey and LeBoeuf, L.L.P. Client Alert 'Class action in Italy' (4 February 2008) citing 'Class Action *per un voto*', in *Il Sole 24 Ore*, 16 November 2007, 3.

[43] Reuters, 9 January 2008.

President Sarkozy, having asked M. Jacques Attali, a former key adviser of the late President Mitterrand, to lead a study of ways to grow the French economy, received his Report on 23 January 2008. Recommendation 191 was to introduce collective actions for consumers brought by their associations, provided that only those consumers opt-ing-in would be included. The Report considered that the introduction of such actions would contribute to the confidence of consumers while at the same time avoiding moving to an American class action system. On 23 January 2008, President Sarkozy seemed to back off somewhat from such a class action proposal saying that he wanted more reflection on the subject 'because I do not want to have all the inconveniences of American society without all the advantages. I see well the intent but I see it only for certain enterprises.'[44]

In a comprehensive analysis of the French law on class actions for the Stanford Conference,[45] Professor Veronique Magnier, commented on the *Vivendi* decision holding that French courts would enforce a US opt-out judgment. She did not specifically dispute the *Vivendi* court's determination that the French concept that the identity of the plaintiff must be known[46] was really for the protection of defendants and should not apply in a securities fraud case.

However, she did question whether the opt-out procedure would be sustained in view of the 'right to be heard' guarantee under French law[47] especially given the 1989 decision of the *Conseil constitutionnel*.[48] There, the *Conseil* ruled in a decision regarding labour unions that can bring actions on behalf of employees, that each employee must be given 'the opportunity to give his assent with full knowledge of the facts and that he remain free to personally conduct the pursuit of his interest'. Professor Magnier concluded that 'the freedom of bringing or not bringing one's own action lies at the heart of this decision . . . [and] most academics have interpreted this decision as condemning any opt-out system'.[49]

An example of the difficulty in France of obtaining damages for injured consumers is the recent mobile phone case. The Competition Commission found a conspiracy to allocate market share among three

---

[44] www.20Minutes.fr, 23 January 2008. Remarks made in the course of commenting on the Report of the Attali Commission.
[45] Stanford Conference on 'The Globalization of Class Actions (2007) ('Magnier Report').
[46] Ibid., *Nul ne plaide par procureur.*
[47] Ibid., *Principe du contradictoire.*
[48] Dec. Cons. Const. No 89–57, 25 July 1989.
[49] Magnier Report, (note 45, above), 12–13.

mobile telephone operators who were fined substantial amounts, but no provision was made by the Commission for the victims. UFC-QUE CHOISIR, a consumer group, wanted to recover damages for consumers. It set up a website where consumers could calculate their damages and sign up for the action. After investing €500,000, less than 1% of those affected signed up.

D. Germany

While the *Vivendi* Court probably correctly excluded German plaintiffs because of the constitutional right of a citizen to be heard in court, contrary to the Court's summary, Germany does have collective actions, in one example going back to the nineteenth century.[50] In general, however, suits by consumer groups and other authorized interest groups cannot seek monetary relief but only injunctive action. There are some minor exceptions where individual consumers can assign their claims for monetary relief to an association. Under another statute, profits from unfair competition violations can be claimed from the perpetrators by certain organizations on behalf of consumers, but the recovery goes to the state not to those injured.[51] In the *CDC* case mentioned above, a lower court has upheld the representation of the claimants by the assignee, but there remain questions under the Legal Advice Act that limits the provision of legal advice to qualified persons or institutions which may be a stumbling block.[52] Another special case is where after a squeeze out, one or more minority shareholders file a challenge via a valuation proceeding (*Spruchverfahren*). The decision of the court is binding on all shareholders irrespective of whether they join the proceedings.[53]

It should also be noted that there are several disadvantages to the Capital Markets Model Case Act. The first is the time it takes for the

---

[50] Unfair Competition Act, UWG §3.
[51] Unfair Competition Act §10.
[52] See, Stanford Conference paper of Dr. Dietmar Baetge of the Max Planck Institute for Corporate and International Private Law, 11.
[53] As in other European countries, where a resolution put to shareholders is contested and a court voids the resolution, all shareholders are affected. In the case of resolutions that must be filed in a commercial registry, such as for share capital increases or mergers, some abuses have arisen in Germany and elsewhere involving significant and potentially harmful delays (e.g. a Nestlé share increase was delayed for two years in Switzerland by the action of some shareholders). In Germany, some legislation has aimed to reduce similar abuses, but not with full success. Here again, the action has a certain collective aspect, albeit not a collective action for damages.

courts to select the model case and have it confirmed on appeal. The second is the fact that counsel for the model plaintiff does not receive any extra compensation albeit has a special burden because it is the model. The third is that the loser pays regime applies albeit the cost is split among all plaintiffs and not just the model case plaintiff. The fourth and possibly most problematic is the fact that once the courts rule in favour of plaintiffs in the model case, other claimants can file their cases knowing there is a kind of *res judicata* in their favour and little risk of having to pay as a loser. One of the advantages of the Model Case procedure is that the court reviews the case at the pleading stage and can shut out weak claims. That Act was expressly intended as a test of that kind of procedure. It is set to expire on 1 November 2010, although Dr. Ditmar Baetge of the Max Planck Institute for Corporate and International Private Law has predicted that it will not only be made permanent but extended more broadly to collective actions of all sorts.[54]

In 1999, Dr Baetge's Institute proposed allowing claims for compensation in most collective actions and some form of opt-out class action for securities and product liability cases. To date these proposals have not been implemented by the legislature.

In March 2007 the German Supreme Court struck down the prohibition on contingent fees as unconstitutional, holding the prohibition of such fees hindered a plaintiff from enforcing his rights. The legislature is supposed to come up with a new law by mid-2008.

E. European Union

EU directives relative to a number of consumer protections include an obligation of Member States to implement collective action measures but only for injunctive relief.[55] As to the future, the EU's paper on Consumer Strategy 2007–2013 included a consideration of collective actions for damages.[56] A Commission Study led by Professor Jules Stuyck on alternative means of consumer proceedings, found that the economic

---

[54] See, Stanford Conference paper of Dr. Dietmar Baetge of the Max Planck Institute for Corporate and International Private Law, 8.

[55] See, for example, Council Directive 93/13/EEC [1995] OJ L95/29, art. 7.1 (unfair terms in consumer contracts). The Office of Fair Trading in the UK was able to get an injunction there against a Belgium catalogue being sent to UK residents, which injunction was then enforced in Belgium. See, Council Regulation on jurisdiction and recognition and enforcement of judgments in civil and commercial matters EC No 44/2001 [2001] OJ L12/1.

[56] COM (2007) 99, 13 March 2007.

literature about cost–benefit justification for consumer collective action did not reach a consensus. The Study identified ECHR Art. 6 and Member State constitutional guarantees of the right to be heard, as obstacles to opt-out class actions.[57]

F. England

In England, two principal methods exist for collective actions: (1) procedural rules, primarily Group Litigation Orders (GLOs);[58] and (2) statutory procedures mostly regulatory in nature in the consumer area. There have been few consumer actions by the organizations authorized to do so largely because of cost considerations. One such consumer organization, 'Which?', brought its first collective action, after a price-fixing charge by the OFT against a T-shirt maker. The defendant had been fined for price fixing by the Competition Appeal Tribunal and appeals were denied – a requisite to the commencement of the consumer organization action. The 'Which?' case will be heard by the same Tribunal. If 'Which?' is successful, consumers will provide proof of purchases to the defendants. If defendants refuse to pay, claimants will have to file their own claims.[59]

In the securities field, the UK Financial Services Authority (FSA) has among its available remedies the right to petition a court to order restitution for investors for violations of securities regulations.[60]

While there is considerable opposition in England to US-style class actions, success fees are allowed in certain circumstances but limited to 100% of the base fee and up to 25% of damages awarded.[61] A big difference from the US, however, is that the loser pays the fees of the winner; in collective actions that represents a significant deterrent to joining the action. One solution to that problem is after-the-event insurance (ATE). ATE is generally sought by claimants and/or third-party funders to insure the loser pays obligation and may in fact be required in certain circumstances. ATE insurance does not cover plaintiff's' counsel

---

[57] Commission Study of Alternative Means of Consumer Proceedings, Professor Jules Stuyck et al., April 2007. See also Professor Christopher Hodges, Summary of European Union Developments, Stanford Conference ('Hodges Report').

[58] Civil Procedure Rules, Part 19 III. The GLO is a procedure for centrally managing numerous cases revolving around similar claims. It is, in effect, an opt-in mechanism of collective action.

[59] The action was brought under the Enterprise Act 2002. See, 'Which? Takes legal action on overpriced replica shirt', *The Guardian*, 9 February 2007.

[60] Financial Services & Markets Act, 2000. ss 382 & 383.

[61] Conditional Fee Agreements Regulations 2000, S I 2000/692. reg. 3 (1) (a).

fees although plaintiffs' counsel will frequently work on the basis of 'no win, no fee'.[62] While obtaining ATE insurance for a group of claimants in commercial litigation would require something more bespoke than standard, there are many providers of such insurance who pride themselves on innovative products and pricing including a number of Lloyd's syndicates.[63]

Towards the end of last year, the giant German insurer, Allianz launched a fund in London to finance litigation in exchange for a percentage of the damage proceeds. And, at least one law firm has set up a working party to consider offering funding to clients. A Clifford Chance partner commenting on the Allianz fund said that third party funding 'could give class action activity in the UK and Europe a boost [and] . . . will start to chip away at the structural differences between UK and US litigation'.[64] Third-party funding in the UK is already becoming a competitive market that has even attracted hedge funds. It should be noted that while the ancient torts of champerty and maintenance are no longer crimes, they still have some viability, despite the lack of strict enforceability.

The principal advantage of third-party funding over US contingency fee class actions initiated by lawyers would seem to be that the latter is lawyer driven and stirs up litigation, whereas the former is claimant driven. Third-party funding separates the issue of lawyers' fees from that of financing the cost of the litigation. Such separation should result in more transparent and better pricing of the two different services. An area where third-party funding has been employed both in the US and England is in insolvency proceedings. There the company liquidator seeks to recover from creditors, management and professionals such as accountants of the defunct enterprise but has limited funds for doing so.

There are currently a number of entities in England ready to offer third-party funding or brokerage services. The latter seek to find the

---

[62] Some countries such as Switzerland prohibit such fee arrangements.

[63] At the request of a third-party funder, the Supreme Court of Switzerland struck down a Zurich cantonal law in 2004 that prohibited third-party funding and lawyers from accepting such funding with the exception of normal liability insurance coverage. The court decided that the freedom to make contracts was important for people like plaintiffs and only incidentally affected the independence of the lawyers. The court cautioned, however, that lawyers should serve the interest of the client in any conflict with third-party funders. See, *L. Gmbh* v. *Kantonsrat des Kantons Zurich*, ATF 131 I 223 (December 2004). A bill (H.R. 5463) was introduced in the US Congress in February 2008 which would make plaintiffs' counsel pay for the fees of the defendant if plaintiffs lose.

[64] www.legalweek.com, 18 October 2007.

best match for a plaintiff or its counsel with a funder who either has special expertise in the type of claim or has the most attractive financial proposal or both. One of the reasons for the activity in third-party funding in England is the support for it from the OFT[65] and the Civil Justice Council.[66] In addition to Allianz, mentioned above, third-party funding has attracted the interest of private equity and hedge funds who, as might be expected have introduced sophisticated methods of financing. In one case, the claimant, a small technology firm suing a larger one for patent infringement sold a zero-coupon note to a private equity fund, Altitude Capital Partners, and agreed to provide the fund with a percentage of the recovery that would be reduced as the amount increased.[67] While a small investor in England would have no incentive to seek out third-party funding for a collective action for securities fraud, an institutional investor might.

Is third-party funding of court litigation or arbitration an important middle-ground solution of the kind Europe has been searching for? It may well be, although there is not yet enough experience with it in England, the US and Germany. In other countries like France it may well not be permissible.[68] Moreover, if there is no structure for collective actions by numbers of claimants, the availability of funding would not matter.

V. Conclusion

The search for a middle ground between the perceived excesses of the US class action system and the current generally ineffective collective action procedures in Europe has accelerated. Class action statutes in Italy and Denmark are effective this year. While they are very European versions and are yet to be tested, they offer a useful model for other countries. The Denmark law goes farthest in (1) providing an opt-out feature if brought by the Ombudsman and approved by the court, (2) that it is applicable in

---

[65] In late 2007 the OFT, in relation to competition law actions, stated: 'The OFT takes the view that third-party funding is an important potential source of funding . . . third-party funding should be encouraged.' See, 'Fighting Funds' 21 January 2008, at www. thelawyer.com.

[66] The Civil Justice Council in a 2007 white paper stated that: 'third-party funding should be recognized as an acceptable option for mainstream litigation.' *Ibid.*

[67] www.legalweek.com, 18 October 2007.

[68] See, Freshfields Bruckhaus Deringer, June 2007 Client Alert, 'Class actions and third party funding of litigation', p. 2.

most areas of the law including securities actions, and (3) that it contains a method for minimizing the loser pays risk.

Other European countries have taken more indirect paths. Germany has a model case procedure. The Netherlands has an opt-out provision, but only for class action settlements not damage actions. England has adopted procedural rules for collective actions (GLOs) but they have not seen much use. On the other hand, actions by authorized consumer organizations for damages have begun and the FSA already has the power to both sanction persons subject to its jurisdiction and order restitution to investors with the approval of a court. And, third-party funding of litigation as well as ATE insurance for the loser pays risk, have become accepted and available in at least some European countries.

In the European Union the issue of the need for some form of collective action for damages has been raised and other countries such as France are debating class actions. Meanwhile, in the securities field France could allow the AMF to affect restitution to investors as proposed in my wife's companion essay, next.

As has often happened in the field of securities law, Europe lags behind the US but sometimes finds different and more moderate solutions. European countries are unlikely to settle on a single model for collective or class actions despite the efforts of the European Union to harmonize national laws. However, as more experience is gained with the variety of approaches already being taken and others that have been proposed, Europe may develop an effective middle-ground procedure for multiparty claims while avoiding the pitfalls in the US class actions system.

12

Some modest proposals to provide viable damage remedies for French investors

MARIE-CLAUDE ROBERT HAWES[1]

This chapter describes the limits of investor damage remedies in securities law actions in France and offers two modest proposals for ameliorating them: (1) utilize the existing injunctive powers of the French securities regulator, the Autorité des Marchés Financier (AMF), to order restitution to investors in lieu of a sanction; and/or (2) obtain additional power from the legislature to allow the AMF to determine and require restitution to investors after the AMF Commission on Sanctions has sanctioned persons subject to their jurisdiction, using the AMF Mediator function to make the determination.

I. Background on existing regulation

The first element of the French system that strikes one is that it was clearly inspired and influenced by the US Securities Act of 1933 and the 1934 Securities and Exchange Act. Similarly, the AMF itself, whose predecessor, the Commission des Operations de Bourse, was created in 1967, is modelled on the US Securities and Exchange Commission (SEC). The AMF has a somewhat broader role than the SEC but with much less power especially in the early days; it not only enforces, administers and proposes new provisions of the securities law to take account of the evolution of the financial markets, it is also perhaps more directly involved in the changes in company and business law. Of course, the integrity of the markets is the main concern of the AMF, and like the SEC, its main tool is disclosure.

---

[1] Former member of the International Faculty for Capital Markets and Corporate Law; retired Mediator of the AMF and former head of the International Department thereof. I wish to acknowledge the help of Alain Hirsch and my husband Douglas Hawes. However, the views expressed are solely those of the author.

The second notable element of our system is that, under the influence of the European Union, it is relatively liberal[2] and seeks to provide freedom of action and choice for companies and investors. Investors are free to choose the best investment for themselves after receiving the fullest information and the best advice from investment professionals. Shareholders are free to elect the directors and dismiss them and vote at shareholders' meetings as well as to approve the annual accounting statements, the amount of dividends, increases in capitalization, and mergers. If investors are defrauded by executives and/or companies they are entitled to sue. That is the theory. The reality is: investors have very few means to affect any of these rights.

Thus, on the one hand shareholders receive from the AMF strong support relative to most aspects of the life of their company: disclosure requirements, corporate governance practices, auditing standards, voting procedures and so on. Most of the rules are designed to discourage misconduct by executives and companies. But when it comes to problems such as auditors who fail to completely check financial statements, misuse of assets, insider trading, misleading prospectuses or other material misstatements and any kind of abuse of the market, virtually the only means of rectification available are administrative or disciplinary sanctions by the AMF or criminal prosecution.

Now, clearly there are such sanctions. They are imposed by the Commission on Sanctions, a separate organism inside the AMF. In 2007, 28 proceedings resulted in sanctions out of 33 cases – 65 persons were sanctioned including 26 entities and 39 physical persons and 40 persons were found not culpable. Among the proceedings, 13 involved violations of the disclosure requirements, 5 insider trading violations, 1 market manipulations; the other proceedings related to investment services providers (5) and portfolio managers (4).[3] However, none of these proceedings involved financial remedies for investors. Investors are free to sue individually but it is very expensive to do so, especially to recover relatively small amounts of individual damages. Moreover, under French jurisprudence, it is practically impossible for an investor to demonstrate, as the law requires direct and different damages from that suffered by the company[4] – so it is not

---

[2] As opposed to a non-liberal system which is governed by bureaucratic rules.

[3] AMF, *Annual Report* (2007), 197–8, www.amf-france.org/documents/general/8333_1.pdf

[4] That is, plaintiffs must show that a direct and personal damage has been suffered by them. In practice such proof is difficult, as the decrease in the value of the stock is not

worth trying. Of course, that is just fine with French executives who are quite afraid of American style class actions being introduced in France.

What then should changes in the law provide to better protect investors? In recent years there have been modest steps to provide collective actions for consumers and, indeed, for investors. In the case of investors, these first steps were important because until then investors had no possibility to collect the funding necessary to commence any proceeding or to authorize a representative to act on their behalf. The only chance they had to recover damages was, if there was a criminal proceeding, they could then attach a civil proceeding to it and seek damages. But in such cases the investors had to join the criminal proceeding individually.

Today, two forms of collective actions by investors have become possible: investor associations and shareholder groups, but they have not been made easy for fear of abuse.[5] The conditions necessary to form an association are so restrictive that there are very few of them and no groups of shareholders (an association is comprised of shareholders in any number of companies whereas a group consists of shareholders all in the same company). To be recognized as an association, the entity must have been in existence for six months and have 200 or more paying members. In addition, they must be authorized by the judge in the proceeding to seek proxies from the member/investors before they can sue.[6]

As noted by the sponsor of a securities bill in the Senate, Philippe Marini, during the 2003 legislative process, even his proposed bill would not solve several problems: (1) how to collect the money necessary for an action; and (2) how to obtain the necessary evidence.[7] Philippe Marini demonstrated the effect of these obstacles under French law by noting that between 1966, the date of the new Company law, and 2003, the date of the new provisions on associations and groups of investors, there were only

---

enough to constitute adequate proof of such an injury. Most of the time, the courts decide that the company itself has been injured, but the investors only indirectly. See also, Stanford/Oxford Conference on 'The Globalization of Class Actions' (December 13–14, 2007, 'Stanford Conference'); Report on France by Professor Veronique Magnier, 14 ('Magnier Report').

[5] Article L 452–1 of the Monetary and Financial Code.

[6] Article L 452–1 of the Monetary and Financial Code. And the association has to be instructed to sue by two members/investors (Article L 452–2 al. 2).

[7] *La Loi de securite financiere, un an après, rapport de* Philippe Marini, 156, *Senat* no. 431, 2003–2004, 156 ('Marini Report').

fifty cases brought by investors in all. And, the new law would not even overcome the two obstacles he mentioned.[8]

Marini also acknowledge that there are two additional obstacles in the French law in that an investor must still demonstrate personal damages which cannot include the loss of value of his or her shares (as noted above) and has to show a fault of an executive which is different and distinct from the fault of the company.[9]

Marini has made three proposals to improve the system: (1) allow proof of personal prejudice more readily; (2) consider that in an action by shareholders against an executive, the separate fault of the executive could be implied; and (3) facilitate actions in the name of the company (*ut singuli*) (which is similar to the derivative action in the US and the recovery also goes just to the company) by obliging the company to pay the expenses of the shareholder in advance.[10] However, it is obvious, even these proposals, which are yet to be incorporated into law, are far from US-style class actions.

The last but not least obstacle to organizing a class action in France is linked to the interpretation made of the European Convention on Human Rights (ECHR), that is, the right of any person to be heard in court.[11] This provision was designed mainly to protect defendants, but has been interpreted by the French courts as requiring each party to an action, including plaintiffs to be personally represented and thus prevents the use of any opt-out system of class action.[12] It is helpful here to distinguish a class action from a collective action. The former involves the opt-out system thus creating a class, whereas a collective action such

---

[8] Since 1992, the date of the creation of the joint representation action, the facility has only been used five times. See Magnier Report, (note 4, above), 14.

[9] The latter point that a distinction must be shown between the fault of the executive and the fault of the company is difficult because, especially in the case of inaction by executives, the French jurisprudence was that the company, but not the executives, were at fault in such case. Now the jurisprudence accepts that executives themselves are liable, for example, when they disseminate inaccurate information, where there were inadequate internal controls or executives did not stop employees from wrongdoing of which they were aware. And, in 2006, the French Supreme Court held that, at least in an administrative proceeding brought by the AMF, both the executive and the company could be found in violation of the securities laws for the same act. See Cass. Com. 11 July 2006 no 05–18728.

[10] Marini Report, (note 7, above), p. 158.

[11] 'Every person is entitled to a fair and public hearing within a reasonable time by an independent and impartial tribunal established by law,' Art. 6–1 of the ECHR.

[12] See D. W. Hawes's chapter in this volume (chapter 11) and Magnier Report, (note 4, above).

as one by an association in France requires an opt-in and does not bar a claimant who does not opt in from bringing his or her own action.

In short, the French securities regulation is strong on prevention and sanction but weak in the matter of remedies for investors. Because of all the obstacles to collective civil actions for damages, to date the main recourse of investors has been to attach a civil complaint to a criminal case (which is a common practice in most areas of law in France) and ride on the coattails of the prosecutor. While the investor benefits from the prosecutor's resources for marshalling the evidence and the decision of the court, the process is long, often taking five to ten years or more. And, most violations of the securities laws do not result in criminal prosecution. There are signs of change. On the one hand the government encourages more company initiative and risk taking with less regulation and a de-emphasis on criminal liability of executives and on the other hand fostering greater help for investors. Thus the problem is to find a way for investors to recover damages for securities fraud without going to the extremes of the American class action system.

The internationalization of companies and of their shareholder bases and of the securities markets as well as the fragmentation of such markets, makes it all the more urgent to find a way in which a French investor won't be disadvantaged merely because of French law and jurisprudence limiting collective actions. As shown by the *Shell* settlement which involved a Dutch company with investors from different countries including France and also the *Vivendi* case involving a French company, what the French investor is reduced to is seeking remedies in a foreign country instead of in France, even from a French company.[13]

One of the reasons it is important for French investors to be compensated for damages, one way or the other, is that if a French investor is a shareholder and is not included in a foreign class action or in a settlement he loses twice: (1) he gets no damages; and (2) his company has to pay damages to the other investors. Why should a French investor risk being treated worse if he buys shares in France than if he bought them in the US?

II. Some modest proposals for France

All of these arguments support the need for a new approach. Certainly the French company representatives (MDEF and AFEP) are hostile to

---

[13]   See, D.W. Hawes's chapter in this volume (chapter 11).

class and collective actions and very much worried about them. They are even opposed to settlements arguing they are also risky for companies and lobby against encouraging them in the legislature.[14]

The AMF could certainly do more in the area of remedies. Two ways for that to happen without the necessity of revolutionizing the French legal system would be: (1) the AMF could use its existing injunctive power which has even recently been broadened[15]; and/or (2) it could authorize the Mediator of the AMF to obtain restitution for defrauded investors after a sanction by the AMF Commission on Sanctions – this latter remedy might require legislation.

The AMF has the power to enjoin any entity or professional under its jurisdiction to stop any activity likely to jeopardize the protection of investors or the proper operation of the markets. For example, if a company wrongly did not respect the pre-emptive rights of shareholders, the Commission on Sanctions of the AMF, after appropriate proceedings, could sanction it with a fine. But the fine goes to the public Treasury and does not compensate the shareholders for the dilution of their shares and the loss of the value of their rights. Alternatively, before any sanction proceeding by the Commission on Sanctions, the AMF could enjoin such a company to: (1) offer the new issue to all the shareholders and postpone the closing of the issue of shares; or (2) propose compensation to shareholders for the loss of their rights. If the company agreed to do so, there would be no sanction proceeding. Thus the injunction, which is different from a sanction and is done by the main AMF Commission, would have essentially the same effect as a consent decree in the US in which the company would agree not to commit such a violation again and would agree to compensate shareholders for the failure to respect their pre-emptive rights. If the company refused, then the AMF would notify the company that it was sending the matter to the Commission on Sanctions of the AMF where the remedy would be a penalty such as a fine.[16]

---

[14] Magnier Report (note 4, above), 19.

[15] 'The Commission of the AMF may, after the person concerned has been given the opportunity to present their defense, enjoin them in France or abroad from violating the obligations imposed by law or regulation or professional rules for the protection of investors against insider trading, manipulation of prices on the market or dissemination of inaccurate information or any kind of infringement aiming at jeopardizing the protection of investors or the good operation of the market.' See Art. L 621–14 1 of the Monetary and Financial Code.

[16] Some years ago, the Swiss Banking Commission found that a mutual fund management company had sold shares of the fund to friends and relatives at a significant discount

Similarly, the AMF could use its jurisdiction over mutual funds and portfolio management companies to mandate compensation to shareholders if it determined after a routine inspection or other investigation that a management company had violated its regulations. These are merely examples of how the AMF could use its existing powers to provide remedies to investors.

The second suggestion I have is that the AMF authorize its Mediator, on a case-by-case basis, to determine compensation for investors following sanctions by the Commission on Sanctions. Here an amendment of the law would be necessary to provide that the AMF Mediator is competent to carry out this task and oblige the companies and professionals subject to its jurisdiction to accept its determination (called a 'settlement') which would be binding on both parties.

I suggest giving this function to the Mediator because as a former AMF Mediator I know the task of calculating the amount of restitution is similar to what the Mediator does in its traditional function except that here it would be acting as a binding arbitrator. The Mediator would have to make it publicly known that restitution would follow the sanction and that investors would have to present their applications for compensation. If the legislature so chose, the proceeding could very well involve, as it does in other areas of the law, a judge who could review the Mediator's determination and could give the Mediator's damage determination binding effect. The Mediator, in its current function has been remarkably successful in finding solutions. In the fiscal year ended April 2006, out of 667 matters handled, an agreement was arrived at in 435 cases.[17] Indeed, if the Mediator was authorized to act following sanctions decided by the Commission on Sanctions, it would have the advantage of an AMF investigation and ruling which is much more than it generally has today. Thus an investor would simply have to prove he was such in the relevant time period found by the AMF.

It is possible that such a new power given by the legislature to become a binding arbitrator would stimulate the AMF to utilize its injunctive

---

from the price to the public a few days later. The Commission ordered the management company to put up a significant bond and published a communiqué to inform the shareholders of their rights to bring an action before a judge or to give a proxy to a representative to act for them. After the fund management appealed arguing that the Commission had abused its authority, the Supreme Court of Switzerland upheld the Commission. The Court said that what the Commission had done was a reasonable exercise of its powers. See, ATF, 'judgment of 21 October 1977, *Anlagerfonds, BGE 103 Ib 303* (1977), www.bger.ch.

[17] AMF, *Annual Report* (2006), 261.

power without the risk of being charged with abuse of power. Such a result could also benefit those subject to investigation in that they could thus avoid sanction.

In the special case, from a juridical point of view, of insider trading, a collective fund of profits made by the insiders would be distributed to the investors who sold or bought securities, as the case may be, during the relevant period as established by the investigation. Since the Mediator function is already funded by the AMF there would be little or no need for funding for the investors (the AMF might need to provide additional funding for the Mediator to take on these additional duties). Another possibility for funding in the case of mutual funds would be for the AMF to mandate a small percentage of the annual management fee or other fees paid by shareholders be used to acquire insurance to pay for processing of claims with the Mediator after an AMF sanction.

There already exists at the European Union level a network, Fin-Net, designed to help investors in cross-border investments seeking compensation where they have been damaged by violations of national securities regulations. If the concept of Mediator-facilitated restitution for investors in France found favour in the EU, perhaps the system could be adopted by other national securities regulators and harmonized by EU directive. It should be noted that the solution of third-party funding suggested in my husband's companion chapter, does not appear to be authorized in France at this time.[18]

III. Conclusion

Using the paths which are already familiar to companies, professionals and investors seems to me more practical than trying to use the limited and ineffective collective action procedures that exist or going beyond my modest proposals to some form of US class action system, which is neither in our financial culture nor compatible with our judicial system. Adopting these modest proposals does not mean that under foreign influences, especially within Europe, our system is not going to evolve, but at least as other countries have evolved their own solutions, we would have set up a method to compensate investors *à la Française*.

---

[18] See Freshfields Bruckhaus Deringer, 'Class actions and third party funding of litigation', June 2007, 24, www.freshfields.com/publications/pdfs/2007/jun18/18825.pdf

13

Pre-clearance in European accounting law – the right step?

WOLFGANG SCHÖN

I. The 'open society' of accounting law actors

The responsibility for the accuracy and reliability of the annual and consolidated acounts of a company has for a long time rested with the members of the board of directors (in some countries also with the members of the supervisory board) and with the auditors who are educated and mandated to scrutinize the financial reports drawn up by the company itself and to testify as to its accordance with the relevant rules and principles under accounting law. This responsibility has been strengthened in recent European legislation. On the one hand, the establishment of an 'audit committee' being part of the company board is held to be necessary for 'public-interest entities' such as listed companies;[1] on the other hand, the standards of auditing for public accountants have been increased by a recently enacted directive, including new levels of public oversight devoted to their work.[2]

Nevertheless, there are additional actors present in the world of accounting. First of all, there are the standard setters as such. In the old days, these used to be national legislators or other national bodies; over time, starting with the directive on annual accounts in 1978, the European Institutions joined this group. Accounting rules were codified during the 1980s in most European countries. This 'legalization' of accounting practice led to an increased scrutiny by the courts. They are competent to decide finally on matters of interpretation of accounting law,[3] although in some Member States of the European

---

[1] Art. 41 of Directive 2006/43/EC of the European Parliament and of the Council of 17 May 2006 on statutory audits of annual accounts and consolidated accounts, amending Council Directives 78/660/EEC and repealing Council Directive 84/253/EEC [2006] 05. L 157/87.

[2] Art. 26 *et seq.* of Directive 2006/43/EC (note 1, above).

[3] Schön, 'Kompetenzen der Gerichte zur Auslegung von IAS/IFRS', *Betriebs-Berater,* 59 (2004), 763 *et seq.*

Union the interpretation of accounting standards is still regarded as a matter of fact rather than as a matter of law. The most prominent example for the examination of accounting issues by the courts is the judgment of the European Court of Justice in the *Tomberger* case[4] which was echoed widely throughout Europe.

For listed companies, accounting law is more and more shaped by the London-based International Accounting Standards Board (IASB), issuing International Financial Reporting Standards (IFRS),[5] and the European Commission, which endorses these standards, thus making them mandatory for listed companies in Europe under the IAS Regulation of 2002.[6] Moreover, the interpretation of these standards is the task of ancillary bodies like the International Financial Reporting Interpretation Committee (IFRIC) in London or domestic standard setters such as the Accounting Interpretations Committee (*Deutscher Standardisierungsrat*) in Berlin.

In recent years, another group of actors has appeared on the accounting scene: capital market authorities and their auxiliary troops such as the UK's Financial Reporting Review Panel or Germany's Federal Reporting Enforcement Panel (*Deutsche Prüfstelle für Rechnungslegung*). They have been entrusted with the task of *ex post* review of financial reports which were disclosed by listed companies. Their work is meant to fill the 'expectation gap' which became apparent in some corporate scandals at the beginning of the new millennium (Enron, Parmalat, WorldCom, FlowTex, etc.).

The introduction of this new enforcement procedure has – for capital market oriented companies – increased the danger of being exposed to a public discussion about the appropriateness of their financial reports. Whereas intra-corporation issues relating to accounting questions only seldom come before a court (e.g. in the context of a shareholder suit) and lawsuits against financial auditors were well nigh unknown till quite recently, the – more factual than legal – pressure effect of the control exerted by the public review panels and by capital market authorities has dramatically changed the scope for action for the accounting of listed companies. It seems understandable against this backdrop, that the big players of the economy voice the desire, that capital market

---

[4] Case 234/94, Tomberger [1996] ECR I-03133.

[5] For further information see www.iasc.org.

[6] Art.3 par.2 of Regulation (EC) No 1606/2002 of the European Parliament and of the Council of 19 July 2002 on the application of international accounting standards [2002] 05. L 243/1.

authorities and their appendices may be enabled – for the sake of preventing accounting law related disputes, i.e. in the run-up to the set-up and adoption of annual and group accounts or even in the run-up of realising the relevant facts – to make clarifying statements vis-à-vis those companies, which are obliged to disclose their accounts to the capital markets.[7] Capital market authorities may be asked for defined (future or already-realized) facts to make individual case-related statements or indicate via 'no action letters', that it would not attack certain accounting measures. By doing so, a provisional assessment of the respective case under the corresponding accounting law rules would take place, in the run-up to the audit certificate by the financial auditor and before the internal involvement of the supervisory board and shareholder bodies.

II. The state of 'pre-clearance' in the US and in Europe

The method of pre-clearance is not unknown in the US-American and European context. The organization of the SEC includes the office of the Chief Accountant, which supports listed companies with clarifying statements[8] encountering ambiguous issues in accounting law when preparing the filing. By doing so the competent statutory auditor and if need be the FASB as standard setter, the Public Company Accounting Oversight Board or other auditing companies are called in by the SEC. The 'no action letter' is typical for the SEC's method, i.e. a personal statement by an SEC employee, which is not legally binding, neither for its commissioners nor for the company in question, but highlights the prospective course of action by the SEC and therefore has great factual importance.[9]

---

[7] See the discussion report on the *Schmalenbach*-Conference 2006 in Hillmer, 'Enforcement in Rechnungslegung und Prüfung', *Zeitschrift für Corporate Governance*, 1 (2006), 39 ff.; that such a competence does not exist under German law is generally recognised, see Gelhausen and Hönsch, 'Das neue Enforcement-Verfahren für Jahres- und Konzernabschlüsse', *Die Aktiengesellschaft*, 50 (2005), 511, at 514.

[8] US Securities and Exchange Commission, *Guidance for Consulting with the Office of the Chief Accountant*, status quo 17 July 2006, www.sec.gov/info/accountants/ocasub guidance.htm; see also US Securities and Exchange Commission, Release N°s 33–8040; 34–45149; FR-60, 12 December 2001, www.sec.gov/rules/other/33–8040.htm.

[9] T.L.Hazen, *Treatise on the Law of Securities Regulation* § 1.4[4] 43 (4th edn.2002) offers a formulation example from the point of view of the competent official in charge: 'This is my view based on the facts as you describe them. You may not rely on it as if it were a Commission decision. If you don't like it, you are at liberty to disregard it and follow your own construction, subject to the risk that I may recommend appropriate action to

Equally in the context of European capital market supervision, openness for the introduction of pre-clarifying methods fundamentally exists. Taking this course of direction, the Standard No.1 on Financial Information by the Committee of European Securities Regulators (CESR) recorded that:

> Some enforcers offer issuers the possibility to obtain pre-clearance, whose aim is only to allow knowledge of the competent enforcer's view on a certain specific accounting or disclosure treatment. In particular, by means of pre-clearances the enforcers that are willing to provide for this possibility will express their view on the fact that a particular accounting treatment may be considered (or not) an infringement to the reporting framework which may lead to enforcer's actions. These pre-clearances should also clearly identify all the circumstances surrounding the specific case submitted by the issuer. [10]

In the meantime the CESR already integrated a few decisions by national enforcement agencies in pre-clearance procedures in its database and published them in due course.[11]

The reaction of the Member States and their domestic authorities is mixed. France[12] is one of the Member States, where the supervisory bodies use the pre-clearance method, whereas the Financial Reporting Review Panel (FRRP) in the UK is not readily available to make such provisional statements and has confirmed this line early in 2008 in its revised operating procedures.[13] In Belgium, there is no general pre-clearance system for accounting rules, but the financial supervisor (CBFA) has a limited power to give 'rulings' regarding certain matters of financial law.[14] In Germany, currently no pre-clearance mechanism

---

the Commission and the Commission may institute proceedings or take other steps if the Commission agrees with my view.'

[10] CESR, Standard N° 1 on Financial Information: *Enforcement of Standards on Financial Information in Europe*, 12 March 2003, § E, www.cesr.eu.

[11] Most recently CESR, Press Release 17 December 2007, 2nd Extract from EEECS's database of enforcement decisions.

[12] *Mémento Pratique Francis Lefèbre*, *Compatble* para 249, (2208); Brown and Tarca, 'A Commentary on Issues Relating to the Enforcement of International Financial Reporting Standards in the EU', *European Accounting Review*, 14 (2005), 181.

[13] FRRP, Operating Procedures, Para.40 (www.frc.gov.uk).

[14] The relevant provision is Art.3 of the Royal Decree of 23 August 2004 (*Moniteur Belge*, 11 Octobre 2004) which refers to Art.12 of the Royal Decree of 31 March 2003 (*Moniteur Belge*, 3 Decembre 2003) which covers the financial reporting obligations of listed companies. This legal basis has recently been replaced by Art.12 of the Royal Decree of 14 November 2007 (*Moniteur Belge,* 3 Decembre 2007). My gratitude for this information goes to Michel Tison, University of Ghent.

exists. Yet some accounting academics have pleaded for the introduction of such a remedy.[15] The Federal Reporting Enforcement Panel would be responsible in a first step; in a conflictual situation the Federal Financial Supervisory Authority (*Bundesanstalt für Finanzdienstleistungsaufsicht*) would have to step in, who has the final say in the hitherto practiced reactive procedures in accounting disputes. One must interpret the most recent press communication by the Federal Reporting Enforcement Panel in this direction, who 'sees itself confirmed to further build the preventive function of the FREP with additional measures'.[16]

III. Allocation of competence in the area of accounting

A. Pre-clearance as an intermediary between rule-setting and application of norms

Even though CESR has indicated in its previous practice a fundamental openness for a pre-clearance mechanism, the same body however formulated in its first standard already significant concerns about the differentiation of the function of such a procedure within the framework of the general competence on interpreting and applying accounting law rules. The doubts hereby focus especially on the delineation between applying and setting norms:

> CESR recognizes that it is important that pre-clearance should not result in enforcers becoming standard setters. [17]

This diplomatically embellished reserve is formulated even more distinctly in the UK. The Institute of Chartered Accountants made clear already in the year 2000, that a pre-clearance procedure encroaches upon both the role of standard-setter and the role of the individual appliers and auditor:

> We recognize that there might be occasions, particularly in the case of new listings, when guidance would be helpful on the compatibility of a proposed accounting treatment with the requirements of the law and relevant accounting standards. However, we believe that it would be undesirable

[15] Böcking, *Zur Notwendigkeit eines Pre-Clearance im Rahmen des Enforcement*, Lecture, Cologne, 27 April 2006, www.wiwi.uni-frankfurt.de/professoren/boecking/downpub/1770.pdf; Böcking and Wiederhold, 'Mehr Sicherheit für Rechnungsleger', *Frankfurter Allgemeine Zeitung*, 31 July 2006, 16.
[16] Deutsche Prüfstelle für Rechnungslegung, Press Communication: Annual Activity Report 2007, 14 February 2008 (2007).
[17] Note 10, above.

for the enforcement agency to provide any form of pre-clearance. This would dilute and even undermine the perceived responsibilities of directors and auditors, as well as encroaching on the standard setter's role by effectively allowing the enforcement agency to issue interpretations of accounting standards. [18]

The basic policy question is thereby already outlined: how should one visualize the role of pre-clearance in the overall system of commercial law and capital market law as a basis for accounting rules and principles? How does the adoption of statements by a capital market authority or a review panel interact with the statements by company bodies, auditors or courts, which are mainly responsible for examining the legality of annual and group accounts?

Already the first decision published by CESR crystallized the problem:[19] as for the fiscal year 2005, a company already requested in 2004 how one ought to deal with intangibles in the conversion from national accounting principles to IAS/IFRS, when these intangibles are completely absorbed by goodwill, for lack of individual tangibility. The accounting issue was particularly focused on the question whether the amortizations on this asset would be carried out in accordance with its effective 'useful life' or whether they could be merely considered in the general impairment test for the goodwill. The domestic review panel endorsed, within the context of a pre-clearance, already in September 2004 the last-mentioned alternative – thus even before the beginning of the authoritative accounting period.

By doing so, the review panel made a statement, which could be just as well formulated within the context of the interpretation of a standard by the IFRIC or by a domestic standard setter such as (in Germany) the Accounting Interpretations Committee. Moreover, this question should be independently assessed by the auditor in the context of the audit certificate or be conclusively judged by a court *ex post*. Evidently, the review panel has made here a general statement on the interpretation of an accounting standard, which can in many cases claim to be applied – and for only this reason has been published by the CESR.

On the other hand, the review panel did not only publish an opinion concerning a question of law. Moreover, at the request of the management

---

[18] Institute of Chartered Accountants in England and Wales (ICAEW), Policy Statement (Tech 23/00) on the Endorsement and Enforcement of International Accounting Standards within the EU, www.icaew.co.uk.

[19] Note 11, above, 3.

of the applicant company, it subsumed the individual case by doing so and told the representatives of this company that it would not interfere if they would proceed according to this standpoint. By doing this, the review panel also reduced the leeway of the company bodies and other involved actors virtually to zero: which board of management will dare take steps against a negative preliminary decision by the review panel, and which supervisory board, audit committee or final auditor will take it upon itself, to raise concerns about a positive decision by the review panel? The pre-clearance by the review panel will – and this is foreseeable – generally represent the final clarification of an accounting problem and thereby preclude both the interpretation competence of the standard setters and the courts and withdraw from the hands of the company bodies and the statutory auditor the concrete application.

B. The institutional framework in the US and in Europe

1. The extensive authority of the SEC in accountancy law

One first important aspect in order to clarify the functional role of a pre-clearance concerns the localization of enforcement in accounting law and capital markets law. Whilst accounting law is in general harmonized in Europe for companies limited by shares (and is equally applied to the domain of some partnerships controlled by corporations), accounting law in the US is plainly focussed on capital markets. By doing so, the SEC's role is from the beginning designed to be considerably stronger than that of a European supervisory body.[20] This is furthermore reflected in the fact that the Securities Exchange Act 1934 allocates the role of standard setting in first instance to the SEC. Although the SEC delegated the development of individual rules to the Federal Accounting Standards Board (FASB) long ago, this did not modify the fundamental reign of the SEC over standard setting. The SEC is furthermore equally the central addressee of all accounts drawn up according to US-GAAP. The enforcement of the SEC inclusive of a pre-clearance therefore corresponds with its extensive authority on standard setting, on interpretation and application in individual cases and implementation. The SEC 'may make laws, may act as a public prosecutor in enforcing these

---

[20] In detail Kiefer, *Kritische Analyse der Kapitalmarktregulierung der US Securities and Exchange Commission*, (Deutscher Universitäts-Verlag, 2003), 50 *et seq.* and 121 *et seq.*, Herwitz and Barrett, *Accounting for Lawyers*, 4th edition (Foundation Press, 2006), 154 *et seq.*

laws, and may then determine the guilt or innocence of the person it has accused'.[21]

The SEC's pre-clearance procedure does not face, against this backdrop, the problem of a separation of powers with another standard setter. The US auditors will equally not be able to moan if the SEC provides 'authentic' interpretations, as a high-ranking source of material accounting rules. And finally, dealings of the courts with the interpretation and application of US-GAAP are virtually unknown in the US; in any case they do not focus on material issues pertaining to correct accounting, but at the most on the applicability of US-GAAP on its merits.[22]

The extension of the SEC's activity in the pre-clearance of accounting law related problems is thus a natural consequence of its extensive decision making and responsibility in the domain of capital markets-oriented accounting.

2. Division of power in European accounting law

The overall situation is however considerably more complicated in Europe. This begins with the allocation of standard setting. The main basics of accounting law are to be found either in the European Parliament's and Council's directives (Annual Accounts Directive, Group Accounts Directive) or in the IAS/IFRS, enacted by the IASB and approved by the European Commission in line with Art.3 of the IAS Regulation. Furthermore, they are fundamentally not founded on capital markets alone, but can also apply to all companies limited by shares (including some applications to partnerships). According to Art.5 IAS Regulation this can also be true for individual and group accounts of non-listed companies which apply International Financial Reporting Standards. The capital market supervisory bodies (or subordinated agencies like review panels) are not integrated in this process of standard setting. At the most, national standard setters – such as the German Accounting Standards Committee (on the basis of § 342 para. 1

---

[21] Lang and Lipton, 'Litigating Administrative Proceedings – the SEC's Increasingly Important Enforcement Alternative', in: *Phillips* (ed.), *The Securities Enforcement Manual – Tactics and Strategies* (American Bar Association), 239, 242 (quoted in: Kiefer, *Kritische Analyse der Kapitalmarktregulierung der US Securities and Exchange Commission*, (note 20, above), 121).

[22] See for example the decision by the US Supreme Court in: *Thor Power Tool Co. v. Commissioner* 439 U.S. (522) on the significance of US-GAAP for the fiscal income determination or the verdict by the US Supreme Court in: *Shalala v. Guernsey Memorial Hospital* 514 U.S. 87 on the relevance of US-GAAP for refunds in the health sector.

Nr.3 German Commercial Code) – are somehow included in the work of international standardization bodies.

Against this backdrop a Member State enforcement unit will not be able to invoke a natural authority for 'authentic' interpretation like the SEC when applying accounting standards. Neither the company bodies nor the statutory auditor will be relieved from making independent and autonomous assessments and the later invoked courts cannot be tied to the statements by the review panel. This is clearly accepted for Belgium and has to be seen in the same way in other countries of the European Union. This problem will not go away if the company bodies or the auditors are given the opportunity to be heard by the review panel in the pre-clearance procedure.

However the factual normativity which would be attributed to the objective content of a pre-clearance statement seems problematic. This is due to the fact that such decisions – as easily apparent in the above-mentioned example from CESR's publication practice – will be attributed, beyond the judged individual case, the effect of a precedent.

As far as the competence of the courts is damaged by such a pre-clearance procedure, it should not go unnoticed that in some European states – such as in the United Kingdom – the introduction, interpretation and application of accounting standards is not considered a task of the courts.[23] Courts must in the tradition of these legal systems treat questions pertaining to correct accounting not as an application of law, but as a factual matter, which in turn refers to the evidence given by experts. Also in Germany, the assessment of 'accounting principles' has for decades followed the prevalent usage of business people in Germany.[24] This line of thinking has not only become obsolete through the juridification of accounting law as a result of the accounting directives of the European Community, but equally through the transfer of the IAS/IFRS to the main body of EC law in the context of the endorsement procedure. Accounting rules – according to general accounting law and capital market oriented IAS/IFRS – are nowadays objective legal rules, whose interpretation is carried out by national courts and the ECJ.[25]

---

[23] See for example Freedman, 'Aligning Taxable Profits and Accounting Profits: Accounting Standards, legislators and judges', *Journal of Tax Research*, (2004) 71, 84 *et seq.*

[24] On the development see Moxter, *Grundsätze ordnungsgemäßer Rechnungslegung* (Düsseldorf: IDW-Verlag, 2003), 10 *et seq.*

[25] Schön, 'Kompetenzen der Gerichte zur Auslegung von IAS/IFRS', (note 3, above), 764.

Neither the capital market authority or the review panel have a decisive function with regard to ensuing lawsuits about the correctness of a balance sheet. Their own later intervention in the enforcement procedure can be resolved by such a pre-clearance, but not other contentions within the company bodies, vis-à-vis auditors or with regard to shareholders. If one follows the US practice, not even the panel itself would be bound by a 'no action letter' issued by one of the employees. However, a company's board of directors will in case of a preparation of balance sheets rely on the panel's statement as a tool to deny any fault of its own in order to fend off ensuing litigations and to neutralize the vulnerability of accounting.[26] The problem of the reliability and tenability of such pre-clearance statements would be thereby again carried over into the ensuing contentions.

Even though the interest of companies in a prompt pre-clearance of individual issues in accounting law cannot be denied, one has to therefore be sceptical about a further extension of pre-clearance mechanisms in European capital market law. Said proposal does not fit into the institutional framework, in which neither the standard setting in accounting nor the legal responsibility for the individual application are to be found with the review panel (or the supervisory body). Factual efficiency and legal competence would not correlate. Therewith, the individual attribution of responsibility to the review panel and the company bodies would be dissolved, which is of paramount importance in the context of efficient corporate governance.

IV. Practical issues of pre-clearance en route towards a new expectation gap

The establishment of review panels in recent years has been legitimized with the necessity of confronting glaring violations of recognized accounting rules with greater fierceness. The new enforcement units should work as an 'accountancy police', which control 'randomly and when suspecting manipulation of accounts'[27] the books of listed companies. The context were 'company scandals at domestic level and abroad', which had shattered 'the trust of investors in the correctness

---

[26] On the characteristic of the 'subjective correctness' of a balance sheet see Schön in: Canaris et al. (ed.), *50 Jahre Bundesgerichtshof – Festgabe aus der Wissenschaft* (München: Beck, 2000), 153 *et seq.*, 155 *et seq.*

[27] Draft of a law on the control of companies' accounts (Bilanzkontrollgesetz), 24 June 2004 (BT-Drs.15/3421, preliminary 1).

of important capital market information'[28]. The review panels have honoured this task with growing success. In a considerable number of addressed cases the panels could correct mistakes; there is in addition a considerable preventive effect, if somewhat difficult to put a number on it.

In contrast, the internal structure as well as the extent of the activity of these review panels would substantially change, if they would receive, alongside the reactive control of individual accounts of selected companies the task of pre-clearance in individual questions pertaining to accounting law. In order to develop the analogy with the police force: it is not easy to transform a criminal investigation unit, operating for special purposes, into a citizen's advice bureau for lawful conduct in road traffic. This begins with the circumstance that the review panels – like also other enforcement units – are designed for their main task of sanctioning evident violations of central accounting rules. The 'scandalous cases', which constitute the actual historical legitimization of the review panels, do not distinguish themselves by difficult issues on the interpretation of accounting standards, but by the glaring non-observance of basic requirements of correct accounting at the level of appreciating facts. The most significant cases in Germany and abroad such as Enron, WorldCom, Balsam, Comroad or Flowtex may be described as mere cases of accounting fraud, whose clarification does not require an innovative development of accounting rules, but necessitates in the first instance a clear improvement in the ascertainment of facts. The 'expectation gap' of the general public related in the run-up to the new legislation not to a further detailing of legal delimitation questions by way of a new interpreting institution, but related to a factual and effective ascertainment and prosecution of deceiving accounting failures. The Supreme Regional Court (*Oberlandesgericht*) Frankfurt defined most recently, in this vein, the target of accounting control: 'to preventively thwart irregularities when drawing up a listed company's financial statements and compiling the report, and to expose irregularities, insofar they still occur and to inform the capital market thereof. Reaching this goal requires a prompt, effective and accelerated review procedure.'[29]

Against this background it was not doubted that the interpretation of accounting rules in the Member States of the European Union would be carried out by companies and their auditors correctly to the largest

---

[28] Statement of reasons, (above, note 27), 18.
[29] OLG Frankfurt, 29 November 2007, Der Betrieb (2008), 629 *et seq.*, 631.

extent possible. In other words, a gap in enforcement is something different than a gap in standard setting and one would misallocate the professional know-how concentrated in the review panels (and their supervisory capital market authorities) if one deployed in future the manpower more to formulate accounting standards and their interpretation and less to prosecute evident accounting violations.

The review panels would also not be able to remedy this, by concentrating on selected cases as already during their control activity. As the responsible body under capital market law, they would be obliged to provide information vis-à-vis all requesting companies in a way which suffers no discriminatory fashion. The same would apply to the liberty of giving information or 'no action letters' as one pleases and without justification.

Against this backdrop it would be difficult for the review panel to shun a factually justified information request, with the allusion to lacking personal capacities. If one considers furthermore that companies subject to disclosure requirements have strict statutory periods for submitting their annual financial reports, a great number of requests can accumulate in the review panels in short periods of time. Boards of management of stock corporations will include in their duties of care a request for information to the review panel to address in time in ambivalent accounting issues. These requests can either only be worked off through a massive increase in personnel (and costs), or a quantitatively high share of 'customers' are not served. A new expectation gap would be foreseeable. Also one cannot simply say, according to which criteria a discretion-conform differentiation between processed and non-processed requests ought to be carried out: within the context of the actual control mission of the review panel, the cases with the highest financially quantitative relevance ought to have priority (in the case of accounting failures, the most extensive damages threaten to arise for investors), whereas the development of accounting rules would suggest a treatment of the legally most significant questions. Finally, the review panel would not have an easy task within the context of its central activity – the reactive control – to take on accounting issues, whose assessment it refused for capacity reasons in the pre-clearance proceedings. The actual 'customers' of the 'accounting police' however, that is those companies who contribute with evident false statements to the deception of financial markets, disappeared at the pace of this development progressively from the focus of the inspection unit, and would probably also not deign to come to a preliminary examination of their fraudulent actions.

In any case, any pre-clearance procedures should be restricted to the correct representation of given facts, from an accounting point of view. Any preliminary information on future facts, which could apply as a basis of business and accounting decisions of the respective company, would go far beyond the target of an adequate hedging of issuers from retroactive accounting claims.

V. Conclusion

The 'open society of accounting law actors' is on the verge of bursting at the seams. The extensive introduction of pre-clearance by capital market authorities and their ancillary bodies – the review panels – would influence the institutional structure within the companies subject to disclosure requirements, their rapport with the statutory auditors and the courts' control function in a sustainable and disadvantageous way. At the same time the accounting 'police' would master less and less its genuine task of effectively persecuting clear violations of rules in the financial statements of listed companies. The SEC's practice can be no example in this case – this body is regarded to be 'omni-competent' both for standard setting and application of standards in US accountancy law and can therefore act as an authentic interpreter of US-GAAP. From the point of view of the European legal system the lasting refusal of the British FRRP to damage the personal responsibility of issuers, their agencies and their statutory auditors by way of an advance clearance seems exemplary.

14

International standards on auditing and their adoption in the EU: legal aspects and unsettled questions

HANNO MERKT

I. Introduction

The Audit Directive of May 2006[1] enforces the use of 'International Standards on Auditing' (ISA) for all statutory audits to be performed in the EU. Aiming at a consistently high quality for all statutory audits required by Community law, the Audit Directive has given implementing powers to the European Commission to adopt the ISA in accordance with the so-called 'comitology procedure'. Moreover, the Commission has recently commissioned a Study on 'The Evaluation of the possible Adoption of International Standards on Auditing (ISA) in the EU'.[2] The object of that Study is to address the incremental direct and indirect costs for EU companies and audit firms, as well as the benefits resulting from the possible adoption by the European Commission of the ISA.

Improving audit quality through the adoption of ISA within the EU has a number of fundamental legal implications that need to be considered in order to comprehensively cover the subject. The following article outlines some of the most important of these issues after an introduction into the genesis of the harmonization process and a brief look at the competence of the EU to adopt ISA.

---

[1] The Directive 2006/43/EC of the European Parliament and of the Council of 17 May 2006 on statutory audits of annual accounts and consolidated accounts, amending Council Directive 78/660/EEC and 83/349/EEC and repealing Council Directive 84/253/EEC [2006] OJ L 157/87, (hereafter, 'the Audit Directive').

[2] Tender Markt/2007/15/F – Study on International Standards on Auditing, Lot 1: Evaluation of the Possible Adoption of International Standards on Auditing (ISAs) in the EU.

II. History of internationalization of auditing standards

A. From IAG to ISA

Not surprisingly, the harmonization of standards of auditing is closely linked to the harmonization of accounting standards.[3] The historical starting point of international harmonization of financial reporting was in October 1972, when during the tenth international congress of accountants in Sydney the International Coordination Committee for the Accountancy Profession (ICCAP) was founded.[4] This congress laid the foundations for the genesis of the International Accounting Standards Committee (IASC), the predecessor of the International Accounting Standards Board (IASB). During the ninth international congress of accountants in 1967 an international working party had been created dealing with the convergence of international best practice in auditing.[5] This decision followed the discussions back in 1962 during the eighth international congress of accountants on the necessity of creating a higher degree of uniformity in accounting and auditing standards.

In October 1977, ICCAP took the initiative, during the eleventh international congress to create the International Federation of Accountants (IFAC).[6] IFAC is the organization that took over the tasks of ICCAP, thereby serving the accounting profession worldwide and having the public interest in mind. The decision to create the International Auditing Practices Committee (IAPC) was taken by the Board of IFAC in 1977.[7] Being one of the most important committees of IFAC, the IAPC developed the International Auditing Guidelines (IAG), which were in fact the predecessors of the International Standards on Auditing (ISA). The IAG represented the best practice within the major audit firms at that time, within the field of auditing and review of historical financial

---

[3] P. Wong, 'Challenges and Successes in Implementing International Standards: Achieving Convergence to IFRSs and ISAs', September 2004, www.ifac.org.

[4] For the following, see D. Schockaert and N. Houyoux, 'International Standards on Auditing within the European Union', *Revue bancaire et financière/Bank- en Financiewezen*, 8 (2007), 515.

[5] IFAC, *News* (February 2007), 12, www.ifac.org.

[6] Sixty-three member bodies signed the official protocol, see Schockaert and Houyoux, 'International Standards on Auditing', (note 4, above), 515 footnote 4; for a critical analysis of IFAC's role in the Internationalization of Auditing Standards see C. Humphrey, A. Loft, S. Turley and K. Jeppesen, 'The International Federation of Accountants: Private Global Governance in the Public Interest' in G. F. Schuppert (ed.), *Global Governance and the Role of Non-State Actors*, (Baden-Baden: Nomos Verlag, 2006) 245–72.

[7] Cf. IFAC, *The First Fifteen Years. 1977–1992*; IFAC, *News* (May 2007), 9, available on www.ifac.org.

information. The first IAG (IAG-1) dealt with the purpose and scope of an audit and was approved in October 1979; they replaced by ISA-1 Objective and General Principles Governing an Audit of Financial Statements in 1992 which in 1994 became renamed ISA 200.

After a period of increased internationalization of business activities and capital markets during the 1980s, the IFAC counted 106 member bodies within 78 countries by the end of 1991, compared to 78 bodies within 55 countries by the end of 1978. In the context of this evolution and the expectation that IAG would shortly be recognized by official securities organizations, IAPC reformed its framework of standards, following IFAC's Constitution created in November 1991. From then on, the 'International Auditing Guidelines' were renamed as 'International Standards on Auditing'. Doing so, the IAPC acknowledged that its standards had obtained a benchmark status[8] for the audit and review engagements related to historical financial information. Therefore, IAPC, being one of the committees of IFAC, had become the auditing standard setter in the international marketplace. In October 1992 the International Organization of Securities Commissions (IOSCO) published a resolution whereby ISA was recognized on capital markets as an acceptable alternative for national auditing standards, in the context of cross-border offerings of continuous reporting by foreign issuers.[9]

In July 1994, IAPC laid the foundations for the structure of an ISA,[10] consisting of basic principles and essential procedures, which were indicated by bold-lettered paragraphs, and explanatory and informative guidance, which were indicated by grey-lettered paragraphs. Furthermore, the ISA were numbered per topic, thereby following the logical sequence of the performance of an audit of financial statements (series 200 on the responsibility of the auditor, until the series 700 and 800 on reporting). In November 2001, IPAC was reformed by the general assembly of IFAC in order to become the 'International Auditing and Assurance Standard Board' (IAASB).[11] Using its new name, this Board intended to spend more time on standards for 'assurance agreements', which from January 2004 on, were named 'International Standards

[8] IFAC, *Annual Report* (1993), 1; and IFAC, *Annual Report* (1995), 2.
[9] Following the reform of the ISA in July 994, IOSCO suspended the resolution. IOSCO never officially withdrew this resolution. Until today, IOSCO discusses within the Consultative Advisory Group (CAG) of IAASB on the evolution of auditing standards in the context of IAASB's Clarity Project.
[10] IFAC, *Annual Report* (1994), 3.
[11] IAASB, *Annual Report* (2002), 8.

on Assurance Engagements' (ISAE). At the same time, a rigorous due process had been set up within IAASB regarding its standard-setting function. By the end of 2004, IFAC counted 163 member bodies within 119 countries, which represented twice the membership from 1978. In the years from 2004 to 2008, IAASB has taken care of its 'Clarity Project' (see infra).

B. From minimum guidelines to benchmark status

The creation of IFAC's constitution in November 1991 had impact on the obligation of member bodies. In the period before November 1991, IAG constituted the 'minimum guidelines' to be followed and promoted by bodies at the national level.[12] After November 1991, IAPC stated that, as far as there was consistency between the IAG and the domestic law and regulations, compliance with these national laws and regulations immediately resulted in compliance with IAG. At that time, IFAC accepted that there were differences between domestic legislation and international standards. When IAG conflicted with national law or regulation, the member bodies needed to comply with the obligations as set out in IFAC's constitution: each member body, in its quality of standard setter, should use its best endeavours to incorporate the international standards (renamed as 'ISA') within the national auditing standard.

In April 2004, the ISA received a benchmark status for the audit of financial statements, namely through the new member obligations[13] imposed by the Statements of Membership Obligations (SMO). In particular, paragraph 4 of SMO 3 stated that member bodies should use their best endeavours to establish convergence with the international standards, thus contributing towards the elimination of the differences of content between national and international auditing standards. Following these obligations, the member bodies of IFAC have considered the ISA as a basis for the national auditing standards. In the European Union, e.g., Belgian, Dutch, Luxembourg, French, and German auditing standards have been subject to a process of transformation ('transposition') of the international 'guidelines' or 'standards'.

---

[12] IFAC, *Towards the 21st Century: Strategic Decisions for the Accountancy Profession*, 3, www.ifac.org.
[13] IFAC, *Handbook of International Auditing, Assurance, and Ethics Pronouncements* (2005), 119–25.

C. The Clarity Project

The so-called 'Clarity Project' of the IAASB has been created following the comments in 2003 on the exposure draft (ED) 'Operations Policy n° 1 – Bold Type Lettering Exposure Draft'. In this ED, the need to use black and grey lettering within the ISA was debated. Significant comments were given by the IOSCO. This project was set up to deal with the comments on the setting of auditing standards that, back in 1994, regardless of IAPC's consideration of these comments, were not followed by a corresponding modification of the ISA.

In September 2004, IAASB issued a Policy Statement 'Clarifying Professional Requirements in International Standards Issued by the IAASB', followed by a Consultation Paper 'Improving the Clarity and Structure of IAASB Standards and Related Considerations for Practice Statements'.[14] Already in October 2005, four EDs were issued, namely ED ISA 300 on planning an audit of financial statements, ED ISA 315 on the auditor's risk assessment, ED ISA 330 on the reduction of the audit risk to an acceptable low level by performing audit procedures further to the auditor's risk management,[15] and ISA 240 on the auditor's responsibilities regarding fraud during an audit of financial statements. In mid 2006, the comment period expired and in December 2006 IAASB issued the final ISA 240, 300, 315 and 330, which, for the first time, were named 'Clarified ISA'. In July 2006, the IAASB approved ISA 600, 'Audit of Group Financial Statements'.

The other ISA will be subject to a 'clarification' process until the presumed final date of the project in 2009. The essence of the 'Clarity Project' can be summarized as follows:

1. The ISA and ISQC 1 are based on clear principles and objectives.
2. The objectives should be met on the basis of a number of requirements representing the essential procedures to be performed by the auditor in 'virtually all' circumstances of the audit engagement.
3. The necessary guidance (application guidance) is given to the auditor in order for him to apply these requirements in all circumstances of the audit engagement, i.e., small and less complex entities, public sector entities, larger entities, public interest entities, etc.

---

[14] Available from the IAASB's website www.ifac.org/iaasb; 'Exposure drafts'.
[15] These standards are the revised versions of the IAASB standards approved in October 2003.

4. In order to clearly distinguish between requirements and application material, IAASB decided in October 2005 to use the word 'shall' within the requirements section, and to use the present tense when dealing with explanatory material within the application guidance. IOSCO's comments, dating back from 1992, have proven to be significant. The difference between requirements and application material will replace the previous difference between bold and grey lettering.

5. Each 'clarified' ISA is set following a uniform structure consisting of a purpose, a requirements section and finally the application material. A short introduction and a set of definitions of key words will be provided at the beginning of each single ISA. Thus, the former 'bold lettering' paragraphs are regrouped at the beginning of each ISA.

All ISA will be subject to this new structure in a progressive way. The more recent standards will be dealt with in the first stage of the project, and the older standards will follow. IAASB will check which of the existing bold and grey lettering paragraphs correspond with the newly created requirements and application guidance sections. A paragraph in a 'to be clarified' ISA will be considered part of the requirement section if: 1) the requirement is necessary to achieve the objective stated in the standard; 2) the requirement is expected to be applicable in virtually all engagements to which the standard is relevant; 3) the objective stated in the standard is unlikely to have been met by the requirements of other standards; and finally 4) the requirement of an ISA as a whole is proportionate to the importance of the subject of the ISA, in order to realize the objective of an audit.

The ISA including ISQC-1 will be clarified following the planning provided by the Clarity Project: eleven standards are to be revised completely (clarified structure and full revision of the content, i.e. 'clarified and revised', namely ISA 260,320 (and 450), 402, 450, 505, 540 (and 545), 550, 580, 600, 620, and 800. The other standards will only be clarified. Part of those standards have been recently rewritten and will thus only be subject to the clarification exercise (e.g. ISA 230, 240, 300, 315, 330, 500, 700 and 701). In the context of the presumed deadline of the Clarity Project in 2009, the remaining standards will only be clarified without the content of those standards being subject to a complete revision (e.g., ISA 210, 510, 520, 530, 710 and 720).

III. Harmonization of auditing standards within the European Union

After a number of financial reporting scandals like Enron and Worldcom in the US and Parmalat in Europe, investors' confidence in capital markets worldwide has weakened considerably and public credibility of the audit profession has been impaired, finally leading to what is widely known as an 'expectation gap'. In response to those scandals and in order to close that expectation gap, the US adopted the Sarbanes–Oxley Act in 2002. Already from 1996, the European Commission developed an approach regarding the statutory audit function, which has been accelerated after these scandals and ultimately led to the approval in the EU of the Audit Directive, ten years later.[16] The initiative of a harmonized approach to statutory auditing in the EU was started by the EC's 1996 Green Paper titled 'The Role, Position and Liability of the Statutory Auditor in the EU'.[17] The policy conclusions which the EU drew from these reflections were included in the 1998 Communication 'The Statutory Audit in the European Union: The Way Forward'.[18] That Communication proposed the creation of an EU Committee on Auditing which would develop further action in close cooperation between the accounting profession and Member States. The objective of this Committee was to improve the quality of the statutory audit by promoting quality assurance, the use of international auditing standards and auditor independence. On the basis of the work of this Committee, the EC issued the 2000 Recommendations on 'Quality Assurance for the Statutory Auditor in the EU'[19] and the 2002 Recommendation about 'Statutory Auditors' Independence in the EU'.[20] In its Communication in 2003 on 'Modernising Company Law and Enhancing Corporate Governance in the EU – A Plan to Move Forward',[21] the Commission defined as its priorities

> strengthening public oversight of auditors at Member State and EU level, requiring ISA for all EU statutory audits … and the creation of an EU Regulatory Committee on Audit, to complement the revised legislation and allow the speedy adoption of more detailed binding measures … The

---

[16] D. Schockaert, 'ISA – Een antwoord op de vertrouwenscrisis', *Revue bancaire et financière/Bank- en Financiewezen*, (2004), 219.
[17] Green Paper of 28 October 1996, [1996] OJ C 321/1.
[18] Commission's Communication of May 1998, [1998] OJ C 143/12–16.
[19] Recommendation of 31 March 2001, [2001] OJ L 091/91.
[20] Recommendation of 19 July 2002, [2002] OJ L 191/22.
[21] Commission's Communication of 21 May 2003, COM (2003) 284 final, [2003] OJ C 236/2–13.

Commission envisaged the use of ISA as a requirement for all EU statutory audits … However, a successful implementation of a binding requirement to apply ISAs in the EU … requires the completion of a number of preliminary actions: the update and completion of the analysis of differences between ISAs and national audit requirements; the development of a set of principles ('framework') for the assessment of ISAs; the availability of high quality translation into all Community languages. As for audit reporting, the Commission plans to use the forthcoming revision of ISA 700 (audit reporting) as a starting-point for analyzing differences between national audit reports by EU professional bodies, facilitated by the European Federation of Accountants (FEE).

Despite those non-binding measures, the Commission required further initiatives in order to reinforce investor confidence in capital markets and to enhance public trust in the statutory audit function in the EU taking into account that auditing is an important part of good corporate governance practice. In May 2006, the European Parliament and the Council adopted the new Directive on statutory audits of annual accounts and consolidated accounts, the 'Audit Directive',[22] which replaces the Eighth Council Directive of 1984. The Audit Directive of 2006 reflects a principles-based approach on auditing matters and aims at reinforcing and harmonizing the statutory audit function throughout the EU. The purpose of the Directive is to reinforce the confidence in the functioning of the European Capital Markets by: 1) clarifying the duties of statutory auditors, the independence and other ethical requirements; 2) by introducing a requirement for external quality assurance; 3) by ensuring public oversight over the audit profession by improving cooperation between competent authorities in the EU; and 4) by enforcing the use of ISA for all statutory audits to be conducted in the EU, through a process of adoption of the ISA, named 'endorsement'.

IV. Competence of the EU to adopt ISA

A core issue in the discussion of adoption of the ISA is the competence of the EU to implement ISA as binding upon Member States. Pursuant to the Audit Dirctive of 2006, statutory audits of annual and consolidated accounts (financial accounts) should be carried out on the basis

---

[22] Directive 2006/43/EC (note 1, above).

of international auditing standards. This, in fact, does imply the adoption of those standards in accordance with Council Decision 1999/468/EC (Comitology Decision).[23] The Audit Directive of 2006 is important in order to ensure a high quality for all statutory audits required by Community law and provides that all statutory audits be carried out on the basis of 'all'[24] international auditing standards.[25] The Directive has given implementing powers to the Commission in order to adopt 'en bloc'[26] the ISA[27] in accordance with the Comitology Decision of the Council dated 28 June 1999. Within this context, the EC will need to be satisfied: 1) that the ISA have been developed with proper due process, public oversight and transparency, and are generally accepted internationally; 2) that they contribute to a high level of credibility and quality in relation to the true and fair view of the annual or consolidated accounts; 3) that they are conducive to the European public good.

In the context of ISA, the basic act is the Audit Directive of 2006, which confers on the Commission implementing powers to adopt ISA (article 26) in accordance with the comitology procedure. Furthermore, the Commission can dispose of the assistance of a committee. According to article 48 (1), the 'Audit Regulatory Committee' (AuRC), composed of the representatives of the Member States and chaired by the Commission, has been set up. Under the comitology procedure it is mandatory for the Commission to consult with the AuRC in relation to the adoption of ISA. The AuRC is then expected to form an opinion on the measures proposed by the Commission. The Audit Directive also introduces a requirement for Member States to organize an effective system of public oversight for statutory auditors and audit firms and to establish coordination of public oversight systems at the community level.[28]

---

[23] See Schockaert and Houyoux, 'International Standards on Auditing', (note 4, above), 521.

[24] It also refers to related standards such as ISQC-1, Legislative Resolution from the European Parliament regarding the proposal for a directive on statutory audit of annual accounts and consolidated accounts and amending Council Directive 78/660/EEC and 83/349/EEC [2005], 5.

[25] Recital 13 of the Audit Directive (note 1, above).

[26] ISQC-1, Legislative Resolution from the European Parliament regarding the proposal for a directive on statutory audit of annual accounts and consolidated accounts and amending Council Directive 78/660/EEC and 83/349/EEC [2005], 5.

[27] Art. 26 (2) of the Audit Directive (note 1, above).

[28] Art. 33 of the Audit Directive (note 1, above); Recital 1 of the Commission Decision of 14 December 2005 setting up a group of experts to advise the Commission and to facilitate cooperation between public oversight systems for statutory auditors and audit firms [2005] OJ L 329/38.

In order to reach the goals outlined in the Audit Directive, the Commission needed to call an expert group, which would contribute to the coordination and the development of public oversight systems within the EU as well as to the technical preparation of the implementing measures.[29] Following the Decision of 14 December 2005, the Commission set up an 'Expert Group of Auditors Oversight Bodies' (EGAOB). The EGAOB is composed of high-level representatives from the entities responsible for public oversight of statutory auditors and audit firms in Member States or, in their absence, of representatives from the competent national ministries.[30] Only non-practitioners are allowed to become members of the EGAOB. The Commission may consult with this group on any question relating to the preparation of implementing measures provided for by the Audit Directive.[31] Furthermore, the task of this group is to contribute to the technical examination of international auditing standards, including the processes for their elaboration, with a view to their adoption at the community level.[32] The EGAOB also created a subgroup dealing with ISA ('ISA subgroup').[33] The objective of this subgroup is to provide technical expertise to the EGAOB and the Commission on items and issues encompassing the need to consider the drafting, the adoption and the use of ISA, and to allow the EC to provide a proactive input into the standard-setting process set up within the IAASB. A small delegation of practitioners is regularly invited to the meetings of EGAOB's ISA subgroup, e.g., representatives from the European Federation of Accountants (FEE).

A. Article 26 of the Audit Directive

According to article 26 (1) of the Audit Directive, Member States may apply a national auditing standard as long as the EC has not adopted an international auditing standard covering the same subject matter. When the EC will adopt the ISA, all standards related to the same subject matter dealt with by the ISA are no longer applicable. However,

---

[29] Recital 2 of the Commission Decision of 14 December 2005 setting up a group of experts to advise the Commission and to facilitate cooperation between public oversight systems for statutory auditors and audit firms [2005] OJ L 329/38.

[30] Art. 3 of the Commission Decision of 14 December 2005 (note 29, above).

[31] Art. 2 of the Commission Decision of 14 December 2005 (note 29, above).

[32] Ibid.

[33] Art. 4 (3) of the Commission Decision of 14 December 2005 (note 29, above).

Member States always dispose of the possibility to adopt a standard on a subject matter that is not related to an ISA adopted by the Commission.

According to article 26 (3)–(4) of the Audit Directive, Member States may impose audit procedures or requirements in addition to – or in exceptional cases, by carving out parts of – the ISA, but only: 1) if the procedures or requirements have not been covered by adopted ISA;[34] 2) if these stem from specific national legal requirements relating to the scope of statutory audits, meaning that those (i) comply with a high level of credibility and quality to the annual or consolidated accounts in conformity with the principles of true and fair view and with the European public good and (ii) shall be communicated to the Commission and the Member States before their adoption.[35] The Directive also provides for a time-limit on 29 June 2010 for the Member States to impose these additional requirements (but not for the carve-outs).[36] If the adopted international auditing standards contain audit procedures that would create a specific legal conflict with national law, stemming from specific national requirements related to the scope of the statutory audit, Member States may carve out the conflicting part of the international auditing standard as long as these conflicts exist,[37] provided that: 1) they communicate the specific national legal requirements, as well as the ground for maintaining them, to the EC and the other Member States at least six months before their national adoption, or in the case of requirements already existing at the time of adoption of an international auditing standard, at the latest within three months of the adoption of the relevant ISA;[38] 2) the carve-outs comply with a high level of credibility and with the European public good.[39] In general, however, carve-outs provide for a dangerous tool in the context of the harmonization of auditing standards within the EU.[40] Carve-outs will impair the credibility of auditing standards as well as the harmonization of auditing standards on a European level. The objective of the Commission is to analyse the content of the ISA in order to determine whether the conditions specified by the Audit Directive

[34] Recital 13 of the Audit Directive (note 1, above).
[35] Art. 26 (3) of the Audit Directive (note 1, above).
[36] Art. 26 (4) of the Audit Directive (note 1, above).
[37] Recital 13 of the Audit Directive (note 1, above).
[38] Art. 26 (3) of the Audit Directive (note 1, above).
[39] Recital 13 of the Audit Directive (note 1, above).
[40] Ibid.

have been met, e.g. the fact whether these standards 'are conducive to the European public good'. In late 2007, the Commission commissioned a study regarding a cost–benefit analysis related to a possible implementation of ISA as well as a study on the differences between the 'clarified ISA' and the PCAOB Auditing Standard.

B. Article 28 (2) of the Audit Directive

As long as the Commission does not adopt ISA 700 and 701 relating to the auditor's report, the Directive confers the powers on the Commission to adopt a common standard for audit reports for (annual or consolidated) accounts which have been prepared in accordance with IFRS as adopted by the Commission.[41] This option for the Commission could provide for the creation of an auditor's report for financial statements prepared in accordance with IFRS that could be different from the auditor's report on other financial reporting framework, other than IFRS as adopted by the EU. This conclusion leads to the question whether an audit will still be an audit after the adoption of ISA. Moreover, the ISA are to be considered as a set of standards, as ISA build on each other, starting with the ISA on the auditor's responsibilities (ISA-series 200–260) and ending with the ISA on reporting by the auditor (ISA-series 700–805). Finally, ISA 700 clearly states that in order to report on the true and fair view of the financial statements in accordance with ISA, all ISA should be applied during the audit.

Therefore, not adopting even one ISA within the European context would necessarily lead to the non-adoption of ISA 700. One might question such a 'non-adoption' by the Commission, in the context of the objective of the Audit Directive to quest for a high level of quality of all statutory audits within the EU, including the audit of financial statements of small entities.

V. Unsettled regulatory issues

Improving audit quality through adoption of International Standards on Auditing within the EU has a number of fundamental legal implications that need to be considered in order to comprehensively cover the

---

[41] Art. 28 (5) of the Audit Directive (note 1, above).

subject. The following text outlines some of the most important of these issues.

A. General legitimacy of harmonizing regulation

First, the discussion of harmonizing auditing standards forms part of the general debate on harmonization of regulation.[42] Accordingly, harmonization of auditing standards, like any regulatory harmonization, requires a careful analysis of arguments in favour and against. Harmonization in general may save costs on one side but, at the same time, may cause new costs because it terminates competition among regulators as an inventive process to steadily improve regulation. Hence, mutual recognition of audits may serve as a viable alternative to full harmonization of auditing regulation.[43] Moreover, it is said that harmonization in general bears the risk of ending up with standards that are not optimal. Harmonized standards, like harmonized regulations in general, tend to petrify and become resistant against reform. Experience shows that it usually turns out to be very hard and complex to change harmonized regulation. Having gone through cumbersome and lengthy negotiations in order to reach harmonization the parties are not really willing to reopen the negotiation process. Also, the role of interest groups in the process of harmonization, like lawyers, the judiciary, members of involved professions and politicians, has to be taken into consideration. All of these groups have individual interests that might be influential in the process of keeping traditional standards or adopting harmonized ones. Accordingly, it is necessary to analyse the specific relevance of the regulatory debate for harmonizing auditing standards.

[42] For a comprehensive overview over the subject see the contributions in G. F. Schuppert (ed.), *Global Governance and the Role of Non-State Actors*, (Baden-Baden: Nomos Verlag, 2006); G. Hertig and J. McCahery, 'Optional rather than Mandatory EU Company Law: Framework and Specific Proposals', *European Company and Financial Law review*, 3 (2006), 341; W. Mattli and T. Büthe, 'Global Private Governance': Lessons from a National Model of Setting Standards in Accounting', *Law & Contemporary Problems*, 68 (2005), 225; R. Michaels and N. Jansen, 'Private Law Beyond the State? Europeanization, Globalization, Privatization', *American Journal of Comparative Law*, 54 (2006), 843; K. Bamberger, 'Regulation as Delegation: Private Firms, Decisionmaking, and Accountability in the Administrative State', *Duke Law Journal*, 56 (2007), 377.

[43] See M. Trombetta, 'International regulation of audit quality: full harmonization or mutual recognition? An economic approach', *European Accounting Review*, 12 (2003), 3.

In addition to these general considerations on harmonization of regulation, there are specific arguments regarding harmonization of auditing regulation that deserve closer investigation.

B. The particular problem of legitimacy of non-governmental regulation

The most important change regarding the adoption by the Commission of ISA is the fact that these standards will become part of a legal system which provides for auditing duties under domestic or harmonized European law. In other words, by adoption through endorsement, ISA will change from voluntary standards to mandatory regulations. However, ISA aren't drafted from a legislative point of view. They represent a benchmark status but not a comprehensive set of rules covering the wide range of possible issues to be regulated in the context of mandatory auditing. The situation is comparable to the adoption of IFRS by the Commission.[44] Accordingly, elevating ISA in their status from benchmark to law requires careful standard-by-standard analysis. At the same time, it is of course of paramount importance for the Commission to communicate its comments as early as possible to the IAASB. It is essential for the success of the harmonization process that ISA do not interfere with corporate law applicable in the individual jurisdictions, such as harmonized European or domestic company law.[45]

While in a more technical sense, endorsement of promulgated international standards by the EU may serve as a suitable mechanism in order to implement those standards into national law, the fundamental question of democratic legitimation of those standards in the process of their development and creation is still open and deserves further research. Specific questions have to be tackled:

- First, who is standing behind the International Standards on Auditing? Who is responsible for selecting and appointing the individuals that

---

[44] See Humphrey, Loft, Turley and Jeppesen, 'The International Federation of Accountants', (note 6, above); R. Delonis, 'International Financial Standards and Codes: Mandatory Regulation without Representation', *New York University Journal of International Law and Politics*, 36 (2004), 563.

[45] European Commission, *Comment on Exposure Drafts Improving the Clarity of IAASB Standards'* (October 2005).

actually formulate the standards? To what extent is independence of standard setters guaranteed?

- Second, do the procedural rules for developing and setting the standards on auditing in fact satisfy basic legal due process requirements with regard to transparency, options for the public to comment, minority protection, and quality assurance?[46]

C. One-size-fits-all versus segmented approach

At the moment, ISA follow a one-size-fits-all approach: all entities, whether listed or not, are audited under the same set of auditing standards. To the extent ISA have not already been adopted in EU Member States or transposed into national auditing standards in those States, adopting ISA in the EU may have significant effects on small and medium-size accounting firms that are mostly involved in rendering accounting services for non-listed entities. Like in the case of International Financial Reporting Standards, the question is whether the audit of small and medium-size entities, i.e., non-listed entities, requires specific ISA for SMEs.[47] In order to answer that question, it is necessary to substantially draw upon the corresponding discussion on IFRS. In the US, the Sarbanes–Oxley Act effectively introduced different standards on auditing for listed entities (PCAOB Auditing Standards) and non-listed entities (US-GAAS).

D. Principles versus rules-based approach

The fundamental 'cultural' difference between the traditional European auditing approach based on principles and objectives and the more rule- and checklist-based auditing approach of ISA mirrors the general divergence between Continental law and Anglo-American statutory law.[48]

---

[46] FEE Issues Paper, *Principles of Assurance: Fundamental Theoretical Issues with Respect to Assurance in Assurance Agreements* (April 2003).

[47] For Denmark see, e.g., Erhvervs- og Selskabsstyrelsen, *Report on the Auditing Requirement for B Enterprises* (March 2005).

[48] For a general reference to the topic see D. Alexander, 'A True and Fair View of the Principles / Rules Debate', *Abacus,* 42 (2006),132; B. Bennett, 'Rules, Principles and Judgments in Accounting Standards', *Abacus,* 42 (2006), 189; G. Benston, 'Principles-versus Rules-Based Accounting Standards: The FASB's Standard Setting Strategy', *Abacus,* 42 (2006), 165; J. Braithwaite, 'Rules and Principles: A theory of Legal Certainty', *Australian Journal of Legal Philosophy,* 27 (2002), 47; W. Bratton, 'Enron, Sarbanes–oxley and Accounting: Rules versus Principles versus Rents', *Villanova Law Review,* 48 (2003), 1023; L. Cunningham, 'A Prescription to Retire the Rhetoric of 'Principles-Based System',

This difference can cause problems in the process of adopting ISA within the EU. If, as proposed, each ISA has an objective that the auditor must demonstrably achieve, there is a very real risk that the objectives will inevitably become input-orientated, detailed and procedural. Only then would auditors be able to defend their actions when judged in hindsight. Therefore, the tendency would be for objectives to focus on procedures and process rather than the aims of the ISA and overall objective of the audit. That risks leading auditors into a tick-the-box mindset – with the risk of negative consequences for audit quality and for the quality of the auditing profession.

E. Single standard objective versus overall objective

The IAASB's Clarity Project started with the modest goal of agreeing on writing conventions that would make auditors' professional requirements abundantly clear – identifying what it is that auditors 'must' or 'shall' do and rewriting 'present tense' sentences so that it is clear whether they are requirements or illustrative guidance only. Very quickly, however, the discussion extended to the structure of the ISA too. In future, ISA are likely to have separate sections for requirements and application guidance. The IAASB's October 2005 exposure draft (ED) on Clarity proposed that each ISA should have a stated objective. The auditor would be expected to achieve the objective of each ISA relevant to the engagement. To do so, the auditor would comply with the requirements set out in the ISA, but would also be expected to perform any other procedures that, in the auditor's professional judgement, were necessary in the circumstances. The IAASB's intention was to focus the auditor's attention on the aims of the engagement, rather than on procedures alone, and to reinforce the need for professional judgement in determining what procedures are necessary in the circumstances. The requirement for the auditor to judge whether all procedures that are 'necessary in the circumstances' to achieve a particular objective, is intended to embrace professional judgement and avoid a tendency for the ISA to try to comprehensively cover all circumstances. However, as drafted, the requirement places strong emphasis on the procedures to be performed rather than the evidence obtained. From a European perspective, the question

in *Corporate Law, Securities Regulation and Accounting, Vanderbilt Law Review*, 60 (2007), 1411; R. Kershaw, 'Evading Enron: Taking Principles too Seriously in Accounting Regulation', *Modern Law Review*, 68 (2005), 594.

should be 'Have I obtained sufficient appropriate evidence and, if not, what can I do to obtain the necessary evidence?' rather than 'Have I performed enough steps?'

Since the beginning of the Clarity Project, regulators, investors, auditors and other stakeholders have been debating the style and structure of the ISA. At stake is not only how the ISA are drafted, but also what is expected to comply with them, including the documentation required. Hence, it is necessary to address the issue of how the objectives of the different ISA fit together to meet the overall objectives of an audit. It might appear helpful for users in understanding how the objectives of the ISA relate to the objective of the audit. It also would be helpful to ensure that the body of the ISA is complete and not duplicative.

F. Sole responsibility versus division of responsibility

Liability for auditing services is another important issue in the context of internationalization of auditing standards. In the *Parmalat* case, division of responsibility among those auditing firms that participated in the audit of the entire corporate group was permissible. As a contrast, German law prohibits division of responsibility and provides for sole responsibility of the auditor even if he or she explicitly relies on the work of other auditors. Unsurprisingly, the reform of ISA 600 'Using the Work of Another Auditor' has triggered a flood of comment letters. Exposure Draft ISA 600 now provides for sole responsibility, whereas under US law division of responsibility is permitted. Note that as a sort of counterbalance, US law prohibits limitation of auditor liability. From a European perspective, it is important to see whether the US will give in on that point and accept sole responsibility.

G. Understandability

Following the Clarity Project of the IAASB, ISA are restructured in order to incorporate an Objective, a Requirements Section and an Application Material section. The authority of the Application Material is described in paragraph 22 of the redrafted preface of ISA: 'While the professional accountant has a responsibility to consider the whole text of a standard, such guidance is not intended to impose a requirement for the professional accountant to perform the suggested procedures or actions.' The adoption of ISA in the EU should not change the authority of the Application Material. Furthermore, the text of an ISA should be read as a whole, including the Application Material, in order to create a consistent application of ISA within the EU. On the other hand, it is obvious that from the perspective of continental law jurisdictions the inclusion of Application Material in the text of ISA might pose questions with respect to the binding force of the ISA as well as the hierarchy between the various parts of ISA. The Clarity Project in that regard is but one first step in order to improve the understandability of ISA.

Another issue in that context is the variable use of words within the auditing standards. For example, in some cases the equivalent requirements in PCAOB-Auditing Standards and ISA use different words: the impact of this different usage needs to be examined. Furthermore, even when the same words are used, the words may have a different meaning due to different definitions or because the words used in the PCAOB-Auditing Standards have a meaning that is commonly understood in US jurisprudence, but for which no such a common understanding exists in ISA. It should also be recognized that the PCAOB-Auditing Standards and US GAAS are written within a certain legal and cultural environment, which means that these factors will be taken into account when evaluating the meaning of the differences between the standards and their impact on auditing practice.

H. Objectives of harmonization of auditing standards

1. Legal security and public trust in auditing

First and foremost, it is said that harmonization of auditing standards would contribute considerably to reduce the current standard overload (PCAOB Auditing Standards / US GAAS, ISA, German IDW-PS and other domestic standards) and, thereby, generally improve legal security and public trust in auditing. At present, the multitude of auditing standards applicable throughout Europe and the world makes it difficult for the auditing profession as well as for professional and non-professional investors alike to apply and understand auditing standards. As in the case of International Financial Reporting Standards (IFRS), International Standards on Auditing would tremendously simplify rendering and understanding the relevant services. This, in turn, would finally reduce capital costs for auditing clients.

2. Improving quality of auditing

Harmonized auditing standards would reduce the complexity of auditing and, thereby, reduce the likelihood of incorrect or incomplete auditing. Differing auditing standards are a most prominent source of problems and mistakes in the course of auditing across borders. This is particularly true in the case of large corporate clients with affiliations and branches in many different countries.

3. Reduction of civil liability risk

Harmonization of auditing standards would reduce the risk of civil as well as criminal liability for auditors. Hence, it would render auditing as a profession more attractive. Accordingly, it would become easier for auditing firms to recruit the personnel required to render in particular large-scale or cross-border complex auditing services.

I. Adaptability of ISA to common European auditing standards

As a precondition for any adoption of International Standards on Auditing, it is necessary to ask for the underlying principles of these Standards. What are the core regulatory subjects, what is the regulatory approach (in terms of regulatory method)? Do these Standards mandate or merely recommend specific action? Do they spell out the regulation in all detail? Do they operate on the basis of sanctions like civil liability? Moreover, the question has to be answered whether and to what extent these principles correspond to traditional Auditing Standards in force within the EU.

J. Problems of transition

On the downside, like in the case of any harmonization, adopting newly introduced uniform auditing standards inherently causes problems of transition. It will definitely take some time until the harmonized standards are applied in a uniform as well as correct manner. Hence, for a transitory period the advantages of harmonized standards have to be counterbalanced against the disadvantages of untested standards.

VI. Conclusion

The European Commission pointed out the need for high quality in all statutory audits required by Community law in order to contribute to the prevention of corporate and financial malpractice. For that purpose, the Audit Directive approved by the European Parliament and the Council in 2006 states clearly that statutory audits be carried out based on ISA.

The Audit Directive reflects a principles-based approach on auditing matters and aims at reinforcing and harmonizing the statutory audit function throughout the EU, thereby building up confidence in the functioning of the European capital markets. To that extent, the Directive provides for the application of ISA for all statutory audits to be conducted in the European Union. For ISA to become part of a legal system, the Commission has to apply the comitology procedure. This procedure sets out the authority of the Commission, the European Parliament and the Council for taking the necessary steps in order to adopt ISA for all statutory audits to be performed within the EU.

ISA are subject to a clarification project of the IAASB, which is one of the most important committees of the International Federation of Accountants, as well as a private body setting international standards. The Clarity Project is an ambitious undertaking designed by the IAASB in order to clarify what exactly is required under the ISA, which purposes are being envisaged within the ISA and how the required audit procedures could be applied in different circumstances of the audit engagement. This article identified a number of issue and questions that deserve closer analysis in order to make sure that harmonizing statutory auditing throughout the EU by adopting ISA will become a success.

15

Corporate governance: directors' duties, financial reporting and liability – remarks from a German perspective

PETER HOMMELHOFF

I. Introduction

The impossible is happening in Germany these days. The management board of Siemens, the jewel in the crown of the German economy, is preparing compensation claims against former management and supervisory board members of the company and thereby supplementing the criminal law investigations which the Munich public prosecutor has instigated against these former executives. That is very embarrassing for those involved! These events are shocking for two reasons: firstly, because management board or supervisory board members have so far hardly ever been made liable in Germany (The sarcastic comment of the former chairman of Deutsche Bank, Hermann Josef Abs comes to mind: 'It is easier to catch a pig by its slippery tail than to make a supervisory board liable.'); and secondly, these proceedings involve Siemens, an icon of the German economy. The former chairman of the supervisory board Heinrich von Pierer was, up to a few days ago, chairman of the Innovation Council, which advises Federal Chancellor Merkel on research strategies of economic significance.

From the point of view of company law, we can here discern the effects of corporate governance and the way it has continued to work better in Germany. And the events at Siemens will certainly significantly increase the already wide acceptance of corporate governance and its mechanisms. In my view, there will soon be a breakthrough in Germany (including a psychological breakthrough) and the regulatory discipline of corporate governance will meet with general approval.

That provides an occasion to trace back the development of corporate governance in Germany and to recall its essential structural elements. This enterprise is dedicated to Eddy Wymeersch with all good wishes.

Years ago, in a group of friends, he introduced me to the still so unfamiliar system of corporate governance; I would like to thank him for that.

II. Development of corporate governance in Germany

Germany initially regarded the concept of corporate governance, as originally developed in Anglo-American circles, with more reservation than interest. The 'principal agent conflict' and its resolution appeared to us to be 'old hat'.

A. Investor protection in company law

In fact, the German legislator, i.e. the Reichsjustizamt and the Reichstag, had considered the economic and therefore highly significant problem of the protection of investors more than one hundred and twenty years ago. Thousands of investors had, in the years after the Franco-German war, invested – and lost – their savings in highly speculative operations. The famous legal scholar Rudolf von Ihering was moved to remark indignantly that there were more criminals gathered together on the boards of German banks than in all the prisons. The German Reichstag responded by passing the major company law amendment of 1884, which is still valid today, making the two-tier system characteristic of German company law.

Even then, the German legislator was concerned to establish the necessary framework for the management structure of listed companies and the effective control of their board members. According to the 1884 amendment, the supervisory board was intended to compensate for the weak position of the numerous investors who were not in a position to genuinely monitor the activities of the management board. That was, and is, investor protection by company law or, in today's terminology, internal corporate governance.

B. Auditor as additional monitor

After 1884, German legislation continued at regular intervals to improve the rights of supervisory boards (and thereby internal corporate governance) in the light of experience gained in practice. The greatest impetus was provided by the Emergency Order of 1931 in reaction to the company failures after 'Black Friday' on the New York stock exchange – one of the major contributors to the growth of National Socialism in Germany.

The Emergency Order converted the 'Liaison Council' or Organ of the hidden Higher Management of the Company into the supervisory board of the company with precise directions on these functions. In addition, so that the supervisory board could effectively perform its tasks, the Emergency Order provided it with especially effective support – the auditor – who pre-audits the accounts of the management board for the supervisory board and reports to the latter on the findings of the audit.

The double function of auditors as guarantors of openness and supporters of the supervisory board, which characterizes their position in Germany, was thereby established. For decades then, auditors permitted themselves in practice to be guided by a third function supplementary to the double function or at least more or less overlapping with it. This consisted of giving friendly advice to the management board, so that the bonds of trust developing between the board and the auditors encroached extensively on their work for the supervisory board. An experienced supervisory board member accurately described the situation regarding the auditor's report: if you compared the draft report discussed in advance with the management board and that presented by the auditor to the supervisory board, you often had the impression that you were dealing with two completely different companies.

The German legislator emphatically remedied this situation in 1998 and ensured by a variety of precisely targeted measures that auditors in their internal company function were entirely directed towards the supervisory board and their bond of trust to the management board was largely loosened. This regime has, in fact, led to change in corporate and auditing practice – not least because the auditor has been recognized as the internal agent of corporate governance. The auditor is now inescapably charged with both functions of reviewing the performance of the management: as guarantor of publicity, and supporting the monitoring by the supervisory board. Advice to the management board has been considerably reduced in importance. This may also be seen from the annual financial statements in the German banking industry at the moment, which, in spite of audits and certificates, still often need to be corrected.

C. German Corporate Governance Code

The auditor and the audited accounts are functional elements of corporate governance in Germany. This is acknowledged in the German Corporate Governance Code of 2002 (now the 2007 version). This Code is the outcome of a carefully graduated process, initiated by private committees of practitioners and academics, and subsequently taken up by the federal government with the appointment of two governmental commissions in 2000 and 2001. The legislator linked the Corporate Governance Code with company law by means of the declaration of conformity: while companies are not bound by the recommendations and suggestions of the Code, if the management board and supervisory board do not wish to accept a recommendation, this must be disclosed. Both organs must make an annual declaration of what recommendations of the Code have been complied with and what not (comply or explain). The declaration must be published along with the separate company or group accounts.

With the German Corporate Governance Code the legislator pursues two objectives: firstly, foreign investors, in particular, are to be made aware of the characteristic duality of the corporate structure of German companies with their management board and supervisory board, and secondly, the legislator sees in the Code the opportunity to ameliorate the extremely strict company law – testified a hundred years ago to have 'the clunking severity of a Prussian senior public prosecutor (*Oberstaatsanwalt*)'. But together with the deregulation and the legislator's retreat from mandatory statutory impositions, another story must also be told. Where companies are resistant and unmoved by mere recommendations, the legislator does not hesitate to strike, and has now forced even Porsche SE to reveal the individual earnings of Wiedeking and other board members in the finest detail in the annual accounts; in Germany, this adds fuel to the flames of political debate on social justice.

D. Corporate governance and shareholder value

All in all, the recommendations of the Code and consequently also its suggestions, enjoy increasing acceptance among companies, in particular the DAX companies, i.e. the top German companies on the Frankfurt stock exchange. The German Corporate Governance Code is contributing significantly to change in the corporate governance practices of German companies. Only four recommendations have met with wide resistance among the DAX companies: the excess in D&O insurance policies; discussing the remuneration structure of the management board in the full supervisory board; ruling out a transfer from the chair of the management board to the chair of the supervisory board; the performance-related remuneration of supervisory board members.

Acceptance by the broader public lags a good way behind this increasing acceptance of the Code among companies. In Germany this is mainly due to the fact that 'corporate governance' is viewed as being linked to 'shareholder value' and that means to the single-minded direction of the management board's actions to the interests of the shareholders and the growth of share value. Such single-mindedness conflicts with widely held values in Germany which are rather aimed at various stakeholder interests and thereby, in particular, those of company employees. In a fairly widespread German view, it is the task of the management board, even of a listed company, to reconcile the various stakeholder interests again and again. That also corresponds to the OECD Principles of Corporate Governance.

It is true that the temperature of this controversy, initially conducted very fundamentally in Germany, has meanwhile noticeably cooled. Even without the one-sided exaggerated pursuit of shareholder interests, increasing company value equally benefits the stakeholders – namely the employees and the security of their jobs. The general approval of corporate governance in Germany is increasing little by little, but the performers are skating on thin ice. The recent description of institutional investors as 'a plague of locusts' is ever present.

III. Duties of organs under the Code

Now let us take a brief look at the obligations, as organs, of the management board and supervisory board as embedded in the German Corporate Governance Code.

A. Interplay between the management board and supervisory board

After a preamble and the first section on shareholders and general meetings, the Code does not immediately go on to deal with the management board and supervisory board: it turns instead to the administrative organs (this strikes German corporate lawyers as unusual) with an introductory section on the interaction between management board and supervisory board. The general prescription of close cooperation of the two organs in the interests of the company is repeatedly broken down into concrete situations: consultation on the strategic direction of the company, and the common concern that the supervisory board is provided with adequate information or the joint corporate governance report of the management board and supervisory board, in which any deviations from the recommendations of the Code over and above company law requirements, must be explained.

For this unusual 'trailer' the members of the commission engage in some self-praise. It is the first time in 'official' regulations that the significance of proper cooperation of both organs for the quality in a two-tier system is so emphatically highlighted. At the same time – and this may be of special interest to British readers – it describes the practical convergence of monistic and dualistic governance models. Well! I have my doubts whether that would convince Paul Davies. Marked out by German company law, the jurisdiction of each of these organs is fenced off from that of the other: management by the management board and supervision by the supervisory board; logically, the supervisory board does not participate in meetings of the management board. Third-party monitoring and division of powers are maintained in the German public company and in the resultant narrowing of the information channels between both organs and their members.

B. Rejection of commandments

Many readers of the Code will expect to find a list of specific duties for the management board, in the manner of 'the ten commandments for proper corporate management' revealing details about the general statutory duty to exercise the care of a proper and conscientious business concern. But they will be disappointed. The detailed duties of the management board referred to by the Code are those stated in any event in the Stock Corporation Act, or they are a matter of course – including the obligation to ensure compliance with the legal provisions and the company guidelines. Instead, the German Corporate Governance Code concentrates intensively on the remuneration of management board members and their conduct in possible conflicts of interest.

The reluctance to give a detailed list of commandments for proper management is to be welcomed. Rules of conduct applicable to all companies in all situations cannot realistically be drafted beyond more or less general platitudes. Management of a company is, in many respects, specific to that company but also specific to the individual. The Code therefore describes and emphasizes for both organs, i.e. equally for the management board and the supervisory board, the application of the business judgement rule – even this is merely the adoption of the statutory provision.

C. Improved supervisory board performance

In principle, these observations apply equally to the Code's recommendations and suggestions to the supervisory board. The statutory provisions are here also repeated – surrounded, however, by many helpful additions and extensions. For example, for the election of supervisory board members, for which the supervisory board itself has, according to statute, to make proposals to the general meeting (AGM), it sets down a qualification profile, compliance with which has already considerably improved the level of German supervisory boards and will continue to do so. Gone are the days when at a general meeting of a major energy company someone could seriously be nominated for the board on the grounds of having successfully worked as a cashier in a church institution. The Code also recommends that each supervisory board member must make sure of having sufficient time to carry out their functions. Logically, it is also recommended (admittedly not mandatory) that the report of the supervisory board to the AGM should state whether a supervisory board member has participated in less than half of the supervisory board meetings in a financial year.

It may be predicted that the quality of the work of the supervisory boards of German listed public companies will improve even more. The proposal in the Code that the supervisory board should regularly review its own efficiency will also contribute. Even today, a remarkable number of supervisory boards have adopted the practice of obtaining the assessment of external third parties. Management consultants and auditing companies offer this evaluation as a well-remunerated service. They apparently find enough retired supervisory board members to conduct the evaluation.

IV. Role of accountancy in the system of corporate governance

In the system of corporate governance, accountancy is in the weld between internal and external corporate governance, i.e. between the company statutes and the capital market. Supplemented and enriched by the specific information instruments of the law of the capital markets, accountancy (meanwhile internationalized) in its published form is designed to support investors' decision-making processes.

A. Function of the intermediaries

Granted, it would be politically false to assume that every small investor could derive and evaluate the necessary information from annual accounts, in particular the figures, in the manner needed to provide a basis for investment decisions. They will not have the necessary expertise and experience which are, at most, the domain of the institutional investors, and even they obtain expert external advice. On the capital markets, and thereby for external corporate governance, the intermediaries are of central importance. Finance intermediaries with their broad range of the most varied services as well as the mere information providers – the financial press, which makes company information, namely the figures in the annual accounts, intelligible for readers. The special significance of the financial press precisely for accountancy was already recognized in Germany almost fifty years ago.

B. Investor information in the management report

Nevertheless, the German and European legislators have not completely lost sight of the small investor, the individual shareholder with special need of information. The management report, setting out the position of the company or the group – independently of the figures in the annual accounts and notes, but nevertheless in conformity with them – is an important element in accountancy both under the EU Directives and the German Commercial Code. The aim of both legislators was that a degree in accountancy law should not be necessary in order to be able to understand the position of the company or the group from the accounts: some financial knowledge must suffice.

The German legislator in 1998 already raised the significance of the verbal element in the annual accounts and logically considerably tightened the standards to which the report and the reporting are subject – admittedly only vis-à-vis the supervisory board and not really in the direction of the shareholders or the general public. The review of the management report therefore affects internal and not external corporate governance.

The EU legislature treats the verbal part of the accounts with even less care – and that in two directions. Firstly, listed companies are completely exempt from providing a management report because international accountancy according to IFRS does not provide for it and the European legislature, in the IAS Regulation, made this form of accountancy mandatory for listed companies. Small investors and the general public are thereby to a great extent excluded from any role in corporate governance. Against this background, it is, secondly, hardly surprising that the remaining verbal section has recently become overloaded with all sorts of additional disorganized information thus weakening even further its effects in relation to corporate governance.

C. Audit committee

None of this means that the European legislator has completely lost sight of the relevance to corporate governance. With the obligatory audit committee in all companies, which (irrespective of their securities) are present on the capital market, the European legislator emphatically strengthened internal corporate governance in the amendment to the Eighth Directive because, apart from prescribing the formation of the audit committee, the Directive imposes special quality requirements on its members: at least one member must be experienced in international accountancy and must also be independent. In German companies without a supervisory board, but which, nevertheless, wish to avail themselves of the capital market (for example, a financing limited liability company without a supervisory board but with listed securities) the audit committee is an additional company organ. A draft Transformation Act dealing with this issue has existed in Germany for some time now.

At the same time, the mandatory audit committee will affect the work of the auditor who has, in the committee, a permanent contact centre with which he or she can discreetly have preliminary discussions about specific 'discoveries' made in the course of the audit. In addition, the audit committee is also in a position to review the quality of the preliminary work provided by the auditor to the supervisory organ. All of this, and more, improves the internal corporate governance and proves generally that, according to the conception of the European legislator, corporate governance in companies accessing the capital market should primarily be further developed internally and emphasis placed on its further professionalization.

V. Mechanism of responsibility

The picture of corporate governance painted up to now would remain incomplete without the mechanisms of individual manager responsibility, based on what I would like to term *Sesselhaftung* (the attachment of board members to their seats). This applies to management board and supervisory board members even before the statutory liability of organs.

A. 'Political' management board responsibility

As is well known, statutory law bars the appointment of a management board member of a German public company for an unlimited period: the appointment can be for five years at most. In addition, the German Corporate Governance Code suggests that, on a first appointment to the management board, this five-year period should not be the rule. On the other hand, a management board member once appointed can be removed prematurely only under specific conditions and not freely, at any time or without grounds. Reappointment then becomes the focus of this provision. A management board member in office will do all in his power to convince the supervisory board by his work, his performance and his success, that his reappointment is in the interests of the company and appropriate in the interests of his stakeholders. This mechanism is backed up by the compulsory annual account the board must give of its work and the obligation to have confidence in it voted on by the general meeting on this basis. If the shareholders withhold their confidence from the management board or one of its members, the supervisory board can remove the member concerned prematurely.

Reappointment and threatened removal are, in the system of allocation of powers in German company law, central pillars of a corporate governance designed to have permanent effects. That applies in the first place to the monitoring of, and feedback from, management board members, but also in a legally less-concentrated form to members of the supervisory board.

B. Enforcement of organ's liability

In comparison to this *Sesselhaftung*, claims for compensation against management board and supervisory board members who may have overlooked some of their obligations, had hardly any practical legal significance in Germany until recently. While the German Stock Corporation Act contains onerous liability provisions, the problem lay rather in their application and enforcement. The enforcing organ, the supervisory board (and management board for former organ members) have had understandable inhibitions against suing their colleagues: 'A crow does not pick out the eye of another crow' (or in an English version: 'dog does not eat dog'). The German Federal Supreme Court, in its programme of action in the Garmenbeck judgment, did not significantly change this.

The German legislator first brought about a legal U-turn by facilitating the power of shareholders to compel action and logically to initiate a special audit. It enables a relatively small (and achievable) minority of shareholders to ensure that measures are actually taken against management board or supervisory board members who have overlooked some obligation. Politically, this was from the outset discussed primarily from the point of view of a really effective corporate governance. In corporate practice, this is beginning to take effect and has, above all, produced a mental transformation: claims for compensation against management board and supervisory board members are no longer taboo. The current debate is proof of that.

C. Role of criminal law

The criminal justice system is developing into a player (admittedly one viewed with reserve and mistrust) in German corporate governance, with proceedings for misappropriation of company assets. The Vodaphone/Mannesmann case already has a place in German legal history. The participation of the prosecution services in the monitoring of company organs is problematic above all because public prosecutors and criminal judges do not rely on typical reasoning processes of civil law or company law but develop these specifically for criminal law. In extreme cases, what is quite permissible in company law may be an offence in criminal law. The discussion of these issues is in full swing in Germany.

VI. Summary

The concept of corporate governance has been adopted widely in German company, accountancy and capital markets law and enjoys general and continuously increasing acceptance among listed companies. But the respect for corporate governance will increase among the public all the more when it is disconnected from the one-sided, exaggerated concept of shareholder value. Outside the circle of listed companies, the major family companies have meanwhile developed a Corporate Governance Code tailored to their specific concerns away from the stock exchange, and the public state companies will follow.

In Germany, corporate governance leads to success. Gone are the days of the banker Fürstenberg with his view that shareholders are stupid and cheeky: stupid because they give their money to companies, and cheeky because, on top of that, they then want dividends in return. Today it is different. Shareholders and their interests have never been taken so seriously in Germany as they are today.

16

Some aspects of capital maintenance law in the UK

JOHN VELLA AND DAN PRENTICE

I. Introduction

The corporate form is used pervasively in the United Kingdom. In 2005 there were 1,968,000 private companies ('Ltd')[1] and 11,600 public companies ('Plc')[2] on the companies' register.[3] In the year 2004–2005 there were 332,700 new private companies incorporated and 1,100 public companies.[4] In 2005, 43,600 companies were struck off the register and 4,200 were wound up.[5] The rate of new incorporations has been significant: it is estimated that since 1997 new incorporations have risen by over 60% and the number of foreign firms incorporating in the UK has more than quadrupled.[6] A salient feature of UK company law is ease of access to the corporate form. No barriers of any substance are placed in the way of obtaining corporate status.[7] There is a 'free market' rationale for ease of incorporation – provided parties are aware that they are dealing with

---

[1] This is the default category, unless a company adopts the public company form it will be a private company: Companies Act 2006, s. 4 (hereafter 'the 2006 Act').
[2] A company must explicitly provide for public company status in its constitution: 2006 Act, s. 4(2).
[3] See DTI, *Companies 2004–2005, Report for the year ended 2005* (DTI, October 2005), Table A2.
[4] See DTI, *Companies 2004–2005*, (note 3, above), Table A2, 14.
[5] The Companies Act 2006, sections 1000–1002, enables the regulatory authorities to have a company struck off the register, normally this is for non-compliance with the regulatory provisions of the Companies Act 2006. This is by far the most common way in which companies are removed from the register. Such companies can be restored to the register: see Companies Act 2006, ss. 1024–34. In 2005, 300 companies were restored to the register (see DTI, *Companies 2004–2005* (note 3, above), Table C1).
[6] Hansard, House of Lords, Vol. 677, at 180 (2006).
[7] The Registrar of Companies offers a one-day incorporation service. It is not uncommon for the large London law firms to incorporate companies in batches so that when the need arises they can take the company off the shelf, hence the common reference to shelf companies. Such companies are treated as 'dormant' companies and are exempted from the regulatory provisions of the 2006 Act until they commence trading; see the 2006 Act, (note 1, above) s. 1134.

a limited liability company they can protect their own interests.[8] To the extent that the corporate form can be abused, control of abusive practices is by means of a liability rule applied *ex post* and by an *ex ante* rule that is designed, for example, to ensure economic viability.[9] Occasionally, UK company law will use a property rule to protect the interests of the *dramatis personae* of company law. One example of this are the provisions on shareholder pre-emption rights,[10] which use a property protection rule, the conferral of a right of pre-emption, rather than a liability rule, that is, an *ex post* legal remedy where a shareholder has been unfairly treated by a particular allotment.[11] Other than in the area of capital maintenance,[12] UK law relies on *ex post* liability rules to curb the misuse of the corporate form, rather than *ex ante* quality control rules.[13]

A second feature of English company law is that it is enabling; that is, it leaves considerable autonomy to the draftsman of a company's constitution as to how the central matters of a company's activities, namely, distribution of profits, allocation of losses, and allocation of control are dealt with.[14] The draftsman of the corporate constitution does not have a completely free hand but there is a larger measure of freedom in drafting a company's constitution that the vast bulk of the Companies Act 2006 would suggest.[15]

---

[8] See Companies Act 1985, s. 349; Griffin, 'Section 349(4) Of The Companies Act 1985: An Outdated Victorian Legacy', *Journal of Business Law*, (1997), 438. This justification is not without its difficulties: it does not address the issue of involuntary creditors (tort victims) or day-to-day normal trade creditors.

[9] For example, the Insolvency Act 1986, s. 212 (misfeasance proceedings by liquidator), s. 213 (fraudulent trading), and s. 214 (wrongful trading) are all *ex post* sanctions. There is no *ex ante* requirement such as minimum capitalization. See D. Prentice, '*Corporate Personality, Limited Liability and the Protection of Creditors*', in Rickett and Grantham, *Corporate Personality in the 20th Century* (Hart, 1998), Ch. 6.

[10] 2006 CA, ss. 574–593. These implement the Second Directive on Company Law (79/91/EEC), Article 29.

[11] See DTI, *The Impact of Shareholders' Pre-Emption Rights on A Public Company's Ability to Raise New Capital* (3 Nov. 2004), DTI, www.dti.gov.uk/cld/current.htm; DTI, *Pre-Emption Rights: Final Report* (Feb. 2005), www.dti.gov.uk/cld/public.htm.

[12] The capital maintenance rules are relaxed for private companies: see 2006 Act, s. 656 (reduction of capital); s. 691 (financial assistance); see *infra*.

[13] It is interesting to note that when limited liability was introduced in 1855 it was initially proposed that limited liability companies should possess a nominal capital of £50,000, but this was rejected: see R.R. Formoy, *The Historical Foundations of Modern Company Law* (1923) at 117.

[14] This assumes that the company is solvent. Insolvency law is prescriptive as regards hierarchy of claims and asset distribution where a company is insolvent.

[15] This Act has 1300 sections and 16 Schedules. There is also subordinate legislation.

The topic of capital maintenance under English law embraces what are standard issues in this area: (i) initial capitalization, (ii) payment for shares, (iii) the acquisition of shares using the company's capital, (iv) reductions of capital and (v) share buy backs. It is proposed to deal with these issues seriatim.

It must be emphasized, at the very outset, that the provisions in the recent Companies Act 2006 (hereafter 'the 2006 Act') dealing with capital maintenance do not fully reflect the preferences of the UK Government. Given the *ex ante* control imposed by this regime and its very prescriptive nature, which as seen does not follow the general approach of UK company law to possible abuses of the corporate form, this might not come as a complete surprise. Reform in this area was in fact constrained by the Second Company Law Directive of 1976 (hereafter 'the SCL Directive') which prescribes a set of minimum requirements Member States must adopt in their national legislation. The UK Government's hands were not, however, completely tied. The Directive only applies to public companies, meaning there was no restriction on the Government's ability to amend the law for private companies; furthermore, it could also remove elements in the previous Act, namely the Companies Act 1985 (hereafter 'the 1985 Act'), which went beyond the requirements of the SCL Directive.

Due to this limited room for legislative manoeuvre, one cannot view the provisions in the 2006 Act in isolation. When considering these provisions we shall thus also look at the extensive consultation that preceded the adoption of the 2006 Act as well as the SCL Directive and the recent work carried out on and around it. The aim, in each instance, will be to present the options that were available to the UK Government and the rationale behind the choices that were made. This exercise should also give us an indication as to what the law might have been if the Government had a completely free hand.

Before dealing with these provisions, we shall set the scene by briefly outlining the processes that led to the production of the 2006 Act and by providing an update on the state of play on the SCL Directive.

II. Reform processes in the UK and the EU

The Company Law Review that led to the 2006 Act was kick-started in 1998 with the publication of the consultation paper *Modern Company*

Law for a Competitive Economy.[16] An independent Steering Group composed of company law experts was given the lead, and its remit was to carry out a thorough and wide-ranging review of core company law. The Steering Group consulted widely and produced a number of consultation documents and reports over a three-year period culminating in the production of its *Final Report* in 2001.[17] The Government's response was contained in a White Paper published in 2002,[18] which was followed by more consultation and the publication of another White Paper in 2005.[19] Following quite an eventful parliamentary process that saw a considerable number of last minute amendments, the new Companies Act was finally enacted in 2006 after no less than eight years of consultation and delay.[20]

It is worth highlighting at this juncture one of the main guiding principles followed by the CLRSG in its review, as this will inform much of what will follow. Rather than adopting prescriptive rules that hinder transactions, the CLRSG preferred granting more freedom and allowing market and other forces, buttressed by transparency requirements, to induce regulation through contract or other means. The CLRSG acknowledged, however, that this presumption against prescription could only be a starting point which would have to yield in circumstances where market and other forces coupled with transparency requirements would not work. Even then, prescriptive intervention must be justified in terms of the costs, benefits and effectiveness. The capital maintenance regime was thus examined under this light, and the proposals made, which we shall examine further on, were thus fashioned by this principle.[21]

As noted, the reform of the capital maintenance regime within the more general company law review process took place in the shadow of the SCL Directive. Under this directive Member States are required to put in place for public companies a regime which regulates the raising of capital, and, once raised, precludes its return to shareholders unless

---

[16] DTI, *Modern Company Law for a Competitive Economy*, (London, March 1998).

[17] DTI, *Final Report*, (London, 2001, URN01/942).

[18] White Paper, *Modern Company Law*, (London, July 2002, Cm. 5533), (hereafter 'White Paper 2002').

[19] White Paper, *Company Law Reform*, (London, March 2005, Cm. 6456), (hereafter 'White Paper 2005').

[20] For a succinct account of this process see G. Morse (gen. ed.), *Palmer's Company Law: Annotated Guide to Companies Act 2006*, (London: Thompson, Sweet & Maxwell, 2007), 49–51.

[21] DTI, *The Strategic Framework*, (London: February 1999, URN 99/654), paras. 2.21–2.23; DTI, *Final Report*, (note 17, above), paras. 1.10–1.11.

specified procedures are followed. This regime, which is meant to protect the interests of creditors, thus links the possibility of a return of value to shareholders to the amount of capital they contributed. In principle, and subject to exceptions, since the capital they contributed is meant to act as a cushion to safeguard creditors' interests, value can only be returned to shareholders to the extent that the company's net assets exceed its capital.

Efforts to amend the SCL Directive were running parallel to the Company Law Review in the UK, however their result ultimately proved to be fairly modest. The first proposals to simplify the directive were made by the SLIM Group in 1999.[22] SLIM was followed by the consultation and work carried out by the High Level Group of Company Law Experts, (hereafter 'Winter Group'), appointed by the European Commission in 2001 to make recommendations on a modern regulatory framework in the EU for company law. In their 2002 report they concluded that reform of the SCL Directive should, as a matter of priority, be carried out along the lines suggested by the SLIM Group with the modifications and supplementary measures suggested by them. They also recommended the undertaking of a feasibility study of an alternative regime that could be offered as an alternative to Member States.[23] The Commission followed these recommendations as it indicated it would in its May 2003 Action Plan for Company Law and Corporate Governance.[24] It thus issued a 'moderately deregulatory'[25] proposal to amend the Directive in October 2004 and finally amended it in September 2006.[26] These amendments did not generate much excitement in the UK. After consultation led by the Department for Business Enterprise and Regulatory Reform (hereafter 'BERR' – formerly the 'Department of Trade and Industry'

---

[22] Company Law SLIM Working Group, *The Simplification of the First and Second Company Law Directives*, Brussells, October 1999, (hereafter 'SLIM Report').

[23] High Level Group of Company Law Experts, *Report on a Modern Regulatory Framework for Company Law in Europe*, Brussels, 4 November 2002, (hereafter 'Winter Report'), 16, 81 and 88.

[24] As signalled in European Commission, *Modernising Company Law and Enhancing Corporate Governance in the European Union – A Plan to Move Forward*, COM (2003) 284 final, Brussels 21 May 2003, 17–18. Most of the EU documentation on this matter can be found at http://ec.europa.eu/internal_market/company/index_en.htm

[25] European Commission, *Proposal for a Directive amending Council Directive 77/91/EEC, as regards the formation of public limited liability companies and the maintenance and alteration of their capital*, COM (2004) 730 final, Brussels, 21 September 2004, 16.

[26] For a critical assessment of this proposal see E. Wymeersch, 'Reforming the Second Company Law Directive', Financial Law Institute Working Paper No. WP2006–15, November 2006.

(hereafter 'DTI')),[27] the Minister for Industry and the Regions declared that one change would be implemented and further consultation would be carried out on another.[28]

Also in line with the proposals of the Winter Group, the Commission engaged KPMG to produce a report on the feasibility of an alternative regime and the impacts of IFRS on profit distribution in October 2006. Prior to the production of this report however, the Commission adopted an updated simplification programme in a bid to reduce administrative burdens and boost Europe's economy. Company law was identified as one of the priority areas within this initiative and the Commission asked in this context, amongst other things, whether the SCL Directive should be partly or wholly repealed or simplified.[29] In December 2007 the Commission produced a synthesis of the reactions it received,[30] which revealed that whilst most respondents took the view that further action should not be taken prior to the completion of the report, a large majority of the respondents who expressed a view on the matter opposed repealing the SCL Directive.[31]

The KPMG report was finally published in January 2008. This report, *inter alia*, compared administrative burdens under the current regime with those under different regimes extant in other jurisdictions or proposed in the literature. One conclusion reached is that the compliance costs of the different regimes, including therefore the regimes based on the SCL Directive, is generally not overly burdensome and so reduction of these costs is unlikely to be a motivation for the transition to an alternative regime. Even if one accepts these findings as robust and significant, it must be emphasized that the focus here appears to be firmly on administrative costs and not on other important considerations which could justify repealing the SCL Directive (such as allowing enhanced

---

[27] DTI, Directive Proposals on Company Reporting, Capital Maintenance and Transfer of the Registered Office of a Company: A consultation document, (March 2005). DTI, Implementation of Companies Act 2006: A Consultative Document, (February 2007). Most of the UK documentation on this matter can be found at www.berr.gov.uk/bbf/index.html

[28] *Written statement – Companies Act 2006: Government response to consultation*, 6 June 2007. This is available on the BERR website.

[29] European Commission, Communication from the Commission on a simplified business environment for companies in the areas of company law, accounting and auditing, COM (2007) 394 final, Brussels, 10 July 2007, 5–6.

[30] European Commission, Synthesis of the reactions received to the commission communication on a simplified business environment for companies in the areas of company law, accounting and auditing, COM (2007) 394, Brussels, December 2007.

[31] Ibid., p.5.

flexibility and removing regulation that has a redundant purpose or a purpose that is achieved more efficiently by other means). The report also examined the impacts of IFRS on profit distribution and explained the effects of the introduction of a new regime.

On the basis of this report, the Directorate General Internal Market and Services concluded, rather disappointingly, that:

> the current capital maintenance regime under the Second Company Law Directive does not seem to cause significant operational problems for companies. Therefore no follow-up measures or changes to the Second Company Law Directive are foreseen in the immediate future.[32]

The momentum for substantially altering or even repealing the SCL Directive thus seems to have been brought to a grinding halt by this report of massive proportion yet narrow conclusions.

The latest developments at an EU level will be met with dismay by many[33] in the UK where a general sense of hostility towards the capital maintenance regime seems to prevail. The dismissive views of many prominent academics are well documented,[34] as are those of the influential Rickford Group.[35] Indeed out of the four regimes proposed in the literature and discussed in the KPMG report,[36] that proposed by the Rickford Group represented the most radical departure from the current regime. More importantly, the UK Government has been clear in its

---

[32] DG Internal Market and Services, Results of the external study on the feasibility of an alternative to the Capital Maintenance Regime of the Second Company Law Directive and the impact of the adoption of IFRS on profit distribution, Brussels, January/February 2008, 2.

[33] Clearly not by all – see the response of the Association of British Insurers, and to a lesser extent, the Confederation of British Industry to the *Communication from the Commission on a simplified business environment for companies in the areas of company law, accounting and auditing,* http://ec.europa.eu/internal_market/company/simplification/index_en.htm

[34] J. Armour, 'Share Capital and Creditor Protection: Efficient Rules for a Modern Company Law?', 63 *Modern Law Review* (2000), 355; J. Armour 'Legal Capital: An Outdated Concept?', *European Business Organisation Law Review,* 7 (2006), 5; E. Ferran, 'The Place for Creditor Protection on the Agenda for Modernisation of Company Law in the European Union', *European Company and Financial Law Review,* 3 (2006), 178.

[35] This group was established on the joint initiative of the Accounting Standards Board and the Company Law Centre at the British Institute of International and Comparative Law. The group produced a report that considers and makes recommendations about reform of the law and practice relating to company capital maintenance regimes. J. Rickford (ed.), 'Reforming Capital: Report of the Interdisciplinary Group on Capital Maintenance', *European Business Law Review,* 15 (2004), (hereafter 'Rickford Report').

[36] See also the FEE's informative discussion paper: FEE, *FEE Discussion Paper on Alternatives to Capital Maintenance Regimes,* September 2007, at www.fee.be.

view that the SCL Directive should be repealed.[37] In a recent publication the BERR in fact explains that 'the existence of outdated and ineffective provision in the Directive significantly constrained the scope for simplifying the capital maintenance and distributions provisions now contained in the 2006 Act'.[38] As will become clearer in the following section, this does not mean that the UK would have completely dismantled the capital maintenance regime if it were not for the Directive. Further relaxations would undoubtedly have been made but these might not have been as extensive as some, especially those viewing the UK debates from the Continent, seem to believe.[39]

III. Initial capitalization

As stated earlier, English company law places no significant barriers to obtaining corporate form. The statistics on initial capitalization of companies in Tables 1–3 graphically illustrate this.[40]

These figures will not, of course, reflect the true 'economic' capital of a company, as opposed to its legal capital, as capital in the form of debt, particularly in the form of bank loans supported by directors' guarantees, plays a major role in the corporate financing of small and medium-sized companies.

As a requirement for registration of a company, the application must in 'the case of a company that is to have a share capital, a statement of capital and initial shareholdings'.[41] The statement of capital must state, *inter alia*, the total number of shares which are to be taken by the subscribers to the company's memorandum[42] and the aggregate value of those shares.[43] This gives a snapshot of the company's capital and the point of registration and it is intended to implement

---

[37] BERR, European Commission consultation on the simplification of EU company law and accounting and audit regulation: Note and Request for Views by the Department for Business, Enterprise and Regulatory Reform. August 2007.

[38] *Ibid.* para. 16. See also *White Paper 2005*, (note 19, above), 42–3.

[39] Ferran notes, for example, that some Continental commentators have tended to erroneously assume that the UK Government is in favour of radical deregulation on distributions. E. Ferran, Book Review of *Legal Capital in Europe* edited by Martin Lutter, *Journal of Corporate Law Studies*, 7 (2007), 357.

[40] DTI, *Companies 2004–2005* (note 3, above), Tables A2, B1 and B2.

[41] CA 2006, s. 9(4)(b).

[42] A company can be formed by one person subscribing to its memorandum: CA 2006, s. 7.

[43] CA 2006, s. 10(2).

Table 1. *Analysis of companies on the register at 31 March 2005 by issued share capital (from Table A7 in DTI, Companies 2004–2005)*

Issued share capital	England & Wales		Scotland		Great Britain	
	No. of companies 000s	Issued capital £m	No. of companies 000s	Issued capital £m	No. of companies 000s	Issued capital £m
No issued share capital	82.0	0.0	4.9	0.0	86.9	0.0
Up to £100	1,509.5	48.8	80.1	2.4	1,589.7	51.2
£100 to £1,000	87.2	29.0	3.9	1.3	91.1	30.3
£1,000 to £5,000	150.2	204.2	7.7	11.3	157.9	215.4
£5,000 to £10,000	25.2	157.8	2.1	13.2	27.3	171.1
£10,000 to £20,000	39.7	462.7	3.8	44.6	43.5	507.3
£20,000 to £50,000	32.9	965.3	3.7	108.9	36.6	1,074.1
£50,000 to £100,000	30.2	1,862.0	2.7	172.9	32.9	2,035.0
£100,000 to £200,000	24.3	3,016.0	2.4	296.3	26.6	3,312.3
£200,000 to £500,000	20.2	6,049.7	1.7	516.1	21.9	6,565.8
£500,000 to £1m	11.1	7,332.9	0.9	605.5	12.0	7,938.4
£1m +	31.8	1,697,378.0	1.8	79,847.8	33.6	1,777,225.8
Total	2,044.4	1,717,506.5	115.7	81,620.3	2,160.0	1,799,126.9

Table 2. *New incorporations of companies with share capital: analysed by amount of nominal capital, 2000–1 to 2004–5 (from Table B1 in DTI, Companies 2004–2005)*

Nominal share capital	2000–1	2001–2	2002–3	2003–4	2004–5
England and Wales					
Up to £100	61.4	57.0	89.8	135.5	112.8
£100 to £1,000	1.2	1.2	2.2	2.4	3.0
£1,000 to £5,000	122.7	117.0	166.6	180.8	154.1
£5,000 to £10,000	0.9	0.8	1.2	1.2	1.7
£10,000 to £20,000	12.8	12.2	17.1	17.7	14.2
£20,000 to £50,000	1.1	0.9	1.5	1.8	1.6
£50,000 to £100,000	2.9	2.3	2.8	2.9	2.4
£100,000 to £200,000	10.2	10.0	13.0	13.2	10.6
£200,000 to £500,000	1.2	0.9	1.4	1.3	1.0
£500,000 to £1m	1.1	1.0	1.4	1.3	1.2
£1m +	5.7	4.6	5.6	5.8	6.4
Companies with share capital	221.2	207.9	302.6	363.9	309.0
Companies without share capital	5.0	5.3	6.2	7.5	8.4

Table 3. *Analysis of companies incorporated in 2004–5 by issued share capital (from Table B2 in DTI, Companies 2004–2005)*

Issued share capital	England & Wales		Scotland		Great Britain	
	No. of companies 000s	Issued capital £m	No. of companies 000s	Issued capital £m	No. of companies 000s	Issued capital £m
No issued share capital	22.2	0.0	0.6	0.0	22.7	0.0
Up to £100	265.0	5.7	14.6	0.3	279.6	6.0
Over £100 & under £1,000	8.4	2.5	0.4	0.1	8.8	2.7
£1,000 & under £5,000	16.5	17.9	0.7	0.7	17.2	18.7
£5,000 & under £10,000	0.6	3.4	0.0	0.2	0.6	3.6
£10,000 & under £20,000	1.3	14.4	0.1	0.6	1.4	15.0
£20,000 & under £50,000	0.6	16.7	0.1	1.6	0.6	18.3
£50,000 & £100,000	0.8	47.7	*	1.8	0.8	48.9
£100,000 & over	1.9	29,532.6	0.1	123.6	2.0	29,656.2
Total	317.3	29,640.4	16.5	128.9	333.7	29,769.3

* Fewer than 50 companies

Article 2 of the SCL Directive.[44] A public company must possess the minimum capital of £50,000 or the Euro equivalent;[45] this is needed to comply with Article 6 of the SCL Directive. What is interesting is the figure has not been altered since the Directive was introduced in 1991. Given the figure was settled over a quarter of a century ago, it is clear is that neither the EU nor the UK makes any serious attempt to ensure that when a company starts life it possesses any significant shareholder capital.

The CLRSG had noted that it was obliged to retain this requirement by the SCL Directive but initially asked whether the amount should be increased, reduced or retained.[46] After consultation, it proposed to retain the same amount subject to the power to vary it. The Winter Group noted that the only function this requirement has is to prevent the light-hearted setting up of public companies, but concluded that since there is no evidence that this constitutes much of a hurdle to business activity it would be wise not to spend too much time considering it. It thus proposed not to alter it.[47] The Rickford Group rightly attacked this approach arguing that useless provisions are always worth repealing.[48]

Under the 1985 Act, public companies were not only subject to minimum capital requirements, they were also required to adopt a limitation on the number of shares they could issue. Indeed, both public and private companies were required to state their authorised share capital in the memorandum of association, and this acted as a ceiling on the number of shares they could issue. The CLRSG proposed abolishing this requirement,[49] and this was taken up by the Government in the White Paper 2005 which noted that this amount is usually set at a higher level than the company will ever need and thus serves no useful purpose. The White Paper also pointed out that companies would still be able to include such a ceiling in their constitutions if it was so desired.[50]

[44]   77/91/EC.
[45]   CA 2006, ss. 761–7.
[46]   DTI, *Company Formation and Capital Maintenance* (London, October 1999, URN 99/1145), para. 3.17.
[47]   *Winter Report*, (note 23, above), 82.
[48]   *Rickford Report*, (note 35, above), 13.
[49]   DTI, *Completing the Structure* (London, November 2000, URN 00/1335) para. 7.6 and DTI, *Final Report*, (note 17, above), para. 10.6.
[50]   *White Paper 2005*, (note 19, above), 43.

IV. Payment for shares

A. Par value – no discount rule

Under the 1985 Act both private and public companies were required to have a fixed par (or 'nominal') value for their shares. Shares could not be issued at a discount to their par, and if they were issued at a price higher than their par, the difference between the two, known as the share premium had to be placed in a share premium account that would be treated for most purposes in the same way as share capital.

These measures are retained in Chapter 17 of the 2006 Act. Section 580 thus prohibits a company from allotting its shares at a discount, a prohibition that was considered to be part of the common law.[51] In *Ooregum Gold Mining Co Ltd* v. *Roper*[52] a company had gone into liquidation but application was stayed because fresh capital was to be introduced into the company. Subscribers were found for 120,000 £1 preference shares. The shares were allotted for 5 shillings (25p in today's currency) with the remaining 15 shillings (75p in today's currency) being treated as having been paid up. The company proved successful and a holder of ordinary shares brought an action broadly to have the allotment declared invalid and that the holders of the preferred shares should be obliged to pay the 15 shillings that had been credited on the preference shares. The action was successful. This, of course, was greatly to the benefit of the ordinary shareholders.[53] However, the price at which the shares were issued was the only realistic one attainable because of the precarious financial state of the company. The ordinary shareholders could have argued, but did not, that it was against their interests in that the dividend payable on the preference shares would be related to the nominal value of the share and not the amount paid up on the preference share;[54] this, however, is an issue relating to dividend policy and not capital maintenance. The reasoning of the court was that the relevant legislation[55] required a company to state in its memorandum 'the amount of capital with which the company proposes to be registered divided into shares of a certain *fixed*

---

[51] *Walworth* v. *Roper* [1892] AC 125 at 145. The courts also held that a company could not purchase its own shares: *Trevor* v. *Whitworth* (1887) 12 App Cas 409.

[52] [1892] AC 125.

[53] There was evidence to suggest that the money was to be used to pay off a debenture.

[54] This was undoubtedly the reason why the shares were issued as £1 shares and not as shares with a nominal value of 5 shillings. Modern drafting of the dividend rights of preference shares normally relates the dividend payable to the amount paid up on the shares. However, partly paid shares of any class are very uncommon in the UK.

[55] Companies Act 1862, s.7 (italics added).

amount' and this entailed that the 'fixed amount' had to be fully paid. The case thus turned on a tightly technical analysis of the relevant statutory language. There was no analysis of the principle. However, the court clearly appreciated that the rule would make it difficult for a company to raise capital where its shares are trading at a discount. More importantly, the court did not address the point that where shares are issued at a discount this cannot ever cause prejudice to creditors as in the event of a company's insolvency shareholders come last so that creditors will inevitably benefit from any shareholder contribution.[56]

This point was noted, however, by the CLRSG in the recent review. The CLRSG also noted that par values rapidly cease to have any significance (as the true economic value of the shares can rise or fall) and merely tended to confuse the layman. It viewed par value requirements as an anachronism and favoured their abolition for both public and private companies,[57] thus allowing companies to issue no par value (NPV) shares, the value of which would simply correspond to a fraction of the economic value of the company as a whole. If such shares were allowed, the no discount rule would obviously also be discarded as would the concept of share premiums. Removing par values could be the first step in dismantling the capital maintenance regime, but, significantly, the CLRSG did not go so far. In fact, it favoured placing the funds subscribed for NPV shares, less the amounts paid out in expenses and commission on the issue of those shares, into an undistributable reserve account.

The CLRSG recognized that the SCL Directive, which indirectly requires shares of public companies to have par or fractional values ('accountable par'), stood in the way of the adoption of this proposal for public companies. It thus proposed the abolition of par value requirements for private companies.[58] Many respondents were 'sympathetic' to this proposal but a large majority opposed it on the ground that it could not be extended to public companies. The CLRSG thus dropped the proposal whilst reiterating its preference for NPV shares[59] and recommending that the DTI (now the BERR) continues to pursue change

---

[56] Existing shareholders may be prejudiced by the potential dilution effect but this is not a concern of capital maintenance rules.

[57] DTI, *The Strategic Framework*, (note 21, above), para. 5.4.27. The possibility of abandoning the par value requirement was raised in the very first document produced in the UK review in 1998. DTI, *Modern Company Law*, (note 16, above), 7.

[58] DTI, *The Strategic Framework*, (note 21, above), paras. 5.4.26–5.4.32; DTI, *Company Formation and Capital Maintenance*, (note 46, above), para. 3.8.

[59] DTI, *Company Formation and Capital Maintenance*, (note 46, above), para. 7.3; DTI, *Final Report*, (note 17, above) , para. 10.7 and 338.

on this issues in the appropriate EU fora.[60] Both the SLIM Group[61] and the High Level Group[62] found NPV shares worthy of further investigation, indeed, the latter noted that wide demand for such shares was being expressed by the financial industry and the legal professions.[63] Unfortunately, however, this did not lead to any amendment of the SCL Directive in this respect.

B. Share premiums

As seen, shares can be issued at price above par, i.e. at a premium; however, the no-discount rule does not require a company to allot its shares at a premium where they are trading in the market at a premium.[64] Directors who fail to obtain the maximum price from subscribers, namely a price that includes any available premium, may be in breach of duty and liable to pay the premium which could have been obtained as damages.[65] Obviously directors can forego a premium in the case of a rights offer, an employees' share scheme, or in offering share options to senior management. All these are seen as providing corporate benefit and can for this reason be defended as providing directors with the necessary flexibility to structure the company's capital. However, it is this very flexibility that the no-discount rule denies.

Curiously, the SCL Directive is silent as to how share premiums are to be treated if shares are issued at a premium. As a result, Member States that did not adopt the UK's logical but gold-plating approach of treating share premiums in almost the same manner as share capital have a much more flexible, if not fully coherent system in place.[66] The Rickford Group appeared to favour taking full advantage of this by allowing more freedom in the use of share premiums,[67] yet the CLRSG actually proposed tightening the regime to make it more coherent. In fact, it proposed removing the possibility available under the 1985 Act of using share premiums for the payment of the initial expenses of the company, commissions or discounts paid or allowed on the issue of other

---

[60] DTI, *Final Report*, (note 17, above), 340.
[61] *SLIM Report*, (note 22, above), 5–6.
[62] *Winter Report*, (note 23, above), 82–3.
[63] Ibid., 82.
[64] *Hilder* v. *Dexter* [1902] AC 474.
[65] *Lowry* v. *Consolidated African Selection Trust Ltd* [1940] AC 648 at 679.
[66] See the *Rickford Report*, (note 35, above), 20–3.
[67] Ibid., 21.

shares or debentures, or to the premium payable on the redemption of debentures,[68] and this was accepted by the Government in the White Paper 2005.[69]

C. Non-cash consideration

One final aspect of the no-discount rule that is worthy of mention relates to the issue of shares for a non-cash consideration, for example, goods or services.[70] Under the common law, this was allowed provided there is no bad faith[71] or the directors failed to place any finite value on the non-cash consideration being exchanged for the shares.[72] As was stated in *Re Wragg Ltd*:[73]

> Provided a limited company does so honestly and not colourably, and provided that it has not been so imposed upon as to be entitled to be relieved from its bargain it appears to be settled . . . that agreements by limited companies to pay for property or services in paid-up shares are valid and binding on the companies and their creditors.

There remains the critical issue of how the non-cash consideration is to be valued. On this the courts deferred to the valuation by the parties:[74]

> The value paid to the company is measured by the price at which the company agrees to buy what it thinks it worth its while to acquire. Whilst the transaction is unimpeached, this is the only value to be considered.

Thus price is value. While it was understandable that courts would not wish to leave embroiled in assessing the commercial merits of a transaction, their severe hands-off approach undermined the no discount principle.[75] Directors are under a duty:

> to consider very carefully how few shares they can issue to achieve the desired acquisition of any particular asset, and, of course, for that purpose,

---

[68] DTI, *Company Formation and Capital Maintenance*, supra n. 46, para. 3.12. DTI, *Completing the Structure*, supra n. 49, 7.8.

[69] *White Paper 2005*, (note 19, above), 42.

[70] See CA 2006, s. 482.

[71] *Hong Kong and China Glass Co. v. Glen* [1914] 1 Ch 527; *Re White Star Line Ltd* [1938] 1 All ER 607.

[72] *Tintin Exploration Syndicate Ltd v. Sandys* (1947) 177 LT 412.

[73] [1897] 1 Ch 796, at 880.

[74] [1897] 1 Ch 796, at 831.

[75] Public companies must now have non-cash consideration valued by an independent valuer. CA 2006, Part 17, Chapter 6.

> to have a very firm idea of what are the respective values of the property being acquired and their own company's shares.[76]

However this does not have the same imperative effect as a capital maintenance rule.

The above still represents the law for private companies. Public companies, on the other hand, are subject to a much stricter regime. Article 7 of the SCL Directive prohibits shares to be issued for an undertaking to perform work or supply services, article 9 prohibits the issue of shares for an undertaking to be performed in more than five years time, and articles 10 and 27 require independent experts to value non-cash consideration received as payment for shares. The CLRSG did not devote much time to this issue. In one of its early consultation documents, it noted that the provisions dealing with these matters in the 1985 Act implemented the requirements of the SCL Directive, and it proposed some minor simplifications and modifications.[77] This issue was not pursued further in the later documents it produced. In contrast, there have been noticeable developments on the EU front. The SLIM Group argued that expert opinions 'were not always useful or necessary, and that the number of cases in which they are not required should be increased'.[78] They thus proposed eliminating this requirement when the consideration consisted of shares traded on a regulated market or a recent valuation was present. The High Level Group agreed, adding that these valuations are expensive and do not offer a total guarantee of the asset's real value.[79] They thus supported the SLIM Group's recommendations to eliminate this requirement in the above instances, adding that it should also be eliminated when the values could be derived from audited accounts.

The Commission followed these recommendations and thus the SCL Directive was amended by eliminating the need for an expert valuation in the above three instances. Minority shareholders are, however, given the right to require a valuation in these instances if

---

[76] *Shearer* v. *Bercain* [1980] 3 All ER 295, at 307.

[77] DTI, *Company Formation and Capital Maintenance*, (note 46, above), 25–26.

[78] *SLIM Report*, (note 22, above), 5.

[79] *Winter Report*, (note 23, above), 83. See also the criticism made by the Rickford Group, *Rickford Report*, (note 35, above), 16–18. The Winter Group also recommended that the Commission review the possibility of allowing, with appropriate safeguards, the provision of services as contribution in kind, which is banned by article 7 of the SCL Directive, as it might be particularly useful for start-ups and technological or professional companies and other companies in which specialized services are important assets.

certain conditions are met.[80] The UK Government welcomed these proposals, yet voiced concerns about the fact that some of the terms used in the proposed relaxations were not defined. It thus believed that there would be uncertainty as to whether the conditions for being exempt from valuation requirements were met, which, when coupled with the possibility that the minority shareholders could still require a valuation, would reduce the take-up of the relaxed provisions.[81] Thus there is no intention to introduce these relaxations in the UK.

V. Financial assistance by company in acquisition of own shares

Since the Companies Act 1929, the companies legislation has prohibited the providing of financial assistance by a company in connection with the acquisition of its own shares or that of its parent company. The prohibition was enacted 'as a result of the previous common practice of purchasing shares of a company having a substantial cash balance or easily realizable assets and so arranging matters that the purchase money was lent by the company to the purchaser'.[82] The prohibition is designed to prevent the resources of a target company or its subsidiaries in a takeover are not 'used directly or indirectly to assist the purchaser financially to make the acquisition'.[83] Obviously, financial assistance could take the form of a gift[84] but normally in a commercial context it would be a breach of director's duties to make gifts. The prohibition is also directed against the entering into of imprudent transactions which could prejudice creditors and minority shareholders who were not participants in the transaction.[85]

The UK ban on financial assistance thus pre-dated the SCL Directive, which requires the imposition of a ban under article 23, but has since become one of the most controversial and criticized parts of UK com-

---

[80] See Directive 2006/68/EC Article 1 (2).

[81] DTI, *Directive Proposals on Company Reporting, Capital Maintenance and Transfer of the Registered Office of a Company: A consultation document*, London, March 2005. It would also not lead to a simplification of the law. DTI, *Implementation of Companies Act 2006 Consultative Document*, (London, February 2007), para. 6.23.

[82] *Chaston* v. *SWP Group plc* [2003] BCC 140, at 150 citing *Re VGM Holdings* [1942] Ch 235, at 239.

[83] *Chaston* v. *SWP Group plc* [2003] BCC 140, at 151.

[84] See CA 2006, s. 677(1)(a).

[85] See CA 2006, s. 677(1)(b)–(d) for other forms of financial assistance.

pany law.[86] The 1985 Act thus curtailed the strength of the ban for private companies by allowing them to provide financial assistance with respect to the acquisition of their shares but only on restricted conditions. In particular the directors of the company giving the financial assistance had to make a statutory declaration[87] broadly to the effect *inter alia* that the company would be able to pay its debts as they fell due during the year immediately following the provision of the financial assistance.[88] Also, in addition the auditors had to make a report that they were not aware of anything to indicate that the director's declaration of solvency was unreasonable.[89] The importance of the Companies Act 1985 provisions on financial assistance is that they embodied two techniques for protecting creditor interests: a solvency declaration of directors which places the responsibility on them for ensuring there is no creditor prejudice and external verification (the auditor's report) that the views of the directors were reasonable.

Despite the relaxation found in the 1985 Act, the provisions dealing with financial assistance were singled out right from the start of the UK review. Financial assistance was in fact targeted in the document that kick-started the review as being 'notoriously difficult'; it was also noted that 'legal and auditing fees are often incurred to ensure that innocent and worthwhile transactions do not breach these rules'.[90] This is not surprising given that the ban on financial assistance was criticized – to varying extents – in reports prepared by various committees in the UK going back to 1961.[91]

Initially, the CLRSG thought the complete removal of the ban for private companies too radical and thus proposed simplifying the whitewash procedure. It also proposed making some minor changes for public companies by, essentially, broadening the exceptions to the prohibition and creating new ones.[92] Emboldened by the responses it received, the

---

[86] See E. Ferran, 'Corporate Transactions And Financial Assistance: Shifting Policy Perceptions But Static Law', *Cambridge Law Journal,* 63 (2004), 225, and *Rickford Report,* (note 35, above), 25–7.

[87] CA 1985, s. 155(6).

[88] CA 1985, s. 156(2)(b). This declaration of solvency had to include contingent and prospective liabilities: s. 156(3).

[89] CA 1985, s. 156(4).

[90] DTI, *Modern Company Law,* (note 16, above), para. 3.3. See also DTI, *Developing the Framework,* (London, March 2000, URN 00/656), para. 7.19.

[91] Jenkins Committee. For a history of the ban see E. Ferran, 'Company Law and Corporate Finance' (Oxford University Press, 1999), 374–6.

[92] DTI, *Company Formation and Capital Maintenance,* (note 46, above), para. 3.42.

CLRSG eventually came down in favour of the complete removal of the ban for private companies,[93] whilst also retaining its proposal for minor changes for public companies.[94] In the White Paper 2005 the UK Government accepted the CLRSG's proposal to remove the ban for private companies, agreeing that abusive transactions could be controlled in other ways, e.g. directors' duties, wrongful trading and market abuse provisions.[95] It declined the proposals to carry out minor changes for public companies, saying that it would give priority to the CRLSG's overarching recommendation for fundamental reform through reform of the SCL Directive.[96] Section 678 of the 2006 Act thus continues the proscription of financial assistance but only with respect to a public company or the subsidiary of a public company providing such assistance. The two regulatory features for protecting creditor interests in private companies (a solvency declaration of directors and external verification) were both jettisoned in the 2006 Act.

Reform at the EU level has also been forthcoming. The SLIM Group proposed that the ban should be reduced to a practical minimum, suggesting that this could be done by either limiting financial assistance to the amount of the distributable net assets or by limiting the ban to assistance for the subscription of new shares.[97] The High Level Group favoured the former solution subject to the introduction of a number of safeguards.[98] The 2004 proposal thus allowed for financial assistance to be given up to its distributable reserves if considerably demanding conditions were met. Once again, the UK Government did not respond enthusiastically to this proposed amendment. It opined that due to the complexity and onerous nature of these conditions, it was unlikely that companies would utilize such a gateway procedure.[99] These conditions have been watered down in the actual amendment to the SCL Directive,[100]

---

[93] DTI, *Developing the Framework*, (note 90, above), para. 7.25; DTI, *Completing the Structure*, (note 49, above), paras. 2.14 and 7.12 and DTI, *Final Report*, (note 17, above), para. 10.6.

[94] DTI, *Completing the Structure*, (note 49, above), paras. 7.13–7.15; DTI, *Final Report*, (note 17, above), para. 10.6.

[95] *White Paper 2005*, (note 19, above), 41. See also DTI, *Developing the Framework*, (note 90, above), paras. 7.18–7.25.

[96] *White Paper 2005*. (note 19, above), 43.

[97] *SLIM Report*, (note 22, above), 7.

[98] *Winter Report*, (note 23, above), 85.

[99] See also E. Ferran, 'Simplification of European Company Law on Financial Assistance', *European Business Organization Law Review*, 6 (2005), 93.

[100] Article 1 (6).

however, this has not been sufficient to move the UK Government to adopt this gateway procedure.

VI. Reductions of capital

Under the 1985 Act companies, both private and public, could reduce their capital by means of a special resolution of shareholders and confirmation by court. Courts were thus entrusted with the role of protecting creditors. Creditors were given a right to object to a reduction even if it would not imperil their claim and they could block the reduction unless their debt or claim was discharged, determined or secured.[101] Courts, however, could dispense with this requirement, and in practice they generally did when reductions were structured to ensure that the creditors' interests would not be adversely affected by the reduction.[102] The CLRSG deemed this procedure inefficient since it could unjustifiably improve a creditor's position (e.g. by obtaining security). It was also known to be costly and time-consuming.[103]

The CLRSG thus proposed a simpler and more efficient approach, which would allow companies to reduce their capital by means of a special resolution of shareholders and a declaration of solvency by directors. Essentially, therefore, this proposal sought to replace an onerous creditor protection mechanism with a less onerous one. Once again the SCL Directive stood in the way of the adoption of this approach for public companies, yet this time only partially so. In fact, the UK had gold-plated the provisions on reductions of capital by requiring court approval for *every* reduction of capital. Under article 32 of the SCL Directive on the other hand, Member States are required to give creditors whose rights antedate the publication of the reduction a right to obtain security for their claims, but this can be set aside if the creditor has 'adequate safeguards' or the latter are not necessary in view of the assets of the company. It is only if a creditor is not satisfied with the above that he must he given a right to apply to a court.[104] Furthermore, under article 33, Member States are not required to apply these creditor protection mechanisms if the reduction is carried out to offset losses

---

[101] CA 85 ss. 136, 137.

[102] E. Ferran, '*Company Law and Corporate Finance*', (Oxford University Press, 1999), 368.

[103] DTI, *Modern Company Law*, (note 16, above), para. 3.2. *White Paper 2005*, (note 19, above), 41.

[104] There has been a recent change in Article 32 of the SCL Directive which shall be discussed further on.

incurred or create an undistributable reserve of not more than 10% of the reduced capital. The CLRSG thus proposed allowing reductions of capital for both private and public companies to take place by means of a special resolution and the production of a solvency statement, subject to the right of creditors of public companies to object. This right would not be available if the reduction was being made to write of losses or to create an undistributable reserve of not more than 10% of the reduced capital. In effect, therefore, the CLRSG was suggesting simplifying this procedure for public companies by dismantling the gold-plating.

At first it was proposed that this procedure would simply replace the old court approval procedure. Following the views expressed by most respondents to the consultation, however, the CLRSG proposed to retain the court approval procedure alongside the new procedure, as an option for companies.[105]

Government put forward the CLRSG's proposals in the White Paper 2002 but in the light of the mixed responses it received, it chose only to proceed with the proposals for private companies.[106] In its White Paper 2005 it explained that whilst many were in favour of simplifying the procedure for reductions, concern was expressed that due to the additional safeguards put in place for public companies few would actually make use of it.[107]

Under the 2006 Act, therefore, a private company may carry out a reduction of capital either by obtaining court approval or by the mere expediency of producing a directors' solvency statement. These two routes involve very different creditor protection mechanisms. In the latter case, the protection will be limited to a mere directors' solvency statement. Initially, it was suggested that solvency statements should here be supported by an auditors' report.[108] Auditors' reports increase time, costs and administration, but provide creditors with greater reassurance. They were required by section 156 of the 1985 Act in support of solvency statements made in connection with financial assistance provided by private companies, and are also required by section 714 of the 2006 Act in support of solvency statements made in connection with a purchase

---

[105] DTI, *Completing the Structure*, (note 49, above), para. 7.9; DTI, *Final Report*, (note 17, above), para. 10.5. For a list of reasons as to why a private company might want to use the court approval procedure see B. Hannigan and D. Prentice (eds.), *The Companies Act 2006 – A Commentary* (London: LexisNexis Butterworths, 2007), 175.
[106] The new procedure is found in ss. 642–646 of the 2006 Act.
[107] *White Paper 2005*, (note 19, above), 42.
[108] DTI, *Company Formation and Capital Maintenance*, (note 46, above), para. 3.30.

of own shares by a private company out of capital. Following its review of responses, the CLRSG came to doubt the need for this requirement and thus dispensed with it, proposing that reductions should take place under these less onerous conditions.[109] Furthermore, one notes that the 2006 Act requires companies to publicize purchases of own shares out of capital in the Gazette and a national newspaper or by written notice to each creditor,[110] but no such requirement is imposed when carrying out a reduction.

One minor change has, however, taken place for public companies. The 1985 Act required authorization in the Articles for a reduction to take place both for private and public companies.[111] The CLRSG proposed abolishing this requirement given that shareholder approval was necessary and that companies could include additional restrictions in their constitutions.[112] Under s. 641 (1) of the 2006 Act, the position has thus been reversed as it simply allows companies to restrict or prohibit reductions by means of a provision in their articles. Further change is also in prospect following the amendment of the SCL Directive. In line with the suggestion of the High Level Group, the SCL Directive was amended to shift the burden of proof that the reduction will prejudice creditors onto creditors themselves.[113] As a result of this amendment, which is meant to avoid creditor hold-ups, the SCL Directive now requires Member States to give creditors the right to apply to court only if they can credibly demonstrate that due to the reduction their claim is at stake and no adequate safeguards have been obtained from the company. The UK Government welcomed this change,[114] yet at first considered its implementation unnecessary. It was noted, in fact, that companies that are concerned that a creditor cannot demonstrate that a reduction would affect the satisfaction of his claim, can ask the court to take this factor into account.[115] Presumably a court would then use its discretion and dispense with the requirement of obtaining the creditor's consent. In the response it received, however, many indicated that an amendment

---

[109] DTI, *Developing the Framework,* (note 90, above), para. 7.26; DTI, *Completing the Structure,* (note 49, above), para. 7.10.

[110] CA 2006, s. 719.

[111] CA 2006, s. 135.

[112] DTI, *Completing the Structure,* (note 49, above), para. 2.15.

[113] Article 1 (9).

[114] DTI, *Directive Proposals on Company Reporting, Capital Maintenance and Transfer of the Registered Office of a Company: A consultation document,* March 2005, London 40.

[115] *Implementation of Companies Act 2006 Consultative Document,* February 2007, London, para. 6.24.

should be made nonetheless for the purposes of clarity, and so the UK is now in the process of adopting this change.[116]

VII. Repurchase of shares and redeemable shares

Under the 1985 Act public companies could purchase their own shares, whether redeemable or not, out of distributable profits or the proceeds of a fresh issue of shares, a system of capital substitution. Private companies could do so out of capital if a prescribed procedure, which included the production of a declaration of solvency, was followed. The CLRSG proposed to retain the substance of these rules subject to technical improvements and the following more significant changes.[117] Firstly, they proposed abolishing, for private companies, the requirement under the 1985 Act for authorization in the Articles to issue redeemable shares. Public companies alone would be subject to this requirement. Secondly, they proposed abolishing the requirement for authorization in the Articles for companies to purchase their own shares.[118] Thirdly, under the 1985 Act the terms and manner of redemption had to be included in the Articles, but the CLRGS proposed that these could be determined by the directors.[119] Finally, they proposed removing the special procedure for purchase of own shares out of capital for private companies given that a much simplified procedure for capital reduction was now being proposed.[120] The Government accepted all proposals save for the last,[121] which was dropped on the grounds that there could still be instances when this procedure would be available but the new reduction procedure would not.

VIII. Conclusion

UK Company Law puts in place a number of mechanisms to protect against abuse of the corporate form. The capital maintenance regime, which is primarily meant to protect creditors, stands out as being the

---

[116] BERR, *Companies (Reduction of Capital Regulations) 2008*, Draft Regulations October 2007. These came into force on 06/04/08.

[117] DTI, *Completing the Structure*, (note 49, above), para. 7.16.

[118] DTI, *Completing the Structure*, (note 49, above), para. 2.15.

[119] DTI, *Completing the Structure*, (note 49, above), para. 7.17.

[120] DTI, *Completing the Structure*, (note 49, above), para. 7.18; DTI, *Company Formation and Capital Maintenance*, (note 46, above), para 3.62; DTI, *Final Report*, (note 17, above) para. 10.6.

[121] The rules on purchase of own shares out of capital are found in CA 2006 Part 18 Chapters 3–6.

one area in which substantial reliance is placed on *ex ante* quality control rules rather than *ex post* liability rules.

At least four types of mechanisms employed in the capital maintenance regime to protect creditors can be identified. The first is the imposition of mandatory rules, such as minimum capital requirements, the no discount rule, the prohibition of certain types of non-cash consideration and the ban on financial assistance. These rules should provide strong protection for creditors due to their mandatory nature; however, their lack of flexibility could, ultimately, have a deleterious effect on creditors. Moreover, as seen, such rules can also be hopelessly misguided, again doing more harm than good.

The second type of mechanism is that of court approval, such as that employed in reductions of capital. Such a mechanism should clearly provide comfort for creditors; however the time and expense entailed for the company might outweigh the benefits for the creditors. On the other hand, companies which obtain court approval then enjoy certainty and finality.

The third type of mechanism employed is that of solvency requirements and statements of solvency. Under the 1985 Act this was used, for private companies, in the context of financial assistance and acquisition of own shares out of capital. The 2006 Act has extended the use of this mechanism to reductions of capital by private companies. This type of mechanism is also found in other related areas of the law, such as in the voluntary winding up of companies.[122] As seen, this mechanism can be tweaked to be more or less onerous on companies, and hence more or less protective of creditors. Further protection can thus be provided by requiring an auditors' report in support of the statement of solvency and imposing publicity requirements. One must not forget that the *ex ante* control provided by statements of solvency are buttressed by rules that impose *ex post* civil and even criminal liability[123] in the event of default by directors in making such statements.

The final protective mechanism is that of directors' duties towards creditors. Directors in the UK do not have a duty to take the interests of creditors into account unless the company is insolvent or on the verge of insolvency,[124] however, certain duties that arise in the context of capital

---

[122] Section 89 Insolvency Act 1986.

[123] See CA 2006 ss. 643 and 715.

[124] *West Mercia Safetyweaer Ltd* v. *Dodd* [1988] B.C.L.C. 250 C.A. The exact position under the common law is somewhat controversial. See now also CA 2006 s. 172 (3).

maintenance might indirectly benefit creditors, such as those relating to the issuing of shares for a non-cash consideration.

As seen, the UK legislator's hands were tied when carrying out the changes now found in the 2006 Act. The consultation documents and the two White Papers reveal that there would have been further changes if the SCL Directive did not stand in the way. There would not have been a complete dismantling of the capital maintenance regime as some might think, but there certainly would have been further relaxations. The balance would probably have shifted towards *ex post* liability, coupled, in some instances, with some light *ex ante* control, particularly in the form of solvency statements. That appears to be the preferred way forward in the UK.

17

Luxembourg company law – a total overhaul

ANDRÉ PRÜM

I. Introduction

After many years of reacting only to new European directives – the best analyses of which are by Professor Eddy Wymeersch, in whose honour the present contribution is made – Luxembourg company law is now undergoing major modernization, as demonstrated by the series of innovative laws that have been adopted over the last two years. The 25 August 2006 Act on the European company (the *Societas europaea* or SE), *sociétés anonymes* (public limited companies or SAs) with management and supervisory boards and single-person private SAs, together with the first Act of 23 March 2007 reforming the mergers and divisions (M&D) regime, and introducing partial asset contributions, transfers of all assets and liabilities, arms of business and professional assets are the key changes in the overhaul. The creation by the 11 May 2007 Act of a separate framework for companies managing family assets is just one further step intended to encourage the formation of companies under Luxembourg law. At the margins of company law, the 19 May 2006 Act on takeover bids transposes Directive 2004/25/EC of the European Parliament and of the Council of 21 April 2004. More modestly, the second Act of 23 March 2007 on international mergers stops a loophole in commercial company law while we await transposal into Luxembourg law of the directive of 26 October 2005 on cross-border mergers of companies with share capital. Of varying scope, these laws all deal with specific matters but do not yet address company law as a whole.

The Luxembourg government is now seeking to move beyond these reforms and to modernize company law in its entirety. It has therefore recently produced a bill amending the 10 August 1915 Act on commercial companies along with several provisions in title IX of the Civil Code that deal with companies. The bill (the Bill), which was submitted to the Chamber of Deputies on 8 June 2007 under number 5730 and is the result of a long-term project by the Ministry of Justice, supported by the *Laboratoire de Droit Economique*,[1] proposes a large number of changes to the Act with the aim of making it clearer and more attractive. The plan for codification à *droit constant*[2] will round off the ambitious reform programme[3]. The Bill consequently adopts the realistic, consensual approach typical of Luxembourg legislative intent in the field of business law.

The small amount of Luxembourg case law, an obvious result of the low number of disputes and limited quantity of doctrine such a small country can produce, denies Luxembourg the luxury of total originality in its approach to the law. Yet while Luxembourg law can of course seek to differentiate itself from other legal systems through its generally liberal philosophy and innovative solutions, natural caution prevents it cutting itself off entirely from Belgian and French law. The Bill recognizes this connection and in the comments on its various sections takes care to point out the inspiration for the new provisions so that their interpretation can benefit from the analyses and decisions that inspiration provides.

The Ministry of Justice has been particularly careful to find out what the legal professions want and to test their reactions to the solutions provided. The dedicated *Commission d'études legislatives* (Legislation Studies Committee) working group within the Ministry, which includes representatives from the government, public authorities and the legal professions that prepared the reform, has been the focal point for all work. The consultation process was further enlarged by canvassing the opinions of a number of eminent lawyers when work began and before the Bill was finalized.

To prevent the huge number of changes involved in a full overhaul of the 10 August 1915 Act producing just a jumbled patchwork of results, the Bill is firmly anchored to the founding principle of the Act, which Professor Nyssens, one of the originators of the initial text, has summarized as, '*contractual freedom for partners and protection for third parties*'. This dual objective, along with the aim of achieving

---

[1] Created under the auspices of the *Centre de Recherche public Gabriel Lippmann* and now attached to the Faculty of Law, Economics and Finance of the University of Luxembourg.

[2] Codification à *droit constant* subsumes the content of all previous relevant laws that are not obsolete and then abrogates the laws themselves.

[3] In the wake of Belgium and France, article IV of the Bill provides the legal basis for statutory codification.

a delicate balance between the sometimes contradictory solutions it can produce, are the key guidelines of the proposed reform and for its analysis.

II. Greater freedom

The overarching purpose of company law is to provide economic operators with a framework in which to share resources – traditionally production resources – so that they can run a commercial or civil business. The framework itself can be more or less flexible in determining authorized formats, the way in which a collective will can be formed and expressed in those formats and how those formats are financed. A liberal approach allows future members the widest possible choice on how their company will be structured, the organization of the powers on which it is based and the ways in which it can issue debt securities.

In these three areas (choice of structure, internal organization and type of finance) the Bill opens new doors.

A. *Greater choice of structures*

In line with recent reforms, the Bill increases firstly the range of company formats available and secondly the number of ways in which an existing company may be transformed or restructured.

1. Increased range of company formats to include the *société par actions simplifiée*

The Bill proposes to introduce, in addition to the traditional company formats and the SE introduced by the law of 26 August 2006, a *société par actions simplifiée (SAS)*. The idea is clearly of French inspiration and derives from European company law in particular, which enables operators to avoid the constraints of the 2nd Directive on company law by setting up an SAS. Since their introduction in 1994, French *sociétés par actions simplifiées* have been a major success.

With the same objective, the Bill defines the *société par actions simplifiée* as a company 'whose capital is divided into shares and that is formed by one or more persons who accept liability up to a limited sum only'.[4] The main characteristic of an SAS is not so much this definition as the

---

[4] Bill: art. 101–18 of the 1915 Act.

very significant freedom it gives shareholders to negotiate and create both its organization and their own inter-relations.

The Bill thus gives shareholders free rein in the articles of association to decide how their company is to be managed,[5] which decisions must be taken collectively by the shareholders and which by management alone. In the case of shareholder decisions, the manner and terms of adoption can also in principle be set out without restriction in the articles of association.[6]

As regards relations between shareholders, the Bill allows the articles of association to prohibit the disposal of shares for up to ten years and to make disposals subject to prior approval by the company or to pre-emptive right. The articles of association may also provide that in some circumstances a member may be required to sell his shares.

These rules, which illustrate the significant freedom allowed to shareholders, should ensure the SAS has a rosy future in many different fields.

2. New transformation solutions

The 27 March 2007 Act has revolutionized merger and demerger law by introducing new, additional ways of restructuring companies. Previously applying to *sociétés anonymes* only, mergers and demergers can now be undertaken by any company with a legal personality of its own and by economic interest groups. A long time coming, full and partial contributions or transfers of assets and liabilities, including of business arms, are a new addition to the range of restructuring techniques allowed. Luxembourg company law therefore now permits companies to use demerger law to transfer assets in the form of a single transfer of all assets and liabilities. They no longer have to make separate transfers of debts and receivables, which are often impossible in practice. At the same time, Luxembourg law has sought inspiration in Swiss law to allow companies, groups and also single-person undertakings to transfer professional assets. No time has been wasted in implementing these new laws, particularly those relating to the transfer of business arms, indicating that they are the answer to what was a pressing need.

---

[5] Bill: art. 101–21 of the 1915 Act, 'the articles of association set out the terms under which the company will be managed'.

[6] Bill: art. 101–25 of the 1915 Act, 'the articles of association set out the decisions that must be taken by the shareholders collectively and the terms and conditions under which this shall be done'.

To complete the picture, the Bill proposes a reform of the company transformation regime which up to now has applied only to the transformation of one commercial company into another and of civil companies into commercial companies but not the reverse, or the transformation of commercial companies into economic interest groups or vice versa.[7] Such restrictions have no justification. The Bill also allows the transformation of any private entity with a legal personality (company or economic interest group) into any other form of company or economic interest group.

The change would be accompanied by a proposed new transformation regime that is largely drawn from Belgian law (which takes quite a liberal approach to the subject).[8] The new measures are specifically intended to protect members against increased liability to which they have not agreed and third-party rights.[9] For example, the Bill would protect capital if the transformation were from a type of company to which the legal definition of 'capital' does not apply to a company based on that very concept.[10] Majority or unanimous voting rules would apply for such decisions, depending on company type. A unanimous vote would always be required to change from a general partnership to another type of company or from a company with limited liability to one with unlimited liability.[11]

B. Greater freedom to organize power within the company

Until the recent reforms, Luxembourg law took a traditional, not particularly innovative approach to the organization and sharing of power within the company. This can be seen firstly in its continuing attachment to the principle of *one share, one vote*, where the only

[7] Bill: art. 3 of the 10 August 1915 Act.

[8] At present the only legislation in the area (apart from that allowing an SE to transform into an SA or vice-versa, as allowed under articles 31–2 and 31–3 of the 10 August 1915 Act) is articles 3 ('The rights of third parties are protected'), 46 (holders of shares that do not carry voting rights acquire them for decisions on whether the company should be transformed), 69(5) ('If the capital reduction would bring the capital below the legal minimum, the meeting of shareholders must at the same time decide either to increase the capital by the appropriate amount or to transform the company') and 137–1(4) ('The provisions relating to the formation of *sociétés coopératives* organised as *sociétés anonymes* apply to the transformation of companies with other forms into *sociétés coopératives* organised as *sociétés anonymes*') of the 10 August 1915 Act.

[9] Bill: art. II, 105, introducing arts. 308bis-15 to 308bis-27.

[10] Bill: art. 308bis-16 to 308bis-20 of the 10 August 1915 Act.

[11] Bill: art. 308bis-21(5), of the 10 August 1915 Act.

exception is non-voting shares that were introduced about twenty years ago, and the system of non-equity *parts bénéficiaires* (income certificates) that do not necessarily carry voting rights. However, the total freedom with which the founders and shareholders of a *société anonyme* can decide the extent of any voting rights and the number of votes attaching to *parts bénéficiaires*, a freedom that distinguishes Luxembourg law from Belgian law, can have a significant effect on the *one share, one vote* principle. The reductive approach to management structures within *sociétés anonymes*, which ignores the management committees that exist in all major companies, is another example of the rather outmoded style of the 1915 Act.

By giving greater scope to the methods for organizing shareholders' rights and powers and to modern types of management within *sociétés anonymes,* while at the same time making it easier for decisions to be taken using modern communication techniques, the Bill increases members' freedom in these areas.

1. Freedom to organize shareholders' rights and powers

The main aims of the Bill are to make it easier to raise capital, to allow more sophisticated allocation of power among shareholders and to allow measures that will encourage a stable share register.

Allowing *sociétés anonymes* to issue shares of differing face value clearly connects to the second objective while at the same time increasing the means they can use to attract new investors. However, since the number of voting rights depends on the size of the stake held, the proportional equality of shareholders would remain protected.[12] Funds could also be raised thanks to the new powers to issue separate subscription rights and shares of less than the fractional value of old shares.[13]

Looking to Belgian law, the Bill would also allow *sociétés anonymes* to give priority rights at capital increases for which pre-emptive rights have been cancelled or reduced.[14] Replacing pre-emptive rights with priority rights should enable third parties to subscribe new shares in public issues at the market price or near market price of the issuer's old shares.

The introduction of shares carrying double voting rights, which already exists under French law, would encourage greater loyalty by rewarding shareholders who retain their shares for at least two years.

---

[12] Bill: art. II, 22) and 43) amendments to arts. 37 and 67 of the 10 August 1915 Act.
[13] Bill: art. II, 17) and 21) amendments to arts. 32 and 32–4 of the 10 August 1915 Act.
[14] New art. 32–3 to the 1915 Act proposed by the Bill.

The Bill would not however adopt the French approach of restricting this option to European shareholders only.[15]

Since the original reason for banning the sale of future shares or bonds has disappeared,[16] the Bill, following in the footsteps of changes in Belgian law in this area, proposes that the restriction should be lifted.[17] Future shares and bonds would therefore be regulated only by ordinary law on the sale of future items as the sale is defined in article 1130 of the Civil Code.

2. Freedom to organize and operate management structures

The Luxembourg legislator has taken advantage of the arrival of the SE to allow all *sociétés anonymes* to opt for a two-tier management system with both a management board and a supervisory board. Few companies appear to have taken up the option so far but a large number have set up management committees with powers far beyond those needed to carry out day-to-day management. In banking the committee is almost unavoidable if there is to be compliance with the 'four eyes criterion' (*Vieraugenprinzip*). At present, under the 1915 Act the board of directors of a *société anonyme* can permanently delegate day-to-day management only.

The Bill proposes that management committees should be officially recognized and be subject to rules close to those adopted in Belgium in 2002, which allow the articles of association to permit boards of directors to delegate their management powers to a management committee without this impinging on the company's general policies or on any of those areas that are by law reserved to the board of directors.[18] Where such delegation occurs, the board of directors is required to supervise the management committee. To prevent objections to a potential conflict of powers, which Belgian law has not prevented, the Bill is careful to point out that powers delegated to a management committee would be exercised by that committee alone. In other words, the board of directors would not be able to reserve any residual authority in those areas. For the protection of third parties, the Bill also states that any restrictions placed on the management powers delegated to a management

---

[15] Proposed new art. 67 para. 4 bis to the 1915 Act.
[16] To prevent agiotage.
[17] By the abrogation of article 43, para. 1 and of article 79 of the 1915 Act.
[18] Proposed new art. 60–1 of the 1915 Act.

committee and any distribution of duties among management committee members could not be enforced against third parties. The conflict
of interests regime that applies to members of boards of directors and
management boards would be transposed to apply also to members of
management committees.[19]

Other sections of the Bill aim to facilitate the running of management bodies and their decision-making processes. For example, it is
suggested that circular resolutions by boards of directors, which are
already common practice, should be formally recognized. Directors,
like the members of the supervisory boards of *sociétés anonymes*, but
unlike the members of management committees, would as a result be
able without fear to take unanimous decisions in writing so long as this
is allowed in the articles of association.[20] There would be no need to
justify the procedure on the grounds of emergency, as is required under
Belgian law.

Preceding the recent EU directive on shareholder rights,[21] the Bill
would enable shareholders outside the Grand Duchy to take part in the
general meetings of Luxembourg companies by videoconference or any
other remote method that ensures effective participation. An original
presumption is that general meetings of shareholders held using these
techniques would be deemed to be held at the company's registered
office. The Bill simply requires that at least one shareholder or his proxy
is physically present in Luxembourg.[22]

C. New freedom to choose finance methods

The most remarkable innovation of the Bill in this area is without any
doubt the right of any company with a legal personality of its own to
raise finance by issuing ordinary bonds,[23] i.e. by issuing bonds that are
not convertible into shares and carry no warrants. To ensure maximum
flexibility, the bonds could be registered or bearer and the issue could be
private or public. The ability to issue bonds would give companies that
are not *sociétés anonymes* new financing options that they will certainly
leap at.

---

[19] Proposed new art. 60–2 of the 1915 Act.
[20] Amendment of art. 64 (1) proposed under the Bill.
[21] Directive of the European Parliament and of the Council of 11 July 2007 on the exercise
of certain rights of shareholders in listed companies 2007/36/EC [2007] OJ L184.
[22] Bill: art. II, 43) and 49) amending arts. 67 and 70 of the 10 August 1915 Act.
[23] Bill: art. 11ter of the 10 August 1915 Act.

The important position Luxembourg accords to the *société à respon-sabilité limitée* (private limited company) has led the government to make an additional suggestion that would allow this type of company, like *sociétés anonymes*, to issue convertible bonds and bonds carrying subscription rights, both of which are particularly appreciated when it comes to financing. The change would not be possible however were it not for the closed nature of *sociétés à responsabilité limitée* that allow new partners only if approved by a reinforced majority of existing part-ners. The new proposal is that anyone wishing to subscribe or acquire a convertible bond or bond carrying a subscription right should be put up immediately for approval. This would give him prior permission to become a partner in the company, after which he could exercise his right of conversion or subscription without hindrance. At the same time, the issue of these bonds would not short-circuit the agreement process.

Another proposal to help *sociétés à responsabilité limitée* is that in future sweat equity contributions would be allowed. While these of course do not create capital and therefore are not a source of financing, they do provide resources of a different kind that can be particularly valuable if the company is micro or medium sized. Following the French model, the government therefore wants to give *sociétés à responsabilité limitée* the right to accept sweat equity so long as this is allowed under their articles of association, which must also set out the acceptance method.

D. Assessment

We expect economic operators will know exactly how to exploit these new freedoms to the full: the increase in the number of available com-pany formats that will follow the introduction of the *société par actions simplifiée,* the new ways of transforming companies and economic inter-est groups, the resources provided for the finer tuning of shareholder powers, the tighter organization of management committees and the ability of any company with its own legal personality to obtain finance by issuing bonds which, in the case of *sociétés à responsabilité limité*, can even be convertible bonds.

Yet modern company law cannot focus only on contractual freedom, it must also seek to ensure that companies operate properly and to give balanced protection to the various interests involved. It is in this area that Luxembourg company law appears to hang back, paralysed by the fear that too much regulation could prevent business expansion. Indeed before the recent reforms, the only changes undertaken were the almost verbatim transposal of Community directives, strictly limited to the mandatory provisions only, although every option to increase shareholder freedom was carefully picked up. At the same time, Luxembourg legislation did not follow the consecutive reforms introduced in Belgium and France, firstly to prevent dilution of the original liberal spirit of the 1915 Act and secondly because Luxembourg remained largely immune to the economic incidents that were often the trigger for change in other countries. Despite the applause this attitude has usually drawn from economic operators, it does present problems. The 1915 Act is now a dated law that is no longer entirely in step with modern economic reality. Its remoteness from the changes in Belgian law and to a lesser extent from French law also prevent it from using the case law and doctrine of these two systems that are so valuable to interpretation.

The Bill in some way seeks to reduce these weaknesses by increasing the intrinsic protection afforded by Luxembourg company law as well as that which it must provide to company members and third parties.

III. Greater protection

The Bill deals with protection in two ways: firstly, by making the effect of company law (i.e. legal protection) clear and transparent; and secondly, by ensuring a proper balance among the interests at stake. The first way removes a number of muddy areas and the second produces the most interesting of the innovations.

Apart from steps to protect creditors, particularly during restructurings, Luxembourg company law has until now been little interested in the 'agency' problems of majority rule or in the relationship between shareholders and management. Today, the position of minorities and the relative independence of management bodies from partners/owners create problems to which, particularly for listed *sociétés anonymes,* the 1915 Act offers no answers. Recent disputes have highlighted these shortcomings. By proposing new rights for shareholders and increasing management duties and responsibilities, the Bill is aiming to counter the potentially negative effects of excessive liberalism. In order better to protect third parties it also suggests that *sociétés à responsabilité limitée* should be subject to some of the capital protection rules that already apply to *sociétés anonymes*. In future, decisions on which of these two company formats to choose should no longer be based on the loopholes in the *société à responsabilité limitée* format.

A. New rights and responsibilities

The biggest problem with the 1915 Act is probably its treatment of minorities and in particular of *société anonyme* minority shareholders.[24] Under the Bill, they would be far better protected. In addition, the concern of shareholders in general that their ownership interests should be properly protected by management acting in a transparent and responsible manner is no longer overlooked, even though the adjustments to the 1915 Act in this respect would be more modest. The Bill proposes to bring *sociétés à responsabilité limitée* in line with *sociétés anonymes* as regards certain provisions on capital protection; this would be in addition to the recommended increase in the protection company law provides to third parties.

1. Majority–minority relations

Under the law as it stands at present, the complex relationship between controlling and non-controlling shareholders is subject to the double democratic principle that each share carries one single vote and that decisions passed by majority vote are binding on all the shareholders. Of course, *parts bénéficiaires* that carry voting rights and non-voting shares can have a (considerable) impact on these rules. Yet the 1915 Act offers little help to minorities seeking to protect themselves against majority shareholders acting primarily in their own sole interests. The theory of 'essential items' or 'accrued entitlement' has had limited success in Luxembourg law.[25] Only decisions that do not increase members' commitments or that change the company's nationality are exempt from the majority rule. Now, in order to facilitate trans-European mobility for companies, the Bill proposes abandoning even the unanimous rule for nationality changes. Minorities who believe they have been treated unfairly by majority shareholders are thus generally forced to rely on abuse of rights as a defence. But in this area actions come up against not only the difficult task of proving that disputed decisions go against the company's interests and have been taken solely in order to benefit the

---

[24] See as an example the recent decision by the Luxembourg Supreme Court, on 21 February 2008 in *Audiolux et al.* v. *Groupe Bruxelles Lambert, RTL Group, Bertelsmann et al.* (case no. 2456).

[25] I. Corbisier and A. Prum, 'Le droit luxembougeois des sociétés, une conception contractuelle et une personnalité morale non obligatoire', in J.P. Buyle, W. Derijcke, J. Embrechts and I. Verougstraete (eds.), *Bicentenaire du code de commerce*, (Brussels: Larcier, 2007), 139 and 183.

majority shareholders to the detriment of the minority shareholders, but also against the sensitivity of the Luxembourg courts on the matter.[26]

The Bill offers a real remedy here by expanding the scope of the *expertise de gestion* (the expert report minority shareholders can demand in the event of disputes with majority shareholders) and introducing the *action sociale minoritaire* (derivative action). But in some circumstances, differences between the huge majority and small minority of shareholders will have to be resolved: either in the interest of one of the two parties or by liquidating the minority shareholding. New exclusion, sell-out and squeeze-out procedures meet this need.

a. Action sociale minoritaire and expertise de gestion   To date the 1915 Act does not allow shareholders acting individually to sue company officers for negligence. This right is reserved to the company alone and is subject to approval by the board of directors and the general meeting of shareholders.[27] The rule is the result of the view that the relationship between directors and the company is similar to a mandate and binds directors to the company alone, not to each shareholder. While logical, the view creates a problem in that liability actions against negligent officers cannot be brought without the agreement of the majority shareholders, who may be reluctant to proceed against people they have themselves appointed. This is probably the reason for the rarity of such actions.

The problem has been overcome in many countries, notably in Belgium and France, by allowing minority shareholders that individually or collectively hold a minimum shareholding to sue officers on the company's behalf if the company itself fails to take such action.

The Bill proposes adopting the same approach by introducing the *action sociale minoritaire* (derivative action).[28] Based primarily on the provisions added to the Belgian companies code in this area, it would allow shareholders and *part bénéficiaire* holders who own at least 1% of the company's voting rights to bring an *action sociale minoritaire*. The holders of non-voting shares could take the same action so long as the negligence imputed to the officer(s) concerned relates to a decision in which they do hold exceptional voting rights, i.e. a decision that might alter the privileges given to compensate for the normal loss of voting rights or one

---

[26] A. Steichen, *Précis de droit des sociétés*, (Luxembourg: Saint-Paul, 2006), n. 335 and quoted case law.

[27] Corbisier and Prum, 'Le droit luxembougeois', (note 25, above), n. 46.

[28] Bill: art. II, 41 introducing arts. 63bis to 63septies to the 10 August 1915 Act.

affecting the substance or survival of the company. As in French law, an *action sociale minoritaire* could be brought not only against directors but also, if the company has a two-tier board structure, against members of the management and/or supervisory board. The procedure would be to appoint a special agent to take charge of the case. To prevent frivolous proceedings, if their action failed, the applicants could be ordered to pay all costs personally plus, if appropriate, compensation to the defendants. However, if they won, all costs reasonably claimed by the applicants and not included in the defendants' costs, would be refunded by the company. These rules should ensure that the *action sociale minoritaire* is as popular as in the countries that have already adopted the system.

Under the present law, the right of shareholders to have management documents examined is very strictly limited: firstly, to shareholders who individually or collectively represent at least one-fifth of the company's capital; secondly, it covers only inspections of the company's books and accounts by auditors appointed by the court; and finally, applications for investigations will be rejected unless there is proof of exceptional circumstances.

This contrasts with the regime that applies in European countries that have already modernized their company law. Based this time on French law, the Bill proposes a total overhaul of the system. The number of people who could request an *expertise de gestion* would be significantly raised to include any member or group of members representing at least 10% of the share capital or 10% of all voting rights. In addition to dropping the threshold by 50%, the Bill also recommends extending the right to all forms of commercial company. Although the proposed threshold is higher than that set under French law, it is the same as that applying to the rights to convene meetings of shareholders, request an item to be placed on the agenda of a meeting of shareholders or, as a result of the Bill, to request an adjournment.

There would be a two-stage procedure when exercising the right. Entitled shareholders could firstly ask the management body for details of one or more transactions or operations by the company or a consolidated subsidiary. If a satisfactory answer is not forthcoming within one month they could then ask the courts to appoint one or more experts to produce a report on the operations in question. The urgent applications judge ordering the report could also order the company to pay the expense and require publication in the manner he decides.[29]

---

[29]   Art. II(76) of the Bill reforming art. 154 of the 10 August 1915 Act.

By making it easier to obtain *expertises de gestion* and extending their scope, the reports themselves become significantly more useful and should encourage the members of commercial companies to make use of a so far very underused facility.

The Bill gives minority shareholders authority by allowing them to sue negligent officers and to demand *expertises de gestion,* thus strengthening their position vis-à-vis the majority shareholders. But these rights will be meaningless unless the minority shareholders, who feel overpowered, can impact on company decisions at least in the medium term. In some cases the dominant position of the majority shareholders will be so all-encompassing that the only solution will be to find some way of enabling the minority shareholder to leave the company.

b. Exclusion, sell-out and squeeze-out   Sell-outs and squeeze-outs first appeared in Luxembourg law at the same time as mandatory general offers (MGOs) – in the 19 May 2006 Act transposing directive 2004/25/EC of the European Parliament and of the Council of 21 April 2004 on takeover bids. But under this Act such operations can be undertaken only if the shares in a company listed on a regulated market in one or more Member States of the European Union are, as a result of an MGO, highly concentrated in the hands of one or more persons acting together.

The Bill relies on the introduction into Luxembourg of sell-outs and squeeze-outs but proposes firstly to expand their scope and secondly to introduce a parallel general exclusion and sell-out procedure to be applied when there is just cause.

In its opinion on the Bill and MGOs, the *Conseil d'État* said it hoped that sell-outs and squeeze-outs would not be used only when the concentration of power was the result of an MGO. Their hope will become a reality if the Bill is passed, since minority shareholders will then be able to demand sell-out of their holdings and majority shareholders will be able to force minority shareholders to sell them their shares (squeeze-out) as soon as 95% of the voting capital and 95% of the voting rights are directly or indirectly in the hands of a single shareholder. The result will be that minorities will have the right to sell their shares if any single shareholder acquires such a dominant position within the company that their own shares almost cease to be liquid. The only condition for sell-outs of this kind is a threshold that is higher than that for sell-outs following an MGO, when the offeror need have obtained only 90% of the company's capital. At the same time, any shareholder who, without any takeover bid, has obtained a hyper majority may buy out the hyper minority shareholders. In both sell-outs and squeeze-outs the right to buy or sell applies not only to voting shares but also to non-voting shares and *parts bénéficiaires*. The Bill refers precise procedures and price-setting methods to a future Grand Ducal regulation.

These proposals apply not only to *sociétés anonymes* all or some of whose securities are traded on regulated markets, but also to those whose securities have been delisted. They do not apply however to securities that have never been listed.

For the latter, the Bill suggests an alternative path by introducing a general exclusion and sell-out with just cause system for all SAs.[30] The idea comes directly from Belgium, where the system appears to have been highly successful ever since its introduction. The aim is to ensure that in the event of disputes between shareholders that have a serious impact on their *affectio societatis* there is an alternative to the extreme solution of winding up with just cause that is allowed under article 1871 of the Civil Code. By bringing an exclusion action, the shareholders who hold a substantial part of the powers within the *société anonyme* (in principle at least 30% of the voting rights) can remove a shareholder with whom disagreements are so great that they compromise the proper running of the company. If the court can be convinced that the just cause they allege in support of their application is relevant, it will order the respondent to transfer his securities to the applicant at a price set by the court. The pendant to this solution is the shareholder's right to demand in law that another shareholder be ordered to buy his securities. There would be no threshold on the number of shares or voting rights held but the applicant would have to prove not only that there is just cause for the action (e.g. by demonstrating serious disagreement) but also that this is imputable to the respondent. As in exclusion, the court would set the transfer price and order the respondent to sell his securities.

It is hard to predict how the Luxembourg courts would react to exclusion and sell-out proceedings since the position of the judge in such actions is the complete opposite of the extremely cautious attitude judges normally adopt in disputes between shareholders, particularly where majority interests are concerned. The duty of setting share or other risk security price that would now be imposed on the judge is likely,

---

[30] Unlike Belgian law, this would also apply to companies with listed securities. See art. II(58) of the Bill which introduces arts. 98bis to 98quinquies to the 10 August 1915 Act. The system would also apply to *sociétés à responsabilité limitée* under art. II(101) of the Bill which introduces arts. 201bis and 201ter to the 10 August 1915 Act.

particularly where unlisted securities are concerned, to cause quite a few palpitations. To make the bringing of such actions easier, articles of association could provide price-setting methods that the court would have to use. They would not be able to rule out either system.

2. Shareholder/management relations

a. Increased liability of directors and members of the management board   The new right given in the Bill to minority shareholders under certain circumstances to bring liability actions against negligent company officers on behalf of the company does expose officers to greater risk of such action.

The Bill not only increases the scope of the right of action, but it also increases the liability of directors and members of management boards if as a result of major loss the company's net assets fall below half its share capital. Officers would then have to convene a general meeting of shareholders to be held within two months to decide whether the company is still a going concern or whether it should be wound up. If it is decided to remain in business, the report presented by management would have to set out the steps recommended for putting the company back on a firm financial footing.

Under the law as it stands at present, failure to convene a shareholder meeting in due time means directors and members of management boards can be sued for serious negligence. In theory, company officers could be ordered to pay all or part of the loss incurred as a result of the failure to call the shareholder meeting but in practice it is hard to prove sufficient causal link between the loss and the alleged negligence of the company officers.

Referring to the Belgian solution, the Bill would remove the problem by creating a simple presumption of sufficient causation between the loss suffered by the company and the failure to call a shareholder meeting.[31]

Serious liability actions could also be brought against directors and members of management committees for violation of the new accounting standards.

b. Better regulation of conflicts of interest   The 1915 Act uses standard prevention methods to regulate situations in which a company officer might put personal interest before that of the company: directors must disclose conflicts of interest to colleagues, they are excluded

---

[31]   Bill: Art. II, 60) reforming art. 100 of the 10 August 1915 Act.

from deliberations on operations and transactions in which the conflict occurs, and they must report the conflict to the meeting of shareholders with a view to *ex-post* approval.

The key change by the Bill in this field is the expansion of the scope of the rule to cover day-to-day management, members of management and supervisory boards and also liquidators.

But the Bill also seeks to make the rules on conflicts of interest more effective.[32] This is achieved by making the rules apply specifically to the direct and indirect interests of the company officer but not to non-pecuniary interests. Other exclusions are current operations entered into under ordinary conditions. The person or body before whom the matter is put will now have to prepare a report on the cause of the conflict, the decision taken and the reason for that decision, along with its impact on company assets. The consequences will also have to be assessed in a report to the shareholders prepared either by the statutory or the internal auditor, depending on circumstances.

If the shareholders do not approve the decision taken by the board of directors on a conflict of interests, they can dismiss the board or bring a liability action against it. This will however not affect the action actually authorized by the board. Under current law, in the event of violation of a required procedure the ability of the company to cancel decisions taken and actions undertaken by the board of directors is unclear.[33] The Bill removes all uncertainty by giving the company the specific right to demand cancellation by the courts if the third party involved in the operation, transaction or decision knew, or ought to have known, that the rules governing conflicts of interests had been violated.

In addition to making conflicts of interest more transparent and introducing more direct procedural sanctions to protect the company, the amendments introduced by the Bill would clarify the scope and operation of this area of law, generally tightening up the 1915 Act.

3. Protection of third parties

The current focus is on the third parties – particularly the creditors – of *sociétés à responsabilité limitée* since although this company format was originally devised as an alternative to the *société anonyme*, it is not covered by the capital protection rules that company law applies to *sociétés anonymes* by virtue of the 2nd Directive.

---

[32] Bill: New art. 57 of the 1915 Act.
[33] A. Steichen, *Précis de droit des sociétés*, (note 26, above), n. 816.

The limitations of the *société à responsabilité limitée* include no duty to have independent appraisals of contributions in kind, no regulation of its subscription of its own shares or of any third-party financing of own share buy-ins.

The Bill would stop these loopholes.

Contributions in kind to *sociétés à responsabilité limitée* would have to be independently appraised along with the valuation method used, to certify that their value is at least equal to the shares issued as consideration. The exceptions currently applying to *sociétés anonymes* would apply to *sociétés à responsabilité limitée* too.

The rules on *sociétés anonymes* are also the model for the terms under which a *société à responsabilité limitée* could buy in its own shares or finance their purchase through third parties.[34] The aim in both cases would be to prevent buy-ins being used by companies materially to reduce unavailable equity without creditors' knowledge. Not all the same rules would apply to *sociétés à responsabilité limitée* however – e.g. the 10% ceiling, the maximum holding period and the duty to obtain the approval of the general meeting of shareholders.

The legal profession is unlikely to be happy about the extension to *sociétés à responsabilité limitée* of the third-party protection until now afforded only by *sociétés anonymes*. But is it reasonable to allow a choice to be made between two company formats on the basis of the weaknesses in the *société à responsabilité limitée* system? In our view, the need to provide reasonable protection to creditors, who must be able to place at least some trust in the declared capital of a company, justifies the restrictions the Bill would place on shareholder freedom.

B. New certainties

The absence of regulation is not necessarily conducive to private initiatives or to contract innovation since the lack of any framework can give rise to considerable uncertainty, particularly in an area as technical as company law, where the ordinary law of obligations does not always provide the reassurances economic operators need as to the legality of the mechanisms they have developed. The lack of a reliable framework can therefore limit contractual freedom.[35]

---

[34] Bill: new articles 190bis to 190octies of the 10 August 1915 Act.
[35] Bill: grounds, 37.

The legislative intent here is clear: ordinary law and contractual freedom in particular are not always able to provide economic operators with the legal security they require.

Doubts remain about the validity of voting agreements, the legality of contract restrictions on the sale of shares or *parts bénéficiaires* in *sociétés anonymes*, the scope of the ban on the use of leonine clauses and the rights of remaindermen and usufructuaries where stripped rights are concerned, to take only the most significant examples.

The Bill would remove these uncertainties.

Voting agreements between shareholders in a *société anonyme* and partners in a *société à responsabilité limitée* would be valid in principle and invalid only if in breach of the company's interests or of the 1915 Act, or if they rendered the person concerned subject to the decisions of the company's officers and bodies. As a precaution, squeeze-out for just cause is also introduced.

The free negotiation of shares and other securities carrying an entitlement to shares could be limited through the articles of association or by agreement, so long as the limitation is restricted in time and is in the company's interests. Any transfer made in violation of such a clause would be invalid.

The ban on leonine clauses imposed under article 1855 of the Civil Code is now too radical because it undermines schemes set up to enable banks and other contributors of funds temporarily to acquire shares or units so that they can support the restructuring of the issuer. Indeed, both the French and the Belgian courts of cassation have relaxed their positions here and have recognized the legality of these carry methods. The Bill would codify the changes in case law by recognizing the legality of the sale or acquisition of company rights '*that do not aim to harm participation in the profits, or contribution to the losses, of the company*'.[36]

The stripping of ownership rights from company rights with attribution to a remainderman and a usufructuary raises many questions about, in particular: who is the partner and who has the right to vote? who owns the right to dividends and to attributed reserves? who has the right to information? What are the rights of the remainderman and the usufructuary in the event of capital increase or sell-out by the company of its shares, capital depreciation etc? The Bill presents a bold, original general solution for the allocation of the rights of the remainderman and the usufructuary of the company rights, based on the assumption that

---

[36] New paragraph 3 of article 1855 of the Civil Code as proposed by the Bill.

in principle the remainderman is the partner. Yet it does not ignore the rights of the usufructuary, particularly where quasi usufruct is involved, or the spirit of fair collaboration with which both must exercise their rights.

To illustrate the government's intention of ensuring company law provides more legal protection, we must add to the above some reference to: the abolition of the invalidity of meetings of partners or bond holders; the amendment of the bans on companies subscribing or buying in their own shares or financing the subscription or buy-in of their own shares through third parties; and the differentiation between *sociétés coopératives à responsabilité limitée* (limited cooperative companies) and *sociétés coopératives à responsabilité illimitée* (unlimited cooperative companies). This article does not unfortunately allow us to go beyond a brief description of the general orientations of the Bill.

The additions with which the Bill fills some of the loopholes in the 1915 Act are not the only corrections it would make to clarify the Act and increase the legal protection it affords. The thirty-eight amendments the Act has undergone since it was brought into law have allowed some inconsistencies in wording to slip in and its architecture in general is not particularly harmonious. By looking at the Act as a whole, the Bill deals with these two weaknesses. If only at a marginal level, it does suggest some adjustment to the terminology used.

More ambitiously, the Bill paves the way for the merger of the 1915 Act with the relevant sections of the Civil Code to produce a new Companies Code to remove '*pointless repetitions, inconsistencies and contradictions*' that would delete '*words, expressions and concepts that are no longer used or are old-fashioned*'.[37] It would also reorganize the whole into a more comprehensive and logical body of work, simplifying the process of access and understanding of its rules.

The modernized substance would thus be reflected also in the form.

---

[37] Bill: grounds, 42.

18

Role of corporate governance reform and enforcement in the Netherlands

JOSEPH A. MCCAHERY AND ERIK P. M. VERMEULEN[*]

I. Introduction

As the recent wave of governance scandals and reforms has focused the public debate on how publicly held corporations should be structured and organized, it is hardly surprising that corporate governance of listed companies has captured the legal imagination. Books, articles and reports on the corporate governance of listed companies abound. Corporate governance reforms in developed countries as well as emerging markets are high on the policy agendas. Proposals have arisen to change, among other things, the role of non-executive directors, executive pay, disclosure, the internal and external audit process, and sanctions on director's misconduct. Suggestions have also been advanced to create new standards of integrity for auditors, analysts and rating agencies. Policymakers and lawmakers are prompted to design measures to protect shareholders from fraud, poor board performance and auditor failure. These most notably include CEO and CFO certification of accounts,[1] imposition of internal controls, the prohibition of company loans to managers and the requiring of firms to establish an independent audit committee.

While the question of the economic effect of the corporate governance regulation on the performance of listed companies has become a leading concern for both lawmakers and investors, the evidence, however, is mixed. On the one hand, it is widely acknowledged that corporate governance rules and standards promote efficiency, transparency and accountability within firms, thereby improving a sustainable economic

---

[*] We would like to thank William Bratton, Stijn Claessens, Florencio Lopez-de-Silanes, and Jaap Winter for their comments. This is an updated and revised version of a working paper on the competitiveness of the Dutch corporate governance regime that was prepared for the Netherlands Ministry of Finance.
[1] CEO: Chief Executive Officer; CFO: Chief Financial Officer.

development and financial stability. On the other hand, some scholars argue that the corporate governance movement has gone too far, entailing nothing more than a box-ticking exercise to ensure compliance with current corporate fashion trends. In this view, companies do not seem to benefit from the spillover effect of the application of disproportionate corporate governance rules and principles that have their origins in the Sarbanes–Oxley regulation.[2]

This paper focuses on the quality of corporate governance which varies widely across countries and firms. In a series of influential papers, La Porta et al.[3] have argued that the level of protection afforded to minority shareholders and creditors is associated with lower concentrations of share ownership positively related to valuable growth opportunities. La Porta et al. found that common law systems tend to outperform civil law systems by adopting legal rules that offer better protection both for expropriation of shareholders by management and the violation of the rights of minority shareholders by large shareholders. It appeared that shareholders and creditors received least protection in French civil law countries, like the Netherlands. The Scandinavian and German countries came somewhere in between. The implication of the work of La Porta et al. is that countries should move toward the more efficient common law system based on transparency and arm's length relationships.[4] However, the legal systems were generally insufficient to deter managerial abuses and misconduct within listed companies at the start of the twenty-first century. Policymakers

---

[2] See *Financial Times* (by Jeremy Grant), 'Sarbox changes welcomed but imitators still abound', 23 March 2007.

[3] R. La Porta, F. Lopez-de-Silanes, A. Shleifer, R.W. Vishny, 'Legal determinants of external finance', *Journal of Finance*, 52 (1997), 1131–50; R. La Porta, F.Lopez-de-Silanes and A.Shleifer, 'Law and finance', *Journal of Political Economy*, 106 (1998), 1113–1155; R. La Porta, F. Lopez-de-Silanes, A. Shleifer, R.W. Vishny, 'Investor protection and corporate governance', *Journal of Financial Economics*, 58 (2000), 3–29.

[4] In their study of forty-nine countries, they classified countries according to the origin of laws, quality of investor protection and quality of law enforcement. Moreover they investigated the extent to which a country adheres to the one-share-one-vote rule. A shareholder protection index was constructed which determined whether proxy voting by mail is allowed, whether minority protection mechanisms are in place and whether a minimum percentage of share capital entitles a shareholder to call for an extraordinary general meeting. Creditor rights are aggregated into an index that is higher when the creditor can take possession of the company in the case of financial distress, when there are no restrictions on workouts and corporate reorganizations and when the absolute priority rule is upheld. Finally, the rule of law index produced by the rating agency, International Country Risk, indicates the country risk and the degree to which laws are enforced.

and lawmakers across the board were forced to call for stricter legal measures that could serve to minimize the managerial agency problem inherent in corporations. Since then the legal landscape has changed rapidly. Part II of this chapter examines the recent and current governance reforms that are designed to lead to the increased accountability, transparency and enhanced performance within firms. We show that substantial progress has been made in corporate governance, bringing improvements from country to country to the legal, regulatory and commercial environments.

Recent empirical work by La Porta et al.[5] found that firms operating in jurisdictions with strong minority shareholder protections tend to have a higher Tobin's Q. The work of Lombardo and Pagano[6] supports the findings of La Porta et al., showing that better legal institutions influence equity rate of returns and the demand for equity finance by companies. They offer two reasons: (1) good laws and efficient courts curtail the private benefits of managers; (2) better law and more efficient courts facilitate the contractibility of corporate relations with customers and suppliers and the enforceability of such contractual relations. As a result, companies are more profitable which hence raise their rates of return and the amount of external financing. In their model, Lombardo and Pagano reduce managerial benefits by introducing legal limits to transactions with other companies that may dilute the income rights of minority shareholders. They also reduce the legal and auditing costs that shareholders must bear to prevent managerial opportunism. Such cost reduction may, for example, result from the introduction of class action suits or voting by mail. They conclude that the size of these effects on the equilibrium rate of return is increasing in the degree of international segmentation of equity markets.[7] This paper seeks to explore which specific corporate governance mechanisms are positively related to firm performance in the Netherlands. The wealth of recent empirical evidence supports the hypothesis of La Porta et al. that good corporate governance is among the most important factors responsible for good corporate performance.[8]

[5] R. La Porta, F. Lopez-de-Silanes, A. Shleifer, and R. Vishny, 'Investor Protection and Corporate Valuation', *Journal of Finance*, 57 (2002), 1147–1170.

[6] D. Lombardo and M. Pagano, 'Legal Determinants of the Return on Equity', in J.A. McCahery et al. (eds), *Convergence and Diversity*, (Oxford University Press, 2002).

[7] Lombardo and Pagano use the dividend yield as measure of the cost of capital.

[8] P.A. Gompers, J. Ishii and A. Metrick, 'Extreme Governance: An Analysis of Dual Class Firms in the United States', Working Paper, Harvard, Stanford and Wharton (2006);

This chapter is organized as follows. Section II takes a brief look at corporate governance in the Netherlands. Special attention is given to the channels through which corporate governance impacts valuation and firm performance in the case of the Netherlands. We focus on how the changes introduced by the Dutch Code are likely to improve the performance of publicly listed firms in the Netherlands. Section III supplies an account of the *ex post* enforcement regime in the Netherlands. Section IV concludes.

II. The Dutch Corporate Governance Regime

In this section, we investigate the quality of the Dutch corporate governance regime, and consider how well the strategy of relying on principles-based measures can encourage transparency, an independent boardroom that monitors management, and a structure through which the company's objectives are met. The approach taken here is to focus on the consequence of the widespread adoption of the best practice code and which *ex ante* corporate governance practices are being implemented and enforced. In this part, our focus is on how effective the current round of *ex ante* measures are in substantially improving the general institutional environment of Dutch firms. Special attention is given to the channels through which corporate governance impacts valuation and firm performance. Our aim is to give directions to intervention to country policy makers and company shareholders. We first give a concise picture of the current status of corporate governance in the Netherlands and argue that recent developments and reforms have altered the rules of the corporate governance game (thereby improving the rights and protection of minority shareholders).

A. Investor protection and corporate governance in the Netherlands

The Netherlands regime lies between the Anglo-American system of diffuse stockholders and the concentrated ownership regime characteristic of many continental European countries.[9] In the Netherlands, share ownership is widely dispersed and the quoted sector is a significant part

L.A. Bebchuk and A. Cohen, 'Firm's Decision Where to Incorporate', *Journal of Law and Economics*, 46 (2003), 383; L.A. Bebchuk, A. Cohen, and A. Ferrell, 'Does the Evidence Favor State Competition in Corporate Law?' *California Law Review*, 90 (2002), 1775.

[9] W.W. Bratton and J.A. McCahery, 'Restructuring the Relationship between Shareholders and Managers', in H. Schenk (ed) *Preadviezen van de Koninklijke Vereniging voor de*

of the economy. The percentage of closely held shares for the average Dutch listed company (7.30%), is much lower than the average European company (19.72%), but is still higher than the average UK (3.29%) or US (1.45%) company (LLSV 2000). However, about 22% of Dutch firms have a dual class structure which is relatively large compared to the European average (17.01%) and the average US (5.00%) and British (less than 1.00%) company. Similarly, research on the direct and indirect ownership of Dutch companies reveals a concentrated ownership structure to the extent that large blockholders (14.30%), pension funds (10.08%) and banks (7.75%) enjoy large stakes.[10] To be sure, whilst there is some evidence that concentrated control has a negative relationship for outside equity, there is some evidence for no effects[11] and positive effects[12].

Historically, the weaknesses in Dutch corporate governance most observers point out centred on limited influence of shareholders on management and extensive takeover defences. A large portion of Dutch listed companies are virtually immune to hostile takeovers. Many Dutch companies adopt one or more anti-takeover provisions, for instance through the use of preference shares. Other firms employ a depository receipt scheme, through which a listed company places its shares with a foundation. The foundation office then issues non-voting depository receipts, thus retaining control with 'insiders', and providing impediments to (hostile) takeovers. For large Dutch companies, shareholders had limited influence on corporate management as compared to the Anglo-Saxon countries. Companies that meet certain requirements for a period of three years are governed by the so-called 'structure regime', which means that a supervisory board is mandatory and able to veto important changes in the identity or structure of the company as well as to appoint the management board. Enactment of the legislation was largely a response to demands for increasing management's accountability to a broader set of stakeholders, and to ensure closer monitoring of managers. The structure regime has three variations: the Full Structure Model, the Mitigated Structure Model and the Common Model. The

Staathuishoudkunde, Herpositionering van Ondernemingen (Utrecht: Lemma, 2001), 63–85.

[10] D. De Jong, G. Mertens and P. Roosenboom, 'Shareholders' Voting at General Meetings: Evidence from the Netherlands', *EMIM Report Series*, Reference No. ERS-2004–039-F&A (2004).

[11] P.A. Gompers, J. Ishii and A. Metrick, 'Extreme Governance: An Analysis of Dual Class Firms in the United States', Working Paper, Harvard, Stanford and Wharton (2006).

[12] R.B. Adams and J.A.C. Santos, 'Identifying the Effect of Managerial Control on Firm Performance', *Journal of Accounting and Economics*, 41 (2006), 55–85.

Full Structure Model is the most prevalent. The function of the supervisory board, which typically holds all voting rights and is granted considerable power, is to evaluate the performance of the top executives, ratify management decisions and reward or penalize performance. Until 1 October 2004, the supervisory board co-opted its own members, which explains historically the predominant position of the supervisory board at the expense of shareholders. In contrast, under new legislation the power to appoint the members of the supervisory board is given to the shareholders. However, the supervisory board retains the power to nominate its own members with the exception that the works council has a right to recommend one-third of the members of the supervisory board. Nevertheless, the general shareholders' meeting is empowered to discharge the entire supervisory board which requires the interference of the Enterprise Chamber in the process of appointing new members.

Even though there is little evidence on the effect of supervisory board control on management performance, there is evidence that contrasts firm performance between shareholder-controlled firms and companies organized under the structure regime. A study by the Netherlands Ministry of Finance[13] evaluated the supervisory board performance of Dutch listed, non-financial firms in terms of market returns, accounting returns and Tobin's Q. The study revealed that for the period of 1993–1997, the sampled firm's market returns were affected by ownership concentration (positive), the size of the supervisory board (negative), depository receipts for shares (negative) and the structure regime (negative). Further, the study showed that companies which voluntarily adopted the structure regime underperformed shareholder-controlled companies. The results in De Jong et al. support the magnitude of these effects of the structure regime on firm performance. Interestingly, they find that the effect is less for Dutch multinational firms that voluntarily adopt the structure regime. We believe that this result is consistent with international competition being an important reason why these firms are better governed and therefore explains why the structure regime has no significant effect on profitability. Our discussion of the structure regime shows that the regime imposes a significant cost on shareholders.

While some groups benefited from the traditional Dutch corporate governance norms, at the same time the increasing focus on

---

[13] Netherlands Ministry of Finance, *Zeggenschapsverhoudingen en Financiële van Beursvennootschappen*, Report prepared by Center for Applied Research (Tilburg University, 2000.

management accountability to shareholders led to the design and implementation of legal measures perceived to increase the rights of shareholders and holders of depository receipts. The actual governance arrangements adopted by Dutch legislators, effective 1 October 2004, include:

- increased powers for shareholders to ratify certain management board resolutions that effect the identity or character of the NV or its businesses;
- a new regulation that gives shareholders a right to vote on the adoption of the company's remuneration policy and an entitlement to vote on a yearly basis to approve the directors' option plans;
- a right to add resolutions to the agenda of a listed company's general meeting for members holding at least 1% of share capital or a stake with a market value of €50 million;
- a measure that gives depository receipt holders in a public company the right to use proxies to exercise their voting rights (except in the context of a hostile takeover);
- an obligation that the board of directors disclose yearly to the supervisory board the main elements of its strategy, business risks and management and control systems; and
- regulation that requires that quoted companies comply with the corporate governance code or explain the reasons for non-compliance.

The common thread running through the reforms is that they increase scrutiny and accountability of directors while providing shareholders with the institutional arrangements that give them the means to exercise their basic rights of voting and economic participation.

So far it is not possible to say what the effect of these reforms have been on the financial performance of Dutch firms. Nevertheless the Dutch government's reliance on disclosure and associated mechanisms appear to have improved shareholder participation in the affairs of quoted companies and induced management to improve performance. The Electronic Means of Communication (Promotion) Act, which came into force on 1 January 2007, enhances shareholder protection by allowing electronic participation in the general shareholders meeting as well as simplifying the issuance of proxies and voting instructions. Under this Act, firms could allow shareholders to cast their votes even before the actual shareholders meeting.

B. *The Dutch Corporate Governance Code*

While there are differences in patterns of ownership and control in Europe and the US, the recent corporate scandals have occurred more in the US than Europe.[14] The Netherlands, however, has not been immune from corporate governance scandals, which attracted the media and regulator attention and highlighted some aspects and weaknesses of the Dutch system. Consistent with Coffee's observations, the Ahold scandal emerged in February 2003, when the company announced that a series of accounting irregularities in its US Food Services subsidiary had led it to overstate more than $500 million in profit booked in the previous two years. Subsequent disclosures revealed that Ahold's reported earnings had been overstated by more than $1 billion and that prior revenues had been overstated by $24 billion. This event focused observers on the state of Dutch corporate governance and prompted the promulgation of a new principles-based code of conduct (the Dutch Corporate Governance Code or Code *Tabaksblat*, hereinafter 'Code') based on a comply-or-explain standard.[15]

The Code contains general principles and detailed best practice provisions related to: the management board (role, remuneration, conflicts of interest); the supervisory board (role, independence, composition, the role of the chairman, remuneration, conflicts of interest); the general meeting of shareholders (powers, depositary receipts, provision of information, responsibility); and financial reporting (internal and external auditors, disclosure). In particular, the Code recommends the appointment of an audit, remuneration and nomination committee, which roles are to prepare the decision making of the supervisory board and supervise the management board. The members of such committees are appointed from among the members of the supervisory board. In case of a one-tier management structure, it advocates the separation between

---

[14] J.C. Coffee Jr., 'A Theory of Corporate Scandals: Why the USA and Europe Differ', *Oxford Review of Economic Policy*, 21 (2005), 198–211.

[15] In order to improve the quality of corporate governance practice of firms, the first Dutch Corporate Governance Committee ('Peters Committee') handed down a report in 1997 that introduced several recommendations designed to strengthen the monitoring role of the supervisory board including that there should be: 1) greater independence of supervisory board members, 2) greater independence of stakeholders associated with the company, 3) more selective procedures for the appointment of supervisory board members, and 4) shareholders should have a more active role in the annual general meeting (Bratton and McCahery, 'Restructuring the Relationship between Shareholders and Managers', 2001).

the Chairman and the CEO and the presence of a majority of independent non-executive directors on the board. On the matter of depositary receipts for shares, the Code states that they should not be used as an anti-takeover measure, but instead depositary receipt holders should have the possibility to exercise their voting rights.

Whilst compliance is not mandated legally, Dutch lawmakers since 2004 require an explanation for non-compliance pursuant to article 391 of Book 2 of the Dutch Civil Code. The Dutch Monitoring Committee's investigations show that there has been widespread adoption of the Code standards by a large majority of Dutch listed companies. However, a significant minority of companies do not explain the reasons for departing from best practice. This percentage is particularly high for the provision related to the anti-takeover devices. Indeed, a quarter of the companies in the survey provide no information about their anti-takeover measures, against the Code requirements. The report of the Monitoring Committee does not explicitly deal with the quality of the explanations provided by non-compliant companies, but it indicates some commonly given explanations, which appear to be standard, general and uninformative. Importantly, a study on the effectiveness of the comply-or-explain system in the UK[16] shows that shareholders should pay attention to the quality of the explanation. UK companies that do not provide any explanation for their non-compliance underperform all others. Conversely, companies which give detailed and narrative explanation in the matters of non-compliance are the best performers, even outperforming the companies that are fully compliant with the UK code of best practice. This could be explained by the fact that such companies, which have carefully considered their governance needs and eventually opted-out from best practice, are able to provide a justification to shareholders, and are well governed to deliver high returns to shareholders.

C. Benchmarking the Dutch corporate governance regime

In this section, we will review the empirical studies assessing the Dutch corporate governance regime. We can look initially to the most well-known indicator of investor protection, the La Porta et al.[17] LLSV

---

[16] S.R. Arcot and V.G. Bruno, 'One Size Does Not Fit All, After All: Evidence from Corporate Governance', Working Paper (2006), http://ssrn.com/abstract=887947.

[17] R. La Porta, F. Lopez-de-Silanes, A. Shleifer, R.W. Vishny, 'Legal determinants of external finance', *Journal of Finance*, 52 (1997), 1131–50; R. La Porta, F. Lopez-de-Silanes and A. Shleifer, 'Law and Finance', *Journal of Political Economy*, 106 (1998), 1113–55.

anti-director rights index, which summarizes the level of protection of minority shareholders in the corporate decision-making process.[18] The Netherlands differs from the other countries in terms of the LLSV anti-director index. The index of investor protection in the Netherlands (3) is in line with the US (3) and Europe (3.1 on average), but it is well below the UK (5). In particular, minority shareholders in the Netherlands seem to have strong powers in challenging resolutions that they fear to be against the company's interests, but have impediments in the exercise of their voting rights.

According to the LLSV index, the law in the Netherlands does not explicitly allow vote by mail or proxy form, allowing shareholders to vote on the items on the agenda in absence.[19] Further, the law requires shareholders to deposit any of their shares prior to a general shareholder meeting. This requirement imposes a cost on shareholders. In addition, the law does not set a default rule specifying the possibility for shareholders to cast all their votes for one candidate for the board or supervisory board (cumulative voting), thus limiting shareholders' monitoring and decisional powers. The LLSV index reveals that the Netherlands shows a mixed corporate governance framework and practices. Compared to companies in other countries, Dutch companies have highly independent boards, but on average have an entrenched board and fewer board committees. In terms of legal regime, the Netherlands ranks relatively low in investor protection index too. Therefore, the corporate governance picture offered by Dutch companies is less favourable due to the presence of entrenched boards, few board committees and low protection of shareholders rights; investors are more cautious about the governance of companies. This gets reflected into lower valuation.

It is important to recall that the LLSV index on the value of investor protection is based exclusively on hard law. Fortunately the recent studies by the Monitoring Committee of the Corporate Governance Code ('Monitoring Committee') on the implementation of the Code allows us to have an idea on the role of the code in promoting best practices in the constitution of board committees, compensation and disclosure. Thus, in terms of actual corporate governance practices prompted by Code changes, the new results of the Monitoring Committee offer a

---

[18] The index has been updated since 1998 and the more recent data are used (see discussion below).

[19] As discussed above, the Electronic Means of Communication (Promotion) Act introduces (1) the electronic convening of a general meeting of shareholders, (2) electronic participation in the meeting, and (3) electronic voting prior to the meeting.

benchmark against which Dutch companies can be compared. The Monitoring Committee established on 6 December 2004 commissioned surveys in order to obtain information on how the Code is complied with in practice. The first report on compliance with the Code was released in December 2005. It shows Dutch companies to have embraced the regulation: the average non-compliance rate per code provision is 12%. This is quite high, although it does not provide comparison with how compliance was prior to the adoption of the Code. The second report was released in December 2006 showing the average application rate and compliance increasing to respectively 92% and 96%. Despite the improvement in compliance overall, the recommendations on internal risk management and remuneration are less than average.

Using the data from the Monitoring Committee Reports, we can begin to assess the impact of the code. While the period of compliance is very short, we can nevertheless assess the role of the Code in promoting best practice. For Part II of the Code, the Management Board, there is an average compliance rate of approximately 80%.[20] Importantly, all compliance percentages are higher than those of the 2004 financial year. Despite the improvements since last year, compliance with two important parts of this chapter of the Code is less than average. These are the provisions on internal risk management and control systems (II.1.3 and II.1.4) and on directors' pay (particularly II.2.9 and II.2.10). The rates of compliance in respect of all these parts are high, namely between 95% (role and procedure and independence) and 100% (one-tier structure). The application rates are on average 4% lower than 2004. The average compliance rates (89% and 91% respectively) are lower than the total average compliance rate of 96%. This lower average figure is caused in particular by the local companies, whose compliance rates are 84% for the powers of shareholders (Part IV.1) and 75% for information and logistics regarding the general meeting (Part IV.3).

In sum, two patterns emerge. First, corporate governance practices are improving dramatically in the short term. Not only is there a high overall compliance and application rate, but key characteristics of the Code have high compliance rates. It may be argued that when companies adopt good governance practices the probability of misconduct decreases and the returns on the stock are better than those with worse corporate governance. Second, some corporate governance practices still deviate in some respects from international best practices. The percentage of

---

[20] See Monitoring Committee (www.corpgov.nl).

companies with a committee dealing with corporate governance issues, for example, only slightly increases over years, from 16.3% in 2004 to 21.2% in 2005. The pattern suggests that companies follow only what the Code recommends, and not other best practices in corporate governance. Moreover, the persistence of control-enhancing mechanisms, such as dual class shares and opaque capital structures, are also likely to affect the governance ratings for Dutch firms.[21]

Finally, there is recent evidence[22] that the degree of investor protection against self-dealing is quite low viewed from a comparative corporate governance perspective. If this is the case, Dutch corporate governance needs to be corrected if the business environment for entrepreneurs is to improve. In the next section, we discuss the anti-self-dealing index of Djankov et al. and we interpret the Netherlands regulations in terms of the protection of investors against self-dealing.

D. Protecting investors against self-dealing

This section looks at the legal rules and their enforcement which have been developed to regulate self-dealing transactions, with particular reference to the Netherlands. Here we look at evidence from other countries when discussing the developments in the Netherlands, which has more in common with other European countries than the UK or the US in this area.

There is widespread agreement about the important role that related party transactions can play in an economy. Concretely, a related party transaction is a situation where there is one man (Mr James) who controlled 60% of company A and proposes that the company buy fifty used vehicles from a company in which he owns 90% of the company. In this context, the price is likely to be higher and Mr James will clearly benefit from the transaction. Such transactions are authorized in many jurisdictions to permit flexibility and to make room for private contractual arrangements that are consistent with the furtherance of corporate objectives and are subject to appropriate checks and balances. In some of these cases, the company's financial situation might preclude it from negotiating arm's length arrangements with third parties.

---

[21] Deminor-rating (2005), *Application of the One Share-One Vote Principle in Europe*, A study commissioned by the Association of British Insurers, available at www.abi.org.uk.

[22] S. Djankov, R. La Porta, F. Lopez-de-Silanes and A. Shleifer, 'The Law and Economics of Self Dealing', NBER Working Paper 11883 (2006).

A key concern about related party transactions is that they can be influenced by the relationship between two sides of a transaction and not undertaken according to market prices. For both controlling shareholders and insiders such as management, related party transactions can be the mechanism for extracting private benefits at the expense of other shareholders. The limited ability of investors to protect themselves against opportunism by insiders and the high cost of regulating such transactions have influenced regulators' strategies. Moreover, the nature of the potential problem varies: in companies with controlling shareholders and with corporate groups the transactions and the measures needed to deal with them differ from those companies where ownership is dispersed and where the board and management are effectively entrenched. Corporate law in many countries allows related party transactions, but also includes a variety of techniques and measures to control the danger of opportunism.

As Djankov, La Porta, Lopez-de-Silanes and Shleifer have showed with their comparative work on protections against self-dealing, common law and civil law countries use similar legal strategies to control related party transactions, namely mandatory disclosure, board approval, the specification of fiduciary duties for the board and shareholder approval. For example, studies show that countries with very different corporate governance systems can achieve similar results in mitigating abusive transactions with different combinations of corporate governance mechanisms.[23] The most common and effective response is disclosure of potentially conflicted transactions. In fact, public disclosure is the predominate pattern around the world. In the US, for instance, publicly listed companies are required not only to publicly disclose all major transactions, but also certain relationships and material transactions between the company and its officers and/or their families and their enterprises. Most jurisdictions rely on board approval to screen conflicted transactions and evaluate whether a related party transaction is at arms length or whether it is detrimental to the company. Authorization for most self-dealing transactions can usually only be given by non-interested directors. Even though lawmakers in common law countries do not typically require mandatory board approval, it functions, nevertheless, to encourage interested managers to obtain approval of conflicted transactions.

---

[23] G. Hertig and H. Kanda, 'Related Party Transactions', in R. Kraakman, P. Davies, H. Hansmann, G. Hertig, K.J. Hopt, H. Kanda and E. Rock, *The Anatomy of Corporate Law, A Comparative and Functional Approach*, (Oxford University Press, 2005), 101–30.

Judging from Djankov's data, countries have made significant progress in establishing measures to protect investors from the wrongdoing of directors. The Netherlands approach of curtailing private benefits and other mismanagement (0.21) is, however, half as low as the average European country (0.40), three times lower than the US (0.65) and almost four times as low as the UK (0.93). This Dutch approach to the enforcement of investor protection from management and large blockholder fraud is based on board disclosure and approval of any conflict of interest or potential conflict of interest that may be of material significance to the company. Shareholders are also required to approve the interested transactions that have obtained board approval and ratification.

In fact, Book 2 of the Dutch Civil Code states in Section 146 (for publicly held corporations) and Section 256 (for closely held corporations) that if directors have a conflict of interest, the corporation shall be represented by the members of the supervisory board. The shareholders' meeting is authorized to appoint another person to represent the company. The Dutch Enterprise Chamber, a division of the Amsterdam Court of Appeals, and Supreme Court have clarified these statutory provisions and decided that the corporation is not bound to a conflicted transaction if the third party did not act in good faith. This 'external effect' is considered to be particularly cumbersome for banks that enter into credit facility agreements with a group of companies as banks run the risk that transactions and payments under the facility will be nullified by subsidiaries in a financially distressed group. Still, even though the legal literature does not approve the *ex post* clarification of the conflict of interest rule, the court's decisions seem to evince the court's intention to enhance shareholder rights by requiring the explicit and immediate approval of conflicted transactions. The following part will highlight the importance of specialized courts in resolving corporate governance related disputes.

III. *Ex post* enforcement in Dutch corporate law

A. *Role of gatekeepers*

An assessment of the corporate governance movement in the Netherlands would be incomplete if it neglected the role of institutions – corporate governance monitoring committees, supervisory authorities, securities regulators, investors' associations, stock exchanges, the judiciary, institutional investors, equity analysts, accountants and a probing media – in safeguarding and promoting the Dutch corporate governance principles.

Arguably these gatekeepers are responsible for interpreting, preserving and developing good governance. At first sight, the interaction of different institutions appears to be conducive to an efficient evolution of the corporate governance framework. Gatekeepers are complementary to each other, and so are more responsive to economic and social change. To see this, let us again look at the Dutch Corporate Governance Code and assess the effect of the code two years after its promulgation. It seems that the enabling ('comply-or-explain') nature of the code could not totally prevent firms from engaging in merely box-ticking, thereby adopting opportunistic strategies to subvert the norm.[24]

Nevertheless, it might be argued that the structure of the game between policymakers and lawmakers on the one side and gatekeepers on the other eventually tends towards a regulatory equilibrium. As noted, policymakers and lawmakers, having promulgated the Code to restore the public confidence in stock markets and to protect the shareholders from managerial opportunism and malfeasance, are compelled to revise, in the next round, their regulatory strategies to induce firm compliance to the stated norms. In response, we can expect gatekeepers to continue to develop innovative interpretations of the principles and give recommendation on how firms should implement the norms in order to be most effective for their own needs. Because the gatekeepers must anticipate being overruled by the necessary update of the policymakers and lawmakers, their explanations and interruptions appear to be consistent with the dictates of efficiency.

In practice, though, the ideal interplay may not prevail. For instance, the corporate governance movement in the Netherlands is more akin to a battleground – in which gatekeepers, preoccupied with their own interests, such as increasing their powers and prestige, strive for market share – than a system of checks and balances. This is evidenced by the

---

[24] EFFECT (VEB-magazine – 'Journal of the Dutch investors' association' – 24 December 2005) mentions ten tricks that firms use to circumvent the code. For instance, (1) firms create their own definitions of 'being independent'; (2) firms state that there are no indications that their internal control systems are not effective (firms do not show explicitly that the internal control systems are optimal); and (3) firms tend to use very general and brief statements, instead of giving the detailed explanations and descriptions as required by the Code. Naturally if all firms were mere box tickers this would lead to a pooling equilibrium. However, since high-quality firms will benefit from sending a signal to the market, firms are more likely to profit where the sophistication of the investors is high and it is more likely that external parties will have the incentives and abilities to benchmark the disclosures.

fact that the corporate governance principles are interpreted broadly by gatekeeper institutions in favour of the (minority) shareholders.

The gatekeepers seem to agree on one thing: so far the Code has resulted in a modest improvement of the diligence in doing business and reporting accurate information. In general, gatekeepers are of the opinion that more must be done to achieve good corporate governance practice in firms. They urge shareholders to be increasingly active and encourage judges and official monitoring agents to contribute to the strict compliance with the code's principles. The result is an avalanche of legal actions for an alleged loss suffered from violations of the corporate governance code, stemming in particular from the inadequate independence of members of the supervisory board in the decision-making process (Versatel and Begemann), the untransparent group structure of the firm (Unilever and ASMI), and the unclear business strategy of the company (Laurus).

B. Reinforcing shareholder rights in the Dutch Enterprise Chamber

Although there is widespread perception that the Dutch Enterprise Chamber has played a long-standing role in the enforcement of corporate governance, the court has only recently made significant progress as the leading institution establishing its authority over the conflict of interest rules, takeovers and the implementation of the code. Under Dutch law, the Enterprise Chamber has jurisdiction in cases where: 1) there are doubts about if a company is properly managed, 2) the decisions of management are challenged as being inconsistent with the code's principles, 3) shareholders voice dissatisfaction with financial reporting, 4) complaints are made about the removal of a supervisory board of a company organized under the structure regime, and 5) squeeze-out procedures are initiated by a shareholder that has at least 95% of the share capital of a company. Judging from the number of cases, the Enterprise Chamber has properly exerted its influence on the governance arrangements in disputes over the way companies are managed.

In Figure 1 we can observe the main steps in an inquiry proceeding. At the first stage, a party can request an inquiry into the affairs of the corporation to determine whether the company has been mismanaged. If the Enterprise Chamber shares plaintiff's concerns, it will appoint one or more persons who will conduct an investigation and file

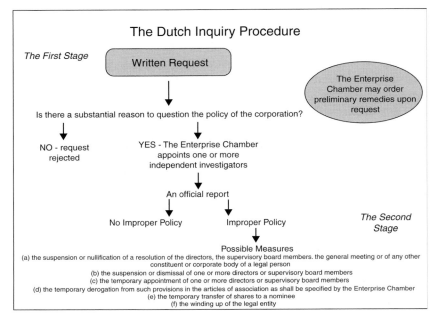

Figure 1 The Enterprise Chamber's Enquiry Procedure

a report with the court. At the second stage, the Enterprise Chamber can, based on the report finding improper conduct, take one or more measures (including dismissal of board members, nullification of board resolutions, appointing temporary directors, temporary transfer of shares) to mitigate the effects of the mismanagement.

1. Takeovers

Increasingly, parties are relying on the Enterprise Chamber to conduct inquiry proceedings in the context of a takeover. The shareholder interest in litigation involving takeovers has peaked recently with shareholders routinely bringing actions to investigate the target company's use of defensive measures. With recent decisions of the court, it is now becoming clearer that the assumption that Dutch law serve to protect the interests of large shareholders and incumbent management is no longer safe.

The Netherlands has a long tradition in defending its domestic companies against foreign acquirers. For instance, Royal Dutch/Shell Group defended itself already in 1907 by giving a 'friendly' foundation enhanced voting powers in order to resist potential 'hostile' buyers.[25] However, over the past decade the mindset towards takeovers has changed in the Netherlands. Firstly, the corporate governance principles that were adopted in 1997 spurred the development of improved shareholder relations. Secondly, the resistance to international acquirers faded (while foreign companies that were incorporated in the Netherlands endeavoured to protect themselves by employing typical Dutch defensive mechanisms, such as the issuance of preference shares to a foundation). The Enterprise Chamber has played an important role in clarifying the acceptance of anti-takeover defences by deciding in the *Gucci* case (1997) and the *Rodamco North America* case (2002) that defensive measures should be proportional, reasonable and temporary.

The Enterprise Chamber continues its responsive role in recent cases involving activist shareholder influence. A recent decision of the Enterprise Chamber, arising out of a shareholder conflict between Stork, a European conglomerate, and two hedge funds, Centaurus Capital of the UK and Paulson & Co of the US, which emerged as its largest investors holding over 31.4% of the company's shares, reinforces the pattern of enhanced shareholder protection in Dutch company law. In 2005, the two hedge funds took up a high profile campaign against the managers of the company, who were content to operate an old-style conglomerate structure consisting of a food systems, technical services and aerospace division. Armed with a study of how Stork could realize shareholder value, the activist funds sought to unbundle Stork's conglomerate structure by reducing the number of unrelated divisions and concentrating solely on the high-value end of its business. Management would reject the hedge funds' advice claiming that the fund managers are merely short-term investors that care more about increasing Stork's share price through unbundling than the long-term interest of the company and its stakeholders. Responding to these allegations, the funds increased their pressure on management by calling a non-binding shareholder resolution that would ask investors to support their divestiture motion. Shareholders overwhelming supported the activists' non-binding resolution, which the board subsequently ignored on the grounds it was not binding legally.

To further underscore its determination to neutralize the activists' threat, Stork's board continued its refusal to discuss strategy with the fund managers. The funds were ultimately forced to call an extraordinary

---

[25] See *The Wall Street Journal* (by Adam Cohen), 'Going Dutch Has New Meaning in Corporate Takeover Battles', 30 May 2006.

shareholders meeting on 17 January 2007 to demand the dismissal of the members of the supervisory board on the grounds of mismanagement. Surprisingly, this action prompted the Stork Foundation, an unrelated but closely aligned entity, to trigger a poison pill device that diluted the hedge funds' interest in the Stork's equity, giving the company's board and its allies effective control of the company. The hedge funds had no choice but to challenge the legality of the poison pill device alleging that the company was guilty of 'mismanagement' by attempting to frustrate shareholders' rights. The Enterprise Chamber found that the use of the poison pill was illegal, but barred the shareholders' planned vote that called for the dismissal of the supervisory board. Instead, the Court decided to appoint three additional independent supervisory board members and to investigate the alleged mismanagement claims of shareholders. The Stork conflict illustrates the core principle of the Dutch Code to enhance the rights of shareholders and shows the ever-increasing important role of the Enterprise Chamber.

Also, another recent case involving a conflict with a majority share-holder in a tender-offer situation appears to show that the Enterprise Chamber will no longer rubber stamp a management protective environment. In Begemann, there was a tender by Tulip (of which company Begemann was the controlling shareholder) for the shares of Begemann, which was supported by the company's boards. Significantly, the tender was undertaken without a fairness opinion or other external support for the tender. Unsurprisingly, the Enterprise Chamber agreed with the minority shareholders and appointed a temporary director and member of the supervisory board in Begemann.

2. Conflict of interest

The other significant area of activity for the Enterprise Chamber is conflicts of interests. The court has for some time attempted to elaborate a standard to prevent the adverse consequences of such actions. Recently, the Enterprise Chamber determined that, in a case involving a struggle for corporate control, a company would be considered mismanaged not only if a potential conflict of interest existed, but if it also failed to take sufficient protections against such a conflict (see Laurus).

Besides setting a standard measure for remedies, the court has recognized a need to set a norm for complying with the code. An especially noteworthy example of the intense battleground shaping the contours of corporate governance in the Netherlands is the recent *Versatel* case. In this case, the Enterprise Chamber of the Amsterdam Court of Appeal decided in favour of minority shareholders, supported by the Dutch investors' association, to forbid the change from compliance to non-compliance with the corporate governance code between two ordinary general shareholders meetings. Swedish Tele2 became the controlling shareholder of Versatel and appointed new 'Tele2-persons' as supervisory board members. According to the Netherlands code, these new members, due to their conflict of interest, would not be able to take part in the decision-making process to approve a merger with the aim to buy out minority shareholders. As a possible solution, Versatel proposed to amend its corporate governance policy by limiting compliance with the conflict of interest provisions of the code. This argument was rejected by the Enterprise Chamber on the grounds that Versatel, having agreed to abide by the Code in their annual accounts of 2004, would respect the expectations of minority shareholders. The effect of the Versatel decision is to dramatically strengthen the rule-based character of the Code.

The foregoing discussions together show that the Enterprise Chamber has reinvented itself, moving from a body engaged in specialized investigations into disputes arising in the context of bankruptcy proceedings to addressing the major governance claims of parties, particularly in the area of takeovers and conflicts of interest. By choosing to intervene in disputes to determine whether misconduct took place, and resolve quickly these actions in a decisive and definitive manner, the court has gradually increased its ability to improve the corporate governance environment in which companies operate. It follows that the Enterprise Chamber has become a leader in the ongoing discussion about the Code and best practices and as a result, has been transformed into the main body responsible for balancing the demands between management and shareholders in the Netherlands.

IV. Conclusion

In this chapter, we discussed the effect of the corporate governance regulation on the performance of listed companies. We reviewed recent analyses that focus on the role of corporate governance rules that tend to promote efficiency, transparency and accountability within firms. With respect to the Netherlands, we identified the various legislative and soft-law measures that have emerged recently and attempted to benchmark the effect of the Dutch reforms. Having explained how corporate governance measures and reform are valued, we then considered if Dutch companies are undervalued relative to their international counterparts in similar industries having similar corporate governance practices. While Dutch firms continue to be undervalued, there are indications that the recent changes introduced by the Dutch Code are likely to improve the performance of publicly listed firms in the Netherlands. Finally, we reviewed the Dutch *ex post* enforcement regime, pointing to a number of key decisions of the Enterprise Chamber that are likely to make minority shareholder protection more effective.

SECTION 3

Takeover law

19

Adoption of the European Directive on takeover bids: an on-again, off-again story

JOËLLE SIMON[1]

The on-again, off-again progress of the takeover Directive began in the 1980s at a time when major economic restructurings were being carried out. The debate on the Directive became less active in 2004 and was thereafter resumed at the beginning of 2005 and came to fruition in March 2006.[2]

This progress corresponds to a series in five episodes:

1st episode (from 1985 to 1999): the rise. Why a takeover directive? What provisions should this directive contain?

2nd episode (from 2000 to 2001): the downfall. Many accidents marred the progress of the directive and led to its rejection by the European Parliament in 2001.

3rd episode (from the end of 2001 to 2003): the reprieve. Mr. Bolkestein did not accept this setback and sought to give a new momentum to these efforts by entrusting a group of experts with the task of finding a way to break the deadlock.

4th episode (in 2004): smoke and mirrors. Adoption in 2004 of a non-directive.

5th episode (starting from 2004): implementation in the domestic laws of the Member States.

---

[1] The author states her personal views in this chapter.
[2] See also, L. Lambert and S. Bedrossian, 'La réglementation des OPA dans l'Union européenne, un chantier plein de surprises', HEC dissertation, May 2002; D. Muffat-Jeandet, 'OPA: l'histoire d'une directive européenne. Le rejet de la proposition de 1989 et de ses versions revises', Revue du Marché commun et de l'Union européenne, 475 (2004), 111; J. Simon, 'OPA: divine surprise ou faux semblant?', Revue européenne de droit bancaire et financier, 3 (2003), 329.

I. 1st episode: Why a takeover directive? What provisions should this directive contain?

In 1985, the Commission published its White Paper (Completing the Internal Market) and announced its intent to propose a directive in order to approximate Member States' legislations on takeover bids. The Commission then launched a four-year works programme.

Upon completion of these works, in 1989, the Commission submitted a proposal for a 13th company law directive concerning takeover bids. This proposal was amended on 10 September 1990 in order to take into account the opinions issued by the ESC and the European Parliament. This ambitious proposal had been drafted in a context in which international takeover bids were becoming more numerous. This proposal was also prepared under the pressure of several Member States that deemed it advisable to create fair-play rules in order to protect all parties concerned by a takeover bid.

The Commission intended to be neutral vis-à-vis takeover bids and saw these bids as a way of contributing to the growth and development of European companies in order to cope with international competition.[3] With the recession that led to a slowdown in M&A activity, the demand from Member States for a takeover directive became less strong, and criticism was levelled against the initial proposal.

In December 1992, during the Edinburgh European Council, the Commission announced that it would revise its text. After lengthy consultations with Member States, the Commission submitted in 1996 a second proposal that was less ambitious and set a number of objectives to be reached by Member States.

After the ESC issued its opinion in July 1996 and after a review by the European Parliament in June 1997, the Commission submitted to the Council a third, amended proposal that integrated a large part of the proposed amendments.

In July 1998, negotiations resumed within the Council.

On 21 June 1999, the Chairmanship brokered a political agreement among the E-15 despite the reluctance of the United Kingdom and the Netherlands.

---

[3] G. Ferrarini, 'Take Over Defences and New Proposal for a European Directive', Second European Conference on Corporate Governance, Brussels, 28–29 November 2002; Lambert and Bedrossian, 'La réglementation des OPA dans l'Union européenne, (note 1, above).

The terms of the agreement were then as follows:

- a framework directive allowing for certain specific local features provided that the same are not incompatible with the principles laid down in the directive,
- a directive aimed at fostering takeovers within the European Union,
- a directive aimed at protecting minority shareholders and providing a measure of information and publicity during the time of the offer,
- a directive asking each Member State to appoint a supervisory authority and enforcing the principles and obligations imposed by the directive.

II. 2nd episode: The downfall. Many accidents marred the progress of the directive and led to its rejection by the European Parliament in 2001

Several incidents hindered the progress of this initiative: the Gibraltar issue and the German opposition.

A. *The Gibraltar issue*

The long-standing dispute between Spain and the United Kingdom concerning the status of Gibraltar blocked the passing of a number of EU provisions. Spain exercised pressure in order to oblige the United Kingdom to reach a general agreement concerning the status of this autonomous territory. Finally, Spain and the United Kingdom reached an agreement in April 2002, and Spain withdrew its reservation concerning the proposal for a directive.

B. *The German opposition*

The German opposition was triggered by the Vodafone/Mannesmann deal: in Germany, the takeover bid launched by Vodafone for Mannesmann seemed like a bolt of lightning out of the blue. Until then, the German industrial community had never voiced any specific opposition to the harmonization of the rules concerning takeover bids. Even though Mannesmann was already controlled by foreign shareholders, this bid came as a shock.

This takeover bid triggered an immediate reaction from the German government. The takeover bill that was being prepared was amended in order to re-introduce anti-takeover bid defences with the *Voratbeschluss*, i.e. the possibility for officers of a company to approve any defence against a takeover bid if shareholders have granted an approval to that end during the eighteen preceding months.

The proposal for a directive then became the focus of attacks by German commentators. The reporter of the Parliament's Legal Affairs Commission, Mr. Klaus Lehne, launched the offensive by targeting mainly Article 9, which laid down the principle according to which general meetings had the final say. Such a provision deprived German companies of any defence, while companies from other Member States and third countries could adopt defensive measures that were henceforth prohibited in Germany, such as multiple voting rights. Mr. Lehne then emphasized the need for a level playing field.

On 13 December 2000, Parliament approved the Council's joint position with fifteen amendments (control threshold, definition of fair price, etc.), one of which aimed at introducing a German-style exception. However, these amendments were eventually dismissed by the Council after receiving the Commission's opinion.

A conciliation procedure then started.

Finally, the German opposition agreed with the German Government, which took a position unfavourable to Article 9 which asserts the general meeting's power as regards takeover bids. Despite Germany's opposition, other Member States decided to maintain their initial position during the negotiation with Parliament and reached a compromise on 5 June 2001.

The EDF case: EDF, which was at the time a public-sector agency and was therefore not subject to the takeover regulations, started buying companies in Spain and Italy, thus triggering an anti-EDF, and thus an anti-takeover, campaign in Italy. The Italian members of the majority then joined all those opposing the directive.

A surprising turn: the directive was rejected by the European Parliament.

On 4 July 2001, the European Parliament surprised everyone by dismissing the compromise by 273 votes in favour and 273 votes against the proposal, the equality of votes resulting in the rejection of the proposal. All German MPs voted against the proposal. It seems that such was also the case for certain French MPs.

III. 3rd episode: The reprieve. A new momentum

Mr Bolkestein, who was at the time Commissioner in charge of the Internal Market, refused to concede defeat. After being encouraged by certain Member States and enterprises from certain countries (MEDEF had supported this directive), he decided to table a new proposal for a directive.

Then, an expert group came into play, comprising seven individuals: Jaap Winter (Netherlands), Jonathan Rickford (United Kingdom), Guido Rossi (Italy), Jose Garrido Garcia (Spain), Jan Christensen (Denmark), Klaus Hopt (Germany) and Joëlle Simon (France).

Already in spring 2001, Mr. Bolkestein had decided to set up an expert group in order to examine the future of European company law in the next few years. Indeed, it is necessary to point out that European institutions had not been very active as regards company law, aside from the last-minute agreement reached at the end of thirty years of efforts in relation to the European company.

Mr Bolkestein took this failure personally and asked the group to deliver to him, on a priority basis, a report by January 2002 concerning the three following issues, which are of unequal importance, but were defined by the European Parliament:

- How is the fair price to be defined in case of a mandatory offer?
- Is it necessary to provide for a mandatory expulsion procedure (squeeze-out and sell-out)?
- Is it possible to create a level playing field and, if so, how?

While the first two issues did not lead to overly heated debates, things went differently for the third question[4].

Fair price: the various existing systems were reviewed, including the French multi-criteria approach, taking into account in particular tangible assets and the affiliation with a group. The group finally approved the definition used in the United Kingdom, i.e. the highest price paid by the offeror during a period preceding the offer, such period being determined by each Member State and ranging between six and twelve months, with possible exceptions. While it is true that this definition has the merit of facilitating the calculation of the fair price and being more favourable to minority shareholders, the application of this test nevertheless leads

---

[4] European Commission, *Report on Issues Related to Takeover Bids, Report of the High Level Group of Company Law Experts,* (2002).

to an increase in the price of takeovers and is not necessarily fair for the offeror in particular at times of sharp and swift share price fluctuations. Thus, by making takeovers more expensive, this test may, in certain cases, be an anti-takeover defence, and this is paradoxical.

Squeeze out and sell out: there is already, in a number of Member States, including France, a procedure for the expulsion of minority shareholders by majority shareholders holding between 90% and 95% of the capital (mandatory withdrawal if the offeror holds 95% of the voting rights). As this procedure restricts minority shareholders' rights, it may seem logical to have it set off by a withdrawal right offered to minority shareholders who may procure the redemption of their shares (under French law, such right exists when the majority shareholder holds 95% of the voting rights, and the minority shareholder does not belong to the majority group; a decision made by the AMF is indispensable), even though the parallelism of these procedures is challenged by certain commentators.

The level playing field: do we need a level playing field? The search for a level playing field, which is a little bit like the quest for the Holy Grail, relies on the following postulate.

Theoretically, when a company taps the market in order to finance its operations, and all or part of its shares are admitted to trading on a regulated market, an offeror should be able to acquire control of the company, without having to face any anti-takeover defences.

However, it is interesting to note that on the two most important financial markets (the US and the UK), the response given is totally different, while the capital structure is similar in both countries, with scattered capital.

US law never barred takeover defences, whether they consisted of poison pills or takeover-proof companies. In contrast, UK law does not allow anti-takeover measures. Thus anti-takeover barriers can survive market laws.

Nevertheless, this does not mean that this issue is not debated in the United States, and certain commentators recommend barring anti-takeover measures. Also, the impact of these measures is assessed in diverging manners. Certain observers consider that they have only a limited impact on the outcome of the bids and only have a marginal impact,[5] while others

---

[5] See, in that sense: J. McCahery and G. Hertig, 'An Agenda for Reform: Company and Takeover Law in the EU', in G. Ferrarini, K. Hopt, J. Winter and E. Wymeersch (eds.), *Modern Company and Takeover Law in Europe* (Oxford University Press, 2004).

conclude that the most frequently used poison pills caused the number of hostile takeover bids to drop by 75% in ten years in the United States.[6]

This raises the very issue of challengeability of control that largely depends on the structure of capital.[7] While it seems that this issue has not been widely debated in Europe, it has been covered by in-depth analyses conducted by US academics.[8]

According to certain US authors, control does not necessarily have negative effects on shareholders, and may even benefit minority shareholders. On the other hand, the *European Round Table* considers that it has not been demonstrated that the challengeability of control increases the target's value, by questioning management. According to those defending this approach, a directive concerning takeover bids in Europe should not be used as an instrument for restructuring European economies: the market alone should decide on where it invests and therefore on the structure of capital. However, because Parliament and the Commission settled this debate by choosing the opposite direction, the Commission entrusted the group of experts with the task of defining the best ways of reaching this goal.

How could this be done? This issue gave rise to arduous and complex discussions, at the end of which the group proposed a relatively complex scheme:

- the general meeting must have the final say, without any possible delegation;
- the risk taking should be commensurate with the control exercised after the launch of the bid: this is the risk-bearing share capital rule according to which shareholders may only vote according to the share of capital that they hold: one share, one vote.
- principle of neutralization of the defence mechanisms after the successful completion of the takeover, i.e. when a certain threshold is reached;
- principle of transparency of structures and control.

Discussions within the group showed how difficult it was to cover all defence mechanisms: thus, do shareholder agreements (which are

---

[6] See: A. Ferrel, 'Why Continental Takeover Law Matters', in Ferrarini, Hopt, Winter and Wymeersch (eds.), *Modern Company and Takeover Law in Europe*, (note 5, above).

[7] For a different opinion, see Guido Ferrarini, '*The challenge of the 13th directive in the EU*', debate organized on 4 March 2003 by the Centre of European Policy Studies.

[8] See: J. Coates, 'Ownership, Takeovers and EU Law: How Contestable Should EU Corporations be', in Ferrarini, Hopt, Winter and Wymeersch (eds.), *Modern Company and Takeover Law in Europe* (note 5, above).

governed by the law of contracts) and pyramid structures avoid the neutralization principle, as well as Dutch foundations. Therefore, the double or multiple voting rights constituted an easy target. Such an approach is not necessarily without guile.

The presentation of the report's conclusions prompted a strongly negative response from many Member States.

The sudden emergence of the debate concerning the level playing field, i.e. on the evenness of the rules of the game applying throughout the European Union in case of a takeover bid, had a considerable impact on the very design of the rules that should apply to takeover bids within the European Union and on the future status of the proposal for a directive. There is no doubt that this rekindled the opposition to a text that was nearly adopted by all Member States, but one.

Most Member States reacted quite harshly to this report, as they considered that the proposals had too much of an impact on company law and were raising constitutional issues because of the lack of indemnification of shareholders whose rights would be neutralized. Thus, if the recommendations contained in this report were to be applied, a voting right would again be attached to formerly non-voting shares, while financial benefits had been granted in consideration for the removal of the relevant voting rights.

Therefore, the Commission did not endorse all of the group's proposals, but asserted very clearly the general meeting's decision-making power, by going one step beyond the earlier text, by removing the possibility of delegating authority to the Board. Also the Commission laid down the principle of neutralization of certain defence measures.

The debate then focused on the two issues below, possibly to the detriment of other technical issues.

1. Board versus general meeting.

The issue that observers believed to be definitively settled in favour of the general meeting of shareholders as a result of the 2001 compromise was reopened again, as Parliament considered that the Board could not be deprived of its powers so long as there was no level playing field between companies of the various Member States.

Even though the Commission, relying on the groups of experts' report and the Member States, confirmed this choice in favour of the general meeting, the debate was not totally closed between those advocating the US system in which the Board has all powers and those willing to give the final say to the general meeting of shareholders. Incidentally, this is shown by the option selected in the text of the directive.

Those promoting, in Europe, a US-style system argued that the vote of shareholders in companies having a scattered capital structure was only an illusion and that it was not certain that the board's neutrality rule would have only positive effects: risks of litigation and difficulty for officers of maximizing shareholders' investment. Three days after the launch of a takeover bid, one third of the shares has already changed hands and is held by arbitrageurs.

In contrast, those opposing a US-style solution considered that such a system could not be imported into Europe, as the Board's omnipotence in the United States was legitimately set off by a liability in tort, on grounds of which shareholders did not hesitate in particular to file class actions. However, such a debate existed also in the United States where shareholders recently submitted to general meetings of US companies draft resolutions under which decisions for the adoption of poison pills were to be submitted for approval to the shareholders.

It is worthy of note that those advocating the Board's decision-making powers include representatives of employees who thus consider that the Board is better placed than the general meeting of shareholders (who represent the capital) to take into account the interests of employees. The idea of freedom of choice between the general meeting and the Board was even brought forward, assuming the creation of an adequate dispute settlement mechanism. However, because of the small likelihood of finding adequate means of effecting such a settlement in Europe, those favouring this idea recommended giving the final say to the general meeting. The future of this provision is indubitably linked to that concerning the neutralization of defence measures.

2. Up to what point is it necessary to neutralize defence measures?

The group of experts proposed to apply the neutralization principle immediately from the launch of the bid as regards the measures departing from the proportionality principle, after the offeror reached a threshold defined according to the threshold required in the Member State concerned, in order to amend the company's articles of association as regards all of the relevant measures.

While the neutralization principle did not per se raise many objections in Europe, such is not the case for the list of measures to which such neutralization may apply. On the contrary, US authors challenge the very usefulness of neutralization measures, in that they doubt their effectiveness in order to create a level playing field and even consider that neutralization measures might create additional costs.

In any event, the neutralization of certain measures, such as the measures preventing free trading in shares (incidentally such measures are often barred as regards companies whose shares are admitted to trading on a regulated market) may not be subject to a serious challenge.

In contrast, and although the scope of the Commission's proposal and the final text of the directive did not finally include double voting rights, we may regret that such double voting rights eventually became the focus of the debate, while other mechanisms were not discussed. Those willing to give double voting rights a bad name had political afterthoughts and knew very well that any attempt to challenge these mechanisms would unavoidably prompt certain Member States to oppose the proposal.

Regardless of our opinion concerning mechanisms departing from the 'one share, one vote' principle, we may deplore that this debate largely contributed to blocking, for months, any significant progress towards the adoption of a directive.

In addition, even if the proportionality principle were to be applied, US authors consider that the neutralization principle would not have any effect on most listed European companies which they see as immune to takeover bids. This principle would then lead to the application of the measures to less transparent systems, such as pyramids.

Finally, US structures show that there is no evidence that structures with double or multiple voting rights have a lower performance and are used in order to support a poor management team.[9] The use of these structures and that of the non-voting shares forms part of enterprises' right to freely choose their organization and management mode in order to gain readier access to capital markets. For the market, the controlling factor is the transparency of the structures and control, proper corporate governance and a high-quality audit process.

IV. 4th episode: Breaking the deadlock through a conjuring trick – the obscuring of the level playing field

Those many years of debate on the harmonization of European takeover bid law were not completely futile, as they are likely to have contributed

---

[9] See in particular Ferrel, 'Why Continental Takeover Law Matters', (note 3, above) and McCahery and Hertig, 'An Agenda for Reform', (note 5, above). It is also necessary to note the change in Mr. Klaus-Heiner Lehne's position in this respect in Revised draft of the report concerning the proposal for a directive of the European Parliament and the Council concerning takeover bids.

to a change in domestic laws: virtually all Member States now have takeover regulations. The last Member State not to have had such regulation, i.e. Luxembourg, adopted takeover rules in connection with Mittal's bid for Arcelor. Therefore was a directive still necessary, as the United States does not have any uniform legislation in this area? It is necessary to answer this question in the affirmative, and not only for symbolic reasons: such was the unanimous decision of the Member States (Spain abstained) and the European Parliament.

A. If so, what should the directive's contents consist of?

Past debates have been marked by the rejection of an overly detailed and technical directive and the adoption of a text that is half political and half technical. Curiously, the final outcome is a directive affording a double option to Member States and, where applicable, to enterprises: nobody would have bet on the chances for success of the so-called Portuguese proposal, i.e. a directive containing an option for Member States and for enterprises. After a few amendments, this proposal was endorsed by the Italian Presidency and was eventually approved.

Finally, the Directive lays down the principle according to which the general meeting of shareholders has the final say (Article 9) and that certain defence measures must be neutralized (Article 11), but offers Member States and enterprises, as the case may be, the possibility of not applying either or both of these Articles (Article 12–3).

B. A first outline of the level playing field

As regards the decision-making body, the text no longer makes it possible, contrary to the draft that was rejected in 2001, for the general meeting to grant, from the outset, authority to the Board. Concerning the neutralization rule, the directive sets forth that its provisions shall apply to restrictions on the free trading of shares, set forth in articles of association or in contractual arrangements, and to provisions of the articles of association or contracts limiting voting rights and governing shares with multiple voting rights.

In addition, the directive sets forth that where, following a bid, the offeror holds 75% or more of the capital carrying voting rights, no such restrictions nor any extraordinary rights of shareholders concerning the appointment or removal of board members provided for in the articles of association of the offeree company or multiple voting rights shall apply during the first general meeting following the bid as convened by the offeree company in order to enable it to amend the company's articles of association or remove or appoint the members of the board. The holders of the said rights must then be entitled to fair indemnification making whole any loss possibly sustained.

However, while the highly complicated text of this compromise eventually ruled for the neutralization of securities with multiple voting rights, the compromise excludes, from the scope of this regulation, securities having a double voting right, because of the definition given to multiple voting securities. Indeed, these securities are defined as securities included in a distinct and separate class and carrying more than one vote each, which is not the case in French law for shares having a double voting right.

Indeed, double voting rights are not vested unless certain objective requirements are satisfied: the shares must be registered and held for no less than two years and no more than four years as regards companies whose securities are admitted to trading on a regulated market. Such double voting right is forfeited in the event of a share sale.

C. . . . with the possibility for Member States, and possibly for enterprises, to provide for exceptions

Member States may reserve the right not to require companies registered on their territory to apply Article 9 (2 and 3) (neutrality of the Board) and Article 11 (neutralization of defence measures). However, in such event, the said Member States may nevertheless authorize the said companies to apply either or both of the said Articles on a voluntary basis.

The decision will then be made by the general meeting of shareholders (this is consistent with Article 9) subject to the quorum and majority rules imposed by the company's articles of association. Notice of this decision shall be given to the supervisory authority of the Member State in which the company has its registered office and to all supervisory authorities of the Member State in which the company's securities are admitted to trading on a regulated market or where such admission has been requested.

Finally, Member States may, under the conditions determined by national law, exempt companies which apply Article 9 (2 and 3) and/or Article 11 from the application of the said Articles, if they become the subject of an offer launched by a company which does not apply the same

Articles as they do or by a company controlled, directly or indirectly, by such a company (Article 12–3).

In the current drafting of this text, it seems that this possibility is granted to all Member States, and therefore even to those Member States that require their domestic companies to apply Articles 9 and 11. In such event, an authorization will have to be granted by the general meeting of the offeree company. Such authorization may not be granted more than eighteen months in advance of the time when the bid is made public. The general meeting may, at any time, withdraw such an authority.

It is interesting to note that the proposal does not provide for the irreversibility of the options, whether as regards Member States or companies, while such irreversibility was a feature of the Portuguese proposal – which is rather fortunate.

Indeed, it is likely that such irreversibility might have created constitutional issues in certain States. Moreover, the irreversibility of the choice made by a company for the application of Articles 9 and 11 is consistent with the spirit of the proposal, i.e. over time to turn such application into a general rule, but is contrary to the company law principle according to which a corporate body must be able to undo any decision that it has made.

Those advocating this system consider that it corresponds to a liberal solution, in that the market should prompt companies to adopt the board's neutrality principle and remove defence measures. Articles 9 and 11 would then constitute the benchmark, even though certain observers characterize these provisions as a half-way benchmark in that they target only certain defence measures.

Although this mechanism is ingenious, it also raises a number of questions, while leaving other questions unanswered.

Certain observers have feared that the system would not reach the assigned objective, in that it might prompt Member States, under pressure from their enterprises, and possibly thereafter these enterprises, to choose the most protective system. This might thus lead to a regression within the Member States currently applying the principles set forth in Articles 9 and 11. This did in fact happen, as we shall see.

This system runs counter to a minimum harmonization of rules applicable to takeover bids. This system is complex to apply, in particular because the option made available to Member States and enterprises may cover either or both of these two Articles.

Even though reciprocity requires a decision of the Member State and the approval of the general meeting of the offeree company, this system lacks consistency and may prove difficult to manage for supervisory authorities and may lack clarity for investors. This reciprocity principle is totally new in EU company law and even seems contrary to the fundamental principles of EU company law: i.e. freedom of establishment and free movement of capital. This may be an unwelcome precedent in EU company law, with a view to the preparation of the action plan prepared by the European Commission.

D. We may therefore question the merits of a 'cherry-picking' directive

Wouldn't it have been preferable to adopt an admittedly less ambitious and more pragmatic solution, i.e. a Directive without Articles 9 and 11? This would have made it possible to dispense with this needlessly complex mechanism that is contrary to EU company law principles. Incidentally, this result will be reached by this complex mechanism whenever the reciprocity rule shall apply on a case-by-case basis. Indeed, a Directive not containing Article 9 or Article 11 would not have been completely without merit, as it would have created a common foundation consisting in the following principles:

- mandatory bid
- protection and information of employees and minority shareholders
- squeeze-out and sell-out procedures
- transparency of structures and control.

Contrary to the opinion of certain commentators, abandoning Articles 9 and 11 would not have been seen as a setback. It is true that the proposal, rejected in 2001 by Parliament, included an Article 9. However, if we take the example of France, it was very unlikely that the country would call into question the affirmed principle of neutrality of the board and the decision-making power of the general meeting or the neutralization of voting right restrictions in the event of a successful bid. This was confirmed by the Act of 31 March 2006. However, it is true that the political process may be driven by reasons that are foreign to law making.

E. Non-optional provisions of the directive:

1. Scope (Articles 1 and 2)

The directive applies to:

- companies governed by the laws of Member States whose securities are admitted to trading on a regulated market in one or more Member States;

- voluntary or mandatory takeover bids leading to the acquisition of control of the offeree company.

2. General principles (Article 3)

Pursuant to the subsidiarity principle, the directive merely sets forth a number of general principles:

- Equality: all holders of the securities of an offeree company of the same class must be afforded equivalent treatment.
- The intended recipients of the offer must have a right to be informed in due time in order to be able to make a decision with full knowledge of the facts.
- The board or management board of the offeree company must act in the interest of the company as a whole and must not deny the holders of securities the opportunity to decide on the merits of the bid.
- An offeror must announce a bid only after ensuring that he/she can fulfil the promises made.
- An offeree company must not be hindered in the conduct of its affairs for longer than is reasonable.

In all cases, Member States may impose more restrictive rules.

3. Supervisory authority and applicable law (Article 4)

Member States shall designate the authority or authorities competent to supervise bids and enforce the rules set forth in the directive:

- public or private authority (AMF),
- requirements: impartiality and independence of all parties to the offer,
- close cooperation among supervisory authorities for cross-border transactions.

4. Rules of conflict for the determination of the supervisory authority and applicable law

The Directive sets forth conflict rules for the determination of the supervisory authority and applicable law in the case of a takeover bid involving one or more Member States. The principle is as follows: the supervisory authority and the applicable law are those of the Member State in which it has its registered office, when the securities are admitted for trading on a regulated market of such Member State.

If the registered office is different from the place of listing, the solution is different depending on the issues raised:

- *company law*: in particular as regards the control threshold, the information provided to employees: the supervisory authority and the applicable law are those of the country in which the company has its registered office;
- *offer procedure and offered consideration*: the rules applied are those of the country in which the securities are listed and, if there are several listing places, the rules of the country in which the shares have been first listed.

In the first case, shareholders are anticipating complying with the rules of the offeree company's home country. In the second case, it is advisable that the offer procedure be governed by the laws of the market on which the bid is launched.

5. Protection of minority shareholders (Article 5)

The best way to protect minority shareholders consists in offering them the possibility of selling their shares at a fair price. This is the objective of the mandatory bid sent to all holders of securities for the purchase of all of their securities at a fair price. We may regret that the Directive no longer defines the percentage of voting rights giving control or the mode of calculation of such percentage.

6. Information (Article 6)

The decision to launch a bid must be disclosed forthwith. The supervisory authority must be informed in order to be able to check whether the information that shall be published meets all applicable requirements. The board of directors or the management board must also inform the employees as soon as the bid has been made public. The Directive lists the minimum information that must be contained in the offer document.

7. Time allowed for acceptance (Article 7)

- such time may not be less than two weeks or more than ten weeks from the date of publication of the offer document;
- such time may not hinder corporate operations for too long a period;
- such time must where applicable enable the offeree company to organize a general meeting concerning the offer.

8. Disclosure (Article 8)

Any information likely to influence the market for the relevant securities must be disclosed, in order to ensure the transparency and integrity of the market for the securities and avoid the publication or circulation of false or deceptive information.

V. 5th episode: Implementation in the laws of the Member States

The implementation of the Directive gave rise to heated discussions in certain Member States and in particular in France where the debate, which was somehow stimulated by Mittal's offer for Arcelor, primarily covered the way in which the options were to be exercised, as most of the provisions of French law were already in line with the Directive. Act No. 2006–387 of 31 March 2006 on takeover bids eventually confirmed the principle of neutrality of general meetings (Article 9), provided for the neutralization of certain control mechanisms (partial application of Article 11), and the implementation of the reciprocity clause (Article 12).

In February 2007, the European Commission published a report on the implementation of the directive in the Member States[10].

Upon publication of the report, seventeen Member States had implemented the Directive.[11]

Board neutrality principle: eighteen Member States have imposed or shall impose the neutrality rule, thus confirming, except for five Member States, a rule already contained in their substantive law. Five Member States, including France, chose to apply the reciprocity exception.

The possibility introduced in French law to issue securities similar to those existing under the US right plans is presented as a negative measure.

Rule for the neutralization of anti-takeover restrictions: the large majority of Member States did not impose or shall not impose such

---

[10] Commission Staff Working Document-report on the Implementation of the Directive on Takeover Bids, Commission of the European Communities, Brussels, 21 February 2007.

[11] The Directive was implemented in French law by Act No. 2006–387 of 31 March 2006 concerning takeover bids. The said Act confirmed the decision-making powers of the general meeting of shareholders during an offer period and chose to partly apply Article 11 consisting in the confirmation of the neutralization of voting right restrictions by the general meeting if the offer is successful and the prohibition of approval clauses in the articles of association of listed companies. The Act also approved the reciprocity clause.

neutralization, which is a mere option available to enterprises. Only Baltic countries, which account for only 1% of EU listed companies, shall impose such neutralization. However, certain Member States have already eliminated the multiple voting rights and/or the other defence measures. Other Member States have already done so for certain measures, such as France and Italy.

Reciprocity: a majority of Member States introduced the reciprocity rule as regards the implementation of (i) the board neutrality rule and/or (ii) the rule for the neutralization of defence mechanisms. This was seen by the Commission as the expression of a certain form of protectionism. Incidentally, the European Commission illustrated its demonstration by citing excerpts from French parliamentary debates. However, the Commission also cites the argument stated in the Lepetit report, according to which the reciprocity rule prompts companies to apply on a voluntary basis the provisions of the directive, if they do not want to have the reciprocity rule used against them in case of an acquisition on foreign markets.

VI. Conclusion

In conclusion, although the Commission does not discount the positive effects of the directive (mandatory takeover bid, information given to shareholders and employees, etc.), it criticizes Member States' reluctance to remove anti-takeover obstacles.

The Commission will closely monitor the implementation of the directive and hold public hearings in 2008, while waiting for 2011 which is the scheduled time for a possible review.

Let us stay tuned . . . while waiting for the next episode.

20

Application of the Dutch investigation procedure on two listed companies: the *Gucci* and *ABN AMRO* cases

LEVINUS TIMMERMAN

In recent years some decisions of the Dutch Enterprise Chamber of the Amsterdam Court of Appeal (and the Dutch Supreme Court) attracted attention in the international financial press. These judgments refer to takeovers of internationally well-known companies which were established according to Dutch company law. All these decisions were issued within the framework of the Dutch investigation procedure. Below I will explain some features of this investigation procedure (which has no equivalent in foreign jurisdictions, as far as I know), and clarify the position of the Enterprise Chamber in Dutch company law. Thereupon I will discuss the *Gucci* and the *ABN AMRO* cases which aroused worldwide interest from the financial world.

The investigation procedure was introduced in Dutch law in 1928.[1] Originally, it was a very simple provision. Minority shareholders were conferred the power to request a court to order an investigation into the matters of the company. The purpose of such an inquiry was to bring to light some facts that could otherwise be difficult for the shareholders to establish. It was up to the parties that asked for the inquiry to seek remedies in accordance with general civil and company law. This provision was not a great success. Only two inquiries in a period of forty years were requested. The unpopularity of the inquiry proceedings may have been caused by the fact that, even when the court ruled that there had been a case of misconduct, it was not capable of attaching any measures to its

---

[1] An excellent overview of the investigation procedure in English has been written by Marius Josephus Jitta, 'The procedural aspect of the right of inquiry' in *The Companies and Business Court from a Comparative Perspective* (Kluwer, 2004), 1–42. I used some of his formulations in this essay. See also L. Timmerman and A. Doorman, 'Rights of minority shareholders', in E. Perakis (ed.), *Rights of Minority Shareholders: XVIth Congress of the International Academy of Comparative Law (Brisbane)*, (Brussels: Bruylant, 2004), 484–609.

decision. In 1971 the investigation procedure was renewed and became an instrument which was extensively elaborated in the Dutch legislation. As from 1971, an investigation procedure consists of two phases. The purpose of the first phase is to get an order for an inquiry into the conduct and policies of the company. An investigation will be ordered if there appear to be well-founded reasons to doubt the correctness of the policies or the conduct of a company. The law grants the right to request an inquiry to *inter alia* shareholders who own 10% of the issued share capital or hold shares with a nominal value of €225,000. It is important to notice that this second threshold is very low, especially when it is applied to a listed company with millions of shareholders. The consequence of this low threshold is that listed companies are often the target of inquiry proceedings if there are problems within the company.[2] The second phase of the procedure aims at establishing whether there has been misconduct and, if so, whether *definitive* remedies should be ordered in order to correct the misconduct. These questions are discussed on the basis of the report of the investigators. Examples of remedies to be deployed are the dismissal of one or more directors and the temporary nomination of a director. When choosing a measure, the Enterprise Chamber is limited to a list which is to be found in the relevant legislation. In 1994, the Dutch legislator added an interim injunction procedure to the investigation procedure. This new provision enables the competent court to order *provisional,* immediate measures once an investigation procedure has been initiated before it. In recent years this interim injunction procedure has turned out to be of extreme importance. The reason hereof is *inter alia* that in company law a provisional measure is often *de facto* definitive because of the high speed at which businesses operate.

In 1971, the Enterprise Chamber of the Amsterdam Court of Appeals has been introduced in the Dutch judiciary as a specialized court for matters of company law for which the Chamber was designated by the legislator as competent court. One of these matters is the investigation procedure. In Dutch company law the Chamber plays a pivotal role. Since its establishment, its competence has been gradually increased by the legislator. It is interesting to note that the chamber is not entirely made up of lawyers. Two of the five judges are layman, usually accountants or former entrepreneurs. Since 1971 the enterprise Chamber has turned to be a court with the traits we normally associate with a

---

[2] Worldwide known companies such as Unilever, Ahold, Heineken, HBG, Rodamco, Corus and DSM were the subject of the investigation procedure.

specialized court.[3] One may expect that specialized courts are activist and not reluctant judges and tend to adopt a rather informal approach to procedural matters. These traits fully apply to the Dutch Enterprise Chamber. The Chamber is a very activist and very informal court and it has for a specialized court the natural tendency to interpret its tasks broadly with all the connected pros and cons. It tends to let substance override form. The Chamber is further helped with the active and informal performance of its tasks by the open structure of the way in which the right of inquiry has been legislated for. For instance, the Chamber can grant provisional immediate measures when these are required in connection with the condition of the company or in the interest of the inquiry. The Chamber is not limited to any specific set of measures, but it can order any provisional measure it deems appropriate. An example of a provisional measure is a prohibition on the directors to act on behalf of the company or to carry out a resolution. It should be noted that the Supreme Court has limited the competence of the Chamber to issue provisional measures to matters of great urgency.[4] Another example of the activist and informal approach is that the Chamber has the power to order an inquiry into broader subjects than that demanded by the plaintiffs. The consequence of all this is that the Chamber has considerable freedom of action. In addition to this, the possibilities of review of decisions taken by the Chamber are limited. The only possibility is to file an appeal in cassation with the Dutch Supreme Court. The Supreme Court only reviews decisions of the Chamber on limited grounds, i.e. whether the law has been correctly applied and whether the decision has been properly reasoned. The Supreme Court is not authorized to review the facts of the case. The Chamber is the only instance which deals with the establishment of the facts.

If one takes the number of decisions under the investigation procedure by the Chamber into consideration, the investigation procedure is a great hit. Since 1971, the Chamber has issued more than 1500 decisions connected with the investigation procedure in approximately 500 cases. The Supreme Court rendered about 100 decisions. A very attractive aspect of the way the Chamber operates is its speed. For instance, the Chamber is prepared to hear the request for an immediate measure within a week and can rule immediately after hearing the case. The popularity of the

---

[3] See on the traits of specialized courts: M. Kroeze, 'The companies and business court as a specialized court', *Ondernemingsrecht* (2007), 86–91.
[4] HR 14 December 2007, *Nederlandse Jurisprudentie* (2008), 105.

investigation proceedings is also caused by the fact that the proceedings contain a cost allocation rule that is beneficial for the plaintiff: the company has to pay the costs of the investigation, ordered by the Court which are sometimes high (a sum of €500,000 is not exceptional). For a plaintiff, the request for an investigation is a good gamble: it costs little and has a high nuisance value for the company that is the subject of the investigation. Another reason for the success of the investigation procedure is that the Chamber has the power to order a provisional measure before it takes a decision on the request for an investigation. The power to order a provisional measure within the framework of the investigation procedure has developed into more or less independent summary proceedings for corporate matters. These summary proceedings are of high importance, as the investigation procedure sometimes ends with a temporary measure, for instance because parties resign with the interim measures. Sometimes, the interim measures and suggestions of the Chamber stimulate the parties to reach a compromise.

A consequence of the practice of the investigation procedure is that judges of the Chamber sometimes interfere in the affairs of a company in an unprecedented manner. The Supreme Court quashed some decisions of the Chamber because these decisions left too little room for the management to pursue policies under its own responsibilities.[5] It is very difficult to assess the contribution the Chamber has delivered to the sound functioning of Dutch corporate life. Without any doubt, the Chamber has contributed to many settlements between the interested parties. Another important fact is that provisional and definitive remedies have often led to a dispute being solved in a certain direction. However, the question remains to what extent judicial interference can really terminate conflicts within companies. This question is legitimate, because the Dutch legislator had certainly an optimistic view on the abilities of the judge in this respect. It was the intention of the Dutch legislator to get a company back on track by restoring sound relations within a company through the investigation procedure. The legislator had in mind conflicts in a company which resulted in a deadlock of the management of the company. However, we know that the resources for all kinds of conflicts within a company are infinite. The investigation procedure has the intention to look forward, i.e. to look into the future

---

[5] HR 21 February 2003, *Nederlandse Jurisprudentie* (2003), 182 (HBG). See on this subject Vino Timmerman, 'Review of management decisions by the courts' in *The Companies and Business Court from a comparative law perspective* (Kluwer, 2004), 43–57.

of the company. I wonder whether this is not a somewhat idealistic trait of the investigation procedure taking into consideration that the business world tends to become more and more antagonistic. Sometimes, the investigation procedure is used by aggressive investors for tactical litigation and not for saving a company. The investigation procedure is in such a case used as one of the instruments to conquer the company. One thing is certain: the investigation procedure offers an interesting tool to Dutch corporate lawyers to further develop Dutch company law. It is a real lawyer's paradise. In the framework of the investigation procedure, litigation over nearly every aspect of company law and procedural aspects thereof has taken place. Against this background, I would like to make some comments on the *Gucci* and *ABN AMRO* cases.

Gucci is a world-famous group of companies specialized in the production and sale of Italian-designed luxury goods. For tax reasons, the listed top holding of the Gucci Group was situated in Amsterdam and established according to Dutch company law and had subsidiaries in Italy, France and several other countries. Gucci Group NV was a Dutch company to which the investigation procedure was applicable. In 1999 LVMH – a French competitor of Gucci, the V in LVMH stands for Vuiton – notified in a public statement that it had acquired an interest of 34.4% in the Gucci Group and that it did not intend to issue a public offer on the shares of the Gucci Group. The management of Gucci Group was not amused. It took countermeasures. Gucci Group issued shares to a newly established foundation 'Employees interests' under an employee stock option plan. The number of shares issued to the foundation was equal to the number which were held by LVMH. Gucci Group lent the foundation the sum it needed to pay up the shares. Some time later, the management of the Gucci Group made public that it had reached an agreement with the white knight PPR – another competitor of Gucci – on a strategic cooperation. Within the framework of this cooperation, Gucci Group issued shares to PPR equal to 40% of its capital without requesting the general meeting of shareholders' approval. Hereafter, LVMH announced a public offer. With the benefit of hindsight, we can conclude that this gentle gesture was too late.

When the management of a Dutch company gets into this kind of mischief, the Pavlov reaction of a shareholder who does not agree with the course of action by the management is to request an investigation into the affairs of the company and ask for immediate, provisional measures. LVMH did not resist this common urge. Immediately after the installation of the stock option plan, it requested an investigation and several provisional measures. The Chamber issued a number of interim decisions. In one of its decrees, the Chamber ordered by way of a provisional measure that LVMH and the foundation were not allowed to vote on their shares. Some weeks later, the Chamber lifted the ban to cast a vote with regard to the shares held by LVMH, because in the meantime, PPR had acquired more than 40% of the capital of Gucci with the willing cooperation of the management of Gucci Group. The Chamber refused to nullify the issuance of shares to PPR because it would be too burdensome to reverse all the consequences of the transaction. On 27 April 1999, the Chamber published its final decision. In this decision, the Chamber denied the request to launch an inquiry into the policies of Gucci Group, it further declared that there was mismanagement on the part of Gucci Group, it quashed the decision by Gucci Group to establish the stock option by way of definitive measure and it ruled that the foundation could not exercise any rights in its capacity of shareholder in the Gucci Group. This decision seems on the face of it obvious. The foundation was a strange corporate creature, as all of its shares had been paid up with the financial help of the Gucci Group. However, this decision belongs to the most audacious decisions the Chamber took since its foundation in 1971. The statutory text clearly states that the Chamber is only authorized to conclude that there is a case of mismanagement and to issue definitive measures on the basis of a report prepared by the designated investigators. In its final Gucci decision, the Chamber determined mismanagement without a report, thereby skipping the inquiry part of the investigation procedure and ruled that a report could not bring to light any further relevant information and that a more detailed investigation would be superfluous and of no use. In this decision, the Chamber set aside a clear legislative text. An appeal in cassation was lodged. The Supreme Court is crystal-clear as well:

> The judgment of the Enterprise Chamber...bears witness to an incorrect interpretation of the law. First, the phrasing and the system of the law bear out that the Enterprise Chamber is not authorized to provide for relief... until 'misconduct has been borne out by the report'. Second it follows from the way in which the stipulations at hand have historically formed... that it was always the legislator's intention that the aforementioned relief could only be provided for once the first proceeding had been concluded with the report on the investigation, in so far as it had been borne out by the report that there had been question of misconduct on the part of the company. Third, it must furthermore be assumed on the basis of the

purport of the law that the Enterprise Chamber has not been authorized independently to judge on the basis of such facts as it has established that it had been borne out that there had been a question of misconduct and provide for relief on the exclusive basis of its own judgment...In so far as there is no reason for launching an investigation...and there is a need for relief, the regular procedure before the civil court with the full complement of related guarantees is always available for this purpose.[6]

In this decision, the Supreme Court underlines the pivotal role of the investigation report in the investigation procedure and quashes the ruling of the Chamber in the *Gucci* case. The effect of the Supreme Court's decision is that the freedom of action of the Chamber has been somewhat diminished. However, I have the impression that the Chamber utilizes to a larger scale the instrument of the provisional measures since the *Gucci* decision of the Supreme Court. The requirement of a previous report does not apply to a provisional measure. By ordering provisional measures, the Chamber can sometimes achieve the same effect as with a definitive measure. The *Gucci* affair ended with a settlement under which PPR acquired all the shares in Gucci.

For Dutch corporate lawyers, the *ABN AMRO* affair is among the most painful that has ever happened. The roots of ABN AMRO go back to a bank that was founded in the beginning of the nineteenth century by our King William I. In the Netherlands, ABN AMRO was considered to be one of the most important companies. The end of the affair is that ABN AMRO has been cut into four pieces, some parts of which have been resold and that ABN AMRO *de facto* has ceased to exist. The reason for this dramatic course of affairs is that, for several years, ABN AMRO did not meet the expectations it had raised. Among shareholders, there was widespread dissatisfaction about the level of the profits ABN AMRO had generated during the last years. Early in 2007, ABN AMRO made public its intention to enter into a share-merger with Barclays Bank in response to this dissatisfaction. Immediately after the announcement, a consortium of three other banks (Fortis, Banco Santander and Royal Bank of Scotland), announced its intention to launch a public offer to ABN AMRO in cash. After several months, the offer of the consortium turned out to be successful, which led to the split-up of ABN AMRO. The *ABN AMRO* case landed with the Enterprise Chamber, because ABN AMRO announced that it had sold its US subsidiary, which represented approximately 25% of the value of ABN AMRO, to an American

---

[6] HR 27 September 2000, *Nederlandse Jurisprudentie* (2000), 653.

bank, while the bid of the consortium was imminent. A Dutch investors' association and some ABN AMRO shareholders requested an investigation by the Chamber and a provisional order to forbid ABN AMRO to sell its American activities. Hereupon, the Chamber deferred its decision on the investigation, but prohibited ABN AMRO bank to sell its American activities without the approval of the shareholders meeting for the duration of the proceedings. It should be noted that ABN AMRO had obtained legal advice that such an approval was not necessary under Dutch company law.

The question of the approval of the shareholders meeting for important transactions is regulated in section 107a of Book 2 of the Civil Code. Section 107a provides as follows:

> Resolutions of the management require approval of the general meeting when these relate to an important change in the identity or character of the company or the undertaking, including in any case...
>
> the acquisition or divestment by it or a subsidiary of a participating interest in the capital of a company having a value of at least one-third of its assets according to its balance sheet and explanatory notes or, if the company prepares a consolidated balance sheet, according to its consolidated balance sheet and explanatory notes in the last adopted annual accounts of the company.
>
> The absence of approval by the general meeting of a resolution...shall not affect the representative authority of the management or the directors.

One may conclude from this text that it is not evident that the approval of the general meeting is required for the sale of American ABN AMRO activities. The Chamber agrees with this conclusion, but solves this problem by interpreting the provision broadly:

> Taking matters into account the Chamber also considers that, in view of the particularities of the case at hand, it cannot be ignored that, even if it cannot directly be brought under the scope of application of section 2:107a Civil Code, it at least represents an occasion which touches on the cases foreseen by this provision (either generically or specifically) to such a degree that it can be virtually equivocated with it, and that the board and supervisory board of ABN AMRO Holding should have felt compelled to put the decision making concerning the sale of LaSalle (i.e. its American subsidiary, LT) before the general meeting. The Chamber points to the following circumstances in this, which should be considered in conjunction: 1. ABN AMRO Holding confirmed at 17 April 2007 to be talking to Barclays on a form of combination of activities; 2. previously – on

13 April 2007 – ABN AMRO Holding announced it would be carefully dealing with a letter from the Consortium, entailing an invitation to hold explanatory talks; 3. LaSalle represents a considerable part of the value of ABN AMRO...; 4. actors such as TCI (*author's note*: The Children's Investment Fund Management, i.e. an investment fund), VEB (*author's note*: Vereniging van Effectenbezitters, i.e. a Dutch investors' association) and the Consortium had let their wishes and plans concerning a possible merger or acquisition of ABN AMRO Holding and the associated sale of LaSalle be known in the period of time concerned; 5. Barclays made the sale of LaSalle...a condition for its intended offer to go ahead. This all means that the sale of LaSalle had become (or had been made) such an issue that the board and the supervisory board of ABN AMRO Holding was no longer at liberty to withhold this, in the circumstances, major and (as talks on the merger and the acquisition of ABN AMRO Holding revealed) critical transaction, from the consultation and the approval of the shareholders meeting.

This consideration is typical for the Chamber. It focuses on the circumstances of the case and does not regard the wording of a statutory provision as decisive. ABN AMRO did not acquiesce in the judgment and lodged an appeal in cassation.

The Supreme Court sings a different tune:[7]

The circumstances cannot, unless the law or the articles of association so provide, result in a right of approval of the general meeting of shareholders of ABN AMRO holding with regard to the sale of LaSalle by ABN AMRO Bank...The Enterprise Chamber rightly assumed that the present case does not fall within the scope of this provision (i.e. section 107a, LT)... The first paragraph of Section 107a cannot, at variance with the findings of the Enterprise Chamber, be applied by analogy...now that the legal history – as set out in... Advocate General's advisory opinion...shows that the legislature, precisely for the sake of legal certainty, wished to deprive this provision from such a broad scope.

The language of the Supreme Court is again crystal-clear and does not need further comments. The Supreme Court quashes the judgment of the Enterprise Chamber. Some months later, the Chamber denied the requested investigation.

What can be learned from the *Gucci* and *ABN AMRO* sagas? I have tried to think deeply on this question, as I was involved in my capacity as Attorney-General to the Dutch Supreme Court. Foreign lawyers could

---

7 HR 13 July 2007, *Nederlandse Jurisprudentie* (2007), 434.

conclude that the Dutch Supreme Court and the Enterprise Chamber disagree about fundamental questions of Dutch corporate law.[8] However, I have concluded something different. I think this is an example of a more general phenomenon of interaction between two courts of justice. If a certain legal court is deciding in an activist and informal way – and, as we have seen, this is the case of the Enterprise Chamber – the higher judicial body that has to review the lower court of justice will take a more distant and formal approach. I am of the opinion that this is an example of a natural interaction between two judicial bodies which will finally lead to a certain state of balance. I am convinced that if the Enterprise Chamber had taken a more distant and formal approach, this would have challenged the Supreme Court to a more active and informal attitude.

[8] See on the jurisprudence of the Dutch Supreme Court in matters of company law: L. Timmerman, 'Company law and the Dutch Supreme Court, some remarks on contextualism and traditionalism in company law', *Ondernemingsrecht* (2007), 91–5.

21

Obstacles to corporate restructuring: observations from a European and German perspective

KLAUS J. HOPT*

In Europe there are still many obstacles to corporate restructuring, even beyond the takeover context. The experience with the implementation of the 13th Directive on Takeovers is sobering indeed. The number of Member States implementing the directive in a seemingly protectionist way is unexpectedly large. This is in line with a growing popular fear of globalization and definite trends toward political protectionism regarding foreign investments in various Member States. Germany is not an exception, as the Risk Limitation Act of July 2008 and the ongoing discussion on further restrictions illustrate. The declaration by Commissioner McCreevy of 3 October 2007 that there will be no European action on the issue of one-share/one-vote should not mean the end of the discussion. The report of the European Corporate Governance Forum Working Group on Proportionality of June 2007 is right in pleading for an enhanced disclosure regime concerning control-enhancing mechanisms. In any case, there is a definite need for more data and further analysis.

I. Introduction

The topic of this chapter is 'Obstacles to Corporate Restructuring', with an emphasis on takeover rules and the market of corporate control. There are two underlying implications to this choice: first, that takeovers play or can play an important role in corporate restructuring; and second, that there are other important parameters for corporate restructuring beyond takeovers. Let me make two preliminary remarks on this.

---

* This essay is dedicated to Eddy Wymeersch, colleague and friend since the 1970s, with whom I had such a longstanding and fruitful cooperation that we pass for academic twin brothers.

As to the role of takeovers in corporate restructuring, one should keep in mind that this is twofold. Takeovers may have synergistic grounds as well as disciplinary reasons. Empirical evidence suggests that there is a certain disciplinary effect on the management of badly performing companies, insofar as functioning markets of corporate control are indeed a means of external corporate governance, as it is sometimes called. But on the whole, takeover targets are not noticeably badly performing companies. This implies that the synergistic reasons for takeovers are more frequent and more important. More details can be found in the ISS report and related studies of the ECGI for the European Commission.[1]

As to the second implication, two other parameters beyond takeovers and takeover law are of key importance for corporate restructuring: the possibility for companies of merging beyond national borders,[2] and the availability of sound rescue procedures before and after formal insolvency. The possibility of merging beyond national borders has been considerably improved by the European directive of 26 October 2005 on cross-border mergers of limited liability companies,[3] which is in the process of being transformed by the Member States. The *Sevic* decision of the European Court of Justice of 13 December 2005[4] has gone even further in opening this door. Company practice in the various Member States is working hard on using both of these new ways of restructuring companies: the way via the directive is narrower but its requirements are more spelled out, therefore making it safer; the way via the ECJ decision is more far-reaching, but it lacks the details of how to go about it and is therefore rather insecure. When things become tighter for companies, the availability of sound rescue procedures becomes paramount. I will just mention in passing that in many of the Member States, both pre- and post-insolvency rescue law reforms have been enacted in the last

---

[1] Institutional Shareholder Services (ISS) in collaboration with Shearman & Sterling LLP and the European Corporate Governance Institute (ECGI), *Report on the Proportionality Principle in the European Union* (18 May 2007); Deutsche Bank AG London, 'Corporate Governance, The control of corporate Europe', *Report* (16 March 2007); see also infra II A.

[2] ECFR Symposium 'Cross-border Company Transactions', Milan, 13 October 2006, *European Company and Financial Law Review*, 4 (2007), 1–172.

[3] European Parliament and Council Directive 2005/56/EC [2005] OJ L310/1.

[4] Case C-411/03, *Landgericht Koblenz* v. *Sevic Systems* AG, [2005] ECR-I-10805, also in *Neue Juristische Wochenschrift* (2006), 425 with many comments in various law reviews, e.g., W. Bayer and J. Schmidt, 'Der Schutz der grenzüberschreitenden Verschmelzung durch die Niederlassungsfreiheit', *Zeitschrift für Wirtschaftsrecht (ZIP)* (2006), 210; C. Teichmann, 'Binnenmarktmobilität von Gesellschaften nach "Sevic"', *Zeitschrift für Wirtschaftsrecht* (2006), 355.

years or are being discussed – for example, in the UK in 2002, in France in 2005, in Germany in 2007, as well as in Italy and elsewhere.[5]

From these two preliminary remarks, it would appear that identifying and overcoming obstacles to corporate restructuring in the takeover context is important, but only as part of a much greater task. If the outcome of our discussion is that not very much can be done on the European takeover front at the moment, then there might be other fields in which the conditions for corporate restructuring in Europe are better, can be used, and should and could be further improved.

Having said this, I shall turn to the obstacles to corporate restructuring in the takeover context. I shall first have a quick look at the implementation of the 13th Directive on Takeover Bids,[6] using the report of the European Commission of 21 February 2007.[7] As we shall see, the findings of the European Commission are not very encouraging, though the overall pessimistic undertone of the report may be exaggerated. Furthermore, the most recent discussions and reform plans in a number of Member States suggest that there is a popular fear of globalization and open markets combined with a new wave of protectionism. I shall illustrate the danger of such a development, even in a traditionally European-minded Member State like Germany, in the second part of my article by taking a short look at the law on limitation of risks of July 2008 and the pending reform of the foreign investment law. In the last part I shall present the findings of the European Corporate Governance Forum Working Group on Proportionality as of June 2007.[8] While there is scepticism about a European one-share/one-vote rule, this group has made some policy recommendations on how to proceed further with deviations from the proportionality principle.

II. The sobering experience with the implementation of the 13th Directive

A. Basic principles of the European 13th Directive on Takeovers

a) The history of the origins, aims, and content of the 13th Directive of 21 April 2004 on takeovers cannot be repeated here. The coming

---

[5] The contributions of a symposium of the ECFR in 2007 in Paris can be found in *European Company and Financial Law Review*, 5 (2008), 135 et seq.

[6] Directive 2004/25/EC [2004] OJ L 142/12.

[7] European Commission Staff Working Document, *Report on the Implementation of the Directive on Takeover Bids* (21 February 2007), SEC(2007) 268.

[8] Infra IV.

about of the directive took decades: it was full of regulatory and political ups and downs, and it was made possible at the end only by a complicated political compromise. The regulatory idea underlying the directive[9] is that in an internal market, takeovers may not be blocked nationally, and that takeovers – including hostile ones – are in general economically useful. This is because a well-functioning market for corporate control strengthens the competitiveness of enterprises and is an important means of external corporate governance. The threat of takeovers tends to discipline managers and encourages them to strive for good share prices. These lie in the interest of both shareholders and management and are the best defence against hostile takeovers. The regulation of takeovers faces three serious principal-agent problems: the first exist between the shareholders and the managers (the board, one-tier or two-tier); the second between the majority shareholders or the parent and the minority shareholders of the target; and the third between the acquirer and the non-shareholder constituencies, in particular labour and other creditors. The first principal-agent problem is particularly relevant in those countries where public companies and dispersed shareholders are the rule, such as the United States and the United Kingdom. The second is prominent in countries with block holders, family enterprises and companies controlled by the state or other public entities; examples are Germany, France and other continental European countries. The regulatory problems for takeover law vary according to these shareholders structures.[10]

b) The 13th Directive tries to solve the first problem apart from disclosure rules through the anti-frustration rule for the board, or, in the case

---

[9] European Commission, High Level Group of Company Law Experts, *Report on Issues Related to Takeover Bids* (10 January 2002), reprinted in G. Ferrarini, K. J. Hopt, J. Winter, E. Wymeersch (eds.), *Reforming Company and Takeover Law in Europe* (Oxford University Press, 2004), Annex 2, 825–924.

A law and economics study on the regulation of takeovers in various countries can be found in: P. Davies and K. J. Hopt, 'Chapter on Control Transactions', in R. R. Kraakman, P. Davies, H. Hansmann, G. Hertig, K. J. Hopt, H. Kanda, E. Rock (eds.), *The Anatomy of Corporate Law, A Comparative and Functional Approach* (Oxford University Press, 2004); the revised and enlarged 2nd edition is to appear in winter 2008/09.

[10] See in more detail Davies and Hopt, 'Chapter on Control Transactions', (note 9, above); Cf. also J. Armour and D. A. Skeel, 'Who Writes the Rules for Hostile Takeovers and Why? – The Peculiar Divergence of U.S. and U.K. Takeover Regulation', *Georgetown Law Journal*, 95 (2007), 1728–94.

of a two-tier board, for the managing board as well as for the supervisory board (Art. 9 on obligations of the board of the offeree company). This rule means that the board of the target company may not engage in defensive actions which may frustrate the bid. Defensive actions are strictly reserved for the shareholders in the general assembly. The reason for this rule is that the directors are tempted to act in their self-interest of keeping their job. The anti-frustration rule is modelled after the example of the English Code on Takeovers and Mergers and is sometimes also called the neutrality principle, though this is not precise since the board is not meant to be strictly inactive, but must give an advisory opinion of its own to the shareholders and may look for a white knight. The anti-frustration rule is supplemented by the breakthrough of certain restrictions in the target, for example on the transfer of securities and on voting rights provided for in the articles of association or in contractual agreements between the target and holders of its securities (Art. 11; in the German version this is wrongly translated as 'Durchgriff', which means 'piercing the corporate veil').

The second principal-agent problem is mitigated by the mandatory bid, which must be made to all shareholders at an equitable price (Art. 5). By such a bid the minority shareholders are enabled to exit at an early stage of acquisition of control or change of controller. This is one of the few European group law rules, i.e., a rule which already takes effect upon entry into the group (group entry control). In contrast, in some countries (like Germany) there is an established group law only during the operation of the group, leading to problems of interpretation, proof and enforcement.[11] Of course, the drawback of the mandatory bid is that it makes the bidder's decision to make a bid more costly, thereby discouraging bids. On the other hand, the successful bidder has the right to squeeze out a small minority left after the bid (from 90% of the voting rights on, Art. 15). This squeeze-out right of the controlling shareholders is balanced by a parallel sell-out right of the small minority (Art. 16).

The third principal-agent problem is dealt with by mere disclosure, as well as the general principle that the board of the target must act in the interests of the company as a whole (Art. 3 (1) (c)).

---

[11] K. J. Hopt, 'Konzernrecht: Die Europäische Perspektive', *Zeitschrift für das gesamte Handelsrecht und Wirtschaftsrecht*, 171 (2007), 199–240.

The above-mentioned compromise that made the directive accept-able in the end consists of a double option of the Member States and an option of the companies concerned. The Member States may opt out of the anti-frustration and breakthrough rules (Art. 9 (2) and (3) and/or Art. 11). But if they do, they must allow the companies with seats in their territory to voluntarily opt in to these rules by a decision of the general meeting (Art. 12 (1) and (2)). In this regard, the Member States may enact a reciprocity rule for companies that have opted in (Art. 12 (3)). Reciprocity means that if such a company becomes the target of a takeover bid by a bidder that is not itself subject to the same restrictions as the target company, the target company is not bound by its option decision, but can defend itself against the bid like any other company in this state.

B. Implementation of the 13th Directive in the Member States

a) The implementation of the 13th Directive by the Member States went rather slowly. A Commission Staff Working Document of 21 February 2007 delivered an interim report on the implementation. The key find-ings of the report are rather sobering. The two major pieces of the 13th Directive on which the document reports are the anti-frustration and breakthrough rules, and the minority shareholder protection by a man-datory bid and a sell-out right that balances the squeeze-out right of the acquirer.

According to the report, the anti-frustration rule has been imposed or is expected to be imposed by eighteen Member States. But what is relevant in this context is that an anti-frustration rule of this or a similar kind already existed previously in all of these Member States, with the exception of only one, namely Malta. Furthermore, five of these Member States have introduced or intend to introduce the reciprocity exception under Article 12 (3).

As to the breakthrough rule, the report says that it is expected to be imposed (or indeed may have been imposed already) only by the Baltic States, and that no other country will obligate its companies to apply this provision in full. Instead, according to the report, all the other countries have made the breakthrough optional for companies under Article 12 (1). Hungary has gone even further and eliminated the partial breakthrough rule it had before. Yet since the publication of the report, Italy has transformed the 13th Directive and now has a breakthrough rule which fully corresponds to Article 11.[12] The report's statement that just 1% of listed companies in the EU will apply the breakthrough rule on a mandatory basis must therefore be corrected. In any case, the majority of Member States have adopted or will adopt the reciprocity rule here as well.

As to minority shareholder protection, most Member States already had the mandatory bid rule previously, but they have used the flexibility granted by the directive to maintain their national exceptions from the mandatory bid rule. These exceptions and far-reaching discretionary powers of the supervisory agencies, for example in the UK,[13] can undermine the effectiveness provided by this rule.

Only as far as the sell-out rule is concerned can clear progress be reported. This rule has been or will be introduced in a large number of Member States for the first time as a consequence of Article 16 of the directive.

b) How should we evaluate these findings? The report concludes on a pessimistic note: 'The number of Member States implementing the Directive in a seemingly protectionist way is unexpectedly large.' The Commission even fears that the new takeover rules of the 13th Directive will have potentially negative effects on the European market. While this is not based on evidence, it is certainly incontestable that there is a strong reluctance among Member States to lift takeover barriers, and particularly to do so in the international context. This is in line with a popular fear of globalization and a general trend in the Member States toward political protectionism.[14]

On the other hand, the facts found by the report should not be evaluated too negatively either. The implementation corresponds to the instructions of the directive, which expressly concedes options and room for discretion. It is quite understandable that the Member States made use of them, in particular if the underlying rules of the directive departed from their national takeover law. Therefore, such

---

[12] Decreto Legislativo 19 novembre 2007, n. 229, *Gazzetta Ufficiale* n. 289 del 13 dicembre 2007, Art.104-bis del decreto legislativo n. 58 del 1998: 'Regola di neutralizzazione.' Cf. M. Lamandini, 'Takeover Bids and 'Italian' Law Reciprocity, *European Company Law* 5 (April 2008) issue 2, 56–7.

[13] It is interesting to confront these far-reaching discretionary powers of the Takeover Panel with the much more legalistic approach taken by the German legislators, which is to be explained by German history and a strict supervision of the German BaFin by the administrative courts. This is a nice example of path dependency.

[14] K. J. Hopt, 'Editorial, Feindliche Übernahmen, Protektionismus, One share one vote?', *Europäische Zeitschrift für Wirtschaftsrecht*, (2007), 257.

implementation is not necessarily only protectionist; depending on the country, it may simply be the preservation of the existing path dependency and a reasonable policy of implementation 'one to one'[15] instead of going further and even gold-plating. This is true for the mandatory bid and the national exceptions from it as well as for the anti-frustration rule.

But most of all, the European Commission and the discussion on implementation in the Member States following it seem to misconceive two important facts. First, the directive represents progress insofar as it contains uncontested and well-implemented rules on many issues other than only those contained in Articles 9 and 11, in particular transparency rules and rules on fair behaviour and procedure in takeovers. Such rules are of key importance for enterprises and shareholders in the EU that need legal certainty and no conflicting legal requirements in the twenty-seven Member States when they make their investment or disinvestment decisions. As far as Articles 9 and 11 are concerned, the directive sets a model that is particularly relevant for those countries and companies with diverse shareholderships. Insofar, the option compromise of the directive in Article 12 is much better than a watered-down version of the anti-frustration rule or even the omission *in toto* of the breakthrough rule would have been.

Second, the reciprocity rule of Article 12 (3) and the fact that the Member States have made use of it so widely is not to be seen only negatively as an exception to the basic rules of Articles 9 and 11. Reciprocity may quite possibly also have positive effects. If a company can be sure not to be taken over by a bidder who himself is not subject to the anti-frustration and/or breakthrough rules, the company may be more willing to opt into these rules itself. As to the latter case, there is no case experience yet, but it is not expected to remain merely theoretical. Certain companies may consider an opting in as a positive signal on the capital market, or they may be under pressure by international, in particular Anglo-American, institutional investors to do so, rather than to fence themselves in by defensive actions. It follows that while reciprocity is an exception of Articles 9 and 11, it may have the positive effect of promoting companies to voluntarily opt in to these rules.

---

[15] In Germany the government made this principle of transformation 'one to one' part of its political programme as reflected in the coalition agreement.

III. Popular fear of globalization and trends toward political protectionism regarding takeovers and foreign investments: the German example

A. Discussion in the member states on unwelcome and potentially dangerous foreign investments

a) As mentioned in the introduction, the globalization movement has led to strong fears among the population of most European Member States, a development that is akin to the fear of international terrorism in the United States. While this fear may be irrational and the challenges and opportunities of larger European and globalized markets outweigh the risks by far, the fear is real.[16] This is so quite apart from the fact that it is an illusion that single states may be successful in the long run in fencing off their markets. In search of popularity and votes, politicians in many Member States are reacting by making general rules that raise the barriers to private investments and takeovers, and by state intervention in specific cases. There are a great many examples for such specific interventions. The French government massively supported the takeover of Aventis by the French Sanofi instead of letting the Swiss group Novartis make the deal. The Spanish government impeded the takeover of the Spanish Endesa by its German competitor E.ON. The French government forced the merger of the French Suez and Gaz de France instead of letting the Italian Enel come in. And the French government started to question the already existing participation of Siemens in the French Areva.[17] Similar cases might be reported from Italy, Poland and other countries.

b) Some pretend that Germany has a much better record. Yet this is doubtful in view of a long list of cases in which takeover fears and takeover defences have influenced the outcome. The 180-degree turnaround of former Chancellor Schröder is unforgotten. In 2001 Schröder defected from the unanimously agreed-upon common standpoint of the Council on the draft 13th Directive of the European Commission that contained an anti-frustration rule which clearly followed the British model.[18] The

---

[16] K. J. Hopt, E. Kantzenbach, T. Straubhaar (eds.), *Herausforderungen der Globalisierung* (Göttingen: Vandenhoek & Rupprecht, 2003); C. Linzbach *et al.* (eds.), *Globalisierung und Europäisches Sozialmodell* (Baden-Baden: Nomos, 2007); R. Howse, 'The End of the Globalization Debate: A Review Essay', *Harvard Law Review 121* (2008), 1528.

[17] For details, see R. von Rosen, 'Die Umsetzung der EU-Übernahmerichtlinie in Europa, Eine erste Bilanz', *Management Zeitschrift für Corporate Governance*, 6 (2007), 241, 243 *et seq.*

[18] See R. Skog, 'The Takeover Directive: An Endless Saga?', *European Business Law Review*, 13 (2002), 301; K. J. Hopt, 'La treizième directive sur les OPA-OPE et le droit allemand',

financial press commented that this was a closing of ranks between Wolfsburg, the seat of the Volkswagen corporation, and Hannover, the capital of Lower Saxony, and pointed at the Volkswagen Act[19] with its right for Lower Saxony to be represented in the Volkswagen board. Indeed, Schröder as Prime Minister of Lower Saxony had been a member of the board of Volkswagen and had gotten so close to the automobile industry that he was nicknamed the 'automobile chancellor'.

In a similar vein, the heated debate on the anti-frustration rule in the German takeover statute ended with the anti-frustration rule as the principle, but subject to four exceptions.[20] The first three are innocuous, including the possibility of an anticipated authorization of the board to engage in defensive actions to be given by the general assembly up to eighteen months before the takeover bid.[21] The Trojan horse is the fourth exception, i.e., the permissibility of all kinds of defensive actions if the managing board gets the consent of the supervisory board. This waters down the anti-frustration rule considerably, since notwithstanding the mandatory separation of the two boards in the German two-tier system,

---

in *Aspects actuels du droit des affaires, Mélanges en l'honneur de Yves Guyon* (Paris: Dalloz, 2003), 529, 537 *et seq.*

[19] In the meantime, see the decision of the Case C-112/05, *Commission* v. *Germany*, [2007] ECR-I-8995, ('Volkswagen-Gesetz,') holding parts of this Act in violation of the EC Treaty. The decision is reprinted and commented e.g., by J. van Bekkum, J. Kloosterman, J. Winter, 'Golden Shares and European Company Law: the Implications of Volkswagen', *European Company Law,* 5 (2008) issue 1, 6–12, as well as in many German law reviews, e.g., *Zeitschrift für Wirtschaftsrecht* (2007), 2068 and *Neue Juristische Wochenschrift* (2007), 3481. The most recent German reaction to this decision proves the point made in this article. The German government intends to maintain the Act with a few changes only insofar as the board delegation rights of the Federal Republic of Germany and of Lower Saxony and the voting cap of 20% combined with a supermajority of 80% for changes of the company statutes are deleted, but the necessity of a supermajority of 80% is to be maintained. In addition, a new requirement for the consent of the supervisory board with a two-thirds majority for important investment decisions is to be introduced. By this the overwhelming influence of labour via the codetermined board is maintained, and restructuring involving changes of plants after foreign takeovers is *de facto* made impossible. An expert opinion for the blockholder Porsche corporation holds that this is in violation of European law, 'Wegen des VW-Gesetzes drohen Zwangsgelder', *Frankfurter Allgemeine Zeitung*, (1 February 2008), No. 27, 14; cf. also F. Möslein, 'Aufsichtsratsverfassung und Kapitalverkehrsfreiheit', *Der Aufsichtsrat* (2008), 72–73; T. Käseberg and F. Möslein, 'Auch die Mitbestimmungsregeln im VW-Gesetz sind fragwürdig', *Frankfurter Allgemeine Zeitung*, (12 March 2008), No. 61, 23.

[20] Section 33 subsection 1 sentence 1 of the German Takeover Act. For a neutrality requirement as to the managing board under company law see Bundesgerichtshof decision of 22 October 2007, *Die Aktiengesellschaft*, (2008), 164.

[21] Section 33 subsection 2.

the German supervisory board cannot be considered to be independent. The practical relevance of the fourth exception is even greater if one considers that in all major German stock corporations, a mandatory system of quasi-parity labour codetermination is forced upon all major corporations. As a matter of experience, in cases of hostile takeovers the best allies for the board of the target are the representatives of labour in its supervisory board. Both stand to lose if the takeover is successful – the former their jobs as directors, the latter their employment in case of restructuring and dismissals.[22] It is telling that when the statutes of the Thyssen Krupp corporation were modified in order to give to the Krupp Foundation three seats in the supervisory board, it was made clear that by this move the corporation would be immune from hostile takeovers, since under such a threat there would always be a thirteen-vote majority (i.e., the three directors delegated by the foundation and the ten labour representatives).

The discussion on defending German enterprises from foreign takeovers reached a new peak in 2005 when foreign hedge funds forced the German Stock Exchange in Frankfurt to change its takeover strategies concerning a friendly takeover offer to the London Stock Exchange, to oust its CEO Seifert, and to overhaul the composition of its supervisory board, including forcing its chairman Breuer to step down. The German financial markets supervisory agency (*Bundesanstalt für Finanzdienstleistungsaufsicht*, BaFin) reacted by starting an inquiry into whether these hedge funds had acted in concert in trying to acquire control of the company, and might even have had the obligation under German law to make a mandatory bid. It is hardly surprising that this inquiry led to nothing and after a while was silently tabled. Many observers believe that the conditions for a mandatory bid had in fact been fulfilled, but that this just could not be proved. Then came the battle over ABN AMRO, which ended with a total victory for the team surrounding 'Fred the Shred' and with the defeat and dismantling of this major bank.[23] In Germany and other Member States, this battle was observed with mixed feelings and afterthoughts on what this might mean for their own national bank and industrial champions. Most recently, the grow-

---

[22] This is essentially the principal-agent conflict between the shareholders and the directors of the target mentioned supra II 1 a. Cf. Davies and Hopt, 'Chapter on Control Transactions', (note 9, above).

[23] G. H. White, A. W. Konevsky and B. Anglette, 'The battle for ABN AMRO and certain aspects of cross-border takeovers', *Butterworths Journal of International Banking and Financial Law* (April 2008), 171–176.

ing activity of huge foreign state investment funds like the one from China has created nervousness in the public and among politicians. These funds have accumulated billions of dollars, and the suspicion is that once they acquire important stakes in key national industries they might use their influence not just for shareholder profit as other private funds, but for political purposes. The consequence of all this was that a draft Risk Limitation Act was drawn up by the Ministry of Finance and plans were made to tighten up the foreign investment law.

B. German Risk Limitation Act of July 2008 and the pending reform of the German Foreign Investment Law

a) The draft Risk Limitation Act was triggered in late summer 2007 by the fact that private equity investment in Germany was lagging and a new risk capital investment law and a reform of the law on participations in enterprises was urgently needed. The draft law on facilitating private equity investment in Germany by tax and other deregulatory measures was meant to contribute to the position of Germany in the international competition for private equity investment. But the left wing of the Social Democratic Party as well as influential parts of the Christian Democratic Party opposed the so-called tax gifts to private equity, and asked for protective measures against what they called 'predatory wild animal capitalism'. At the end, such burden easing for capital was politically unacceptable without being matched by 'limitations of the risk' allegedly presented by this. In order to keep these limitations at a level which would not endanger the attractiveness of Germany as an investment place, the German Ministry of Finance asked the Hamburg Max Planck Institute to compare what other states do in limiting the predatory activities of private equity, hedge funds and state funds. Though the result of this inquiry was that basically the free internal market concept still prevailed internationally, the Ministry reacted with the draft of the so-called Risk Limitation Act in late September 2007. To begin with, it can be observed that while the expectation of getting real deregulation and a sensibly better tax environment for the investment industry was not met, the draft Risk Limitation Act was not eased up correspondingly.

As of December 2007 the draft law contains a whole set of technical reforms, among them disclosure rules. An investor with 10% or more must tell the issuer on demand whether he intends a long-term strategic investment and whether ultimately he even might aim at acquiring control of the company. To be sure, this is not a one-shot obligation; changes of intention must also be disclosed. The investor must also disclose to what extent he is financing his acquisition by his own means or by outside financing. Furthermore, the true owners of the shares will be more easily identifiable by the company in the future. The banks are supposed to find out and disclose to the company the true ultimate owner of a block, thereby piercing through the chain of street name registrations. The draft does not say how these duties will be enforced against non-national banks and nominees, but it is intended to withhold the voting rights in case of non-compliance. It is quite obvious that this would create considerable uncertainty on the final outcome of shareholder voting and would encourage the so-called predatory shareholders to blackmail the corporations by contesting the votes before the courts,[24] quite apart from costly and probably fruitless inquisition efforts of the banking community. Furthermore, the information rights of the employees of the company against block investors are to be reinforced.[25]

Yet the most important and controversial draft reform concerns the considerably stiffened rules on acting in concert as compared with the old text.[26] Under the proposed rule, acting in concert presupposes an acting in concert by the owners of shares with a view toward a common enterprise policy.[27] In the future, the concerted acquisition of blocks of shares will already be relevant. By this, a restrictive decision of the German Bundesgerichtshof would be set aside which had interpreted the law in the sense that it covers only acting in concert within the general

---

[24] This is a peculiarity of the German corporate reality quite unlike that which exists in other countries; see T. Baums, A. Keinath and D. Gajek, 'Fortschritte bei Klagen gegen Hauptversammlungsbeschlüsse? Eine empirische Studie', *Zeitschrift für Wirtschaftsrecht*, (2007), 1629; T. Baums and F. Drinhausen, 'Weitere Reform des Rechts der Anfechtung von Hauptversammlungsbeschlüssen', *Zeitschrift für Wirtschaftsrecht*, (2008), 145.

[25] Together with presenting the draft Risk Limitation Act, the government announced that it would examine whether to take legislative action concerning the sale of credit claims, a controversial consumer protection reform. G. Nobbe, 'Der Verkauf von Krediten', *Zeitschrift für Wirtschaftsrecht*, (2008), 97.

[26] Section 30 subsection 2 sentence 1 of the German Takeover Act says that votes of a third party are to be counted as votes of the bidder 'if thereby the bidder or his subsidiary act in concert as to the target either by agreement or else; agreements on voting in single cases are excepted'. A. Raloff, *Acting in Concert* (Gottmadingen: Jenaer Wissenschaftliche Verlagsgesellschaft, 2007).

[27] The formula of the draft act is: 'There is acting in concert, if the bidder or his subsidiary and a third party act in concert in a way which is apt to permanently or considerably influence the entrepreneurial line of the target.'

assembly.[28] Furthermore, the exception under the old law that acting in concert in single cases remains legitimate is meant to be done away with. In the discussion there is even talk about *de facto* presumptions of concerted action under certain circumstances. Because of the drastic possible consequence of a mandatory bid, this proposed change is by far the most controversial reform measure in the public discussion.

The draft Risk Limitation Act met with a criticism that was stronger and more widespread than anything the Ministry of Finance had experienced before. This criticism was articulated not only in the press, but in particular in a public hearing of the Committee of Finance of the German Bundestag in January 2008. The protocols of this hearing are available[29] and need not be taken up here in more detail. It suffices to mention the critical but moderate comments by the German Share Institute,[30] which had organized a seminar on the draft the day before; by the commercial law committee of the German Attorneys Association;[31] and by the leading German shareholder association, the German Association for Protection of Securities.[32] It is hardly surprising that the observations made by the institutional investors were most critical, such as those made by Christian Strenger, a director of the supervisory board of DWS, the investment arm of the Deutsche Bank, or from abroad by Hermes, the well-known British pension fund with around €100 billion in assets. On the other side, the German Trade Union Confederation[33] and some academics were in favour of the new law and even asked for further restrictions for fear of a sell-out of German industry, of losing jobs, and of nurturing further, as it has been called, 'neo-liberal market ideology'.[34] Academic critique was made in more detail at the biannual

---

[28] Bundesgerichtshof decision of 18 September 2006, case 'WMF,' *Entscheidungen des Bundesgerichtshofes in Zivilsachen* 169, 98 *et seq.*, no. 17.

[29] German Bundestag, 16th Voting Period, Committee of Finance, 23 January 2008, Berlin, Protocol No. 16/82.

[30] Deutsches Aktieninstitut (DAI) Frankfurt am Main, Comments of 18 January 2008.

[31] Handelsrechtsausschuss des Deutschen Anwaltsvereins (DAV), 'Stellungnahme zum Regierungsentwurf eines Risikobegrenzungsgesetzes', *Neue Zeitschrift für Gesellschaftsrecht*, (2008), 60.

[32] Deutsche Schutzvereinigung für Wertpapierbesitz, Comments of 9 January 2008.

[33] Deutscher Gewerkschaftsbund (DGB).

[34] Cf. R. Stürner, *Markt und Wettbewerb über alles? Gesellschaft und Recht im Fokus neo-liberaler Marktideologie* (Munich: C. H. Beck, 2007). But see, e.g., H. Siebert, *Jenseits des sozialen Marktes, Eine notwendige Neuorientierung der deutschen Politik* (Munich: Deutsche Verlags-Anstalt, 2005); H.-W. Sinn, *Ist Deutschland noch zu retten?*, 3rd edition, (Munich: Econ, 2003); S. Empter and R. B. Vehrkamp (eds.), *Soziale Gerechtigkeit – eine Bestandaufnahme* (Gütersloh: Bertelsmann, 2007).

symposium of the leading German company law journal by Holger Fleischer[35] and at the yearly meeting of the working group on economics and the law by Peter Mülbert.[36] These criticisms are well-founded in several respects:[37]

(1) Transparency is one thing and – as a general rule – positive, though details of the proposed disclosure rules are critical. Yet a too harsh mandatory bid rule frightens off potential bidders, takes away choices for the shareholders, and weakens the takeover market. It follows that it would be better to dissolve the parallelism between the rules on acting in concert in the German Securities Exchange Act and the Takeover Act.[38]

(2) More generally, the consequences of the new rule on corporate governance must be taken into consideration. Investors must be able to discuss investments to be made among themselves. Active shareholders are welcome. Board members are controllers and need to be able to act together in pursuing this task. A well-functioning takeover market supplements this internal control from outside and is an important part of external corporate governance.

(3) For example, shareholders who intend to jointly prevent a too-risky policy of their corporation (standstill), or want to oust a chairman whose entrepreneurial policy they do not support, or who are ready to jointly rescue the corporation in case of financial crisis, must be able to do this without running the risk of facing a mandatory bid requirement. These and similar situations should at least be mentioned as a safe harbour in the motives of the Act.[39]

It remains to be seen what the legislators will finally decide in the near future. It might be that the old exception for acting in concert in single cases will be maintained, or that the proposed alternative of being apt

---

[35] H. Fleischer, 'Finanzinvestoren im ordnungspolitischen Gesamtgefüge von Aktien-, Bankaufsichts- und Kapitalmarktrecht', *Zeitschrift für Unternehmens- und Gesellschaftsrecht*, 2–3 (2008), 185.

[36] Arbeitskreis Wirtschaft und Recht, 25 January 2008. See also G. Spindler, 'Acting in Concert – Begrenzung der Risiken durch Finanzinvestoren?', *Wertpapier-Mitteilungen*, (2007), 2357.

[37] See K. J. Hopt, 'Viel zu defensiv', *Handelsblatt*, (30 January 2008), No. 21, 19.

[38] The same view has been taken expressly by the statement of DAI (note 30, above), 3.

[39] See also the statement of the DAI (note 30, above), suggesting to make clear in the motives that an exchange of opinion between investors on entrepreneurial topics is safe provided its result is still open, and that it must remain possible to try to win others over to one's own position.

to exercise a 'permanent or considerable' influence will be replaced by 'considerable' influence only. But it is pretty certain that acting in concert, even outside the general assembly, and also with others than group members, will be caught by the new provision. On the other hand, if the text stays as it is now or is not relativized by safe-harbour remarks in the motives, there will be a serious danger for internal corporate governance, i.e., active shareholdership, as well as for external corporate governance, i.e., an active market for corporate control.[40]

The latest news is that on 25 June 2008 the Financial Committee of the German Bundestag reached the following difficult compromise: 'There is acting in concert, if the bidder or its subsidiary and the third party come to an agreement with each other as to the exercise of votes or if they otherwise cooperate with the aim of reaching a permanent and considerable change of the enterpreneurial direction of the target.' The German Parliament has accepted this version and enacted the Risk Limitation Act on 27 June/4 July 2008. The final outcome is a tightening up with which one can live.

b) The pending reform on the German foreign investment law[41] goes too far as well, at least in its present form which contains only a vague general clause instead of concrete formulas that could guarantee legal certainty for the companies of M&A deals or those involved in takeovers. This reform has its origins in two situations: the decision of the People's Republic of China to establish a US$200 billion state fund company which would also seek investment opportunities in foreign corporations; and the interest of the Russian gas producer Gazprom in looking for investments in the German transport sector and in the distribution of natural gas. A list consisting of the more than forty most significant worldwide state funds shows that the state funds of the Arab Emirates, Singapore, Norway, Saudi Arabia and Kuwait have still higher assets than the new Chinese state fund, with the Arab Emirates holding assets of US$875 billion.[42]

---

[40] Some even see a violation of European law, cf. R. Schmidtbleicher, 'Das „neue" acting in concert – ein Fall für den EuGH?', *Die Aktiengesellschaft*, (2008), 73.

[41] Federal Ministry of Economics and Technology, Draft 13th Act Modifying the Foreign Investment Act and the Foreign Investment Ordinance as of 5 November 2007.

[42] Abu Dhabi Investment Authority (ADIA) with US$ 875 billion <Milliarden>. A list of the largest state funds can be found in: State Experts Council for Evaluation of the Economic Development at Large (Sachverständigenrat zur Begutachtung der gesamtwirtschaftlichen Entwicklung), *Annual Expert Opinion* (2007/08), table 55, 396. According to a more recent study of the London International Financial Services Institute the total assets held by the state funds is estimated to increase dramatically by 2015, 'Neue Macht aus

Since it is technically difficult to single out hedge funds, and politically unwise to openly hit state investment funds, the draft foreign investment law reform plans a rule under which any foreign (now from outside the EU) investment of 25% or more in a German corporation may be forbidden if public security is concerned. Originally even the strategic infrastructure was included in this protection. This is very vague indeed, since specific sectors of industry – such as energy and armament, to name just two – are not mentioned in the proposal. Even worse, while there is no requirement of state permission for such investments, the government may take up such transactions within three months, ask for full information and, after having received it, forbid it within another two months (though not longer). Originally there were even plans to extend the time frame for state intervention up to three years retroactively, and the reform would have extended to all foreign investors, i.e. also those from within the European Union.[43] The European Commission and members of the European Parliament have criticized these reform plans. While the original version ('strategic infrastructure') would certainly have infringed on the freedoms of establishment and capital of the EC Treaty, it is still doubtful whether such a general clause is compatible with European law since such a general clause lacks the clarity needed by foreign investors and thereby impedes the investment flow.[44]

dem Osten', *Handelsblatt* (1st April 2008), No. 63, 24. See also S. Butt, A. Shivdasani, C. Stendevad and A. Wyman, 'Sovereign Wealth Funds: A Growing Global Force in Corporate Finance', *Journal of Applied Corporate Finance* 19 (2007), 73–83.

[43] See the draft new section 7 subsection 2 No. 6 of the Foreign Investment Act: 'Transactions on the acquisition of enterprises having their seat in Germany as well as of participations in such enterprises, if the acquisition endangers the public order or security of the Federal Republic of Germany'. See also the draft new section 53 subsection 1 sentence 1 of the Foreign Investment Ordinance: 'Acquisition of an enterprise having its seat in Germany or of a direct or indirect participation in such an enterprise by a foreigner or a national enterprise in which a foreigner holds at least 25% of the votes...'. In the meantime the Minister of Labour demanded to have a say in the decision with the clear aim of protecting domestic labour. Fortunately this protectionist move was not accepted. The compromise as of 11 July 2008 is that the decision to take up the affair shall be made by the Minister of Economics alone, while a decision to prohibit the transaction is up to the federal government after having heard the various ministries. 'Federführung bei Staatsfonds entschieden', *Handelsblatt* (14 July 2008), No. 134, 5.

[44] 'EU-Kommission lehnt Regeln für Staatsfonds ab', *Frankfurter Allgemeine Zeitung* (28 February 2008), No. 50, 12. Unfortunately in the meantime the European Commission yielded to the political pressures by Germany as transmitted by the German industry Commissioner Verheugen and by other Member States: 'EU billigt Vorgehen gegen Staatsfonds', *Handelsblatt* (13 March 2008), No. 52, 6. See W. Bayer and C. Ohler, 'Staatsfonds ante portas', *Zeitschrift für Gesellschaftsrecht* (ZGR), (2008), 12–31 and most recently M. Nettesheim, 'Unternehmensübernahmen durch Staatsfonds:

The State Experts Council in its yearly report 2007/8[45] severely criticized the reform plans. According to the Council, other less intrusive alternatives are available, in particular antitrust and competition law measures and the possibility of the state keeping or acquiring a majority participation in the industries concerned (to be sure, not just a golden share that gives votes out of proportion to the actual shareholding of the state).[46] The German Council denies, at least at present, that the state funds present a danger since their aim is to build up a capital stock for future generations and to help to stabilize prices of natural resources in case of price fluctuations. It is true that more transparency is needed, but this would be sufficient. Also the elaboration of a Code of Conduct for these state funds as planned under the auspices of the International Monetary Fund is useful. The OECD and the European Commission declared to be willing to cooperate with the IMF in this matter, and the European Parliament is preparing a transparency initiative too[47]. Deliberations on the code are under way with the aim that the state funds commit themselves to make their investment decisions irrespective of any political influence. It is expected that the Code could be ready by October 2008.[48] As a countermove to such a Code the Western industrial nations should be expected to refrain from their protectionist moves and to keep their markets open for foreign investments including those made by state funds.[49]

The German Council is well aware of the fact that the US has a new Foreign Investment and National Security Act (FINSA) since October 2007 which gives the basis for a very restrictive and insecure treatment of foreign investments in the United States.[50] Yet the Council is fully right in stating that this example is leading in the wrong protectionist direction

Europarechtliche Vorgaben und Schranken', lecture given at the 150 Years Anniversary Symposion of the *Zeitschrift für das gesamte Handelsrecht und Wirtschaftsrecht* on 6 June 2008 in Berlin.

[45] State Experts Council, (note 42, above).

[46] State Experts Council, (note 42, above), ch. 7, 385–437 with dissenting opinion by Bofinger. Similarly J. B. Donges et al. (Kronberger Kreis), *Staatsfonds: Muss Deutschland sich schützen?* (Berlin 2008).

[47] European Parliament, Committee on Legal Affairs, Klaus-Heiner Lehne, 'Transparency of the Institutional Investors', *Working Document* (22 January 2008); the final version by the European Parliament is expected by autumn 2008; cf. also the short report by Fischer zu Cramburg, 'Hedgefonds und Private Equity', *Finanzplatz* 2 (March 2008), 28.

[48] 'Neue Macht aus dem Osten', *Handelsblatt* (1 April 2008), No. 63, 24.

[49] M. Maisch, 'Staatsfonds, Die neue Macht', *Handelsblatt* (2 April 2008), No. 64, 10.

[50] State Experts Council, (note 42, above), 432 *et seq.* Australia seems to go into the same direction: 'Australien rüstet sich gegen Staatsfonds', *Frankfurter Allgemeine Zeitung*

and should not be followed by Germany. Germany is an export-oriented nation, not only as far as products and services are concerned but also as to capital. Indeed, if Germany were to protect its own industry from capital inflows, this would be inconsistent with its own capital export record and could lead to retaliation. Furthermore, it is probable that the planned reform would also frighten off those investors and investments that are clearly useful and welcome. Protection is needed only for a very few specific sectors, such as armament, the atomic industry, and the energy sector. Catching all kinds of foreign investment under the vague general clause of 'public order and security' is going too far, since no M&A deal could be sure any longer whether or not there will be state intervention.

The general conclusion as to the foreign investment reform plans is that Germany has an elementary interest in keeping the capital market open. Germany has a large capital balance surplus[51] and cannot afford restrictions that would backfire. Foreign investments – also from state funds – create jobs and may rescue enterprises in difficulties, as illustrated quite clearly in the current finance crisis of American banks such as Citibank, Merrill Lynch and even Morgan Stanley. Measures taken specifically against state funds and/or hedge funds are problematic. As to the latter, single-handed efforts are bound to fail. International efforts – such as better transparency for hedge funds[52] and possibly further requirements for banks that finance these funds[53] – are more promising alternatives.

(4 March 2008), No. 54, 16. Russia has followed, T. Wiede, 'Russland verschärft die Regeln für Investoren', *Handelsblatt* (26 March 2008), No. 58, 6.

[51] For statistical information see State Experts Council, (note 42, above), at 389 *et seq.*

[52] The fourteen largest European hedge funds under the lead of Andrew Large have agreed to set up a code of conduct according to which there will be more transparency, control of the development of the investments by independent experts, and no more voting in the general assemblies with shares that are only lent and not owned. See Hedge Fund Working Group (HFWG), *Hedge Fund Standards: Final Report (Large Report),* London (January 2008) and, 'Hedge-Fonds öffnen sich', *Handelsblatt* (23 January 2008), No. 16, 22. From the USA see the two private-sector committees reports to the President's Working Group on Financial Markets: Asset Managers' Committee, *Best Practices for the Hedge Fund Industry,* and Investors' Committee, *Principles and Best Practices for Hedge Fund Investors,* Washington (April 15, 2008).

[53] See the path-breaking study by M. Kahan and E. B. Rock, 'Hedge Funds in Corporate Governance and Corporate Control', *University of Pennsylvania Law Review,* 155 (2007), 1021–93; see also from Germany: H. Eidenmüller, 'Regulierung von Finanzinvestoren', *Deutsches Steuerrecht,* (2007), 2116; H. Eidenmüller, 'Private Equity, Leverage und die Effizienz des Gläubigerschutzrechts', *Zeitschrift für das gesamte Handelsrecht und Wirtschaftsrecht* 171 (2007), 644; C. Kumpan, 'Private Equity und der Schutz deutscher Unternehmen', *Die Aktiengesellschaft,* (2007), 461; C. Kumpan, *DAJV Newsletter*

IV. One-share/one-vote discussion and recommendations of the European Corporate Governance Forum Working Group on Proportionality of June 2007

A. One-share/one-vote discussion and the reply of Commissioner McCreevy

In this section, I move to the European discussion on proportionality. The outcome of the one-share/one-vote studies by ISS Europe, the ECGI and Shearman & Sterling which were published by the European Commission on 4 June 2007 are well known.[54] On 3 October 2007, Commissioner McCreevy reacted, declaring before the European Parliament that he had made a deliberately provocative statement when announcing his plans to bring about a European one-share/one-vote rule. He acknowledged that there is no economic evidence of a causal link between deviations from the proportionality principle and the economic performance of companies, and concluded that there is no need for action at the EU level on this issue. Unfortunately, he also declared that he does not intend to propose any action in this context, not even concerning more transparency.

I belong to those experts and investors who, even in light of the economic evidence brought forward in the aforementioned studies, plead for more transparency in the need for and use of control-enhancing mechanisms. This is what the recommendations of the European Corporate Governance Forum Working Group on Proportionality of June 2007 say.[55]

(2007), 166, concerning the US; G. Spindler, 'Die Regulierung von Hedge-Fonds im Kapitalmarkt- und Gesellschaftsrecht', *Wertpapier-Mitteilungen*, (2006), 553 *et seq.* and 601 *et seq.*; A. Graef, *Aufsicht über Hedgefonds im deutschen und amerikanischen Recht* (Berlin 2008). As to the European initiatives see Athanassiou, 'Towards Pan-European Hedge Fund Regulation? State of the Debate', *Legal Issues of Economic Integration*, 35 (2008) 1, 1–41.

[54] European Commission, Institutional Shareholder Services ISS, Shearman & Sterling, European Corporate Governance Institute ECGI, *Report on the Proportionality Principle in the European Union* (18 May 2007); M. Burkhart, S. Lee, 'One Share – One Vote: The Theory', *Review of Finance*, 12 (2008), 1–49; R. Adams, D. Ferreira, 'One Share – One Vote: The Empirical Evidence', *Review of Finance*, 12 (2008), 51–91.

[55] IV B-D are closely following the Paper of the European Corporate Governance Forum Working Group on Proportionality of 12 June 2007. This group was headed by Jaap Winter, the former chairman of the High Level Group of Company Law Experts (note 9, above) and comprised both members of the High Level Group (among them myself) and some outside members, including Eddy Wymeersch.

B. Variety of control-enhancing mechanisms, the repudiation of a general one-share/one-vote rule and the need for better understanding

To begin with, the group makes a distinction between four different disproportionality dimensions: l) corporate institutional arrangements directly affecting shareholder rights, 2) corporate institutional arrangements indirectly affecting shareholder rights, 3) other corporate institutional entrenchment mechanisms, and 4) non-corporate institutional mechanisms. Examples for these four rings are 1) multiple voting rights and voting ceilings, 2) priority shares conferring an exclusive right to nominate board members, 3) share transfer restrictions, staggered board provisions and certain codetermination arrangements, and 4) pyramids and cross-shareholdings as well as market techniques that allow for decoupling of voting rights from cash flow rights, resulting, for example, in votes being exercisable without any economic investment (so-called 'empty voting')[56]. In light of these wide variations, the group concluded that an overall European proportionality rule is neither useful nor feasible. Shareholder democracy is a misleading catchword that draws unfounded analogies to politics and democracy of the people.

On the other hand, the group sees a need for an objective framework for further analysis of control-enhancing mechanisms, with due consideration of the differences of the instruments used in the four rings just mentioned – in particular, whether or not they are furthering the entrenchment of the board and the controlling shareholder, and whether they might function as obstacles to corporate restructuring. In this context, competing objectives should be examined, such as monitoring by the controlling shareholder,[57] easier access to capital markets, long-term orientation and stakeholder protection, and last but not least, freedom of contract and efficient competition. Only under three conditions – namely, if certain mechanisms are to be judged negatively on balance, if such mechanisms inhibit the achievement of EU policy objectives and if regulatory intervention at the EU level seems desirable – should the following possible regulatory tools be discussed and possibly prove useful.

---

[56] See most recently H.T.C. Hu and B. Black, 'Equity and Debt Decoupling and Empty Voting II: Importance and Extension', *University of Pennsylvania Law Review*, 156 (2008), 625–739.

[57] See most recently A. M. Pacces, *Featuring Control Power* (Rotterdam Institute of Law and Economics, 2007).

C. Toward an enhanced disclosure regime concerning control-enhancing mechanisms

In this light and in view of the many open questions found by the two ECGI studies, the group recommends in the short term an enhanced disclosure regime.[58] This disclosure regime might include the following four building blocks[59] to be discussed:

First, in addition to the disclosure obligations pursuant to Article 10 of the 13th Directive and the disclosures under the Transparency Directive, companies could be required to provide more detailed transparency on disproportionate mechanisms applied by them.

Second, shareholders who derive a voting position from such mechanisms exceeding, say, 10% of the total votes that can be cast in a meeting, could be required to provide insight into the size and nature of their shareholdings and their policy on the exercise of the relevant powers.

Third, companies and shareholders could also be required to provide more transparency on the actual use of disproportionate mechanisms – for example, in respect to specific related party transactions not entered into on an arm's length basis.

Alternatively, the Commission could ask the Member States to provide it annually with comparable information regarding application of disproportionate structures in their jurisdictions to the aforementioned extent. This would be an extension of the reports due by the Member States under Article 20 of the 13th Directive.

D. Particularly pressing problem areas and the need for more data and further analysis

The Forum Working Group further identified a number of particularly pressing problem areas in the field where it believes that, as a matter of principle,[60] a more substantial approach than mere disclosure is needed. Among them are:

---

[58] For a survey of the use of disclosure in European law, see S. Grundmann and F. Möslein, *European Company Law, Organization, Finance and Capital Markets* (Antwerpen/ Oxford: Intersentia, 2007), § 9. As to the disclosure principle for enterprises in a historical, economic and legal perspective see H. Merkt, *Unternehmenspublizität* (Tübingen: Mohr Siebeck, 2001).

[59] For the building block system in European law making, cf. Forum Europaeum Group Law, 'Corporate Group Law for Europe', *European Business Organization Law Review*, 1 (2000), 165–264.

[60] With due respect to the context, see supra IV B last paragraph.

First, instances where full board entrenchment is achieved. According to the group, the European Commission should make it clear in a recommendation that as a matter of principle this is unacceptable from a corporate governance perspective.

Second, the group is concerned by the decoupling of voting rights and economic ownership through mechanisms such as securities lending, contracts for difference, and call/put options whose mechanisms may affect the effective exercise of proportionate voting rights.[61] This point has also been made forcefully by the ECGI paper on empirical evidence concerning one-share/one-vote.

In addition to better disclosure, the EU should concentrate on the role of securities intermediaries in the voting process of their clients. The role of these intermediaries is crucial.

Overall there is a clear need for more data and further analysis. Part of this could be brought to light by the enhanced disclosure regime mentioned above. In addition, empirical studies are needed on the various control-enhancing mechanisms, their functions and implications, and the economic pros and cons. These studies should be supported morally as well as financially because they are in the public interest.

V. Conclusions

In Europe there are still many obstacles to corporate restructuring in the takeover context and beyond. According to an Interim Report of the European Commission, the experience with the implementation of the 13th Directive on Takeovers in the Member States is sobering indeed. As the Commission Report says, even though too pessimistically, the number of Member States implementing the directive in a seemingly protectionist way is unexpectedly large. This is in line with a growing popular fear of globalization and definite trends toward political protectionism regarding foreign investments in various Member States. In many, the legislators are tempted to raise the barriers to private investments and takeovers from abroad, and the governments tend to interfere when they see their national banking or industry champions threatened by takeovers from abroad. Germany is not an exception, as the legislative history of the Risk Limitation Act of July 2008 and the ongoing discussion on further restrictions of the foreign investment law illustrate. The far-reaching plans of Commissioner McCreevy of mandating

---

[61] Note 56, above.

a one-share/one-vote rule by European law could not be upheld in the light of the results of the Commission-mandated studies by ISS Europe, the ECGI and Shearman & Sterling. Yet the conclusions drawn from them by the European Commission are too pessimistic, and the declaration by Commissioner McCreevy of 3 October 2007 that there will be no European action on the issue of one-share/one-vote should not mean the end of the discussion. While there is a definite need for more data and further analysis, the report of the European Corporate Governance Forum Working Group on Proportionality of June 2007 sees a need for further development of the European internal market and pleads for an enhanced disclosure regime concerning control-enhancing mechanisms.

22

Protection of third-party interests under German takeover law

HARALD BAUM

During the legislative proceedings of the German Takeover Act, the interests of third parties – i.e. persons only indirectly concerned by but not actively involved in the takeover process as such, e.g. individual shareholders of a target company – did not figure prominently. However, this changed dramatically once the Act came into force. Numerous court decisions dealt with this question, launching an intensive and still ongoing discussion.

I. Introduction

The protection of (minority) shareholders confronted with a takeover of the company they are invested in has been an issue of lasting concern and interest for *Eddy Wymeersch*. He has long been a high-profile promoter as well as a critical commentator of the pertinent European developments.[1] This is especially true with respect to the Takeover

---

[1] See K. J. Hopt and E. Wymeersch (eds.), *European Takeovers. Law and Practice* (London: Butterworth, 1992); E. Wymeersch, 'The Mandatory Bid: A Critical View', in Hopt and Wymeersch (eds.), *European Takeovers*, 351–68; E. Wymeersch, 'Problems of the Regulation of Takeover Bids in Western Europe: A Comparative Survey', in Hopt and Wymeersch (eds.), *European Takeovers*, 95–131; E. Wymeersch, 'European Takeovers: The Mandatory Bid', *Butterworths Journal of International Banking and Financial Law* (1994), 25–33; E. Wymeersch , 'The Regulation of Takeover Bids in a Comparative Perspective' in R. Buxbaum, G. Hertig, A. Hirsch and K. J. Hopt (eds.), *European Economic and Business Law* (Berlin: de Gruyter, 1996), 291–323; E. Wymeersch, 'The Proposal for a 13th Company Law Directive on Takeovers: A Multi-jurisdiction Survey, Part 1', *European Financial Services Law* (1996), 301–307; 'Part 2', *European Financial Services Law* (1997), 2–7; E. Wymeersch, 'Les défenses anti-OPA après la treizième directive – commentaires sur l'article 8 de la future directive', *Financial Law Institute Working Paper Series*, (Jan. 2000); E. Wymeersch, 'Übernahme- und Pflichtangebote', *Zeitschrift für Unternehmens- und Gesellschaftsrecht*, 31 (2002), 520–45; G. Ferrarini, K. J. Hopt, J. Winter and E. Wymeersch (eds.), *Reforming Company and Takeover Law in Europe* (Oxford University Press, 2004).

Directive, whose main goal is the protection of the interests of holders of securities of companies that are the subject of takeover bids or of changes of control (Recital 2).[2] As a framework directive, the 13th Directive provides for basic principles to adhere to, but leaves ample scope for the Member States in other areas. A prominent example of this is the right of the Member States to determine how the protection prescribed in the Directive should be enforced, and whether rights for individual shareholders are to be made available at all. These may be asserted in administrative or judicial proceedings, either in proceedings against a supervisory authority or in proceedings between parties of a bid (Recital 8). Additionally, Article 4 (6) clarifies that the Directive neither affects the power of Member States to regulate whether and under which circumstances parties to a bid are entitled to bring administrative or judicial proceedings, nor does it affect the power of the Member States to determine the legal position concerning the liability of supervisory authorities or litigation between the parties to a bid. In sum, it is by and large left to the national laws of the Member States to determine how individual shareholders of a target company – the exemplary 'third parties' in the takeover proceedings besides the bidder and the target[3] – may or may not pursue their own interests in the context of a takeover or change of control situation.

This solution appears somewhat surprising from a regulatory point of view – though less so from a public choice perspective, given the previous thirty years of political bargaining about the Directive – because the question of whether and how individual shareholders may pursue their own interests in these situations is without doubt an issue of central importance for implementing the Directive's goals. Typical conflicts arise if a bidder, in spite of getting control of the target and thus being obliged to make a mandatory bid to acquire all outstanding shares, refuses to do so, or if the Supervisory Authority mistakenly exempts the bidder. Also, the target's shareholders may not be content with the price offered (and approved by the authority), especially when there are different classes of shares with different price tags attached by the bidder. These are but a few situations where the shareholders may want to have the legislative means to pursue their own interests. The German takeover law, however, at least in principle, does *not* grant many of these. Instead,

---

[2] Directive of the European Parliament and of the Council of 21 April 2004 on Takeover Bids 2004/25/EC [2004] OJ L142/2.

[3] Other 'third parties' are e.g. potential competitive bidders.

it is very restrictive with respect to the enforcement of third-party interests and offers surprisingly little protection on the procedural level. However, this outcome is highly disputed as will be discussed hereafter. The analysis is structured as follows. To frame the discussion, it begins with an overview of the legislative framework and institutional setting in Germany (part II). It then deals with the question of whether individual shareholders may assert their rights against the German supervisory authority (part III). Thereafter it discusses whether, as an alternative, civil law remedies are available in judicial proceedings between parties of a bid (part IV). Part V summarizes the findings.

II. Legislative framework and institutional setting

A. *The Takeover Act*

The relevant German legislative source is the 'Securities Acquisition and Takeover Act' (*Wertpapiererwerbs- und Übernahmegesetz*), the WpÜG of 2001.[4] The Act was the end of the German self-regulatory takeover regime based on the Takeover Codex of 1995.[5] The Codex had some functional shortcomings and mainly failed because it was not accepted by a sufficient number of listed companies.[6] The WpÜG was enacted on 1 January 2002, and thus predates the Takeover Directive. But given the freedom of choice discussed above that the Directive provides for national lawmakers, the German legislators rightly did not see a necessity under Community Law to amend the restrictive pertinent provisions of the WpÜG when implementing the Directive in 2006.[7] Therefore, case

---

[4] *Gesetz zur Regelung von öffentlichen Angeboten zum Erwerb von Wertpapieren und von Unternehmensübernahmen (WpÜG)*, Law of 20 December 2001, Federal Gazette I (2001) 3822, as amended; the law was accompanied by four ordinances dating from 27 December 2001, Federal Gazette I (2001) 4263 *et seq.*, as amended. English translations can be found with M. Peltzer and Voight, *German Securities Acquisition and Takeover Act* (Cologne: O. Schmidt, 2002); G. Apfelbacher, S. Barthelmess, T. Buhl and C. von Dryander, *German Takeover Law – A Commentary* (Munich: C.H. Beck, 2002).

[5] *Übernahmekodex der Börsensachverständigenkommission beim Bundesministerium der Finanzen* of 14 July 1995, amended 1 January 1998; see S. Schuster and C. Zschocke, *Übernahmerecht / Takeover Law* (Frankfurt: F. Knapp, 1996).

[6] *Cf.* C. Kirchner and U. Ehricke, 'Funktionsdefizite des Übernahmekodex bei der Börsensachverständigenkommission', *Die Aktiengesellschaft* (1998), 105–116.

[7] Act for Implementing the Takeover Directive (*Gesetz zur Umsetzung der Richtlinie 2004/25/EG des Europäischen Parlaments und des Rates vom 21. April 2004 betreffend Übernahmeangebote [Übernahmerichtline-Umsetzungsgesetz]*), Law of 8 July 2006, Federal Gazette I (2006) 1426.

law and discussion predating the implementation is still of unchanged relevance for the question of how third-party interests may be enforced.

The enactment of the WpÜG was triggered by what was – for most observers – the totally unexpected hostile takeover of Mannesmann AG, a traditional German manufacturer successfully turned into a mobile phone operator, by the British Vodafone plc, a foreign bidder, in 1999/2000. This was the biggest hostile takeover ever, amounting to more than €150 billion. It sent shock waves down the spine of corporate Germany, and the German government went into red alert. Accordingly, the ensuing legislative proceedings attracted wide public attention in Germany. Academia as well as practitioners were intensely involved in the discussion on the different drafts of the Takeover Act. However, again somewhat surprisingly, not much attention was paid to the question of whether and how individual shareholders and other third parties might pursue their own interests in the context of a takeover, though obviously this is an issue of high practical relevance. This situation changed dramatically once the WpÜG came into force. An unforeseen number of court decisions were forced to deal with this question, launching an intensive and still ongoing discussion.[8]

According to the official legislative texts, in substance – though not in form and structure – the WpÜG is modelled after the British City Code and thus has been, in principle, in accordance with the later Takeover Directive from the beginning. A core element of the WpÜG is the mandatory offer a bidder has to make if he has gained control of the target company.[9] The relevant threshold is 30% of the voting rights.[10] Based on the price regulation of the bid – the average share price or a higher price paid by the bidder during the previous six months[11] – minority shareholders participate in a possible control premium. To secure this outcome, the WpÜG – like the City Code – is necessarily characterized by a high regulatory intensity. Nevertheless, as in Britain, one of the official goals of the German legislators was to provide for a legislative framework that allows for speedy takeover procedures.[12] WpÜG § 3 (4) stipulates that the bidder and the target company must implement the procedure quickly, and the Act includes various provisions that oblige the parties to act without undue delay.

---

[8]　These developments will be addressed below in Section III.

[9]　§ 35 (2) WpÜG.　　[10]　§ 29 (2) WpÜG.

[11]　§ 31 WpÜG, §§ 3–7 of the WpÜG Offer Ordinance (*WpÜG-Angebotsverordnung*), Ordinance of 27 December 2001, Federal Gazette I (2001) 4263 as amended.

[12]　Legislative Materials, *BTDrucksache* 14/7034, 35.

However, in contrast to the British role model, the WpÜG is not an act of self-regulation but a body of public law whose actions may be and already have been challenged rather frequently in the courts, even though the Act has only been in force for a few years. This outcome differs markedly from the British experience, where due to the specific institutional setting takeover-induced litigation is extremely rare.[13]

B. Supervision in the public interest

Furthermore, the takeover-related supervisory structure in Germany differs fundamentally from the British. Power to carry out the supervision of *all* segments of the German financial markets lies with the 'Federal Financial Supervisory Authority' (*Bundesanstalt für Finanzdienstleistungsaufsicht*), the BaFin, established in its present form in 2002.[14] Since the enactment of WpÜG, its supervision includes takeovers. The BaFin is a major federal government agency somewhat similar to the SEC in the USA but different from the British 'Panel on Takeovers and Mergers', which was established in 1968 by the industry as an independent self-regulatory body and whose main functions are (only) to issue and administer the 'City Code on Takeovers and Mergers' and to supervise and regulate takeovers and other matters to which the Code applies.

According to § 4 (1) WpÜG, the BaFin shall carry out the supervision of takeover bids and other public bids for the acquisition of shares in accordance with the provisions of the Act. Within the scope of the tasks allocated to it, it has to counter any irregularities that may impair the orderly execution of bids or that may have materially adverse effects on the securities market in general. The Federal Authority may issue orders which are appropriate and necessary to eliminate or prevent such irregularities. Its exclusive competence to enforce and interpret the WpÜG as well as its exclusive right to grant exemptions secures a powerful position for the BaFin.

---

[13] G. Rosskopf, *Selbstregulierung von Übernahmeangeboten in Großbritannien* (Berlin: Duncker & Humblot, 2000), 191 *et seq.*; in general M. Button (ed.), *A Practitioner's Guide to the City Code on Takeovers and Mergers* (Surrey: Old Woking, 2004); M. A. Weinberg, M.V. Blank and L. Rabinowitz, *Weinberg and Blank on Takeovers and Mergers,* 5th edn, (London: Sweet and Maxwell, 2002).

[14] Information about the BaFin is supplied at www.bafin.de; see also H.-O. Hagemeister, 'Die neue Bundesanstalt für Finanzdienstleistungsaufsicht', *Wertpapiermitteilungen* (2002), 1773–9.

This quasi-monopolistic position is enhanced by the fact that the Authority is to perform the tasks and exercise the powers assigned to it under the Act *solely* in the interest of the general public, but *not* of individual investors (§ 4 (2) WpÜG), who are accordingly regarded by many as lacking the standing to challenge the Authority's decisions.[15] The BaFin's supervisory activities are aimed *only* at maintaining investor confidence in the processing of public takeovers in general; the legislators regarded this as essential but sufficient for the functioning of the market.[16]

This kind of restriction was first introduced in the Banking Act[17] after the German Supreme Court, the *Bundesgerichtshof*, decided in a shift of opinion in 1979 that the provisions of that Act describing the tasks of the former supervisory agency were meant to protect not only the public, but individual investors as well.[18] As a consequence, the government could be held liable under § 839 of the German Civil Code[19] in combination with Article 34 of the German Constitution to customers of failed banks if the damages these incurred were caused by faulty banking supervision. However, to principally exclude any state liability vis-à-vis the *individual* customers of banks, insurers, investment funds, or exchanges active in a financial market supervised by a government agency, all pertinent laws now include a provision which expressly stipulates that the supervision is carried out in the public interest only. Provisions identical to § 4 (2) WpÜG can be found in § 4 (4) of the Act Concerning the Federal Financial Supervisory Authority,[20] § 3 (3) of the Stock Exchange Act,[21] and § 81 (1) of the Act on the Supervision of Insurance Undertakings.[22]

Since their introduction, these restrictions have been disputed on constitutional and public policy grounds.[23] However, though the

---

[15] See the discussion hereafter at III.

[16] Legislative Materials, *BTDrucksache* 14/7034, 36.

[17] *Kreditwesengesetz*, Law of 10 July 1961 Federal Gazette I (1961), 881, as amended.

[18] BGHZ 74, 144 *et seq.*; BGHZ 75, 120 *et seq.*

[19] *Bürgerliches Gesetzbuch*, Law of 18 August 1896, newly publicized 2 January 2002, Federal Gazette I (2002), 42 and 2909, Federal Gazette I (2003), 738, as amended.

[20] *Gesetz über die Bundesanstalt für Finanzdienstleistungsaufsicht*, Law of 22 April 2002, Federal Gazette I (2002), 1310, as amended.

[21] *Börsengesetz*, Law of 21 June 2002, Federal Gazette I (2002), 2010, as amended.

[22] *Gesetz über die Beaufsichtigung der Versicherungsunternehmen*, Law of 17 December 1992, Federal Gazette I (1993), 2, as amended.

[23] For a detailed discussion, see e.g. B. Rohlfing, 'Wirtschaftsaufsicht und amtshaftungsrechtlicher Drittschutz', *Wertpapiermitteilungen* (2005), 311–19; L. Giesberts in H. Hirte and T.M.J. Möllers (eds.), *Kölner Kommentar zum WpHG* (Cologne: Carl Heymanns Verlag, 2007), § 4, marginal notes 34 *et seq.*; L. Giesberts in H. Hirte and

German Constitutional Court, the *Bundesverfassungsgericht* (BVerfG), has not yet decided on this question,[24] the Supreme Court held in 2005 that the former pertinent provision in the Banking Act – meanwhile replaced without any change in substance by § 4 (4) of the Act Concerning the Federal Financial Supervisory Authority – did not violate the Constitution.[25] Also, the Takeover Senate of the Frankfurt High Court, the *Übernahmesenat des Oberlandesgerichts Frankfurt am Main*, to which § 62 WpÜG assigns a special jurisdiction for takeover-related administrative proceedings, regarded § 4 (2) WpÜG in two decisions of 2003 as constitutional.[26] With respect to the aforementioned former provision of the Banking Act (and the accordingly restricted tasks of the pertinent agency acting as a precursor of the BaFin), the Court of Justice of the European Communities confirmed in 2004 that a Member State may assign the supervision over financial institutions to a government agency that acts solely in the public interest without violating Community law.[27]

With the various courts squarely backing the German legislators' attempts to avoid state liability for faulty supervision of their agencies, an intense discussion has arisen among academia and practitioners over what consequences this legislative policy has for third parties who want to assert their rights in the context of a takeover.[28] Two different

C. von Bülow (eds.), *Kölner Kommentar zum WpÜG* (Cologne: Carl Heymanns Verlag, 2003), § 4, marginal notes 24 *et seq.*

[24] In a decision of 2 April 2004 the BVerfG refused to deal with this question as not being relevant in that specific case; see BVerfG, *Wertpapiermitteilungen* (2004), 979.

[25] Decision of 20 January 2005; see *BGHZ* 162, 49 *et seq.*

[26] Decisions of 27 May 2003 and 4 July 2003; see *Neue Zeitschrift für Gesellschaftsrecht* (2003), 731, 1122 *et seq.*, respectively.

[27] Decision of 12 October 2004 – Rs C-222/02; see *Zeitschrift für Wirtschaftsrecht* (2004), 2039 *et seq.* (*Paul et al. v. the Federal Republic of Germany*).

[28] See C. Aha, 'Rechtsschutz der Zielgesellschaft bei mangelhaften Übernahmeangeboten', *Die Aktiengesellschaft* (2002), 160–169; A. Barthel, *Die Beschwerde gegen aufsichtsrechtliche Verfügungen nach dem WpÜG* (Cologne: Carl Heymanns Verlag, 2004); B. Berding, 'Subjektive öffentliche Rechte Dritter im WpÜG', *Der Konzern* (2004), 771–838; A. Cahn, 'Verwaltungsbefugnisse der Bundesanstalt für Finanzdienstleistungsaufsicht im Übernahmerecht und Rechtsschutz Betroffener', *Zeitschrift für das gesamte Handelsrecht und Wirtschaftsrecht,* 167 (2003), 262–300; M. Hecker, 'Die Beteiligung der Aktionäre am übernahmerechtlichen Befreiungsverfahren', *Zeitschrift für Bankrecht und Bankwirtschaft* (2004), 41–56; H.-C. Ihrig, 'Rechtsschutz Drittbetroffener im Übernahmerecht', *Zeitschrift für das gesamte Handelsrecht und Wirtschaftsrecht,* 167 (2003), 315–50; A. Möller, 'Das Verwaltungs- und Beschwerdeverfahren nach dem Wertpapiererwerbs- und Übernahmegesetz unter besonderer Berücksichtigung der Rechtsstellung Dritter', *Zeitschrift für das gesamte Handelsrecht und Wirtschaftsrecht,* 167 (2003), 301–314; Nietsch, 'Rechtsschutz der Aktionäre der Zielgesellschaft im

venues are being pondered: enforceable public rights against the German Supervisory Authority and, alternatively or additionally, civil law remedies against the bidder. As indicated in the text of the Directive cited at the beginning, both venues are available under Community law, but both are problematic with respect to the legislative design of the WpÜG.

III. Enforceable public rights against the German Supervisory Authority?

If a party involved in a takeover is the *addressee* of an administrative act by the BaFin, it may, as in any normal administrative procedure, appeal the decision (§ 48 WpÜG); if the appeal is unsuccessful, it may file an administrative suit against the Authority with the Frankfurt High Court, which has a special jurisdiction for these matters (§ 62 WpÜG). There are at least no major differences in comparison with general administrative proceedings.[29] Also, if a faulty order of the Authority caused damage for the addressee, it is not disputed that this kind of damage – though it may be rather rare – has to be compensated by the State in accordance with § 839 of the German Civil Code and Article 34 of the German Constitution.

But if individual investors who are *not* the addressees of the specific administrative Act but are only *indirectly* affected by the incriminated decision of the Authority want to challenge a decision of the BaFin, this central question arises: does the restriction to the public interest to avoid

---

Übernahmeverfahren, *Betriebs-Berater* (2003), 2581–2588; P. Pohlmann, 'Rechtsschutz der Aktionäre der Zielgesellschaft im Wertpapiererwerbs- und Übernahmeverfahren', *Zeitschrift für Unternehmens- und Gesellschaftsrecht*, 36 (2007), 1–36; von Riegen, 'Verwaltungsrechtschutz Dritter im WpÜG', *Der Konzern* (2003), 583; B. Rohlfing, 'Wirtschaftsaufsicht', (note 23, above), 311–19; Y. Schnorbus, 'Rechtsschutz im Übernahmeverfahren', *Wertpapiermitteilungen* (2003), 616–25 (Part I), 657–64 (Part II); Y. Schnorbus, 'Drittklagen im Übernahmeverfahren – Grundlagen zum Verwaltungsrechtschutz im WpÜG', *Zeitschrift für das gesamte Handelsrecht und Wirtschaftsrecht*, 166 (2002), 72–118; C. H. Seibt, 'Rechtsschutz im Übernahmerecht', *Zeitschrift für Wirtschaftsrecht* (2003), 1865–1877; B. Simon, *Rechtsschutz im Hinblick auf ein Pflichtangebot nach § 35 WpÜG*, (Baden-Baden, Nomos, 2005); B. Simon, 'Zur Herleitung zivilrechtlicher Ansprüche aus §§ 35 und 38 WpÜG', *Neue Zeitschrift für Gesellschaftsrecht* (2005), 541–544; M. Uechtritz / G. Wirth, 'Drittschutz im WpÜG – Erste Entscheidungen des OLG Frankfurt a.M.: Klarstellungen und offene Fragen', *Wertpapiermitteilungen* (2004), 410–417; D. A. Verse, 'Zum zivilrechtlichen Rechtsschutz bei Verstößen gegen die Preisbestimmungen des WpÜG', *Zeitschrift für Wirtschaftsrecht* (2004), 199–209.

[29] The legislators have expressly stated this in the legislative materials to the WpÜG; see *BTDrucksache* 14/7034, 36.

state liability *necessarily* have the negative effect of denying these *any* standing? For example, do individual shareholders of the target company have the standing to request the BaFin to take action against the bidder who, in spite of getting control of the target, refuses to make a mandatory bid? Or do they have the standing to challenge an administrative act by the Authority that mistakenly exempts the bidder from doing so?

The BaFin and the courts have taken a clear position. The Authority has consistently decided *against* a standing of individual shareholders under these circumstances. In its view, shareholders lack the individual and direct rights necessary for any action because of the express restriction of its activities to the public interest in § 4 (2) WpÜG. The Frankfurt High Court has repeatedly confirmed this view and dismissed all pertinent suits filed by shareholders of targets against the BaFin.[30] The High Court argues that although various provisions of the WpÜG indeed do have the potential to favour the interests of shareholders, this fact as such does not imply that the legislators intended to create a regime of individual enforceable *public* rights to assert their interests by way of an active participation in the formal takeover proceedings.[31] Nor were they obliged to do so on constitutional grounds. As the High Court sees it, the legislators instead had the freedom to design the present regime restricted to the protection of the public interest only without violating any constitutional rights of third parties.[32] Instead of administrative remedies against the BaFin, the High Court refers shareholders to potential *civil* remedies against the bidder.

The High Court quotes legislative history in its argument. In fact, earlier drafts of the Takeover Act did contain a provision that provided for damages in the case of an abusive use of third-party rights. The existence of that provision clearly shows that, originally, the legislators must have planned to grant those rights. That would have made a lot of sense from the regulatory logic of the WpÜG, which requires that the Act, as well as the Securities Trading Act and other financial market-related laws, serve a dual purpose: protection of the functioning of the market in general as well as protection of individual investors.[33] However, in the course of

---

[30] See the decisions cited supra, note 26, and the decision of 9 October 2003; see *Neue Zeitschrift für Gesellschaftsrecht* (2004), 240 *et seq.*

[31] See Decision of 4 July 2003; see *Neue Zeitschrift für Gesellschaftsrecht* (2003), 1121 *et seq.*

[32] See Decision of 4 July 2003, see *Neue Zeitschrift für Gesellschaftsrecht* (2003), 1122 *et seq.*

[33] K.J. Hopt, 'Grundsatz und Praxisprobleme nach dem Wertpapiererwerbs- und Übernahmegesetz', *Zeitschrift für das gesamte Handelsrecht und Wirtschaftsrecht*, 166 (2002), 386 ('... Funktionen- und Anlegerschutz').

the legislative proceedings, actually at its very end, that provision was scrapped because the Financial Committee of the Parliament in charge of politically renegotiating the Act did not see any practical necessity for it; according to the Committee, third parties do not have any individual rights in this regard that they could possibly abuse.[34] In this view, protection of individual investors is but a mere 'legislative reflection' of the general protection of the market function.

The reasoning of the BaFin and the High Court is disputed on various grounds. Though the majority of commentators accept the constitutionality of § 4 (2) WpÜG – notwithstanding their criticism of the legal solution on policy grounds – some do so only under the precondition that the provision is at least interpreted in a constitutional manner which would exclude a complete denial of third-party rights.[35] This approach, however, is problematic. The legislative order of the provision – to act in the public interest only – is unequivocal.[36] Thus it does not seem permissible to circumvent the clearly expressed legislative intention by way of constitutional interpretation.[37]

Others promote a restrictive interpretation of § 4 (2) WpÜG. In this view the provision aims only at excluding state liability for faulty administrative acts or a failure to act by the BaFin, but does not say anything about the rights of third parties and their standing vis-à-vis the Authority.[38] However, this interpretation too is problematic. The exclusion of state liability is dependent on the assumption of non-existence of according individual rights against the Authority. Thus, if § 4 (2) WpÜG excludes state liability under the provisions of the Act, these cannot be contradictorily interpreted as simultaneously granting individual public rights enforceable against the BaFin with respect to other matters.[39]

---

[34] See Legislative Materials, *BTDrucksache* 14/477, 70; the technical conception of the WpÜG has been criticized strongly in this regard; see e.g. Y. Schnorbus, 'Drittklagen', (note 28, above), 117.

[35] See e.g. L. Giesberts, in H. Hirte and C. von Bülow (eds.), *Kölner Kommentar zum WpÜG* (note 23, above), § 4, marginal notes 62 *et seq.*, 75; Aha, 'Rechtsschutz der Zielgesellschaft', (note 28, above), 162 *et seq.* Others plainly deny the constitutionality; see e.g. B. Berding, 'Subjektive öffentliche Rechte Dritter im WpÜG', (note 28, above), 774 *et seq.*

[36] A. Möller, 'Das Verwaltungs- und Beschwerdeverfahren', (note 28, above), 306.

[37] B. Simon, *Rechtsschutz*, (note 28, above), 117 *et seq.*

[38] See e.g. A. Cahn, 'Verwaltungsbefugnisse der Bundesanstalt', (note 28, above), 284 *et seq.*

[39] P. Pohlmann, 'Rechtsschutz der Aktionäre', (note 28, above), 20; M. Uechtritz and G. Wirth, 'Drittschutzim', (note 28, above), 414.

Also, it is not permissible, as some have attempted, to disregard the unequivocal legislative will to exclusively restrict the Act's regulatory aim to the protection of the market function by assuming that this does not actually mean a total exclusion of individual investor protection because some provisions of the Act expressly refer to their interests.[40] An example of this is § 37 (1) WpÜG. According to this provision, the BaFin may exempt bidders who have acquired a controlling stake from their duty to make a full bid for all outstanding shares only if this exemption would not be contrary to the interests of the other target's shareholders.[41] However, this reference to the shareholders' interests cannot be interpreted as a means to grant them individual and direct public rights. It is simply a legislative order addressed at the BaFin to balance the interests of the bidder with those of the other shareholders in general under specific circumstances.[42]

The above considerations can be summarized in the – not altogether happy – finding that the current German takeover legislation does not make available any direct public rights for third parties involved in a takeover that might be enforced in an administrative proceeding against the BaFin. Instead, third parties are forced to rely on the Authority's zest to supervise the country's takeover market. The only alternatives, if any, are civil law remedies against the bidder that might possibly provide some direct relief for the shareholders of the target and other third parties.

IV. Civil law remedies against the bidder?

From this perspective, the following questions are of specific practical interest: does § 35 WpÜG – stipulating the obligation to publish and to make an offer in the case of an acquisition or change of control – provide a legal basis for the other shareholders of the company against a shareholder that has acquired a controlling stake[43] to make an offer for all outstanding shares? If not, or if an offer is made but the consideration offered is insufficient, may the shareholders sue such a person for damages?

Once more, the issue is highly disputed. In principle, the WpÜG is conceived as a market surveillance law showing the typical mix of public

---

[40] See e.g. A. Barthel, *Die Beschwerde*, (note 28, above), 109 *et seq.*
[41] For details, see H. Krause and T. Pötzsch, in H. Assmann, T. Pötzsch, and U. H. Schneider (eds.), *Wertpapiererwerbs- und Übernahmegesetz* (Cologne: Otto Schmidt, 2005), § 37, marginal notes 31 *et seq.*
[42] B. Simon, *Rechtsschutz*, (note 28, above), 127 *et seq.*
[43] I.e. at least 30% of the target's voting rights, as defined in § 29 WpÜG.

law regulations, administrative powers, quasi-criminal sanctions and civil law consequences. Within this regulatory framework, the question of which provisions of the Act can be qualified as civil law in substance and what legal consequences are attached to this qualification can only be answered on a case-by-case analysis.[44] With respect to the market surveillance-oriented character of WpÜG, there is no underlying assumption that the provisions of the Act are intended to have civil law consequences in principle; instead, as an exemption this has to be shown for each individual provision.[45]

In the decisions cited, the Frankfurt High Court has (expressly) left open the question as to whether § 35 WpÜG actually provides a legal basis for shareholders to demand an offer for their shares from a controlling shareholder in accordance with the pertinent provisions of the Act and the WpÜG Offer Ordinance.[46] [47] The literature is divided, but a clear majority of commentators answer the question in the negative.[48] There is indeed no room for a different interpretation. The wording of § 35 does not mention shareholders at all but (only) stipulates a general duty for the controlling shareholder to publish an offer. This general order matches the market-oriented character of the provision. Any other understanding would lead to a plethora of difficulties when applying the rule in a civil law context. Additionally, a broad interpretation would be problematic on constitutional grounds, as the resulting far-reaching consequences for the controlling shareholder would have to be based on a narrowly defined rule.[49] Also, allowing for individual claims would be hard to reconcile with the Act's overarching aim to provide for a regulatory framework that guarantees speedy takeover procedures.[50] In other words, the legislators obviously did not intend to grant shareholders a direct civil law claim against a controlling shareholder under § 35.[51]

---

[44] Y. Schnorbus, 'Rechtsschutz', (note 28, above), 663.

[45] Y. Schnorbus, 'Rechtsschutz ', (note 28, above), 663.

[46] § 31 WpÜG, §§ 3–7 *WpÜG-Angebotsverordnung*, see supra note 11.

[47] See the decisions cited supra, note 26 and note 30.

[48] See e.g. H. Krause and T. Pötzsch, in H. Assmann, T. Pötzsch and U.H. Schneider (eds.), *Wertpapiererwerbs- und Übernahmegesetz* (Cologne: Otto Schmidt, 2005), § 35, marginal notes 252 *et seq.*; P. Pohlmann, 'Rechtsschutz der Aktionäre', (note 28, above), 11 *et seq.*; B. Simon, *Rechtsschutz*, (note 28, above), 206 *et seq.*

[49] H. Krause and T. Pötzsch, in H. Assmann, T. Pötzsch and U.H. Schneider (eds.), *Wertpapiererwerbs- und Übernahmegesetz* (Cologne: Otto Schmidt, 2005), § 35, marginal note 252.

[50] Legislative Materials, BTDrucksache 14/7034, 35.

[51] P. Pohlmann, 'Rechtsschutz der Aktionäre', (note 28, above), 12.

Even if the shareholders do not have a primary claim against the controlling shareholder, they may nevertheless possibly have a secondary claim in the form of damages based on § 823 (2) Civil Code in combination with § 35 WpÜG. § 823 (2) Civil Code provides for a general liability in damages in combination with specific protective provisions of other codes. The precondition for this is a violation of a rule that intends to protect not only the market as such but the individual claimant as well.[52] According to a minority view, the denial of direct *public* rights of individual shareholders as third parties under the WpÜG automatically implies that *none* of the provisions of the Act can be regarded from a *civil* law perspective as a protective norm in the sense of § 823 (2) Civil Code in order to prevent a contradictory policy interpretation.[53] This view, however, is not convincing. There is *no* compelling connection between a public law and a tort law evaluation.[54] Rather, the two questions – whether a person has an administrative claim against a state agency and/or whether that person, cumulatively or alternatively, has a tort claim against a controlling shareholder – have to be clearly distinguished and, accordingly, different answers to each do not constitute a contradiction in the evaluation of that norm.

The relevant question is thus whether § 35 as it stands may serve as a protective norm in the sense of § 823 (2) Civil Code. This again is controversially discussed.[55] As has been argued with respect to a possible primary claim against the controlling shareholder, there is also no indication in the wording of the provision (nor in the legislative materials)

---

[52] See in general H. Sprau, in Bassenge et al. (eds.), *Palandt. Bürgerliches Gesetzbuch*, 67th edn (Munich: C.H. Beck, 2008), § 826, marginal notes 56 *et seq.*

[53] Y. Schnorbus, 'Rechtsschutz', (note 28, above), 663; B. Berding, 'Subjektive öffentliche Rechte Dritter im WpÜG', (note 28, above), 777; H. Krause and T. Pötzsch, in H. Assmann, T. Pötzsch and U. H. Schneider (eds.), *Wertpapiererwerbs- und Übernahmegesetz* (Cologne: Otto Schmidt, 2005), § 35, marginal note 253 with respect to § 35 WpÜG.

[54] P. Pohlmann, 'Rechtsschutz der Aktionäre', (note 28, above), 21; D. A. Verse, 'Zum zivilrechtlichen Rechtsschutz', (note 28, above), 203 *et seq.*; H.-C. Ihrig, 'Rechtsschutz', (note 28, above), 338; C. H. Seibt, 'Rechtsschutz ', (note 28, above), 1868.

[55] *Pro:* e.g. C. von Bülow in H. Hirte and C. von Bülow (eds.), *Kölner Kommentar zum WpÜG* (Cologne: Carl Heymanns Verlag, 2003), § 35, marginal note 199; T. Baums and M. Hecker in T. Baums and G. F. Thoma (eds.), *WpÜG – Kommentar zum Wertpapiererwerbs- und Übernahmegesetz* (Cologne: RWS Verlag), § 35, marginal notes 297 *et seq.*; H.-C. Ihrig, 'Rechtsschutz', (note 28, above), 349. *Contra:* besides those cited supra at note 52, see e.g. P. Pohlmann, 'Rechtsschutz der Aktionäre', (note 28, above), 12 *et seq.*; Hommelhoff and C.-H. Witt in W. Haarmann and M. Schüppen (eds.), *Frankfurter Kommentar zum Wertpapiererwerbs- und Übernahmegesetz*, 2nd edn. (Franfurt am Main: Verlag Recht und Wirtschaft, 2005), § 35, marginal note 109; B. Simon, 'Zur Herleitung zivilrechtlicher Ansprüche', (note 28, above), 542.

that the legislators intended § 35 to serve as a protective norm for the individual shareholders as a basis for secondary damages claims. But such an expressed intent would be necessary. It is a common view that the mere fact that a norm may (also) have beneficial consequences for a person involved as such is not sufficient to assume a protective *purpose* of that norm. Furthermore, allowing for a secondary claim for the shareholders would in effect undermine the legislators' decision not to grant them a primary claim in the first place: according to § 249 (1) Civil Code, persons who are liable in damages must restore the position that would exist if the circumstance obliging them to pay damages had not occurred. This would mean that the claimants could require the controlling shareholder to make an offer to buy their shares as damages.

Instead of allowing for either a primary or a secondary claim in the form of damages, the legislators have created a unique system of triple sanctions against the controlling shareholder who failed to make a bid pursuant to § 35 WpÜG: (i) § 60 WpÜG provides for an administrative fine, (ii) § 59 WpÜG regulates the loss of rights for controlling shareholders as long as they do not comply with their duties, and (iii) § 38 WpÜG obliges them to pay the shareholders of the target company, for the duration of the contravention, interest on the amount of the consideration of five percentage points per year above the relevant base interest rate pursuant to § 247 Civil Code. Whether shareholders have a direct claim against the controlling shareholder based on § 38 WpÜG, and how this provision is to be characterized dogmatically – as a civil law claim or sanction – is once again controversial.[56] But this will no longer come as a surprise for the patient reader.

Less disputed, however, is the standing of the target's shareholders with respect to § 31 WpÜG. This provision is of central importance in the context of a mandatory bid. As already mentioned, it sets out the standards for an appropriate consideration which the bidder has to offer, and ensures that all shareholders get the same price.[57] To these ends, the average stock market price and purchases of shares up to six months prior to the publication of the bid have to be taken into consideration.[58]

---

[56] See B. Simon, 'Zur Herleitung zivilrechtlicher Ansprüche', (note 28, above), 543; P. Pohlmann, 'Rechtsschutz der Aktionäre', (note 28, above), 18 *et seq.*; Hommelhoff and C.-H. Witt in W. Haarmann and M. Schüppen (eds.), *Frankfurter Kommentar zum Wertpapiererwerbs- und Übernahmegesetz*, (note 55, above), § 38, marginal notes 1 *et seq.*, 31 *et seq.*; Y. Schnorbus, 'Rechtsschutz', (note 28, above), 663.

[57] Details are regulated in §§ 3–7 WpÜG Offer Ordinance; see supra note 11.

[58] § 31 (I) WpÜG together with § 4 WpÜG Offer Ordinance.

In addition, purchases made during the offer period for a higher price as well as purchases made within one year after the closing have to be considered.[59] If the price offered by the bidder violates these standards, the shareholders who have accepted the bid are entitled to file a claim against the bidder demanding the price difference. Though the dogmatic questions involved are again somewhat controversial, the fact that § 31 WpÜG provides for a direct civil law remedy against the bidder is generally acknowledged.[60] Thus, at least with regard to a consideration offered, the shareholders might take the initiative to assert their rights.

V. Conclusion

Perhaps the *tour d'horizon* above has unearthed more questions than it has answered. Indeed, the German takeover regulation shows a surprising amount of legal uncertainty and unresolved dogmatic questions. This complexity results partly from the fact that the WpÜG is to a significant degree a legal transplant whose imported features do not always fit seamlessly into the traditional German legal order. However, at least for commentators, this has obviously been a bone of contention. The numerous commentaries, the multitude of dissertations, and the countless academic articles on the German takeover regulation have assembled together to form an incredible amount of literature within a few years that some may regard as somewhat out of proportion with the *actual* number of takeovers in Germany. In this regard as well, the German takeover regime seems to differ significantly from its British role model.[61]

Third-party rights are but one example of the intense discussion. These have also been the cause of an unexpected – and rather 'un-British' – spat of litigation soon after the WpÜG was enacted. However, in most cases shareholders of target companies have tried to sue in vain. As they have discovered the hard way, though it is disputed, the current German takeover legislation does not make available any direct public rights for third parties involved in a takeover that can be enforced in an administrative proceeding against the BaFin in its capacity as supervising authority over the German takeover market.

---

[59] § 31 (4) (5) WpÜG.
[60] See e.g. D. A. Verse, 'Zum zivilrechtlichen Rechtsschutz', (note 28, above), 200 *et seq.*; Pohlmann, 'Rechtsschutz der Aktionäre', (note 28, above), 14 *et seq.*
[61] For a structural comparison, see H. Baum, 'Funktionale Elemente und Komplementaritäten des britischen Übernahmerechts', *Recht der Internationalen Wirtschaft* (2003), 421 *et seq.*

Thus the attention has shifted to civil law remedies as a possible alternative. But here, too, the picture is sobering. As a rule, the provisions of the WpÜG do not provide for directly enforceable rights against a bidder. This is especially true with respect to the mandatory bid. Shareholders do not have the means to force a shareholder who gained control to make a bid for all outstanding shares of the target company as required under the WpÜG. Some consolidation may come from the fact that, at least with respect to a consideration offered, shareholders may hold the controlling shareholder accountable.

23

Takeover defences and the role of law: a Japanese perspective

HIDEKI KANDA[1]

I. Introduction

Today, takeovers of publicly held business firms are understood as an effective and speedy means of resource allocation. Yet the legal framework surrounding takeovers, particularly hostile ones, is not simple. It appears to vary significantly from country to country.

With regard to takeover defences, the United States is rich both in its practical experience and academic literature. In contrast, Japan was poor at least until 2005. While courts in Delaware in the United States have shaped the law in this area over the past twenty-five years, Japanese law is not clear despite the existence of several statutory provisions of the Japanese Company Act and certain well-known cases in recent years. Although the United States is rich in its practical experience and academic literature, evidence seems to be inconclusive. Moreover, there is so much debate among commentators that opinions are quite divided among reasonable people. As a result, this area has produced (and still today produces) one of the most difficult issues in US corporate law.[2] First, while empirical studies generally show that hostile takeovers are good for the economy in the sense that they generally enhance the value of the target firms, it is unclear from the past empirical studies whether defence measures adopted by target boards, in particular 'poison pills', are good or bad for the target firms (and thus for the economy). Second, normative arguments in academic literature about what defensive measures should be legally permitted or prohibited, and to what degree, are quite split in the United States. In Delaware, however, the standard of

---

[1] Professor of Law, University of Tokyo. An earlier version of this chapter was written for a project by the Korean Development Institute.
[2] The text draws on H. Kanda, 'Does Corporate Law Really Matter in Hostile Takeovers?: Commenting on Professor Gilson and Chancellor Chandler', *Columbia Business Law Review*, 67 (2004).

judicial review for takeover defences (including poison pills) has already been established. Delaware courts today apply the 'enhanced business judgment rule' and require 'proportionality' in reviewing takeover defences. Thus, the takeover defences upheld by the courts in Delaware fall within a certain range, and the law is predictable as to whether a particular defensive measure (including poison pill attempts) to be taken would be upheld or denied by Delaware courts.

In contrast, in Japan, until recently, no one could tell what the law was with respect to takeover defences. However, beginning in 2005, several well-known hostile takeover attempts took place in Japan, and a few cases were brought into court rooms. To date, more than three hundred public firms have introduced the 'Japanese version' of the poison pill since 2005. Discussion as to what should be the criteria with which a particular hostile bid is judged good or bad has been immense. Correspondingly, a few amendments to the relevant statutes have been made in 2005 and 2006.

In this chapter, I describe these developments and experiences in Japan: Section II describes the recent developments; Section III shows characteristics as found in the recent developments; finally, Section IV is my preliminary conclusion and offers implications from preceding sections.[3]

II. Developments

As Professor Curtis Milhaupt stated, 'the unthinkable has happened'.[4] In 2005, a battle for control over Nippon Broadcasting occurred. In response to the takeover attempt by Livedoor, the board of Nippon Broadcasting adopted a defence measure by issuing stock warrants (*shinkabu yoyaku ken*) to its de facto parent, Fuji TV in order to dilute Livedoor's stake. The Tokyo District Court enjoined the issuance and its decision was affirmed by the Tokyo High Court.

---

[3] For articles on the Japanese situation in English include S. Kozuka, 'Recent Developments in Takeover Law: Changes in Business Practices Meet Decade-Old Rule', *Zeitschrift für Japanisches Recht*, 21 (2006), 5; K. Osugi, 'What is Converging? Rules on Hostile Takeovers in Japan and the Convergence Debate', *Asian-Pacific Law and Policy Journal*, 9 (2007), 143.

[4] C.J. Milhaupt, 'In the Shadow of Delaware? The Rise of Hostile Takeovers in Japan', *Columbia Law Review*, 105 (2005), 2171. See also J.B. Jacobs, 'Implementing Japan's New Anti-takeover Defense Guidelines, Part II: The Role of Courts as Expositor and Monitor of the Rules of the Takeover Game', *University of Tokyo Journal of Law and Politics*, 3 (2006), 102.

Nippon Broadcasting, a radio broadcaster, is part of the Fuji Sankei media group and was a de facto subsidiary of Fuji Television Network, Inc. ('Fuji TV'), Japan's largest media company. Somewhat anomalously, however, Nippon broadcasting held 22.5% of the outstanding shares of Fuji TV while Fuji TV held only 12.4% of Nippon Broadcasting's shares. In part to rectify the situation, on 17 January 2005, Fuji TV announced a cash tender offer for all of the outstanding shares of Nippon Broadcasting. The bid was approved by the board of Nippon Broadcasting.

In the midst of this tender offer, on 8 February 2005, Livedoor, an internet service provider, made a sudden announcement that it had just acquired approximately 29.6% of Nippon Broadcasting's shares. Livedoor acquired these shares through market purchase.[5] In combination with the shares previously owned, Livedoor's stake reached 38% of Nippon Broadcasting's shares. On the same day, Livedoor informed Nippon Broadcasting of its intent to acquire all of its outstanding shares.

In response, on 23 February 2005, Nippon Broadcasting announced that its board had decided to issue stock warrants to Fuji TV exercisable into 47.2 million shares of Nippon Broadcasting stock. If exercised, the warrants would give Fuji TV majority control and dilute Livedoor's stake to less than 20%. Livedoor by that time had acquired approximately 40% of Nippon Broadcasting stock. The board decision was unanimous. Four outside directors voted for the decision and four directors affiliated with Fuji TV abstained from participation in the decision. The warrants were exercisable at 5,950 yen, the price offered in Fuji TV's tender offer. Nippon Broadcasting announced that the purpose of the issuance of warrants was to remain within the Fuji Sankei group, which would provide long-term benefits to its shareholders.

Livedoor sued to enjoin the issuance of warrants. The Tokyo District Court enjoined the warrant issuance as 'significantly unfair' under the Commercial Code. The court held that its primary purpose was to maintain control of the firm by incumbent management and affiliates by the Fuji Sankei Group. The Tokyo High Court affirmed.[6] Accordingly, Nippon Broadcasting and Fuji TV abandoned the warrant issuance. Livedoor eventually obtained a majority of shares of Nippon Broadcasting.

---

[5] The method of purchase deployed by Livedoor, called off the floor, after hour trading, was permitted during the period when a tender offer was pending. This method was much criticized, and the law was amended in July 2005 so as to make such a trading method unlawful.

[6] Tokyo District Court Decisions on 11 March 2005 and on 16 March 2005. Tokyo High Court Decision on 23 March 2005, 1899 *Hanreijiho* 56.

The battle ended in a somewhat peaceful way. On 18 April 2005, Livedoor agreed to sell its Nippon Broadcasting shares to Fuji TV at 6,300 yen per share, approximately the average price it paid for the shares. In return, Fuji TV obtained a 12.5% stake in Livedoor for a capital infusion of approximately $440 million, and the three companies established a joint committee to explore related ventures.

The rationales in the two decisions of the Tokyo District Court and the Tokyo High Court are not identical, but they have many common elements. To cite from the decision of the High Court, the court stated a basic principle of the 'power allocation doctrine'. Under this doctrine, shareholders elect directors. The board of directors has the power to issue stocks and warrants only for the purpose of funding new capital, paying incentive-based compensations and others. However, the board does not have power to take defensive measures against hostile bids. The decision of who should take control over the company must be delegated to shareholders. This, however, permits exceptional situations where the board is permitted to take defence actions as an emergency. Those situations are found where the bidder attempts to disrupt the firm. The court did not find such exceptional situation in the battle for control over Nippon Broadcasting.

This case was enough to call the serious attention of managers of all publicly held firms in Japan and market participants. The Corporate Value Study Group, established by the Ministry of Economy, Trade and Industry ('METI') in 2004, released its interim report on 27 May 2005[7] and on the same day, guidelines for defensive measures were released jointly by METI and the Ministry of Justice ('Guidelines').[8] It must be noted that while the Nippon Broadcasting case involved a 'post-bid' defence, these documents are for 'pre-bid' defensive measures, and public firms began to introduce a variety of pre-bid defensive measures beginning in mid 2005.

The Guidelines, although they are not the law, list three basic principles for the validity of pre-bid defence measures.[9] First, the purpose of such defence measure must be to enhance corporate value and thus shareholders' value as a whole. Second, the adoption of such a defence plan must be based on the shareholders' will. Finally, such defence

---

[7] Ministry of Economy, Trade and Industry, *Corporate Value Study Group Report* (27 May 2005).

[8] Ministry of Economy, Trade and Industry and Ministry of Justice, *Guidelines regarding Takeover Defenses for the purposes of Protection and Enhancement of Corporate Value and Shareholders' Common Interests* (27 May 2005).

[9] Ibid.

measure must be necessary and satisfy proportionality, namely, they must be a reasonable and non-excessive means to accomplish the purpose. Also, the Guidelines specifically discuss the issuance of stock warrants. They provide that if such warrants are issued by a decision at the shareholders' meeting, its validity or compliance with the three principles would be presumed. If such warrants are issued by a board decision without a shareholders' meeting, necessity and proportionality would have to be strictly required.

In the course of these quick developments, a couple of changes in the relevant statutes were made. First, the Ministry of Justice ('MOJ') promulgated a disclosure rule for defensive measures, effective on 1 May 2005. A joint-stock company is required to disclose its fundamental policy for its management in its annual business report.[10] This rule applies to the fiscal year ending on or after 1 May 2005, and it means that most public firms began to disclose such policy in 2006. Second, the Subcommittee on Corporate Governance at the Liberal Democratic Party discussed this area in the first half of 2005 and released an important report on 7 July 2005.[11] This report endorsed one type of poison pill using a trust scheme by making clear of its tax implications. In addition, the report called for a few changes of tender offer regulation. The bill for wide-range reform of the Securities and Exchange Act ('SEA') (which includes the tender offer regulation) was passed in the Diet in June 2006, and the proposed changes by the Subcommittee were included. The relevant part of the regulation became effective on 13 December 2006. In this connection, the Financial Services Agency ('FSA'), which has jurisdiction over tender offer regulation, made detailed rules under the amended SEA. Among others, when a tender offer is commenced, the target board has the legal right to ask questions to the bidder and the bidder must answer them in their public documents. A European-style mandatory bid rule (which requires the bidder to bid for all outstanding shares) was introduced, but only where the bidder attempts to acquire two-thirds or more of the target shares. Finally, Tokyo Stock Exchange ('TSE') has been serious in promulgating rules and guidelines to avoid possible confusions in the stock market it operates as a result of possible hostile battles and unexpected measures that might be taken by both sides. TSE is still in the process of writing rules and guidelines, but to

---

[10] See Article 127, Ministry of Justice Companies Act Implementation Rule (2005).
[11] Report of the Subcommittee on Corporate Governance, Liberal Democratic Party (7 July 2005).

date, it has made several important announcements concerning a few specific items.[12] It is clear that 'golden shares' or other 'dead hand' poison pills are not permitted for the companies listed on the TSE.

In the course of these developments, two further court decisions were made. First, a pre-bid defensive scheme using stock warrants, adopted by the board of Nireco, a provider of various controlling and measuring systems, was enjoined by the Tokyo District Court and Tokyo High Court in June 2005.[13] Second, a post-bid defence adopted by the board of Nippon Gijutsu Kaihatsu (Japan Engineering Consultants Co., 'JEC'), a consulting firm in construction, was approved by the Tokyo District Court in July 2005.[14] In the latter case, on 20 July 2005, Yumeshin, a construction firm, launched a hostile tender offer for all outstanding shares of JEC. In response, JEC announced a stock split. JEC asserted that it adopted an advance warning defence plan (see below) and Yumeshin violated the process asked for by the plan. At that time, it was unclear whether the bidder was permitted under the SEA to change the bid price during the bid period if an unexpected thing happened, such as a stock split, but eventually, the FSA permitted such change. This means that a stock split would have no effect in frustrating Yumeshin's hostile bid. Under the situation, on 29 July 2005, the Tokyo District Court decided not to enjoin the stock split. On the same day, JEC announced an issuance of stock warrants. After this, JEC found a white knight, which launched a competing bid with a higher price. Yumeshin's bid turned out to be unsuccessful (as Yumeshin ended up with holding 10.59% of JEC stock). Eventually, JEC withdrew the issuance of warrants, and the battle ended.

With these court decisions and related discussions, many publicly held firms in Japan moved to adopt two types of pre-bid defence measures. One is a poison pill scheme using a trust or similar structure, and the other (more popular one) is a scheme known as advance warning. As of 25 May 2007, 359 listed firms (out of total of approximately 3,900 listed firms in Japan) have pre-bid defence plans. For listed firms on the TSE Section One, 283 firms out of total 1,753 have adopted such plans. Among 359 firms, 349 have adopted some form of advance warning plan, and 10 have trust-type or similar warrant schemes.[15]

---

[12] See generally Tokyo Stock Exchange, *Interim Report of the Advisory Group on Improvements to TSE Listing System*, 27 March 2007.

[13] Tokyo District Court Decisions on 1 June 2005 and on 9 June 2005. Tokyo High Court Decision on 15 June 2005, 1900 *Hanreijiho* 156.

[14] Tokyo District Court Decision on 29 July 2005, 1909 *Hanreijiho* 87.

[15] See the material submitted to the METI Corporate Value Study Group on 29 May 2007.

Under a typical trust based scheme, the firm issues stock warrants to a trust bank with designated shareholders as beneficiaries of the trust. When a hostile bid occurs, the pill is triggered, and the trust bank transfers the warrants to the shareholders. The warrants have a discriminatory feature and the bidder has no right to exercise them, as the terms and conditions of the warrants usually provide that the warrants are not exercisable by the shareholders who own 20% or more of the firm's outstanding stock.

The advance warning plan varies from company to company but its typical style is as follows. The board, sometimes with approval of the shareholders' meeting, makes a public announcement that if a shareholder attempts to increase its stake to 20% or more of the firm's outstanding stock, before the shareholder does so, the shareholder is required to disclose and explain, in accordance with the details specified in the announcement, its intent to hold such stake and what the shareholder would do for the firm. If the shareholder does not answer these questions or the target board thinks the shareholder's explanation to be unsatisfactory, then a defence measure would be triggered. Such defence measure is typically to issue stock warrants to all shareholders but the shareholder having 20% or more cannot exercise the warrants. Instead, such shareholder's warrants can be redeemed at a fair price at the option of the company. Thus, typically, warrant issuance has an effect of 'cashing out' the hostile bidder.

In most plans (304 plans out of total 359), judgment for triggering is to be made by a special committee composed of independent individuals. In some companies' plans, such defence measures are to be triggered after approval at the shareholders' meeting.

Because the Tokyo High Court decision on Nippon Broadcasting and the METI-MOJ Guidelines emphasize shareholder decision, most public companies adopt defence schemes which ask for a decision at the shareholders' meeting either when it introduces a pre-bid defence plan and/or when it triggers such a plan.[16] In practice, in most companies, the board proposal for introducing an advance-warning-type defence measure was put for approval at the shareholders' meeting, and in fact obtained shareholder approval. For those companies who introduced advance-warning defence plans, it is unknown whether they will survive a judicial review

---

[16] Out of 359 advance warning plans, 307 plans were introduced by approval at the shareholders' meeting. The remaining 42 plans were introduced by board decisions only. See supra note 12.

when such a plan triggers the pill, because to date, there has been no case in which that has happened, except in the JEC case noted above.

In May 2007, Steel Partners, a US buy-out fund, commenced a hostile tender offer for all outstanding shares of Bulldog Sauce, a Worcester sauce producer.[17] Bulldog Sauce did not have any pre-bid defence plan. As a post-bid defence, the board of Bulldog Sauce intended to issue stock warrants to all stockholders, including Steel Partners and its affiliates (collectively 'SP'), with the condition that SP cannot exercise the warrants. The warrants have a redemption feature, by which the warrant holders other than SP receive common stocks in exchange for turning the warrants into the company whereas SP receives cash. Thus, the scheme was structured as a scheme diluting the voting right of SP without an economic loss to SP ('economic' does not include the value of voting right). The Bulldog board introduced the proposal at the annual shareholders' meeting on 24 June 2007, and the plan was approved by more than 80% of the shares. SP sued to enjoin the issuance of the warrants. The Tokyo District Court held on 28 June 2007 that the scheme was valid.

The court held that strict judicial scrutiny adopted by the High Court decision on Nippon Broadcasting case does not apply here because the defence measure was approved at the shareholders' meeting. The court also held that since the defence measure provides 'just compensation' to the hostile bidder, it does not violate the proportionality principle. In other words, the court's position is that 'necessity' is presumed because shareholders decided and 'proportionality' is subject to judicial review (and it was held to be satisfied in this case). Steel Partners appealed, but the Tokyo High Court affirmed on 9 July 2007. Tokyo High Court found that SP was an 'abusive bidder' and held that the defence measure was lawful.

Steel Partners appealed to the Supreme Court. On 7 August 2007, the Supreme Court affirmed. The Supreme Court's opinion was somewhat similar to that of the Tokyo District Court. The highest court held that because the defence measure was approved by shareholders, the necessity requirement was met, and because it provided SP with just compensation, the proportionality test was satisfied. It also held that because the measure satisfied the proportionality test, it did not violate the purpose of the principle of equal treatment of shareholders.

---

[17] For a detailed description and analysis of this case and the court decisions, see S. Osaki, 'The Bull-Dog Sauce Takeover Defense', *Nomura Capital Market Review*, 10 (2007), No.3, 2.

The Steel Partners' tender offer ended on 23 August 2007. Only 1.89% of all outstanding shares were tendered. On 30 August 2007, Bulldog Sauce introduced an advance warning style pre-bid defence plan.

In a similar fashion, in May 2007, Steel Partners launched a hostile tender offer for all outstanding shares of Tenryu Saw Mfg. Co. ('Tenryu'), a saw blade manufacturer. In response, Tenryu adopted an advance warning defence plan with approval of more than 80% shares at the shareholders' meeting.[18] Steel Partners' bid was unsuccessful because only 2.69% of all voting shares were tendered (Steel Partners ended up with 11.73% of all voting shares of Tenryu).

III. Characteristics

The developments described above show a few characteristics in this area in Japan. First, the rule in the statute is not clearly written and as a result whether and when a given defensive measure is legal is relegated to proper interpretation of the relevant statutory revisions.[19] The most relevant are the provisions under the Companies Act, Articles 210 and 247, which provide that the issuance of stock or stock warrants is enjoined if such issuance is significantly unfair. The courts have been struggling to find an appropriate test of judicial review.

Second, the Japanese discussion and judicial development emphasize shareholder decision. However, Bulldog Sauce and Tenryu are exceptional companies in that they apparently have many shareholders friendly to the management. Usually, it seems not easy to obtain

---

[18] This pre-bid plan explicitly stated that the plan does not apply to the tender offer by Steel Partners which was pending at that time. It applies to all future tender offers and other stock acquisitions.

[19] Under the Companies Act of 2005, defence plans using the class of shares are possible. For instance, a firm may issue a special class of shares which does not have voting power for the part of the shares exceeding the 20% stake of all outstanding shares. To issue such shares, the firm's charter must state its content. A firm issuing common shares may convert them into such special class shares by a charter amendment, which requires two-thirds approval at the shareholders' meeting. However, in practice, no company has introduced such class shares yet. There is discussion in academia as to whether such shares are always lawful, and the Tokyo Stock Exchange takes the view that such shares are not appropriate for existing listed firms, as opposed to firms making IPOs. In November 2004, an oil company issued a 'golden share' (a special class share) which gave the holder of the share a veto right over all proposals submitted to its shareholders' meetings. However, the share was issued to the government, and it was understood that the oil company should be permitted to issue such shares to the government from a national public policy standpoint.

two-thirds approval at a shareholders' meeting. What happens if the firm obtains simple majority approval at a shareholders' meeting? What if the firm introduces a pre-bid defence plan without shareholders' approval? Indeed, certain firms did introduce such defence plan without shareholders' approval, but as noted above, those plans have not yet been triggered, and thus it is not clear whether the plan will be held valid by the courts if triggered.

Third, with the important exception of the emphasis on shareholder decision, the rule developed in recent years is similar to the one which was shaped in the United States, particularly in Delaware, in the past twenty-five years. 'Necessity and proportionality' is the standard of judicial review. However, to date, the scope of permitted discretion of a target board seems much narrower in Japan than in the US.

Finally, there has been almost no proposal to clarify the rule, or improve the situation, by introducing new legislation. The only proposal that was made in the past was the one to introduce a European style 'mandatory bid' rule, and as noted above it was partially recognized in the amendments to the SEA as effective on 13 December 2006. However, most of this area has been relegated to judicial development.

IV. Preliminary conclusion

What implications can we draw from all of these developments? In theory, it is often said that there can be both good and bad takeovers (although economists might say that distinction between these two cannot be made). Good or bad must be judged from an economic perspective. In this sense, the position of the Guidelines is correct in that takeovers enhancing corporate value are good ones and those reducing corporate value are bad ones. Correspondingly, defences for frustrating hostile bids are justified if the defence enhances corporate value and they are not justified if the defence decreases corporate value. A far more important question, however, is who should be the ultimate decision maker on this point? The board, shareholders or judges?

Rules in this area vary from country to country. They are, however, within a reasonable range in all jurisdictions. What is different is who the ultimate decision maker is. Today, for Japan, the most important question that remains to be resolved is to what extent a target board can act to frustrate or stop hostile takeover attempts without asking shareholders' approval.

PART II

Perspectives in financial regulation

SECTION 1

European perspectives

24

Principles-based, risk-based regulation and effective enforcement

EILIS FERRAN

Enforcement intensity may impinge on capital market competitiveness. It also has implications for the development of international securities regulation, which is increasingly likely to depend on determinations of equivalence as between different national (or regional) regimes.

The UK Financial Services Authority is not enforcement-led and, in tune with its principles-based, risk-based approach, it employs a range of compliance-promoting strategies. Its measured approach to enforcement divides opinion and particular controversy surrounds its application in relation to market abuse. This chapter reviews the Financial Services Authority's enforcement record in this difficult area and identifies challenges that lie ahead.

I. What does principles-based, risk-based regulation mean?

The essence of the distinction between rules and principles lies in their specificity.[1] At opposite ends of the spectrum lie: a 'rule' which is written

---

[1] A rich body of jurisprudence examines this distinction, whether it is meaningful, and the factors influencing the choice between a rule or a principle as the form in which a particular requirement is stated. It includes: J.B. Braithwaite, 'Rules and Principles: A Theory of Legal Certainty', *Australian Journal of Legal Philosophy*, 27 (2002), 47–82; F. Schauer, 'Prescriptions In Three Dimensions', *Iowa Law Review*, 82 (1997), 911–22; F. Schauer, *Playing By The Rules: A Philosophical Examination of Rule Based Decision Making in Law and Life* (Oxford: Clarendon Press, 1991); D. Kennedy, 'Form and Substance in Private Law Adjudication', *Harvard Law Review*, 89 (1976), 1685–1778; L. Alexander and K. Kress, 'Against Legal Principles' in A. Marmor (ed.), *Law and Interpretation: Essays in Legal Philosophy* (OUP, 1995), 279, reprinted in *Iowa Law Review*, 82 (1997), 739–86; J. Raz, 'Legal Principles and the Limits of Law', *Yale Law Journal*, 81 (1972), 823–54; R. Dworkin, *Taking Rights Seriously* (Cambridge, MA: Harvard University Press, 1977), 22–3.

in such detailed and precise terms that all questions about what conduct is permissible are settled in advance leaving only factual issues for later judgment; and a 'principle' (or 'standard') written in open-textured language that leaves open both specification of what conduct is permissible and judgment on factual issues.[2] Many, if not most, regulatory requirements will occupy the space between these endpoints showing more (or less) of the characteristics of a rule (or principle), being as Cunningham has put it, 'hybrids along a continuum'.[3] The combination of principles, rules and all points in between within a legal system can, in jurisprudential terms, be seen as a compromise between two social needs: 'the need for certain rules which can, over great areas of conduct, safely be applied by private individuals to themselves without fresh official guidance or weighing up of social issues, and the need to leave open, for later settlement by an informed, official choice, issues which can only be properly appreciated and settled when they arise in a concrete case'.[4]

In recent years, principles-based regulation has come to mean more than just the form in which regulatory requirements are written. At the level of regulatory theory, it has been associated with a new style of governance that spans the public/private divide, where the regulator defines polices and goals, cooperates with the regulated industry in determining how those goals are to be achieved, and leaves room for industry to innovate whilst still being accountable for its actions.[5] New governance is said to be characterised by collaborative, pragmatic, open-ended methods and robust communication mechanisms between public and private actors.[6] In the UK financial services context, this extended concept of what principles-based regulation entails has been hardwired into the institutional culture of the Financial Services Authority (FSA), which emphasizes a style of supervision that focuses on outcomes rather than the details of the processes that regulated firms use to achieve them, and places considerable responsibility on senior management of firms to develop their own internal compliance policies (rather than being

---

[2] This definition is derived from L. Kaplow, 'Rules Versus Standards: An Economic Analysis', *Duke Law Journal*, 42 (1992), 557–629.

[3] L. Cunningham, 'A Prescription to Retire The Rhetoric Of "Principles-Based Systems"' in 'Corporate Law, Securities Regulation, and Accounting', *Vanderbilt Law Review*, 60 (2007), 1411–1493, at 1492.

[4] H.L.A. Hart, *The Concept of Law* (Oxford: Clarendon Press, 1961), 127.

[5] C.L. Ford, 'New Governance, Compliance, and Principles-Based Securities Regulation', *American Business Law Journal*, 45 (2008), 1–60.

[6] Ibid.

told what to do by the regulator).[7] This style of supervision is designed to foster open and cooperative, perhaps more grown-up, relationships between the regulator and those it regulates.

Risk-based regulation is said to 'complement' principles-based regulation.[8] Being risk-based in relation to supervision and enforcement implies prioritizing resources in areas that pose the biggest threat to the regulator's regulatory objectives.[9] Thus, in the enforcement context, the regulator may eschew the temptation to achieve easy gains by going after the 'low hanging fruit' and decide against taking formal enforcement action against less serious forms of misconduct in areas that are not strategically important. Working in combination with principles-based regulation, it may enable the regulator in some cases where a contravention has occurred to conclude that the issue can be resolved through open dialogue with the relevant parties or through a firm's internal disciplinary procedures, and that public disciplinary action to impose more severe penalties is not needed. The FSA explains its 'strategic' use of enforcement tools in these terms:

> We are selective in the cases we choose to investigate. Our considerations include: whether the misconduct poses a significant risk to our objectives; if it is serious or egregious in nature or both; if there is actual or potential consumer loss or detriment; if there is evidence or risk of financial crime; and whether it is an FSA priority to raise standards in that sector or issue.[10]

The regulatory model developed by the FSA has enjoyed high approval ratings for a considerable period of time. Within the UK, it fits squarely within the current government strategy of promoting 'better regulation': a risk-based, proportionate and targeted approach to regulatory inspection and enforcement is a central part of that agenda;[11] so too is the idea that regulations should be clear and simple.[12] Internationally, in

---

[7] J. Black, M. Hopper and C. Band, 'Making a Success of Principles-based Regulation', *Law and Financial Market Review*, 1(3) (2007), 191–206. For the FSA's own account of what it means by principles-based regulation: Financial Services Authority, *Principles-based Regulation: Focusing on the Outcomes That Matter* (2007).

[8] J. Tiner, 'Chief Executive's Report', *FSA Annual Report* (2006/7).

[9] R. Baldwin and J. Black, 'Really Responsive Regulation', *Modern Law Review*, 71 (2008), 59–94, at 65–68.

[10] Financial Services Authority, *Enforcement Annual Performance Account 2006/07*, para. 8.

[11] BERR, *Regulators' Compliance Code: Statutory Code of Practice for Regulators* (December 2007).

[12] 'The Five Principles of Good Regulation', Annex B to Better Regulation Task Force, *Regulation – Less is More: Reducing Burdens, Improving Outcomes* (2005).

a number of reports published in the United States in 2006/7, the UK's principles-based, collaborative regulatory environment and its measured approach to enforcement were singled out as positive features that appeared to enhance the competitiveness of its capital markets.[13] Ben Bernanke, the Chairman of Federal Reserve, added his voice to this favourable assessment with a speech in May 2007 urging US financial regulatory authorities to look at the UK as a model for the way markets might be better regulated.[14] Also in 2007, the Japanese Financial Services Agency was reported to have come out in favour of a shift towards a more UK-style principles-based regulatory model, to strengthen the country's competitiveness as a financial centre.[15]

The FSA's reputation was undoubtedly dented by the run on Northern Rock in late 2007, circumstances that according to one official report revealed that the FSA 'systematically failed in its regulatory duty to ensure that Northern Rock would not pose a systemic risk'.[16] The Authority is now on the back foot in defending itself against the view that principles-based regulation is flawed.[17] Whilst full-scale dismantlement

[13] McKinsey & Co, *Sustaining New York's and the US' Global Financial Services Leadership* (report commissioned by M.R. Bloomberg and C.E. Schumer, January 2007); Commission on the Regulation of US Capital Markets in the 21st Century, *Report and Recommendations* (March 2007); Committee on Capital Markets Regulation, *Interim Report* (November 2006).

[14] J. Grant, 'Bernanke Calls for US to Follow UK's "Principles-based" Approach', *Financial Times*, 16 May 2007, 1.

[15] M. Nakamoto, 'Tokyo Eyes Move Towards UK-style Financial Regulation', *Financial Times*, 25 October 2007, 7. See further Financial Services Agency, *Plan for Strengthening the Competitiveness of Japan's Financial and Capital Markets*, (December 2007), Pt III, provisional and unofficial translation at www.fsa.go.jp/en/news/2007/20071221/01.pdf (accessed March 2008).

[16] House of Commons Treasury Committee, *The Run on the Rock* (5th Report of Session 2007–8, HC 56-I, 56-II, January 2008).

[17] 'Northern Rock does not mean principles-based regulation is flawed. Indeed, we believe that a full analysis of the events will support our principles-based approach to regulation, and in particular the importance of both us and firms' management focusing on the consequences of their actions rather than rigid adherence to detailed rules.' C. Briault, 'Regulatory Developments and the Challenges Ahead', speech by FSA Managing Director, Retail Markets, Compliance Institute Annual State of the Nation Conference 30 January 2008. Text available at www.fsa.gov.uk/pages/Library/Communication/Speeches/2008/0130_cb.shtml (accessed March 2008).
Briault, who led the team overseeing Northern Rock, left the FSA 'by mutual consent' in April 2008. The FSA's internal audit report on Northern Rock supported the general risk-based approach and high-level, principles-based framework but found failings in the manner in which it had been applied: *FSA Moves to Enhance Supervision in Wake of Northern Rock* (FSA/PN/028/2008, 26 March 2008) (www.fsa.gov.uk/pages/Library/Communication/PR/2008/028.shtml, accessed 20 October 2008).

of the current system is not likely, the challenges of a changing economic climate give a new urgency to questions about its overall robustness.

II. Effective enforcement

A successful principles-based regulatory strategy that relies heavily on *ex ante* compliance-promoting strategies can reasonably be expected to produce fewer formal enforcement actions than a system that emphasizes the deterrent effect of *ex post* sanctions. Likewise, relatively little formal enforcement is consistent with a risk-based approach given that it implies that the regulator should concentrate on enforcement where it will have the greatest impact and should not pursue wrongdoers merely in order to generate more demonstration cases. The influential theory of responsive regulation moreover teaches that a crude polarization between persuasion and deterrence strategies is misconceived and that an escalation in enforcement intensity is a function of failure of lower-level compliance-promoting strategies.[18] It would thus be rash to extrapolate from a comparatively low level of formal enforcement activity by the FSA that non-compliance is endemic in the UK financial services sector. Not only would such an assessment arguably fail to capture fully the implications of the FSA's regulatory culture and style, it is also open to the criticism that it ignores other compliance-promoting factors that are at work in the UK, including the role played by other public oversight and enforcement bodies and the influence of a powerful institutional investor community, underpinned by certain legal powers for shareholders that can be more formidable than those found elsewhere.[19]

---

[18] The 'enforcement pyramid' developed by Ayres and Braithwaite has persuasion at its base and criminal penalties and other punitive sanctions at its apex: I. Ayres and J. Brathwaite, *Responsive Regulation* (OUP, 1992).

[19] The power for shareholders to remove directors from office by simple majority of those voting (Companies Act 2006, s. 168) is a powerful control mechanism. L.A. Bebchuk, 'The Myth of the Shareholder Franchise', *Virginia Law Review*, 93 (2007), 675–732 advocates a system for the US in which shareholders have more power to replace or remove directors and uses the example of the UK (which, he states, 'has long had such a system') to counter 'doomsday scenarios' painted by critics of his proposals.

That there is this wide range of public and private forces at work suggests that, in theoretical terms, it may be more appropriate to think of a 'three-sided' pyramid embracing control exerted by bodies other than State agencies: N. Gunningham and P. Grabosky, *Smart Regulation* (Oxford: Clarendon Press, 1998); Baldwin and Black, 'Really Responsive Regulation', (note 9, above). Baldwin and Black also emphasise the importance of taking account of the constraints and opportunities presented by institutional environments in shaping enforcement activities.

The fact that there is a complex interplay of public and private forces at work means that whilst it may be the case that, in some countries, formal enforcement intensity impinges significantly on market competitiveness (although this is highly debatable),[20] it does not follow that the UK would necessarily derive competitive advantages from a policy shift by the FSA in favour of more aggressive enforcement.[21]

This is not to suggest that the implications of principles-based, risk-based regulation for enforcement do not need to be taken seriously.[22] Some empirical work suggests that the utility of less specific forms of regulation decreases the more that enforcement depends on formal prosecution but that where the chosen regulatory strategy relies heavily on firms engaging cooperatively and collaboratively with the regulator in fashioning compliance procedures and practices, short simple requirements are more desirable than those focusing on precision and prosecutability.[23] Open-textured principles may put an enforcement agency into a position where its officers have to make difficult judgement calls on whether there is sufficient evidence to prove a breach of principles alone. However, the FSA is adamant that its move away from detailed, prescriptive rules to principles-based regulation does not undermine its ability to be tough in appropriate cases, has emphasized its willingness to take enforcement action based on breach of a principle alone, and has brought a number of cases on that basis.[24] And in much of the debate thus far around its principles-based regulation agenda, the FSA has had to defend itself not from accusations that this will mean a less tough

[20] J.C. Coffee, 'Law and the Market: The Impact of Enforcement', *University of Pennsylvania Law Review*, 156 (2007), 229–311. However, note Committee on Capital Markets Regulation, *The Competitive Position of the US Public Equity Market* (December 2007), which examines the erosion in US market competitiveness. This Report reviews closely a paper on listing premiums by C. Doidge, G.A. Karolyi and R.M. Stulz, 'Has New York Become Less Competitive in Global Markets? Evaluating Foreign Listing Choices over Time' (Fisher College of Business Working Paper No. 2007-03-012, July 2007), available at http://ssrn.com/abstract=982193) that (in an earlier version) is an important part of the evidence on which Coffee builds his enforcement matters thesis. The Committee identifies a number of concerns with the work.

[21] I. MacNeil, 'The Evolution of Regulatory Enforcement Action in the UK Capital Markets: A Case of "Less is More"?', *Capital Markets Law Journal* 2(4) (2007), 345–69.

[22] R. Baldwin, 'Why Rules Don't Work', *Modern Law Review*, 53 (1990), 321–37, at 328.

[23] *Ibid*. Note also M. Hopper and J. Stainsby, 'Principles-based Regulation – Better Regulation?', *Journal of International Banking Law and Regulation*, 21 (2006), 387–91, where the authors note that proving breach of a principle may be more challenging that establishing breach of a specific rule.

[24] See below.

approach to enforcement but from concerns coming from precisely the opposite direction and which reflect long-recognized and much debated fears about principles-based enforcement – that it may lead to over-zealousness and unfair *ex post* rule making because the open-textured nature of principles generates uncertainty and unpredictability that the enforcer may exploit to its advantage when judging conduct with the benefit of hindsight.[25]

Does the ability to bring action on a basis of breach of a principle alone promote effective, credible enforcement? What does being risk-based in relation to enforcement actually mean in sensitive areas where there are considerations pulling in different directions? These questions can be examined by looking at recent FSA enforcement activity cases relating to market misconduct. Market misconduct, in the form of insider trading, has been the focal point of recent comparative discussion of enforcement intensity, with the UK appearing to come out badly by comparison to the US on some measurements, to the extent that it has been suggested that the existence of significant listing premiums on the major US exchanges and none on the London Stock Exchange may be attributable to 'the failure of the UK to effectively enforce its own insider trading restrictions'.[26] This comment needs to be handled with care because there is evidence of a listing premium in fact being available on markets other than the major US exchanges, including on the London Alternative Investment Market (AIM), which often bears the brunt of comments about weak enforcement in the UK.[27] However, even though the links between enforcement of insider trading in the UK and competitiveness may not be fully understood, there are other grounds for focusing on market misconduct cases to examine the effectiveness of principles-based, risk-based enforcement in the UK.

Maintaining confidence in the financial system and reducing financial crime are fundamental, symbiotically related, regulatory objectives.[28] It

---

[25] Major critiques of rulemaking though enforcement are: R.S. Karmel, *Regulation by Prosecution: The Securities and Exchange Commission Versus Corporate America* (New York: Simon & Schuster, 1982); H.L. Pitt and K.L. Shapiro, 'Securities Regulation by Enforcement: A Look Ahead at the Next Decade', *Yale Journal on Regulation* 7 (1990), 149–304. A recent resurgence in principles-based enforcement in the US has been noted: J.J. Park, 'The Competing Paradigms of Securities Regulation', *Duke Law Journal*, 57 (2007), 625–89.

[26] Coffee, 'Law and the Market', (note 20, above), 240.

[27] Committee on Capital Markets Regulation, *The Competitive Position of the US Public Equity Market* (December 2007) makes the point about the AIM listing premium.

[28] Financial Services and Markets Act 2000, s. 3 and s. 6.

is thus crucial from a public interest perspective for the FSA to prioritize market cleanliness and to accommodate within its measured risk-based approach to the imposition of penalties or other formal sanctions a credible commitment to cracking down on insider dealing and other forms of deliberate misconduct.[29] Although a risk-based approach implies that some instances of even deliberate wrongdoing may not be prioritized because they are too low-level to have strategic repercussions, this has to be balanced against the danger that tolerance could lead to some forms of malpractice becoming so widespread that their cumulative effect is strategically dangerous.[30] Recent research on market cleanliness that involves measuring price movements preceding market announcements by FTSE 350 issuers and price movements prior to takeover announcements makes rather uncomfortable reading for the FSA in that the measurements suggest that the incidence of informed trading prior to takeover announcements is not lower than it was before the upgrading of the regulatory framework by the Financial Services and Markets Act 2000, and even increased slightly in part of the post-2000 period.[31] Whilst the fact that it has supported the publication of this work reflects well on the credibility of FSA's commitment to transparency and to devising well-informed regulatory solutions,[32] the substance of the data prompts obvious questions about whether the FSA has yet struck the right balance so that

---

[29] D. Mayhew and K. Anderson, 'Whither Market Abuse (in a More Principles-based Regulatory World)?', *Journal of International Banking Law and Regulation*, 22(10) (2007), 515–31.

[30] Baldwin and Black, 'Really Responsive Regulation', (note 9, above).

[31] B. Dubow and N. Monteiro, *Measuring Market Cleanliness* (FSA Occasional Paper No 23, March 2006): research on FTSE 350 issuers' announcements up to 2004 suggested no change in market cleanliness that could be related to the timing of the new statutory powers; research on takeover announcements indicated a small but statistically significant increase in informed price movements prior to takeover announcements in the period up to 2004. N. Monteiro, Q. Zaman and S. Leitterstorf, *Measuring Market Cleanliness* (FSA Occasional Paper No 25, March 2007) revised the technical methodology and updated the findings to take account of 2005 market data. The new FTSE 350 analysis indicated that the measure of informed trading was very low in the years 2004 and 2005 and was statistically significantly lower than in the period 1998–2000 before FSMA was introduced, which could suggest that markets had become cleaner. Results for the takeovers analysis still showed a significant increase in the measure of informed trading between 2000 and 2004, as reported in the first paper; there was a decline in the measure between 2004 and 2005, but the level of the measure remained high (23.7% of takeover announcements in 2005 were preceded by informed price movements, compared to 32.4% in 2004) and it was not lower than it was in 2000 before FSMA came into force.

[32] M. Hopper and J. Stainsby, 'Measuring Market Abuse: Cleaning Up?', *Practical Law for Companies*, 17(4) (2006), 6–7.

actors who are unlikely to respond to the incentives embedded within strategies that rely on cooperation and dialogue or who are outside its reach because they are not part of the regulated community are held in check effectively through strong deterrence mechanisms. [33]

Do high-intensity enforcers perform better? According to a study conducted by the *Financial Times* of trading data for the top 100 US and Canadian deals since 2003, suspicious trading occurred ahead of 49 per cent of all North American deals. This study employed different methodologies from that used in the UK surveys and the results are therefore not directly comparable. Furthermore, since the headline figure does not distinguish between the US (an outlier in terms of enforcement intensity) and Canada, too much significance should not be attached to the fact that the percentage of suspicious trades is somewhat larger than that identified in the UK. Yet, even with these caveats, the survey does indicate that devising effective enforcement strategies to stamp out improper informed trading is a problem that is not exclusive to the UK.[34]

III. Pursuing market misconduct through criminal prosecutions: preliminary general comments

It has been argued that because securing convictions on complex charges that involve financial market malpractices is notoriously difficult, criminal prosecutors may for strategic reasons choose to focus on relatively straightforward aspects of wrongdoing, such as document shredding, or frame their charges in narrow terms of basic fraud.[35]

---

[33] As Sally Dewar, then director of the FSA's markets division, acknowledged: 'The figures for takeover announcements, although moving in the right direction, remain a cause for particular concern. There will be no let up in our efforts to tackle the problems in this area'. Quoted in J. Quinn, 'Insider Trading Hits One in Four Deals', *Daily Telegraph*, 8 March 2007, 1 (City section).

Similar quantitative research on market cleanliness conducted by the Netherlands Authority for the Financial Markets on the effects of the Market Abuse Directive has shown that implementation of the Directive has resulted in a cleaner and more well-informed market: 'Netherlands Publishes Study on Effects of Market Abuse Directive', *Company Lawyer*, 29 (2008), 19.

[34] V. Kim and B. Masters, ' "Suspicious Trading" Ahead of 49% of North American Deals', *Financial Times*, 6 August 2007, 19.

[35] D. McBarnet, 'After Enron Will "Whiter than White Collar Crime" Still Wash?', *British Journal of Criminology*, 46 (2006), 1091–109. A. Alcock, 'Five Years of Market Abuse', *Company Lawyer*, 28 (2007), 163–71, notes: 'Even when prosecutions for market misconduct were pursued, the authorities preferred to use more general charges like conspiracy

There is a downside to this strategy in that it can mean that the enforcement strategy fails to send out official messages about issues of concern in relation to complex practices.[36] From a principles-based perspective, even a successful criminal case may thus be a 'missed opportunity' to use enforcement as a mechanism for deepening real learning about the root causes of compliance failures.[37] Another drawback of a prosecution strategy is that, if it is pursued in an imbalanced way, this is likely to inculcate the regulated community with a sense that the system of oversight is adversarial, punitive and legalistic, which may, in turn, mean that people are less willing to engage in open dialogue and cooperation, thereby making it harder for voluntary compliance strategies to operate effectively.[38] Furthermore, the imposition of disproportionate criminal sanctions may give rise to perverse incentives for wrongdoers to engage in more egregious forms of misconduct.[39] This implies that optimal stringency in enforcement may well lie somewhere below maximum stringency.[40]

IV. Criminal prosecutions in relation to insider dealing and other forms of market abuse

Insider dealing is a criminal offence under Part V of the Criminal Justice Act 1993 and the FSA has power to prosecute (in England and Wales).[41] Other bodies with power to prosecute in respect of insider dealing are the Department for Business, Enterprise and Regulatory Reform,[42] the

---

to defraud by rigging a market or provisions of the Theft Act for fear of the technicalities of the specialist crimes.' But note K.F. Brickey, 'Enron's Legacy', *Buffalo Criminal Law Review*, 8 (2004), 221–76, who argues that the vast majority of post-Enron corporate fraud prosecutions did not focus on peripheral issues.

[36] McBarnet, 'After Enron', (note 35, above).

[37] On the importance of 'enforcement learning': Ford, 'New Governance', (note 5, above).

[38] Baldwin and Black, 'Really Responsive Regulation', (note 9, above).

[39] Law Commission, *Company Directors: Regulating Conflicts of Interests and Formulating a Statement of Duties* (Consultation Paper No 153, 1998), para. 3.81.
See also R.A. Booth, 'What is a Business Crime?' (November 2007). Available at SSRN: http://ssrn.com/abstract=1029667 (arguing for reliance on the criminal law only when all else fails).

[40] Ayres and Brathwaite, *Responsive Regulation*, (note 18, above), 52.

[41] Financial Services and Markets Act 2000, s. 402.

[42] As between the Department for Business and the FSA, the FSA is the primary enforcer and the Secretary of State's powers will be used only rarely in cases which it would be inappropriate for the FSA to investigate: Department of Trade, *Companies in 2003–2004*, 22.

Crown Prosecution Service and the Serious Fraud Office. General guidelines are in place to establish principles to assist these bodies in deciding which of them should act in cases where there are overlapping powers.[43]

Between 1987 and 1997 there were thirteen successful convictions relating to insider dealing.[44] However, not all of those cases were upheld on appeal. From 1997 to February 2006 criminal proceedings were brought against fifteen individuals, of which eight were successful.[45] Among the successful cases were one in 2005 where the former compliance officer of an investment firm was jailed for five years and a 2004 case where a proofreader at a financial printers pleaded guilty to leaking inside information and was imprisoned for twenty-one months.[46] All of the completed cases to date were brought by prosecuting authorities other than the FSA. In January 2008 the FSA brought its first criminal prosecution; the case is ongoing at the time of writing.

Misleading statements and practices can also be pursued through the criminal law: Financial Services and Markets Act 2000, section 397 (previously the Financial Services Act 1986, section 47). The FSA and the Department for Business are among the bodies that have power to institute proceedings under this section.[47]

The Department of Business (more accurately its predecessor the Department of Trade and Industry but this paper will use the Department's current name) has brought a number of prosecutions under this section over the years.[48] In the most recently reported case, the CEO of a company admitted to trading on OFEX (now PLUS Quoted) was sentenced to eighteen months' imprisonment and disqualified from holding the office of director for ten years (reduced to seven years on appeal).[49] His offence took place in an interview with a journalist during which he made a number of statements and forecasts about the company which were false. The Department also recently used this section to

---

[43] Financial Services Authority, *Enforcement Guide*, Annex 2.

[44] C. Conceicao, 'The FSA's Approach to Taking Action Against Market Abuse', *Company Lawyer*, 28 (2007), 43–45.

[45] On 13 February 2006, the Department of Trade and Industry issued a Written Answer to House of Commons Parliamentary Question No. 2005/3120 from Austin Mitchell MP (*Hansard*, vol. 442, col. 1635W), which sought information regarding the (a) prosecutions and (b) successful prosecutions for insider trading since 1997.

[46] R. Burger and E. King, 'An Inside Job?', *New Law Journal*, 158 (2008), 390.

[47] Financial Services and Markets Act 2000, s. 401.

[48] For an overview see *Palmer's Company Law* (London: Thompson, looseleaf), paras. 11.138–11.145.

[49] *R* v. *O'Hanlon* [2007] EWCA Crim 3074.

prosecute financial journalists who bought shares they were about to tip in their newspaper column. In this case custodial sentences of between three and six months were imposed on two of the defendants and a community service order was made against the third.[50] In 2005 the FSA secured convictions in its first criminal prosecution under the section against the CEO (and Chairman) and CFO of a company listed on the London Stock Exchange who had issued a false trading statement to the market. However, the FSA's success in this case was later tempered when the original custodial sentences of three and a half years and two years were reduced on appeal to eighteen months and nine months, respectively, and the defendants also appealed successfully against confiscation orders.[51] In February 2008 the FSA secured a conviction and a fifteen-month prison sentence against an unauthorized stockbroker, on a number of charges under the Theft Acts, the Financial Services Act 1986 and Financial Services and Markets Act 2000, with a further thirty-four offences taken into consideration. He was also disqualified from being a company director for five years.[52]

The FSA has been quite open at a senior level in acknowledging the difficulties in prosecuting insider dealing and other forms of market abuse: the absence usually of a smoking gun and the need therefore to rely heavily on circumstantial evidence; practical problems in presenting complex and often highly technical evidence to a jury; and the challenge of persuading a jury that they can be satisfied to the criminal standard that the elements of the crime, in particular that the accused knew that he had inside information and dealt on that basis, are present.[53] For a risk-based regulator that emphasizes efficiency in its choice of enforcement options and which has limited resources, such considerations militate strongly against bringing a criminal case, notwithstanding that it is only a criminal prosecution that offers the possibility of 'the showcase effect of getting business leaders behind bars'.[54] The FSA is not pursuing an idiosyncratic line in adopting a measured approach in relation to criminal enforcement of insider dealing and other forms of market abuse: general principles applicable to all criminal prosecutors in the

---

[50] *R* v. *Hipwell* [2006] EWCA Crim 736.

[51] *R* v. *Bailey, Rigby* [2005] EWCA Crim 3487 and [2006] EWCA Crim 1653.

[52] FSA/PN/011/2008.

[53] M. Cole, 'Insider Dealing in the City'. Speech by FSA Director of Enforcement, 17 March 2007. Text available at www.fsa.gov.uk/pages/Library/Communication/Speeches/2Cole (accessed March 2008).

[54] McBarnet, 'After Enron', (note 35, above), 1100.

UK provide that the prosecutor must be satisfied that there is enough evidence to provide a 'realistic prospect of conviction' and, if not, it must drop the prosecution.[55] However, there are suggestions that the FSA is at a particular disadvantage because the range of covert investigative powers available to it is less extensive than that available to other bodies.[56] Senior FSA officials have indicated that it is hampered by not having power to offer immunity from prosecution to whistleblowers or to enter into plea bargains.[57]

There is a perception that the 'fear factor' is missing from financial regulation in the UK because the FSA has not made sufficient use of criminal sanctions.[58] The very low incidence of successful prosecutions certainly presents the FSA and the UK's financial regulatory system more generally with at least a credibility problem that needs to be addressed, including by giving the FSA the appropriate range of powers that it needs to operate effectively as a criminal prosecutor in such a complex area. The FSA itself acknowledges a need to escalate its deterrence-oriented work and that the criminal law has a meaningful role to play in this, albeit as part of a 'multi-pronged' approach and not as the exclusive or even, necessarily, the primary tool.[59] Considerations identified in this section suggest that this is a defensible and pragmatically sensible stance: the well-known difficulties of securing convictions; the need for care not to lose the benefits of a principles-based approach though unwarranted over-reliance on aggressive and adversarial prosecution-oriented strategies; and the continuing elusiveness, notwithstanding advances in empirical research, of the additional degree of criminal enforcement intensity that *might* causally make all the difference in deterrence terms.

---

[55] CPS, *Code for Crown Prosecutors*.

[56] C. Conceicao, H. Hugger and S. Riolo, 'Deciphering the FSA's Declining Caseload', *European Lawyer*, 73 (2007), 10–11.

[57] L. Saigol and P.T. Larsen, 'FSA Boss Admits Defeat', *Financial Times*, 3 July 2007, 18, reporting on speech by John Tiner, then the FSA's CEO. Brickey, 'Enron's Legacy', (note 35, above), 264 notes that all but four of the seventy-three defendants who pleaded guilty in federal fraud prosecutions between 2002 and 2004 became cooperating witnesses.

[58] 'But while these [market surveillance] tools may help Mr Sants and his team at the FSA, they are unlikely to enhance the fear factor. When he leads one of these dealers away in glinting handcuffs in front of an array of photographers, then terror might finally sink into the City's psyche': L. Saigol, 'City Must Join Insider Trading Fight', *Financial Times*, 23 April 2007, 19.

[59] M. Cole, 'The FSA's Approach to Insider Dealing'. Speech by FSA Director of Enforcement, FSA, American Bar Association, 4 October 2007. Text available at: www.fsa.gov.uk/pages/Library/Communication/Speeches/2007/1004_mc.shtml (accessed March 2008).

This conclusion derives support from the first-ever report on the FSA's performance by the UK National Audit Office, published in 2007, which concluded that there was no need for the FSA to increase significantly the proportion of its resources spent on combating financial crime (although there was room for it to improve the effectiveness with which it used the current level of resources).[60]

V. Administrative enforcement of the market-abuse regime

The Financial Services and Markets Act 2000, Part VIII contains provisions that enable the FSA to impose unlimited financial penalties on, or to censure publicly, those who engage in market abuse or who encourage such behaviour, including persons who are not part of the regulated community. The FSA can also apply for an injunction restraining market abuse or seek restitution. The administrative regime was introduced to complement the criminal law and to cover a wider range of serious misconduct.[61] According to one senior FSA official: 'It was anticipated that a civil process with the accompanying benefits like a civil burden of proof, a jury not being required, the ability to settle, a quicker process with non-custodial outcomes and the ability to have a specialist Tribunal for difficult issues of fact and law would result in more successful actions against insider dealing.'[62] However, this is not exactly how things have turned out.

Charges under Part VIII are often described as 'civil' offences but it is clear that proceedings are regarded as 'criminal' for the purposes of safeguards in respect of human rights under the European Convention on Human Rights (such as the admissibility of statements made to investigators).[63] When it was first enacted, there was considerable discussion as to whether the standard of proof under Part VIII was criminal (beyond reasonable doubt) or civil (on a balance of probabilities) as

---

[60] National Audit Office, *The Financial Services Authority: A Review under Section 12 of the Financial Services and Markets Act 2000* (2007).

[61] Joint Committee on Financial Services and Markets, *Draft Financial Services and Markets Bill: First Report* (HL Paper 50-I, HC 328-I, 1999, vol I) para. 255; Alcock, 'Five Years', (note 35, above).

[62] Cole, 'Insider Dealing in the City', (note 53, above).

[63] *Davidson and Tatham* v. *FSA*. That this would be the case was anticipated during the Parliamentary passage of the Financial Services and Markets Bill, and ECHR-related safeguards were added: s. 174(2) (admissibility of statements); s. 134 (legal assistance scheme).

this matter is not dictated by the Convention. Decisions of the Financial Services and Markets Tribunal have since established that the standard is properly described as the balance of probability,[64] but that the concept requires some refinement in its application because there is, in effect, a sliding scale that implies that: 'The more serious the allegation the less likely it is that the event occurred and, hence, the stronger should be the evidence before the court concludes that the allegation is established on the balance of probability.'[65] The Tribunal has indicated that where the charge is 'grave', in a practical sense it may be difficult to draw a meaningful distinction between this standard and the criminal standard.[66]

The FSA concluded its first Part VIII case in 2004 and by 2007 it had brought sixteen successful cases with total fines in the region of £19.5 million.[67] Eleven of these cases related to the misuse of information, three related to false and misleading impressions and two were distortion cases.[68] The £17 million fine imposed on Shell/Royal Dutch in 2004 for misstating its proved reserves stands out as the single biggest fine to date. In relation to insider dealing, the FSA's most notable success thus far under Part VIII came in 2006 in proceedings against Philippe Jabre, a hedge fund manager, who was fined £750,000 for market abuse and breach of the FSA Principles for Approved Persons.[69]

However, in 2006 the FSA also suffered a high-profile setback in *Davidson and Tatham*, where the decision of its Regulatory Decisions Committee that Davidson and Tatham had engaged in market abuse in relation to spread betting activity to create a misleading impression of the demand for, and value of, shares to be admitted to trading on AIM was overturned by the Financial Services and Markets Tribunal. The Tribunal also awarded costs against the FSA, which, by implication, constituted a finding that the FSA had acted unreasonably because the Tribunal has power to make costs orders only in exceptional circumstances.[70] The Tribunal, which has an original, rather than purely supervisory, jurisdiction and

---

[64] *Mohammed* v. *FSA* (2005); *Davidson and Tatham* v. *FSA* (2006); *Parker* v. *FSA* (2006).

[65] *H (Minors) (Sexual Abuse: Standard of Proof)*, *Re* [1996] 1 All ER 1 at 16, *per* Lord Nicholls.

[66] *Parker* v. *FSA* para. 35.   [67] Conceicao, 'The FSA's Approach', (note 44, above), 44.

[68] Ibid.

[69] His firm, GLG Partners LP, was also fined £750,000 for breach of Principles.

[70] Financial Services and Markets Act 2000, sch. 13, para. 13. For comment on this case, see A. Hart, '*Paul Davidson and Ashley Tatham v FSA* [2006] – The Case and its Implications', *Journal of International Banking Law and Regulation*, 22 (2007), 288–92; C. Band and M. Hopper, 'Market Abuse: A Developing Jurisprudence', *Journal of International Banking Law and Regulation*, 22 (2007), 231–9.

which can therefore determine itself on the basis of the evidence available to it whether there is market abuse and, if there is, what the appropriate penalty should be, disagreed with the FSA both with regard to the interpretation of the factual position and on certain of the requirements needed to satisfy the statutory tests that were in force at that time.[71]

There is room to believe that the *Davidson and Tatham* experience dented the FSA's confidence in relying on its Part VIII powers as an enforcement tool. Alcock has pointed out: 'Whether coincidental or not, there have been no further market abuse cases reported since the costs decision in *Davidson* and *Tatham* and it could be that the FSA may become more cautious about all but the most straightforward cases of insider dealing or deliberate lying to the market.'[72] Whilst the *Jabre* case was completed in 2006, it was one of only two market abuse cases under Part VIII that year and it related to activities that took place several years before.[73] In 2007, furthermore, there was no successful market abuse case apart from one instance where the FSA obtained an injunction to freeze the proceeds of suspected market abuse.[74] At a senior level, the FSA has been quite candid in admitting that concessions in respect of ECHR protections and the application of a near-to-criminal standard of proof have not made its life easy:

> It was anticipated that a civil process with the accompanying benefits like a civil burden of proof, a jury not being required, the ability to settle, a quicker process with non-custodial outcomes and the ability to have a specialist Tribunal for difficult issues of fact and law would result in more successful actions against insider dealing… We have found, in reality, that a number of the same evidential challenges face us for civil cases.[75]

---

[71] As discussed in the articles in the previous note. The Tribunal agreed that the behaviour was in relation to qualifying investments traded on a relevant market (shares trading on the grey market prior to admission to AIM). However, the Tribunal disagreed on whether the behaviour would be likely to be regarded by a regular user of AIM as a failure to observe the standard of behaviour reasonably expected of persons in such a position in relation to the market. The Tribunal's view was that, given that there was no regulatory obligation to disclose the behaviour, market abuse had not taken place.

[72] Alcock, 'Five Years', (note 35, above).

[73] Conceicao, Hugger and Riolo, 'Deciphering', (note 56, above).

[74] *Ibid.* Details of this action are not publicly available, a fact which has been criticized from a transparency of justice perspective: Mayhew and Anderson, 'Whither Market Abuse', (note 29, above).

[75] S. Dewar, 'Market Abuse Policy and Enforcement in the UK': speech by FSA Director of Markets Division, BBA and ABI Market Abuse Seminar, 22 May 2007. Text available at www.fsa.gov.uk/pages/Library/Communication/Speeches/2007/0522_sd.shtml (accessed March 2008).

It is against this background that the shift to enforcement on the basis of principles alone is to be assessed. Principles-based enforcement is more limited in scope than enforcement under the criminal law or the administrative regime for market abuse because it can only be pursued against those who are within the regulated community. On the other hand, it has the advantage of appearing to circumvent high burdens of proof and other legal requirements that makes it hard to succeed on other bases. However, whatever its relative merits, principles-based enforcement must operate within the rule of law and therefore actions taken and sanctions imposed must be proportionate and fair.

VI. Sanctions in respect of breach of principles

The FSA Handbook contains certain specific sets of principles, including those that apply to regulated firms (Principles for Businesses), persons performing certain functions (Principles for Approved Persons), listed entities (Listing Principles) and sponsors (Principles for Sponsors). In addition, the FSA is shifting to a more principles-based approach to regulation throughout its activities, although it continues to recognize the need for prescriptive rules in particular areas and sometimes (i.e. where this is necessary to implement EC Law) it has no option but to adopt that form.[76]

Of forty disciplinary cases in 2006/07, twelve (30%) were based on principles alone and almost all of the remaining cases were based on a combination of principles and rules.[77] These included in the area of market protection: *Citigroup Global Markets Limited* (2005) (the 'Dr Evil' trades in European government bonds, £13.96 million financial penalty); *Deutsche Bank AG* (2006) (proprietary trading while book-build exercise in progress, £6.36 million financial penalty); *Pignatelli* (2006) (individual disseminating information believed to be inside information, £20,000 financial penalty); *Casoni* (2007) (selective disclosure of information, £52,500 financial penalty). All of these cases were settlements with the FSA, under executive settlement powers introduced in October 2005.

From a risk- and efficiency-based perspective the incentives to settle that are now built into the FSA's enforcement framework, whereby

---

[76] Financial Services Authority, *Principles-based Regulation: Focusing on the Outcomes That Matter* (2007), para. 2.2 and para. 3.1.

[77] Financial Services Authority, *Enforcement Annual Performance Account 2006/07*, para. 10.

the amount of a financial penalty is discounted by between 30% and 10% depending on when in disciplinary proceedings settlement is reached, have advantages because settlements support prompt redress in consumer-related cases, send timely messages to the industry and achieve swift and effective outcomes, with associated cost savings.[78] Between 1 April 2006 and 31 March 2007, thirty-four cases were concluded by executive settlement and the FSA's expectation for the future is that 'most' cases will settle via executive settlement.[79] However, the quality of the messages sent to the market though this process is open to question because settlement notices show signs of being heavily negotiated compromises, which diminishes their clarity and precedent value.[80] There is an echo here of the concern noted in relation to criminal proceedings of how strategic choices with regard to enforcement options may constitute missed opportunities for the transmission of clear signals and for the deepening of regulatory learning.

Does principles-based regulation and enforcement satisfy the rule of law? Lord Bingham, the distinguished Law Lord, has identified eight sub-rules into which the rule of law can be broken down.[81] Of these, the two that have particular relevance in this context are: the law must be accessible and so far as possible intelligible, clear and predictable; and questions of legal right and liability should ordinarily be resolved by application of the law and not the exercise of discretion. Principles have at least superficial merits in terms of accessibility and intelligibility – they offer scope for slimming down voluminous and complex rule books that are a barrier to entry and to compliance[82] – but they are more vulnerable with regard to certainty and predictability. The European Court of Human Rights has made the point: 'a norm cannot be regarded as a "law" unless it is formulated with sufficient precision to enable the citizen to regulate his conduct: he must be able – if need be with appropriate advice – to foresee, to a degree that is reasonable in the circumstances, the consequences which a given action may entail'.[83] And, with regard to the second sub-rule, Lord Bingham himself has observed: '[t]he

---

[78] Financial Services Authority, *Enforcement Annual Performance Account 2006/07*, para. 29.

[79] *Ibid*, paras. 27–31.

[80] Mayhew and Anderson, 'Whither Market Abuse', (note 29, above); Band and Hopper, 'Market Abuse', (note 70, above).

[81] Lord Bingham, 'The Rule of Law', *Cambridge Law Journal*, 66 (2007), 67–85.

[82] A.M. Whittaker, 'Better Regulation – Principles vs. Rules', *Journal of International Banking Law and Regulation*, 21 (2006), 233–7.

[83] *Sunday Times* v. *United Kingdom* (1979) 2 ECHR 245, 271, 149.

broader and more loosely-textured a discretion is, whether conferred on an official or a judge, the greater the scope for subjectivity and hence for arbitrariness, which is the antithesis of the rule of law'.[84]

The outcomes-oriented focus of principles-based regulation and the onus that it places on firm to develop their own compliance strategies expose it to the charge that it provides little in the way of legal certainty.[85] However, a counterargument is that principles, when taken together with the shared sensibilities between the regulator and regulated on what it is expected in particular situations that are fostered by the collaborative and cooperative style implied by principles-based regulation, can deliver more legal certainty than detailed rules in complex situations.[86] This shared understanding can also serve to constrain the wide discretion that less precisely formulated requirements may appear to give to those responsible for overseeing their application and enforcement. With regard to predictability, again there are competing arguments: one of the regularly cited benefits of principles is that their flexibility minimizes the scope for 'creative compliance' practices that thrive by exploiting the gaps left by rigidly prescriptive detailed rules; but the risk of hindsight basis in enforcement decisions, which may fall to be taken in a politically-charged atmosphere where they relate to high-profile problems, is a consideration that pulls in the opposite direction as it implies a high risk of *ad hoc* enforcement arbitrariness.[87] The FSA is, of course, fully aware of its responsibilities as a public body and, unsurprisingly therefore, regularly acknowledges the fundamental nature of the requirement for predictability – '[i]n order for consequences legitimately to be attached to the breach of a principle, it must be possible to predict, at the time of the action concerned, whether or not it would be in breach of the principle'[88] – but there is a risk that

---

[84] Lord Bingham, 'The Rule of Law' (note 81, above), 72.

[85] C. Band and K. Anderson, 'Conflicts of Interest in Financial Services and Markets. The Regulatory Aspect', *Journal of International Banking Law and Regulation*, 22 (2007), 88–100. This view is supported by academic writing on legal theory: Raz, 'Legal Principles', (note 1, above).

[86] Braithwaite, 'Rules and Principles', (note 1, above). See further the ideas of 'interpretative communities' and 'regulatory conversations developed by Black, in particular: J Black, *Rules and Regulators* (Oxford: Clarendon Press, 1997).

[87] J. Patient, 'Treating Customers Fairly: the Challenges of Principles Based Regulation', *Journal of International Banking Law and Regulation*, 22 (2007), 420–25; Black, Hopper and Band, 'Making a Success', (note 7, above).

[88] Whittaker, 'Better Regulation', (note 82, above) (the author is the FSA's chief lawyer). To similar effect: Financial Services Authority, *Enforcement Annual Performance Account 2006/07*, para. 10; Financial Services Authority, *Principles-based Regulation: Focusing on the Outcomes That Matter* (2007), para. 3.2.

its actual practice will fall short of this standard. Its emphasis on 'guidance' as a predictability-enhancing mechanism is also potentially problematic.[89] The range of materials that is to be regarded as guidance in this context is so broad that it can reasonably be asked whether in reality this will provoke a tension with meeting accessibility and intelligibility goals because people will still need to consult a large volume of paperwork to understand the FSA's thinking on any particular point.[90]

Other potential certainty/predictability problems flow from the fact the open-textured nature of principles allows for different interpretations, which raises the possibility of inconsistent decisions between the FSA and the Financial Services and Markets Tribunal or the Financial Ombudsman Service (which can award compensation to consumers on the basis of its own opinion as to what would be fair and reasonable in the circumstances of the case). The inter-relationship of 'outcomes'-oriented principles and enforcement is also unclear in certain key respects: e.g. as to the basis for determining whether a firm has failed to achieve a particular outcome, and as to the relevance of fault in that determination.[91]

VII. Risk-based regulation and European supervisory convergence

The European market integration agenda is another source of tension for the development of principles-based, risk-based regulation. Risk-based regulation is not embraced wholeheartedly across Europe: for example, the FSA's policy of only investigating instances of suspected market abuse where justified on a risk-based assessment is almost unique among European regulators.[92] The FSA has made it clear that it will strongly resist any tendency for European regulation to fetter its legitimate discretion of action, particularly in the areas of monitoring and enforcement, or to compromise its ability to pursue risk-based supervision.[93] At the moment, it is clear that notwithstanding considerable efforts to

---

[89] Financial Services Authority, *Principles-based Regulation: Focusing on the Outcomes That Matter* (2007), para. 3.1 outlines the wide range of FSA material that is to be regarded as 'guidance' in this context. Industry guidance also has a role in enabling firms to determine how best to meet FSA expectations under principles-based regulation: ibid.

[90] Hopper and Stainsby, 'Principles-based Regulation', (note 23, above).

[91] Black, Hopper and Band, 'Making a Success', (note 7, above).

[92] Conceicao, 'The FSA's Approach', (note 44, above).

[93] J. Tiner, 'Principles-based Regulation: The EU Context'. Speech delivered at APCIMS Annual Conference Hotel Arts, Barcelona, 13 October 2006. Text available at www.fsa.gov.uk/pages/Library/Communication/Speeches/2006/1013_jt.shtml.

harmonize the supervisory powers available to national authorities, some differences remain and that, furthermore, a significant degree of continuing disparity is found in how the authorities actually exercise their powers,[94] with enforcement of market abuse singled out as an area where there are particularly noticeable differences between Member States.[95] However, pressure is undoubtedly building for greater consistency in pan-European oversight and enforcement of EC laws[96] and this puts in doubt the extent to which the FSA can maintain its distinctive, risk-based, stance.

VIII. Conclusion

A recent paper exploring the possible links between competitiveness and enforcement intensity refers to the FSA's 'relative distaste for enforcement'.[97] Coffee, the paper's author, is not the first to ponder the low level of formal enforcement in the UK in relation to insider dealing and other forms of market misconduct. Indeed, quite independently of the Coffee article, the FSA itself has recognized the need to make a greater inroad into this difficult area and is employing a number of compliance-promoting and enforcement strategies with this aim in mind. It has also invested significantly in upgrading its fraud-detection system (Surveillance and Automated Business Reporting Engine (Sabre)), which uses complex software with a view to monitoring transactions and detecting insider trading and other market abuses as they occur.

The FSA's first successful prosecution for insider dealing is likely to have a strong symbolic value. Yet, whilst it is clearly desirable for the FSA to be a credible prosecuting body (and it should be equipped with all of the powers that investigating and prosecuting bodies need to operate effectively), there are many good reasons why criminal sanctions should play only a limited role in the UK's overall risk-based, compliance-promoting strategy. The part played by principles-based enforcement may prove to be more controversial. Whether principles-based enforcement will enable the FSA to take effectively tough action and, if it does,

[94] CESR, *An evaluation of equivalence of supervisory powers in the EU under the Market Abuse Directive and the Prospectus Directive A report to the Financial Services Committee (FSC)*, (CESR Ref: 07–334), para. 9.

[95] ESME Report, *Market Abuse EU Legal Framework and its Implementation by Member States: A First Evaluation*, (2007), 19.

[96] N. Moloney, *EC Securities Regulation,* 2nd edn (OUP, 2008) ch 12.

[97] Coffee, 'Law and the Market', (note 20, above), 311.

how this will be balanced against the need for fairness and proportionality are key issues for which responses will need to be hammered out on the anvil of practical experience. Managing the tension between distinctive features of the British approach and the strong forces now pushing in favour of greater consistency in pan-European oversight and enforcement of EC laws will also be one of the main challenges that lies ahead.

25

The Committee of European Securities Regulators and level 3 of the Lamfalussy Process

NIAMH MOLONEY

Professor Wymeersch's long and distinguished career, and his remarkable influence on EU securities regulation, is well-reflected in his Chairmanship of the Committee of European Securities Regulators (CESR). CESR can now be argued to be one of the (if not the) dominant influences on the recent and explosive development of EU securities regulation. This chapter seeks to assess the nature of CESR's activities at level 3 of the Lamfalussy process and, in particular, whether the burgeoning reach of its influence poses accountability and legitimacy risks or whether CESR has the potential to construct a discrete accountability model which supports its rapidly developing range of activities.

I. Introduction

It is a truisim to state that the Financial Services Action Plan (FSAP) period has wrought massive regulatory, institutional and supervisory change on EC securities markets. One of the main drivers for change has been the Lamfalussy process for delegated law-making.[1] As is well known, under the Lamfalussy process, the Commission adopts 'level 2' rules, which are frequently, although not always, detailed and technical, based on mandates in the related 'level 1' measure (either a directive or a regulation) which is adopted under the Treaty-based inter-institutional procedures. The Commission is advised by the Committee of European Securities Regulators (CESR, composed of national regulators) and supervised by the European Securities Committee (ESC, composed of Member State representatives). Level 3 of the Lamfalussy process concerns convergence and consistency in the application of level 1 and 2 rules. Level 4 concerns enforcement. The Lamfalussy process

---

[1] Final Report of the Committee of Wise Men on the Regulation of European Securities Markets (2001).

has supported an exponential increase in the content of EC securities regulation over the FSAP period – whether the quality of the regulatory regime has increased equally dramatically is less clear.[2] But it is clear that the Lamfalussy process has brought an actor of central importance to the policy stage in the shape of CESR. This chapter addresses CESR and its burgeoning influence on EU securities regulation which raises significant accountability and legitimacy questions.

CESR's activities at level 2 have, temporarily, come to a close. The FSAP stage of the level 2 process is now complete with CESR noting its move from level 2 advisory activities to level 3 supervisory convergence in its June 2006 annual report.[3] A vast range of level 2 rules have been adopted under all of the key measures including the Markets in Financial Instruments Directive (MiFID),[4] the Market Abuse Directive,[5] the Transparency Directive,[6] the Prospectus Directive[7] and the pre-FSAP 1985 UCITS Directive.[8] The evidence which has recently emerged on the CESR/Commission/ESC dynamic during the adoption of the first generation of level 2 rules (during the FSAP period) suggests that CESR's advice is heavily influential on the shape of the rules ultimately adopted by the Commission. But the constitutional controls on level 2 in terms of Commission, ESC and Parliament oversight of CESR's advice and the location of rule-making power in the Commission, appear reasonably robust. [9] The evidence also suggests that CESR is acutely aware of the

---

[2] For a critique of the effectiveness of the capital-raising rules see E.V. Ferran, *Building an EU Securities Market* (Cambridge University Press, 2004).

[3] CESR, *Annual Report* (2005), 5. All CESR references are available on www.cesr-eu.org.

[4] Commission Directive 2006/73/EC [2006] OJ L241/26 and Commission Regulation (EC) No 1287/2006 [2006] OJ L241/1.

[5] Commission Definitions and Disclosure Obligations Directive 2003/124/EC [2003] OJ L339/70, Commission Investment Recommendations Directive 2003/125/EC [2003] OJ L339/73, and Commission Regulation (EC) No 2273/2003 on Buybacks and Stabilisation [2003] OJ L336/33.

[6] Commission Directive 2007/14/EC [2007] OJ L69/27.

[7] 2004 Prospectus Regulation (EC) No 809/2004 [2004] OJ L149/1. It sets out the detailed information which must be included in public offer prospectuses. It has been amended to reflect the decision to postpone the equivalence determination with respect to third country accounting systems (Commission Regulation (EC) No 1787/2006 [2006] OJ L337/17). A second revision addresses disclosure by issuers with complex financial histories (Commission Regulation (EC) No 211/2007 [2007] OJ L61/24).

[8] In 2007 the Commission adopted level 2 rules concerning the definition of the 'eligible assets' in which a UCITS fund can invest under the UCITS III regime for UCITS investment. Commission Directive 2007/16/EC [2007] OJ L79/11.

[9] For discussion see N. Moloney, *EC Securities Regulation*, 2nd edn (Oxford University Press, 2008), Ch. XIII. The Commission has, e.g., reinforced the importance

constitutional limitations of its position as an advisory body at level 2 and is not prepared to act outside the level 1 mandates, even where there is strong market support for level 2 action on a particular issue.[10]

But the level 2 controls do not apply at level 3 where, in the troublesome sphere of supervisory convergence, CESR is increasingly exercising direct influence over the financial markets. Level 3, which is strongly associated with supervisory convergence, is designed to support convergence and consistency in the implementation and application of level 1 and level 2 rules. It was initially envisaged by the Lamfalussy Report as producing guidelines on implementation, developing recommendations and standards on issues not covered by EU law (a controversial element which has not been pursued by CESR), and defining best practice. It was characterized by CESR in its 2004 Level 3 Report as having three strands: coordinated implementation of EU law; regulatory convergence; and supervisory convergence.[11] As the FSAP shifts from regulation to operation, level 3 is now commanding attention at the highest political and institutional levels as the Community's response to the challenges raised by supervision of the post-FSAP marketplace and it was at the centre of the recently concluded 2007 Lamfalussy review.

The recent dramatic evolution of the level 3/supervisory convergence aspect of CESR's activities is perhaps best described as organic. Through its level 3 activities, CESR has acquired a degree of influence over the financial markets which is remarkable given its establishment in 2001 and given the resource commitment the level 2 advice process

---

of the level 1 delegation on occasion. This was the case with its rejection of CESR's advice that the MiFID level 2 regime address the content of the investment firm/investor contract on the grounds that, in addition to the national sensitivities and risk of disruption to national contract-systems, the level 1 delegation did not support such measures. It also rejected CESR's advice in relation to the level 2 market-abuse regime that investment recommendations by journalists be subject to a specific regime given the need to respect the difficult level 1 compromise achieved on this issue with the European Parliament. The market-abuse regime also saw the Commission reject CESR's advice that credit-rating agencies become subject to the investment research rules of the market abuse regime.

[10] A notable example relates to the MiFID level 2 consultation on the suitability regime and CESR's refusal to treat derivatives as 'non-complex' products and as within the 'suitability-free' execution-only regime, given the exclusion of derivatives at level 1, in the face of strong market demands for their inclusion. Similarly, CESR refused to give advice on expansion of the Market Abuse Directive Art 8 stabilization and buy-back regime beyond its level 1 limits.

[11] CESR, *The Role of CESR at 'Level 3' Under the Lamfalussy* Process (2004), CESR/04–104b.

demanded. This has occurred through a range of quasi-regulatory\ supervisory mechanisms, discussed in the following sections, none of which are specified in CESR's founding Decision.[12]

Issuer disclosure provides a good example of CESR's burgeoning influence. CESR's role has developed from providing level 2 advice on the Prospectus and Transparency Directives, to establishing own-initiative level 3 guidance on the prospectus regime,[13] to developing an innovative Q and A device to support supervisory convergence, [14] to quasi-enforcement activity with respect to supporting the implementation of IFRS and consistency in the enforcement of IFRS by national authorities,[15] to liaising with the SEC on US GAAP/IFRS reconciliation,[16] to driving operational innovation and supporting market initiatives with respect to the electronic network of Officially Appointed Mechanisms (with respect

[12] Commission Decision 2001/527/EC OJ [2001] L191/43.

[13] CESR/05–054b.

[14] CESR/07–852. The Q and A is regularly updated (three times over the course of 2007). It is designed to 'provide market participants with responses in a quick and efficient manner to 'everyday' questions which are commonly posed to the CESR secretariat or CESR members', CESR/05–054b.,1.

[15] See e.g., CESR's recommendations on the adoption of Alternative Performance Measures (CESR/05–178b) and its exhortation that issuers provide clear disclosure on their use of options in the reporting regime (CESR/05–758). CESR also produced a road map for the IFRS transition (CESR/03–323e) and has continued to exhort supervisory authorities to remain vigilant in ensuring compliance with the new regime (CESR/07–121b). Through CESR-Fin, which promotes convergence in the application of IAS/IFRS and has a strongly operational orientation, CESR produces non-binding standards for the enforcement of IAS/IFRS at national level and supports coordinated enforcement by providing a forum within which dialogue and cooperation can occur. In 2003, for example, it recommended basic principles for the robust and consistent enforcement of IAS/IFRS by the Member States (Enforcement Standards on Financial Information in Europe). This was followed in 2004 by a standard on coordination of national approaches to enforcement (Co-ordination of Enforcement Activities) which led to a framework for coordinating enforcement mechanisms and, in particular, to the European Enforcers Co-ordination Sessions. The Sessions, which support discussion of enforcement decisions and emerging issues, are designed to support the development of a high level of convergence on enforcement practices. In a key enforcement initiative, CESR has also established a database which includes national enforcement decisions on IAS/IFRS application in order to support supervisory convergence on the application and enforcement of the standards and consistency in the use of the standards on the marketplace.

[16] CESR/06–434. The work programme was established to promote the development of high-quality accounting standards, the high quality and consistent application of IFRS worldwide, consideration of international counterparts' positions regarding application and enforcement, and the avoidance of conflicting regulatory decisions on the application of IFRS and US GAAP. Consistent application of IFRS is a central concern of the work programme which includes discussion by the SEC and CESR of issuer-specific matters in an attempt to avoid diverging interpretations.

to issuer disclosure)[17] and, potentially, providing a supervisory capacity with respect to the electronic network.[18] All of this occurred without any substantive change to CESR's founding Decision and Charter.[19] It might appear to be but one step from here to prospectus-approval capacity – a role which CESR had earlier identified in the Himalaya Report.[20] But it is also clear that CESR is acutely sensitive to the accountability and legitimacy risks and is developing a multi-faceted response (discussed later in this chapter) which, the 2007 Lamfalussy Review suggests, enjoys institutional and political support.

II. Range of activities at level 3

A. Agenda-setting and quasi-regulatory activity

CESR's range of activities at level 3 is becoming formidable and its rhetoric, of considerable symbolic importance,[21] is increasingly that of an established regulator/supervisor. Its 2005 Annual Report noted that 2006 would 'witness CESR's metamorphosis from being primarily a regulatory advisory body to becoming a body which is well on its way to becoming an operational network of supervisors.'[22] The 2006 Annual Report adopted a similar tone and asserted that CESR 'was entering a new phase'.[23] Its 2007 Work Programme was similarly ambitious and

---

[17] The Commission described CESR as pivotal to the development of the network during ESC discussions on the Recommendation which governs the electronic network (Commission Recommendation 2007/657/EC on the electronic network of officially appointed mechanisms for the central storage of information referred to in the Transparency Directive [2007] OJ L267/16): ESC Minutes 13 September 2007. CESR's generally pragmatic and market-facing advice on the design of the network (CESR/06–292), which followed an earlier orientations document (CESR/05–150b), was reflected in the Recommendation.

[18] The Commission suggested in the Recommendation that the network could be supervised by a college of supervisors (either CESR or a specially constituted body) but rejected this solution as being outside the scope of the level 2 powers granted to the Commission under the Transparency Directive with respect to the storage of regulated information.

[19] CESR 06/289c.

[20] CESR, *Preliminary Progress Report, Which Supervisory Tools for the EU Securities Market? An Analytical Paper by CESR* (2004), CESR 04–333f.

[21] This point has been well made by Professor Langevoort in connection with the US SEC. See e.g., D. Langevoort, 'Structuring Securities Regulation in the European Union: Lessons from the US Experience' in G. Ferrarini and E. Wymeersch (eds.), *Investor Protection in Europe. Corporate Law Making, the MiFID and Beyond* (Oxford University Press, 2006), 485.

[22] CESR, *Annual Report* (2005), Foreword by the Chairman, 5

[23] CESR, *Annual Report* (2006), Foreword by the Chairman, 3.

was sharply directed towards level 3 activities, with CESR noting the 'marked shift in focus' towards operational activities.[24]

The range of guidelines adopted at level 3 (adopted without a formal mandate) stands out as a striking example of the reach of CESR's influence. They now cover the UCITS regime with respect to eligible assets[25] and the transition to the UCITS III regime[26], the prospectus regime[27], and, in some detail, the market abuse regime.[28] The MiFID regime is strongly characterized by amplification at level 3 and includes guidelines on the MiFID passport[29], on inducements[30], on best execution[31], and on the MiFID record-keeping regime.[32] CESR has also produced guidance on MiFID's transaction-reporting regime.[33] Standards have been adopted in conjunction with the European System of Central Banks with respect to clearing and settlement,[34] although these have proved particularly troublesome, generated considerable tensions with the Parliament, and have yet to be formally adopted. Standards have also been adopted with respect to financial reporting,[35] in support of the enforcement of the IFRS reporting regime.[36]

These guidelines have in common their considerable level of detail, extensive consultation, market support (for the most part), as well as a (generally) practical, market-facing, and operational orientation which points to CESR's ability to build consensus and develop pragmatic solutions to problems generated by the regulatory regime.[37] But, and aside from concerns as to their effectiveness (given their tendency to increase the opacity of the regime and their non-binding status), the guidelines also share considerable accountability and legitimacy risks, not least given CESR's tendency to use level 3 to achieve solutions which were subsequently either rejected, or regarded as not appropriate for level 2.[38] While guidance is formally

---

[24] CESR, *2007 Work Programme for the Committee of European Securities Regulators* (2006), CESR 06–627, 2.

[25] CESR/07–44.　　[26] CESR/04–434b.　　[27] CESR/05–054b.

[28] CESR/04–505b and CESR/06–562b.

[29] CESR/07–337 and CESR/07/337b.

[30] CESR/07–228b.　　[31] CESR/07–320.　　[32] CESR/06–552c.

[33] CESR/07–301.　　[34] CESR/04–561.

[35] CESR/03–073 and CESR/03–317B.

[36] See note 15, above.

[37] As was the case, e.g. with respect to its resolution of double reporting by branches under MiFID's transaction reporting regime under CESR's Branch Protocol (CESR/07/672).

[38] There are elements of this in CESR's level 3 guidance on the UCITS III eligible assets regime e.g., and in its 2007 level 3 guidance on the determination of inside information under the market abuse regime. In the latter, CESR included guidance on the definition of inside information in the form of examples of how inside information might arise;

non-binding, regulatory guidance has traditionally been regarded by the market as tantamount to regulatory fiat. CESR has also recently become more confident in its assertions as to the potential effects of level 3 and in seizing the initiative as to the appropriate characterization of level 3, which remains elusive.[39] It has suggested, in the context of the MiFID Q and A project, that while level 3 is not legally binding its 'legal effects' could include: being used by courts and tribunals in interpreting level 1 and 2 measures; being 'of relevance' in enforcement action taken by a competent authority; and 'creating relevant considerations and legitimate expectations', particularly with respect to the predictability of actions taken by competent authorities.[40] Given that the MiFID level 3 matrix includes best execution Q and A guidance by CESR to the effect that connection by an investment firm to one execution venue might meet the best execution obligation, which seems, optically at least – firms remain subject to competitive pressures – to subvert the concentration-abolition principle on which MiFID is based, this is not an assertion to be taken lightly. Similarly, it has suggested that its level 3 guidance on the transparency regime might provide a safe-harbour for market participants.[41] While the ambitious reach of CESR's characterization of its guidance may represent a degree of wishful thinking by CESR, it is also unlikely that CESR's pronouncements, as authoritative statements from Europe's regulators, will be ignored in judicial and enforcement proceedings.

But the guidance is generally rooted in the level 1 and 2 regime (although this was not the case with the ill-fated clearing and settlement initiative), is typically stated not to conflict with or subvert level 1 and 2 rules, and level 2 discussions have seen the Commission and ESC negotiations move particular standards to level 3, as was the case with the UCITS III regime. CESR's efforts to bolster the legitimacy of the guidelines are also clear, as discussed later in this chapter. A more tentative approach to the adoption of guidance also appears to be emerging. CESR's July 2007 Call for Evidence on the Transparency Directive level 3 regime suggested some reluctance to engage in an extensive

these are closely based on the additional guidance provided by CESR in its earlier level 2 advice and which was not adopted at level 2.

[39] See e.g., City of London Group, *Level 3 of the Lamfalussy Process. Submission to the Inter-Institutional Monitoring Group By a Group in the City of London* (2007), www.cityoflondon.gov.uk.

[40] CESR/07–704c, 3.

[41] CESR/07–043.

programme,[42] while its post-consultation Feedback Statement (February 2008) was similarly restrained, reflecting some market support for no action at level 3 given the premature state of the regime.[43]

Perhaps in a reflection of the accountability risks of its guidance, as well as CESR's growing sophistication in developing level 3 tools, it has also embraced softer forms of intervention. The prospectus regime, for example, has seen the adoption of a regularly updated and well-received Q and A document which allows CESR to respond rapidly to market and supervisory concerns.[44] It does not require a consensus CESR position and identifies dissenting opinions – although, in a reflection of CESR's potential to build supervisory convergence, these are reducing. A FAQ document has also been used to explain the Accepted Market Practice regime which is of central importance with respect to the determination of market manipulation under the market abuse regime.[45] The development of a MiFID Q and A is a priority for CESR's MiFID level 3 agenda.[46] But while FAQ initiatives carry considerable benefits in terms of speed and practicality, they also, in common with level 3 guidance more generally, have the potential to complicate further the already dense regulatory environment and obscure the distinction between binding and non-binding measures, increasing legitimacy and accountability risks.

CESR's influence over regulatory policy extends beyond level 3 guidance and level 2 advice. It has been closely involved in the preparation of the reviews and reports required of the Commission with respect to controversial MiFID provisions under MiFID Article 65 and which will frame future revisions to MiFID. In particular, it has been a significant actor in the sensitive discussions on whether MiFID's transparency regime should be extended to the debt markets. Although CESR has adopted a measured approach,[47] in principle the risks attached to CESR's legitimacy are added to the momentum risks which already attach to Article 65.

Although the Commission has shown some signs of avoiding over-reliance on CESR, perhaps in an attempt to limit its influence, it has also turned to CESR to develop new policy solutions, notably with respect to the reforms to the UCITS summary prospectus in which CESR is playing a key role in developing and, importantly, market testing disclosure formats. Most notably, perhaps, the turmoil in world credit markets in

---

[42] CESR/07/487.   [43] CESR/08–066.   [44] CESR/07–852.   [45] CESR/05–365.
[46] CESR/07–704c, 2.   [47] CESR/07–284b.

2007 saw the Commission turn to CESR for policy advice, particularly with respect to the rating by credit rating agencies of structured products.[48] While this development augurs well for the quality of new policy design post-FSAP, it also deepens CESR's influence and the legitimacy risks it poses.

B. Agenda-setting and policy activities

In the level 3 policy sphere, CESR is, notwithstanding the lack of a specific mandate, fast-developing a distinct policy towards the retail investor, including outreach activities to encourage investor involvement in law-making and investor education.[49] This development sees CESR acting independently as quasi-policy-maker and supporting the nascent retail investor interest. It also points to its ambitions in the policy sphere and its ability to take ownership over a high-profile policy area which carries considerable potential for institutional and political influence.

CESR has also been quick to exploit the blurred boundaries between securities market regulation and corporate governance, perhaps in a reflection of the current political high profile of corporate governance reform. It has drawn cross-border takeovers, which carry considerable potential for political sensitivity, into its ambit through its, thus far, relatively benign discussions on the practical operation of the takeover regime.[50] Auditors have also come within its ambit, with CESR's own-initiative activities including a survey of its members with respect to the relationship between the auditor and the public which asked, provocatively, whether direct communications between auditors and the public should be enhanced.[51]

Less controversially, CESR has also developed a monitoring role with respect to EC financial markets more generally. Its 2006 Report contains

---

[48] Commissioner McCreevy requested that CESR examine the rating of structured-finance products as a 'matter of urgency': letter from Commissioner McCreevy to CESR (11 September 2007), attached to CESR's 12 September 2007 Press Release on the Commission's Additional Request to Review the Role of Credit Rating Agencies, CESR/07–608.

[49] CESR's 2007 Work Programme, e.g., highlighted 'engaging retail investors more effectively' and 'investor information' as specific priorities: CESR/06–627. Notable initiatives include CESR's MiFID guide for retail investors: CESR, *A Consumer's Guide to MiFID. Investing in Financial Products* (2008).

[50] CESR, *2007 Interim Report on the Activities of CESR* (2008), CESR/07–671, 27.

[51] CESR, *2007 Interim Report on the Activities of CESR* (2008), CESR/07–671, 14.

an extensive discussion of overall market trends and risks.[52] While this might appear to be among the less glamorous and contentious of its level 3 activities, it nonetheless cements CESR's position as an authoritative voice on financial market policy.

Chief among its general policy initiatives, however, are those in support of supervisory convergence and, in particular, the development of a European 'supervisory culture'. CESR has been charged with reporting on progress on supervisory convergence to the Council's Financial Services Committee, which places it at the heart of the efforts to support convergence. More mundane practical CESR initiatives, but which should reap considerable convergence benefits, include the development of staff exchange-programmes between CESR members and the development of a joint-training programme, which the 3L3 committees are developing under their Joint Steering Committee on Training.[53]

C. Monitoring and quasi-enforcement

CESR's monitoring activities are directed towards its members, in support of supervisory convergence, but they are also, and more controversially, market-facing.

In one of its most notable institutional contributions to supervisory convergence, CESR's Peer Review Panel, established in 2003 but recommended by the Lamfalussy Report, reviews the implementation by CESR members of CESR guidelines and standards and, where requested by the Commission, of Community rules. The Panel, which represents an innovative, self-disciplining technique for monitoring CESR members, has the potential to drive strong convergence, although only as long as peer pressure and reputational dynamics are effective.

But there is also a more troublesome market-facing dimension to CESR's quasi-enforcement activities. Notably, it reviews compliance by credit rating agencies with the 2004 IOSCO Code of Conduct for Rating Agencies. This innovative joint venture between CESR and the industry, based on a voluntary agreement, gives CESR the colour of a European regulatory and supervisory agency. Its first report in January 2007 included, for example, a warning to the industry concerning the lack of progress in the separation of rating business from other business lines in order to manage conflicts of interests.[54] CESR also carries out a more

---

[52] CESR, *Annual Report* (2006), 10–19.   [53] CESR, *Annual Report* (2006), 26.
[54] CESR/06–545.

indirect and lighter monitoring role, in conjunction with other actors, with respect to the Code of Conduct on Clearing and Settlement through the Code's Monitoring Group.

D. Supporting supervision, enforcement action, and institutional innovation

CESR's supervisory-convergence activities are supported by its rapidly developing operational structures which support supervision and the coordination of national enforcement strategies. The MiFID regime, for example, is notable for the practical initiatives adopted by CESR to support passport notifications and the supervision of branches.

With respect to enforcement, the market abuse regime is notable for the operational structures which have been developed by CESR-Pol, a permanent operational group within CESR which addresses the surveillance of securities markets and cooperation concerning enforcement and information exchange. Key operational developments include the establishment of the Urgent Issues Group and the Surveillance and Intelligence Group and the construction of an enforcement database. Operational innovation is also evident in the financial reporting sphere where CESR-FIN, a permanent operational group which coordinates enforcement of IFRS by CESR members, has established the European Enforcers' Co-ordination Sessions as well as a database on enforcement decisions. In a significant move towards the promotion of stronger supervisory convergence, CESR has also developed a mediation mechanism to support supervisory convergence and resolve supervisory disputes between national authorities.[55] Particular care appears to have been taken here to respect institutional sensitivities. A concern not to subvert institutional competences, particularly with respect to the interpretation of rules, can be seen in the development of the mechanism.[56]

E. Operational initiatives: supporting trading transparency and issuer disclosure

One of the most striking features of post-FSAP securities regulation has been the extent to which EC securities regulation has begun, slowly, to encompass operational measures in support of regulatory objectives. While the operational regime is, as yet, embryonic, CESR has

---

[55] CESR/06–286b.
[56] CESR, *Annual Report* (2005), 48–9 and CESR, *Annual Report* (2006), 53–4.

considerable potential to provide an operational capacity which supports the post-FSAP regulatory regime and to provide a focal point for the articulation of industry and regulatory interests.

In particular, CESR has emerged as a key player in the development of the electronic network of Officially Appointed Mechanisms, which is designed to consolidate the distribution of ongoing issuer disclosure. CESR has also supported the development of a pan-EC dissemination system for trading transparency disclosures (under MiFID) by adopting level 3 guidelines which govern dissemination channels and, significantly, are designed to support the consolidation of information flows. Both initiatives are characterized by their hybrid nature: high-level principles are designed to support market-led innovation. While the success of this approach remains to be seen, it represents an important sea-change in the regulatory orientation of EC securities regulation.

MiFID's transparency and transaction reporting regime has also seen considerable operational innovation led by CESR-Tech. Notably, the TREM (the Transaction Reporting Exchange Mechanism) project, although problematic, has seen the construction of a system which allows CESR members to exchange reports and adopts particular format and coding standards for reports.[57] CESR also maintains a series of databases which support MiFID obligations, chief among them the Database on Shares Admitted to Trading on a Regulated Market,[58] which includes the important list of 'liquid shares' which are key to the application of MiFID's transparency regime.

F. A distinct supervisory capacity?

CESR's level 3 activities thus far have been confined to supporting supervisory convergence within the network of home and host supervisors which police EC securities regulation. The scale of these activities alone gives some pause. But, and leaving on one side the debate as to the appropriateness of a Euro-SEC, there have been some straws in the wind which, given CESR's tendency to acquire influence organically, and its broadly

---

[57] CESR/07–739 and CESR/07–627b. TREM is used to exchange reports between CESR members but the project also acts as a platform for trialling technical issues concerning national transaction reporting, particularly with respect to the technical codes used by firms. For a discussion see CESR, *Annual Report* (2006), 46.

[58] CESR/07–718. CESR has also published a guide on how the database can be used (CESR/07–370b).

positive relationship with the market, might, if only tentatively, point to a more formal, limited supervisory capacity were political conditions to change.

The development of the issuer-disclosure dissemination regime, for example, saw some suggestions that CESR might act as the supervisor of the new electronic network, although the Commission ultimately resiled from this approach in favour of a 'workable solution' based on network supervision. CESR initially harboured far-reaching ambitions in this regard. Although the Himalaya Report rejected the central supervisor model, it initially floated whether CESR should acquire a capacity for 'EC decision making', including with respect to pre-clearance of innovative products and approval of, for example, standardized UCITS and the supervision of trans-European infrastructures.[59] More recently, however, a sharper awareness of the legitimacy risks to its position, and perhaps, a realization of the possibilities afforded through level 3, appears to have reduced its enthusiasm for the political maelstrom any such transfer of power would generate.[60]

G. Institutional and market links

CESR's influence and capacity to drive supervisory convergence is only likely to increase as cross-sector links strengthen, new advisory bodies are developed post-FSAP, and as the institutional structure which supports financial market policy development fragments, thereby increasing CESR's influence as the actor with policy links across all the major actors. It has, for example, observer status on the European Securities Markets Expert Group which advises the Commission on financial market policy. It has close links with the European Central Bank, as is clear from its clearing and settlement activities. It sits on the Monitoring Group which oversees market implementation of the novel Code of Conduct on clearing and settlement. The level 2 process has seen it develop close links with the Commission and the Parliament. Formal links have been made with its parallel 3L3 committees in the banking and insurance/pensions area through the 3L3 Joint Work Programme on issues of common concern, such as credit rating agencies, financial

---

[59] Himalaya Report 2004, 17.
[60] In its 2007 Securities Supervision Report CESR stated clearly that it was 'not advocating for the creation of an EU single regulator embedded within the Treaty': CESR, *A Proposed Evolution of Securities Supervision Beyond 2007* (2007), CESR/07–783, 6.

conglomerates and regulatory arbitrage in product regulation.[61] CESR is also developing considerable political influence and contacts. It increasingly acts as a high-level adviser to the Council by reporting to its Financial Services Committee on supervisory convergence and to the Financial Stability Table of the Council's Economic and Financial Committee on issues related to the overall stability of the EU financial system.[62]

Through its extensive consultation procedures, CESR has driven largely national, if vocal and well-resourced, market interests to adopt more sophisticated and networked pan-EC lobbying models.[63] It now has strong links to the markets which are only likely to intensify. This is all the more the case as it seems to be in the very early stages of developing a quasi-lobbying role for market interests under the level 3 prospectus regime, where CESR has suggested that market reaction to the Q and A could act as a driver for supervisory convergence.[64] Support from the market could also act as a bulwark against accountability charges,[65] although there are some indications of nervousness in some quarters as to the extent of CESR's reach, particularly with respect to its market abuse initiatives.[66] Tellingly, CESR engaged in an extensive consultation over 2007 on the industry's and stakeholders' assessment of CESR's activities from 2001–7.[67]

---

[61] See, e.g., CESE, CEBS, CEIOPS, *3L3 Medium Term Work Programme. Consultation Paper* (2007) (CESR/07–775).

[62] CESR's FST reports have covered market conditions as well as cross-sector reviews (with CEBS and CEIOPS) of the bond markets, financial conglomerates, regulatory arbitrage, and offshore financial centres (CESR, *Annual Report* (2006), 65, 74).

[63] See e.g. the London Investment Banking Association's (LIBA) construction of networks with other European trade associations in order to engage more effectively with CESR's MiFID consultations. LIBA, *Annual Report* (2005), Chairman's Statement.

[64] This is clear from the dissenting views of competent authorities on particular questions which were identified in the 2006 Q and A (along with the Commission's position in some cases). The 2007 Q and A, by contrast, did not contain any dissenting opinions in the new material included, suggesting that CESR's view that publication of the dissenting views would 'foster a wider debate among market participants which the CESR members with diverging views might find useful in considering their previous positions' was well-founded: CESR, *CESR's Report on the Supervisory Functioning of the Prospectus Directive and Regulation* (2007), CESR/07–225, 9.

[65] See e.g. market support for further CESR convergence activities under the prospectus regime: Supervisory Functioning of the Prospectus Report 2007, 3.

[66] See e.g. the response by APCIMS to CESR's 2006 consultation on what would become the 2007 level 3 guidance in which it expressed a wish that no further guidance be adopted and noted a general view to that effect. Available on www.cesr-eu.org.

[67] CESR/07–499.

Although the consumer interest remains lamentably and dangerously under-represented in financial market consultations, CESR is also building links to the nascent retail investor lobbying community through initiatives such as its MiFID Consumer Day, its commitment to preparing consumer-friendly versions of consultation papers, and its recent initiatives to develop investor governance and education.

CESR's growing stature and influence also reflects deepening transatlantic links. Although high level and increasingly successful political contacts between the Commission and the SEC occur through the US–EU Financial Markets Regulatory Dialogue,[68] CESR is emerging as the main point of contact for regular, operational SEC negotiations and has entered into an agreement with the SEC on cooperation and collaboration on market risks and regulatory policy.[69] It has also entered into a formal agreement with the SEC on the enforcement of IFRS application, which placed it close to the highly sensitive but ultimately successful EU/US negotiations on IFRS/US GAAP reconciliation. Its links with IOSCO are also deepening, as its January 2007 report on credit rating agencies makes clear. CESR's ambitions in this sphere are considerable. It regards itself as increasingly the 'advocate of common interests' of CESR members internationally and has called for a more direct role in international negotiations, in order to limit supervisory competition with respect to third country market access in particular. Notably, it has called for a role in the developing negotiations with the SEC on the mutual recognition of supervisory regimes – one of the most significant recent developments in international securities regulation – and suggested that it play a more direct role in the US–EU Financial Markets Regulatory Dialogue.[70]

CESR therefore sits at the centre of an increasingly complex institutional web and is developing strong links to market and consumer interests. It looks set to have a unique institutional and market perspective and influence on policy formation.

---

[68] For a review of its current activities see Commission, *Single Market in Financial Services Progress Report 2006,* SEC (2007) 263, 7–9. The resolution in early 2007 of the dispute concerning the de-listing of EU issuers from US exchanges in the wake of Sarbanes-Oxley, as well as the November 2007 decision by the SEC to lift the US GAAP reconciliation requirement for accounts prepared in accordance with IFRS, count as major successes of the Dialogue.

[69] CESR, *Annual Report* (2006), 70.   [70] CESR, *Securities Supervision Report* (2007), 6.

III. Accountability and legitimacy risks

All this has developed organically from the original 2001 Commission Decision which established CESR as part of the Lamfalussy process and as an independent advisory group on securities, to advise the Commission, either on the Commission's initiative or on its own initiative, in particular with respect to level 2 measures (Article 2). The Decision does not refer directly to supervisory convergence activities, although they are covered in CESR's Charter.[71] The Lamfalussy Report simply recommended that level 3 produce guidelines on implementation, develop recommendations and standards on issues not covered by EU law, and define best practice. CESR has deepened and widened this initial characterization of level 3 through its 2004 Level 3 Report and the Himalaya Report and, more tellingly, by its recent practice. Although both 2004 Level 3 reports were, for the most part, accepted by the institutions,[72] recent practice suggests that CESR's influence now has an organic and dynamic character. But there is no formal legal basis for CESR's activities.

CESR's formal accountability is minimal.[73] It is not formally accountable to the Member States or the EU institutions and sits somewhat adrift in the institutional structure. It declares itself as independent[74] and the foundation Decision establishing CESR simply required CESR to present an annual report to the Commission (Article 6) and to maintain close operational links with the Commission and the ESC (Article 4).

---

[71] Art. 4 provides that CESR is to 'foster and review' common and uniform day-to-day implementation and application of Community legislation, issuing guidelines, recommendations and standards to be adopted by CESR members in their regulatory practices on a voluntary basis (Art. 4.3). It also provides for the establishment of the Review Panel. Level 3 is also reflected in Art. 4.4 which provides that CESR is to develop effective operational network mechanisms to enhance day-to-day consistent supervision and enforcement of the single market for financial services.

[72] See e.g.: Commission, *The Application of the Lamfalussy Process to EU Securities Market Legislation* (2004), 10; European Parliament, *Van den Burg Resolution on the Current State of Integration of EU Financial Markets* (2005), T6–0153/2005 (based on the Economic and Monetary Affairs Committee, *Van den Burg Report* (2005) (A6–0087/2005)), B.12; and ESC Minutes 15 December 2004, albeit that all, presciently, expressed reservations as to accountability.

[73] For a recent exploration of accountability in the context of the comitology process (which CESR engages in at an early stage through its level 2 advice to the Commission) see D. Curtin, 'Holding (Quasi-) Autonomous EU Administrative Actors to Public Account', *European Law Journal,* 13 (2007), 523.

[74] CESR's Annual Report for 2004 describes CESR as 'an independent Committee of European Securities Regulators': CESR, *Annual Report* (2004), 66.

Very little is known as to the dynamics of CESR decision-making at level 2. This difficulty persists at level 3 (and with respect to the adoption of CESR guidance in particular) where consensus (unanimity minus one or two)[75] dominates. This opacity as to its regulatory philosophy and decision-making dynamics therefore obscures the interests and traditions which inform the quasi-regulatory and supervisory choices it makes for the integrated financial market. The stakes are high as the constitutional controls exerted by the level 2 process and Commission/ESC/Parliament oversight are removed and given the rate at which CESR has acquired influence over the markets.

The institutions have, however, become more alert to the growing influence of CESR,[76] with concern that CESR may operate in a 'grey zone where political accountability is unclear'.[77] The European Parliament was the most vocal in the initial calls for greater CESR accountability. In the 2005 Van den Burg Resolution, and in order 'to guarantee democratic accountability', it called for CESR (and CEBS and CEIOPS) to report semi-annually to the Parliament.[78] Somewhat more aggressively, Parliament attached the utmost importance to 'guaranteeing the political accountability of the supervisory system' and noted 'gaps in parliamentary scrutiny and democratic control particularly with respect to work undertaken at level 3'. It urged all 3L3 committees 'to pay the utmost attention to providing a sound legal basis for their actions, avoiding dealing with political questions and preventing prejudice to upcoming Community law'.[79] Given the relatively limited reach of level 3 in 2005, Parliament's hostile reaction can be linked to its severe criticism in 2005 of the CESR-ESCB Standards on Clearing and Settlement which launched an inter-institutional fracas, given the attempt to embue the Standards, which do not derive from a level 1 or level 2 measure, with a quasi-binding quality, and which saw the Parliament deliver a stinging rebuke to CESR as to the need for its actions to have a legal base and for stronger accountability. [80]

---

[75] CESR, *Securities Supervision Report* (2007), 4.
[76] Prior to the explosion in level 3 activities, the reaction was more sanguine. The Council's Economic and Financial Committee reported in 2002 that accountability mechanisms employed by CESR (in the form of reporting obligations and consultation procedures) were adequate: EFC, *Report on Financial Regulation Supervision, and Stability* (2002), 19
[77] As described by certain (unidentified) ESC delegations: ESC Minutes 15 December 2004.
[78] Van den Burg Resolution 2005, B.14.   [79] Van den Burg Resolution 2005, B.19.
[80] *European Parliament, Resolution on Clearing and Settlement in the EU* (2005), P6_TA(2005)0301, paras 18–22.

The Commission also, albeit less vocally, has raised accountability concerns, as has the European Central Bank.[81] In its 2004 Report on the Lamfalussy Process, for example, the Commission expressly addressed level 3 accountability risks and called for a clearer articulation of the role of level 3, particularly with respect to protecting the institutional prerogatives of the Council, Parliament and Commission.[82]

IV. Constructing an accountability model

A. Institutional links

But CESR's political antennae appear to be sensitive. It clearly feels the need to develop a model for its accountability and legitimacy, perhaps in order to avoid the imposition of an unattractive model. Recent Annual Reports, for example, contain repeated references to CESR's efforts to develop accountability structures.[83]

CESR initially responded by 'establish[ing] clearer accountability links with Council Committees and with the European Parliament' over 2005. A new accountability framework with the Parliament was formalized in September 2005 which is, in essence, based on frequent reporting by CESR to the Parliament. Parliamentary relations are a recurring theme of CESR's annual and interim reports.[84] Annual and half-yearly reports are addressed to the Commission, as required in CESR's founding Decision, but also to the Parliament and the Council. CESR has also developed close links with Council's Financial Services Committee through its supervisory convergence reports. CESR regards these reports as strengthening its accountability,[85] although they might be

---

[81] European Central Bank, *Review of the Application of the Lamfalussy Framework to EU Securities Market Legislation* (2005), 7–8.

[82] Commission Lamfalussy Process Report 2004, 4. Writing in 2005 Internal Market Director General Schaub warned that level 3 could not prejudice the political process: A. Schaub, 'The Lamfalussy Process Four Years On', *Journal of Financial Regulation and Compliance,* 13 (2005), 110–16.

[83] The 2005 Annual Report contains a section on accountability and reporting to the EU institutions (CESR, *Annual Report* (2005), 72–3, while accountability is prominent in the Chairman's statement (at 5). The 2006 Report contains extensive discussion of CESR's reports to the European Parliament: CESR, *Annual Report* (2006), 75.

[84] The 2007 Interim Report e.g. notes the concern of CESR's Chairman to build on the good relationship established with the European Parliament: CESR, *Interim Report* (2007), 30.

[85] See e.g. CESR, *First Progress Report on Supervisory Convergence in the Field of Securities Markets for the Financial Services Committee* (2005), CESR/05–202, 2.

better regarded as opportunities for CESR to extend its political influence: CESR has publicly characterized the 2006 ECOFIN conclusions on supervisory convergence[86] as 'explicit support for the work of CESR'.[87]

As discussed below with respect to MiFID, it also now appears to be anxious to engage the Commission more fully in its decision making and to capture, albeit informally, the legitimacy which may flow from the Commission's tacit approval, if not endorsement, of its activities. This approach may be wise. Recent evidence from the Commission's approach to the development of policy in new and sensitive areas such as bond market transparency, hedge funds and private equity, sees the Commission drawing on a wide range of market and institutional opinion and reducing the risks of over-reliance on CESR. The Commission's somewhat benign public statements on CESR's problematic accountability model (certainly by comparison with the Parliament's trenchant views) appear to have been counter-balanced by an institutional determination in practice not to yield too much power to CESR. In its initial strategy report on the highly-sensitive extension of MiFID's transparency regime beyond the equity markets,[88] the Commission's consultation strategy included advice from CESR but also from ESME, FIN-USE (on retail interests) and other expert groups. Although CESR has since become the first port of call for large-scale regulatory design questions (such as the UCITS disclosure review) and live policy challenges (with respect to the 'credit crunch'), the Commission now has a variety of expert groups as its disposal.

B. The MiFID example

Attempts to build an accountability model can also be traced in CESR's recent level 3 activities which represent a more careful attempt to address the legitimacy of its actions than earlier pronouncements.[89] Although

---

[86] 2726th ECOFIN Meeting, 5 May 2006, Press Release 8500/06.

[87] CESR, *Interim Report* (2006), 24.

[88] Commission, *Call for Evidence, Pre- and post-trade transparency provisions of MiFID in relation to transactions in classes of financial instruments other than shares* (2006).

[89] CESR initially related the legitimacy of its level 3 role, rather tenuously, to the 'fact that CESR members take decisions on a daily basis that create jurisprudence. This bottom-up approach relates to the normative nature of concrete decision-making activities of the supervisors. The impact of precedents on decisions is determined by the law and cannot be fully controlled by legislators. In addition, in an integrated European market, the jurisprudence created by supervisors produces effects that cannot be limited to national jurisdictions and therefore must be considered at EU level: A.-D. Van Leeuwen, (first CESR Chairman) and F. Demarigny, (CESR Secretary General), 'Europe's

CESR is clearly anxious to protect its level 3 agenda (it has stated in uncompromising terms that it is 'master of its own agenda' at level 3)[90] it appears acutely aware of the accountability risks of its level 3 guidance and seems to be developing a response. The MiFID level 3 regime is particularly instructive in this regard.

In October 2006 CESR presented its first MiFID level 3 agenda,[91] following an earlier consultation which revealed considerable market unease as to its scale.[92] The MiFID level 3 process has emerged as largely driven by the Commission and by 'cascades' from level 1 and level 2, rather than by CESR-driven initiatives. A substantial proportion of the initial level 3 agenda concerned the extensive reporting and review obligations required of the Commission under MiFID Article 65. Cross-sector convergence was also a dominant theme; the initial agenda included a number of initiatives of common concern to the banking, pension, insurance and securities sectors.

The more troublesome quasi-regulatory standards or guidance also formed a central part of the initial MiFID level 3 agenda. But it yields intriguing evidence as to CESR's approach to legitimacy risks. The inducements regime, in particular, saw CESR harnessing the Commission to its cause and thereby cloaking its quasi-regulatory activities with the mantle of the Commission's authority. The Guidance notes that the Commission participated in CESR's development of the recommendations on inducements as an observer, that CESR discussed the interpretation of relevant MiFID legal obligations with the Commission, and that the Commission agreed with CESR's interpretations and considered that the recommendations did 'not go beyond the MiFID regime but flow[ed] from a normal, natural reading of MiFID and the Level 2 Directive'.[93] This might be tentatively described as a quasi-endorsement process had CESR not already vehemently rejected any institutional endorsement of its level 3 standards under the market abuse regime.[94] It might be better

---

securities regulators working together under the new EU regulatory framework', *Journal of Financial Regulation and Compliance*, 12 (2004), 206 (at 4 of the online version).

[90] CESR, *2006 Report on Supervisory Convergence in the field of Securities Markets* (2006), CESR/06–259b, Summary (in the context of the market abuse regime).

[91] CESR/550b.

[92] See the joint response of a group of leading financial market trade associations to CESR's consultation (12 September 2006). It expressed concern that the work programme was 'more extensive and ambitious than necessary'.

[93] CESR/07–228b, 3.

[94] One respondent to CESR's initial consultation on the market abuse level 3 guidance suggested that the AMP list being drawn up by CESR members in accordance with CESR's

described as an aspect of the multi-level, evolutionary, and pragmatic accountability model which CESR is beginning to develop. It also reflects CESR's concern to bolster the validity of its guidance in the face of fierce market hostility, particularly where questions arise as to the legal base of its activities. The inducements regime generated severe market hostility as to its scope and its relationship with the MiFID regime (in particular its basis in the Article 19(1) 'best interests' obligation rather than in the narrower MiFID conflict-of-interest regime) and appears to have led CESR to rely on the Commission to buttress its authority.

CESR's October 2007 Protocol on the Supervision of Branches, adopted just prior to the application of MiFID in November 2007, is also revealing.[95] In an example of a developing dynamic between CESR and the Commission which supports accountability, and under which the Commission provides additional guidance on the scope of legal obligations and CESR develops operational responses (the best execution regime, discussed below, provides another example), CESR asked the Commission for an interpretation as to the meaning of Article 32(7), and the division of responsibilities between home and branch Member States, on which it could build a practical mechanism for the supervision of branches.[96] This followed in the Commission's June 2007 advice on Article 32(7).[97] But CESR's heightened sensitivity to accountability risks, and its concern to maintain its independence, are both apparent in its subsequent Protocol. It took some care to distance itself from the Commission's advice and to place the Protocol in the context of its previous level 3 guidance on the passport. CESR noted that the Commission's advice was a 'helpful contribution' that set out various scenarios and which it used as background in developing the Protocol, but that the advice did not form part of any CESR arrangements. A concern to avoid a perception of over-reaching its competences at level 3 seems implicit in the robust statement that it was not for CESR to address the legal interpretation of Article 32(7) and that it neither endorsed nor challenged the Commission's advice.[98] The Protocol does not therefore address the difficult questions as to which competent authority is responsible for branch

---

level 3 procedures be approved by the European legislature. CESR trenchantly responded that there was no legal or other justification for this: CESR/05–274, 9.

[95] CESR/07/672.

[96] CESR/07–337, 7.

[97] Commission, *Supervision of Branches under MiFID* (2007), MARKT/G3/MV D (2007).

[98] CESR/07–337, 2.

activity in specific cases, but establishes a cooperation framework which supports close coordination between competent authorities.

Although the Branch Protocol might suggest some distance between CESR and the Commission, evidence has emerged from the best-execution guidance of workman-like dialogue between the Commission and CESR in the construction of level 3 standards, which supports accountability. CESR made clear in its early position paper on best execution in February 2007 that its objective was 'supervisory convergence and not the making of new rules'.[99] Following deadlock in CESR as to the treatment of dealer markets, it also sought and received clarification from the Commission on the scope of the MiFID best-execution regime to anchor its work.[100] In addition, rather than adopt additional formal guidance in a highly controversial area which is already heavily regulated at level 1 and 2, CESR proceeded through a 'process-driven'[101] Q and A format which is designed to 'present [CESR's] views in a user-friendly way that facilitates compliance by firms and convergence among competent authorities...it presents CESR's answers to practical questions raised by firms and competent authorities'.[102] This is a practical and, in principle, 'light touch' response to the best execution issue and is designed not to impose additional obligations but to 'explain CESR's views on how firms can comply with the [MiFID regime] in the particular circumstances and situations that stakeholders have raised'.[103] In practice, however, market participants are likely to treat this guidance as a binding rule to reduce regulatory risk.

A restrained approach continued in CESR's 2007–8 MiFID work programme.[104] Notably, CESR's approach to the sensitive 'thematic' workstream which covers level 3 guidance and standards was economical and reflective of market concerns. Noting that the market and supervisors required time to adjust to the recent regulatory changes, it de-emphasized the guidance strand, focusing only on those areas highlighted by stakeholders as requiring guidance, including conflicts of interest, best execution, and soft commissions and unbundling. CESR has also

---

[99] CESR/07–050b, 4.
[100] CESR/07–050b, 4. The Commission responded at length. Letter from David Wright, Commission to CESR Chairman (19 March 2007), http://ec.europa.eu/internal_market/securities/isd/mifid_en.htm.
[101] CESR, *Interim Report* (2007), 18.
[102] CESR/07–320, 3.
[103] CESR/07–320, 3.
[104] CESR/07–704c. An earlier consultation took place (CESR/07–704).

frequently cautioned against moving measures from level 2 to level 3, even though level 3 gives more freedom to CESR. It was particularly concerned during the MiFID level 2 discussions that level 3 not be used to escape from political decisions at levels 1 and 2 and, in a clear concern to avoid legitimacy risks, that any transfer from level 2 to level 3 be made explicit in the level 2 measure 'in order to have the political backing of the EU institutions'.[105]

C. Consultation

Accountability is also enhanced through CESR's increasingly sophisticated consultation procedures. More indirectly, CESR has prompted market interests to adopt more sophisticated and networked lobbying models which should ensure that genuine European market expertise and legitimate concerns are reflected in its initiatives – as long as CESR remains uncaptured by the market interests which dominate consultations. The recent strengthening of its resources and capacity for cost–benefit analysis through the establishment of ECONET in summer 2006[106] should act as a counter-balance. CESR is also actively promoting the development of a retail lobby through its governance and education initiatives. The striking move by CESR into retail policy may, indeed, give considerable political weight to CESR's activities in the long term as well as dilute the risk that the well-organized market lobby could engender a market-facing bias in CESR's activities.

D. Tests for level 3 intervention

CESR has also voluntarily adopted a suitability test for deciding which activities it will undertake at level 3. It will only undertake work which meets three 'rigorous criteria': (i) a risk threshold (in that the issue addressed at level 3 represents a significant market failure or a repeated or major regulatory or supervisory failure); (ii) an EU threshold (in that the issue is likely to have an EU-wide impact on market participants or end-users and on the smooth functioning of single market); and (iii) an effectiveness threshold (in that CESR can contribute positively by

---

[105] ESC Minutes, 23 February 2005.
[106] ECONET was established in August 2006 as part of the wider reforms to CESR's operation. It is to evaluate, develop and maintain CESR's approach to impact analysis, in line with CESR's commitment to more extensive use of economic analysis and evidence-based methodologies.

creating change or through 'collective direct action' by CESR members).[107] Internal limits have therefore been imposed on the reach of level 3.

E. Charter reform

July 2006 saw CESR make the first changes to its Charter since its inception and a major change to CESR's decision-making structure.[108] The most important reforms concern CESR decision making. Article 5 of the CESR Charter[109] now provides for qualified majority voting with respect to level 2 advice. But the Charter also now provides that level 3 work which is expressly requested by Community legislation, or is directly related to Community legislation, must be subject to a unanimous vote where one or more members so requests. Where unanimity cannot be reached, the Commission must be informed.[110] Although this reform suggests the possibility of formal vetoes in limited circumstances, consensus is likely to remain the primary method for addressing level 3.

V. The 2007 Lamfalussy Review

The accountability and legitimacy of the level 3 process emerged again in the important 2007 Lamfalussy Review which saw input from the market,[111] think tanks[112] and the institutions.[113] Although radical institutional changes to the supervision structure were not suggested,[114] important reforms designed to strengthen accountability were proposed.

---

[107] CESR, *Supervisory Convergence Report* (2006), 2–3.

[108] CESR, Press Release 2 August 2006, CESR/06–303.

[109] CESR, *Charter of the Committee of European Securities Regulators* (2006), CESR/06–289c. Further reforms followed in 2008 after this book went to press.

[110] Charter, Art 5(7).

[111] See e.g. City of London Group 2007 and Deutsche Bank, *Towards a New Structure for EU Financial Supervision*, EU Monitor 48 (2007), 3.

[112] See e.g. E. Ferran, and D. Green, *Are the Lamfalussy Networks Working Successfully?* (A Report by the European Financial Forum) (2007) and the opinions issued by EUROFI for its December 2007 conference on Achieving the Integration of Financial Markets in a Global Context.

[113] The major reports and reviews included: Parliament Van den Burg Resolution 2007 (P6_TA (2007) 0338); the Commission, *Review of the Lamfalussy Process. Strengthening Supervisory Convergence* (2007); Inter Institutional Monitoring Group, *Final Report Monitoring the Lamfalussy Process* (2007) (which was based on consultation with the institutions and other key stakeholders, including market interests); and CESR, *Securities Supervision Report* (2007).

[114] The Commission e.g. argued that more ambitious institutional changes, such as the granting of independent rule-making power to the level 3 committees were not

But the essential legitimacy of the level 3 process and of CESR's activities was supported.

Reinforcement of the status of the level 3 committees, including CESR, was a recurring theme of the review which saw discussion of a possible strengthening of the level 3 committees through the regulatory framework[115] and through voting reforms – in particular greater use of qualified majority voting – although positions varied.[116] Related accountability concerns were also prevalent. Proposed reforms included the adoption by the institutions of general mandates for the 3L3 committees,[117] institutional endorsement of 3L3 work programmes by the EU institutions, and the submission of progress reports and reasons for failure to meet objectives.[118] The accountability discussion was also, and for the first time, framed in terms of national supervisors, with support for national supervisory mandates to refer to supervisory convergence obligations.[119]

CESR's approach to the Review warrants some attention given its earlier attention to developing its own accountability model. Despite its care to address accountability sensitivities, it has recently become more assertive in pointing to the limits of its non-binding level 3 guidance and the related threat to its credibility, particularly on the marketplace.[120] But it has opted for an approach which builds on peer

---

feasible given lack of agreement among Member States and stakeholders: Commission Lamfalussy Report (2007), 3.

[115] Inter Institutional Monitoring Group (2007), 14; Commission Lamfalussy Report (2007), 8; Van den Burg Resolution 2007, 55.

[116] The Inter Institutional Monitoring Group supported consensus as the default voting method, but suggested that the 3L3 committees operate under QMV in respect of specific delegations under level 1 and 2: Inter Institutional Monitoring Group (2007), 18. The Commission was more radical, concerned as to the difficulties posed by consensus decision making, and suggested that QMV be used for any measure aimed at fostering convergence: Commission Lamfalussy Report (2007), 9. The Parliament also supported QMV decision-making: Van den Burg Resolution 2007, para. 55.

[117] Commission Lamfalussy Report (2007), 7; Van den Burg Resolution 2007, para. 55.

[118] Inter Institutional Monitoring Group (2007), 17; Commission Lamfalussy Report (2007), 7; and Financial Services Authority and HM Treasury, *Strengthening the EU regulatory and supervisory framework: A Practical Approach* (2007), 7.

[119] Inter Institutional Monitoring Group (2007), 18; and Commission Lamfalussy Report (2007), 8.

[120] CESR argued that 'there is a gap between an informal (de facto) EU mandate given to CESR creating the expectation that rules will be applied in the same manner in the market, and the legal national accountability obligations of each CESR member that governs their daily activities. Uniform supervisory behaviour should not be expected by market participants within the current framework as CESR members may have no

pressure dynamics, and which reflects its generally nuanced approach to accountability risks, rather than calling for binding status to be, somehow, afforded to its guidance. It has maintained its commitment to consensus-led decisionmaking for level 3 initiatives.[121] But in addition to supporting the comply-or-explain technique with respect to findings of non-compliance by the Review Panel, it has also suggested that it adopt enforcement instruments, 'fundamentally reputational' in design.[122] Any 'enforcement-style' decisions would be subject to a qualified majority vote. This represents a significant hardening of CESR's peer pressure mechanisms. CESR has also called in aid from the enforcement powers of the Commission, suggesting that the Commission indicate that it would not ignore the existence of level 3 when exercising its enforcement powers. Building on its earlier attempts to establish a tailored accountability model, CESR also called for national supervisory mandates to include compliance with supervisory convergence – a shrewd move which allows CESR to strengthen compliance with its level 3 initiatives without opening the Pandora's Box which embuing level 3 guidance with binding force would involve.

The review process culminated with the important December 2007 ECOFIN Conclusions[123] which broadly reflect these themes and CESR's proposed reforms. The Conclusions did not support major institutional change, but represented a strong statement of political support for supervisory convergence/level 3 and for the work of the 3L3 committees. The key accountability recommendations included ECOFIN's call for the Commission to clarify the role of the 3L3 committees and to consider 'all options' to strengthen them – but with the caveat that the institutional structure must not be unbalanced.[124] Accountability was further addressed by the traditional reporting model developed by CESR, with ECOFIN inviting the 3L3 committees to submit a draft work programme to the Council, Commission and Parliament and to report annually on the achievement of the objectives set.[125] The non-binding effect of level 3 guidance, the voluntary nature of convergence, and the extent to which national supervisors could be bound against their will were also

---

alternative but to respect legitimate national discretions': CESR Securities Supervision Report 2007, 2.

[121]   CESR, *Securities Supervision Report* (2007), 4.
[122]   CESR, *Securities Supervision Report* (2007), 5.
[123]   2836th ECOFIN Meeting, 4 December 2007, Press Release 15698/07.
[124]   December 2007 ECOFIN Conclusions, 17.
[125]   December 2007 ECOFIN Conclusions, 17.

major themes of the Conclusions. ECOFIN took a compromise position and requested the 3L3 committees in order to enhance the efficiency and effectiveness of their decision-making procedures, to introduce the possibility of qualified majority voting. But it also acknowledged that decisions would remain non-binding and suggested that, as proposed by CESR, the comply-or-explain model be used to drive compliance.[126] ECOFIN also supported the adoption of supervisory-convergence mandates in national supervisory mandates, although it was not prescriptive and simply recommended that Member States consider including in the mandates of national supervisors the task of cooperating within the EU and working towards supervisory convergence.[127]

CESR's careful attempts to address accountability risks appear therefore to have reaped dividends as, overall, CESR has emerged strengthened from the 2007 Review (not least given the ECOFIN commitment to strengthening its funding model and addressing the severe resource strain under which CESR now operates). The Commission's strong support for supervisory convergence, and its enthusiasm for CESR's decisions to be afforded akin-to-binding authority (through its support of qualified majority voting in particular) during the Review, suggests that it had reached an accommodation with CESR's burgeoning powers, while the European Parliament also appears more sanguine as to accountability and legitimacy risks.[128] The 2007 Review also saw strong political support for CESR's activities which suggests that CESR members should not face too many domestic political conflicts. The risk of a change in the political climate cannot, however, be ruled out. Although some tensions persist, notably with respect to CESR's voting mechanisms and its role in international relations, the scale of CESR's activities at level 3 now appears to have institutional backing.

The range of CESR's activities, and its key role as the driver of supervisory convergence, raises complex accountability and legitimacy issues which reflect the wider complexities of the dynamic process whereby the disciplines of the financial markets are established by a range of actors. CESR's accountability model looks set to develop as a hybrid, based for the most part on indirect, reporting and consultation accountability

---

[126]   December 2007 ECOFIN Conclusions, 17.
[127]   The FSC and EFC were mandated to consider this issue.
[128]   The 2007 Van den Burg Resolution 'welcomed' the work of the 3L3 committees at level 2 and their progressing of the convergence agenda 'without overstepping their remit' or attempting to replace the legislators, and argued that their work must be encouraged: Van den Burg Resolution 2007, para. 53.

links, but also placed cleverly within national supervisory and accountability structures. The current dynamic period may well see the emergence of an optimal model which reflects the particular functions CESR exercises and the particular accountability risks it poses. The indications also continue to suggest that CESR will remain careful to tread lightly in expanding the boundaries of level 3. Notably, CESR members appear to be uncertain as to the wisdom in seeking binding status for level 3,[129] reflecting a grasp of political realities which augurs well for its future stability.

[129] CESR, *Securities Supervision Report* (2007), 7.

26

Market transparency and best execution: bond trading under MiFID

GUIDO FERRARINI

The relationship between best execution and market transparency deserves careful consideration in an analysis of MiFID.[1] Best execution has mainly been studied with respect to equity trading, which is generally exchange based and widely regulated also with respect to market transparency.[2] In this chapter, however, I focus on bond trading, which takes place predominantly over-the-counter (OTC) and is not subject to MiFID's transparency provisions. After introducing the topic (Section I), I offer a critical view of the transparency requirements applicable to equity trades and their formation (Section II). I then examine the recent policy discussion on non-equities market transparency, as reflected in the Report issued by the European Commission under Article 65 (1) of the MiFID,[3] examining whether the requirements for pre-trade and post-trade information should be extended to non-equities markets (Section III). I finally consider the role of best execution in bond markets, focussing on the impact of transparency on order execution for retail investors (Section IV). In Section V, I draw some conclusions.

[1] See Directive 2004/39/EC of the European Parliament and of the Council on markets in financial instruments (MiFID) [2004] OJ L 145.

[2] See R. Davies, A. Dufour and B. Scott-Quinn 'The MiFID: Competition in a New European Equity Market Regulatory Structure', in G. Ferrarini and E. Wymeersch (eds.), *Investor Protection in Europe: Corporate Law Making, the MiFID and Beyond*, (Oxford University Press, 2006), 163–97; G. Ferrarini, 'Best Execution and Competition between Trading Venues – MiFID's Likely Impact', *Capital Markets Law Journal*, 2 (2007), 404–13; C. Gortsos, MiFID's Investor Protection Regime: Best Execution of Client Orders and Related Conduct of Business Rules, in E. Avgouleas (ed.), *The Regulation of Investment Services in Europe under MiFID: Implementation and Practice* (Haywards Heath, West Sussex: Tottel Publishing, 2007), 101–37; for the US, J. Macey and M. O'Hara, 'The Law and Economics of Best Execution', *Journal of Financial Intermediation*, 6 (1997), 188–233.

[3] DG Internal Market and Services, Working Document, *Report on non-equities market transparency pursuant to Article 65 (1) of Directive 2004/39/EC on Markets in Financial Instruments (MiFID)* (3 April 2008).

I. Introduction

A few introductory remarks may help to set this study in context. First of all, the type of instrument traded and the structure of the relevant market have an impact on best execution, as also recognized by the MiFID and its implementing Directive.[4] Shares, to start with, are generally traded in order-driven and centralized markets, such as stock exchanges (and, to a lesser extent, MTFs).[5] Only a fraction of listed shares are traded frequently, mainly in small sizes.[6] Liquidity is high and continuous for the most traded shares, while price formation is based around a dominant trading venue (usually an exchange).[7] Bonds, on the contrary, are mainly traded off-exchange, in quote-driven and decentralized markets.[8] Only a minority of bonds are traded frequently, while trading sizes are large in a majority of cases.[9] Liquidity depends on issuer, size of issue, rating, etc., while price formation occurs through competitive 'requests for quotes' (RFQs) in OTC markets, which are closely correlated with credit derivatives markets.[10] Therefore, best execution criteria shall be implemented differently for shares and bonds, to the extent that, for instance,

---

[4] See Article 21 of Directive 2004/39/EC on markets in financial instruments (MiFID) and in particular its para. 1, which defines the best execution obligation as requiring that 'investment firms take all reasonable steps to obtain, when executing orders, the best possible result for their clients taking into account price, costs, speed, likelihood of execution and settlement, size, nature or any other consideration relevant to the execution of the order'. See also the 70th *considerandum* of Commission Directive 2006/73/EC of 10 August 2006, implementing Directive 2004/39/EC of the European Parliament and of the Council as regards organizational requirements and operating conditions for investment firms and defined terms for the purposes of that Directive (the MiFID's Implementing Directive), which states: 'The obligation to deliver the best possible result when executing client orders applies in relation to all types of financial instruments. However, given the differences in market structures or the structure of financial instruments, it may be difficult to identify and apply a uniform standard of and procedure for best execution that would be valid and effective for all classes of instrument.'

[5] See CESR, *Response to the Commission on non-equities transparency* (June 2007), 4; L. Harris, *Trading and Exchanges. Market Microstructures for Practitioners* (Oxford University Press, 2003), 32 *et seq.*

[6] See Harris, *Trading and Exchanges,* (note 5, above), 45.

[7] See CESR, *Response to the Commission on non-equities transparency*, (note 5, above), 4.

[8] See the Report of the Technical Committee of IOSCO, *Transparency of Corporate Bond Markets* (May 2004), 3: 'Trading in many corporate bond issues has tended to remain predominantly bilateral between dealers and their clients. Even when bonds are listed, the majority of trading frequently occurs off-market'; CEPR, *European Corporate Bond Markets: Transparency, Liquidity, Efficiency,* report by B. Biais, F. Declerk, J. Dow, R. Portes and E. von Thadden (City of London, May 2006), 28 *et seq.*

[9] CESR, *Response to the Commission on non-equities transparency*, (note 5, above), 4.

[10] Ibid.

most shares have a dominant trading venue, whereas bonds are traded exclusively or predominantly OTC.[11]

Furthermore, market transparency has an impact on best execution. Firstly, transparency contributes to price discovery making markets more efficient, to the extent that prices fully reflect the information available.[12] As argued with respect to equity markets, transparency enhances liquidity: the more price setters know about the order flow, the better they can protect themselves against losses to insiders, so allowing them to narrow their spreads.[13] The role of informed traders, however, is less important in bond markets.[14] Moreover, there are situations in which transparency may have a negative impact on liquidity. For instance, in the case of a block trading of securities, immediate publication of the relevant data may expose the dealer to an adverse market movement, as other market participants will try to exploit the relevant information.[15]

Secondly, transparency can improve liquidity if customers have to search for the best quotes:[16] since it is costly to search for quotes, in opaque

[11] See again the 70th *considerandum* of the MiFID's Implementing Directive, which specifies: 'Best execution obligations should therefore be applied in a manner that takes into account the different circumstances associated with the execution of orders related to particular types of financial instruments. For example, transactions involving a customized OTC financial instrument that involve a unique contractual relationship tailored to the circumstances of the client and the investment firm may not be comparable for best execution purposes with transactions involving shares traded on centralized execution venues'.

[12] See the report by the Division of Market Regulation of the SEC, *Market 2000: An Examination of Current Equity Market Developments* (Jan. 1994), IV-17, also highlighting that transparency contributes to the fairness of markets, as all investors have access to information.

[13] See M. Pagano and A. Röell, 'Transparency and Liquidity: A Comparison of Auction and Dealer Markets with Informed Trading', *Journal of Finance,* 51 (1996), 579–611. These authors argue that transparency also depends on market microstructure, to the extent that order-driven markets are 'inherently' more transparent than quote-driven ones. Requiring transparency from the latter markets may force changes to their microstructure, as was sometimes argued in the discussion which finally led to the regulation of equity market transparency in the Investment Services Directive: see G. Ferrarini, 'The European Regulation of Stock Exchanges: new Perspectives', *Common Market Law Review,* 36 (1999), 569–98, 580.

[14] See CEPR, *European Corporate Bond Markets,* (note 8, above), 9, arguing that the optimal financial contracting literature has shown that corporate bonds are designed to minimize adverse selection, relative to stock.

[15] Ibid., 7, noting that an argument used against transparency is that it could deter liquidity. In transparent markets, once a trader has purchased shares, his competitors may opportunistically quote a high price for liquidity, making it difficult for the trader to unwind its inventory.

[16] See the 76th *considerandum* of the MiFID's Implementing Directive, stating *inter alia*: 'Availability, comparability and consolidation of data related to execution quality

markets customers may end up choosing to trade with a dealer even if it does not have the best quotes.[17] Competition between dealers is reduced as a result. Recent empirical research[18] concerning TRACE[19] finds that transparent bonds have lower transaction costs than non-transparent bonds and that transaction costs decrease when bonds become price transparent.[20] One of these studies suggests that in 2003, when $2 trillion in bond issues were traded for which prices were not published on a contemporaneous basis, investors would have saved a minimum of $1 billion per year had the relevant prices been TRACE-transparent.[21]

Thirdly, if significant post-trade information is not readily available, investors have difficulties in assessing best execution by their brokers.[22]

provided by the various execution venues is crucial in enabling investment firms and investors to identify those execution venues that deliver the highest quality of execution for their clients.'

[17] See X. Yin, 'A Comparison of Centralized and Fragmented Markets with Costly Search', *Journal of Finance,* 60 (2005), 1567–90.

[18] See A. Edwards, L. Harris and M. Piwowar, 'Corporate Bond Market Transaction Costs and Transparency', *Journal of Finance,* 67 (2007), 1421–51; H. Bessembinder, W. Maxwell and K. Venkataraman, 'Market Transparency, Liquidity Externalities, and Institutional Trading Costs in Corporale Bonds', *Journal of Financial Economics,* 82 (2006), 251–88; M. Goldstein, E. Hotchkiss and E. Sirri, 'Transparency and Liquidity: A Controlled Experiment on Corporate Bonds', *Review of Financial Studies,* 20 (2007), 235–73.

[19] TRACE (Trade Reporting and Compliance Engine) was created in 2002 by the National Association of Securities Dealers (NASD), under pressure from Congress, buy-side traders, and the SEC by requiring dealers to report all OTC bond transactions through it. As a result, within two and a half years after the start of TRACE operations, prices from about 99 per cent of all trades representing about 95 per cent of the dollar value traded were disseminated within 15 minutes: see A. Edwards, L. Harris and M. Piwowar, 'Corporate Bond Market Transaction Costs and Transparency', (note 18, above), at 1422, citing SEC Release No. 34–49920 and File No. SR-NASD-2004-094, with the specification that this figure does not include the trades of the Rule 144a market, which is still opaque.

[20] See Edwards, Harris and Piwowar, 'Corporate Bond Market Transaction Costs and Transparency', (note 18, above), at 1425, stating that their study complements the results of at least three other studies: G. Alexander, A. Edwards and M. Ferri, 'The Determinants of Trading Volume of High-yield Corporate Bonds', *Journal of Financial Markets,* 3 (2000), 177–204 (transparent high-yield bonds can be fairly liquid); Bessembinder, Maxwell and Venkataraman, 'Market Transparency, Liquidity Externalities, and Institutional Trading Costs in Corporale Bonds', (note 18, above) (declines in transaction costs for insurance company trades in corporate bonds after the introduction of TRACE); Goldstein, Hotchkiss and Sirri, 'Transparency and Liquidity', (note 18, above) (declines in transaction costs due to transparency for all but the smallest trade size groups in a matched-pair analysis of BBB bonds).

[21] See Edwards, Harris and Piwowar, 'Corporate Bond Market Transaction Costs and Transparency', (note 18, above), 1423.   [22] Ibid.

I will develop this intuition in Sections IV and V, arguing that market transparency is also needed for best execution and its enforcement, particularly with respect to retail investors, whose presence is substantial in some countries and could be enhanced in others by EU-wide post-trade transparency.[23]

II. MiFID'S equity market transparency

Market transparency was regulated for the first time at EC level with the ISD,[24] which included minimum standards for post-trade transparency in regulated markets and provided considerable latitude for Member States in the implementation of those standards, particularly with respect to bonds and other debt instruments.[25] Moreover, the Directive allowed Member States to require transactions in equity securities to be carried out on a regulated market.[26] As a result, some Member States, such as France, Italy and Spain, maintained 'concentration rules', i.e. rules mandating exchange execution of listed securities trades as a requirement for the best execution of transactions by investment intermediaries.[27] However, these domestic provisions were frequently criticized as anticompetitive by market participants and policy makers, whilst stock

---

[23] On the retail market for corporate bonds in Europe, see CEPR, *European Corporate Bond Markets*, (note 8, above), 32, stating that direct holdings of fixed income securities by households vary a lot across countries in Europe: 'While in Italy they can be as high as 20% of total financial holdings or even higher, in Germany they are between 10% and 15%, and in other countries they will typically be lower than 5%.' In the latter countries, investments in fixed income securities take place primarily through funds. See FSA, 'Trading Transparency in the UK Secondary Bond Markets', Discussion Paper 05/5 (September 2005), 9 *et seq.*

[24] Directive 93/22/EEC of 10 May 1993, on investment services in the securities field [1993], OJ L 141. See, for diffuse analysis, N. Moloney, *EC Securities Regulation,* (Oxford University Press, 2002), 295 *et seq.*

[25] See Article 21 (2) ISD, providing *inter alia:* 'The competent authorities may also apply more flexible provisions, particularly as regards publication deadlines, for transactions concerning bonds and other forms of securitized debt.' On the ISD implementation, E. Wymeersch, 'The Implementation of the ISD and CAD in National Legal Systems', in G. Ferrarini (ed.), *European Securities Markets: The Investment Services and Beyond* (London: Kluwer, 1998), 3–44.

[26] See Article 14 (3) ISD.

[27] See Ferrarini, 'The European Regulation of Stock Exchanges: new Perspectives', (note 13, above), 583, noting that other Member States, such as the UK, did not provide for the mandatory concentration of transactions on exchanges, leaving the investors and their intermediaries free to transact off-board.

exchanges took advantage of the same to consolidate their market power in domestic equities trading.

Throughout the MiFID's formation political agreement was reached, despite strong opposition from some exchanges and banking circles in the Continent, to dismantle national barriers and promote competition in the offer of trading services between regulated markets, MTFs and intermediaries internalizing trades of listed securities.[28] As a result, the new Directive allows internalization of orders and, at the same time, regulates this practice with provisions concerning transparency, order handling, conflicts of interest and best execution.[29] Transparency obligations, in particular, are aimed at remedying the fragmentation of markets which derives from competition in the offer of trading services.[30] As listed shares can now be traded through multiple venues (or entities), information concerning both on- and off-exchange transactions must be published by the relevant venue (or entity) under MiFID's post-trade transparency requirements. These requirements are similar for regulated markets,[31] MTFs[32] and investment firms that execute transactions in shares admitted to trading on

---

[28] See G. Ferrarini and F. Recine, 'The MiFID and Internalisation', in Ferrarini and Wymeersch (eds.), (note 2, above), 117, 120 *et seq.*, analysing the MiFID's formation and the interplay of interest groups either favouring concentration of trades or opposing the same as anticompetitive.

[29] See Ferrarini and Recine, 'The MiFID and Internalisation', (note 28, above), 139 *et seq.*; J. Köndgen and E. Thyssen, 'Internalisation under MiFID: Regulatory Overreaching or Landmark in Investor Protection?', in Ferrarini and Wymeersch (eds.), *Investor Protection in Europe*, (note 2, above), 271–96; N. Moloney, 'Effective Policy Design for the Retail Investment Services Market: Challenges and Choice Post FSAP', in Ferrarini and Wymeersch (eds.) (note 2, above), 381–442.

[30] On post-trade transparency as a remedy to market fragmentation, see the Report from the Technical Committee of IOSCO, *Transparency and Market Fragmentation* (November 2001).

[31] See Article 45 (1) MiFID stating that Member States shall, at least, require regulated markets to make public the price, volume and time of the transactions executed in respect of shares admitted to trading. Article 45 (2) specifies that the competent authority may authorize regulated markets to provide for deferred publication of the details of transactions based on their type or size, in particular of those that are large in scale compared with the normal market size.

[32] See Article 30 (1) MiFID stating that Member States shall, at least, require that investment firms and market operators operating an MTF make public the price, volume and time of the transactions executed under its systems in respect of shares which are admitted to trading on a regulated market. Article 30 (2) specifies that the competent authority may authorize investment firms or market operators operating an MTF to provide for deferred publication of the details of transactions based on their type or size, in particular of those that are large in scale compared with the normal market size.

a regulated market outside a regulated market or MTF.[33] Common requirements as to post-trade transparency are also foreseen by the Commission Regulation implementing the MiFID.[34]

Pre-trade transparency proved to be a much more controversial subject, as already seen for the ISD.[35] However, political agreement was not too difficult to reach for MiFID concerning regulated markets and MTFs,[36] probably reflecting increased consensus on the merits of organized markets' transparency and also the fact that market micro-structures are today mainly order-driven. The real controversy centred around whether pre-trade transparency should be imposed upon inter-nalizers. Answers to this question largely depended on attitudes taken towards national concentration rules and their impact on competi-tion. Those supporting similar rules (including Continental exchanges and banking associations) advocated that internalization should in any case be subject to rigorous pre-trade transparency requirements. Those objecting to trading concentration also objected to the introduc-tion of pre-trade information requirements as unduly interfering with markets.[37]

---

[33] See Article 28 stating that Member States shall, at least, require investment firms which, either on own account or on behalf of clients, conclude transactions in shares admitted to trading on a regulated market outside a regulated market or MTF, to make public the volume and price of those transactions and the time at which they were concluded.

[34] See Article 27 (Post-trade transparency obligation), Commission Regulation (EC) No 1287/2006 of 10 August 2006, implementing Directive 2004/39/EC of the European Parliament and of the Council as regards record-keeping obligations for investment firms, transaction reporting, market transparency, admission of financial instruments to trading, and defined terms for the purpose of this Directive [2006], OJ L 241/7 (MiFID's Implementing Regulation), which applies to investment firms, regulated markets, and investment firms and market operators operating an MTF. See also Article 28 (Deferred publication of large transactions) of the same Regulation.

[35] The following text reflects Ferrarini and Recine, 'The MiFID and Internalisation', (note 28, above), 246 *et seq.*

[36] See Articles 29 and 44 of the MiFID, concerning pre-trade transparency requirements respectively for MTFs and regulated markets.

[37] See Ferrarini and Recine, 'The MiFID and Internalisation', (note 28, above), 240, describing the MiFID's 'political economy' as follows: 'On the one hand, stock exchanges (particularly those operating in Continental Europe) fight to defend their national fran-chises, which are in some Member States protected by concentration rules. On the other, investment banks (often belonging to American groups or European financial conglom-erates) seek wider territories of action. The business model is that of the City of London, where the Stock Exchange, ATS and internalising firms offer different trading func-tionalities to institutional and retail investors. On the whole, investment banks defend the rents generated by internalised trades against the stock exchanges protecting their quasi-monopolies in the trade of domestic equities.'

The European Commission, in its 2002 consultation document on the ISD revision, suggested that internalized market orders and limit orders left unexecuted by internalizers should not be reported.[38] However, in its proposal for a directive published later that year,[39] the Commission accepted, through a last-minute *coup de scène*, the opposite view and included provisions mimicking the US pre-trade transparency rules.[40] The 'quote rule', in particular, was adopted by the SEC in 1978 requiring broker-dealers who maintain quotes for a security to promptly disseminate and honour the same; in 1996, the SEC extended this rule to apply to Nasdaq market makers who posted quotes in ECN.[41] The 'limit order display rule' was adopted in 1996 with the Order Handling Rules[42] and requires dealers who accept limit orders and specialists to display these orders, including their full size, when the order is placed at a price

---

[38] See European Commission, 'Revision of Investment Services Directive (93/22/EEC), Second Consultation'; for an analysis of this document, E. Wymeersch, 'Revision of the ISD', *Financial Law Institute, Ghent University, Working Paper 2002–11* (August 2002).

[39] See the Proposal for a Directive of the European Parliament and of the Council on Investment Services and Regulated Markets, and amending Council Directive 85/611/EEC, Council Directive 93/6/EEC and European Parliament and Council Directive 2000/12/EC, 19 November 2002, COM(2002) 625, 8.

[40] According to the press, the change was due to the personal intervention of Mr. Prodi, president of the European Commission: Lex Column 'The Prodi Plot', *Financial Times* (19 November 2002). Indeed a Commission informal draft widely circulated on 3 September 2002 did not envisage any pre-trade transparency obligation for investment firms.

[41] SEC Rule 11Ac1-1. Prior to 1978, the quotes disseminated on Nasdaq by market makers did not specify the number of shares to which the quote applied. In addition, market makers did not always honour their quotes, refusing to trade at the specified price. See J. Coffee and J. Seligman, *Securities Regulation,* 9th edn. (New York: Foundation Press, 2003), 652–3.

[42] The Order Handling Rules were an important step in the development of the National Market System (NMS), envisioned by the 1975 Securities Acts Amendments (which also contemplated the abolition of fixed commission rates), that would ensure investors competitive markets and best execution of their trades: see Coffee and Seligman, *Securities Regulation,* (note 41, above), 650–653; for early analysis of the NMS from a European perspective, E. Wymeersch, *Le contrôle des marches de valeurs mobilières dans les États membres de la Communauté européenne. Rapports sur les systèmes de contrôle nationaux. Partie II,* (Commission des Communautés Européennes, Série concurrence – Rapprochement des legislations, 1981), 219–308. The Amendments fixed five basic goals for the SEC to pursue in implementing the national market system: (i) economically efficient execution of transactions; (ii) fair competition among broker-dealers, among exchanges and between exchanges and other markets; (iii) ready availability of quotation and transaction information to broker-dealers and investors; (iv) ability of broker-dealers to execute orders in the best market; (v) opportunity for investors to execute orders without the participation of a dealer (Section 11A).

superior to the market maker or specialist's own quotations.[43] Therefore, if the prices quoted by market makers left an artificially wide spread, a new source of competition would be introduced by allowing customers to introduce a price quotation that would narrow the bid/ask spread. As a result, brokers holding market orders from their clients would be required by their duty of best execution to execute their trades against these limit orders.[44]

The Commission's proposal of rules similar to the American provisions just cited generated an intense political debate. Investment intermediaries, often based in the City of London, insisted that the abolition of concentration rules could be effective only in the absence of other hindrances to off-exchange trading. On the contrary, banks in the Continent supported the imposition of pre-trade transparency obligations on dealers in order to create a level playing field between trading venues or entities. The stock exchanges hit by the abolition of concentration rules defended pre-trade transparency requirements as a means to achieve efficient price discovery in fragmented markets. A compromise solution was found, at last, in the European Parliament. The proposed European 'limit order display rule' was limited to share trading. The 'quote rule' was restricted to cases of 'systematic internalization' and to transactions of a 'standard market size', while the duty to quote was referred only to the internalizing firm's clients.

As a result, Article 22 (2) MiFID requires investment firms to make public, in a manner that is easily accessible to other market participants, limit orders concerning shares admitted to trading on a regulated market, which are not immediately executed under prevailing market

---

[43] Coffee and Seligman, *Securities Regulation,* (note 41, above), 653, make the following example: if the market maker's quotation were $18 bid and $19 asked, and a customer placed a limit order with him to buy at $18.50, the market maker's bid quotation would become $18.50 bid and $19 asked. If $18.50 were the highest bid price submitted to Nasdaq and $18.75 the lowest asked quotation, then the NBBO (National Best Bid and Offer) would become $18.50 and $18.75, and all transactions would be done at this price until the orders were exhausted or a still superior price were quoted.

[44] Ibid. The Order Handling Rules were introduced after a pricing collusion was discovered amongst Nasdaq's market makers, under which they avoided odd-eighths quotes. An empirical study by W. Christie and P. Schultz, 'Why Do Nasdaq Market Makers Avoid Odd-Eighth Quotes', *Journal of Finance,* 49 (1994), 1813, examined an extensive sample of bid-ask spreads for 100 of the most active Nasdaq stocks in 1991 and found that spreads of one-eighth were virtually non-existent for a majority of this sample. In the authors' opinion, the fact that market makers enforced a minimum spread of $0.25 for a majority of large stocks could partially explain why previous research had found trading costs to be higher for Nasdaq than for the New York Stock Exchange.

conditions. As CESR explained, this provision should facilitate and accelerate the execution of client limit orders, whilst contributing to price discovery.[45]

Concerning the 'quote rule', Article 27 MiFID requires internalizers to publish firm quotes only if a number of conditions are met. Firstly, the relevant instruments must be shares admitted to trading on a regulated market and for which there is a liquid market. Secondly, the internalizing firm must be a systematic internalizer for shares, i.e. 'an investment firm which, on an organized, frequent and systematic basis, deals on own account by executing orders outside a regulated market or an MTF'. Thirdly, the transaction size must be up to standard market size. Moreover, Article 27 (3) requires systematic internalizers to execute their clients' orders at the price quoted when receiving the order. However, in the case of orders from professional clients, systematic internalizers may execute those orders at a better price, provided that such price falls within a range close to market conditions and the orders are of a size bigger than that customarily undertaken by a retail investor. One of the main criticisms of the quote rule throughout the MiFID's preparatory works was the potential exposure of investment firms to credit risks towards unknown counterparties. Article 27 (5) aims to avoid this occurrence by allowing systematic internalizers to choose 'on the basis of their commercial policy' which investors should have access to their quotes, provided that they proceed 'in an objective non-discriminatory way'. In essence, systematic internalizers are charged with a duty to deal

---

[45] See CESR, *Technical Advice on Possible Implementing Measures of the Directive 2004/39/EC on Markets in Financial Instruments* (April 2005), 72. However, the European context is profoundly different from that in the US, where following the 1975 Securities Acts Amendments transaction and quotation information from different markets was consolidated into a single stream of data available to all market participants and investors. In Europe, a similar consolidated information system is lacking, whilst stock exchanges often perform a similar function at national level. Under MiFID, also trade information and execution systems other than regulated markets and MTF could be used by internalizers: for example, a bilateral system operated by the same internalizing firm or a trade execution system operated by an information provider. See Article 31 of the MiFID's Implementing Regulation, stating that an investment firm shall be considered to disclose client limit orders that are not immediately executable if it transmits the order to a regulated market or MTF that operates an order book trading system, or ensures that the order is made public and can be easily executed as soon that market conditions allow. This would make it often difficult for investors to find the relevant information, save that efficient consolidation systems would develop at the initiative of information vendors. See Article 32 of the MiFID's Implementing Regulation, stating amongst others that any arrangement to make information public must facilitate the consolidation of the data with similar data from other sources.

with all market participants and can derogate from this duty only for reasons concerning the credit and counterparty risks deriving from their internalization activities. Therefore, systematic internalizers are placed in a position similar to other 'trading venues' such as regulated markets and MTFs, which are also subject to principles of non-discrimination with respect to investment intermediaries.[46]

The reasons for a similar treatment of internalization are made clear by the formation process of the MiFID: on the one side, the rules just examined (including those on transparency) have satisfied the incumbent exchanges' request for a level playing field; on the other, the internalizers' duty to deal with all investment intermediaries in a non-discriminatory fashion has reduced the fear (typical of small- and medium-sized intermediaries in Latin countries) that internalization by large investment banks may subtract liquidity from the stock exchanges thereby forcing local intermediaries out of their traditional markets. However, the limits of the MiFID's response to internalization are apparent: first, the relevant duties are subject to restrictive conditions, such as the requirement for internalization to be 'systematic' and for shares to be 'liquid'; second, the content of these duties has been diluted through the MiFID's negotiation to the point that their regulatory bite is relatively modest (even the 'antidiscrimination' rule admits for exceptions which can be not too difficult to invoke in practice).

III. Should MiFID's transparency requirements be extended to bond markets?

The MiFID's transparency rules examined in the preceding paragraph do not include debt instruments in their scope; also the policy debate which led to the transplant of the US 'quote rule' and 'limit order rule' into European law was limited to share trading. No doubt, the interest groups involved in the discussion were different for bonds, which are predominantly traded OTC, with transactions on listed instruments mainly occurring off-exchange.[47] The stock exchanges, therefore, had small interests at stake with respect to bond trading, whilst investment and commercial banks joined forces to defend

---

[46] See Ferrarini and Recine, 'The MiFID and Internalisation', (note 28, above), 263.
[47] See IOSCO, 'Transparency of Corporate Bond Markets', (note 8, above), 4–6, specifying that in Europe the majority of corporate bonds are listed on exchange and yet are traded off-exchange to a significant proportion.

the rents that opaque trading allows them to extract.[48] As a result, the question whether transparency requirements should also apply to bond markets was set aside under Article 65 (1) MiFID, which provides that 'the Commission shall, on the basis of public consultation and in the light of discussions with competent authorities, report to the European Parliament and Council on the possible extension of the scope of provisions of the Directive concerning pre- and post-trade transparency obligations to transactions in classes of financial instruments other than shares'.[49] In order to comply with this provision the Commission published, in June 2006, a call for evidence that posed a range of questions relating to possible policy rationales for mandating transparency.[50] In August 2006, the Commission requested CESR to provide initial assistance by conducting a fact-finding exercise in relation to cash bond markets. Having been requested for further assistance,[51] CESR conducted a public consultation which led the same to issue, in June 2007, an advice reflecting the comments received.[52]

The core question dealt with by CESR in its advice, also in light of the consultations conducted by the same Committee and the Commission, was whether there would be 'convincing evidence of a market failure with respect to market transparency in any of the instrument markets under

[48] On rents for dealers see CEPR, *European Corporate Bond Markets*, (note 8, above), 20, assuming that bond dealers privately acquire information, which results in differences of information as 'some dealers end up with better signals than the others. This creates a winner's course problem for the latter. They risk getting a better fill rate for less profitable trades. To make up for these losses, relatively uninformed dealers will widen their spreads. This, in turn, reduces the competitive pressure faced by the better informed dealers, who also widen their spreads. Such wide spreads generate rents for the dealers'. For a similar analysis, see R. Bloomfield and M. O'Hara, 'Can Transparent Markets Survive?', *Journal of Financial Economics*, 55 (2000), 425–59.

[49] See also the 46th *considerandum* of MiFID's Preamble stating: 'A Member State may decide to apply the pre- and post-trade transparency requirements laid down in this Directive to financial instruments other than shares …'.

[50] European Commission, *Call for Evidence: Pre- and Post-trade Transparency Provisions of the Markets in Financial Instruments Directive (MiFID) in Relation to Transactions in Classes of Financial Instruments Other than Shares* (12 June 2006). See also the DG Internal Market and Services working paper including the Feedback statement concerning this consultation (13 November 2006).

[51] See the Commission's Mandate to CESR for technical advice on possible extension of the scope of the provisions of Directive 2004/39/EC concerning pre- and post-trade transparency obligations to transactions in classes of financial instruments other than shares (27 November 2006). A similar mandate was given to the European Securities Markets Expert Group (ESME) on the same date.

[52] CESR, *Response to the Commission on non-equities transparency*, (note 5, above). A similar report was published by ESME, *Non-equity Market Transparency* (June 2007).

review'.[53] The vast majority of the respondents in the consultations felt that there was no market failure affecting wholesale participants in the secondary bond markets that could be attributed to transparency levels. However, a number of respondents, particularly the private investors group, noted that bond markets might be a difficult environment for direct retail investors, who have no access to transparency information on the same basis as other participants: 'They might receive less data, or the data they did obtain might be more delayed, meaning they would be a step behind other participants.'[54] The low level of transparency might indeed be the cause of the low level of direct retail involvement in bonds. CESR further specified that the extent of information asymmetry may differ depending on the instruments traded. For more liquid bonds (such as government bonds, supranational and large corporate issues) the ability to access trading information tends to be greater.[55] As transparency levels reduce, market failures may become more likely: 'Price discovery, and thus the ability to assess prices for best execution purposes, will tend to become more difficult, particularly for smaller players.'[56] CESR's general answer to the core question at issue was that there is no evident market failure in respect of market transparency in bond markets. Yet, smaller participants, including retail investors, might benefit from receiving access to greater trading transparency, which could also encourage higher levels of retail participation in the markets.[57] Nonetheless, 'any increase in transparency would need to be carefully tailored to ensure that liquidity provision and levels of competition were not damaged as a result of dealers reducing or withdrawing their commitment to the markets'.[58]

The Commission's Report, which was subsequently published under Article 65 (1) MiFID, reached similar conclusions.[59] With respect to

---

[53] CESR, *Response to the Commission on non-equities transparency*, (note 5, above), 6, where possible market failures (such as information asymmetry and market power) are considered. See also, for an analysis of possible market failures, the ESME's Report to the European Commission, (note 52, above).

[54] CESR, *Response to the Commission on non-equities transparency*, (note 5, above), 8.

[55] Ibid., this being due to higher levels of multilateral trading and the greater number of two-way quotes made available by dealers.   [56] Ibid.

[57] Ibid., 9. See, for a similar conclusion, ESME, *Non-equity Market Transparency*, (note 52, above), 13, identifying some evidence of sub-optimality with respect to market transparency in retail bond markets.

[58] Ibid., also noting (at 11) that the perspective of mandated pre-trade transparency caused concern for the risk of a negative impact on dealers' willingness to provide the markets with liquidity.

[59] DG Internal Market and Services, Working Document, *Report on non-equities market transparency pursuant to Article 65 (1) of Directive 2004/39/EC on Markets in Financial Instruments (MiFID)* (3 April 2008).

the retail bond markets, the Commission services accepted CESR's and ESME's view that investors have 'sub-optimal' access to price information: 'Clearly, without ready access to bond market prices retail clients are in no position to check the quality of execution they receive from their intermediaries, including the competitiveness of the prices they are quoted.'[60] With respect to wholesale markets, the Commission services similarly accepted the argument that no convincing case of a market failure has been made out.[61] As a general conclusion, the Commission argued that there does not seem to be, at this time, a need for expanding the MiFID's transparency requirements to financial instruments other than shares.[62] Assuming, however, that there is an issue with respect to retail access to bond market prices, the Commission services accepted that market participants appear to be well-placed to address the same through self-regulatory initiatives. Moreover, the Commission encouraged 'all designers and implementers of self-regulatory solutions, including ICMA and SIFMA, to consider carefully the design parameters so that retail access to realistic and up-to-date prices is broadened and deepened to the fullest extent possible consistent with ensuring that liquidity is not impaired'.[63]

A few comments may help to better understand the consultations' outcome. Firstly, a majority of interventions came from trade associations of banks, securities firms and other professionals.[64] This suggests some degree of caution in assessing the view that wholesale bond markets would be immune from market failures. No doubt, also buy-side participants, such as investment fund managers, often concurred in this view.[65] However, they may have acted strategically, fearing that the costs of regulation, including the potential loss of liquidity from dealers, could be higher than the benefits deriving from increased market transparency. Secondly, almost all participants shared the view that retail investors might suffer from information asymmetry, even though the concept of 'sub-optimality' seemed more appropriate than that of market failure. Broad consensus emerged, however, on the need for remedying this asymmetry through a market-led disclosure mechanism similar to TRACE. The Commission's final recommendation was in the

---

[60] Ibid., 10, also specifying that 'for many retail customers it would be totally impractical in terms of transaction costs to engage multiple intermediaries and secure competing quotes prior to each transaction, as institutional investors tend to do'.
[61] Ibid., 10–11.   [62] Ibid., 13.   [63] Ibid.
[64] See CESR, *Response to the Commission on non-equities transparency*, (note 5, above), 7.
[65] See DG Internal Market and Services, (note 50, above), 2.

same direction, suggesting self-regulation of post-trade transparency. Pre-trade transparency did not appear fit for regulation, which would also require the introduction of an obligation to quote for price information to be meaningful. A similar obligation would create problems like those already seen for the MiFID's quote rule[66] and would adversely impact bond markets' microstructures. Thirdly, best execution emerged as one of the key arguments supporting enhanced market transparency, which would improve retail investors' ability to control order execution by their intermediaries, in addition to helping the latter to comply with best execution requirements. I will try to develop this argument in the rest of the chapter, by examining the interaction between transparency and best execution.

IV. Best execution in transparent bond markets

MiFID is aimed at enhancing competition between trading venues. As seen with respect to equity markets, the Directive's opposition to domestic concentration rules was motivated by competitive concerns. Moreover, mandatory transparency was introduced to remedy the negative impact of market fragmentation on price discovery;[67] also best execution was regulated in view of promoting competition between trading venues, in addition to protecting individual investors. However, as I tried to show in another paper, the principle of best execution was specified in ways which could make competition in share trading more difficult for new entrants and in the end protect the incumbent exchanges.[68] After summarizing the core arguments of my previous paper (a), I will analyse three examples of bond trading from a best execution and transparency perspective (b).

(a) MiFID offers a broad definition of best execution[69] which deserves approval, for it is often acknowledged that order execution should be

---

[66] See the preceding paragraph.

[67] See Section III.

[68] Ferrarini, 'Best Execution and Competition between Trading Venues – MiFID's Likely Impact', (note 2, above), 404–13.

[69] Under Article 21 (1) MiFID, investment firms are required to 'take all reasonable steps to obtain, when executing orders, the best possible result for their clients taking into account price, costs, speed, likelihood of execution and settlement, size, nature or any other consideration relevant to the execution of the order'. This is a best endeavour obligation, which is met by complying with the provisions foreseen in the following paragraphs of Article 21. See the AMF, *Enforcing the Best-execution Principles in MiFID and its Implementing Directive* (25 July 2006), 7, speaking of a 'best efforts' obligation.

assessed also on the basis of criteria other than price.[70] A flexible concept of best execution makes competition between trading venues easier, to the extent that exchanges, MTFs, internalizing firms and other liquidity providers compete both as to price and other aspects of trading. As a result, new execution venues or entities will emerge and offer trading functionalities different from those already provided by exchanges. However, other provisions of the MiFID and the implementing Directive constrain the flexibility of best execution by making its requirements more specific.[71] Particularly in the case of execution of orders for retail clients, the best execution factors enumerated by Article 21 (1) of the MiFID are incorporated, at level 2, in the narrower criterion of 'total consideration'.[72] Reference to 'total consideration' is justified on two counts. First, it is an easy test to apply for retail clients wishing to monitor the quality of order execution by an investment firm. Second, retail orders are generally small and relatively easy to execute. Therefore, getting the best price for an instrument and the lowest costs for trading the same should suffice for best execution purposes. This approach has

[70] See FSA, *Best Execution,* Consultation Paper 154 (October 2002); J. Macey and M. O'Hara, 'The Law and Economics of Best Execution', *Journal of Financial Intermediation,* 6 (1997), 188.

[71] First, the order execution policy (offering information on execution venues and how to choose among them) 'shall at least include those venues that enable the investment firm to obtain on a consistent basis the best possible result for the execution of client orders' (Article 21 (3) MiFID). It is not enough for investment firms that, for example, internalize execution of orders to refer to the prices made in the exchange where the securities are listed. Their execution policy should also 'include' this exchange (assuming it assures 'on a consistent basis' the best possible result for the firm's clients). Therefore, the investment firm should be ready to trade on the relevant exchange and, in any case, should monitor the prices of internalized trades by periodically comparing the same with those made in the exchange at issue. Secondly, investment firms should obtain the 'prior consent' (which could also be tacit)[71] of their clients to their execution policy and inform the same about the possibility, when foreseen by this policy, to execute their orders outside a regulated market or MTF. Moreover, investment firms should obtain the 'prior express consent' of their clients before proceeding to execute their orders outside a regulated market or MTF. Similar requirements protect the incumbent exchanges by alerting clients against the risks of off-exchange transactions. At the same time, they underline that exchange markets offer liquidity and price efficiency. In brief, domestic concentration rules are replaced by 'consent' requirements and by the duty to include the best performing exchange in a firm's execution policy.

[72] Article 44 (3) of the Commission Directive requires, in similar cases, to determine the best possible result in terms of total consideration 'representing the price of the financial instrument and the costs related to execution, which shall include all expenses incurred by the client which are directly related to execution of the order, including execution venue fees, clearing and settlement fees and any other fees paid to third parties involved in the execution of the order'.

an impact on competition between trading venues, to the extent that reference to the traded instruments' price puts established and more liquid venues at a competitive advantage.[73]

The impact on competition of a narrow best execution concept, such as that embodied in the total consideration criterion, is manifest when considering the possibility of including a single execution venue in a firm's policy. As argued by CESR in a consultation document, 'there may be circumstances in which only one particular execution venue or entity will deliver the best possible result on a consistent basis for some instruments and orders'.[74] It may also be that for other instruments or orders there are other potential venues. However, the cost of accessing more than one execution venue directly, to the extent that it would be passed on to clients, 'may outweigh any price improvement an alternative venue might offer'.[75] CESR considered that, in similar circumstances, it may be 'reasonable' to decide not to connect to these other venues; nonetheless, the investment firm should always consider also the advantages of indirect access (i.e. transmitting its client orders to another execution intermediary rather than executing those orders itself).[76] In its final document CESR, whilst confirming that an investment firm may include a single entity in its policy, adopted a more general stance by asking the same 'to show that this allows it to satisfy the overarching best execution requirement'.[77]

(b) Three examples show the complexity of best execution analysis in bond trading. The first refers to bonds which are only traded OTC, with liquidity provided by one or more dealers. When the retail customer asks her broker to buy similar bonds, the latter will look for the best offer available and execute the transaction with the relevant dealer.[78] Given the transaction's likely small size, there will generally be no negotiation of the price with the dealer. If there is no pre-trade transparency, as presently is generally the case in OTC markets, the broker will ask the dealers for a quote and possibly compare the same with quotes from other

[73] No doubt, total consideration also includes transaction costs and, where there is more than one execution venue, the trading firm's commissions and costs for executing an order on each of the eligible venues shall be taken into account (Article 44 (3) Commission Directive).

[74] CESR, 'Best Execution under MiFID', Public Consultation (February 2007), 10.

[75] Ibid.   [76] Ibid.

[77] CESR, 'Best Execution under MiFID', Questions and Answers (May 2007), 8.

[78] See, for more information on the microstructure of the European corporate bond market, CEPR, (note 14, above), 29.

dealers through an information provider (such as Bloomberg). If there is post-trade transparency, as is sometimes the case in domestic bond markets also for OTC transactions[79] and was suggested by the Commission, the broker will find his task easier and the customer will be able to exercise better monitoring on her order's execution by the broker. The situation gets more complex when either the broker is also a dealer for the security in question or the dealer and the broker belong to the same group of companies. In similar cases, the relevant provisions on conflict of interests will also have to be complied with.[80]

The second hypothetical case refers to bonds which are admitted to trading on a regulated market and are actually traded on the same market and on another venue (regulated market or MTF). Assuming that the broker has access to both venues and that they offer both pre-trade and post-trade transparency, as often happens with regulated markets and MTFs also for bond trading,[81] compliance with best execution will be relatively easy, with order execution taking place in the venue offering the best price. However, the broker might also choose to trade bonds on a single venue, in which case best execution is satisfied by trading on this venue, provided that the performance of the same is periodically compared with that of the other venue, so as to check the possibility for the broker to keep only one venue in his execution policy.[82]

The third hypothesis is a combination of the previous two. Assume that bonds are admitted to trading on a regulated market and are traded both on- or off-exchange. Further assume that the regulated market offers pre-trade and post-trade transparency, whilst off-exchange transactions are not published under the applicable rules. Briefly, this is a case of competition between a transparent and an opaque market. Economic theory predicts that the opaque market will prevail, as dealers in this market exploit their informational advantage to quote narrower spreads and earn more profits than their more transparent competitors. In addition, most dealers choose to be of lower transparency, if allowed to do

---

[79] See CESR, *Response to the Commission on non-equities transparency*, (note 5, above), Annex 'Existing trading transparency in Europe for listed bonds'.

[80] See Articles 13 (3) and 18 MiFID, and Ch. II, sec. 4, MiFID's Implementing Directive. For a critical view, see L. Enriques, 'Conflicts of Interest in Investment Services: The Price and Uncertain Impact of MiFID's Regulatory Framework', in Ferrarini and Wymeersch, *Investor protection in Europe*, (note 2, above), 321–338.

[81] See the Annex, 'Existing trading transparency in Europe for listed bonds', (note 79, above).

[82] See CESR's criteria, (notes 74 and 77, above), and accompanying text.

so.[83] From a best execution perspective, the broker in our example will choose the best offer from either market; assuming that opaque dealers quote the best prices, the broker will transact off-exchange. However, the broker is not bound to ask all dealers, if there are information costs. Moreover, the client will have difficulties in assessing the quality of order execution, if the off-exchange market is opaque and the exchange prices are often worse that those made for off-exchange transactions. If post-trade transparency were mandated for all transactions, the two markets would compete on a level playing field and the clients would better monitor the quality of their brokers' order execution.

V. Conclusion

The examples just analysed confirm that transparency is important for best execution in bond trading and that market-led solutions directed to enhance post-trade transparency deserve approval. In the case of regulated markets and MTFs, both pre-trade and post-trade transparency are often already available. For OTC transactions pre-trade transparency is more difficult to obtain, as changes to the market microstructure may be needed. Post-trade transparency, on the contrary, is feasible for OTC markets. However, a crucial question needs to be answered, concerning the time when the relevant information should be published.[84] In view of the Commission's consultation, the International Capital Markets Association (ICMA) sent a questionnaire to its members concerning possible market-led mechanisms for bond market transparency.[85] The questionnaire set out two non-mutually exclusive options, which were designed to help retail investors, while avoiding liquidity problems for firms: 'Option 1 is a Price Service, which would involve publishing, at the end of the day, an average of the closing bid and offer quotes for each reportable security and the high, low and average prices for each bond trade which has been reported to ICMA. Option 2 is a Single Trade Publication Service, which would involve publishing trades in large investment grade bonds above a specified minimum level and below a specified upper size limit.'[86]

These proposals show some of the core questions to be addressed when setting-up post-trade disclosure for debt securities. First, should

---

[83] See Bloomfield and O'Hara, 'Can Transparent Markets Survive?', (note 48, above).

[84] See, for an analysis, CEPR, *European Corporate Bond Markets*, (note 8, above), 68–69.

[85] 'The ICMA Bond Market Transparency Questionnaire: Assessment of Responses' (21 May 2007).

[86] See, for details of these options, Annex B of the Questionnaire.

real-time or end-of-day publication of data be chosen? No doubt, delayed publication is favoured by most dealers; however real-time (or close to real-time) information would be more helpful from a best execution perspective.[87] Second, should post-trade transparency only apply to liquid bonds or also to illiquid ones? Again, dealers tend to favour limiting transparency to markets which are already liquid; yet, from an investor's perspective, the benefits of transparency would emerge particularly in the case of illiquid markets.[88] Third, what size of transactions should be covered? If the principal aim is to protect retail investors, information should also be published for relatively small sizes, while trade information concerning blocks is less needed (and dealers would no doubt object to real time publication of the same). The Commission, despite being aware of the numerous trade-offs between transparency and liquidity, restrained from doing more than suggesting a 'careful' design for self-regulatory initiatives.[89] It remains to be seen, however, whether market participants will be able to solve their collective action problems and strike the right balance between transparency and liquidity, without regulators intervening either to 'inspire' self-regulation informally or to set a general framework for market-driven solutions.[90]

---

[87] See, however, ESME, *Non-equity Market Transparency*, (note 52, above), 16, stating that 'it does not appear that there would be significant additional benefit to retail investors from the provision of real-time publication'.

[88] See however CEPR, *European Corporate Bond Markets*, (note 8, above), 65, arguing that for less liquid bonds the impact of transparency on liquidity could be a real issue; ESME, *Non-equity Market Transparency*, (note 52, above), 16, stating that 'information is unlikely to be of much value [to retail investors] in illiquid markets where a bond may go for weeks or months without being traded'.

[89] See the text accompanying note 63, above.

[90] This is the case of Consob in Italy, which requires regulated market operators and MTFs to include in their market rules 'adequate' provisions on pre- and post-trade transparency for non-equity instruments (Article 32 of Consob's Markets Regulation), and systematic internalizers to similarly adopt transparency mechanisms differentiated depending on market microstructure, type of instrument and type of investor (Article 33). On the Italian approach to bond market regulation, see C. Salini, 'Bond Markets in Italy: Transparency and Regulatory Issues' (19 March 2007), available at www.consob.it.

27

The statutory authority of the European Central Bank and euro-area national central banks over TARGET2-Securities*

PETER O. MÜLBERT AND REBEKKA M. WIEMANN

I. Introduction

As an academic as well as a banking and securities regulator, the dedicatee of this volume has made significant contributions to the integration of European financial markets. Accordingly, the topics of his publications reflect the ongoing integration process of European financial markets and of European securities markets, in particular. While, at the outset, his interests focused on securities regulation in Europe,[1] he has recently turned to studying the various initiatives to render clearing and settlement in Europe more efficient.[2] Indeed, while safe and efficient clearing and settlement systems are universally acknowledged as being an essential factor in the creation of an integrated European financial market,[3] numerous obstacles still exist that render cross-border securities transactions costly and less efficient than ultimately possible.

TARGET2-Securities (in financial jargon 'T2S') is one of the most advanced steps towards a more efficient and sound clearing and settlement infrastructure for the European securities market. The project

---

* May 2008. Any subsequent developments could not be taken into account.
[1] E. Wymeersch, 'Securities Market Regulations in Europe' in A.M. George, and I.H. Giddy (eds.), *International Finance Handbook* (New York: Wiley, 1982), 1–51; *idem*, 'Europese Effectenreglementering', in J. R. Schaafsma and E. Wymeersch (eds.), *Bescherming van beleggers ter beurze, Vereniging Handelsrecht* (Zwolle: W.E.J. Tjeenk Willink, 1986), 271–392; *idem*, 'The EEC and the Eurosecurities Markets', *Singapore Conference on International Business Law* (1987).
[2] E. Wymeersch, 'Securities Clearing and Settlement: Regulatory Developments in Europe', in G. Ferrarini and E. Wymeersch (eds.), *Investor Protection in Europe*, (Oxford University Press, 2006), 465 et seq.
[3] See the European Commission, *Financial Services: Implementing the Framework for Financial Markets: Action Plan* (1999), http://ec.europa.eu/internal_market/finances/docs/actionplan/index/action_en.pdf).

undertaken by the Eurosystem, i.e., the European System of Central Banks (ESCB) known as 'the European Central Bank (ECB) and the national central banks (NCBs) of those Member States whose currency is the euro'[4], aims at creating a settlement service for securities transactions linked to the existing Europe-wide cash settlement system known as TARGET2. The project is praised as being 'ground-breaking'[5] or even as an 'opportunity to jointly shape the future',[6] but has also met with severe criticism,[7] sometimes to the point of outright rejection.

One of the controversial issues raised almost at the outset was whether European law confers the statutory authority on the euro-area central banks (CBs), i.e. the ECB and the euro-area NCBs, to develop a securities settlement infrastructure. Although those denying the Eurosystem's legal power – in practice critics doubted the ECB's power in particular – have become fewer and most market participants seem to accept the Eurosystem's initiative, the question of whether the euro-area CBs can claim a sufficient legal basis for setting up and operating such a facility remains essential for the realization of the entire project.

This chapter, in seeking to provide a definite answer, is organized as follows. Starting with a brief overview of the other initiatives in the field of clearing and settlement (Section II), it goes on to give a brief description of TARGET2-Securities and to explain some pertinent key features (Section III). The main section (Section IV) then examines whether the euro-area CBs are empowered to implement TARGET2-Securities. It first sets out basic assumptions offering *inter alia* some clarifications as to the relationship between the ESCB and the Eurosystem, on the one hand, and the interplay between the Eurosystem and the ECB/NCBs, on the other hand. Building on that analysis, it then examines in some detail the relevant provisions that might confer the authority on the euro-area CBs to set up and operate TARGET2-Securities. The essay ends by offering some concluding remarks (Section V).

---

[4] Hence, the term 'Eurosystem' is not only a shorthand for 'the ECB plus the euro-area NCBs', but denotes a particular version of the ESCB. As to this interpretation, see infra IV.A. in more detail.

[5] M. Godeffroy, 'Ten frequently asked Questions about TARGET2-Securities' (available at www.ecb.int/paym/t2s/defining/outgoing/html/10faq.en.html).

[6] J. Tessler, 'An Opportunity to jointly shape the Future', *TARGET2-Securities Newsletter* No. 2, August 2007, 3 (available at www.ecb.int/paym/t2s/pdf/T2S_Newsletter_070829. pdf).

[7] E.g., J. Mérère, 'The Devil is in the Detail', *Finanzplatz* (January 2007), 18.

II. Overview of other initiatives in the field of clearing and settlement[8]

Taking existing EU legislation as a starting point, some directives contain provisions relevant for certain aspects of securities clearing and settlement activities. This is particularly true for the Settlement Finality Directive (SFD) of 1998,[9] but also for the Collateral Directive of 2002,[10] and – to a certain extent – the (recast) Banking Directive of 2006[11] and the (recast) Capital Adequacy Directive of 2006.[12] Even some provisions of the Markets in Financial Instruments Directive (MiFID)[13] have an effect on the clearing and settlement infrastructure, e.g. Article 34, which gives a right of access to an investment firm in one Member State, on a non-discriminatory basis, to the clearing and settlement system of another Member State. However, these provisions do not constitute a comprehensive framework for securities clearing and settlement activities, but rather form a partial patchwork regulating only specific problems.

The European Commission, following its Financial Services Action Plan of 1999,[14] set up a group of financial market experts, chaired by Alberto Giovannini, to analyse the status quo of the European financial market. The Giovannini Group, in its first report on clearing and settlement within the EU, identified fifteen barriers rendering cross-border securities transactions inefficient (often called Giovannini barriers), and, in its second report on the same topic, suggested a set of actions to eliminate these barriers.[15] Building

---

[8] For more details see Wymeersch, 'Securities Clearing and Settlement', (note 2, above), 470–83; K.M. Löber, 'The Developing EU Legal Framework for Clearing and Settlement of financial Instruments', *European Central Bank, Legal Working Paper Series*, No. 1, February 2006; H. Beck, 'Clearing und Settlement im Fokus europäischer Rechtspolitik', in K.P. Berger, G. Borges, H. Heermann, A. Schlüter, and U. Wackerbarth (eds.), *Zivil- und Wirtschaftsrecht im Europäischen und Globalen Kontext* (Berlin: De Gruyter, 2006), 669–95.

[9] Directive 98/26/EC [1998] OJ L 166/45.

[10] Directive 2002/47/EC [2002] OJ L 168/43.

[11] Directive 2006/48/EC [2006] OJ L 177/1.

[12] Directive 2006/49/EC [2006] OJ L 177/201.

[13] Directive 2004/39/EC [2004] OJ L 145/1.

[14] European Commission, *Financial Services: Implementing the Framework for Financial Markets: Action Plan* (note 3, above).

[15] The Giovannini Group, *Cross-Border Clearing and Settlement Arrangements in the European Union, Brussels* (November 2001); *idem, Second Report on EU Clearing and Settlement Arrangements*, Brussels, April 2003, http://ec.europa.eu/internal_market/ financial-markets/docs/clearing/second_giovannini_report_en.pdf.

on the second Giovannini report, the European Commission in its Second Consultative Communication on Securities Clearing and Settlement[16] proposed the preparation of a framework Directive on Clearing and Settlement and the establishment of three groups of experts: the Clearing and Settlement Advisory and Monitoring Expert Group (CESAME), the Legal Certainty Group (LCG) and the Fiscal Compliance Expert Group (FISCO).[17]

In the meantime, since the former goal of removing the Giovannini barriers within a time period of three years has proved to be unrealistic, the European Commission has reversed its approach. Instead of pursuing the preparation of a framework Directive, the Commission has asked the market participants to agree on a Code of Conduct[18] that contains specified commitments of trading and post-trading infrastructure providers. According to the European Commission's report to the ECOFIN in July 2007,[19] the Code of Conduct has already had a positive impact. However, this does not imply that further activities are unnecessary. Quite the contrary, the FISCO report of October 2007[20] will serve the Commission as a basis for further discussions with Member States on future EU initiatives to simplify and modernize tax procedures applied to financial assets. Likewise, the LCG report, due in mid-2008, is expected to outline proposals for substantial EU legislation – probably either in the form of a Directive or a Regulation – dealing with substantive legal aspects of clearing and settlement.

A working group was established by the European System of Central Banks (ESCB) in collaboration with the Committee of European Securities Regulators (CESR) to elaborate common standards or recommendations for securities settlement systems and to enhance the safety

---

[16] *Clearing and Settlement in the European Union – The way forward*, Communication from the Commission to the Council and the European Parliament, COM(2994) 312 final.

[17] For further information on the expert groups, see http://ec.europa.eu/internal_market/ financial-markets/clearing/index_en.htm.

[18] European Code of Conduct for Clearing and Settlement of 7 November 2006, http:// ec.europa.eu/internal_market/financial-markets/docs/code/code_en.pdf.

[19] Improving the Efficiency, Integration and Safety and Soundness of Cross-border Post-trading Arrangements in Europe, Report to the ECOFIN, 25 July 2007, http://ec.europa. eu/internal_market/financial-markets/docs/clearing/ecofin/20070725_ecofin_en.pdf.

[20] The Fiscal Compliance Experts' Group, *Solutions to Fiscal Compliance Barriers Related to Post-trading within the EU, Second Report 2007*, http://ec.europa.eu/internal_market/ financial-markets/clearing/compliance_en.htm.

and efficiency of cross-border securities clearing and settlement activities within the EU. Building on the CPSS/IOSCO recommendations,[21] but seeking to adapt these global recommendations to European circumstances, the group elaborated the Standards for Securities Clearing and Settlement within the European Union,[22] nineteen standards aimed at rendering securities clearing and settlement systems within the European Union safer, more efficient and sound.[23]

Still further initiatives within Europe are undertaken by the European Financial Markets Lawyers Group (EFMLG), a group established in 1999 following a Eurosystem initiative and composed of European lawyers working for major credit institutions active in the European financial market. The EFMLG's work aims at promoting the harmonization of EU financial market activities through legal initiatives. In its report 'Harmonisation of the legal Framework for Rights evidenced by book-entries in respect of certain financial Instruments in the European Union'[24] the EFMLG observed barriers to cross-border securities transactions similar to those identified by the Giovannini Group. The EFMLG formulated recommendations calling for further EU legislation in the form of directives and supporting the (as it was called at the time) EU Securities Account Certainty Project, proposed by the Giovannini Group.

Looking beyond Europe, some global initiatives show parallels to the work currently being undertaken in the EU, e.g. the 'Convention on the Law Applicable to certain Rights in respect of Securities held with an Intermediary'[25] concluded by the Hague Conference in 2002 and signed by two signatories – Switzerland and the US – in 2006 (dealing with matters that are addressed albeit differently within the EU by the SFD and other EC legal acts). Another initiative is UNIDROIT's project on Intermediated Securities. The original text of the 'Preliminary draft

---

[21] CPSS/IOSCO, *Recommendations for Securities Settlement Systems*, November 2001, www.bis.org/publ/cpss46.pdf.

[22] The ESCB-CESR Standards for Securities Clearing and Settlement in the European Union, www.ecb.int/pub/pdf/other/escb-cesr-standardssecurities2004en.pdf.

[23] Critical, then, Bundesverband Deutscher Banken, *Europäische Wertpapiermärkte – Konsolidierung des Rechtsrahmens*, Berlin, January 2006, 34.

[24] European Financial Markets Lawyers Group, *Harmonisation of the legal Framework for Rights evidenced by book-entries in Respect of certain financial Instruments in the European Union*, European Central Bank, June 2003.

[25] Hague Conference on Private International Law, 'Convention on the Law Applicable to Certain Rights relating to Securities held with an Intermediary', 5 July 2006, www.hcch.net/index_en.php?act=conventions.text&cid=72.

Convention on harmonized substantive Rules regarding Securities held with an Intermediary' of 2004 was further developed during the international negotiation process that took place between May 2005 and May 2007. In September 2008, a diplomatic conference is planned to be held in Geneva to adopt a 'Convention of substantive rules regarding intermediated securities'.[26]

III. TARGET2-securities: main features of the project[27]

On 7 July 2006, the ECB's Governing Council announced that the Eurosystem is evaluating opportunities to provide settlement services for securities transactions. Having drafted the project's rough features, the Eurosystem launched feasibility studies which came to the conclusion that the project was operationally, legally, economically and technically feasible.[28] A first consultation paper, that framed the cornerstones of TARGET2-Securities by setting up twenty principles and sixty-seven high-level proposals, was published in March 2007[29] on which market participants could comment by June 2007.[30] Working groups, designed to allow a variety of institutions to participate, elaborated the user requirements which were fully articulated by the end of 2007.[31] A second public consultation was launched in December 2007. Market participants were invited to comment on the TARGET2-Securities user requirements

---

[26] For the Preliminary Draft and further information on Study 78 on intermediated securities, see www.unidroit.org/english/workprogramme/study078/item1/main.htm.

[27] As to the following, cf. Godeffroy, 'Ten frequently asked questions about TARGET2-Securities' (note 5, above); ECB, *TARGET2-Securities, The Blueprint* (8 March 2007), www.ecb.int/pub/pdf/other/t2sblueprint0703en.pdf; ECB, *T2S Progress Report* (26 October 2007), www.ecb.int/pub/pdf/other/t2s-progressreport200710en.pdf.

[28] The feasibility studies are available at www.ecb.int/paym/t2s/decisions/html/nextphase.en.html.

[29] ECB, *T2S Consultation Paper: General Principles and high-level Proposals for the User Requirements* (26 April 2007), www.bundesbank.de/download/zahlungsverkehr/t2s_us_070426.pdf.

[30] For an overview of the market participants' reactions see I. Terol, 'How have the Principles and Proposals been reviewed after the Consultation?', presentation, T2S info session 29 August 2007, www.ecb.int/paym/t2s/pdf/outgoing/t2s_infosession_070829_presentation1.pdf.

[31] ECB, *T2S – The User Requirements* (12 December 2007), www.ecb.int/ecb/cons/shared/files/T2S_urd_chapters.pdf; a summary of the user requirements can be found at www.ecb.int/ecb/cons/shared/files/T2S_urd_management_summary.pdf. For a description of the TARGET2-Securities governance structure cf. TARGET2-Securities Newsletter No. 1, June 2007, www.ecb.int/paym/t2s/pdf/T2S_Newsletter.pdf, 3 *et seq.* or the (shorter) overview at www.ecb.int/paym/t2s/defining/html/index.en.html.

and the methodology for the assessment of the economic impact of the project by April 2008.[32] The ECB assumes the project will be concluded by 2013, at the latest.[33]

The objective of TARGET2-Securities is to maximize safety and efficiency in the settlement of euro-denominated securities transactions. The main features of the project, as so far determined, are as follows:

TARGET2-Securities will be a single, purely technical platform providing harmonized IT settlement services to central securities depositories (here below referred to as 'CSDs') based on the TARGET2 platform,[34] a technical platform for the settlement of payment instructions. It will be established as well as fully owned by the Eurosystem[35] and technically operated on behalf of four of the Eurosystem NCBs (Bundesbank, Banque de France, Banca d'Italia and Banco de España).[36] TARGET2-Securities will allow the simultaneous (real-time) booking of both legs of a transaction in securities , i.e. the payment in (exclusively) central bank money and the transfer (of title) of the securities on a single IT-platform (integrated model). In more detail:

The ECB/Eurosystem will not operate as a CSD[37] since it will not legally maintain securities accounts for CSDs,[38] or even less for banks that are clients of such a CSD. Instead, the account and legal relationships remain exclusively between CSDs and their clients, i.e. the banks holding securities accounts with the CSDs also manage the account relationships among the different CSDs (the legal arrangements between CSDs will, however, be affected by the harmonized terms and conditions governing the settlement services provided by TARGET2-Securities)[39]. From this it follows that cross-border and cross-CSD securities transactions will still be effected by book entries in securities

---

[32] ECB Press Release of 18 December 2007, www.ecb.int/press/pr/date/2007/html/pr071218.en.html.

[33] Speech by G. Tumpell-Gugerell, Member of the Executive Board of the ECB at the *Journal of Financial Transformation* dinner London, 27 September 2007, www.ecb.int/press/key/date/2007/html/sp070927.en.html.

[34] *General Principles* (note 29, above), 4, principle 2.

[35] ECB Press Release 7 July 2006, www.ecb.int/press/pr/date/2006/html/pr060707.en.html; *General Principles* (note 29, above), 4, principle 1.

[36] Questions and Answers on TARGET2-Securities, 8 March 2007, www.ecb.int/press/pressconf/2007/html/is070308.en.html#t2s.

[37] *General Principles* (note 29, above), 4, principle 3.

[38] *General Principles* (note 29, above), 5, principle 4.

[39] *General Principles* (note 29, above), 7, principle 15.

accounts held by CSDs' clients with CSDs or by CSDs with one another. Moreover, the question of whether the T2S's booking of a security from one account to another perfects a transfer of title, and at what point in time it does so, lies outside the scope of TARGET2-Securities, and is determined solely by the national law(s) applicable to the transaction. In this respect TARGET2-Securities will neither alter the present situation nor will national legislative adaptations be necessary for the implementation of TARGET2-Securities (even if legal harmonization would be desirable to improve integration).[40] However, T2S may increase (even in the absence of legal harmonization of substantive law) the predictability of and legal certainty on the completion of the legal transfer, due to the transfer order finality on both sides of a cross-system transaction and the standardized simultaneous settlement in T2S in the accounts of both CSDs involved resulting in the legal exchange of cash and securities.

What the ECB/Eurosystem will provide is the TARGET2-Securities platform, i.e. the integrated IT-platform allowing for the simultaneous booking of cash transactions in cash accounts held with the Eurosystem central banks by CSDs or their customers, as well as securities transactions in securities accounts held with the CSDs. The database functionality required will be restricted to the basic role of collocating and electronically storing account-related data in a common technical location.[41] All CSDs are eligible under equal-access conditions[42] to participate in TARGET2-Securities,[43] but not required to do so. TARGET2-Securities will operate on a non-profit-making basis.[44] As regards the relationship between cash transactions and securities transactions, TARGET2-Securities is planned to operate following the so-called Delivery versus Payment (DVP) model 1, which in T2S means simultaneous real-time delivery versus payment settlement in central bank money for domestic *and* cross-border transactions of securities.[45]

---

[40] TARGET2-Securities, *Legal Feasibility Study* (8 March 2007), 6. Admittedly, the study assumes that the soundness and efficiency of TARGET2-Securities could be strengthened by further harmonization in this respect (available at www.ecb.int/pub/pdf/other/t2slegalfeasibility0703en.pdf).

[41] TARGET2-Securities, *Legal Feasibility Study* (note 40, above), 1.

[42] *General Principles* (note 29, above), 7, principle 14, principle 12.

[43] *General Principles* (note 29, above), 7, principle 13.

[44] *General Principles* (note 29, above), 8 principle 18.

[45] TARGET2-Securities, *Legal Feasibility Study* (note 40, above), 2.

IV. Legal assessment

A. Basics

The starting point for a legal analysis of TARGET2-Securities is a seeming puzzle. On the one hand, as mentioned above, the Eurosystem is said to be the full owner and operator of TARGET2-Securities, whereas, on the other hand, critics have disputed the legal authority of the ECB (and the NCBs) to operate the system.

These divergences obviously beg the question whether the Eurosystem is a separate actor from the ECB and the NCBs, or whether the term is just an abbreviation for denoting the ECB and the NCBs. The problem is compounded by the fact that the EC Treaty as well as the Statute of the European System of Central Banks and of the European Central Bank ('ESCB/ECB Statute') only deal with the ESCB but do not employ the term Eurosystem at all. Moreover, both the EC Treaty as well as the ESCB/ECB Statute invest the ESCB with tasks and, in order for these tasks to be carried out, confer certain legal powers on the ECB and the NCBs.

Against this backdrop, any meaningful discussion of the question whether the EC Treaty and/or the ESCB/ECB Statute actually confer the legal authority required on the actor owning and operating TARGET2-Securities presupposes some prior clarifications as to the nature of the Eurosystem and its relationship with the ESCB on the one hand and the ECB on the other hand.

1. ESCB and the Eurosystem

The Eurosystem according to the definition given in Article 9 Sentence 2 of the Rules of Procedure of the ECB[46] means 'the European Central Bank (ECB) and the national central banks of those Member States whose currency is the euro'. By contrast, the EC Treaty and the ESCB/ECB Statute only refer to the European System of Central Banks defined by Article 107 (1) EC Treaty as being 'composed of the ECB and of the central banks' of all Member States.

However, this neither implies that the Eurosystem lacks a legal foundation in primary community law nor that the ESCB and the Eurosystem form two different organizations existing alongside one another. In particular, it would be misleading to conceive of the Eurosystem as a subset of the ESCB. Rather, it is more appropriate to say that the EC Treaty as

---

[46] Decision ECB/2004/2 [2004] OJ L 080/33.

well as the ESCB/ECB Statute – despite the definition given by Article 107 (1) EC Treaty – attribute two different meanings to the term 'ESCB'. Depending on the Article in question, the term 'ESCB' must be construed either in the sense of Article 107 (1) EC Treaty as 'the ECB and the NCBs of all Member States' or, as is most often the case, in the sense of Article 9 Sentence 2 of the Rules of Procedure of the ECB, i.e. as 'the ECB and the euro-area NCBs'. Moreover, the term 'Eurosystem' does not denote any distinct organization existing apart from the ESCB but denotes the ESCB in its latter quality, i.e. the ESCB comprising the ECB and euro-area NCBs.

Art. 122 (3) and (4) EC Treaty and Art. 43 (1), (3) and (4) ESCB/ECB Statute determine for the provisions of the EC Treaty and the ESCB/ECB Statute respectively whether those provisions address the ESCB in the sense of Art.107 (1) EC Treaty or in the sense of the 'Eurosystem'. The reading depends on whether those provisions according to the definition given by Art. 122 (3) and (4) EC Treaty and Art. 43 (1), (3) and (4) ESCB/ECB Statute refer to (the NCBs of) all Member States or only to (the NCBs of) euro-area Member States.

2. Legal nature of the ESCB/Eurosystem

The ESCB/Eurosystem, as is universally admitted, has no legal personality of its own. This follows *a contrario* from Article 107 (2) EC Treaty and Article 9.1 ESCB/ECB Statute which, both, award legal personality only to the ECB.

Most commentators even assert that the ESCB/Eurosystem has no existence of its own, i.e. that it does not exist as a separate organization. Instead, the ESCB/Eurosystem is labelled as being an institutional framework of rules establishing a link between the ECB and the (euro-area) NCBs,[47] or even reduced to the status of being nothing more than an abbreviation denoting the ECB and the (euro-area) NCBs.[48]

On the other hand, according to the ECB's presentation, TARGET2-Securities will be fully owned and operated by the Eurosystem. In line with this, recital 4 of the ECB's guideline on a Trans-European Automated Real-time Gross settlement Express Transfer system (TARGET2) provides for the ECB, '[a]cting on the Eurosystem's behalf', to enter into a

---

[47] H.K. Scheller, *The European Central Bank – History, Role and Functions*, 2nd edition (Frankfurt: ECB, 2006), 42.

[48] W. Kahl and U. Häde, 'Art. 107 EC Treaty' in C. Callies and M. Ruffert, *Das Verfassungsrecht der Europäischen Union*, 3rd edition (Munich: Beck, 2007), No. 2 (with further references).

contract with a service provider.[49] Both documents strongly hint at the ECB's willingness to accept the Eurosystem as an organizational actor in its own right, even though these statements would not be in line with the primary Community law just described if they meant to attribute to the Eurosystem a legal personality of its own.

Indeed, primary Community law, i.e., the provisions of the EC Treaty and those of the ESBC/ECB Statute, the latter being a Protocol to the EC Treaty and therefore also part of primary Community law,[50] is rather ambiguous as to the nature of the ESCB/Eurosystem.

At a first glance, the ESCB/Eurosystem seems to form an organizational entity, being endowed with certain tasks, members, and decision-making bodies which, for the lack of a legal personality of its own, cannot as such enter into any legal relationship with third parties, i.e., non-members. According to this interpretation, the tasks are set out in Article 105 (2) EC Treaty as well as in Article 3 ESCB/ECB Statute, whereas Article 107 (1) EC Treaty determines membership. With regard to the system's own decision-making bodies, Article 107 (3) EC Treaty entrusts the decision-making bodies of the ECB with governing the ESCB/Eurosystem, as well. Thus, while the ESCB/Eurosytem arguably lacks institutions ('*Organe*') of its own, it is governed (cf. Art. 105 (1) EC Treaty) internally through the pertinent decision-making bodies of the ECB. Whereas, the operational tasks are carried out by the central banks forming part of the Eurosystem (Art 9.2., Art 16 et seq. ESCB/ECB-Statute) putting, under the principle of decentralization, an emphasis on the NCBs with regard to the fulfilment of operational tasks (Art 12.1 (3) of the ESCB-Statute). Put differently, with regard to inner-organizational decisions the ESCB/Eurosystem – as opposed to the ECB – takes decisions by relying on the latter's decision-making bodies. By contrast, with regard to activities vis-à-vis third parties, Articles 18 *et seq.* ESCB/ECB Statute confer the power to act on the ECB and euro-area NCBs as legal persons.

Serious doubts still remain. Even if one were to conceive of the ESCB/Eurosystem as an organizational entity in its own right, the existence

---

[49] Guideline ECB/2007/2 [2007] OJ L 237/1.

[50] R. Smits, 'Art. 105 EC Treaty', in H. von der Groeben and J. Schwarze (eds.), *Vertrag über die Europäische Union und Vertrag zur Gründung der Europäischen Gemeinschaft, commentary*, 4 vols., 6th edn (Baden-Baden:, Nomos, 2003), vol. III, No. 20; B. Kempen, 'Article 105 EC-Treaty', in R. Streinz (ed.), *EUV/EGV Vertrag über die Europäische Union und Vertrag zur Gründung der Europäischen Gemeinschaften, commentary* (Munich: Beck, 2003), No. 15 (referring to Article 311 EC-Treaty).

of such a system would not entail any practical consequences, at all. To begin with, any decisions taken on behalf of the ESCB/Eurosystem are at the same time decisions taken by the ECB, since the latter's decision-making bodies also govern the ESCB/Eurosystem. Article 110 (1) EC Treaty is testimony to this, since it explicitly stipulates that, in order to carry out the tasks entrusted to the ESCB, the ECB shall make regulations, take decisions and make recommendations. Moreover, the actions of the system's members, i.e. of the ECB and the NCBs, are not governed by the decision-making bodies of the ESCB/Eurosystem, but by those of the ECB. With respect to the NCBs, Article 14.3 ESCB/ECB Statute provides for the ECB (by way of its decision-making bodies) to issue guidelines and instructions for the NCBs to follow when acting in their capacity as an integral part of the ESCB/Eurosystem.

On balance, then, in line with the prevailing interpretation, the ESCB – and the same holds true for the Eurosystem, as well – is to be understood as shorthand meaning 'the ECB and the (euro-area) NCBs'. Hence, for present purposes, whether any actor is empowered to implement TARGET2-Securities is to be discussed solely with respect to the ECB and the euro-area NCBs.

B. Statutory power of the ECB/euro-area NCBs over TARGET2-Securities

Before embarking on a detailed analysis of whether the EC Treaty and/ or the ESCB/ECB Statute confer the legal authority to set up and operate TARGET2-Securities on the ECB and the euro-area NCBs, it seems worthwhile to briefly point out that the settlement of securities transactions is a not uncommon function of central banks. Currently, for example, the central banks of the United States, Japan, Belgium, Greece and Portugal are active in this field.[51] In addition, in the last twenty years the central banks of France, the UK, Spain,[52] Italy, Ireland, the Netherlands and Finland (as major shareholders) were involved in securities settlement but gave up their involvement in the context of the de-mutualization and privatization of their securities exchanges during the 1990s.

---

[51] G. Tumpel-Gugerell, 'Speech at the EU Commission's Conference on The EU's new Regime for Clearing and Settlement in Europe', 30 November 2006, Brussels, www.ecb. int/press/key/date/2006/html/sp061130_1.en.html.

[52] Godeffroy, 'Ten frequently asked Questions about TARGET2-Securities', (note 5, above).

Admittedly, the involvement of other central banks in the settlement of securities does not predicate anything about whether any of the actors just mentioned is empowered to execute such actions given the current legal regime. However, it illustrates by way of example that this field of activity is not alien to the operation of a central bank (some of which are in fact euro-area NCBs). Indeed, in comparison with TARGET2-Securites, most of these central banks assert a much more substantive role in securities settlement, e.g. the US Fedwire System also acts as CSD.[53]

1. Principle of limited transfer of powers to the ECB/euro-area NCBs

The starting point for an analysis of whether the EC Treaty and/or the ESCB/ECB Statute confer the authority to implement TARGET2-Securities on the euro-area CBs, i.e. the ECB and the euro-area NCBs is the principle of limited transfer of powers.

The EC does not possess comprehensive jurisdiction, but can only act insofar as sovereign rights have been transferred by Member States in accordance with the principle of limited transfer of powers from Member States to the EC ('*compétence d'attribution*'). The principle of limited transfer is not only applicable as far as the regulatory power of the EC is concerned (Article 5 (1) EC Treaty), but also with respect to the EC institutions ('*Organe*') (Article 7 (1) EC Treaty). Thus, each institution can only act insofar as it has been assigned authority.[54]

The ECB is arguably not an institution of the EC (see Article 7, Article 8 EC Treaty) since it was established and given a legal personality of its own by Article 107 (2) EC Treaty.[55] Its exact legal nature is controversial.[56] However, since its powers are formed on a similar basis to an institution of the EC,[57] any action by the ECB requires a basis of authorization, i.e. a legal basis. This applies for any kind of action – lawmaking as well as other forms of acting. From this it follows that for the ECB

---

[53] E.M. Jaskulla, 'Zukünftige Regelung des Clearing und Settlement von Wertpapier- und Derivategeschäften in der EU', *Zeitschrift für europarechtliche Studien*, (2004), 497, at 509.

[54] R. Geiger, *Vertrag über die Europäische Union und Vertrag zur Gründung der Europäischen Gemeinschaft, commentary*, 4th edn (Munich: Beck, 2004), Art. 7 EC Treaty, No. 15.

[55] Case C-11/00: *Commission v. ECB ('OLAF')* [2003] ECR I-7215, para. 92.

[56] Cf. amongst several others U. Häde, 'Zur rechtlichen Stellung der Europäischen Zentralbank', *Wertpapiermitteilungen* (2006), 1605 *et seq.*

[57] C. Schütz, 'Die Legitimation der Europäischen Zentralbank zur Rechtsetzung', *Europarecht* (2001), 291–2; A. Decker, Die Organe der Europäischen Gemeinschaft', *Juristische Schulung* (1995), 883–4.

to be empowered to set up and operate TARGET2-Securities requires a provision that goes beyond empowering the EC in general by vesting the ECB in particular with the authority to undertake such a project.

Moreover, since the euro-area NCBs are an integral part of the ESCB and, as such, act in accordance with the guidelines and instructions of the ECB to carry out the tasks entrusted to the ESCB/Eurosystem (Article 14.3 ESCB/ECB Statute) the principle of limited transfer of powers applies to the euro-area NCBs, when acting as an integral part of the ESCB/Eurosystem, too.

2. Criteria for the choice of a legal basis

The legal basis is to be chosen according to objective, legally verifiable circumstances, especially the purpose and content of the legally relevant act.[58] Given the features of TARGET2-Securities described above, any legal provision that may serve as a legal basis for the euro-area CB's authority for TARGET2-Securities has to empower the ECB/euro-area NCBs to carry out payments for securities transactions and to book securities held by CSDs from one account into another in order to settle securities transactions.

Since the Statute of the ECB, as part of the ESCB/ECB Statute, forms a part of primary Community law,[59] one or several Articles of the Statute may empower the ECB/euro-area NCBs to establish and operate TARGET2-Securities.

3. Provisions in the EC Treaty?

Neither Articles 56 *et seq.* EC Treaty nor Articles 94 *et seq.* EC Treaty supply a legal basis for any action on the part of the ECB in general, or for the setting up of TARGET2-Securities in particular.

In contrast, Article 105 (2) EC Treaty has been invoked as a legal basis. Indeed, as just mentioned, Article 105 (2), fourth indent, of the EC Treaty and Article 3.1, fourth indent, of the ESCB/ECB Statute attribute to the ESCB the basic task *inter alia* of 'promot[ing] the smooth operation of payment systems'. However, these provisions only define the framework of the ESCB's activities.[60] The specific operations that the ESCB and – since the ECB and the NCBs form part of and may carry out functions

---

[58] Case 45/86, *Commission v. Council APS* [1987] ECR-1493, para. 11.
[59] Supra IV.A.2. at note 50, above.
[60] R. Smits, *The European Central Bank, Institutional Aspects* (The Hague: Kluwer Law International, 1997), 179.

of the ESCB – the ECB and the euro-area NCB's respectively are empowered to pursue tasks as regulated in the ESCB/ECB Statute.[61] These detailed provisions would be circumvented, if Article 105 (2) EC-Treaty on its own could serve as a legal basis for TARGET2-Securities.

4. Article 18.2 ESCB/ECB Statute?

Pursuant to Article 18.2 ESCB/ECB Statute, the ECB is to establish general principles for open market operations and credit operations carried out by itself or the NCBs.

For obvious reasons, this provision on its own does not authorize the ESCB to set up TARGET2-Securities: general principles within the meaning of Article 18.2 are legally non-binding rules i.e. rules that do not bind third parties (except euro-area NCBs),[62] not a technical platform. The general principles referred to in this provision include *inter alia* the preconditions which market participants willing to enter into transactions with the ECB or euro-area NCBs have to fulfil in order to qualify as an eligible counterparty[63] and set out the criteria under which the ECB and euro-area NCBs enter into binding relationships and execute transactions with such eligible counterparties. Thus, establishing these principles, on the one hand, provides important information to the market and, on the other hand, serves to limit the power of the ECB/euro-area NCBs to discriminate among market participants in selecting counterparties to operations pursuant to Article 18.2. It also provides for the binding framework under which the ECB and euro-area NCBs conduct transactions, including the eligible ways of settling such transactions, for instance, regarding the cross-border settlement of collateralized credit.[64]

5. Article 18.1 in conjunction with Article 17 ESCB/ECB Statute?

According to Article 18.1 second indent ESCB/ECB Statute, the ECB and euro-area NCBs may conduct credit operations with market participants,

[61] Kempen, 'Article 105 EC-Treaty', in Streinz (note 50, above), Art.107 EC-Treaty', No. 8, 15; Smits, 'Article 105 EC-Treaty', in von der Groeben and Schwarze (eds.) (note 50, above), No. 4, 5; Smits, *The European Central Bank,* (note 60, above), 179.

[62] Smits, *The European Central Bank* (note 60, above), 274; cf. also the examples given in Weenink, 'Art. 18 ESCB Statute', in von der Groeben and Schwarze (eds.) (note 49, above), No. 41 *et seq.*

[63] Weenink in von der Groeben and Schwarze (eds.) (note 50, above), No. 41.

[64] See e.g. Chapters 3 and 6 of the General Documentation on the Eurosystem monetary policy instruments and procedures, September 2006 (Annex 1 to Guideline ECB/2000/7 as amended) (available at www.ecb.int/pub/pdf/other/gendoc2006en.pdf).

with lending being based on adequate collateral. By way of clarification, Article 17 ESCB/ECB Statute authorizes the ECB and NCBs to 'accept assets, including book-entry securities, as collateral'.[65] The term 'assets' is rather wide, and thus covers any legal method of transferring securities,[66] including *inter alia* the pledging of securities, the fiduciary transfer of claims on third parties and the institution of a lien.[67]

Even read in conjunction, Articles 18.1 and 17 do not provide for a legal basis for TARGET2-Securities in its entirety. As a purely technical platform, the system will not alter the existing securities accounts structure. CSDs will still hold accounts with each other, whereas other market participants will hold accounts with a CSD. As a consequence, the ECB under TARGET2-Securities acts on behalf of the CSDs even if, in a purely technical sense, holders of a securities account with a CSD could send their settlement orders directly to the settlement platform. In contrast, the ECB and NCBs, when carrying out the tasks entrusted to the ECB by conducting lending operations based on accepting adequate collateral with market participants, act for themselves when taking book-entry securities. From this it follows that Articles 18.1 and 17 cannot serve as a legal basis for the TARGET2-Securities project insofar as the establishment and operation of a securities settlement platform on behalf of market participants, i.e. CSDs, are concerned.

Arguably, the situation is somewhat different as far as the lending by the ECB and euro-area NCBs based on collateral in the form of book-entry securities is concerned (which is required for all central bank credit operations). Admittedly, Articles 18.1 and 17 do not explicitly state whether the ECB/euro-area NCBs are empowered to establish and operate technical facilities aimed at facilitating the secure and efficient settlement of lending against collateral transactions. However, the Eurosystem does have a vital interest in the efficient and secure functioning of securities settlement systems since, otherwise, its ability to pursue monetary policies by lending against collateral transactions will be severely hampered. Therefore, one may indeed interpret Article 18.1 in conjunction with Article 17 to the effect that *a fortiori* the ECB/

---

[65] It has been argued that the legal basis for the cash leg of the system or the collateralization of central bank credit by securities could be found in Article 17. However, this approach disregards the complex structure of TARGET2-Securities. In any case, it does not supply a legal basis for the entire project.

[66] Weenink, 'Art. 17 ESCB Statute', in von der Groeben and Schwarze (eds.) (note 50, above), No. 11.

[67] Smits, *The European Central Bank*, (note 60, above), 263.

euro-area NCBs are empowered to set up the technical (IT) infrastructure required for the purpose of effectively operating lending against collateral transactions. Put differently, the establishment and operation of a platform providing services conducive to the more effective conduct of the Eurosystem's credit operations falls within the mandate of the ECB and the NCBs (notwithstanding the fact that such operations are currently conducted without such a platform having been established, albeit in a less effective and less secure manner). On the other hand, this interpretation only holds true for those book-entry securities which the ECB and the euro-area NCB's are willing to accept as collateral, at least in principle.

6. Article 23 ESCB/ECB Statute?

Article 23 ESCB/ECB Statute empowers the ECB and euro-area NCB's to acquire and sell spot and forward all types of foreign exchange assets – including securities as clarified by the regulation itself – as well as to hold and manage the assets and conduct all types of banking transactions in relations with third countries.

It has been argued that the provision furnishes a legal basis for TARGET2-Securities, because the ECB and the euro-area NCB's have been granted such a wide scope of operations in the external field and therefore authority cannot be denied to the ECB/euro-area NCBs domestically. Admittedly, the ECJ has developed external powers of the EC by drawing a parallel to its internal powers as an example of implied powers.[68] According to this ruling, the EC is not only entitled to conclude international treaties if the EC Treaty explicitly stipulates a regulatory power to do so, but also if the EC has the corresponding inner authority.[69] However, as regards the ECB and the euro-area NCBs, their internal powers are regulated in Articles 17–22 ESCB/ECB Statute and thus implied powers can only be derived from these detailed regulations. Article 23 only refers to external operations as its headline and its content expressively state.

Still, it would be inconsistent if the regulation granted external powers to the ECB/euro-area NCBs to a much greater extent than internal

---

[68] A. Haratsch, C. Koenig and M. Pechstein (eds.), *Europarecht*, 5th edn (Tübingen: Mohr-Siebeck, 2006), 430.
[69] Case 22/70: *Commission v. Council (AETR)* [1971] ECR 263, para. 72 *et seq.*; Joined Cases 3, 4 and 6/76: *Kramer* [1976] ECR 1279, para. 30, 33.

powers.[70] Therefore, Article 23 ESCB/ECB Statute indicates that the provisions dealing with the internal powers, i.e., Articles 17–22 ESCB/ECB Statute are to be construed extensively.

7. Article 22 ESCB/ECB Statute

Pursuant to Article 22 ESCB/ECB Statute, (i) '[the] ECB and national central banks may provide facilities',[71] and (ii) 'the ECB may make regulations, to ensure efficient and sound clearing and payment systems within the Community and with other countries'. With respect to 'facilities', the provision empowers the ECB as well as the euro-area NCBs.

a. Providing facilities for a securities settlement system on the basis of Article 22?   According to the ECB, the term 'clearing and payment systems' in Article 22 also refers to securities settlement systems because of the following arguments:[72]

- the inclusion of the term 'clearing system' would not have been necessary if Article 22 referred only to payment systems;
- the potential for a major disturbance in a CSD's operation, that could spill over to payment systems and endanger their smooth functioning, is likely to have increased in recent years because of the increased importance of secured lending as money market instruments, the increased use of securities collateral to control risks and increase liquidity in payment systems through collateralized intraday credit lines, and the rapid growth of securities settlement volumes':[73]

---

[70] Smits and Gruber, 'Art. 23 ESCB Statute', in von der Groeben and Schwarze (eds.) (note 50, above), No. 24; Smits, *The European Central Bank,* (note 60, above), 312.

[71] According to some commentators, the euro-area NCBs are empowered with respect to payment systems operating within their country, whereas the ECB is empowered with respect to payment systems operating cross-border within some or even all Member States of the ESCB (cf. Smits and Gruber, 'Art. 22 ESCB Statute', in von der Groeben and Schwarze (eds.) (note 50, above), No. 21). However, neither the EC Treaty nor the ESCB/ECB Statute explicitly stipulate that there is a geographic limitation to the powers of NCBs, if they act on behalf of the Eurosystem.

[72] For most of the following arguments see ECB, 'The role of the Eurosystem in payment and clearing Systems', *ECB Monthly Bulletin* (April 2002), 52, www.ecb.int/pub/pdf/mobu/mb200204en.pdf.

[73] See Bank for International Settlements, *Cross-border Securities Settlement* (Basle, 1995), 6. Also, in the Introduction of the CPSS/IOSCO Recommendations for securities settlement systems it is pointed out that 'securities settlement systems (SSSs) are a crucial component of the financial markets' and that 'weaknesses in SSSs can be a source of systemic disturbances to securities markets and to other payment and settlement systems'.

- real-time cross-system DVP in central bank money can only be achieved in a single integrated set-up and nobody but the Eurosystem as the sole statutory provider of euro central bank money is able to provide this service;
- the application of the term 'system' for payment systems as well as securities settlement systems in the Settlement Finality Directive.[74]

However, none of these arguments is convincing.[75] To begin with, 'clearing' is understood as a mechanism for transferring value in a particular way, usually by way of 'netting'. Strictly speaking, 'clearing' excludes the settlement phase as well as systems where no clearing is used, such as 'gross' settlement systems where value is transferred immediately via accounts held with the settlement agent. In addition, a large variety of clearing systems exist in the financial market infrastructure, but they are also used in many other (non-financial) areas of the economy. Put more generally, 'clearing' is not a specific feature of securities transfer systems. Second, even granting that Article 22 vests the ECB with the power to make Regulations in the Community law sense of the word,[76] the (purported) necessity for a uniform legal treatment of delivery versus payment systems cannot override the lack of a pertinent legal basis, but simply prevents the realization of a system which – and this is crucial in this context – is not mandated by the ESCB/ECB Statute. In addition, TARGET2-Securities has no bearing on the legal framework, i.e. the set of legal rules governing cross-border securities transactions. Third, the use of a word in secondary and (!) subsequent EU legislation does not allow any inference as to the meaning of the same word used in preceding primary EU law. Moreover, Article 22 explicitly qualifies the systems meant by adding the word 'payment'.

In order to refute these arguments, it is sometimes said that, because of the close functional relationship between payment systems and securities clearing and settlement systems, the ECB/euro-area NCBs will only be able to carry out the ESCB's task of contributing to the stability of the financial system (Article 3.3 ESCB/ECB Statute) to perfection if they have

---

[74] Directive 98/26/EC (note 9, above).

[75] As to the following, in the same sense, see C. Keller, Regulation of Payment Systems', *Euredia* (2002), 455, 460–3.

[76] Some authors even argue that the term 'clearing' in Art. 22 is not specific enough to grant any authority for taking measures to promote the operation of 'securities settlement and payment systems'; cf. A. von Bogdandy and J. Bast, 'Scope and Limits of ECB Powers in the Field of Securities Settlement', *Euredia* (2006), 365, 382.

also powers with respect to securities systems.[77] However, this argument neglects the distinction enshrined in Article 3 ESCB/ECB Statute between the ESCB's basic task of promoting the smooth operation of payments systems (Art. 3.1 fourth indent) and its more limited role of contributing to the stability of the financial systems (Article 3.3). Article 22 empowers the ECB and the euro-area NCBs 'to ensure efficient and sound clearing and payment systems', i.e. attributes authority only in regard of its basic task to promote the smooth operation of payment systems.

Finally, to clutch at straws, one may want to point to Article 2 (1) of the German statute implementing The Headquarters Agreement between the Government of the Federal Republic of Germany and the European Central Bank concerning the seat of the European Central Bank.[78] According to this provision, the ECB participates as the central depository for securities in the commercial intercourse of the CSDs. However, the agreement is not a binding interpretation of the EC Treaty or the ESCB/ECB Statute respectively. The regulation just shows that the Member State, Germany, acted on the assumption of an ECB authority for the settlement of securities transactions.

b. Designing TARGET2-Securities as a (facility for a) payment system Since Article 22 does not cover securities settlement systems as such, the ECB/euro-area NCBs would only be empowered to establish TARGET2-Securities if, at least given a certain design, the system would qualify as a facility for a payment system.

(i) The meaning of 'payment systems' in Article 22 is hardly ever spelled out in any detail. The ECB provides the following useful definition: 'a set of instruments, banking procedures and, typically, interbank funds transfer systems which facilitate the circulation of money'.[79] Put differently, payments systems combine legal regulations, technical norms and standards, and hardware for the primary goal of facilitating the transfer of money.[80]

---

[77] Smits and Gruber, 'Art. 22 ESCB Statute', in von der Groeben and Schwarze (eds.) (note 50, above), No. 21.

[78] Gesetz zu dem Abkommen vom 18 September 1998 zwischen der Regierung der Bundesrepublik Deutschland und der Europäischen Zentralbank über den Sitz der Europäischen Zentralbank, 19 December 1998, BGBl. II 1998, 2995.

[79] ECB, 'The role of the Eurosystem in payment and clearing Systems', *ECB Monthly Bulletin,* (April 2002), (note 72, above), 47.

[80] The term 'payment' contained in Art. 22 is thus not limited to its meaning in Art. 56 (2) EC, where payments constitute the consideration within the context of an underlying

(ii) Article 22 does not limit the power of the ECB/euro-area NCBs to provide facilities for payment systems of a particular design. Indeed, the wording to 'provide facilities' in order 'to ensure efficient and sound clearing and payment systems ...' does not even require that the facility has to be part of a payment system.

Admittedly, existing payment systems, e.g. TARGET, do not interlink the transfer of payments and the corresponding transfer of securities. However, payment systems could also be designed to provide for 'contingent' payment messages by participants, i.e. messages to effectuate the cash transfer only on condition that the corresponding book entries in the participants' securities accounts have already been made or will, at least, be made simultaneously. The operator of such a payment system could even choose whether to allow orders to the effect that a payment is only to be made provided that the transfer of title with respect to the securities in question has taken effect or, less demanding on the operator, whether just to allow orders subject to the condition that the respective book entries have been made, regardless of their effect with respect to the ownership of the securities.

Regardless of the final design, for the ECB/euro-area NCBs to provide (facilities for) such a payment system would fall within the scope of Article 22. Clearly, such a system would contribute to the smooth operation of payments systems, at least with respect to linked payments/(cross-border/cross-CSD)securities transactions.

(iii) TARGET2-Securities lends itself to be designed as such a second-generation payment system[81] for at least two reasons. First, while CSDs would continue to serve as such and would still hold securities settlement accounts with one another, the ECB would not act as a CSD but would operate the technical platform for the clearing and settlement of the securities transactions taking place, including those between the CSDs. Second, the booking on a single technical platform would facilitate the interlinking of the settlement of the cash leg and the securities leg of a transaction. The design of TARGET2-Securities according to the increasingly common

---

transaction, but it also includes money transfers forming part of the 'movement of capital' in the sense of Art. 56 (2) EC; see von Bogdandy and Bast, 'Scope and Limits of ECB Powers in the Field of Securities Settlement', (note 76, above), 371.

[81] Likewise, the Legal Committee of the Eurosystem (Legal Feasibility Study (note 40, above), 2 (dating from 20 December 2006) states that 'T2S is conceived as a feature that supplements the operation of TARGET2,' i.e. a payment system.

model[82] for securities settlement systems – DVP, i.e. booking is only carried out after payment has been made – does not constitute a restriction, because what is envisaged is delivery-versus-payment model 1, which means settlement in real time of the cash leg of a securities transaction in central bank money alongside *simultaneous* settlement of the securities leg (a novelty for cross-system transfers which can only be provided through the active involvement of central banks as the sole supplier of central bank money). Thus, the delivery of securities takes place simultaneously with the payment and is – as a consequence – compatible with the model of a 'contingent' payment.[83]

(iv) It has been argued that Article 22 ESCB/ECB Statute can only serve as a legal basis for TARGET2-Securities if current securities settlement systems are either inefficient or unsound, but neither the wording of the regulation nor its intention justify such a restrictive interpretation. Both also cover actions by the ECB/euro-area NCBs destined to improve even further the workings of an already largely sound and efficient clearing and payment system as well as actions intended to prevent currently sound and efficient systems from becoming inefficient or unsound. However, even those who postulate this additional requirement come to the conclusion that it is met, due to the inefficiency of the current systems.

(v) The final question of whether Article 22 even empowers the ECB/euro-area NCBs to establish and operate the particular part of an IT platform where the booking of the securities is carried out can also be answered in the affirmative. This follows from the fact that the easiest, most effective and most secure way to promote the smooth operation of an Eurosystem payment system which allows for contingent payment orders, i.e. for the payment orders of CSDs to be executed on condition that the corresponding securities transaction has taken place or takes place simultaneously, is for the ECB/euro-area NCBs to operate a technical platform which allows the ECB/

---

[82] See Standard No. 7 of the ECB-CESR Standards for Securities Clearing and Settlement in the European Union (note 22, above).

[83] It could even be argued that a payment system permits payment messages on the condition that the corresponding book entries in the securities account will be made in the future. However, this conflicts with the principle of settlement finality since future cancellations of payments could be necessary.

euro-area NCBs to effectuate the book entries in the CSDs' securities accounts as well – exactly the gist of TARGET2-Securities.[84]

The upshot is that a legal basis for TARGET2-Securities can be derived from the term 'payment system' in Article 22 ESCB/ECB Statute having regard to the euro-area CBs' role as defined by Articles 105 (5) EC Treaty, Article 3.3 ESCB/ECB Statute.

8. Principle of subsidiarity pursuant to Article 5 (2) EC Treaty

Since Article 22 is a concurrent competence,[85] Article 5 (2) EC Treaty applies. Due to the regulation's transnational character, this requirement is not problematic.

9. Principle of competential proportionality pursuant to Article 5 (3) EC Treaty

According to the ECJ, the principle of competential proportionality is only violated by manifestly inapt measures, apparently erroneous evaluations or if it is obvious that a less encumbering measure proposed by the persons involved is equally effective,[86] which is not the case in this context.

V. Conclusion

The question whether the euro-area CBs, i.e., the ECB and the euro-area NCBs, have authority to develop TARGET2-Securities can be answered in the affirmative. The legal basis, which is required according to the principle of a limited transfer of powers from EU Member States to the ECB/euro-area NCBs, is furnished by Article 22 ESCB/ECB Statute having regard to the ECB's role, as defined by Articles 105 (5) EC Treaty, Article 3.3 ESCB/ECB Statute.

However, because of the limited competence of the Eurosystem under Art 22 ESCB/ECB Statute (referring only to facilities for payment and clearing systems) TARGET2-Securities should not constitute a facility

---

[84] However, as it has been argued correctly, this does not include the legal authority that would permit the ECB to constrain CSDs to use exclusively TARGET2-Securities.

[85] C. Eser, *Die Außenkompetenz Europäischen Zentralbank im Spannungsfeld zur Europäischen Gemeinschaft in der Endstufe der Wirtschafts- und Währungsunion* (Regensburg:, 2005), 134; Smits and Gruber, 'Art. 22 ESCB Statute', in von der Groeben and Schwarze (eds.) (note 50, above), No. 17.

[86] Case 280/93: *Germany v. Council ('Bananenmarktordnung')* ECR [1994] I-5039, para. 90 *et seq.*

for a securities settlement system, but should qualify as a variation or a feature ancillary to the operation of a payment system. This should be possible, because Article 22 ESCB/ECB Statute does not limit the euro-area CBs' power to provide facilities for payment systems of a particular design. Although existing payment systems do not interlink the transfer of payments and the corresponding transfer of securities, payment systems could also be designed to provide for 'contingent' payment messages by participants, i.e. messages to effectuate the cash transfer only on condition that the corresponding book entries in the participants' securities accounts have already been made or will be made simultaneously. Thus, the initial design of TARGET2-Securities as a mechanism enabling the delivery-versus-payment model 1, i.e. settlement in real time of the cash leg of a securities transaction in central bank money alongside simultaneous settlement of the securities leg, would fall within the ambit of Article 22 ESCB/ECB Statute. Alterations of and additions to the initial model are of no relevance as long as TARGET2-Securities will be a functionality that is ancillary and subordinate to the main operation of the Eurosystem, i.e. to the running of its payment system TARGET2. However, if TARGET2-Securities were to provide a comprehensive service to CSDs comprising the full post-trade production chain (similar to a 'Single Settlement Engine' as conceived by other market participants) this might be considered tantamount to a circumvention of Art 22 ESCB/ECB Statute. Given that, TARGET2-Securities should limit itself to a technical module allowing the coordination of book entries by the CSD and by the Eurosystem to ensure delivery versus payment (DvP). As a minimum, this would require TARGET2-Securities to take recourse to TARGET2 for the settlement of the cash legs. Otherwise, the required supportive character of TARGET2-Securities vis-à-vis TARGET2 would be in doubt.

SECTION 2

Transatlantic perspectives

28

Learning from Eddy: a meditation upon organizational reform of financial supervision in Europe

HOWELL E. JACKSON

With the March 2008 release of the US Treasury Department's Blueprint for a Modernized Financial Regulatory Structure, the reorganization of financial regulation in the United States is, once again, an issue of public debate in American policy circles. Fortunately, this is also a subject which Eddy Wymeersch recently addressed in *The Structure of Financial Supervision in Europe: About Single Financial Supervisors, Twin Peaks and Multiple Financial Supervisors*. Like much of Professor Wymeersch's academic writing, this article offers American readers a unique and illuminating view into European regulatory practice, combining the theoretical sophistication of an accomplished academic with the pragmatic insights of a senior regulatory official. My goal in this chapter is to meditate upon Professor Wymeersch's description of the evolving supervisory practices in Europe and draw out potentially useful implications for policy issues raised in the Treasury Department's *Blueprint* and how regulatory reform might be implemented in the United States.

At the outset I should acknowledge the envy with which I regard my academic and regulatory counterparts working in other jurisdictions. While the United States prides itself in having a dynamic economy that fosters innovation and invention, the country's capacity to reform the structure of its regulatory institutions pales in comparison to the ability of member states of the European Union – or other developed countries such as Japan and Australia – to modernize their regulatory bodies. As has often been noted, the American system of financial regulation is a product of nearly two centuries of bureaucratic accretions, dating back to the free banking statutes of the 1830s. Over the generations, numerous oversight bodies have been added and few eliminated with the resulting maze of supervisory bodies incomprehensible to those familiar with the supervisory systems of other leading economies and a source of extraordinary cost and unnecessary complexity for regulated firms and practicing attorneys in the United States.

With effort and patience, one can come to understand how and why the American regulatory structure has evolved in the way it has and a large portion of any academic course on financial regulation in the United States is typically dedicated to unpacking the mysteries of regulatory jurisdiction in this country.[1] A national taste for federalism explains why we have overlapping systems of state oversight in banking and securities. Anachronistic and long-abandoned interpretations of the Commerce Clause of the US Constitution allowed insurance regulation to develop exclusively at the state level in the late nineteenth and early twentieth centuries. An aversion to concentrated sources of governmental power has led American politicians to retain sectoral division of supervisory agencies – that is, separate regulatory bodies for banking, insurance and securities – and also our even more fragmented oversight of depository institutions (Federal Deposit Insurance Corporation (FDIC), Comptroller of the Currency (OCC), Office of Thrift Supervision (OTS), and Federal Reserve Board), securities/futures (Securities and Exchange Commission (SEC) plus the Commodities Future Trading Commission (CFTC)), and insurance (distinguishing freestanding insurance companies regulated at the state level from employer-provided pensions and health insurance covered by the Employee Retirement Income Security Act of 1974 at the federal level). On top of these latent political preferences and historical accidents, the political impediments inherent in our divided and increasingly partisan political system make it difficult to effect financial reform, at least as compared to the parliamentary systems of government found in most other developed nations. Finally, add in a national predilection to review any idiosyncratic aspect of governmental structure as a manifestation of American exceptionalism, and one can develop a relatively rich though not always inspiring explanation of why the American system of financial regulation has strayed so far from the models of supervisory oversight upon which the rest of the world is converging.

But whatever the explanation of the Rube Goldberg complexity of regulatory oversight in the United States, there is still much to learn from the experience of other countries in reforming their own supervisory

---

[1] H.E. Jackson and E.L. Symons, *The Regulation of Financial Institutions: Cases and Materials* (West Publications, 1999).

systems. My purpose in reflecting upon Professor Wymeersch's article is to consider how the regulatory reforms with European members states over the past decade might inform our understanding of the Treasury Department's recent proposal and, more specifically, to consider how that experience can help us evaluate the many conflicting arguments that have been made for and against more radical proposals to consolidate financial regulation in this country.

I.

In modern debates over regulatory reform, the issue is typically framed in terms of a question of the degree to which and the manner in which traditional sectoral agencies should be consolidated into a smaller number of regulatory bodies. There are two basic approaches to consolidation. The first and simpler approach is to combine two or more sectors of the financial services industry under a consolidated regulatory body, such as the British Financial Services Authority.[2] Alternatively, existing agencies can be reconstituted into new and specialized organizational units designed to advance specific regulatory objectives, like ensuring the fairness and transparency of interactions between financial firms and their customers (sometimes called market conduct) or safeguarding the safety and soundness of financial institutions (often denominated prudential supervision). Adopting terminology coined by Michael Taylor, this second approach is often labelled a 'twin peak' or 'multi-peaked' model, depending on how many different regulatory objectives are specified and assigned to separate agencies.[3] The Treasury Department's recent *Blueprint* contains elements of both approaches. In terms of combinations, the Department recommends in the relatively near future the merger of the SEC and CFTC as well as the consolidation of banking supervisory bodies, including its proposed merger of the Office of Thrift Supervision with the Comptroller of the Currency and also its more obliquely recommended combination of the currently divided FDIC and Federal Reserve oversight of

---

[2] H.E. Jackson, 'An American Perspective on the FSA: Politics, Goals & Regulatory Intensity', in L. J Cho and J. Y. Kim (eds.), *Regulatory Reforms in the Age of Financial Consolidation: The Emerging Market Economy and Advanced Countries* (Korean Development Institute, 2006), 39–71 (avail. at www.kdi.re.kr/kdi_eng/database/report_read05.jsp?1=1&pub_no=00009931).

[3] M.W. Taylor, *Twin Peaks: A Regulatory Structure for the New Century* (London: Centre for the Study of Financial Innovation, 1995).

state banks.[4] Over the longer run, the proposal envisions the creation of multi-peaked objective-oriented agencies, focusing on prudential regulation, market conduct and market stability, an objective centred on minimizing systemic risks. As the Treasury also envisions the creation of two smaller regulatory units – one for oversight of corporate issuers and the other to contain government guarantee funds – the Blueprint's long-term recommendations might best be labelled a 'three peak, two foothill' model of regulation.[5]

Within policy circles, the debates over the reform of financial regulatory systems have been well-rehearsed at this point, and the basic trade-offs are fairly well understood.[6] The combination of single-sector agencies offers the promise of greater efficiency and efficacy, as consolidated agencies enjoy economies of both scale and scope. The advantages are, it is argued, capable of simultaneously improving the quality and lowering the cost of financial supervision, while also benefitting regulated firms by offering a single point of supervisory contact and eliminating sources of regulatory duplication and inconsistency. The on-going consolidation of the financial services industry is often cited as further justification for the combination of supervisory functions, as an integrated regulatory supervisor is said to be better equipped to oversee conglomerates that offer a full spectrum of financial products

---

[4] United States Department of the Treasury, *Blueprint for a Modernized Financial Regulatory Structure* (Mar. 2008), 89–100 (avail. online at www.treas.gov/press/releases/reports/Blueprint.pdf).

[5] United States Department of the Treasury, *Blueprint for a Modernized Financial Regulatory Structure* (note 4, above), 137–80.

[6] For more extensive treatments of the subject, see R.J. Herring and J. Carmassi, 'The Structure of Cross-Sector Financial Supervision', *Financial Markets, Institutions & Instruments*, 17 (2008), 51–76; United States Government Accountability Office, 'Financial Regulation: Industry Trends Continue to Challenge the Federal Regulatory Structure', GAO-08-32 (Oct. 2008); E.F. Brown, 'E Pluribus Unum – Out of Many, One: Why the United States Needs a Single Financial Services Agency', *University of Miami Business Law Review*, 14 (2005), 1–101; L.T. Llewellyn, 'Institutional Structure of Financial Regulation and Supervision', in J. Carmichael, A. Flemming, and L.T. Llewellyn (eds.), *Aligning Financial Supervisory Structures with Country Needs* (World Bank Institute, 2004), 17–92; D. Masciandraro and A. Porta, 'Single Authority in Financial Markets Supervision: Lessons for EU Enlargement', in D. Masciandaro (ed.), *Financial Intermediation in the New Europe* (2004), 284–320; C. Briault, 'Revisiting the Rational for a Single National Financial Services Regulator', FSA Occasional Paper Series No. 16 (Feb. 2002); T. Di Giorgio and C. Di Noia, 'Financial Regulation and Supervision in the Euro Area: A Four-Peak Proposal', Wharton Financial Institutions Center Working Paper 01–02 (Jan. 2001); R.K. Abrams and M.W. Taylor, 'Issues in the Unification of Financial Sector Supervision', IMF Working Paper WP/00/213 (Dec. 2002); H.M. Schooner, 'Regulating Risk Not Function', *University of Cincinnati Law Review*, 66 (1998), 441–88.

and manage their own risks on an organization-wide basis. The growing dominance of financial conglomerates in global markets also raises the costs of single-sector supervision, as consolidated firms are thought to be more capable of exploiting opportunities for regulatory arbitrage – that is, instances in which different regulators establish different substantive rules to deal with functionally similar products or activities – which single-sector agencies have difficulty identifying and correcting. Relatedly, consolidated agencies are thought to be better equipped to identifying regulatory gaps, that is, pockets of economic activity that fall outside the remit of traditional financial sectors, with hedge funds and perhaps sub-prime mortgage lending activities and securitization activities being prominent examples in recent times.

The case against regulatory consolidation is also multi-faceted. To begin with, there is the absence of irrefutable evidence that consolidated agencies are any more efficient than their single-sector predecessors, at least in terms of total regulatory costs.[7] More substantively, critics of consolidated supervisory functions argue that the goals of supervision differ across industry sectors and that a combination of regulatory functions may actually dilute the quality of supervision by imposing a standardized model of oversight on all sectors of the industry. Combined oversight may also diminish market discipline as government guarantees traditionally limited to certain sectors, like banking, may be assumed to extend more broadly in a country where all sectors have a common supervisory agency. In addition, there is concern that regulatory consolidation produces a governmental monopoly, less likely to respond to changing market conditions and potentially more prone to wholesale regulatory capture or at least a supervisory posture tilted in favour of large conglomerates at the expense of smaller more specialized firms.

Regulation by objective, the third multi-peaked model of regulatory organization, is a bit of a hybrid approach and thus shares some of the advantages and disadvantages of the two other models.[8] By reducing the number of supervisory units, regulation by objective offers potential efficiency advantages over traditional sectoral regulation, and it also addresses

---

[7] See M. Čihák and R. Podpiera, 'Is One Watchdog Better than Three? International Experience with Integrated Financial Sector Supervision', IMF Working Paper 06/57 (Mar. 2006) (finding evidence of quality improvements not cost savings from consolidated supervision).

[8] J.J.M. Kremers, D. Schoenmaker and P.J. Wierts, 'Cross-Sector Supervision: Which Model', in R. Herring and R.E. Litan (eds.), *Brookings-Wharton Papers on Financial Services* (2003), 225–43.

concerns of regulatory arbitrage as functionally similar products and services are under the jurisdiction of the same supervisory body. But, like fully consolidated oversight, regulation by objective risks imposing one-size-fits-everyone rules, which discount unique characteristics of traditional sectors and subsectors. Moreover, multi-peaked models generate new problems of coordination, duplication and gaps, as the lines between functions such as market conduct, prudential regulation and market stability are not clear, and many regulatory structures, like disclosure or even capital requirements, advance all three objectives. With regard to concerns over governmental monopolies and supervisory rigidity, multi-peaked models again constitute an intermediate case, less centralized than fully consolidated operations but less attuned to sectoral differences than traditional sectoral oversight.

Another much discussed dimension of regulatory consolidation is the appropriate supervisory role of central banks. Oftentimes, reorganization entails the movement of bank supervision away from the central bank, as happened in the United Kingdom when the supervisory powers of the Bank of England were transferred to the new Financial Services Authority in the late 1990s. Less frequently, but occasionally, the central bank itself becomes the consolidated regulatory, thereby expanding its jurisdiction as a result of reorganization. Finally, in certain multi-peaked models, including perhaps the Treasury Department's *Blueprint*, the central bank may itself be designated the 'peak' responsible for market stability. The often-voiced concern about this aspect of regulatory reorganization is the possibility that moving direct supervisory oversight out of a central bank diminishes the bank's ability to effect appropriate monetary policy and maintain financial stability.

Like many important issues of public policy, the debates over regulatory reorganization rest on numerous, conflicting claims regarding the consequences of various kinds of reforms. Seldom do policy analysts have unambiguous empirical evidence to validate their intuitions. But, in the case of the financial regulation, we do have the benefit of looking to the experiences of the dozens of European jurisdictions which have engaged in regulatory reorganizations over the past two decades, as well as Professor Wymeersch's very helpful synthesis of what we might learn.

II.

In many respects, Professor Wymeersch's portrayal of European regulatory consolidation covers familiar arguments for and against regulatory consolidation, with the growth of financial conglomerates pushing supervisors towards sectoral consolidation and the creation of amalgamated agencies posing concerns over the homogenization and dilution of supervisory oversight. But where Professor Wymeersch's analysis covers new territory is in its explication of how the process of financial consolidation has actually occurred in the twenty-five EU Member States his article surveys.

A.

Consider, for example, Professor Wymeersch's description of modern regulation within the traditional sectors. Typically, one discusses sectoral oversight in terms of the regulatory structure applicable to the core lines of business: banking, securities and insurance. But a recurring theme of Professor Wymeersch's article is the accretion of numerous cross-sectoral regulatory regimes that are already in place in most industrialized countries – money-laundering rules, privacy requirements, anti-terrorism measures, and measures to police tax avoidance.[9] As is true in the United States, regulations addressing these over-arching issues of public policy tend to be imposed uniformly across the financial services industry – that is, on a consolidated basis – and then implemented on a sector by sector basis. Thus, in even the most fragmented of modern supervisory systems (that is, in the United States), we observe many elements of consolidated regulation, albeit implemented in a haphazard, diffuse and likely inefficient manner.

Another theme of Professor Wymeersch's description of European practices is the incremental and variegated manners in which member states have transitioned to consolidated financial services oversight. While foreign observers tend to focus on the fact that a substantial majority of EU Member States now maintain consolidated supervisors, Professor Wymeersch's front line reporting reveals that many countries have made the transition only haltingly and often have only gone partway down the path. Moreover, if one looks closely at the organizational structure within the regulatory apparatus of different EU member states, one can often observe that old sectoral models of oversight have not disappeared even within jurisdictions that maintain a single financial services agency.

[9] E. Wymeersch, 'The Structure of Financial Supervision in Europe: About Single Financial Supervisors, Twin Peaks and Multiple Financial Supervisors', *European Business Organization Law Review*, 8 (2007), 245–6.

Consider first the initial stages of financial reform. In many jurisdictions, reform has often been a gradual process. The front end of regulatory consolidation is sometimes accompanied by ad hoc efforts to coordinate sectoral bodies, such as the creation of a coordinating council in the Netherlands and several other jurisdictions or the use of memoranda of understanding to coordinate existing bodies in Germany and the United Kingdom.[10] While Professor Wymeersch reports that these preliminary efforts typically lack sufficient strength to effect significant changes in regulatory practices, they often serve as the first step in a complex supervisory quadrille that ultimately results in legislated reforms enacted through parliamentary procedures. If true, then perhaps the much-publicized memorandum of understanding between the SEC and CFTC in the spring of 2008 will someday come to be marked as the opening movement of this process in the United States as would be subsequent efforts to achieve written agreements between the SEC and Federal Reserve Board

Also of potential interest to US observers is Professor Wymeersch's discussion of the role of industry conglomeration in regulatory consolidation. Within the United States, the merger of banking and securities firms – facilitated by the passage of the Gramm–Leach–Bliley Act in 1999 – has long been recognized as a reason to develop better coordination between banking and securities regulators. And the decision of the Federal Reserve Board to extend credit to Bear Stearns and subsequent actions with respect to AIG have only reinforced the need for this coordination. Within parts of the EU, one sees similar developments, particularly in the London markets, where the lines between major banks and securities firms have long been blurred. But what is interesting about Professor Wymeersch's account of industry consolidation is his emphasis on the combination of banks and insurance companies in many continental European jurisdictions and his assertion that the regulatory objectives in these two areas are actually quite closely aligned, focused as they are on prudential oversight and thus highly likely to benefit from integrated supervision. For American financial analysts, less attuned to insurance regulation which is largely regulated to state bodies, the notion that there are serious benefits to be gained from combining banking and insurance regulation is eye-opening, but upon reflection not wholly implausible.

Perhaps the greatest lesson to be learned from Professor Wymeersch's survey of regulatory practices in Europe is the array of organizational

---

[10]   Ibid., 262.

arrangements currently in place within the EU. Putting aside the several countries that have not yet combined all three core sectors into one body, one still sees ample variation in approaches. On the one hand, many jurisdictions maintain separate sectoral divisions for front line oversight within integrated regulatory structures. This practice is quite common in the Nordic states but exists elsewhere around the world, most notably in Japan. In contrast, other consolidated agencies, such as the British FSA, organized their chief supervisory units into retail and wholesale markets (a sort of mini-twin-peaks approach within integrated agencies) but also have something of a sectoral matrix approach that maintains expertise along traditional lines but with a special unit for complex organizations. Perhaps not surprisingly, integrated supervision does not in practice consist of an undifferentiated blob of civil servants loosed upon the financial service industry. Rather, in many jurisdictions, operations are divided into supervisory units that would be readily intelligible to one versed only in traditional sectoral oversight.

B.

A commonly cited, but as yet not well-documented virtue of consolidated financial oversight is cost savings in government payrolls. Although Professor Wymeersch alludes to these financial savings, as well as even greater savings accruing to regulated firms that need only deal with one supervising body,[11] his emphasis is on the qualitative improvements that consolidated supervisory agencies provide – an aspect of integrated supervision that has been explored elsewhere but not with nearly as much institutional detail as Professor Wymeersch is able to offer.[12]

To begin with the most mundane, many administrative functions are common to all regulatory bodies: personnel offices, information technology departments, various support personnel at all levels, and even top positions such as the executive director or governing board.[13] Aside from the elimination of redundant offices, consolidated departments have inherently larger mandates, which are apt to attract more experienced and senior personnel. Oftentimes, expanded scope will afford increased

---

[11] Wymeersch, 'The Structure of Financial Supervision in Europe', (note 9, above), 263.

[12] For supporting views, see M. W. Taylor and A. Fleming, 'Integrated Supervision: Lessons of Northern European Experience', *Finance and Development*, 36 (1999), 18; Ćihák and Podpiera, 'Is One Watchdog Better than Three?', (note 7, above).

[13] Wymeersch, 'The Structure of Financial Supervision in Europe', (note 9, above), 260.

flexibility, allowing examiners or enforcement staff to be transferred from one sector to another depending on changing conditions.

In terms of substantive expertise, there are to begin with the mounting number of topics – money laundering, tax avoiding, privacy, and financial education – that in many jurisdictions apply to all sectors of the financial services industry and must be staffed repeatedly and inefficiently under traditional sectoral regulation.[14] With integrated agencies, policy making can be combined and streamlined. But if one looks inside the substance of traditional sectoral regulation, there are many more instances of highly comparable matters of substantive expertise: fitness qualifications for new owners or controlling shareholders; suitability standards for investment products (and exemptions for qualified parties); limitations on transactions with affiliated parties; diversification requirements; disclosure obligations of various sorts; and licensing procedures for new firms.[15] Most modern systems of financial regulation share these same core elements. While the technical requirements (and even terminology) often differ from sector to sector, the differences are often more the product of historical happenstance than major distinctions in substantive policy. Attorneys, economists and other policy analysts trained up to deal with these matters in one sector could quite easily apply their expertise in other sectors. Very plausibly, they would do their jobs better and make life substantially easier for regulated parties if they had the broader remit afforded under a consolidated supervisor.[16]

An excellent example of the benefits of a cross-sectoral purview is capital requirements. Much attention has focused on the reform of bank capital requirements under the Basel II process, which has attracted the attention of some of the world's most talented financial economists and been supported by literally hundreds of working papers and dozens and dozens of academic conferences and symposia. Many of the issues that have been explored in the Basel II process – value-at-risk models, internal ratings, back-testing procedures – are potentially applicable to other types of financial institutions, such as securities firms and insurance companies. Within the more integrated European system, these connections are more easily drawn. In fact, securities firms in Europe are subject to the Basel II capital requirements (and not the different SEC net capital rules applicable to broker

---

[14] Ibid., 245–56, 248–9.
[15] Ibid., 270–1.   [16] Ibid., 275.

dealers in the United States). As Professor Wymeersch explains, even the new insurance Solvency II directive is heavily informed by the Basel II capital rules.[17] Thus the oversight of insurance companies in Europe indirectly draws on the expertise of the Basel process in a way that would be difficult to imagine in the United States, where insurance capital rules fall within the bailiwick of the NAIC and state insurance commissions, which have few formal connections to banking regulators and the large number of highly trained economists housed in the Federal Reserve regional banks.

C.

Another insight available in Professor Wymeersch's account concerns the persistence of jurisdictional and substantive conflicts within consolidated regulatory frameworks and the manner in which those conflicts are resolved. Regulatory reorganizations within the financial services industry do not so much eliminate the existence of conflicts, as they alter the dimension on which conflicts arise and change the locus of their resolutions.

Take the case of the classic form of twin-peak regulation, where market conduct is delegated to one agency and prudential oversight is given to another. While this division of authority works well in theory, in practice it entails considerable potential overlap in regulatory design. To begin with, market conduct rules can have prudential implications, as, for example, improper lending practices can give rise to private claims and enforcement actions, which in the extreme can threaten institutional solvency. On the other hand, ample capital reserves – the core of prudential regulation – can have market conduct implications, as well-capitalized concerns are more likely to police their own business activities in order to prevent reputational losses and diminution of franchise value. For these reasons, prudential regulators may have different views on market conduct issues that conflict with the views of the market conduct regulator and vice versa. Sometimes, a policy that advances market conduct regulation – say enhanced disclosure of financial weakness – can actually conflict with prudential considerations or even market stability. Thus one regulatory body may oppose additional disclosures whereas another opposes it, and the issue of the proper hierarchy of regulatory functions is called into question.[18]

---

[17] Ibid., 269.   [18] Ibid., 245, 249.

In the early years of twin-peak regulation in Australia, there were many examples of regulatory conflicts of this sort and it took a number of years (and several memoranda of understanding) to devise a practical system for implementing this form of divided regulatory authority. Professor Wymeersch suggests that similar problems have arisen in multi-peaked regulatory structures in the European context.[19]

With a fully consolidated regulatory structure, similar conflicts arise. If the agency is organized around traditional sectoral divisions, then the same inter-sectoral conflicts arise across divisions. For consolidated agencies organized around functional divisions – that is, replicated multi-peak models within a single agency – the same overlaps and potentially divergent views described above will arise in this context too. What is different about the consolidated agency, as Professor Wymeersch notes, is where these inevitable conflicts will be resolved, and that is within the agency itself, presumably at the highest level.[20] Conflict resolution in the United States and in other jurisdictions where regulatory jurisdictions is divided across numerous regulatory bodies is more complex. In some instances, cross-agency compromises, typically in the form of memoranda of understanding, can be used to reconcile disagreements. But, as Professor Wymeersch notes, these are complicated to negotiate and tend to leave important issues unresolved or unforeseen.[21] The alternative is resolution in courts or through legislative intervention.[22] But these solutions – as exemplified in the United States – tend to be time-consuming and unreliable, with many inter-jurisdictional conflicts allowed to drag on for years.[23]

In this light, one of the less well understood virtues of consolidated regulatory structures is their built-in ability to resolve through internal mechanisms the inevitable conflicts that arise across industry sectors and regulatory functions. Of course, this advantage carries with it an amplification of one of the greatest potential problems with consolidation: the centralization of excessive governmental authority within a single administrative body, a topic to which I now turn.

[19]   Ibid., 247, 267.
[20]   Ibid., 243; R. M. Kushmeider, 'Restructuring US Financial Regulation', *Contemporary Economic Policy*, 25 (2007), 337.
[21]   Ibid., 267–8.
[22]   Ibid., 281–2.
[23]   H.E. Jackson, 'Regulation of a Multisectored Financial Services Industry: An Exploratory Essay', *Washington University Law Quarterly*, 77 (1999), 319–97.

D.

Perhaps the most vexing questions surrounding the consolidation of financial regulatory functions concern issues of accountability and maintenance of appropriate regulatory focus. Especially in the United States, where concerns over aggregation of governmental authority have a special and historic salience, regulatory consolidation is often portrayed as almost un-American on the grounds that divided government is inherently better than centralized authority, at least in this hemisphere. On a more instrumental dimension, the benefits of regulatory competition among diverse and overlapping regulatory agencies are thought to prevent governmental stasis, to combat regulatory capture, and to ensure appropriate regulatory reforms in light of market and technological developments. European experience with consolidated supervision, as Professor Wymeersch recounts, offers a somewhat different perspective on all of these lines of argument.[24]

To begin with, a number of European jurisdictions have attempted to hardwire political accountability into the enabling statutes for their consolidated regulatory bodies. The best example of this is the British FSA, for which Parliament set forth a clear set of regulatory goals and principles of good regulation to which the agency is expected to abide.[25] To ensure fidelity to these statutory guidelines, the FSA prepares annual reports, holds annual meetings, works with a larger number of advisory groups populated with different public constituencies, and – for at least its first decade of existence – seems to have honed fairly tightly to the guidelines that the British legislative process established. According to Professor Wymeersch's account, similar mechanisms of accountability are found in other European statutes.[26]

Another lesson of Professor Wymeersch's analysis is that domestic regulatory competition of the sort illustrated by SEC versus CFTC conflicts is not the sole source of competitive pressure on regulatory agencies. Within an increasingly globalized economy, regulatory

---

[24] Wymeersch, 'The Structure of Financial Supervision in Europe', (note 9, above), 277–86.

[25] For a more detailed discussion, see M. W. Taylor, 'Accountability and Objectives in the FSA', in M.C. Blair et al. (eds.), *Blackstone's Guide to the Financial Services and Markets Act 2000* (Blackstone Press, 2001), 17–36. See also E. Hüpkes, M. Quintyn and M.W. Taylor, 'The Accountability of Financial Sector Supervisors – Principles and Practice', *European Business Law Review*, (2005) 1575–620; Briault, 'Revisiting the Rational for a Single National Financial Services Regulator', (note 6, above).

[26] Wymeersch, 'The Structure of Financial Supervision in Europe', (note 9, above), 277–9, 281.

competition across international boundaries offers a quite plausible substitute for the kind of regulatory competition that once only existed within
nation states. (Indeed, within the quite permeable national boundaries
of the European Union, Professor Wymeersch seems to see an excessive
amount of regulatory competition.) But the key point for policy analysts
fearful of the aggregation of regulatory functions within a single national
regulatory body is that cross-border regulatory competition is now an
important dynamic, which will put a natural constraint on the ability of
a domestic consolidated regulator to fall behind in regulatory innovations.[27] And, of course, in most jurisdictions, not all regulatory functions
are moved into consolidated agencies, with central banks and Ministries
of Finance (such as the US Treasury) usually also retaining some market
oversight role and offering a source of domestic checks on consolidated
agencies.

Another and somewhat surprising insight from Professor Wymeersch's
survey is the reportedly diminished role of regulatory capture with consolidated regulatory bodies. Among US academics, one of the principal
failings of administrative agencies is their tendency to fall under the influence of the firms they oversee.[28] A potential concern about consolidated
supervision is that the dangers of regulatory capture could be multiplied as
the jurisdiction of the regulatory agency is expanded. But what Professor
Wymeersch reports from Europe is that the relative power of any sector of
the financial services industry is diminished with respect to consolidated
agencies and so the ability of any single sector to capture the agency is
diminished.[29] To be sure, this portrayal does not ensure that a coordinated
effort on the part of the entire financial services industry would not be successful in having undue influence on regulatory authorities. But it does
suggest that in at least some instances consolidated agencies may be more
resistant to regulatory capture than their single-sector predecessors.

E.

A final insight to be drawn from Professor Wymeersch's description of
current EU practices concerns the distinction between regulation – that

[27] In a similar vein, interaction with multilateral organizations, such as ISOCO or the Basel
Committee on Banking Supervision, provides further checks on any single countries
regulator getting too far out of line of evolving international standards.

[28] J.R. Macey, 'Administrative Agency Obsolescence and Interest Group Formation: A
Case Study of the SEC at Sixty', *Cardozo Law Review*, 15 (1994), 909–49.

[29] Wymeersch, 'The Structure of Financial Supervision in Europe', (note 9, above), 265,
278–9.

is, the articulation of regulatory requirements – and supervision – the application of those legal requirements to various sectors of the financial services industry through oversight, examination and inspection, and both formal and informal enforcement activity. While financial supervision in Europe is increasingly implemented through consolidated agencies, financial regulation in the region is often still effected along traditional sectoral lines. The EU directives governing the financial sector are the best example of this phenomenon, structured as they are around securities sector (e.g. the prospectus directive, the transparency directive or MiFID), the banking sector (e.g. the capital adequacy directive and the second banking directive), and insurance sector (the solvency directive).[30] [31] As Professor Wymeersch explains, this fragmented lawmaking process produces many of the problems common in the United States. Functionally similar insurance and securities products are subject to different conduct of business rules, creating regulatory anomalies and opportunities for regulatory arbitrage.[32] Thus, while much attention has been focused on the supervisory consolidation within many EU Member States, many of the benefits of this consolidation are not fully realized as long as regulatory standards are largely set on a sectoral basis. Here seems to be an area where Brussels needs to catch up with the Member States.

Another idiosyncrasy of the EU regulatory structure is the dispersion of supervisory authority across member states, whether to consolidated regulatory units of the sort found in the United Kingdom or to more traditional sectoral bodies of France and Spain. This phenomenon raises serious questions as to whether regulatory policy established at the community level is being implemented and enforced consistently across the region, issues which the Lampfalussy process was designed to address, but which still has not been fully resolved, at least judging from Professor Wymeersch's account.[33] Perhaps ironically, the principal organizational mechanism being employed to monitor and correct uneven implementation or enforcement is sectoral-based coordinating councils, such as the Committee of European Securities Regulators (CESR), which Professor Wymeersch has chaired. Thus, the fully consolidated regulatory agencies, such as the British FSA or Professor Wymeersch's

---

[30] The financial conglomerate directive would be a counterexample (ibid., 260), as would the privacy directive.
[31] Ibid., 244.
[32] Ibid., 254 and n. 37.
[33] Ibid., 288.

own Belgium Banking, Finance and Insurance Commission (CBFA), find themselves operating under sectoral directives established at the EU level and then coordinating with the authorities of other member states through sectoral counsels such as CESR. It is apparently the fate of consolidated supervisors to have to operate, at least initially, in a world built upon sectoral structures.

While the institutional details of European regulatory organization reflect many conditions peculiar to the evolution of the European Union and larger issues of constitutional structure, certain aspects of European practice do, perhaps, have lessons for the United States and other jurisdictions. The distinction between regulation and supervision is an important one. Within the United States there is intense political resistance toward consolidation of traditional supervisory units, whether across sectoral lines, such as banking or securities, or even among depository institutions (such as banks, thrifts and credit units) or functionally similar products such as securities or futures. But European practice reveals that it is possible to distinguish regulatory consolidation from supervisory consolidation. The United States might possibly proceed with regulatory consolidation – establishing uniform national standards across sectoral boundaries – and still retain supervision and enforcement within our traditional sectoral-based oversight units, at least for a transitional period. In many areas, such as money laundering, privacy safeguards and truth in lending, this is already the state of affairs although these rule-making functions are currently located in different administrative units. Recent initiatives to broadening the Federal Reserve Board's authority over issues of market stability could be seen as a continuation of this process. As I explore in greater detail elsewhere, one could easily imagine the creation of another industry-wide regulatory unit – perhaps built upon the current President's Working Group for Financial Markets – to develop consistent American regulation and associated policy-making functions for other areas of financial regulation, including consumer protection, the mechanical aspects of regulation such as fitness standards or affiliated party transactions, and other rules common to all sectors of the financial services industry. In this way, the United States could begin to achieve many of the benefits of consolidated supervision, but without disrupting our traditional supervisory structure and taking on all of the quite formidable political challenges that consolidation of those units would entail.

If the United States were to head down this path, it would become the converse of the current European model. Whereas the EU system now largely depends on sectoral regulation at the EU directive level with mostly consolidated supervision and enforcement among member states, the path toward consolidation that I imagine for the United States would consist of moving towards consolidated regulation through congressional legislation as well as a newly devised regulatory agency to articulate most forms of financial regulation and perhaps the Federal Reserve Board for issues related to market stability, but could retain for some years sectoral supervision and enforcement along current lines. The United States and the European Union could then engage in a quite interesting form of regulatory competition over which form of financial regulatory consolidation works best.[34]

* * * * *

For many years, financial regulation was a national affair, and regulatory structures evolved in response to national conditions and domestic constituencies, with little attention to developments beyond national borders. Today, however, financial regulation is inherently a global undertaking, with an ever-increasing volume of cross-border transactions and an ever-escalating mobility of financial firms. Nowhere in the world can financial regulators proceed without attention to evolving supervisory practices in other jurisdictions. For a number of decades now, American legal academics have had the great good fortune to be able to look to the work of Professor Wymeersch for a lucid and insightful window into the European regulatory perspectives. All of us very much look forward to many more years of this most important and illuminating work.

---

[34] One of the challenges of devising a more integrated form of financial regulation in the United States is dealing with the fact that the scale of the US economy and its regulatory operations is so much greater than that of other jurisdictions, (Jackson, 'An American Perspective on the FSA', (note 2, above), 39–71). For an argument that scale factors should not inhibit full consolidation of financial regulatory functions in the United States, see Brown, 'E Pluribus Unum – Out of Many', (note 6, above), 1–101.

29

The SEC embraces mutual recognition

ROBERTA S. KARMEL

I. Introduction

The traditional approach of the United States Securities and Exchange Commission (SEC) toward foreign (non-US) issuers, financial intermediaries and markets has been national treatment rather than mutual recognition. In the view of the SEC, mutual recognition was appropriate only when there was harmonized securities regulation between the US and a foreign jurisdiction. Accordingly, although the SEC made accommodations to foreign issuers, it rarely engaged in mutual recognition, the one important exception being the multi-jurisdictional disclosure (MJDS) regime with Canada. This exception actually proved the rule because the Canadians amended their securities laws to harmonize their securities regulations with US law, and to the extent that this was not the case, with regard to generally accepted accounting principles (GAAP), Canadian issuers were required to reconcile Canadian GAAP to US GAAP.

More recently, however, the SEC has been taking a new look at mutual recognition, and in the case of international financial reporting standards (IFRS) it now allows foreign issuers to use IFRS rather than US GAAP based on a theory of convergence rather than a requirement of harmonization. Furthermore, with regard to the prospect of foreign exchange and broker-dealer access to the US capital markets, the SEC is contemplating mutual recognition based on a theory of regulatory equivalence rather than a requirement of harmonization. On 1 February 2008, SEC Chairman Christopher Cox and European Union Commissioner for the Internal Market and Services Charlie McCreevy met in Washington, DC and agreed to a goal of an EU–US mutual recognition arrangement for securities regulation, declaring that 'mutual recognition offers significant promise as a means of better protecting investors, fostering capital formation and maintaining fair, orderly, and efficient transatlantic securities markets'.[1]

This chapter will discuss the differences between mutual recognition based on securities law harmonization, securities law convergence and securities law equivalence, and suggest that changes in the international capital markets are forcing the SEC to reconsider its long-standing insistence on harmonization as a predicate for mutual recognition. By accepting IFRS from foreign issuers, the SEC based its rule-making on convergence between US GAAP and IFRS, rather than insisting on full harmonization. In considering allowing foreign trading screens into the US, the SEC may base new rules on regulatory equivalence. In order to remain a leading securities regulator, the SEC is engaging in discussions with foreign regulators to achieve regulatory comparability, whether called harmonization, convergence or equivalence, and the promise of mutual recognition may well act as an incentive to realizing high international standards for investor protection.

II. National treatment

A. Public companies

Generally, the most common approaches to regulating foreign issuers which sell securities to domestic investors are: requiring them to comply with host country laws (national treatment);[2] creating special host country rules for them;[3] developing harmonized international standards;[4] and accepting compliance with home country standards (mutual recognition).[5] The US historically approached this problem through national treatment, with some special rules to ameliorate the problems of compliance for foreign issuers. By contrast, the EU has a

---

[1] SEC Press Release 2008–9, 'Statement of the European Commission and the US Securities and Exchange Commission on Mutual Recognition in Securities Markets', www.sec. gov/news/press/2008/2008–9.htm, at 2 (last accessed 1 February 2008).

[2] See R.C. Campos, 'Speech by SEC Commissioner: Embracing International Business in the Post-Enron Era', speech at the Centre for European Policy Studies in Brussels (Belgium), www.sec.gov/news/speech/spch061103rcc.htm (last accessed 11 June 2003).

[3] Ibid. This has been the SEC's approach to some extent.

[4] See M.G. Warren III, 'Global Harmonization of Securities Laws: The Achievement of the European Communities', *Harvard International Law Journal*, 31 (1990), 191.

[5] Ibid.

regime of mutual recognition, at least within the EU.[6] While there is no international securities regulator with the ability to impose a disclosure or other regulatory regime on all issuers worldwide, the International Organization of Securities Commissions (IOSCO) has developed a template for basic disclosure standards and the International Accounting Standards Board (IASB) has developed international accounting standards (formerly known as IAS and now known as international financial reporting standards or IFRS).[7]

When the Securities Act of 1933 ('Securities Act') was passed, Congress contemplated that foreign issuers might make offerings into the United States, and provided a special disclosure regime for sovereign debt.[8] Further, the jurisdictional reach of the law extended to interstate and foreign commerce.[9] The US courts have given the SEC authority to impose its disclosure obligations on any foreign company that sells shares to US nationals.[10] Under the federal securities laws, any foreign issuer which makes a public offering into the US must then become an SEC registered and reporting company. A company wishing to list its securities on a US exchange also must register its listed securities with the SEC under the Securities Exchange Act of 1934 ('Exchange Act') and become subject to the SEC's annual and periodic reporting and disclosure requirements.[11] Although the SEC could require any foreign issuer with more than 500 shareholders worldwide, of which 300 are US investors, and which has $10 million in assets, to register its equity securities pursuant to the Exchange Act,[12] the SEC has not exerted its jurisdiction to this extent. Foreign issuers which would be required to file under the Exchange Act because they have $10 million in assets and 300 out of 500 US shareholders can file for an exemption from such registration.[13]

---

[6] See M.I. Steinberg and L.E. Michaels, 'Disclosure in Global Securities Offerings: Analysis of Jurisdictional Approaches, Commonality and Reciprocity', *Michigan Journal of International Law*, 20 (1999), 255–61.

[7] See M.I. Steinberg, *International Securities Law: A Contemporary and Comparative Analysis*, (Kluwer Law International, 1999), 27–38.

[8] Securities Act, Schedule B, 15 U.S.C. § 77aa (2008).

[9] Ibid. § 77b (7) (2008).

[10] See *Europe and Oversees Commodity Traders, S.A.* v. *Banque Paribas London*, 147 F.3d 118 (2d Cir. 1998), *cert. denied*, 525 U.S. 1139 (1999) (suggesting that the Securities Act applies when both the offer and sale of a security are made in the United States); *Consol. Gold Fields PLC* v. *Minorco, S.A.*, 871 F.2d 252, *modified*, 890 F.2d 569 (2d Cir.), *cert. dismissed*, 492 U.S. 939 (1989).

[11] 15 U.S.C. § 78a (2008), *et seq.*

[12] See 15 U.S.C. ' 78*l*. The SEC has under consideration rule-making to make this exemption more difficult to claim and maintain. See note 53, *infra*.

[13] Exchange Act Rule 12g3–2 (b), 17 C.F.R. § 240.12g3–2 (b).

The attitude of the SEC staff long was that if a foreign issuer was going to tap the US capital markets then it should play by the SEC's rules. In the mid 1970s the SEC requested public comment on improving the disclosure required by foreign issuers, noting that the registration forms used by them required substantially less information than required of US domestic issuers.[14] The SEC then adopted Form 20-F as a combined registration and annual reporting form,[15] but, since corporate governance regulation generally was left to the states under US law, it was similarly left to the national law of foreign issuers. Among other things, foreign issuers were exempted from SEC proxy solicitation regulations and short-swing insider transaction reporting requirements.[16] Further, in Form 20-F, the SEC bowed to some of the objections of foreign issuers and deleted certain proposed disclosures relating to corporate governance.[17] Additionally, following a policy of international cooperation during the 1980s and 1990s, the SEC fashioned special exemptions for foreign issuers relating to private offerings to institutional investors,[18] and amended its foreign issuer disclosure forms to comply with disclosure standards endorsed by IOSCO.[19]

In 1991 the SEC adopted the MJDS whereby qualified Canadian issuers could issuer securities in the US based on their filings with Canadian securities regulators.[20] This regime was based on harmonization of securities law requirements between the SEC and the Canadian securities regulators and was a mutual recognition system. Canadian issuers could use the same prospectus for offerings in the US as they had

---

[14] Means of Improving Disclosure by Certain Foreign Private Issuers, Exchange Act Release No.13,056, 41 Fed. Reg. 55,012, at 55,013 (16 December 1976).

[15] 17 C.F.R. § 249.220 (f). This continues to be the primary reporting form for foreign issuers.

[16] 17 C.F.R. § 240.3a12–3.

[17] Specifically, the disclosure of the business experience and background of officers and directors, the identification of the three highest paid officers and directors and the aggregate amount paid to them; and conditioned a material transactions disclosure to the requirements of applicable foreign law. Rules, Registration and Annual Report Form for Foreign Private Issuers, Exchange Act Release No. 16,371, 44 Fed. Reg. 70,132, at 70,133 (6 December 1979). See also Adoption of Foreign Issuer Integrated Disclosure System, Securities Act Release No. 6437, 47 Fed. Reg. 54,764 (6 December 1982).

[18] See Regulation S, 17 C.F.R. §230.901–905; Rule 144A, 17 C.F.R. §230.144A; Rule 12g3-2 (b), 17 C.F.R. §240.12g3-2(b).

[19] International Disclosure Standards, Securities Act Release No. 7745, 64 Fed. Reg. 53900 (5 October 1999).

[20] Multijurisdictional Disclosure and Modifications to the Current Registration and Reporting System for Canadian Issuers Securities Act Rule 29354, 56 Fed Reg 30096 (1 July 1991).

used in Canada, except that they were required to reconcile their financial statements to US GAAP.[21] After the MJDS was put into effect, the SEC considered establishing a mutual recognition regime with other jurisdictions, in particular, the United Kingdom, but this effort was abandoned. Among other reasons, the British authorities were advised that the SEC could not establish a mutual recognition regime with only one and not other EU countries.

Another area in which the SEC established a mutual recognition regime was with respect to tender offers and rights offers.[22] Because of complaints from US investors holding foreign securities who were deprived of the opportunity to participate in foreign issuer takeover and rights offerings by reason of SEC protections they did not desire, the SEC established a principle of mutual recognition for these types of cross-border offerings. These rules were adopted at about the same time that the SEC revised its disclosure standards for foreign private issuers based upon the international disclosure standards endorsed by IOSCO. The SEC was also going forward at this time on a program to harmonize US and international accounting standards through the IASB. Unfortunately, this spirit of international cooperation between the SEC and foreign regulators was undermined by the enactment of the Sarbanes–Oxley Act of 2002 ('Sarbanes–Oxley').[23]

Although foreign issuers had become used to a regime under which US corporate governance standards did not apply to them, Sarbanes–Oxley did not exempt foreign issuers from its new corporate governance requirements. Foreign issuers viewed the context for Sarbanes–Oxley to be US financial scandals and failures, and argued that the SEC should not be imposing corporate governance regulations on corporations that functioned in very different corporate finance systems and with very different structures than US firms.[24] Congress and the SEC retreated to the view that if foreign issuers wish to tap the US capital markets, they needed to play by US rules. Financial scandals in Europe, including the Royal Ahold, Parmalat and Vivendi cases,[25]

---

[21] Ibid. at 30101.

[22] Cross-Border Tender and Exchange Offers, Business Combinations and Rights Offerings, Securities Act Release No. 7759, 64 Fed Reg. 61382 (10 November 1999).

[23] Sarbanes-Oxley Act of 2002, Pub. L. No. 107–204, 116 Stat. 745 (2002) (codified in scattered sections of 11, 15, 18, 28 and 29 U.S.C.).

[24] See K.S. Lehman, 'Recent Development: Executive Compensation Following the Sarbanes–Oxley Act of 2002', *North Carolina Law Review*, 81 (2003), 2132–33.

[25] See L. Enriques, 'Bad Apples, Bad Oranges: A Comment From Old Europe on Post-Enron Corporate Governance Reforms', *Wake Forest Law Review*, 38 (2003), 911; E. Mossos,

strengthened this view and made the SEC unwilling to craft exemptions for foreign issuers. Although the SEC did exempt foreign issuers from the requirement that their audit committees have independent directors if their governance structures achieved the same goals as the Sarbanes–Oxley audit committee provisions,[26] the SEC required foreign issuers to comply with other provisions such as the CEO-CFO certification requirements[27] and the internal control provisions of Section 404 of Sarbanes–Oxley.[28] After some difficult negotiations, the SEC and foreign regulators came to an accommodation regarding regulation of audit firms.[29]

B. Foreign exchanges and broker-dealers

Pressure from the EU on US policy makers to allow foreign trading screens in the US has been ongoing for some time.[30] A response to this pressure was expressed by SEC Commissioner Roel C. Campos, who explained that the SEC 'imposes significant regulatory requirements on exchanges, as well as on issuers who list on those exchanges, whether foreign or domestic. The exemptions being requested by some foreign

'Sarbanes-Oxley Goes to Europe: A Comparative Analysis of United States and European Union Corporate Reforms After Enron', *Currents: International Trade Law Journal*, 13 (2004), 9; C. Storelli, 'Corporate Governance Failures – Is Parmalat Europe's Enron?', *Columbia Business Law Review*, 3 (2005), 765.

[26] Final Rule: Standards Relating to Listed Company Audit Committees, Securities Act Release No. 8220, 68 Fed. Reg. 18788 (16 April 2003).

[27] Sarbanes-Oxley, §§ 302, 906.

[28] 15 U.S.C. § 7262 (2008).

[29] Sarbanes–Oxley, which created the Public Company Accounting Oversight Board (PCAOB), directed public accounting firms that participate in audits of SEC reporting companies to register with the PCAOB and become subject to PCAOB audit rules and inspection (§§ 102–104, 15 U.S.C. § 7212 (2004)). These provisions applied on their face to foreign auditors, a situation which created conflict between the SEC and foreign regulators. In order to ameliorate these problems, the PCAOB stated its intention to cooperate with non-US regulators in accomplishing the goals of the statute without subjecting non-US public accounting forms to unnecessary burdens or conflicting requirements. *See* Final Rules Relating to the Oversight of Non-US Public Accounting Firms, PCAOB Release No. 2004–005, www.pcaobus.org/Rules/Docket_013/2004–06–09_Release_2004–005.pdf, at 2–3 (last accessed 9 June 2004).

[30] See F. Bolkestein, 'Towards an Integrated European Capital Market', Keynote Address at Federation of European Securities Exchange Convention, London', (13 June 2003); F. Bolkestein, 'Press Conference with EU Internal Market and Taxation Commissioner Frits Bolkestein, Washington, D.C.', http://europa.eu/rapid/pressReleasesAction.do?reference=SPEECH/03/297&format= H TML&aged=1&language=EN&guiLanguage=en (last accessed 29 May 2002).

exchanges would create access to US investors on different terms than those available to US Exchanges. This, in turn, puts considerable stress on our system of regulation, disrupting the level playing field we have created for all market participants.'[31]

There are two problems with regard to giving foreign securities exchanges access to the United States. One is how to fit such exchanges into national market system (NMS) regulation. Domestic electronic communications networks (ECNs) or alternative trading systems (ATSs) have been brought into the NMS regulatory framework through the adoption of Regulation ATS and a revised definition of the term 'exchange' under the Exchange Act.[32] In its Concept Release proposing that ATSs should either register as exchanges or undertake new responsibilities as broker-dealers, the SEC addressed the problem of foreign exchanges wishing to access the US capital markets.[33] Since then, the SEC and the EU have put in place comprehensive and probably incompatible regulations governing trading on regulated markets.[34] The second major problem preventing foreign stock exchange access is that thousands of foreign securities that are not registered with the SEC and whose issuers do not meet SEC disclosure and accounting standards, would become tradeable in the US.[35] The SEC has suggested several possible solutions to this problem. First, the SEC could subject foreign exchanges to registration as 'exchanges' under the Exchange Act and prevent them from trading any securities not registered with the SEC under the Exchange Act.[36] Second, the SEC could limit cross-border trading by ECNs, ATSs or foreign exchanges seeking US investors to operate through an access provider which would be a US broker-dealer or ECN.[37] Third, the SEC could limit trading in foreign securities by foreign exchanges to transactions with sophisticated US investors so that some exemption from Securities Act registration

---

[31] R.C. Campos, 'Speech by SEC Commissioner: Embracing International Business in the Post-Enron Era', speech at the Centre for European Policy Studies, Brussels, www.sec.gov/news/speech/spch061103rcc.htm (last accessed 11 June 2003).

[32] See Exchange Act Rule 3b-16, 17 C.F.R. § 240.3b-16 (2000).

[33] Concept Release, Regulation of Exchanges, Exchange Act Release No. 38672, 62 Fed. Reg. 30485 (4 June 1997) [hereinafter 'ATS Concept Release'].

[34] See R.S. Karmel, 'The Once and Future New York Stock Exchange, The Regulation of Global Exchanges', *Brooklyn Journal of Corporate, Financial and Commercial Law*, 1 (2007), 370–79.

[35] See ATS Concept Release, *supra* note 33, at 30529.

[36] Ibid. at 30488.

[37] Ibid. at 30488.

might be available.[38] Fourth, the SEC could limit trading to world-class foreign issuers.[39]

C. Marketplace changes

Marketplace developments in recent years have made a US listing less attractive for foreign issuers. The European markets have matured to a point where capital can be raised there to meet the needs of most companies.[40] Foreign, and even some US companies, engaging in IPOs or stock exchange listings have done so in Europe, rather than in the US. In 1999 and 2000, foreign IPOs on US exchanges exceeded $80 billion, ten times the amount raised in London, but in 2005 London exchanges raised over $10.3 billion in foreign IPOs compared to $6 billion on US exchanges.[41] In 2004, only three out of the twenty-five largest IPOs were listed on US exchanges, in 2005 none of the twenty-five largest IPOs were listed on US exchanges, and during the first half of 2006, only two of the largest twenty-five international IPOs were listed on US exchanges. By contrast, in 2000, eleven of the twenty-five largest IPOs were listed on US exchanges.[42]

Another possible factor in the SECs new attitude toward mutual recognition probably was the merger of the New York Stock Exchange, Inc. with Euronext, NV in 2007.[43] In order for this merger to be accomplished, it was necessary for the SEC to assure European regulators that the SEC would not attempt to impose provisions of Sarbanes-Oxley upon companies listed on Euronext.[44] In addition, it was necessary for

---

[38] Ibid. In 2003 the staff of the Ontario Securities Commission recommended a new approach to the recognition of securities in foreign based stock exchange indexes based on mutual recognition. *See* Regulatory Approach for Foreign-Based Stock Exchanges, www.osc.gov.on.ca/Regulation/Rulemaking/Current/Part2/sn_21–702_for.

[39] J.W. White, 'Speech by SEC Staff: "Corporation Finance in 2008 – International Initiatives", Remarks Before PLI's Seventh Annual Institute on Securities Regulation in Europe', www.sec.gov/news/speech/2008/spch011408jww.htm, at 15–16 (last accessed 14 January 2008).

[40] See K. Betz, 'Former SEC Official Sees New Realities For Foreign Issuers Seeking to Raise Capital', 38 *Sec. Reg. & L. Rep. (BNA)*, (15 May 2006), at 852.

[41] See S. Fidler, 'How the Square Mile Defeated Prophets of Doom', *Financial Times (London)*, (10 December 2005), at 11.

[42] See A. Lucchetti, 'NYSE, Via Euronext, Aims to Regain Its Appeal for International Listings', *Wall Street Journal*, 30 June 2006, at C1.

[43] See NYSE Euronext At-a-Glance, www.nyse.com/pdfs/NY7_3_p44_45InSide.pdf.

[44] C. Cox, 'Speech by SEC Chairman: Remarks on Acceptance of the Atlantic Leadership Award from the European-American Business Council', www.sec.gov/news/speech/2008/spch020108cc.htm, at 3 (last accessed 1 February 2008).

the SEC to be assured of regulatory cooperation by European regulators. In order to facilitate this merger, the SEC and the College of Euronext Regulators therefore negotiated a comprehensive arrangement to facilitate cooperation in market oversight.[45]

III. The converge concept and the IFRS roadmap

At the end of last year, the SEC determined to allow foreign issuers to report their financial statements in IFRS, rather than US GAAP, without a US GAAP reconciliation.[46] This step was a significant breakthrough in a step toward mutual recognition by the SEC in circumstances where regulatory standards are sufficiently converged (although not completely harmonized) to protect investors. Of equal importance to the decision by the SEC to accept IFRS in filings by foreign issuers, the SEC proposed to allow US issuers to report their financial statements in IFRS.[47]

The recognition of IFRS has been a long time in coming. In 1988, the SEC explicitly supported the establishment of international accounting standards to reduce regulatory impediments resulting from disparate national accounting standards.[48] Nevertheless, the SEC determined not to adopt a process-oriented approach to IASB standards, recognizing them as 'authoritative' and therefore comparable to US GAAP standards promulgated by the Financial Accounting Standards Board. Rather, it intended to assess each IASB standard after its completion, and then recognize acceptable standards. In 1991 and 1993, it did so with respect to IASB standards on cash flow statements, business combinations and the

---

[45] SEC Press Release 2007–8, SEC, Euronext Regulators Sign Regulatory Cooperation Arrangement, www.sec.gov/news/press/2007/2007–8.htm (last accessed 25 January 2007).

[46] Acceptance from Foreign Private Issuers of Financial Statements Prepared in Accordance with International Financial Reporting Standards Without Reconciliation to US GAAP, Securities Act Release No. 8879, 73 Fed. Reg. 986 (4 January 2008) [hereinafter 'Acceptance of IFRS Final Release'].

[47] Concept Release on Allowing US Issuers to Prepare Financial Statements in Accordance with International Financial Reporting Standards, Securities Act Release No. 8831, 72 Fed. Reg. 45599 (14 August 2007), corrected 72 Fed. Reg. 53509 (19 September 2007).

[48] C.W. Hewitt and J.W. White, Testimony Concerning Globally Accepted Accounting Standards, Before the Subcomm. On Securities, Insurance, and Investment of the Sen. Comm. On Banking Housing and Urban Affairs, www.sec.gov/news/testimony/2007/ts102407cwh-jww.htm, at 2–3 [hereinafter 'Hewitt Testimony'] (last accessed 24 October 2007).

effects of changes in foreign exchange rates.[49] But the SEC then suspended this approach of recognizing one standard at a time and decided instead to consider all IASB standards after the IASB completed its core standards work program.[50] This program was completed in March 2000, and the SEC then issued a Concept Release as part of the assessment process possibly leading to the SEC's acceptance of IFRS. IOSCO, as well as the SEC and others, were working on financial disclosure harmonization, and by May 2000, IOSCO had assessed all thirty core standards in the IASB work program and recommended to its members that multi-national issuers use the core standards, supplemented by reconciliation, disclosure interpretation where necessary.[51] But in its 2000 Concept Release on accounting disclosure for foreign companies, the SEC continued to reject a mutual recognition approach except for the MJDS with Canada.

At this time, the SEC was not concerned about particular IFRS standards, with a few exceptions, but it questioned whether these standards could be rigorously interpreted and applied.[52] In particular, the SEC had criticized the structure and financing of the IASB and took a heavy hand in restructuring this organization. A new constitution was adopted in May 2000, which established this body as an independent organization with two main bodies, the Trustees and the Board, as well as the Standing Interpretations Committee and Standards Advisory Council.[53] The Trustees appoint the Board Members, exercise oversight and raise the funds needed, whereas the Board has sole responsibility for setting accounting standards. The founding Chairman of the Board of Trustees for the restructured IASB was Paul A. Volker, Former Chairman of the US Federal Reserve Board.[54] It appeared that, despite SEC staff reservations about IFRS, a momentum for mutual recognition of accounting standards, based on convergence, if not harmonization, was moving along. But the spirit of cooperation that had been established between

---

[49] International Accounting Standards Concept Release, Securities Act Release No. 7801, 65 Fed. Reg. 8896 (23 February 2000), at 8903, n.33 [hereinafter 'IAS Release'].

[50] Ibid. at 8899.

[51] See Press Release, IOSCO, IASC Standards, http://iosco.org/news/pdf/IOSCONEWS26.pdf (last accessed 17 May 2000).

[52] See IAS Release, (*supra* note 49), at 8901–02.

[53] See Acceptance From Foreign Private Issuers of Financial Statements Prepared in Accordance With International Financial Reporting Standards Without Reconciliation to US GAAP, Securities Act Release No. 8818, 72 Fed. Reg. 37962, (11 July 2007) [hereinafter 'Acceptance of IFRS Proposing Release'], at 37964.

[54] Hewitt Testimony, (*supra* note 48), at 5.

the SEC, the EU and the IASB was unfortunately overtaken by the stock market collapse of 2000–1 and the enactment of Sarbanes–Oxley.

The EU was then able to seize the initiative with respect to international accounting standards by turning those European issuers which had been considering reporting in US GAAP rather than their home country GAAP, to IFRS, by mandating that all listed companies report in IFRS as of the year end 2005 and threatening to make US EU-listed companies also report in IFRS. Moreover, Asian and other issuers also began looking at IFRS, rather than US GAAP, as an alternative to reporting in their national GAAPs for offerings in the international capital markets.[55] As the markets in Europe and Asia strengthened, relative to the US markets, New York was no longer the only place where multinational corporations could raise capital and the SEC was no longer a regulator which could force its regulations on foreign issuers.

In April 2005, the Chief Accountant of the SEC set forth a roadmap for eliminating the need for non-US companies to reconcile to US GAAP financial statements prepared according to IFRS.[56] This roadmap was explicitly affirmed by SEC Chairman William Donaldson in a meeting with EU Internal Market Commissioner Charlie McCreevy in April 2005,[57] and then reaffirmed by SEC Chairman Christopher Cox in February 2006.[58] On 6 March 2007, the SEC held a Roundtable on IFRS as a prelude to issuing a proposed rule on 2 July 2007 to accept from foreign private issuers financial statements prepared in accordance with IFRS.[59]

In that release, the SEC pointed out that almost a hundred countries, including the twenty-seven EU Member States, were using IFRS, with more countries considering adopting IFRS.[60] The SEC made two arguments in favour of allowing foreign issuers to report in IFRS, a somewhat

---

[55] D. Tweedie and T.R. Seidenstein, 'Setting a Global Standard: The Case for Accounting Convergence', *Northwestern Journal of International Law and Business,* 25 (2005), 593.

[56] D.T. Nicolaisen, 'Statement by SEC Staff: A Securities Regulator Looks at Convergence', www.sec.gov/news/speech/spch040605dtn.htm (last accessed April 2005).

[57] SEC Press Release 2005–62, Chairman Donaldson Meets with EU Internal Market Commissioner McCreevy, www.sec.gov/news/press/2005–62.htm (last accessed 21 April 2005).

[58] SEC Press Release No. 2006–17, Accounting Standards: SEC Chairman Cox and EU Commissioner McCreevy Affirm Commitment to Elimination of the need for Reconciliation Requirements, www.sec.gov/news/press/2006–17.htm (last accessed 8 February 2006).

[59] Acceptance of IFRS Proposing Release, (*supra* note 53).

[60] Ibid. at 37965.

remarkable turnabout from its prior resistance to the use of any foreign GAAP in SEC filings. First, the SEC asserted that it had long advocated reducing disparity between US accounting and disclosure regulations and other countries as a means to facilitate cross-border capital formation; second, the SEC asserted that an international accounting standard may be adequate for investor protection even if it is not the same as the US standard.[61] Therefore, based on increasing convergence between US GAAP and IFRS, and cooperation between the SEC, IOSCO and the Committee of European Securities Regulators (CESR), the SEC proposed amendments to its rules that would allow a foreign private issuer to file financial statements without reconciliation to US GAAP, if those financial statements are in full compliance with the English language version of IFRS as published by the IASB.[62] The SEC adopted final rules on permitting foreign issuers to report in IFRS, substantially as proposed, based primarily on the progress of the IASB and the FASB toward convergence, their expressed intention to work toward further convergence in the future and a finding that IFRS are high-quality standards.[63] Yet, significant differences between IFRS and US GAAP continue to exist, and questions remain about the funding and independence of the IASB, as well as how IFRS will be interpreted and the lack of convergence on auditing standards between US and EU regulation.

Nevertheless, the SEC's decision to end the requirement that foreign issuers reconcile financial statements to US GAAP was extraordinarily important from a philosophical and political standpoint, and showed the rest of the world the US was serious about global accounting standards.[64]

IV. Equivalence as a predicate for mutual recognition

A serious change in the tone and content of the SEC–EU dialogue on foreign exchange access was marked by the publication in 2007 of an article by Ethiopis Tafara, Director of the SEC's Office of International Affairs suggesting 'substituted compliance' as a basis for permitting foreign stock exchanges to place their screens in the United States and also

---

[61] Ibid. at 37965–66.
[62] Ibid. at 37970.
[63] Acceptance of IFRS Final Release, (*supra* note 46).
[64] S. Marcy, 'End of Reconciliation Requirement Big Step to Common Accounting, IASB Member Says', *39 Sec. Reg. & L. Rep.* (BNA), (10 December 2007), at 1915.

for permitting foreign broker-dealers to solicit US customers without being registered with the SEC.[65] Although the SEC as a matter of policy disclaims responsibility for statements by an SEC staffer, this article nevertheless was a trial balloon of a new approach to a policy of mutual recognition. Tafara's proposal was a system of bilateral substituted compliance for foreign screens and foreign financial service providers based upon four steps: (1) a petition from a foreign entity to the SEC seeking an exemption from registration; (2) a discussion between the SEC and the entity's home regulator to determine the degree to which the trading rules, prudential requirements, examinations, review processes for corporate filings and other securities regulatory requirements are comparable; (3) a dialogue between the entity and the SEC which would include an agreement to submit to SEC jurisdiction and service of process with regard to the anti-fraud laws; and (4) public notice and an opportunity for comment on the petition.[66] An important part of this proposal was collaboration between the SEC and an entity's home jurisdiction, including a memorandum of understanding (MOU) between the two regulators and their ability to share inspections reports, conduct joint inspections and therefore enable them to share enforcement-related information.[67] In this connection, it should be noted that the SEC has MOUs with the EU, CESR and a number of individual European securities regulators.[68]

Following the publication of the Tafara article and favourable comments upon it,[69] the SEC held a Roundtable on Mutual Recognition.[70]

---

[65] E. Tafara and R.J. Peterson, 'A Blueprint for Cross-Border Access to US Investors: A New International Framework', *Harvard International Law Journal,* 48 (2007), 31.

[66] Ibid. at 58–9.

[67] Ibid.

[68] See US Securities and Exchange Commission, International Enforcement Assistance, www.sec.gov/about/offices/oia/oia_crossborder.htm#bilateral; US Securities and Exchange Commission, Cooperative Arrangements with Foreign Regulators, www.sec.gov/about/officies/oia/oia_cooparrangments.htm#enforce.

[69] See E.F. Greene, 'Beyond Borders: Time to Tear Down the Barriers to Global Investing', *Harvard International Law Journal,* 48 (2007), 85; E.F. Greene, 'Beyond Borders Part II: A New Approach to the Regulation of Global Securities Offerings', www.corporateaccountability2007.com/02.pdf (last accessed 2007); H. E. Jackson, 'A System of Selective Substitute Compliance', *Harvard International Law Journal,* 48 (2007), 105. *But see* G.W. Madison and S. P. Greene, 'TIAA-Cref Response to A Blueprint for Cross-Border Access to US Investors: A New International Framework', *Harvard International Law Journal,* 48 (2007), 99.

[70] See SEC Press Release No. 2007–105, SEC Announces Roundtable Discussion Regarding Mutual Recognition, www.sec.gov/news/press/2007/2007-105.htm (last accessed 24 May 2007).

The purpose of the Roundtable was to discuss selective mutual recognition, described as 'the SEC permitting certain types of foreign financial intermediaries to provide services to US investors under an abbreviated registration system, provided those entities are supervised in a foreign jurisdiction with a securities regulatory regime substantially comparable (but not necessarily identical) to that of the United States'.[71] Mutual recognition of foreign markets and broker-dealers was also promoted in speeches by the SEC Director of the Division of Market Regulation.[72]

The SEC Director of the Division of Corporation Finance also has embraced mutual recognition based on mutual recognition of foreign securities regulatory regimes as a means to permit foreign financial intermediaries and broker-dealers to access US markets based on equivalent regulatory standards.[73] He made clear, however, that in his view, such a regime should apply to trading of world-class securities, not to capital raising by foreign companies. Furthermore, he suggested that with regard to foreign issuers with a significant US shareholder following, the SEC might alter its long-standing exemption for foreign issuers from the reporting requirements of the Exchange Act.[74]

V. The way forward

On 1 February 2008, SEC Chairman Cox and EU Commissioner McCreevy met in Washington and agreed to implement a mutual recognition regime in order to better protect investors, foster capital formation and maintain fair, orderly and efficient transatlantic securities markets. They jointly declared that since the US and EU comprise 70% of the world's capital markets, they had a common interest in developing a cooperative approach to securities regulation.[75]

---

[71] Ibid.

[72] See E.R. Sirri, 'Speech by SEC Staff: A Global View: Examining Cross-Border Financial Services', http://sec.gov/news/speech/2007/spch081807ers.htm (last accessed 18 August 2007); E.R. Sirri, 'Speech by SEC Staff: Trading Foreign Shares', www.sec.gov/news/speech/2007/spch030107ers.htm (last accessed 1 March 2007).

[73] J.W. White, 'Speech by SEC Staff: "Corporation Finance in 2008 – International Initiatives" Remarks Before PLI's Seventh Annual Institute on Securities Regulation in Europe', www.sec.gov/news/speech/2008/spch011408jww.htm, at 16 (last accessed 14 January 2008).

[74] Ibid.

[75] SEC Press Release 2008–9, Statement of the European Commission and the US Securities and Exchange Commission on Mutual Recognition in Securities Markets, www.sec.gov/news/press/2008/2008–9.htm (last accessed 1 February 2008).

Hopefully, future cooperation between the SEC, the EU and CESR will lead to improved investor protection regimes that can form the basis for mutual recognition initiatives based either on convergence or substantial equivalence, thus reducing compliance costs for issuers and financial intermediaries, and making capital formation more efficient. Both the SEC and the EU are facing regulatory competition from other securities regulatory regimes around the world. Working together they can continue to act as leaders in the field of financial regulation and attract both investors and issuers into their markets.

30

Steps toward the Europeanization of US securities regulation, with thoughts on the evolution and design of a multinational securities regulator

DONALD C. LANGEVOORT

I. Introduction

The United States currently faces a set of regulatory issues that are profoundly important to the future of its form of securities regulation and hence its place in the global capital marketplace. Calls for extensive reform have come from a well-publicized set of studies that question the ability of the US to be competitive worldwide because of excessive regulation and an overdeveloped litigation culture.[1]

One of the principal moves being considered takes the form of mutual recognition.[2] The likely first stage of this would be the invitation to foreign stock exchanges and securities firms to have a presence in the US without registration with the SEC as a domestic exchange or broker-dealer firm, upon the determination that adequate home country regulation exists and can be relied upon as a substitute for direct SEC oversight. As part of this, however, would be some attention to a bigger project: the potential for mutual recognition of issuer disclosure and governance rules. Foreign trading screens and foreign broker-dealer presence in the US is meaningful largely as a means of making foreign securities more readily available to US investors, and the potential for increased competition and lower costs will hardly follow if making such securities available means intense US regulation of the issuers of those securities. Some mutual recognition of issuer disclosure standards is thus inevitable if

---

[1] Committee on Capital Markets Regulation, Interim Report, 30 November 2006, www. capmktsreg.org/research.html.
[2] E. Pan, 'The New Internationalization of US Securities Regulation: Improving the Prospects for an Trans-Atlantic Marketplace', *European Company Law*, 5 (2008), 1; E. Tafara and R. Peterson, 'A Blueprint for Cross-Border Access to US Investors: A New International Framework', *Harvard International Law Journal*, 48 (2007), 31–68.

the project is to succeed, and the SEC has already taken steps in this direction with the recent determination that foreign issuers do not have to reconcile their financial reporting to US generally accepted accounting principles.[3] Because financial reporting is at the heart of issuer disclosure, toleration of different sets of rules would presumably signal a willingness to do the same with respect to other aspects of disclosure.

Of course, we do not yet know that this willingness to experiment in mutual recognition will continue. There have been Republican chairmen of the SEC for the last eight years, and a shift in political control of the chairmanship and majority of the Commission might lead to a pull-back. Nor do we yet know the details of what might emerge even under the current administration. Quite possibly the eventual steps in the direction of mutual recognition will be small and disappointing to its adherents.

Because of this political uncertainty, my aim in this essay is not to explore mutual recognition in depth. Rather, it is to connect this and a number of other issues to what I regard as a deeper shift in the style and substance of US securities regulation that is likely to continue no matter who exercises political control. That shift comes as a result of the increasing institutionalization of both holdings and trading in stocks of widely-followed companies, or what Brian Cartwright, the SEC's general counsel, recently termed the resulting 'deretailization' of the US securities markets.[4]

Mutual recognition and the issues arising out of 'deretailization' have much in common. What makes them particularly appropriate to consider in this volume of essays in tribute to Eddy Wymeersch's masterful contributions both as regulator and scholar is that they both represent ways in which the US is increasingly open to a more European style of securities regulation, where institutionalization has long been dominant and mutual recognition a long-standing project within the EU.[5] I am not suggesting a perfect analogy, of course. Europe has determined that greater retailization of its capital marketplace is a worthwhile goal,[6]

---

[3] J. White, 'Corporation Finance in 2008 – International Initiatives,' London, England, 2008, www.sec.gov/news/speech/2008/spch011408jww/htm.

[4] B. Cartwright, 'The Future of Securities Regulation', University of Pennsylvania, Philadelphia, Pennsylvania, 24 October 2007, www.sec.gov/news/speech/2007/spch102407bgc.html.

[5] E. Ferran, *Building an EU Securities Market* (Cambridge University Press, 2004).

[6] N. Moloney, 'Building a Retail Investment Culture Through Law: The 2004 Markets in Financial Instruments Directive', *European Business Organization Law Review*, 6 (2005), 341–421.

so that what we may be seeing is movement toward a more mixed investor demography on both continents. And mutual recognition as it is developing in the US, at least, may actually be a form of deregulation aimed mainly at the more sophisticated, wealthy end of the market, not something that makes significant changes for the average American household.

But it does seem clear that US securities regulation is today willing to concede that for well-known issuers, the market is truly institutional, and that forms of regulation of these issuers (and their trading markets) that exceeds what institutional investors want or need does risk driving some business away to the detriment of the securities industry and its ancillary service providers such as lawyers and accountants. The fear in the US is that Europe's ability to focus on market building without the heavy baggage of historically large-scale retail participation is a competitive advantage in this respect.

Thus, I want first to think about how US securities regulation might change so as to become more European in style – that is, more consonant with institutional investor demands and preferences – with respect to the securities of larger issuers. (To be clear, I am not suggesting that Europe has built its markets and regulatory regime at the behest of institutional investors; rather, it has built its markets and regulatory regime in an environment where there has not been a strong, competing political voice by retail investors). It is important to emphasize that 'deretailization' does not imply a drop in the percentage of US households who hold securities, but just that more of those households have interests in securities held by institutional intermediaries. The political fact that still makes the US different from most of Europe is that far more US households see themselves as active investors, and hence the beneficiaries of relatively intense securities regulation. Thus the political demand for strong securities regulation will not change. What will change is the focus. There will still be emphasis on those segments of the market (e.g. microcap stocks) that remain largely retail, and – of course – greater emphasis on the need for protection of investors who participate in institutional portfolios of various sorts. The SEC will still have plenty of work to do in the name of retail investors. But where the interests of retail participants are relatively well aligned with those managing the institutional portfolios, the SEC is likely to defer increasingly to the professional investors' articulation of how they would like to see the law structured.

There is one additional form of Europeanization of US securities regulation that also strikes me as at least a strong possibility. It is probably still a fair assessment that Europe treats the public responsibilities of large corporations more seriously than the US does as a matter of corporate governance. There is more emphasis on disclosure of labour and environmental practices, and more strings that European governments can pull to rein in the private, competitive impulses of larger firms located within their jurisdictions. I have written elsewhere that even though the norm of shareholder primacy still officially holds in the US, there have been reforms in both securities law and corporate governance that hint strongly of greater public-regarding expectations with respect to the process of corporate decision making, which strikes me as a bit more like the European model. Sarbanes-Oxley is a good illustration, insofar as it introduces more transparency, accountability and public voice into the boardroom in order to check both excessive risk taking and private aggrandizement.[7] The effects of many of these rules (i.e. strong internal controls) are at best ambiguous in terms of value to investors, but that does not appear to be the test – the value to society in general from more open corporate decision making seems to be the point. Although its effects will not always dominate the political landscape, this increasing 'publicization' of the US corporation will persist. Such political demand is independent of any trend toward deretailization, and – at least through the voices of public pension funds, the most vocal of institutional investors – may actually be enhanced by it.

In the following pages, then, I want to look at a number of conceptual issues in securities regulation to see how a more European approach to US law might play out. The list of issues is not meant to be exhaustive of the important possibilities, but simply illustrative.

II. Jurisdiction and mutual recognition

The mutual recognition discussion that is on-going in the US is really the continuation of a much longer-running debate over the subject-matter jurisdiction of US securities law as applied to cross-border activity. In principle – and assuming a relatively high degree of market efficiency – it is easy to imagine a regime of issuer choice, where the issuer commits to a particular regulatory regime by some state or country.[8] It would then be

[7] D. Langevoort, 'The Social Construction of Sarbanes-Oxley', *Michigan Law Review*, 105 (2007), 1817–55.

[8] S. Choi and A. Guzman, 'Portable Reciprocity: Rethinking the International Reach of Securities Regulation', *Southern California Law Review*, 71 (1998), 903–52.

able to offer securities or trade in the capital markets in any other country based on its adherence to its 'home country' law. Sophisticated investors would assess the risks, costs and benefits associated with the chosen regulation and the markets would price the securities accordingly.

This, however, is not the European way. Though committed to a passport system of mutual recognition, the EU has insisted that Member States adhere to certain fairly demanding standards of regulation so that what is exported has a high degree of regulatory credibility. Many of the institutions of contemporary EU securities law are meant to force Member States into a stronger and more uniform commitment to regulation and enforcement so as to support a safer form of mutual recognition.[9]

The US does not have the same institutional tools to work with, and so mutual recognition would take a somewhat different form. Apparently, what would happen is that the US would set its own minimum standards for the quality of 'home country law' that would have to be satisfied before the SEC would allow the foreign exchange, securities firm or issuer to enter the US without the full application of US law. Importantly, there would be no deference to home country law with respect to instances of securities fraud that occur or have significant effects in the US.

Let us assume, as is likely, that this form of mutual recognition is limited to securities or services where the institutional presence dominates. It seems to me that institutional investors would have little reason to oppose this kind of liberalization. It offers somewhat lower transaction costs associated with doing business in foreign securities because of enhanced competition and disintermediation. To be sure, institutions that value the higher level of disclosure required by US law might prefer that it be available, but the evidence is that many foreign issuers are choosing to avoid listings in the US rather than submit to such requirements, and so that might not really be the choice.

The key to any workable system of mutual recognition is in assessing both *ex ante* and on an on-going basis the quality of the home country's securities regulation. Initially, it would seem, the EU would be the place to start: countries that indeed adhere to the requirements in the various Directives could be presumed to have acceptable regulation. No doubt more work needs to be done (as Europe already recognizes)

[9] N. Moloney, 'Innovation and Risk in EC Financial Market Regulation: New Instruments of Financial Market Intervention and the Committee of European Securities Regulators', *European Law Review*, 32 (2007), 627–63.

to bring the enforcement capacity of Member States' laws up to speed, but this is already on the agenda. So long as US and European regulators coordinate their demands appropriately, mutual recognition by the US could be helpful in moving the European efforts along. And with this experience as a guide, mutual recognition could be extended to other major capital marketplace countries.

What may be more difficult is in addressing the specific issues that are likely to arise *after* mutual recognition is granted. Suppose, for instance, that a particular problem were to arise, with disagreement about the home country's willingness to be as aggressive in applying its laws as the SEC would like. There is, of course, the possibility of withdrawal of mutual recognition, but this seems unlikely except in the most extreme circumstances. Instead, the likely response to a breakdown is that the US would invoke its reserved authority over fraud to act unilaterally. In fact, for a variety of reasons having to do with the way the federal securities laws were originally drafted, the SEC and private plaintiffs have learned numerous ways to turn virtually any form of misbehaviour into fraud.

If that happens frequently enough, however, it is unlikely that mutual recognition will succeed, because foreign participants will foresee this and find little comfort in entering the US under home country law that can so easily be displaced. For mutual recognition to succeed, then, there must be some dispute resolution mechanism that helps mediate these disputes before the US defects by unilaterally bringing fraud claims. Here is another place where the European experience may be a guide. The creation of CESR and other institutions of pan-European cooperation in securities regulation have many justifications, but one is their role as a dispute resolution mechanism where Member States might disagree about what the basic Directives requirements mean.[10]

Mutual recognition on a global scale requires a dispute regulatory authority on a comparable scale. This need not be a formal administrative body, but does need to be a reliable mechanism whereby skilled 'neutrals' are able to pressure individual countries and their regulators into either action or forbearance. One could imagine any number of forums that could be so designated, including some growing out of existing structures such as IOSCO. My prediction would be that the success of mutual recognition – and the willingness of countries such as the US to embrace broader versions of it, not simply limited to the institutional setting – is wholly dependent on this. To be sure, as is currently

---

[10] Moloney, 'Innovation and Risk in EC Financial Market Regulation', (note 9, above), 646.

an issue in the EU, the emergence of any mediator would raise questions of legitimacy and accountability, but these are familiar problems with respect to nearly all efforts at harmonization short of treaty-based formal authority.

In turn, the creation of such a global administrative body, even if advisory only, could become a platform for other tasks that are likely necessary for mutual recognition to succeed. As I have written about elsewhere in a volume that Eddy Wymeersch and Guido Ferrarini edited, cross-border securities enforcement is likely to be problematic unless some institutions of enforcement cooperation are created that overcome the 'home bias' of domestic regulatory authority.[11] Although the creation of a 'global SEC' may be beyond the politically practicable, it is not beyond imagination that if a group of major capital marketplace countries could agree on an informal dispute resolution mechanism authority, that that authority could also be a place where professional staff could guide a team of enforcement personnel from each of the participating countries in order to launch joint investigations and enforcement proceedings that invoke the existing laws of those countries in a coordinated fashion. To be workable, this would have to be limited to cases of fraud and manipulation about which there is no substantive disagreement. But with the growth of the dispute resolution process in the application of minimum global standards, a consensus on enforcement is itself more likely to evolve.

Mutual recognition, if successful in its earliest stages, naturally raises the question of how far it should extend. To what extent should it be extended to retail investors, or more thinly capitalized foreign issuers? Obviously, we can expect gradual extension insofar as there is strong confidence in home country regulation in terms of its ability to respond to issues and problems that arise. As a well-known and long-standing academic debate in the US has considered, one could eventually take mutual recognition to the point at which there is near-total 'issuer choice' – any issuer could simply choose its home jurisdiction, which would lead to competitive rewards to countries whose regulation that is most attractive, and competitive penalties to jurisdictions that either over- or under-regulate.

The vehicle through which mutual recognition would most likely evolve in this direction is exchange-based listings. To the extent that the

---

[11] D. Langevoort, 'Structuring Securities Regulation in the European Union: Lessons from the US Experience', in Ferrarini and Wymeersch (eds.), *Investor Protection in Europe: Corporate Law Making, the MiFID and Beyond* (Oxford University Press, 2006), 485–506.

world is willing to accept that the appropriate securities regulator is the jurisdiction of the exchange on which the issuer has voluntarily chosen to list its securities for trading, then there will be a de facto regime of issuer choice.[12] Arguably, this is what is going on right now – New York is losing its relative position as a favourable site for cross-listings, and other jurisdictions are gaining. The call in the US is for relaxing the intensity of its regulation as a response, which if successful would presumably reverse the trend. That is exactly as it should happen.

But before getting carried away with this as the vision for global securities regulation generally, it is important to remember that this vision is one for cross-listings only, not listings generally. In fact, I am not convinced that listings will continue to play a pivotal role in securities regulation at all. They can to the extent that trading is centralized on a single exchange, which then has the incentive to seek regulatory enforcement to bond the credibility of the listing commitment. But if global securities trading instead moves in the direction of fragmentation rather than consolidation – with many different trading sites around the world sharing in the order flow – the incentive for any one exchange or regulator to devote the necessary resources to enforcement diminishes. In a fragmented trading environment, it is unlikely that any single country has good reason to devote adequate resources to the regulatory task, unless its own citizens are disproportionately at risk.

Whether or not there is continued fragmentation, however, there is a second reason to doubt that listings can truly be the primary jurisdiction nexus. The test is to consider the extent to which a country like the US would permit its own domestic issuers to migrate away from US regulation simply by listing solely on a foreign stock exchange, as a few have done. In fact, the issuer accomplishes relatively little by so doing. To be sure, the burdens of the Securities Act and its regulation of the public offering itself are removed, so long as the issuer submits to the heavy lock-ups required by Regulation S. But registration under the Securities Exchange Act – the on-going corporate disclosure obligations and resulting litigation exposure – are triggered whenever a domestic issuer comes to have 500 or more shareholders and more than $10 million in assets. For domestic issuers, there is nothing comparable to the reporting relief given to unlisted foreign issuers under Rule 12g3–2.

What we are observing, then, is an increasingly 'territorial' basis to jurisdiction. That is, there are two levels in terms of the intensity of

---

[12] C. Brummer, 'Stock Exchanges and the New Market for Securities Law', *University of Chicago Law Review* 75 (2008), 1435.

securities regulation. For those issuers with a strong territorial nexus with the US – essentially, domestic issuers – there is a high level of regulation, and largely inescapable. For widely traded foreign issuers, there is increasingly less regulation.

My sense is that this is a stable equilibrium, which will eventually result in near-complete deregulation of such foreign issuers via a strong regime of mutual recognition if they choose to list in the US. In a marketplace characterized by high institutional holdings, the pricing efficiency and risk-absorbing feature of portfolio diversification make it reasonably safe to defer to competent foreign regulatory regimes, especially if aided by the kind of global inter-jurisdictional 'mediator' I described earlier.

What about the predilection of US retail investors to react to issuer misbehaviour and demand reforms in the face of scandal? What, in other words, will happen in the aftermath of the next large issuer meltdown involving a well-known foreign company that triggers losses by US investors? Mutual recognition is fairly well suited to weather foreign issuer scandals without triggering a Sarbanes–Oxley kind of reaction. First, the percentage of US investors affected by a foreign issuer scandal is less than for a domestic one, and there is less political potency for this reason alone. And those affected are more likely to be through diversified portfolios, so that the effects are even more softened. But the biggest difference – to me, explaining much about Sarbanes–Oxley and US regulation generally – is that the spillover effects of the foreign issuer scandal on other important constituencies, such as employees, company pensioners, local communities and the like, are dramatically smaller.[13] To the extent that these effects are what creates the political motivation for dramatic regulatory responses, the motivation will almost always be lacking when the main locus of the fraud is elsewhere. Conversely, this also explains why a listings-driven (as opposed to cross-listings-driven) regulatory regime would be unstable: the US will not give issuers with so great an ability to harm multiple US constituencies an ability to opt out from its preferences about the proper level of transparency and accountability.

I do not want to make too much of the analogy with Europe here. The EU, of course, has struggled with the right balance among sovereignty, subsidiarity and the free flow of economic activity – the desire of certain Member States, at least, to maintain 'home country' regulatory control

---

[13] D. Langevoort, 'The Social Construction of Sarbanes–Oxley', *Michigan Law Review*, 105 (2007), 1828–9.

over their domestic business entities is strong, presumably for reasons similar to those in the US. My simple point is that the compromises made in the US will increasingly resemble those made in Europe as the investment marketplace in the US becomes more heavily institutional and the institutional investor voice comes to dominate the retail voice in important segments of the capital markets.

III. Institutionalization and the litigation culture

By all accounts, the most troubling difference in terms of competitive appeal between the US and European approaches to securities regulation comes in terms of enforcement and litigation. On the public enforcement side, there are difficult questions regarding intensity: whether the US overdoes both criminal prosecution and agency (SEC) enforcement. This is another area where the relative degree of institutionalization makes a difference. With respect to repeat players, knowledge sharing among institutions and the need for regular access to the capital markets makes reputation a more formidable check on misbehaviour compared to retail markets in which new naïve investors regularly appear and old ones too often forget. But even in institutional markets, reputation is an imperfect check (last period problems, etc.) and so a reasonable degree of *ex post* enforcement is needed. It is certainly possible that European countries have found strategies, such as prudential oversight, that obviate the need for even this. But I am not aware that there has been any well-grounded explanation for precisely what forces would be at work that would lead to behaviours consistent with anything but the classical economic calculus: that what works in deterrence is the balance between the probability of detection and severity of sanction upon discovery. Given the immense profits that can be made by cheating in the securities markets, and the difficulties of detection, one is forced to believe that significant enforcement intensity is required. I am open to the possibility that other extra-legal influences (business culture, moral suasion, etc.) have some power, and that the close-knit nature of certain European money centres – the City of London being the most notable example – may utilize these more effectively than is practicable in a more diffuse capital market such as the US. If this is an explanation, then the interesting question becomes whether it is sustainable as these money centres gain greater geographic and cultural reach, becoming world markets in which it is harder for local elites to impose extra-legal discipline simply by invoking locally established behavioural norms. My suspicion is that

Europe will gradually adjust by intensifying public enforcement, while the US will more likely shift the focus of when and how public enforcement occurs.

The much more interesting question has to do with private securities litigation, which operates in the US in ways simply not replicated anywhere else in the world. The exercise, once again, is to think through how US attitudes toward private litigation might change, based on a shift to a more completely institutionalized market for the securities of well-known issuers. Some imagination is necessary because the voices of certain institutional investors are affected by conflicts of interest that make it hard to disentangle the economic from the political. Public pension funds have led aggressive litigation, but perhaps (though they certainly deny it) for reasons having to do with the interests of those in state governments. Conversely, the silence of mutual funds in the litigation area may be explained by their role in administering employer-sponsored retirement funds, which may be put at risk if they take on a visible plaintiff-side litigation posture.

The economics of private securities litigation are complicated, and by all accounts, differ depending on whether we are considering a lawsuit against a company that has directly benefited from an alleged fraud (as is the case in a public offering in which the company raises funds through a false or misleading prospectus) or not (as in the case of a typical 'fraud on the market' lawsuit). To be sure, the line between these two kinds of cases is blurred, but we can assume that at least a substantial portion of fraud was meant to enrich only the managers of the firm, not the firm itself.

In the latter instance, there is good reason to suspect that well-diversified institutional investors lose more than gain from litigation.[14] There are two well-known points here. First, consider that – apart from insider trading or other extractions of wealth by the wrongdoers – fraud is close to a zero-sum game for investors. Those fortunate enough to sell stock when the price is artificially inflated win, while those unlucky enough to buy lose. Over time, for well-diversified active investors, one would expect the gains and losses to even out – indeed, for active traders, we would expect some evening out because the investor both bought and sold during the class period. Absent a theory about why any given investor would expect systematically to be a loser over time (which is

[14] J. Coffee, 'Reforming the Securities Class Action: An Essay on Deterrence and its Implementation', *Columbia Law Review*, 106 (2006), 1534.

especially difficult to imagine for a professionally managed portfolio), it is not clear that institutions in general would demand much at all in litigation rights if the gains and losses are internalized within the capital markets. Certainly, they would not pay heavily for any such protection.

The second point is related. The vast majority of all payouts in private securities litigation come from the issuer, either directly or (to a far greater extent) insurance paid for by the issuer and for which the issuer is the named beneficiary. In essence, then, payments in settlement or judgment come largely from the pockets of some investors to the pockets of others, which merely reallocates funds rather than transfers money from the guilty to the innocent. Recent research has confirmed that the insurer's role in private securities regulation comes with little benefit in terms of doing justice.[15] Insurers do not vary their price much to reflect the corporate governance risk, nor are they particularly sensitive to the merits of the underlying claims. They settle when their customers (company management) ask them to settle.

This system has some benefits, to be sure. Investors do receive some compensation, which may be significant when the investor was insufficiently diversified or otherwise systematically or especially unlucky. It also has a somewhat greater rationality from a deterrence perspective when the fraud was intended to benefit the company as well as its managers, although even this is negated when the payments come entirely from the insurers. The key point comes in the costs: the very high legal fees paid to both plaintiffs' and defendants' law firms, plus the profits made by the insurance companies for funding such a system of transfer payments.

The problem is a collective action one, once again. Even if investors lose more than gain from the system in general, they will invoke whatever rights they are given in those circumstances when they are hurt by fraud. In turn, the compensation recovered is tangible and visible, whereas the costs paid over time are diffuse and largely invisible. My suspicion is that on an entirely rational calculus, institutional investors have little reason to support such a litigation system, and that the political support for it comes mainly from retail investors much more affected by the differences in saliency between costs and benefits and inclined to see litigation as an exercise in retribution.

If so, then this should be another area where the increasing voice of the institutional investor should lead to a shift in regulatory attitude.

[15] T. Baker and S. Griffith, 'The Missing Monitor in Corporate Governance: The Director and Officer's Liability Insurer', *Georgetown Law Journal*, 95 (2007), 795–845.

We know that private securities litigation is effectively limited to highly institutionalized settings, both because courts require a showing of high market efficiency to afford the class a presumption of reliance, and because plaintiffs' law firms tend only to target high-capitalization issuers because that is the only setting where there is enough money to be found. The so-called 'Paulson Committee' report recommends that issuers be allowed to opt out of class action exposure by placing limitations on the right to sue in a company's charter or articles.[16] The hypothesis is that this will lead to forms of alternative dispute resolution, such as arbitration, as an alternative. Whether this is plausible depends on whether there are forums that can handle large-scale, fact-intensive inquiries; the current models for arbitration in the securities area (e.g. customer-broker disputes) are not suited for this. Nor is it clear that it would be easy to design an incentive structure that would encourage good actions to be brought, given the expenses associated with such actions. A reasonable fear is that no adequate alternative system would emerge, and that the opt-out would be in the direction of no significant deterrence at all.

There are others changes that would be more investor-friendly. Remember that an important objective from the standpoint of the sophisticated investor is to recoup the fruits of fraud from insiders who do capture the benefits. Some investors in the US are pushing revisions in executive employment contracts that allow for clawbacks of incentive compensation and trading profits after the discovery of significant corporate misconduct. There are ways the law could be revised to encourage greater use of disgorgement and other equitable remedies that target such insider gains, which institutional investors might well also find appealing.

One of the most interesting lingering questions in the building of a more institution-friendly litigation system has to do with public offerings. If we think in terms of an initial public offering, the idea of a lawsuit seems relatively efficient: the money raised in the first stage of public financing is a transfer from public investors (including many institutions) to the promoters, backers and other insiders of the start-up firm. Recapturing this money in the event of fraud resembles the disgorgement of insider gains from fraud-on-the-market, rather than simple pocket-shifting. This, however, becomes less so with respect to

---

[16] Committee on Capital Markets Regulation, *Interim Report*, 30 November 2006, www.capmktsreg.org/research.html.

distributions by seasoned firms. Moreover, it is not clear that sophisticated investors would necessarily want to base recovery on the current standards in US law: strict liability for the issuer (assuming that the stock price drop that triggers the lawsuit can be associated with discovery of some material misrepresentation) or due diligence liability for directors, underwriters and others who, especially with respect to some kinds of financing, have little practicable ability to discover the truth. This liability arguably leads either to under-pricing of the deal or higher fees charged by deal participants. Hence, this is another area where reform might be supported by unconflicted institutional investors.

The potential roadblock to reform here is that, thus far, it appears that US retail investors see themselves as beneficiaries of the current litigation system. In this sense, they are political allies with those – plaintiffs' law firms and public pension funds – who have staked the clearest claims to the efficacy of strong private rights of action. Overcoming this requires stronger empirical evidence that retail investors as a whole lose more than they gain, and that the hidden costs associated with the meagre recoveries that occasionally occur are significant. Politically, even if institutional investors as a group were persuaded, selling this to broader segments of market participants probably requires that there be evidence that some alternative mechanisms will emerge to address the need to target wrongdoers,[17] and to gain compensation for those retail investors (e.g. pensioners with portfolios heavily weighted with the stock of a single issuer) where the costs of issuer fraud are most vivid.

IV. Conclusion

My hypothesis is that US securities regulation as it relates to foreign issuer disclosure, corporate governance and litigation will gradually shift in the direction of policies that sophisticated institutional investors find comfortable, which will mean significant shifts from the legacies created during the times (from the 1930s through to the early 1980s) when the US had a more thoroughly retail investment culture. It is interesting to think of how many of the rules and procedures in US laws that are currently under criticism – the structure of the two main securities statutes and the fraud-on-the-market lawsuit, for instance – date from

---

[17] D. Langevoort, 'On Leaving Corporate Executives "Naked, Homeless and Without Wheels": Corporate Fraud, Equitable Remedies, and the Debate Over Entity Versus Individual Liability', *Wake Forest Law Review*, 42 (2007), 627–61.

this time period. Once again, however, I would emphasize that even a strong institutional voice will not check the demand for regulation that comes from domestic stakeholders when serious negative externalities result from a US-based breakdown in corporate governance.

Mutual recognition is a healthy exercise through which to wean US law away from these legacies in the settings in which the markets are sufficiently institutional. In turn, as this occurs, those segments of the US market will take on a more European character. To be sure, not all forms of investing in the US are making this shift: there will always be a robust retail presence in the markets for smaller stocks. And just as in Europe, the retail nature of the markets *for* institutionalized investments will continue to pose regulatory challenges and a demand for significant protections. The more complicated the portfolio strategies of institutional investors, the more opaque and potentially risky the individual accounts.

My prediction, then, is that US securities regulation will significantly reduce its intensity vis-à-vis foreign issuers, and partially reduce its intensity vis-à-vis domestic issuers. The reduction will take place with respect to litigation as to both domestic and foreign issuers so long as some 'safety-valve' remains in place for disciplining and recouping wealth from insiders who cause serious economic damages to investors and other stakeholders. This would be a distinctly European turn. As to retail investor interests, the shift will be towards seeing the ultimate problem in securities regulation as addressing the relationship between public investors and those who manage large portfolios. I make no claim to see Europeanization coming here – rather, regulators on both continents will find this the common challenge in coming decades.

31

The subprime crisis – does it ask for more regulation?

FRIEDRICH KÜBLER[1]

I. Introduction

The creation and sale of asset-backed securities (ABS) is an established practice of financial management. It offers benefits to all participants. The original lender (originator) can sell the loans made to the original borrowers although they are correctly qualified as 'imperfectly marketable assets'. In a normal sale the information asymmetry between the selling bank, who knows the borrower, and the acquiring institution, who does not know her that well, will result in a considerable discount from the nominal value of the loan. This outcome is avoided by the securitization procedure. The claims (assets) are collected in a pool, held by an independent and bankruptcy-remote 'special purpose vehicle' (SPV), which is often organized in the form of a trust. The SPV issues debt instruments – notes or commercial paper (CP) or bonds – to the public, mostly to institutional investors. Their information problems as to the credit or default risk affecting the pooled assets are greatly reduced by the analysis and the evaluation of the pool by a credit rating agency (CRA). In many transactions the rating is improved by the 'credit enhancement' (CE) provided by the arranger of the programme or by the arranger's bank; this is a guarantee that a set percentage of the losses generated by defaulting assets will be borne by the arranger or the bank.

Such a transaction allows the original lender to transform its highly illiquid assets into cash and to significantly reduce the amount of required capital under the capital adequacy rules.[2] The lender removes risky assets from the balance sheet and thus reduces capital requirements.

---

[1] The assistance of Justin Gross is gratefully acknowledged.

[2] For a general description of the mechanism and the advantages it offers to participants, see H. Scott, *International Finance: Transactions, Policy and Regulation*, 14th edn. (New York, Foundation Press, 2007), 530 *et seq.*

At the same time the lender can use the cash to engage in more lending transactions, and this again increases the availability of credit for borrowers. The investors receive considerably higher returns from their CP compared to bank deposits; at the same time they enjoy the liquidity of a security traded on an organized market. And the arranger is benefited by the fees derived from setting up the scheme, from providing credit enhancement, and possibly from underwriting the securities issued by the SPV.

The generation of mortgage-backed securities (MBS) follows very much the same pattern. This practice is even older; it dates back to the 1960s, and the amounts outstanding appear to be considerably higher than those for ABS. At a first glance MBS look like more stable instruments compared to ABS. ABS are mostly based on pools of credit card and car loan receivables; these assets are directly exposed to the considerable risk of consumer insolvency. MBS appear to provide much more safety as the pooled home owner loans are collateralized by mortgages. Whenever the borrowing home owner fails, the creditor can look for satisfaction from the mortgage which is backed by the value of real estate.

There appears to be ample evidence that this mechanism of securitizing or restructuring debt has worked quite well until recently. The amounts outstanding increased from year to year,[3] and the contractual instruments were refined by the joint efforts of banks and law firms. Larger-scale problems were unknown.

The subprime crisis came obviously as a surprise. It appears that there have been some market participants or observers who at an early stage were concerned by some of the specific practices used more recently. But the dimensions of the problems became evident only step by step; and at the moment, when this contribution is written, it is generally assumed that still more will come to the surface. But some facts are uncontroversial. Very experienced financial institutions like Merrill Lynch, Citibank or UBS had to disclose losses from investments in ABS amounting to volumes close to or even exceeding $20 billion.[4] A number of smaller institutions like Century in the US, Northern Rock in the UK or Industriekreditbank (IKB) and Sächsische Landesbank in Germany either failed or had to be rescued by merger or by huge capital injections

---

[3] For Europe it is assumed that in 2006 the outstanding amount of European securitization deals exceeded $1 trillion; see P. Aguesse, 'Is Rating an Efficient Response to the Challenge of the Structured Finance Market', *Autorité des Marchés Financiers (AMF)*, *Research Department, Risk and Trend Mapping*, 2 (2007), 7.

[4] *New York Times*, 1 February 2008, C 6.

from controlling shareholders. This again has affected the stock markets globally; and there appears to be a threat that the world economy will sink into a recession.

In this situation lawyers interested in the regulation of financial markets and institutions have good reasons to ask not only what went wrong but also whether there are regulatory responses which might prevent similar outcomes in the future. This preliminary investigation is organized in five steps. The first question, discussed in Section II, is to what extent the planned securitization of mortgage debt has influenced the contracting process between the borrower and the lender which generates the securitized assets. In a next step, in Section III, it will be asked to what extent the continued leveraging of MBS and CDO debt has contributed to the problem. In particular with regard to highly complex financial instruments, it can be asked to what extent the incentives provided by the internal structure of financial institutions discourage or prevent participants from applying adequate due diligence, this is discussed in Section IV. In Section V, it has to be asked whether the observed practice of rating structured finance products is appropriate or should be improved. Finally, some preliminary conclusions will summarize the observations in Section VI.

II. Impact of securitization on the origination: predatory lending and borrowing

One source of the problem appears to be the contracting process between the borrower (mortgagor) and the lending bank (originator). It is credibly reported that in many cases the documentation as to the borrower has been very weak.[5] There is no documentation of the income and the assets of the borrower; this makes it difficult to determine whether the borrower honestly disclosed her situation to the lender. It is assumed that this was not always true: that there have been cases of 'liar loans' and of predatory borrowing.

But there is evidence that in many cases the lending institution did not care about the financial situation of the borrower. Many of the borrowers had weak FICO scores and little or no equity. Many of them had faced bankruptcy in the last five years and/or foreclosure during the last two years and/or two or more thirty-day delinquencies in the last twelve

---

[5] R. Herring, 'From Subprime Mortgages to ABS to CDO to SIVs and ABCP: The Darker Side of Securitization' (slides 2007, on file with author).

months.[6] Many of the loans had very specific features. They provided the borrower with a 'five-year interest-only option', during which time no repayments of capital were due. For the first two or three years there was a 'teaser' interest rate, lower than the interest rate for fixed-rate mortgages. After this time nearly 90% of the loans became 'adjustable rate'. The interest rate was now determined by the market.[7] For many of the borrowers this structure entailed a continuing and very steep increase of their mortgage costs over a period of only a few years.[8] It could be that in the beginning they had to use about 40% of their income to service the mortgage, and that this ratio had climbed to 80% after five years. Under these circumstances foreclosure appears to be inevitable. And there was mostly less than 10% of equity or none at all; thus the loan would not be fully repaid once real estate prices started to decline.

These are transactions implying a degree of default risk which would under normal circumstances exclude them from being done by a financially rational and responsible bank. They were obviously acceptable for no other reason than to sell them in securitized form to an anonymous market. This impression is confirmed by the procedures used for making these loans.[9] New Century Financial, a company which filed for bankruptcy protection on 2 April 2007, had established an automated internet-based loan submission and pre-approval system called *FastQual*. Under this system, subprime lending by New Century grew at an annual rate of 59% between 2000 and 2004; in 2006 the firm originated $51.6 billion of mortgage loans.

These facts suggest that there are flaws in the securitization process; this will be discussed later. They have also triggered requests for additional regulation, e.g. for federal legislation which would prohibit predatory lending. At this point it is much less than clear that this would have any significant impact. The Truth in Lending Act (TILA) and other (state) rules already address unsafe lending and borrowing practices. They may be helpful where they address and sanction misrepresentations used to defraud the other party. But this is not the major problem

---

[6] A. Ashcraft and T. Schuermann, 'Understanding the Securitization of Subprime Mortgage Credit' (typescript 2007, on file with author), 19; IMF, *Global Financial Stability Report* (October 2007), 7, note 7.

[7] Ashcraft and Schuermann, 'Understanding the Securitization of Subprime Mortgage Credit', (note 6, above), 20.

[8] The offer of 'affordable products' expose borrowers to later payment shocks, See IMF, *Global Stability Report* (April 2007), 6.

[9] Ashcraft and Schuermann, 'Understanding the Securitization of Subprime Mortgage Credit', (note 6, above), 18.

here. The agents operating for the lending institutions must have been aware that many of the loans were extremely risky. They did not care as they were not affected by the likely defaults. It is to be assumed that they were motivated by a compensation structure rewarding the conclusion of the deals regardless of the consequences they would entail. This is a more general problem affecting the way financial markets work, it will be discussed in Section IV.

III. Leveraging

A second aspect of the present crisis is the amazing practice of leveraging mortgage debt. In an MBS transaction the pool of the collected assets is normally cut into several tranches.[10] There is a senior tranche, mostly rated AAA, which pools the mortgages presenting the lowest default risk. This tranche would back bonds or commercial paper sold to institutional investors. In addition there can be more junior 'mezzanine' tranches pooling more risky mortgages and therefore backing lower-rated commercial paper or notes designed for more sophisticated investors.[11] At the low end of the spectrum there are tranches which do not receive a rating as they are backing highly risky debt or equity securities. This separation and subordination presents a method of providing credit enhancement to the most senior tranches. But it also raises the question of what to do with the tranches at the lower end. The originating bank could keep them: this would improve risk sharing as the bank would continue to have an interest in keeping the lending operations within the limits of sound banking practice.[12]

But this is not what has happened recently. To a large extent the first loss pieces have been transferred to entities which would repackage them into pools serving again as collateral for the issuance of securities, mostly asset-backed commercial paper (ABCP).[13] The first loss pieces and junior tranches have been mostly repackaged into Collateralized Debt Obligations (CDOs). They can have different features: they can be

[10] See Herring, 'From Subprime Mortgages to ABS to CDO to SIVs and ABCP', (note 5, above) and IMF, *Global Stability Report* (April 2007), 8.

[11] G. Franke and J. P. Krahnen, 'Default Risk Sharing Between Banks and Markets: The Contribution of Collateralized Debt Obligations' in M. Cary and F. Stulz, *The Risk of Financial Institutions* (2007), 603–8.

[12] Franke and Krahnen, 'Default Risk Sharing Between Banks and Markets', (note 11, above), 625.

[13] The face value of the debt instruments pooled in ABCP vehicles amounts to $1.4 trillion; IMF, *Global Financial Stability Report* (October 2007), 19.

fully funded by the transfer of ABS or they can be 'synthetic'; in this latter case the bank retains the securities and buys a credit default swap on behalf of the CDO vehicle.[14]

The CDO vehicles can and often did repeat the process of cutting its pool into tranches which would represent different categories of risk and therefore bear different rating grades. The most senior tranches were sold to the market, the most junior ones securitized again. The vehicles now could be CDOs again, or Structured Investment Vehicles (SIVs), which would also receive and pool other assets, or Security Arbitrage Conduits (SACs), which would collect preferably higher-rated ABS.[15] And with their ABCP the process could be repeated again and again. The rated securities were sold mostly to hedge funds and to banks.[16]

It is not too difficult to see how this process of leveraging increases the risk for the holders of the ABCP. It is always the tranches containing the most risky assets which are securitized again. When the new pool is divided again and the best assets are put into a senior segment rated AAA, this method of credit enhancement does not appear to reduce the risk and to improve the quality of the original assets, which continue to be needed to satisfy the claims of the holders of the ABCP. That is to say, each new securitization of MBS products considerably increases the default risk for the holders of the leveraged securities.

Again it is to be asked whether this practice of leveraging securitized debt could and should be contained by new regulation. And again this is difficult to determine. Leveraging can be a useful technique of risk allocation. This is no less true where it is combined with asset securitization; any ban or constraint of these transactions is not likely to improve the efficiency of financial markets. What is striking, however, is the complexity of the arrangements and the intransparency and opaqueness of the process used to put together the CDOs, SIVs etc.[17] In December 2004, the Securities and Exchange Commission (SEC) adopted Regulation AB providing for major changes to the disclosure regime for public offerings of ABS.[18] Regulation AB requires information explaining the

---

[14] Franke and Krahnen, 'Default Risk Sharing Between Banks and Markets', (note 11, above), 606.

[15] IMF, *Global Financial Stability Report* (October 2007), 18.

[16] Ibid., 15.

[17] J. R. Mason and J. A. Rosner, 'How Resilient are Mortgage Backed Securities to Collateralized Debt Obligation Market Disruption?', Working paper (2007), http://ssrn.com/abstract=1027472.

[18] Release No. 33–8518; 34–5095, (22 December 2004).

characteristics of the pool, the background, experience, performance and role of the parties, and the legal structure used for the SPV. But this applies only to public offerings and not to private placements. Where ABCP are exclusively sold to institutional investors like hedge funds or banks the gathering and evaluation of the material facts is left to their exercise of due diligence. This is to be further discussed in Section IV.

Another element of the existing regulatory framework to be taken into consideration at this point are the rules on capital adequacy. The rules introduced by Basle I certainly encouraged securitization. Whenever a bank replaced a loan to a customer by sponsoring and enhancing an ABS project originated by this customer the bank was able to considerably reduce the amount of required capital.[19] This would not be dramatically different under Basle II. The new rules increase the amount of required capital for banks pooling and securitizing their own receivables. The most interesting change occurs with regard to banks investing into ABS originated and sponsored by other institutions. Basle I provided for risk categories which would normally imply a risk weight of 100%. Basle II – for the Standardized Approach – refers to credit rating: for ABS in a senior tranche with an AAA rating the risk weight factor would be reduced to 20%. Now we are faced with the question: how good is the process of rating ABS or other structured credit products? This is to be discussed in Section V.

IV. Complexity and due diligence

Another aspect of the current crisis is that these highly leveraged ABCP have been bought to an amazing extent by highly sophisticated financial institutions. For 2007 Merrill Lynch had to write down $24.5 billion, Citigroup $22.1 billion, UBS $18.4 billion and HSBC $10.7 billion.[20] This may include some losses which are not connected to high-risk home loans, but there is no doubt that the problems result primarily from the

---

[19] Assume a bank lends $100 million to a car manufacturer who needs to finance loans made to the buyers of the cars. The loan has a credit weight of 100%. The capital ratio mandated by Basle I is 8%. This means that the bank has to support this transaction by using $8 million of its capital base. Providing credit enhancement of 5% to a $100 million pool of car loan receivables generates a potential – and therefore off-balance-sheet – liability of $5 million. As a standby type of guarantee it carries a conversion factor of 100% and (again) a risk weight of 100%. In other words, the required capital amounts to 8% of $5 million or $400,000. This is just 5% of the $8 million required for the loan to the car manufacturer. Even if we assume a credit enhancement for 20% of the pool the required capital is only one-fifth of what it would be for the loan.

[20] *New York Times*, 1 February 2008, C 6.

collapse of the subprime mortgage market. Thus we are faced with the question of why and how these and other financial firms did accumulate such enormous amounts of highly problematic securities. One answer could be that they trusted favourable ratings. This certainly has to be taken into account, but it does not fully explain the lack of in-house analysis before making these huge investments.

There are other indications that the observance of due diligence has declined.[21] Clayton Holdings is a firm specialized in rendering due diligence reports to investment banks with regard to residential mortgage loans; it is the biggest provider of this service in the US. Clayton reported that starting in 2005, it observed a significant deterioration of lending standards, and that with the growing demand for the residential loans, mortgage companies were in a strong enough position to stipulate that investment banks have Clayton and other consultants look at fewer loans. It appears that the lenders wanted due diligence to find fewer problem loans which would be sold at a discount. Clayton reported in addition that investment banks did not give the due diligence reports to the rating agencies.[22]

This story suggests a somewhat paradoxical situation. On the one hand, the instruments of structured finance have become inherently less safe for investors, and the increasing risks were disguised by more and more complex and opaque arrangements. On the other hand, due diligence has been systematically reduced.

There are several ways to explain this phenomenon; they are not mutually exclusive. Many of the players in the field are big institutions characterized by complex organizational structures, a high degree of specialization to perform very specific services, incentive compensation based on short-term results, and significant job mobility.[23] Such an arrangement generates incentives to increase volume regardless of the medium- or long-term consequences: when the losses occur, the responsible agents have cashed their bonuses and been moved to other functions. Another explanation is 'disaster myopia', the often-observed tendency to underestimate the probability and the consequences of low-frequency

---

[21] This appears to be equally true for other functions in the process; see Ashcraft and Schuermann, 'Understanding the Securitization of Subprime Mortgage Credit', (note 6, above), 10.

[22] J. Anderson and V. Bajaj, 'Loan Reviewer Aiding Inquiry Into Big Banks', *New York Times*, 27 January 2008, 1 and 10.

[23] R. Herring, 'Credit Risk and Financial Stability', *Oxford Review of Economic Policy*, 15 (1999), 63–73 *et seq.*

shocks.[24] And we may also see the consequences of 'herding' behaviour: the fact that others have done exactly the same thing serves as a defence against *ex post* recriminations.[25] These phenomena are interconnected: disaster myopia and herding behaviour can be supported and reinforced by institutional arrangements.[26]

This experience raises the question of whether and to what extent top management and possibly the board of financial institutions should be held responsible for inadequate organizational structures which discourage employees from observing adequate due diligence and risk assessment practices. This would not be a completely new approach. Section 404 of the Sarbanes–Oxley Act requires management to establish and maintain effective internal controls with regard to corporate governance. Bank supervisors could be allowed and encouraged to have a closer look into the organizational implications of sound risk management.

V. Rating structured finance products

It is obvious that there have been considerable problems with the rating of MBS, CDOs and other structured finance products. Top executives of major rating agencies have conceded in public that significant mistakes have been made.[27] Changes in the methods of MBS and CDO rating[28] led to considerable downgrading of already-issued ABCP.[29] This again has negatively affected the reputation and credibility of rating agencies.[30]

It is less obvious why the rating process failed to such an extent. There are several explanations (which are again not mutually exclusive):

1. There is some evidence that the rating agencies have not been fully informed by the issuers and underwriters of ABCP.[31] It is less obvious

---

[24] R. Herring and S. Wachter, 'Real Estate Booms and Banking Busts – An International Perspective', Group of Thirty, *Occasional Paper*, No. 58 (1999), 9 *et seq.*

[25] R. Herring, 'Credit Risk and Financial Stability', (note 23, above), 73.

[26] J. Guttentag and R. Herring, *Disaster Myopia in International Banking*, (Princeton University International Finance Section, 1986), 5; R. Herring, 'Credit Risk and Financial Stability', (note 23, above), 73.

[27] F. Norris, 'Moody's Official Concedes Failure in Some Ratings', *New York Times*, 28 January 2008, C 13.

[28] J. Mason and J. Rosner, 'Where did the Risk Go? How Misapplied Bond Ratings Cause MBS and CDO Market Disruption', Working paper (2007), http://ssrn.com/abstract=1027475, 21.

[29] *Ibid.*, 80 *et seq.*

[30] C. W. Calomiris, 'Not yet a 'Minsky Moment'' (typescript 2007, on file with author), 3.

[31] Anderson and Bajaj, 'Loan Reviewer Aiding Inquiry Into Big Banks', (note 22, above), 15, report that investment banks did not give their due diligence reports to the rating agencies.

why the agencies either did not find out this lack of disclosure or abstained from sanctioning them. Traditionally rating agencies have enforced disclosure by downgrading issuers who had proved to be unwilling to come forward with all the required information.

2. Another aspect may be derived from the special relationship between the rating agencies and the ABCP issuers (and their investment banks and law firms). It is argued that the number of relevant issuers has declined and that this form of concentration impairs the market position of the rating agencies; they become more dependent on specific issuers and therefore more inclined to accommodate to their wishes.[32] At the same time the revenues of rating agencies are increasingly derived from evaluating structured finance products.[33] And the complexity of these products asks for closer cooperation between rating agencies and investment banks; this is plausibly viewed as a new source of conflicts of interest.[34]

3. Another concern is the use of ratings by regulators.[35] It is true that the rating agencies are mostly compensated by the issuer. This does not necessarily imply a conflict of interest as they are normally chosen by the institutional investors who are or may be interested in acquiring the securities. In these cases the rating agencies depend on the goodwill they enjoy among institutional investors. Their reputation and their success are closely linked to the accuracy and the reliability of their evaluations and their forecasts, they are thus disciplined by the market. This is not necessarily true with ratings for regulatory purposes as regulators normally do not insist that the rating be made by the agency of their choice. This can modify the incentives, such that rating agencies may be more inclined to respect the wishes of the issuers.

4. Finally it has been correctly observed that the rating of structured finance products differs significantly from the rating of corporate bonds.[36] In assessing the default risks of corporate bonds the rating agency evaluates the financial stability and the future cash flows of

---

[32] Aguesse, 'Is Rating an Efficient Response to the Challenge of the Structured Finance Market', (note 3, above), 8 *et seq.*

[33] Mason and Rosner, 'Where did the Risk Go?', (note 28, above), 8.

[34] Ibid., 31.

[35] Calomiris, 'Not yet a 'Minsky Moment'', (note 30, above), 18 *et seq.*

[36] Ashcraft and Schuermann, 'Understanding the Securitization of Subprime Mortgage Credit', (note 6, above), 48 *et seq.*; Mason and Rosner, 'Where did the Risk Go?', (note 28, above), 36 *et seq.*

the issuing firm. MBS and CDO ratings are different; they refer to a static pool and not to a dynamic corporation; they rely on quantitative models and not on the judgement of analysts.[37] In addition, rating agencies have difficulties assessing the risk of whether a mortgage will be prepaid by the borrower.[38] And these aberrations tend to increase with every step of leveraging the original pool.[39]

Do these weaknesses and deficiencies in the process of rating structured finance products present good reasons to ask for changes in existing regulation? First of all, it has to be remembered that in the US, rating agencies are regulated.[40] Since 1975, the SEC has determined who is a 'Nationally Recognized Statistical Rating Organization' (NRSRO).[41] In 1997, the SEC defined the formal criteria for becoming an NRSRO. The Credit Rating Agency Reform Act from 2006[42] has officially confirmed the regulatory and supervisory powers of the SEC; the Act states that the SEC can revoke NRSRO status of a rating agency for lack of financial or managerial resources.[43] In December 2004, the International Organization of Securities Commissions (IOSCO) released a code of conduct for the rating agencies.[44] And the Committee of European Banking Supervisors (CEBS) has issued 'Guidelines on the Recognition of External Credit Assessment Institutions',[45] following largely the example of American legislation. The promulgation of these rules obviously overlaps in time with the emergence of the problems described in this contribution. For all these reasons the push for new regulations at this moment should not be supported; the effectiveness of the existing framework should be carefully assessed before additional rules are enacted.

A separate issue is the proposal to eliminate the use of ratings for the purpose of regulation.[46] This would affect and probably eliminate the

---

[37] Ashcraft and Schuermann, 'Understanding the Securitization of Subprime Mortgage Credit', (note 6, above), 48.

[38] Mason and Rosner, 'Where did the Risk Go?', (note 28, above), 55.

[39] Ibid., 66 et seq.

[40] US regulation is essential since the most important rating agencies are located in the US.

[41] Ashcraft and Schuermann, 'Understanding the Securitization of Subprime Mortgage Credit', (note 6, above), 43.

[42] S. 3850, 109th Congress § 2 (E) (2006).

[43] Mason and Rosner, 'Where did the Risk Go?', (note 28, above), 29.

[44] IOSCO, Press Release, 'IOSCO Releases Code of Conduct Fundamentals for Credit Rating Agencies', (23 December 2004).

[45] Available at www.bundesbank.de/download/bankenausicht/pdf/cebs/GL07.pdf.

[46] Calomiris, 'Not yet a 'Minsky Moment'', (note 30, above), 18 et seq.

core element of the Basle II regime of capital adequacy which refines the risk weighting of bank assets by the use of ratings. Before such a revolutionary (or reactionary) step is taken it should be considered whether there are less far-reaching options likely to improve the rating process. One possibility would be to distinguish between ratings which have been asked for by investors and are in addition used for risk weighting, and ratings which are exclusively used for regulatory purposes. The first category should be less of a problem as the selection of the agency continues to be controlled by the market. In the other case the choice should not be left to the issuer or the underwriter: the decision should be made by the regulatory agency which is charged with the supervision. This might eliminate or at least reduce the temptation of the rating agency to pay too much attention to the interests of the issuer.

VI. Preliminary conclusion

There can be no doubt that some of the consequences of the subprime crisis are serious. They may justify measures taken for the protection of individuals who are facing particularly harsh consequences like the loss of their family home through foreclosure.[47] But this cannot be achieved by the hasty introduction of new regulation for the financial markets. So far there is no evidence that any risk affecting the safety of the global financial system cannot be addressed by existing tools like the provision of liquidity by the central banks. It should also be remembered that we cannot expect financial markets to move consistently on a path of regular and balanced growth; there appears to exist no reasonable method to prevent business cycles by regulatory intervention. At the same time we should acknowledge that individual behaviour on financial markets is not completely determined by rational motives; and this appears to be true not only for small investors but also for the professionals who are running major financial institutions like banks and insurance companies. It is not likely that their performance will be improved by new regulation. Yet there is evidence that some of the irregularities – disaster myopia, herding, and extreme short-termism – are at least partially due to the internal structures and the compensation schemes of financial institutions. This

---

[47] This is, however, far from uncontroversial; see e.g. the warnings by the (American) Shadow Financial Regulatory Committee, 'Treasury Department's Mortgage Foreclosure Program', *Statement No. 250* (10 December 2007).

could and probably should be addressed by the supervision of these firms within the existing regulatory framework. At the same time it should be remembered that there are strong indications that financial markets are already overregulated.[48] New rules should not be enacted unless there is at least some evidence that the benefits will outweigh the costs.

---

[48] For the US, see Committee on Capital Markets Regulation, *Interim Report* (30 November 2006) and 'The Competitive Position of the US Public Equity Market', *Report* (4 December 2007).

32

Juries and the political economy of legal origin

MARK J. ROE[*]

I. Introduction

Legal origin – common law versus civil law – is important to the past decade's finance theory. Peculiarly, the theory has not had traction in the academic legal literature, which might be surprising given academic disciplines' understandable tendency to see their own issues as central and determinative. What legal academic commentary that the theory has provoked has either been sceptical that the legal origins channels that the law and finance literature promotes are really so important or sceptical that origin could be as important as modern political economy considerations. That is, while the legal literature hardly denigrates law's importance, it has doubted the importance of legal origin to financial development. Mahoney,[1] although sympathetic in part (particularly to the idea of a detrimental statist nature of civil law), denigrates the idea that civil law codification can be as important as the legal origin theory had hypothesized, since so much of American corporate and commercial law is codified. Coffee[2] sees the propensity of some countries to disrupt their stock markets, which would have provided the needed investor protections regardless of underlying legal institutions, as central. Roe indicates that while property rights and investor protection are important, legal origin differences cannot explain the institutional differences, since common law countries use non-common-law institutions, such as securities regulators, and not just common-law-oriented fiduciary duties: modern political economy forces are likely to explain modern financial and investor protection differences in wealthy nations better than legal origin.[3]

[*] This article was originally published in the *Journal of Comparative Economics*, 35 (2007), 294–308.
[1] P.G. Mahoney, 'The common law and economic growth: Hayek might be right', *Journal of Legal Studies*, 30 (2001), 503–25.
[2] J.C. Coffee, 'The rise of dispersed ownership', *Yale Law Journal*, 111 (2001), 1–82.
[3] M.J. Roe, 'Political preconditions to separating ownership from corporate control', *Stanford Law Review*, 53 (2000), 539–606; M.J. Roe, 'Legal origins, politics, and modern stock markets', *Harvard Law Review*, 120 (2006), 460–527.

In *Legal Origin?* Klerman and Mahoney [4] investigate central elements of Edward Glaeser and Andrei Shleifer's [5] analysis of how differences between common and civil law emerged in the thirteenth century, critiquing a paper called, simply enough, 'Legal Origins.' There, Glaeser and Shleifer said that the English judiciary was decentralized relative to the French and that political differences between England and France at the time best explained that relative decentralization. The relative power of the king in each nation differed, the barons feared the king more than one another in one nation (and one another in the other nation), and each nation's economic structure differed, with large contiguous land holdings in France giving the thirteenth century French barons more power and autonomy than the British barons.

I had much admired Glaeser and Shleifer's investigation and explanation, because it focuses on power and politics in the thirteenth century as explaining legal structure outcomes; despite that I am not a fan of the legal origins strand in the law and finance literature overall, as the citations in the first paragraph of this note suggest. I am sceptical of their big picture story because, first, it exaggerates the impact on financial outcomes of differences in legal style, when there are much more important – and more modern – explanations for the differences than legal origin. It also privileges corporate legal institutions in finance, which while important, are usually less critical than whether the polity has an ongoing antagonism to, or affinity for, capital markets. If the polity likes capital markets, then capital markets will tend to get the supporting institutions that they need. While older legal institutions are important, they are only part of the story and probably not the central one. Equally important, the differences in institutions between the legal origins are not so wide that either one is disabled or privileged in achieving the goals sought, such as investor protection primarily and property protection more broadly. Indeed, common law countries use regulators, such as the Securities and Exchange Commission, and codes, such as the securities regulations and the uniform commercial code, to deal with commercial disputes among investors and merchants. When we use those kinds of institutions, we forgo whatever advantages common law institutions, such as fiduciary duties, could have provided. Investor

---

[4] Daniel M. Klerman and Paul G. Mahoney, 'Legal Origin?', *Journal of Comparative Economics*, 35 (2007), 278–93.

[5] E. Glaeser and A. Shleifer, 'Legal origins', *Quarterly Journal of Economics*, 117 (2002), 1193–1228.

protection can be achieved through institutions available to both legal traditions. The big picture issue is more likely to lie in whether the polity is ready to accept and promote financial markets, not which institutional forms it classically preferred.

But I admired the 2002 'Legal Origins' piece because it convincingly focused on the issues of power and politics in the thirteenth century, cogently analysing how differing political configurations in England and France then seemed to have yielded strong juries in England and centralized judging in France. I also admired the 2002 piece as a sustained effort to link legal origins institutions to outcomes in a tight way; the legal origin literature displays many regressions but few extended inquiries beyond the 2002 piece linking origins to outcomes theoretically and historically. So, it is disappointing to see that Klerman and Mahoney view the history there as not fully accurate, with the actual structures (English courts were quite centralized, they say, and under the king's thumb in the twelfth century and for centuries thereafter) the opposite of what Glaeser and Shleifer described. Since both sides rely on standard sources, perhaps there is an uncertain historical record. It is also possible that some of Glaeser and Shleifer's jury decentralization story can be preserved if we move beyond their jury story, which Klerman and Mahoney say is inaccurate, to a more general explanation for thirteenth century English decentralization. I shall explain how below.

Here I make three points about the interplay between the emergence of the jury in thirteenth century England and modern finance. The first is that legal origins proponents should have paused in their other work in which they assert that legal origin has a major impact on financial outcomes around the world, because the jury is not central to financial regulation in many important common law nations. Indeed, its existence on the periphery of finance may be detrimental to financial development. If it is the jury that needs to be explained to understand differences in legal origin, but the jury is not important to finance (or is in fact detrimental), then that suggests legal origin differences may be less important to modern finance than the origins literature has it.

Second, for the jury story to resonate with the overall legal origin story, Britain would have had to have generally transferred the jury system to its colonies. As Glaeser and Shleifer state, in the thirteenth century:

> France went in the direction of adjudication by royally controlled professional judges, while England moved toward adjudication by relatively independent juries. Over the subsequent millennium, the conditions in

England and France reinforced the initial divergence in the legal systems. Moreover, the transplantation of the two legal systems ... may account for some crucial differences in social and economic outcomes in countries that are reported in empirical studies. [6]

But *did* Britain uniformly transplant the jury to its colonies? While the jury has had a long, deep and important role in the United States and Britain, it seems that most British colonies did not usually use the jury for civil trials and many, perhaps close to a majority, did not for criminal trials. The jury clashed with British colonial policy: decentralization and local empowerment was not something that the British sought, particularly after its experience with the jury in Ireland. Britain's wariness in transferring the jury around the world exemplifies a general and deeper point – it illustrates the bigger concept that legal origin institutions are trumped, and perhaps trumped easily, by modern political economy forces. Britain was in the business of running a colonial empire. If the jury conflicted with its colonial strategy, then out it went.

Third, the structure of the legal origins jury argument is in tension with the overall, bigger picture legal origins thesis. The overall legal origin thesis is that differences in French civil law and common law legal origin determine (or strongly influence) differences in modern financial markets. Why are there differences in institutions? The answer lies, the theory has it, in important part in differences in the political economies of thirteenth-century England and France: powerful barons with contiguous land holdings in France, a strong king in England. Differing legal institutions emerged then based on the differing political configurations of the time – so far, so good, those institutional differences persisted, and those persisting differences in institutions determine differences in financial markets in the twentieth and twenty-first centuries.

It is the conclusion in that chain that the legal origins' authors ought to have been more wary of: if the political economy of the thirteenth century explains thirteenth-century outcomes, why should we not look as well to twentieth-century political economy explanations to explain twentieth-century outcomes? Should we not look to historical experiences more recent than the thirteenth century as well? If political economy differences were important in the thirteenth century, might political economy differences of the twentieth century also be important, perhaps even dominant?

I explore some of these issues below.

---

[6]   Glaeser and Shleifer, 'Legal origins', (note 5, above), 1194.

II. Emergence of juries in the thirteenth century

A. *Thirteenth-century political differences*
between England and France

Medieval, thirteenth-century France was unstable, while England was at peace. England's king decentralized judicial decision making, while the French king centralized it. A key piece of English decentralization was the emergence of the jury, say Glaeser and Shleifer.

According to Glaeser and Shleifer, the relative power of the king in Britain and France induced centralized French courts, because this was the only way that the relatively weak French king could control proceedings and because the rivalrous barons acceded to the king's control since they feared one another more than they feared the king. Meanwhile, the more confident English monarch in the more peaceful realm could allow for decentralized juries and courts that could counter the local barons. Glaeser and Shleifer focus in particular on bullying, with the powerful French barons more likely to bully local juries successfully than would the weaker English barons.

B. *The Klerman–Mahoney reconsideration*

Klerman and Mahoney say this story just was not so: British courts were, they report, centralized in the twelfth century and for centuries thereafter. Indeed, this is as one might expect (and indeed Glaeser and Shleifer expected that the powerful English king would have centralized judicial power and were surprised to conclude that he had not): the powerful monarch tries to, and succeeds in, centralizing authority, while the weaker monarch cannot. Moreover, the doctrines and institutions that emerged then that could have had later pro-investor effects seem to have emerged from the most centralized, most 'French-like' features of the English courts, say Klerman and Mahoney. If there is a true institutional difference between the common law and the civil law, say Klerman and Mahoney, it emerged centuries later.

Klerman and Mahoney point out that rather than dispersing the English judiciary, the English kings, from Henry II onward, kept the judges on a short leash. Physically the king kept them close at Westminster, that is, close to the king. Typically when they travelled through England, they did so with the king. And the English judges were a small group that the king controlled more easily than he could have controlled a larger group of judges. And, yes, the king's judges sought to build a common law, but common in the sense of *uniform* through-out the king's lands. Moreover, they point out, doctrines and institutions like fiduciary duties – useful to modern outside investors in enterprises – emerged not in the law courts that practiced the common law, but in the king's chancery courts, which emerged in the fourteenth century as the most centralized of the English courts, the most under the king's control, and the least tied to juries. Hence, they say, whatever differences there are today between common and civil law emerged after the thirteenth century and, hence, the thirteenth-century history does not give one the opportu-nity to reject the basic idea that law and social/economic/political institu-tions are largely determined simultaneously in favour of a legal origins theory. Whatever emerged in the thirteenth century does not seem to have determined later institutions, mostly because England was centralized in the thirteenth century. Perhaps, they say, the divergence occurred later, when British merchants obtained more political power in the seventeenth century and then got the kind of court system they preferred. And, they suggest, perhaps the later, continuing divergences had much to do with the continuing ascendancy of the Whig commercial interests in England, an ascendancy that presumably allowed the Whigs to get – and keep – a legal system that was not antagonistic to their interests.

III. Legal origin theory's bigger picture

Let us take a step back from Klerman and Mahoney's critique. For the moment, let us take Glaeser and Shleifer's view of the thirteenth-century differences as accurate, despite Klerman and Mahoney's criticisms. What impact should that analysis have on the legal origins bigger pic-ture? The jury analysis in 'Legal Origins' does not fit well with the legal origins big picture on several important margins.

First, the historical record does seem to be contestable here, since both sides use standard sources. Not being a legal historian or even someone who consults legal histories of the English thirteenth cen-tury regularly, I am not well positioned to arbitrate. Moreover, even if Glaeser and Shleifer's sources are inaccurate, perhaps enough of their basic thirteenth-century story could still be preserved to be useful. That is, Glaeser and Shleifer interpret the Magna Carta's judgment by one's peers as guaranteeing a jury trial. Klerman and Mahoney point out that the jury trial was not so used, that 'judgment' required judging not jury-ing. The Magna Carta did not guarantee jury trials, they argue using standard historical sources. However, the core of Glaeser and Shleifer's specific argument here could be saved if they view the judgment of one's peers as a decentralizing move, one that reduced the king's power, even if King John never agreed to give the barons a true jury. Still, Klerman and Mahoney say that the next phrase in the Magna Carta – or the law of the land – reasserts the king's authority. Here Glaeser and Shleifer might argue that this still confined the king to avoid actions based on caprice, requiring consistency with prior rulings.

So, let us consider the implications if Glaeser and Shleifer's thirteenth-century view is, on the whole or in important part, correct. How does it fit with the bigger legal origins picture? It still fits awkwardly.

A. What is the bigger picture?

The bigger picture is straightforward: legal origin is important to modern finance because common law nations protect outside investors in firms better than do French civil law nations. Common law nations use fiduciary duties to protect outside investors *ex post*, after transactions occur; they also prefer transparency and property rights; and they are relatively decentralized and non-statist. The emergence of the thirteenth-century jury – in the version Glaeser and Shleifer promote – fits the bigger picture, they say, because the jury decentralizes power, reflecting and promoting the barons' independence from the English king. The less-centralized state allowed institutions that could protect property rights to emerge in a way that a centralized state might not have allowed. They state:

> Starting in the twelfth and thirteenth centuries, the relatively more peaceful England developed trials by independent juries, while the less peaceful France relied on state-employed judges to resolve disputes. It may also explain many differences between common and civil law traditions with respect to both the structure of legal systems and the observed social and economic outcomes.

English systems promote commerce, French systems promote state power, and some important packet of those differences trace back to the thirteenth century.

B. How important for modern commerce?

One can see how the jury *could* be important to commerce. With the jury drawn from the populace, the state would find it harder to dominate decisions left to the judiciary. Judicial decentralization would facilitate commerce. Property owners would be less fearful of state incursion. In contrast, a system of state-appointed judges operating without juries could promote state power at the expense of property interests in medieval times and business interests generally in modern times.

On the surface, there's something appealing in the idea. But some facts cause problems, problems that should induce us to rethink the idea and possibly reject it. First, the facts. The key on-the-ground American lawmaking institutions that affect outside investors are the Delaware Chancery Court and the Securities and Exchange Commission. The SEC operates without a jury, of course. It is staffed by government-appointed officials. But – and here is the problem for this arm of the legal origins theory – so does the Delaware Chancery Court. Yet the absence of the jury is regularly seen by legal commentators to be an *advantage* of the Delaware courts over others.[7] A lively literature in legal academic circles has arisen on why American firms incorporate away from their original place of business and what the consequences of that movement are. It is quite plausible and consistent with the range of that literature that American corporations are incorporating into Delaware in part, perhaps in major part, to *escape* the jury.[8]

Moreover, English civil courts do *not* use juries, Klerman and Mahoney point out. Hence, the jury idea could have induced legal origins theorists to re-think whether the core common–civil law differences are really important to finance. If the jury is a key characteristic of the common law, but if financial interests try to *escape* the jury and often prefer (French-like) expert judges to juries, then it is open to question whether the common law generally, or this feature of traditional American and British law, is basic to finance.

C. Is the jury uniformly important in common law nations?

For the jury story to resonate with the overall legal origin story, Britain would have had to have generally transferred the jury system to its

---

[7] M. Kahan and E. Kamar, 'The myth of state competition in corporate law', *Stanford Law Review*, 55 (2002), 708–709.

[8] To be sure here, other states' corporate laws are often dealt with via jury trials and when the SEC sues wrongdoers it usually needs to operate before a jury. Trials for securities damages go to juries, but my understanding is that players consider the jury's awards to be erratic. And recall that Britain hardly uses the jury at all in non-criminal trials.

colonies. But did it? It is true that juries have had a long and storied role in English and American jurisprudence. But it appears that many, perhaps most, former British colonies do *not* use juries for civil trials and perhaps a majority do not for criminal trials. For Britain, a colonial jury clashed with British colonial policy: decentralization and local empowerment was not something that the British sought, particularly after their difficult experience with the jury in Ireland. This is not a secondary point – it fits with the bigger concept that political economy considerations trump legal origin institutions.

American colonists used the power of the jury to subvert the authority of royal governors and the Crown. Jury nullification resulted in the acquittal of John Peter Zenger (tried for criminal libel against British interests), smugglers prosecuted under the Navigation Acts, rioters against the Stamp Act, and participants in the Boston Tea Party, as Vogler retells.[9] One royal governor complained that a 'Customs House Officer has no chance with a jury let his cause be what it will,' Moore reports.[10] Irish juries were reluctant to enforce the law, which they saw as a tool of English domination. Their reluctance led to lower conviction rates for all crimes in Ireland than in England and Wales, Johnson states,[11] such that Britain suspended Irish juries during periods of unrest.[12] As a nineteenth-century colonial power, the British had reason from experience not to deeply embed the jury in its new colonies. As Young concludes, even if the French origin systems had more centralizing and less litigious potential than the British:[13]

> By the time of the British imperial occupation of African territory, the dangers to colonial hegemony in indiscriminate transfer of British legal practices was well recognized. Thus, there was no question of application of the jury system of criminal law, which had so undermined the effectiveness of the law as a vehicle for colonial control in Ireland and the North American colonies.

[9] R. Vogler, 'The international development of the jury: The role of the British Empire', *International Review of Penal Law*, 72 (2001), 528.

[10] L.E. Moore, *The Jury: Tool of Kings, Palladium of Liberty*, (Cincinnati: W.H. Anderson Co., 1973), 110.

[11] D. Johnson, 'Trial by jury in Ireland, 1860–1914', *Journal of Legal History*, 17 (1996), 273–277.

[12] K. Quinn, 'Jury trial in Republic of Ireland', *International Review of Penal Law*, 72 (2001), 200.

[13] C. Young, 'The African colonial state and its political legacy', in D. Rothchild and N. Chazen (eds.), *The Precarious Balance: State and Society in Africa*, (Boulder, CO: Westview Press, 1988).

The British did introduce the jury trial to India, extended it haltingly, but never fully embedded it throughout India. They used it in India to convince Europeans to feel safe working and living there, because trial by a jury (of one's European peers) protected *Europeans* from answering for crimes against Indians;[14] India abolished it after independence,[15] presumably because Indians saw it as a tool of hegemonic power. African encounters with the jury are parallel: Britain limited its use and, where used, used it primarily to protect Europeans against native Africans.[16] This illustrates the complexity of context: the jury might well have been a *decentralizing* institution in thirteenth-century England. But, in some colonies Britain used it to *centralize* power by freeing colonizing Europeans from native justice.

To be specific here and current, several representative common law countries do not seem to systematically use juries: Botswana, Kenya, India, Nigeria, Pakistan, and South Africa. Others do, but usage is by no means uniform. Hence, if the purpose of examining the jury's emergence in England is to find a foundation for jurisprudence and decentralization in English legal origin countries, that showing has not been made. And a preliminary look at the legal history suggests it would not have been easy to find that jury foundation throughout the common law world.

D. Rebuilding Glaeser and Shleifer's jury-decentralization view

Legal origins theorists might have re-thought the jury's impact in the following way: the current *direct* presence or absence of the jury in corporate and commercial cases is not really so important (recanting some of the implications of the 2002 article), they might concede. But, overall the jury represents a decentralized system that protects property. It is an example of decentralization but not intrinsic to it.

Here is how, they might say: for governments (or the powerful, such as landowners in the thirteenth century and corporate insiders in the twentieth) to take property from another, they needed to get courts to

[14] A.G.P. Pullan, 'Trial by jury in India', *Journal of Comparative Legislation and International Law*, 28 (1946), 109, 3d series.

[15] Vogler, 'The international development of the jury', (note 9, above), 532.

[16] R.K. Mawer, 'Juries and assessors in criminal trials in some commonwealth countries: A preliminary survey', *The International and Comparative Law Quarterly*, 10 (1961), 892–8; Vogler, 'The international development of the jury', (note 9, above), 525–52.

approve or acquiesce. But, the argument would run, if property owners are well distributed through the populace – or at least among those who could be selected for jury service – property would be protected. If the judge – appointed by the legislature, the king or those in authority – acted alone, civil-law-like, the judge might run roughshod over property rights if the judicial institution lacked a check from a property-sympathizing jury, one composed typically of property owners. Hence, the ubiquity of common law jury trials protected property, with the operational tool being that the jury would be chosen from a populace of property holders.[17]

Though plausible, that argument gets tied up in knots when we try to tie it to the bigger legal origin theory. What makes that kind of jury work is that property is well-enough distributed that property owners dominate juries, or the rules for jury selection make property ownership a likely characteristic of the median jury member. But the same pro-property result would be reached if property owners dominate the *legislature* (or, again, if the rules for legislative composition favoured property owners). If property owners dominate the legislature, then it will produce property-oriented legislation. It will set up rules for its courts that protect property. But if so, then the *judicial system* derives from the composition of society (or, better, from the composition of its legislative commanders). Even if the polity had *no* jury, if the *legislature* (or the electorate or the relevant decision-makers) were dominated by property owners, then that society's rules would protect property and the composition of the jury would not matter, because even if there were no jury, *judges* would have to respect property.

Hence, it is *not* whether a nation uses a jury that matters but whether the nation's *political institutions* support or denigrate property rights. If the legislature supports property and the legislature is powerful, then in the end even judges without juries will protect property. If they would not protect property, the legislature (or the executive, or the electorate) would not let them be appointed. If property-disrespecting judges did somehow get appointed, the legislature would take away their authority. Most likely, severe conflict would not arise, because judges and legislators would come from the same milieu – the same law schools, for example – and have similar world views. If property

---

[17] Or, if they gave up their jury argument, Glaeser and Shleifer might say that the Magna Carta, by providing for judgment by one's peers, protected property owners enough in the thirteenth century that the baronial property owners would invest in improving their property.

is not well distributed among the jury population (and if the jury did thwart property rights), then the property-oriented legislature would disband or control juries (so as to protect property). Or courts would adapt to the legislative realities, in the way Spiller and Gely suggested.[18] Perhaps through happenstance, this sequence occurred in the United States: a property-oriented polity allowed a corporate law institution – Delaware Chancery Court judges operating without a jury – to emerge and become important because it would protect corporate property better than a jury-based court would.

And the converse is true as well: if the legislature is antagonistic to property, then, first, the composition of the jury pool probably would not be property protecting and, second, even if it is, the rules and institutions would not last long against a property defiling but powerful legislature.

Thus, the common law jury argument standing on its own is a dead-end.

This sequence parallels Klerman and Mahoney's hypothesis that the history of British property protection emanates not from the thirteenth century jury but from the seventeenth-century legislature. Their conjecture seems plausible, because that is when commercial interests asserted themselves and came to dominate the British power structure. It also parallels[19] Roe's[20] arguments that twentieth-century politics could have overturned prior property protection, and did in some nations. When those in power were not interested in supporting financial markets, financial markets did not develop. Nations' legal traditions were less important than their contemporaneous political economy features.

This is not just history. The process of legislative property protection is happening here and now, in the United States. Consider the *Kelo* case, which the United States Supreme Court decided in 2005.[21] The court said that state legislatures were free to define what the public purpose was when they took property from property owners for economic development. (There is more detail here for a law school property course, but

---

[18] P.T. Spiller and R. Gely, 'Congressional Control or Judicial Independence: The Determinants of U.S. Supreme Court Labor-Relations Decisions, 1949–1988', *RAND Journal of Economics*, 23 (1992), 463–92.

[19] Roe, 'Political preconditions to separating ownership from corporate control', (note 3, above), 539–606.

[20] M.J. Roe, 'Delaware's competition', *Harvard Law Review*, 117 (2003), 588–646; Roe, 'Legal origins, politics, and modern stock markets', (note 3, above), 460–527.

[21] United States Supreme Court, *Kelo v. City of New London*, 125 S. Ct. 2655 (2005).

we need not go into it.) This decision would not be a good one for a legal origin theory that sees fundamental importance in common law judicial property protection. But then the issue became a public one, going on the ballot in eleven states, with nine of them confining their decision makers from expanding the notion of property that could be taken.[22] Today it is the American property-oriented polity, not the judges, that restricts takings.

IV. Juries' interaction with the bigger picture

There's another interaction between the Glaeser–Shleifer article and the bigger picture of the legal origin analysis – and it may well be more important. Let us pursue it here and see how it could lead us to higher ground and better insights. That higher ground is the ascendancy of political economy considerations in understanding the foundations for financial markets.

A. Political economy foundations in the thirteenth century

First, let us analyse the core legal origins perspective, step by step.

The central argument in this literature is that law that protects investors is important for financial markets. (Few would dispute this in its ordinary form.) Law though is not primarily the creation of modern political and economic forces, the legal origin theorists assert, but the result (primarily, largely, in important measure) of long-standing legal traditions that date back centuries. Figure 1 illustrates the view that modern property protection is rooted in medieval institutions.

What caused the common and civil law legal systems to diverge? Well, political differences in the twelfth, thirteenth, and perhaps the seventeenth centuries; political differences having to do with the relative power in England and France of the king and of the complementary relative power of the barons in each nation. I illustrate with Figure 2.

With these two sequences in mind, we can, in the legal origins theory, understand much of modern finance.

---

[22] Castle Coalition, www.castlecoalition.org/legislation/ballot-measures/index.html (2006); C. Cooper, 'Court's eminent-domain edict is a flashpoint on state ballots', *Wall Street Journal*, August 7 (2006), A4.

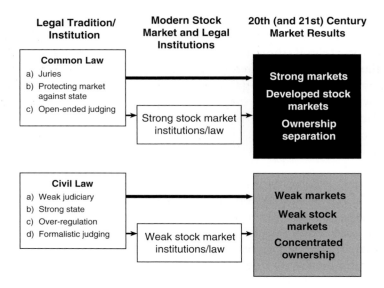

Figure 1 From medieval legal origin to modern financial markets

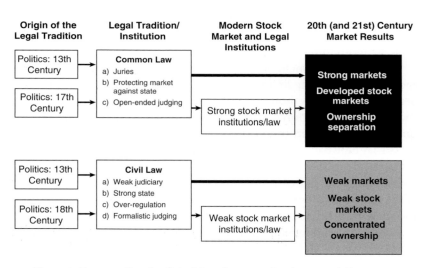

Figure 2 From medieval political foundations to legal origins differences

B. Political economy foundations in the twentieth century?

So in the legal origins theory, politics is indeed important, but its importance is in how it induced institutional differences to arise in the twelfth, thirteenth, and maybe the seventeenth centuries. Modern politics in the theory is relatively unimportant. For example, in one legal origins piece, Botero et al.[23] argue that left–right power and the relative importance of labour interests are not as important to European labour legislation in the past few decades as legal origin. One might – dropping the theory's transmission institution of legal origin – call the thesis one of the medieval origins of modern financial markets. I illustrate with Figure 3 the legal origin advocates' rejection of modern politics as a key determinant of financial markets. (Surely the authors would not deny that modern politics has some effect, but their idea would be that its effect is smaller than legal origin, or interacts so closely with legal origin that it is really origin that determines the lion's share of the political economy configurations and the financial outcomes.)

An alternative view, one that I illustrate with Figure 4, is that modern politics *is* quite important to modern financial markets. Some polities favour capital markets; others are hostile to financial markets. The first will build supporting institutions; the second will not. And even if the second does build those institutions at times – or does allow them to emerge privately – they will not do much good in developing deep financial markets because capital owners are wary of letting go of their capital in a hostile (or indifferent) political environment. Roe develops this theory.[24]

The point here is not to deny that institutions, particularly legal institutions, are sticky. They are. And their stickiness can persist for years, even decades, impeding some changes.[25] But stickiness does not mean that, once constructed, they are impervious to subsequent influences. If history had ended in the thirteenth or seventeenth centuries in Europe, then it is plausible that the institutional objects, having been set in motion, would persist. And if those institutional differences were central to financial differences (a view disputed in part by Klerman and Mahoney here and Mahoney[26] and Roe elsewhere – because both sets of institutions can achieve the same investor protection ends if the political

---

[23] J. Botero, S. Djankov, R. La Porta, F. Lopez-de-Silanes and A. Shleifer, 'The regulation of labor', *Quarterly Journal of Economics*, 119 (2004), 1339–1382.

[24] Roe, 'Political preconditions to separating ownership from corporate control', (note 3, above), 539–606; Roe, 'Delaware's competition', (note 20, above), 588–646; Roe, 'Legal origins, politics, and modern stock markets', (note 3, above), 460–527.

[25] M.J. Roe, 'Chaos and evolution in law and economics', *Harvard Law Review*, 109 (1996), 641–68; L.A. Bebchuk and M.J. Roe, 'A theory of path dependence in corporate ownership and governance', *Stanford Law Review*, 52 (1999), 127–69.

[26] Mahoney, 'The common law and economic growth', (note 1, above), 503–25.

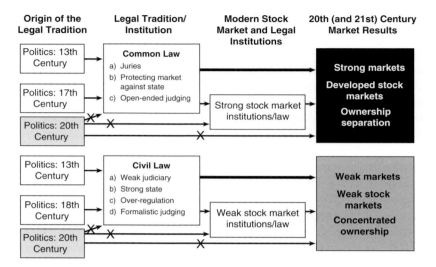

Figure 3 Medieval legal origins and the unimportance of modern politics to modern financial markets

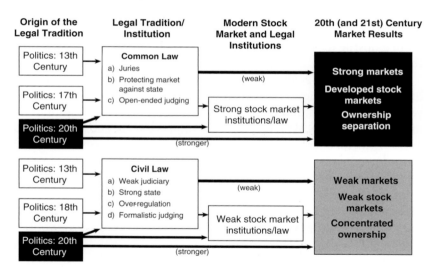

Figure 4 The importance of modern politics to modern financial markets

will is there), then modern finance could well have been determined by centuries-old institutions. More plausibly, other institutional differences arose in the interim, replacing, strengthening and changing earlier ones. The residue of events from the thirteenth century was certainly an input, but only one and probably not the determinative one. Certainly the English Civil War and the Glorious Revolution were central to English history, substantially influenced the English economy in the seventeenth century, and had continuing influence into the eighteenth century and beyond. Certainly the welfare state's rise in the twentieth century and its intensity in continental Europe could have affected finance and property. The point is not that institutions are not sticky, but that the events that influence them occur more frequently than once every seven centuries.

C. Differences due to wars and insecurity

A parallel analysis of the legal origins argument can be made – parallel in the sense that the influence of thirteenth century (or seventeenth century) institutional differences has strong modern parallels, forcing us to wonder whether it's the medieval influence or the modern one that is the stronger one. Starting in the twelfth and thirteenth centuries, Glaeser and Shleifer state (at 1194):

> France went in the direction of adjudication by royally controlled pro-
> fessional judges, while England moved toward adjudication by relatively
> independent juries. Over the subsequent millennium, the conditions in
> England and France reinforced the initial divergence in the legal systems.
> Moreover, the transplantation of the two legal systems ... may account for
> some crucial differences in social and economic outcomes [around the
> world].

Glaeser and Shleifer say that this happened because the French situation in the thirteenth century was unstable, while the English enjoyed (relative) tranquillity. This – relative order and tranquillity in England – induced differential institutional development. As Glaeser and Shleifer plausibly state (at 1208):

> We estimate that between 1100 and 1800, France had a war on its soil dur-
> ing 22 per cent of the years, whereas England only 6 per cent (one can also
> argue that the wars on English soil were relatively bloodless). The constant
> war on the French soil meant that weapons and warriors were readily
> available to anyone who wanted to subvert justice.

Glaeser and Shleifer focus on the stability of the jury system:

> It is not entirely surprising...that tight state control of adjudication has
> often been introduced as part of national liberation or unification, often
> in the aftermath of national liberation or civil war and other disorder.

Without internal peace to begin with, a system of juries may simply not work. [27]

Again, the jury system might not be so central to modern finance, for the reasons I gave a few pages ago, and may not have been transplanted around the common law world, but one could stick with the basic elements of the Glaeser–Shleifer argument by substituting the consequence as being one of a decentralized state, one amenable to local, property interests (for which the jury could have been a manifestation, but not a necessary one) and which internal and external disorder would weaken.

Some of this relative order arose, I shall add to give some texture to Glaeser and Shleifer's argument, from the differences of geography: the open areas of the European continent put differing, often hostile, populations next to one another. The English had the advantage of being separated by a channel of water, with the Scots and Welsh as the only immediate hostile neighbours. (Invasions of England, like the Norman one in 1066 and what could be characterized as the Dutch one of 1688, were difficult to pull off.) The contrasting geography of the thirteenth century gave a geographic impetus to a powerful prince in Europe in general and France in particular, one who could fend off hostile neighbours. The English had an easier time thinking of suppressing a standing army and decentralizing power than would most states on the continent.

From these differences in internal and external order, in the Glaeser and Shleifer perspective, it is plausible that a centralized civil law system emerged on the continent in France, perhaps as early as the thirteenth century, and a less centralized one emerged in England. Centuries later, these contrasts affected finance, with the English courts better equipped institutionally to protect property, shareholding and creditor interests than the centralized, statist civil law systems, as Figure 5 illustrates.

But the problem is that this kind of continental European disorder did not end once and for all in the thirteenth century, or even in the seventeenth century. This contrast persisted up to 1945 and the end of World War II, or perhaps until 1989 and the collapse of traditional communism and the Berlin Wall. Figure 6 illustrates. Proponents of the legal origin story may simply be seeing in medieval legal origins the back reflections of more modern – and more important – political economy differences of the twentieth century, differences arising in large measure from the

---

[27] Glaeser and Shleifer, 'Legal origins', (note 5, above), 1211.

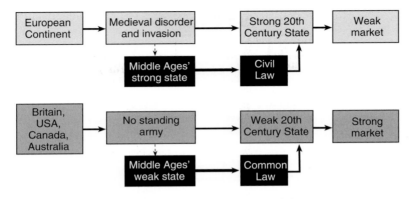

Figure 5 Medieval disorder and stability

contrasting levels of twentieth-century disorder and destruction, and their political consequences. And that, I suspect, is where, for modern financial outcomes, the real political economy story begins in earnest.

V. Conclusion

Legal origin has been brought forward as a key influence on modern finance, with the perspective being advanced that common law institutions are intrinsically better adapted to protect investors than civil law institutions. Glaeser and Shleifer offer a creative inquiry into the early emergence of the jury in common law nations and its relative unimportance in civil law nations.[28] They offer it as one of the significant continuing differences between common and civil law, one dependent on the differences in relative power between the English monarch and the French one in the thirteenth century, with the powerful British monarch able to forgo centralization, while the weaker French monarch needed to assert control over localities via a more powerful judiciary. Daniel Klerman and Paul Mahoney provide an excellent analysis of the difficulties of doing this kind of historical work, as it turns out that much evidence indicates that the powerful British monarch in fact centralized judicial authority.[29] If differences emerged, say Klerman and Mahoney, they emerged later on. Moreover, they say that one cannot yet reject the possibility that law is determined simultaneously with social, political

---

[28]   Glaeser and Shleifer, 'Legal origins', (note 5, above), 1193–228.
[29]   Klerman and Mahoney, 'Legal Origin?', (note 4, above).

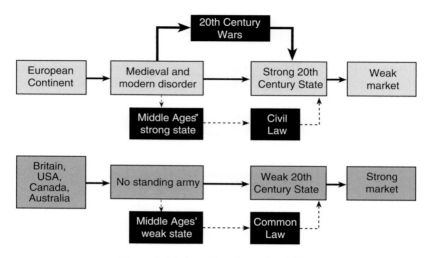

Figure 6 Modern disorder and stability

and economic facts, as the thirteenth century structures did not seem to predetermine the later ones. If by simultaneous, we mean over the course of decades, with multiple feedback effects, their thesis is one I'd sympathize with and indeed put forward.[30]

And the basic investigation here of the jury should give pause to those promoting the overall legal origin thesis. The first reason to hesitate is that the jury is not central to protecting outside investors in common law nations. Indeed America's premier corporate court – the Delaware Chancery court – sits without a jury and the usual view in legal circles is that the jury's absence (which results in decision making by expert judges, not juries) is a strength of the court, not a weakness. The second reason is that Britain often did not transfer the jury to its colonies. The transplantation assumption in the legal origin literature is weaker, maybe much weaker, than the law and finance literature has it. The third reason is that the analysis for the jury differences between civil and common law nations depends on political economy differences of centuries ago. But if political economy differences determined institutional differences in the earlier centuries, it is plausible that political

[30] Roe, 'Political preconditions to separating ownership from corporate control', (note 3, above), 539–606; Roe, 'Delaware's competition', (note 20, above), 588–646; Roe, 'Legal origins, politics, and modern stock markets', (note 3, above), 460–527.

economy differences in intervening centuries *also* have affected financial outcomes. Indeed modern and contemporary political economy differences that lead some nations to support capital markets and some to denigrate them could be as important to modern financial outcomes as thirteenth and maybe even seventeenth century political differences. Perhaps more so.

PART III

Miscellaneous

33

The practitioner and the professor – is there a theory of commercial law?

JEAN NICOLAS DRUEY

Of course, my title indicates a reverence to Eddy Wymeersch. He has shown that in commercial law both practical and theoretical functions of a highest level can be united in one person. And the lesson he teaches goes one step further: he certainly did not undertake all the burdens simply for honours, but because he saw a professional need to follow both tracks. Practice requires guidelines from theory and theory the feedback from practice.

But I am hesitating: what exactly does theory offer to commercial practice? In our actual world, is not the flow going more and more the other way in that innovative practice gets faster and faster, and, be it just for the changing allocation of forces, theory slower and slower? The two seem to become increasingly unequal, the one trying breathlessly to run behind the other.

My question has two branches. First, it applies a sociological view on those having to do with commercial law. This is kind of an outward look. Then, the inward look has to follow, i.e. an analysis of the actual state of commercial legal theory, its possible deficits and chances. All that will necessarily be limited to some observations and ideas from one of many possible viewpoints.

But before all, let us start by an *example*. It will allow a closer view to the problem, and will set more players into the field than the professor and the one applying the law in commercial practice; in particular lawmakers and courts have to come into the picture. On the other hand, the retarding factors in the evolution of theory will be better seen. The introductory example which I choose is the one which has particularly brought Eddy and me together.

I. The law on corporate groups as an example

Groups of companies being directed by a common policy determined by a parent company are a phenomenon going back to the nineteenth century. Since then they have continuously increased – maybe not so much in application fantasy, but in size and number, the multi-corporate structure having become organizational routine everywhere in the world.

The legal world reacted quite promptly. Typically, in a country like the United States the reaction was aimed at particular issues such as accepting the group as not being a conspiracy in restraint of trade, whereas the *Deutscher Juristentag* of 1902 placed the subject of groups *as such* on its agenda. Sixty-three years later, the Federal Republic promulgated a chapter in the *Aktiengesetz* titled '*Verbundene Unternehmen*' (related companies), thus claiming to systematically regulate the group phenomenon (if composed by companies limited by shares). Some other countries followed to a various extent. 'The rest is silence' – incredibly enough after more than a century!

Having been, like Eddy Wymeersch, one of those sitting over this group law subject for innumerable hours, be it reading and writing at my desk, teaching in the classroom, or listening and discussing in many, many conferences, seminar and meetings, I ask myself: Was all that fruitless? I would insist on the statement that we tried hard from the side of theory and that none of these hours was dull. But the point of departure and the object of interest were *facts* and *phenomena*. Legal theory tried to cope with the inventions of commercial practice – and failed to cope with itself!

What I mean is a failure to get the new legal tools ready, which always are necessary to grasp a new phenomenon. Without that, all is mere subsumption; all is measured by the pre-existing standards. Groups thereby are an issue under minority protection, under creditors' protection, workers' protection, contract law or whatever: legal action about groups is, then, instigated by the view that groups might create a danger under such aspects. The German *Aktiengesetz* of 1965 is the protagonist for some of these purposes. This kind of legal thought, however, runs a serious risk to be counterproductive, creating injustice instead of justice. Subjecting groups to a cumbersome minority protection, for example, raises the question whether the situation is actually better or worse in others than affiliated companies, and whether it is for those concerned even more of an advantage than a disadvantage to be integrated in a group etc. This is to say that, truth being on both sides, general rules in favour of one side will soon prove to be a Procrustian bed. In other words, to have no group law might be the better solution than *this* group law. One way or the other, the start from pre-existing concepts is too rough because theory lacks the patience to analyse the group as a phenomenon of its own, as a mix of centripetal and centrifugal tendencies which requires its proper institutions.

This example indicates a need and, at the same time, a deficit, of a switch in paradigm. Legal thought tends by nature to be positivistic, and lets others do the work of conceiving policies and preparing new laws. However, groups of companies, like most issues in commercial law, are a problem of *insufficiency* of the existing law, and lawyers therefore as the 'users' of law would have a primordial signalling function. But practice has not the time and the systematic approach to produce such signals. So the problem is: if practice sees no problem, it is by far not certain that there is none.

II. The power of practice

This brings me to my question. There is in commercial law a strong interrelationship between the phenomena and the law. Our times are more and more departing from the one-sided perspective that there are facts ruled upon by laws, in favour of a cybernetic approach viewing facts as law producers by themselves in the sense of feedbacks given to the law. Thus, when we speak of a *system* this is not only the question of whether there is, and what is, the system of commercial law, but of the system *generating* the law.

I am well aware that describing the situation in this manner implies a statement of *weakness* of the law. It certainly would be worth an indepth investigation – none is known to me from my angle – to show the various manifestations of this position-loss in politics, in legislative, legal or academic practice etc. This is not necessarily to blame our guild of lawyers, but may equally well indicate a courageous opening towards the *non-legal* considerations, from economic theory to statistics, or from great scandals to innocent day-to-day-practice, and to a *global* or at least *European* view. An opening always is a concession of weakness, but who does it first might be the final winner.

And this is also to say that, within the legal professions, the role of the practitioner has been enhanced. Practice has become the focus on which these various perspectives converge. And practice, in turn, has not only the option to consider them, but it *must* find its way in order to eliminate the major risks coming from any side whatsoever. This creates an autonomy increasingly enlarging the gap to legislated law. Commercial practice builds its own world by establishing standard contracts, by concentrating know-how in certain places (a merger between two middle-sized Swiss companies is normally managed from downtown Manhattan) or by developing its own, usually abbreviated, language or its rules of thumb.

I do not think that we *must* accept this evolution forever, and neither that we *should* do so. Let me somewhat elaborate on these two questions.

III. Securing the connection of theory and practice

If, referring to the authority of established law, one does not accept the autonomy of practice, one must show how the two can be tied together. Essentially, there are two ways: either the gap is bridged over by *persons* or by *procedures*. The first is to have persons available who are in hybrid positions, having functions on both sides, being practitioners and simultaneously, say, professors – I would mean by 'professors' any legal professionals having the overview over the existing body of law and the theory behind it. The second is to offer channels of understanding between the practitioners and the professors, such as common seminars, periodicals publishing the views of both sides, a severe legal education of the future practitioners safeguarding a lifetime interest for the legal basics, or, to the contrary, trainings of professors in practice – I am serious on that too!

Both ways have their specific advantages and specific cost. To unite all aspects in one person is to avoid all transferring and processing of information; what is available is so at any time. But all the more restricted are the capacities and thus the available quantities of information. Of course, I would not dare to express a formal choice in my few thoughts presented here. Generally speaking, it is not entirely a matter of voluntary choice, not an issue of strategy of whomsoever. Rather it is rooted in *traditions* which will not follow an order to change, and, in varying proportions, there will always be a *mix* of both. Thus, I will limit myself to some considerations related to this weighing. These will favour a separation of powers, specifically suggesting to let professors just be professors. That may appear to be more daring than any other proposal when I write this precisely to the honour of Eddy Wymeersch. But I trust he will understand what I mean.

Looking at those traditions, we might observe a difference between bigger and smaller countries. I am not able to make final statements on this, my view being to a great deal limited to my home country,

Switzerland. But there is a chance of more parallels to Eddy's country, Belgium, than for example to Germany, England or the United States. Smaller countries are more limited in their personal resources and therefore tend to attribute to their best people a plurality of functions. I do not overlook that other European countries like France or Italy, although being important, also have a tendency to combine advocacy and (full) professorship; I will not discuss their particular motives.

IV. The trend toward double-bind positions

If I consider the developments in Switzerland, the trend in the field of commercial law clearly is in favour of the combination. To be sure, professors in this area used to write opinions, to be a part in arbitration courts or in legislative commissions in prior times as well. But today an increasing number even of *ordinarii* actually mix functions particularly by being partners in a legal office. On the other hand, members particularly of big law firms tend to undertake an academic kind of tasks by teaching courses and/or being active in publishing.

The reasons for this trend have to do, as I see it, with the better awareness for career planning, both on the side of the young people and of their potential employers. The brilliant law students and graduates are looked for by their academic teachers and also by the big law firms, and to ride on both tracks is for the young candidates sort of a natural way of solving the dilemma, or rather of avoiding a solution. Differences are merely gradual, depending on how well the inner academic fire survives the immense challenge which is encountered in a glamorous legal business. The amount of energy and time-management skills shown by the runners of such hybrid careers is admirable.

Now, the *evaluation* of this double-bind as a bridge between practice and theory raises positive but also negative aspects. The tie to theory secures, I may say, a certain cleanness of practical arguing referring it to the legal bases, but also inspires the fantasy to find maybe unusual lines of argument, which is in the interest of the case *and* of the evolution of law as such. The familiarity with practice also protects theory against growing grey and contributes to the authenticity of academic teaching. On the negative side I see mainly the problem that this kind of career cannot, by simple limitations of time and attention, focus on theory as such; the thinking is either pragmatic or positivistic. Theory, then, is a body more or less well conserved since the times of studying and thesis writing, and not itself the object of elaboration. In publications and courses, the choice of topics and the answers given are often preceded by work on specific cases, which serve clients and, even if they are not biased, there is a natural tendency to stick mentally with those cases.

However, all this starts from one presumption, namely that there is a value in developing legal theory. The impression is rather the opposite: commercial law practice seems to have learned to swim, to stay at the surface without need of a solid bottom, and does so for the sake of being faster and more flexible. We have to consider that now.

V. Commercial law in need of a theory

I understand a legal theory to be a system of sentences lying behind the specific rules prescribing any kind of behaviour. The assertion is that law cannot do without, and that commercial law is no exception. Quite to the contrary: the more flexible the law is, the stronger has to be the construction holding it together. And a theory is not just a purpose, because purposes never can be followed up to their end, but are subject to a legislative dosage which is a matter of policy, not of theory. And theory also is more than denominating a field of action. To say that Sarbanes-Oxley is aimed to improve corporate governance does not relate the substance of the rules to their conceptual roots, thus has no theoretical leverage.

Theory is a guideline for interpretation and to determine the inherent limits of legal rules. And lack of theory may therefore be of great cost. For example, we should have more theory on the requirement of *independence* of decision makers. As a concept, independence bears hardly a limitation in itself; however, it is clear that our segmented business world needs an immense number of decision makers and that we may not exclude, for reasons of bias, any friend of a friend of any person possibly interested in the outcome of a decision. The law has to draw a line, it has to sort out the forbidden from the acceptable cases, but it cannot specifically name all cases which should not be tolerated. Theory could help to prepare the selection, it could systematically analyse the causes of bias and show, as a first thing, that there are many other sources of unwanted influences beside proper interest and relations to interested parties, such as opinions previously expressed, political or religious views, informal quid-pro-quos etc. Then, theory could systematize the countervailing virtues of double-bind positions. And clarity should be elaborated on a general level about the consequences for the decisions taken with the collaboration of excluded persons: are they invalid? Is the election of the person invalid from the outset or only the respective contribution (vote etc.)? Or is all valid under the provision of liability for damages? What about confidential information given to excluded persons? And so on.

It is not without purpose that I am going into some length with this example: uncertainties on points like those mentioned may have an important destabilizing effect. And by no means can we expect that the insular provisions in laws or governmental or private regulations will actually cover the subject in the multitude of its aspects. Nor are the short-cut methods satisfactory which usually are applied in legal uncertainty, such as weighing of interests or conclusions by analogy. Weighing of interests is by far not able to give the precise guidelines required in advance on issues of independence. And analogy blurs the limits which, as stated, always are necessary in matters of incompatibility. It cannot do without a theory indicating in turn the limits of arguing by analogy.

It would be easy to multiply the examples of areas of strong, but too pragmatic evolution of modern commercial and economic law. Probably the most important today would be the world of financial reporting, but we could also revert to the corporate groups and show how creditors and shareholders of Sabena could have been helped against Swissair by a more solid state of theory.

Why is there no uproar of practice against so much uncertainty, so much imprecision in core issues of commercial law? Why do the practitioners, being the professional wolves in their cases, behave like lambs in face of issues of legal development?

VI. Commercial law theory in need of professors

Is there at all something which may be called a body of theory of commercial law? Every commercialist anywhere in the world might give the ready-made answer 'Yes, of course' and will with pride point to the company law. I am not so sure. History of companies, especially of those with limited liability, might with good reasons rather be called a distorting of theory, a fruit of marketing more than of legal doctrine, in that investors of desperately needed risk capital were called 'members' or 'shareholders', although others were clearly the entrepreneurs conceiving and initiating the business. Time worked with respect to such initial shortcomings of theory more in the sense of forgetting than clearing. For sure, there are other examples, where the long time available helped steady improvement of the institution like in case of bills of exchange:

here, precision was the goal since the beginnings in the late Middle Ages, and led to an admirable mechanics of rules spread over the world thanks to its clarity.

More recent institutions such as capital market law often do have their underlying theories, but the discussion got out of breath too soon. The parallelism of market and investors' protection, which seems to be the prevailing answer with respect to the purpose of capital market law, is not much of a statement. Naturally, legislators tend to give to their products a broad scope, such as drugs are claimed to cure from top to toe. Theory is all the more asked to indicate the unavoidably necessary limitations.

One point is clear, however: *economic* theory is not by itself legal theory. Law can obviously not neglect what economic science is asserting and opening the law for this kind of reflection has been one of the most deserving efforts in legal theory of the last decades. But economic theories are models based on certain assumptions; they start with an 'If …', and law has to look behind such 'Ifs', and this always brings contrary considerations into light. For example, market theory calls for transparency, but a firm only can work when privacy is granted to its internal developments. Maybe that economic theory itself will deal with such conflicting aspects, possibly by taking into the picture behavioural economy, but legal theory at least has to ask the questions and usually has to care for finding the equilibrium. And there will always be considerations flowing exclusively from the legal system. Law is based on fundamental rights which are not derived from any-where else. In this sense, conceptions of social values put forward by economic theory have necessarily to be complemented by individual values and freedoms. Property rights, for example, will never be suf-ficiently explained by functions ascribed to them in the general eco-nomic process.

VII. Professorship or practice

In the networks of the legal professions, theory is allocated with the professors. They are not freed from this task by the fact that nobody cares for theory, but it makes it all the more cumbersome. For one thing, it puts the additional burden on them to awake the need for theory as such, i.e. to make the community again sensible for the indispensabil-ity of theory, to profess a 'theory on theory'. Theoretical statements, if they are good, have little rhetoric power and thus little chance to have a direct impact on practice. Theory, therefore, must grow in the seclusion of pondering and discussing, and requires the recognition of the value of theory per se.

Secondly, we observe an intriguing phenomenon of divergence: whereas awareness of theory diminishes, the fields of theory are becoming more and more large. My observations above have alluded to economics, but the same is true for sociology or psychology. The classical task of ascertaining the law in the respective field can no longer restrict itself to collecting judicial precedents and scholarly opinions under the applicable keywords, but has to look into constitutional, procedural and other branches of law, into linguistic, historical and philosophical aspects as constituents of the law. And all that should not be limited to one country or one language area. On top of this, working on theory calls for an effort of synthesis, not just accumulating an immense pile of materials, but extracting therefrom generalized statements, which is no fast business.

This sounds utopian, taking into account the very small number of professors as compared with other legal professions. But there lies no justification for doing nothing. Thus, I plead in favour of *professorship to be a pure professorship*, and of selecting professors in view of their ability and willingness to dig into the bases of their legal fields.

Of course, theory under circumstances whatsoever will not die. People wanting to look into larger contexts will continue to show up. But we should be afraid of the *dissociation* of theory and practice. Practice and theory must understand and watch each other. Both are subject to fashions, and even a theory working in the unnoticed 'underground' may, due precisely to its one-sidedness, one day get sufficient power to break into a practical environment inspired by a very different culture. We lived this after World War II with radical ideas on antitrust law, and we continue to observe it with claims for transparency.

As stated before, the 'purity' of professorship therefore implies the introduction of other institutional warranties to safeguard the contacts with practice. My own way was to stay in practice for some years between the termination of studies and entering a full professorship. It proved to be a good experience, but it has periodically to be brushed up. Without looking at other options, I should eliminate at least one source of misunderstanding: an important role in filling the gap lies certainly with those part-time university teachers who not only provide the students with a sense of the practical impact of legal regulations, but also are active as legal writers making known successes and failures of the law.

I think I have sufficiently distinguished my case from that of Eddy Wymeersch. When an academic career as his, fully devoted to teaching and research, is crowned by one of the highest practical functions which his country has to offer, he has deserved it – among others by his academic merits.

34

A short paean for Eddy: Clever, Wise, August, Funny and European*

RUBEN LEE

When archaeologists finally unearthed the foundation stone of the ruins of the modernist building close to the Arc de Triomphe with the unknown logo 'ESEC' on its fascia, they were surprised to discover underneath it the following short text:

> *Efficiency with our Head, Protection with our Heart, Stability with our Soul.*
> We are One, We are Many.
> We Change, We Remain the Same.

> *Efficiency with our Head, Protection with our Heart, Stability with our Soul.*
> No Process, No Substance.
> No Justification, No Action.

> *Efficiency with our Head, Protection with our Heart, Stability with our Soul.*
> No Controls, No Freedoms.
> No Consensus, No Decisions.

> The Facts are the Facts.
> The Vision is the Vision.
> *Know which Must Triumph.*

If there is one thing that has been universally accepted about this intriguing and ancient text, it is that the language seeks to capture the essence of what is now believed to have been a widely followed cult from the early twenty-first century, promoting a range of private and public securities and services at the heart of a series of cultural, social, economic and financial exchanges.

There is little doubt that the repeated chorus of *efficiency, protection,* and *stability* reflects the three inner goals the cult's regulators or gods were mandated to achieve. The first verse is also broadly viewed as representing the essence of the contradictions at the heart of the movement: the union requires sublimation of the individual state to the one, yet at

---

* With great thanks and apologies to Ursula and her Acacia Seeds.

the same time, the many must remain; to meet the future the union must be in a continuous flux of change, yet at the same time it must remain true to itself and never abandon its underlying philosophy.

It is over the interpretation of the subsequent verses, however, that a passionate controversy has raged for many centuries. Two major opposing schools of thought have developed. There are the *idealists*, those who believe that the unknown author of the ESEC manuscript depicted the world as he viewed it should be. The text is viewed as a mantra that should lead to utopian harmony, if only it were followed and repeated often enough. Its meaning is clear: no substance is possible without due process; no action can be taken without justification; no freedoms are possible without appropriate controls; no decisions can be taken without consensus.

The opposing school of analysis is composed of the *realists*, those who maintain that the poet must have written the ode to depict the world as it was, rather than as it should be. For them, rather than being a mantra to follow, the text is the author's description of the harsh and forbidding environment as then existed. The meaning of the language is also clear, and, in this instance, relentlessly nihilist: there is no worthwhile process; there is no substance; there is no justification; there is no action; there are no controls; there are no freedoms of movement; there is no consensus; there are no decisions that cannot be challenged.

The final verse provides no respite to this battle of wills. For the idealists, everything is true to itself and consistent. So, the facts are accepted as facts, the vision is accepted as a vision, and there is no need to determine which will triumph. The vision can only triumph if it responds appropriately to the facts. For the realists, in contrast, the facts and the vision are a world apart. While they know that the facts should be determinative in deciding what is to be done, they also know it is the vision that will always triumph in the end, irrespective of the facts.

Will it ever be possible to reconcile these two opposing views? The strength with which they are held, and the certainty of each school that only their explanation is correct, is without question. If only we could travel to this fascinating and distant period, and ask the mysterious author where the truth lay and how to resolve the perpetual enigma.